Outsmarting Deer & Other Critters

Outsmarting Deer & Other Critters

FOOLPROOF TIPS FOR DETERRING PESKY MAMMALS AND PROTECTING YOUR YARD AND GARDEN

Deer ▪ Rabbits and Hares ▪ Voles ▪ Squirrels ▪ Skunks ▪ Raccoons
Moles ▪ Chipmunks ▪ Gophers ▪ Rats and Mice ▪ Bears ▪ Peccaries
Woodchucks ▪ Armadillos ▪ Porcupines ▪ Muskrats ▪ Beavers ▪ Opossums

BY NEIL SODERSTROM

Photos by author, except where noted

This book is being published simultaneously by Rodale Inc. as *Deer-Resistant Landscaping*.

© 2008 by Neil Soderstrom

Rodale books may be purchased for business or promotional use or for special sales. For information, please write to: Special Markets Department, Rodale Inc., 733 Third Avenue, New York, NY 10017

Printed in the United States of America

Rodale Inc. makes every effort to use acid-free ♾, recycled paper ♻.

Book design by Anthony Serge

Illustrations by Michael Gellatly; range maps by Anthony Serge and Sandy Freeman

Map outline of North America © Map Resources

Photographs by author unless otherwise noted

Library of Congress Cataloging-in-Publication Data

Soderstrom, Neil.
    Outsmarting deer & other critters : foolproof tips for deterring pesky mammals and protecting your yard and garden / Neil Soderstrom.
       p.   cm.
    Includes bibliographical references and index.
    ISBN-13 978-1-59486-908-2 hardcover
    ISBN-10 1-59486-908-1 hardcover
    1-59486-909-X paperback
    978-1-59486-909-9 paperback
    1. Deer—Control. 2. Wildlife pests—Control. I. Title. II. Title: Outsmarting deer and other critters.
  SB994.D4.S63   2008
  635'.0496—dc22   2008048436

Distributed to the trade by Macmillan

2 4 6 8 10 9 7 5 3   hardcover
     4 6 8 10 9 7 5 3   paperback

RODALE
LIVE YOUR WHOLE LIFE™

We inspire and enable people to improve their lives and the world around them

For more of our products visit **rodalestore.com** or call 800-848-4735

For my wife, Hannelore, and our son, Nikolai

Contents

About This Book

SHARING OUR BOUNTY

After moving into our present New York farmhouse in 1988, Hannelore and I broke ground for a 20 × 200-foot garden plot. There we planted vegetables, herbs, and berries that flourished in the rich sandy loam, further enriched by goat manure we bartered for. Plants in the first two years suffered virtually no insect damage and no damage from deer or other mammals, even though the garden had no fence.

In the spring of our third year, Hannelore offered garden samples to the chef at our regionally famous Drover's Inn. The chef liked those samples and brought the inn owner to inspect the garden. Both enthusiastically invited Hannelore to begin weekly deliveries.

However, before departing, the inn's owner inquired, "Don't you have deer trouble?"

"Not yet."

"You will!"

Indeed, we were naïve to the potential for damage by deer and other mammals. Luckily for us, the previous owners had planted mainly deer-resistant ornamentals near the house.

Actually, our first problems began when raccoons destroyed our corn patch the night before our planned harvest. The following spring, four woodchucks caused havoc before being dealt with. That summer, voles wiped out our potato crop. Even though deer had discovered our daylilies near the house and our yew bushes along the foundation, they hadn't yet learned to recognize our vegetables as food.

DEER AND OTHER MAMMALS

As challenging as deer alone can be, other mammals sometimes cause greater combined landscape damage, including lawn damage. Other mammals undermine house foundations and chew electrical wires that can cause house fires and disable vehicles. Many mammals, including deer, have injured and killed pets and people. Some rodents have caused catastrophic flooding. And virtually all mammals can spread serious diseases and parasites. Yet, despite such problems, most of these mammals play vital roles in nature.

This book concentrates initially on deer and then devotes chapters to more than 20 other mammals. In each chapter, I introduce problems that each mammal causes, relative to each mammal's role in its ecosystem. Next follow factors that will help you identify culprits based on damage, tracks, and other signs. As important, you'll learn each mammal's year-round behaviors, which can help you decide on seasonally adjusted options for exclusion, eviction, frightening, and either live trapping or lethal measures. I discourage use of poisons because they are inhumane, besides being dangerous for kids, pets, and the environment.

Besides deer, the list of problem mammals includes armadillos, black bears, beavers, chipmunks, collared peccaries (javelinas), hares as well as rabbits, marmots, mice, moles, muskrats, pocket gophers, opossums, porcupines, rats, and skunks, as well as tree squirrels and ground squirrels—in all, representing hundreds of species that are often unique to tiny regions.

My research included consultations with experts continentwide. In order to understand problems that western mammals cause, I traveled there for firsthand observation and interviews. In that process, I found many of my original perspectives changing. Rather than routinely fencing out (or going so far as to kill) pesky mammals, I realized that we need to try to live in greater harmony with wildlife (outside the home, that is).

DEER: A COMPLICATED COMMUNITY ISSUE

Deer overpopulation and the resulting overbrowsing of understory plants can destroy native ecosystems, as well as gardens. In response, people at one end of the philosophical spectrum argue for increased hunting harvests. In contrast, animal rightists insist that we "let nature take its course." But to let nature take its course, as it did before the Pilgrims landed, we'd need to stock dwindling wild lands with wolves and cougars, a prospect that gives most people pause.

Ironically, even the fences we erect to exclude deer can increase our problems with other mammals, such as moles, voles, mice, rats, gophers, and rabbits. That's because tall mesh deer fencing can also exclude foxes, coyotes, skunks, owls, and hawks that help keep pest populations in check.

What plants don't deer eat? The answer isn't simple because plant species change in their appeal to deer throughout the year, largely due to their changing chemical and physical defenses. Research on deer-resistant plants is in early stages, in part inspired by pioneering studies on grazing habits of livestock by Utah State's Frederick Provenza. Fred found that young ruminants such as cattle, sheep, and goats learn from Mom what's good to eat and when, or else pay "post-ingestive consequences" that can be temporary, though instructive, or fatal. Continuing research into the foraging behaviors of ruminants, like cattle and deer, will teach us much. On the other hand, when too many deer populate a small area, they try to subsist on whatever plants are available, even if those plants would otherwise rank low on their preference list.

Important to note, many so-called deer-resistant plants are also invasive aliens that can undermine native ecosystems. Invasives that are deer resistant crowd out native plants on which entire ecosystems depend. For example, they do this by denying palatable food to butterfly-producing caterpillars on which nesting birds depend to feed their young.

To put it mildly, the solutions to deer problems and problems with most other mammals can be complex. In solving one problem, we often create others for ourselves and surrounding ecosystems.

May this book increase your appreciation and respect for deer and other mammals, informing your options for avoiding or reducing conflicts. These marvelous creatures came first historically, and they're struggling to survive on the edges of the small––often shrinking—patches of habitat we've left them.

Acknowledgments

Principal Photo Contributors: Although this book contains more than 400 of my own photos, its visual impact largely depends on the remarkable photos of deer and other wildlife by Lennie and Uschi Rue, husband/wife photojournalists. Lennie and Uschi first met on a remote wilderness road in Alaska's Denali National Park. When my longtime friend Lennie inquired what Uschi was doing so far from civilization, she replied, "I'm looking for grizzly bears." Something clicked, in addition to their camera shutters.

Leonard Lee Rue III pioneered 35mm wildlife photography and is one of the most widely published wildlife photographers in the world. In fact, Lennie was the first to capture tack-sharp photos of airborne flying squirrels, as featured on page 183. For his more than 30 books on deer and other wildlife, the University of Colorado awarded Lennie an honorary doctorate. It was my privilege to serve as Lennie's editor on some of those books and more recently read his manuscripts-in-progress on whitetails and on his life. His books and manuscripts provided valuable research and insights for this book. For more, visit ruewildlifephotos.com.

Manuscript Contributors: Author of 10 excellent books on gardening and 5 more as coauthor, Miranda Smith served as the principal manuscript editor. She also cowrote most of the book's profiles on deer-resistant plants. There, she focused on plant descriptions and growing needs, while I focused on reputations for deer resistance and toxicities that often determine if a plant repels deer. Longtime friend, Miranda has been a market gardener in Vermont, Massachusetts, and New York.

Also thanks to Kathleen Nelson, ardent advocate of native plants over invasive aliens that can undermine native ecosystems. Kathy's frank opinions enliven the listing of deer-resistant plants beginning on page 235. As a Connecticut nursery owner, garden writer, and lecturer, Kathy has become both a gardening mentor and friend.

Thanks to garden author and friend Anne Halpin for plant insights and "catches" as this book was going to press.

AVOIDING EASTERN BIAS

To better acquaint myself with deer and mammal problems that Westerners face, I undertook what became the most exciting and instructive photo safari of my life.

In Oregon: George Guthrie Jr. led me to dozens of plants that blacktails snub as they patrol the perimeter fencing of the state-owned Shore Acres Garden on the Pacific Coast near Coos Bay, Oregon, where George is superintendent. When I mentioned that I next planned to visit Forest Farms nursery (forestfarm.com), George praised its owners and the quality and variety of their plants. There, Ray and Peg Pagg welcomed me to their nursery—which is indeed inside a forest—before Marla Cedar conducted the plant ID tour. Later that day, Peg took me to the newly created Pacifica Botanic Garden, with scenery right out of the old "Bonanza" TV show, where plants prove resistant to deer or they vanish.

In California: In the foothills of the Sierra Nevadas, Carolyn Singer specializes in deer-resistant landscape design. Upon our meeting, Carolyn presented the deer-resistant flower arrangement shown on page 219. She then conducted a tour of a magnificent garden she'd designed for friends before turning me loose to photograph it. Days later, Carolyn showed me her hillside home garden and nursery, where she's been testing deer resistance for decades, while also contending with ground squirrels (new to me), raccoons, black bears, and rumors of nearby sightings of mountain lions. Carolyn's excellent book series on deer-resistant plants, *Deer in My Garden,* can be ordered at her Web site (www. gardenwisdompress.com).

In Sonoma County's Kenwood, I visited legendary blacktail-fawn rescuer Marjorie Davis. Then age 87, Marj was in the process of passing the directorship of her nonprofit Fawn Rescue organization to Melania Mahoney (see page 28). During my visit, fawns that were 3 and 4 months old roamed in bonded groups just prior to release. Among Marj's key guidelines to anyone coming upon fawns are these:

■ Never assume a lone fawn is abandoned. A mother deer doesn't abandon her fawn even if it's been handled. If the mother is alive, she will return for her fawn after people depart.

■ If the mother has been killed, avoid feeding a fawn cow's milk, which can kill it. Instead wrap it gently in a blanket and bottle-feed with warm water, after enlarging the nipple opening, until delivery to an authorized rehabilitation center. Fawn rehab centers stock powdered fawn-milk formula high in fats and nutrients. On that formula, newborn fawns double their weight in 2 weeks.

You won't regret a visit to fawnrescue.org, which provides inspirational and instructive reading. Donations are tax-deductible. Note: For a listing of rehabilitators throughout the United States and Canada, visit the National Wildlife Rehabilitators Association at nwrawildlife.org; if that doesn't turn up a nearby rehabilitator, check with regional veterinarians.

Marj and Melania also led me to a herd of Columbian blacktails that were beginning the fall breeding season, known as the rut. Resulting photos appear later in this book. Two days later, I arrived in Yosemite National Park where California mule deer had not yet begun the rut. There, bucks had the largest antlers I'd ever seen on live deer, and those guys were grooming one another like pals. They seemed unaware that their testosterone levels would soon skyrocket, converting pals to mortal enemies, willing to battle to the death for breeding rights.

Too early for lunch at the home of friends Dillard and Cheryl Hunley, I killed time by driving nearby streets in hopes of spotting my first gopher. From her police-car window, an officer looked at me incredulously, "You ain't seen a gopher?" Turns out, the piles of lawn dirt I'd been overlooking concealed gopher holes shown on page 99. After lunch, Dill showed me a battery-powered, sonic device that resembled a small rocket. It was designed to be inserted nose first into the soil and emit sonic vibrations to keep rodents away. Little wonder Dill saw potential in the rocket shape. As a retired NASA historian, Dill is author of three fine books on rocket technology. (Added thanks for gopher insights from the Hunley's daughter, Kelly Overacker, and for Dill's link to an old national newspaper story, suggesting that tunneling rodents caused a catastrophic canal collapse, as recounted in the gopher chapter.)

Thanks, too, for post-trip black-bear insights from the Tahoe Basin's Ann Bryant, as recounted in that chapter.

In Arizona: Son Nikolai helped hunt for collared peccaries as recounted in that chapter and was the first to point out my first-ever rock squirrel, shown on page 172. Good times, Nik!

MINNESOTA PERSPECTIVES

Thanks to Minnesota cousin Karen Spooner for news clips on controlling deer inside Duluth's city limits. To cousin Kathy Goedel for her bear and mice experiences. To cousin Sharon Holbeck for her astounding report on her deer-defying hostas.

Row 1: Ann Bryant and friend Marvin, Carolyn Singer (photo by Alicia Berardi), Karen Spooner, Sharon Holbeck, and Kathy Goedel (photo by Jim Spooner), Dill and Cheryl Hunley. Row 2: Nikolai Soderstrom, Miranda Smith (photo by Sharon Turex), George Guthrie, Jr. Row 3: Lynn Rogers (photo by Donna Rogers), Hannelore Soderstrom, Douglas Tallamy (photo by Cynthia P. Tallamy). Row 4: Lennie and Uschi Rue III, Kathy Nelson, Anne Halpin (photo by Lynn Tolsdorf), Marj Davis and Melania Mahoney.

The four of us grew up in Two Harbors, Minnesota, on the North Shore of Lake Superior. There, deer watching and bear watching were favorite entertainments, greatly enriched by deer and bear stories told without detectable exaggeration by our forebears.

Just 70 miles north of Two Harbors, in Ely, Lynn Rogers has conducted the longest-running black-bear study on record. Known as "The Man Who Walks with Bears," Lynn provided invaluable anecdotes and perspectives for the bear chapter, as well as jaw-dropping photos.

BACK HERE IN THE EAST

In Emmaus, Pennsylvania, at Rodale Books, thanks to this book's initial advocate and my ever-encouraging editor, Karen Bolesta. To photo editor Marc Sirinsky, whose budgetary skills allowed my trip out West. To senior project editor, Nancy Bailey, who managed manuscript processing and updates, some of it after hours. To highly talented book designer Anthony Serge, layout specialist Jennifer Giandomenico, and imaging coordinator Caroline McCall. Finally, thanks to freelancers all—copy editors Amy Kovalski and Claire McCrea, illustrator Michael Gellatly, and cartographer Sandy Freeman.

Thanks to Adirondack friend Ed Kanze whose book *Over the Mountain and Home Again* provided hilarious tips on locating mouse access points in house foundations. For insights on the astounding range of toxins that find their way into our food and water, thanks to friend Jerry Gibbs.

For permission to cite from their lists of deer-resistant native plants, thanks to Pennsylvania's Ian Caton of larryweanerdesign.com and to Larry himself. For interviews on deer resistance, photo opportunities, and public access to their plant lists, thanks to New York's Norbert Lazar at phantomgardener.com and to Brad Roeller at ecostudies.org.

For helping me photograph their line of wildlife control equipment, thanks to Connecticut's Alan Huot, Carol Oliver Huot, Dan Bouchard, and Mandy Nurge at wildlifecontrolsupplies.com. For extended interviews on wildlife control, thanks to Connecticut's Ed Machowski and to Duchess County's sanitarian Rich Robbins, Hyde Park's Colin Burgess, Millbrook's Tony DeBonis, Beekman's Dermott O'Connor, and Mahopac's Kristen (Cricket) Creary. For donation of a raccoon-proof pet door, thanks to David Ritterling of moorpet.com and to Stephanie Weaver who tested it.

Thanks to Connecticut's Mary Ann McGourty for her marvelous vole anecdote, to Lorraine Ballatto (ladygardner.com) for her insights on handling rodents, to Angela Dimmitt for demonstrating her vole-trapping methods for my camera, and to Bob and Jean Cunningham for the referral that became the book's raccoons-in-the-kitchen story and to Stephanie Weaver, who told it.

These good folks allowed me to photograph their gardens, later helping with plant IDs:

■ In Connecticut: Lee and Diana Bristol (bloomingfieldsfarm.com, Sherman); Sal Gilberti, Gilberti's Herb Gardens (Easton); Eugene Reelick, Hollandia Nursery and Garden Center (Bethel).

■ In New York: Duncan and Julia Brine (hortdesign@gardenlarge.com, Pawling); George Fenn (Amenia), Petronella Collins (Innisfree Garden, Millbrook); Jonathan Meigs (director of Trevor Zoo, Millbrook School, Millbrook); and Ellen and Eric Petersen (Stormville). And special thanks to neighbor Bill Bonecutter for opportunities to photograph his three Vizsla dogs when they treated me like a deer approaching their invisible fence, announced by shock collars.

Thanks to Frederick Provenza for his pioneering research on the feeding habits of ruminants; James Layne for vetting the armadillo chapter; Dwight Kuhn for mole advice and extraordinary photography; and Stephanie Sexton at Premier 1 Supplies for review of the electric fence section.

Thanks to Douglas Tallamy, professor of entomology and wildlife ecology at the University of Delaware, Newark. Doug's book, *Bringing Nature Home,* opened my eyes to the vital ecological role native plants can play on one's own property. Doug also vetted portions of this manuscript and provided two photos of his method of protecting young trees from deer.

Thanks to Apple Store genius Krag Lehmann and lead creative tutor Dave Fuller for life support as deadlines loomed.

Finally, thanks to wife Hannelore and son Nikolai, for your endless support, patience, and love.

Neil Soderstrom

PART 1

Outwitting Deer

CHAPTER 1

Deer

One sunny morning in late June, my wife, Hannelore, and I were enjoying breakfast on our garden porch. Were the daylilies twitching? No. The twitching came from the ears of twin whitetail fawns in the daylilies, completing their own breakfast.

One of the twins emerged and pranced playfully in our direction. Upon drawing alongside the porch, it sensed our presence and wheeled to face us. Uncertain what we were, it stomped a front hoof before dashing back to its twin and leading it up the hill into the woods.

A few days later, I sighted the twins in our neighbor's meadow—again with no mother. Contacted by phone, friend and deer authority Leonard Lee Rue III agreed that the fawns must have been orphans. That is, mother deer don't allow their fawns to be abroad by themselves, certainly not by day.

PROBLEMS FOR PEOPLE

Deer are a hot topic among gardeners, as well as homeowners who simply want to protect whatever plants they have. Besides damaging plants, deer cause car accidents and introduce ticks to residential areas.

All deer can become accustomed to human activity, but mule deer tend to be calmer and more trusting of people than blacktails and whitetails. As a result, mule deer are more likely to be seen by day raiding gardens.

Lectures on deer-resistant strategies bring standing-room-only audiences, especially gardeners, for good reason. People can lose vegetable and

Deer-Vehicle Collisions

In the United States, deer are annually involved in a million or more vehicle collisions that usually result in more than 50 human deaths and more than 20,000 injuries. Collisions peak in fall, during the breeding season, known as the rut, because deer are more active and less cautious then. Near residential areas throughout the year, deer become most active after sunset.

Highway departments can often reduce deer-car collisions by removing plant cover at traditional highway crossing points. As an alternative, broad grass-covered highway overpasses allow deer and other wildlife to cross without dodging traffic. And well-marked crosswalks for deer in some places have reduced vehicle collisions by about 40 percent. Alas, "deer whistles" that attach to front bumpers to emit sounds above the range of human hearing aren't effective in keeping deer out of harm's way, according to State Farm Insurance.

ornamental gardens overnight. As ruminants, deer feed until their rumen (the first of four stomach chambers) is full before retiring to chew their cud. The rumen can hold roughly 2 gallons of plant material, which author Rue has determined can weigh 16 to 18 pounds. So during a single visit to your hostas or daylilies, one deer can do a devastating job.

In a short time, deer browsing on trees and shrubs can require costly replacements and greatly reduce property values. Although these problems

Order: Artiodactyla ■ **Suborder:** Ruminata ■ **Family:** CERVIDAE ■ **Genus:** *Odocoileus* ■ **Species:** 2 ■ **Subspecies:** 24

Deer overpopulation results in overbrowsed wild plants, forcing deer to risk daytime feeding in residential areas. Where wild food is more plentiful, deer usually avoid residential areas until after sunset when people and pets are indoors. The doe shown at the birdfeeder had grown so accustomed to people that it was willing to be enclosed by deck fencing while being photographed. (Photos by Lennie and Uschi Rue III)

have a common thread throughout North America, they often differ somewhat from region to region and from season to season.

Prior to the fall breeding season, bucks rub velvet from their antlers by violently sparring with shrubs, breaking many branches. Bucks also rub tree trunks, removing enough bark to mortally wound most trees, but these rubs seldom occur near residences.

In many regions, deer overpopulation is a bigger problem in wild areas than it is in residential areas. Ironically, encroachment of houses on former wildlands establishes ideal habitat by creating open feeding areas near woodsy cover that harbors no natural deer predators and is off-limits to hunters.

ROLE IN THE WILD

Over millions of years, deer in the Americas have served an important role. In many regions, they've been a major link in the food chain between plants and larger predators.

Deer predators include carnivores such as timber wolves, red wolves, cougars, bobcats, lynx,

These five photos show distinctions among the four members of North America's deer family. All males grow and shed their antlers annually. Top right to bottom are bull moose, elk, and caribou; females are called cows. The two left-hand photos illustrate some differences between the two genera of deer we call "deer." Their males are bucks, and their females are does (pronounced DOZE). Shown during the fall breeding season, the top pair are whitetails; note the buck's forward-curving main antler beam on each side. At bottom left, a Rocky Mountain mule deer buck courts a doe. His antlers form double Ys on each side. (Photos by Lennie and Uschi Rue III)

coyotes, and feral dogs. Fawns sometimes fall victim to bears, foxes, wolverines, fishers, eagles, and alligators. The most efficient predator of blacktails and mule deer is the cougar, which may routinely consume a deer per week. Over millennia, as deer populations increased, predators helped keep those populations in relative balance with plant resources—that is, at the land's ideal biological carrying capacity. Absence of natural predators has since thrown deer populations and their supporting habitat way off balance.

Today, deer overpopulation among whitetails has proven almost disastrous in many wild areas. Deciduous forestlands with good fertility are usually capable of supporting up to about 15 deer per square mile. Beyond that number, whitetails tend to overbrowse understory plants essential to that ecosystem. In overbrowsed areas, amphibians and insects have no cover. And insects that are dependent on a particular plant species have no palatable food. Birds and other wildlife dependent on those same insects must move on or starve.

Today, some forestlands and other areas are afflicted by more than 200 whitetails per square mile. There, pathetically malnourished deer devour virtually all plants to a height of 7 feet. In winter, many of these weakened deer die of starvation. In addition, overcrowding leads to the spread of diseases and parasites.

THE DEER FAMILY

Technically, the Deer family (Cervidae) in North America includes caribou, elk, moose, and the smaller cousins we call *deer*—the principal subject of this book. North of Mexico, the total population of the two species we call deer averages about 40 million.

Caribou range in the Far North in large migrating herds that don't browse home gardens. Elk live mainly on wildlife refuges but can venture off the refuge to cause problems for gardeners and commercial growers. Although both elk and moose sometimes ravage home gardens,

their populations are spotty and small within limited ranges. Even so, many of the same strategies for outwitting deer can succeed in outwitting elk and moose.

THE DEER WE CALL "DEER"

North America's two deer species are in the same genus: *Odocoileus* (pronounced *oh-dough-COY-lee-us*). In his *Deer of North America,* Rue explains that the genus name, *Odocoileus,* arose from a spelling mistake. That is, in 1832, French-American naturalist Constantine Samuel Rafinesque meant to describe the deer's fossilized concave (hollow) tooth in Greek, and so should have spelled it "Odontocoelus" instead. But first names stick. The species name, *virginianus,* acknowledges Virginia because Rafinesque found that fossilized tooth there.

Of the two species of deer, the more populous is known as whitetail (*O. virginianus*), today numbering about 30 million. There are 17 officially recognized subspecies north of Mexico, depending on who is officiating. Whitetails inhabit all contiguous states and all provinces, though principally east of the Rockies. The other roughly 10 million native deer are of the same species: *O. hemionus.* In Greek, *hemionus* means "mule" or "part-ass," an apparent reference to the large ears. These deer are westerners known either as mule deer or blacktails. Of the seven subspecies, five have "mule deer" in their common name, and two have "blacktail" in their name.

Whitetails. Maps and captions on the next page indicate the 17 traditionally recognized subspecies of whitetails north of Mexico. However, relocation efforts by game commissions in the early 1900s mixed gene pools significantly, tainting "pedigrees" and blurring regional boundaries.

Which species came first? Based on DNA testing of fossilized bones, scientists believe that the deer we call the whitetail, or a very similar species, first appeared more than 3 million years ago on the Central Plains of North America. That's more than 1 million years before Hawaii's Oahu arose from the Pacific.

(continued on page 8)

Understanding Deer Ranges

These range maps show distributions of the two genera of deer we call "deer." Subspecies are identified by a third Latinized scientific name, usually also by a unique common name that often identifies the region.

The first species in each genus to be named scientifically is known as the "type species." Its subspecies name repeats the species name, as in *Odocoileus virginianus virginianus.*

In the 20th century, many taxonomists recognized 17 subspecies of whitetails (*Odocoileus virginianus*) north of Mexico. However, translocation efforts by game commissions in the early 1900s mixed gene pools, significantly blurring deer "pedigrees" and regional boundaries.

Depending on the taxonomist, there are five to eight subspecies of blacktails and mule deer (*Odocoileus heminonus*).

The genus/species ranges in each map are based on maps in *Wild Mammals of North America,* second edition; George A. Feldhamer, Bruce C. Thomson, Joseph A. Chapman, editors (Johns Hopkins University Press, 2003). Mid 20th-century ranges of whitetail subspecies are based on *The Outdoor Life Deer Hunter's Encyclopedia,* Neil Soderstrom, editor and producer (Outdoor Life Books, 1985).

RANGES OF DEER SPECIES IN NORTH AMERICA

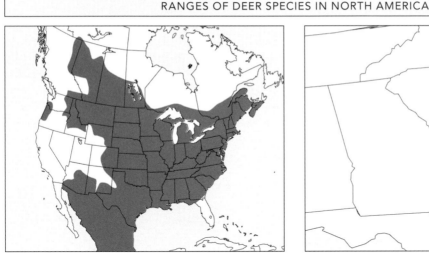

WHITETAIL SPECIES (*Odocoileus virginianus*)

WHITETAIL SUBSPECIES	
	Blackbeard Island whitetail (*Odocoileus v. nigribarbis*)
	Bull's Island whitetail (*O. v. taurinsulae*)
	Hilton Head Island whitetail (*O. v. hiltonensis*)
	Hunting Island whitetail (*O. v. venatorius*)

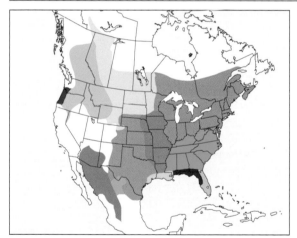

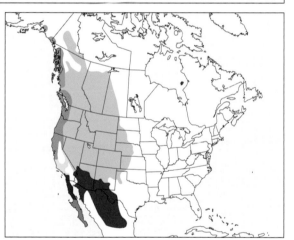

Left: *These New Jersey whitetails carry DNA from multiple subspecies because of translocations in the 1900s. (Photo by Lennie and Uschi Rue III)* Right: *Regardless of deer species, young trees need the protection of wire surrounds anchored by rebar or else diligent applications of repellent. (Photo by Douglas W. Tallamy)*

RANGES OF DEER SPECIES IN NORTH AMERICA

WHITETAIL SUBSPECIES
Avery Island whitetail (*Odocoileus virginianus mcilhennyi*)
Carmen Mountain whitetail (*O. v. carminis*)
Columbia whitetail (*O. v. leucurus*)
Coues or Arizona whitetail (*O. v. couesi*)
Dakota whitetail (*O. v. dakotensis*)
Florida coastal whitetail (*O. v. Osceola*)
Florida Key whitetail (*O. v. clavium*)
Florida whitetail (*O. v. seminolus*)
Kansas whitetail (*O. v. macrourus*)
Northern woodland whitetail (*O. v. borealis*)
Northwest whitetail (*O. v. ochrourus*)
Texas whitetail (*O. v. texanus*)
Virginia whitetail (*O. virginianus virginianus*)

MULE DEER AND BLACKTAIL SPECIES
Sitka black-tailed deer (*Odocoileus hemionus sitkensis*)
Columbian black-tailed deer (*O. h. columbianus*)
California mule deer (*O. h. californicus*)
Rocky Mountain mule deer (*O. h. hemionus*)
Desert mule deer (*O. h. crooki = O. h. emericus*)
Peninsula mule deer (*O. h. penisulae*)
Southern mule deer (*O. h. fuliginatus*)

That earliest whitetail is considered a marvel in evolutionary design and adaptability. It managed to survive essentially unchanged over those millions of years in spite of the advance and retreat of major glaciers; in spite of extreme changes in climates and weather; in spite of enormous wildfires; and in spite of giant carnivores that failed to survive the Continent's megafaunal extinctions of 7,000 to 12,500 years ago.

Which species came second? About 2 million years ago, whitetails in what's now the California region must have become isolated by glaciers, according to Valerius Geist, in his *Deer of the World.* No doubt the glacial isolation was reinforced by the already present Rocky Mountains.

In isolation, species often evolve traits and appearances that are distinct from those of their ancestors. Speculating now, it seems logical that those isolated "California whitetails" of 2 million years ago in rocky, mountainous terrain would have been at a disadvantage when fleeing predators if they continued to use the long, leaping escape stride of today's whitetails. That leaping stride is better suited for plains and woodlands.

Those isolated mountain deer had to escape large carnivores by dashing up rocky slopes, which would favor a rock-hopping running style. Rock-hopping also requires sudden zigzags, which must have thrown big predators off stride. To rock-hop well, all four hooves need to land essentially at once before the next sudden bounce at any trajectory in any direction. Deer that mastered this pogo-stick, boing-boing escape style lived to breed. And they taught their skills after passing the "skill genes" to their offspring. This running style is today known as *stotting,* and it evolved as the predominant running style of deer in the California region that are today called blacktails.

In addition, the relatively open, rocky terrain may have rewarded bucks with higher and wider antlers than are practical for escape in dense cover of woodlands. Importantly, higher and wider antlers help bucks assert dominance and thus breeding rights over other bucks. Coincidentally, larger display antlers usually improve a buck's appeal to does interested in breeding.

Whatever the reasons for those two major evolutionary modifications, DNA tests show that a deer much like today's blacktails evolved in the California region.

And this DNA revelation overturned 20th-century rationale for species classification of western deer. Until just recently, blacktails were assumed to be a small subspecies of mule deer. Instead, DNA testing has shown that mule deer began as hybrids of whitetails and blacktails where their ranges overlapped a mere 10,000 years ago, not 2 million years ago. Perhaps not just coincidentally, that hybridization occurred during the great North American megafaunal extinctions of giant carnivores, allow-

Evolutionary Time Line It's fun to consider these time perspectives.	
Years Ago	
70–40 million	Rockies are formed.
65 million	Dinosaurs disappear.
4–3 million	Whitetails appear on the Central Plains.
2,000,000	Blacktails appear in today's California region, as Hawaii's Oahu rises from the Pacific.
1.5 million	First humans appear in Africa.
12,500–7,000	Major extinctions of giant predators occur in North America.
10,000	Mule deer appear (actually hybrids of whitetail bucks and blacktail does).
600	Total North American deer population is 40 million.
100	Total North American deer population is less than 1 million.

ing the earliest hybrids time and space to evolve escape skills, which modern hybrids often lack.

WHITETAILS

Whitetails are considered a marvel in evolutionary terms because they have changed so little in 3 million years. They changed little because they could adapt to extremes of climate, habitat, weather, and fire, as well as the changing cast of predators that evolved with them. However, by the early 1900s, the world's most efficient predators—human hunters—had almost caused the whitetail's extinction.

Why the name? Whitetail subspecies all have a large pendantlike tail with a snowy-white underside, which they "flag" upright when agitated and when fleeing. The white underside appears even larger and brighter because white hairs on the rump patch become flared as well.

The magnificent white "flag" has helped whitetails survive millennia of fleet-footed predators in many ways: (1) The flag provides a silent "alert" signal to fawns and other feeding herd members. (2) It helps mothers with hidden newborns decoy predators away. (3) The white flag helps traveling fawns and yearlings keep track of their mother, especially at night, when fleeing through dense vegetation. (4) And, this is my guess, the white tail continually rises above low, dense vegetation during leaping strides, helping the also leaping fawns and yearlings see the flag that low-running wolves, coyotes, and cougars have a hard time seeing through vegetation.

Running escape styles. Whitetails can adapt their running style to the current need. They can employ a rotary gallop in short bursts much like a quarter horse and reach speeds up to 40 miles per hour. They often use this racehorse speed to reach open areas where they can easily gain distance between themselves and far slower wolves and dogs.

Whitetails can then switch to graceful leaping through vegetation and over fallen trees with strides approaching 30 feet in length. In this case, the rear hooves land after the front hooves, before relaunching the forequarters. Scientists call this leaping stride *saltatorial,* like that of grasshoppers.

When agitated and during flight, whitetails usually "flag" their namesake tail, revealing its white underside, while simultaneously flaring their rump patch. (Photo by Lennie and Uschi Rue III)

This alerted yearling is looking and listening for the source of camera sounds. Deer often have difficulty distinguishing a motionless person from a busy background. (Photo by Lennie and Uschi Rue III)

These leaps often slow pursuers that need to course forth and back to pick up widely spaced hoof imprints and their scent. Great leaps also carry whitetails through marshes and shallow rivers that further break up their scent trail. During these leaps, deer use their wide-set eyes to see behind them without needing to turn their heads.

When a whitetail flees into the home ranges of other whitetails, its tracks can create a confusing matrix of scent trails for wolves and dogs to follow, in effect passing the pursuers along to neighboring deer. Wolves, on the other hand, need to be cautious about entering the home ranges of competing wolf packs and so may give up the chase at that invisible boundary.

Whitetail running styles are far better suited to plains, marshes, and woodlands than to rocky, mountainous slopes where the stotting, *boing-boing,* stride of mule deer and blacktails has proven vital to their survival.

Antlers. Male whitetails, called bucks, annually grow and then shed a pair of antlers, each of which has a single forward-sweeping main beam from which points project upward.

Yearling bucks usually grow a small set of antlers with just two points, consisting of the point of its eventual main beam and the antler's first upward point. Each ensuing year, bucks grow a larger, more massive set of antlers, though not always a new point, until the fifth to seventh year.

Ears. A whitetail's ears are about one-third the length of the head, much smaller than the ears of mule deer and Columbian blacktails.

Whitetail subspecies. In the early 20th century, taxonomists recognized more than 17 subspecies of whitetails ranging north of Mexico and another dozen or so exclusively south of the Mexican border. They based subspecies distinctions on the regional differences they found, such as body size and tail length, that are sometimes obvious to lay persons. They also based distinctions on dentition, skull structure, and bone structure that only specialists could determine in postmortems.

Comparison of Whitetails to Blacktails and Mule Deer

These illustrations show physical differences among adult male deer in North America and support Valerius Geist's theory that blacktails evolved about 2 million years ago from whitetails that had become isolated by glaciers along the West Coast. Those earliest blacktails closely resembled present-day Sitka blacktails, which still today resemble whitetails more closely than mule deer. In fact, says Geist, mule deer evolved as hybrids of whitetails and blacktails a mere 10,000 years ago, after the last Ice Age and the extinction of giant wolves, lions, and bears.

On whitetails, antler points project from each forward-sweeping main beam. But on Columbian blacktails and on mule deer, each antler is bifurcated—branched like a Y. (We show only three mule deer of five to seven subspecies, depending on who's counting.)

Whitetails have a large pendant-shaped tail that flags upright when they suspect danger, which reveals a snow-white underside and a flared white rump patch. Tails on blacktails and mule deer have distinctive black-and-white patterns and don't flag upright. Last to evolve, the Rocky Mountain mule deer has a dangling ropelike tail. Also, mule deer have much larger ears than whitetails.

These illustrations are closely based on those by Geist in his Deer of the World: Their Evolution, Behavior, and Ecology, *with gracious permission of the publisher, Stackpole Books.*

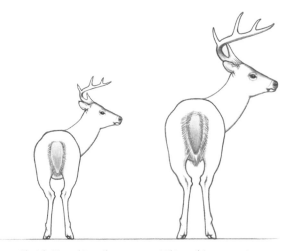

Florida Key whitetail   Whitetail (representing northern subspecies)

Argument arose whether so many subspecies of whitetail could be justified on grounds of small physical differences. During the 20th century, taxonomists who argued for fewer subspecies classifications became know as Lumpers, and those who insisted on small physical distinctions became known as Splitters.

The Splitters began losing their case in the early 1900s, when game commissions began importing whitetails from far distant regions to restock herds decimated by overhunting. Some translocations were undertaken for the sake of hunters with a goal of introducing deer with larger bodies and larger antlers. Of course, these imported deer began altering native gene pools. So today, except for a few relatively isolated regional strains of whitetails, local populations may carry genes and bone features from mid-20th-century ancestors imported from more than 1,000 miles away.

DNA testing now allows scientists to trace evolving family histories at the cellular level. As a result, many thousands of animals and plants are being reclassified as to species, genus, family, and order. Rather than attempting to pretend that the traditional 17 whitetail subspecies north of Mexico all still possess the DNA of the 1800s, it's more useful to compare sizes and weights north and south. Deer in the South tend to be far smaller than in the North, as explained at some length on page 12.

For example, in southern latitudes, two whitetail subspecies have largely retained the distinction of being the lightest in weight. These two are the diminutive Key deer (*O. v. clavium*) of the Florida Keys and the Coues deer (*O. v. couesi*) of Arizona and New Mexico. Bucks in the Keys weigh only 50 to 80 pounds, roughly the weight of Labrador retrievers. And the Southwest's Coues bucks weigh only about 100 pounds. By comparison, adult whitetail bucks in northern regions routinely reach weights of 150 to 200 pounds, with some bucks topping 300 pounds. Mature bucks in all subspecies usually weigh about 35 percent more than does.

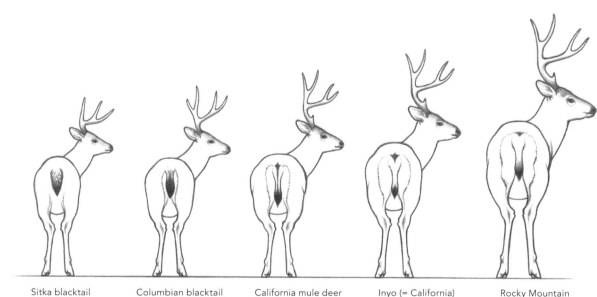

Sitka blacktail (northwestern British Columbia into coastal Alaska)

Columbian blacktail (northern California into southwestern British Columbia)

California mule deer (western Sierra Nevadas)

Inyo (= California) mule deer (eastern Sierra Nevadas)

Rocky Mountain mule deer

Mule deer and blacktails usually run with all four hooves landing and lifting off at the same time in a boing-boing gait known as stotting. (Photo by Len Rue Jr.)

Whitetails usually flee in long, graceful leaping strides. Their hind hooves land ahead of the front hooves before relaunching the forequarters. (Photo by Lennie and Uschi Rue III)

MULE DEER AND BLACKTAILS

All adults of the seven *Odocoileus hemionus* subspecies have ears that are about one-half the length of their heads and thus far longer than the ears of whitetails. In fact, the fawns have ears longer than their heads.

Because mule deer and blacktails have tails of various shapes and coloration, early explorers couldn't devise a single name to characterize their varied tails, as they could for whitetails. On the other hand, "mule-eared" seems to me a disparaging characterization of the large, beautiful ears of these subspecies, especially beautiful on the fawns. Yet the ears are the most consistent feature that distinguishes these subspecies from whitetails.

This section is a challenge to write because, before DNA testing, blacktails were thought to be a subspecies of mule deer, rather than an ancestor. So let's focus first on mule deer that have "blacktail" in their common name, the ones thought to date back 2 million years.

In his *Deer of the World,* Valerius Geist speculates that the Sitka blacktail (*O. hemionus sitkensis*) of coastal British Columbia and Alaska is the earliest of current subspecies because it is most like the whitetail. Its ears, antlers, body, and tarsal glands inside the hind legs are smaller than those of mule deer. And its tail is more pendantlike, broader at the base than the tails of mule deer. The Sitka blacktail lives near sea level in a cool, moist climate with old-growth conifers that Geist suggests were common on the California coast during glaciation. Geist believes the somewhat larger Columbian blacktail (*O. hemionus columbianus*) of California and coastal Oregon, Washington, and the Vancouver region evolved next. It, too, is smaller and shorter legged than the mule deer hybrids that evolved from whitetail and blacktail interbreeding 10,000 years ago. The two blacktails also tend to stick to their home ranges, like whitetails, rather than roaming widely and migrating from summer and winter ranges. Like whitetails, blacktails also maintain a system of trails leading to feeding and bedding sites. And Valerius Geist feels "stotting is less evolved in blacktails than in mule deer. . . . Unlike mule deer, fleeing black-tailed deer elevate the tail during running or stotting," perhaps harking back to genetic whitetail memory.

Conveniently for mule deer, that recent period saw massive countrywide extinctions of huge predators, including the dire wolf, the giant short-nosed bear, saber-toothed cats, and cheetahlike cats. And this helped hybrid deer survive and evolve far more easily than if those large predators had survived.

Interestingly, blacktails and mule deer are more trusting of humans. This makes them more likely than whitetails to move into cities and national parks with low predator densities, often showing themselves in the daytime, unlike whitetails.

Running escape style. Like whitetails, blacktails and mule deer can run with a fast rotary gallop of up to 40 miles per hour. Yet when fleeing a predator, they puzzlingly often resort to the slower stotting gait that cuts speed to only 18 to 31 miles per hour. Stotting requires that the four hooves lift off and land almost together, creating a bounding motion reminiscent of the boing-boing of a pogo stick. Still, the jump can measure 26 feet in length. I was amazed to see it in general use, not just for escaping, first in blacktails near Sonoma, California, and then in mule deer at Yosemite.

In relatively open terrain, the mule deer is more susceptible to coyotes and dogs that hunt in packs. On the other hand, the stotting gait is ideal for escaping up obstacle-laden rocky slopes, as well as through broken terrain and dense chaparral. When stotting uphill, the leap requires hardly any descent, greatly accelerating flight compared to the time needed between jumps on level ground. By contrast, whitetails approached by predators on hillsides usually head downhill, gathering speed for flight on flatter terrain.

In stotting uphill, the mule deer can create obstacles for the predator to address—rocks more than 4 feet tall and drop-offs more than 20 feet wide. The living pogo stick can also change directions and trajectories at will, also twisting its body in the air to fit through openings. Rather than attempting to pursue mule deer through their chosen obstacle courses, the cougar often lies in wait for the mule deer's approach or stalks from above and leaps onto the deer's back.

In terrain in which they feel secure, mule deer tend to be more tolerant of predators than whitetails. Then, if they feel the need to escape for a short distance, mule deer usually stop to see whether their predator has given up the chase. This pause no doubt can save energy. But it often proves fatal if the predator is a human hunter patiently waiting for an unhurried shot.

I photographed these Columbian blacktails in early October on the first day of the breeding season. In the photo at right, the doe was evading the advances of the herd's biggest buck. The next day, I spotted them lying companionably away from the rest of the herd.

Today's Hybrid Deer

Where their ranges overlap, whitetails sometimes breed with mule deer and blacktails. Normally, the whitetail bucks breed with blacktail does and mule deer does. This is so partly because fleet-footed whitetail does easily escape interested mule deer bucks.

But as expected among what are known as F1 hybrids (initial offspring), male hybrids are often sterile. And hybrid males and females have physical characteristics of each parent. The hybrids tend to be among the first taken by predators because they run and jump awkwardly, according to University of Calgary wildlife researcher Valerius Geist, PhD. Geist also says that hybrids are too "tame and inquisitive" for their own good. For example, in a test enclosure with pursuing dogs, whitetails instantly fled. Instead, the mule deer often chose combat by attacking the dogs as a group. The hybrids, on the other hand, approached the dogs naively and stared. Even so, absence of natural predators often allows these female hybrids to breed with whitetail bucks, threatening the pool of survival genes that evolved in mule deer over the last 10,000 years. Mule deer, explains Geist, are being expected to survive on steep-walled islands within a sea of whitetails.

When males of a species need to compete for breeding rights, they are usually much larger than females, says Lennie Rue. Mature bucks weigh about 35 percent more than females. This phenomenon is known as sexual dimorphism. (Photo by Lennie and Uschi Rue III)

DEER SIZES NORTH TO SOUTH

Whitetails and mule deer tend to be larger in the North than in the South. In the North, mature bucks commonly exceed 200 pounds in fall, and females commonly exceed 150 pounds.

By contrast, whitetails of the Florida Keys are tiny, the bucks weighing less than 80 pounds. Many other mammal species with extensive north-south ranges reflect this size disparity, too, consistent with Bergmann's Rule.

Christian Bergmann was a 19th-century German biologist. He noticed that northernmost members of a species with an extensive north-south range tend to be larger than those at the southern end of their range. From this, he concluded that larger members survive extreme cold better because their larger body mass results in less heat loss per square inch of skin surface. Conversely, he observed that smaller seemed better in hot, dry climates, where heat must be dissipated quickly, helping those mammals survive a variety of "heated situations" better than their larger brethren could if transplanted south.

Bergmann's Rule went largely unchallenged throughout most of the 20th century. But in 1987, Geist observed that body sizes of moose and caribou tend to increase northward before decreasing at about 60 degrees north latitude (roughly in a horizontal line between Anchorage, Alaska, and middle Hudson Bay). Geist also noted that body size is smaller at low and at high altitudes and on coastal islands.

Almost undermining his own challenge of Bergmann's Rule, Geist created a chart that shows relatively steady increase in body size for whitetails from the equator well into Canada. Thus it appears that Bergmann's Rule holds true for continental whitetails, at least. In disputing Bergmann, Geist contends that a key factor is extended good foraging in autumn in the North, enhanced by frost. Geist asserts that besides the "pulse of maturing seeds and fruits (mast). . . . Sharp frosts kill the herbaceous vegetation and allow fungi and bacteria to ferment . . . tough-fibered and poisonous vegetation. . . .The plants then lose their toxicity and ferment into nutritious natural silage. This adds weeks of good foraging and, consequently, many days of body growth for the young."

Agreeing with Geist in part, deer authority and author Leonard Lee Rue III, has always contended that "for northern animals, bulk is better." His Rue's Addendum to Bergmann's Rule reads thus: "Distance from the equator tends to result in larger members of the same species, as long as their preferred food is abundant and meets their nutritional needs; body size decreases in direct proportion to decreasing food availability."

I'd be reluctant to dispute Geist's emphasis on frost's ability to create nutritious forage in nature's selection for larger animals in the extreme North. But it seems to me that Bergmann's Rule deserves at least partial credit for larger members of a given species in the North for these reasons.

■ **Bergmann's Rule resuscitated:** It seems logical that greater body mass in extreme cold must help reduce heat loss per square inch of skin surface. And this should slow the loss of body fat on which whitetails and mule deer largely depend for internal heat and energy until spring.

■ **Herd competition in winter:** In the coldest regions with heavy snow, whitetails often congregate in areas sheltered from wind. In these "yarding areas," larger does especially, as well as bucks, would be able to drive smaller deer away from meager nearby browse, this is, leaves and tips of twigs. On starvation rations in winter, does will even drive their own offspring from scarce browse. Also, larger deer on hind legs can rear up higher for woody browse than smaller deer.

■ **Big-buck disadvantage:** Contrary to what most people might assume, as Rue has pointed out, the largest bucks often have a disadvantage during long, severe winters after their antlers have fallen off. That's because these biggest, most dominant bucks usually have done the most fighting and breeding during the fall rut. Fighting and breeding, rather than eating, these large bucks often begin winter with too little body fat to maintain energy

and body heat into spring. Even so, by then, they usually will have passed along their larger-body genes during the rut, helping nature in the North select for larger bucks as well as larger does.

■ **Back to Rue's "for northern animals, bulk is better":** It appears to me that various factors reward larger body size in cold climates and smaller body size in hot climates. Just as Bergmann's Rule seems to hold true for continental whitetails, it seems to hold true for raccoons and smaller mammals that aren't dependent on frost-induced silage in order to lay on winter fat reserves.

Larger deer can rear up higher in winter for scarce browse than smaller deer, partially explaining why whitetails, especially, tend to be larger in the North. (Photo by Lennie and Uschi Rue III)

MOM IS BOSS

As with many other mammals, whitetail and mule deer society is divided for most of the year between male groups from various families and female groups based on the dominant mother's bloodlines. Grandmothers, actually, are usually accompanied by daughters of previous years as well as by male and female fawns of that year. Yearling males disperse during their second spring. Mothers may help enforce male dispersal—a good thing, because it reduces chances of inbreeding.

Expectant mothers become territorial prior to giving birth and some weeks after, driving off even their own daughters. Hannelore and I witness this phenomenon indirectly every spring during our morning constitutional up a nearby mountain road. In early spring, we invariably see three or four females traveling together. But by late May, birthing time, we see them only singly, browsing along widely spaced roadside stretches before returning to their hidden fawns. These females may rejoin with family after their fawns can travel.

In contrast, blacktails of Olympic National Park "form group territories defended by both sexes," according to Valerius Geist.

Stomping a front hoof, this whitetail mom alerts her often less wary fawns to potential danger. Mothers and lead does in larger groups often approach what bothers them to get a better look. (Photo by Lennie and Uschi Rue III)

Why Bucks Are Bigger Than Does

Deer authority and author Leonard Lee Rue III explained the phenomenon to me this way: "There is very little body size difference in monogamous animals such as the wolf, coyote, and fox. However, for species in which the males need to compete for breeding rights, there is a great difference in size between females and the males."

Biologists use the term *sexual dimorphism* to indicate significant differences in body size between males and females. In the case of whitetails, females reach maximum body weight at 3 to 4 years old. Males don't usually reach theirs until 4 to 5 years old. At these maximum weights, bucks tend to weigh about 35 percent more than does.

HISTORICAL DEER SLAUGHTER

Beginning in the 1700s into the early 20th century, year-round hunting for venison and deerskins took an increasingly heavy toll on deer populations. Slow-loading flintlock rifles from Revolutionary days gave way to single-shot breechloaders and then to repeating rifles that allowed hunters to fire more quickly, more accurately, and at greater distances.

In *The Outdoor Life Deer Hunter's Encyclopedia*, the revered conservation writer John Madson wrote, "America literally grew up eating venison and wearing buckskin. Buckskin was scraped, oiled, and stretched over cabin windows when there was no glass; venison was oiled and given to babies when there was no bread. Deer hides were a medium of exchange where money was scarce, as it usually was along the frontier; they were even part of the salary of some public officials."

Madson continued with a staggering litany of numbers on deer commerce. As early as 1753, one company in North Carolina shipped 30,000 deer hides to England. Between 1755 and 1773, a Georgia company shipped England 600,000 deer hides. But by the late 1800s, Madson adds, "Americans were not wearing as much buckskin and did not depend on venison for sheer survival, but both buckskin and venison were still cash crops." Thousands of tons of venison were loaded onto railroad cars bound for metropolitan markets. During that time, one team of hunters in California sold 3,000 deerskins in a single year.

Yet commerce wasn't the greatest cause of herd depletion, according to Madson: "Hunting by full-time professionals was bad enough, but it probably wasn't a patch on the toll of deer exacted by countless backwoods families that still depended heavily on wild game for meat, hides, and trade goods. Hunted with increasing intensity and skill, deer were given no quarter. During the Massacre Winter of 1856–57, Iowa settlers butchered the last of their deer and elk as the animals broke through deep, crusted snow. The helpless animals were slaughtered with knives and axes.

"Georgia backwoodsmen, with packs of fine hounds, wiped out their deer in the mountain coves, and mountaineers in the Great Smokies set iron deer traps in game trails. Southern slaves devised ingenious knife traps for deer, and northern woodsmen cruised lakes and rivers at night in canoes, jacklighting the deer Indian-style with torches and panfuls of glowing coals.

"Then, it ended. The close of the 19th century also saw the close of the Great American Deer Hunt, for the deer were almost gone."

RESTORING DEER POPULATIONS

By 1900, hunters had reduced the continent's estimated original 30 million whitetails to about 350,000. And they had reduced the West's estimated 5 to 8 million blacktails and mule deer to similarly small numbers as well. Deer became so rare in some Eastern states that sightings were reported on the front pages of newspapers.

Public outrage over the decimation of deer populations, as well as those of elk and bison, resulted in legislation intended to protect the populations so they could rebound. Some legislation and practices were good for deer, and some were

bad—though well intended. For example, bad legislation placed bounties on predators. And some states began importing deer from other regions, a controversial practice that states continued until recent decades, when it was apparent that translocations could also spread major diseases among the herds.

Back in the early 1900s, restricted hunting seasons proved the most effective means of stimulating the growth of deer populations. Laws banned year-round hunting and instead postponed hunting until after the fall breeding season. Laws also established bag limits and banned the sale of venison in meat markets and in restaurants. One of the most effective laws banned the shooting of "antlerless deer," which ensured that virtually all fertile does became pregnant each fall.

In some ways, hunting laws since the early 1900s and increasingly sophisticated game management since the 1950s have been stunning successes. Today's deer populations have returned to the nearly 40-million level when the Pilgrims landed. But is that good?

Too much success? Alas, today's restored 40-million deer population is a misleading success because that 40 million, along with virtually all native mammals and plants, have been forced onto smaller and smaller parcels of land. Many such parcels now serve like far-flung islands capable of supporting limited numbers of wildlife and plants.

Exacerbating that problem, thousands of invasive alien plants have jumped garden fences and established themselves in wild areas. Many of those aliens are unpalatable to native insects and herbivores, leaving far less food for native wildlife than the green landscape might suggest.

This loss of habitat has proven disastrous for many native plants—and has even caused extinctions of some native insects. Loss of these species also reduces availability of food and shelter for animals in the rest of the food chain—including many now-threatened songbirds.

Ironically, in many regions, habitat loss and absence of larger predators have often helped deer. For example, suburban sprawl and gentrification of the countryside often establish ideal deer habitat by providing open feeding areas and garden plants with nearby woodsy cover, free of natural predators and off-limits to hunters.

Yet in many regions of the country, deer "are eating themselves out of house and home," to use the old cliché, while also eating hundreds and thousands of other species of wildlife out of house and home.

Ironically, it turns out, the ban on "antlerless deer" hunting that helped restore deer populations to their level when the Pilgrims landed in the New World may be one of the most promising considerations when deciding how to return populations to levels that the land can support. This fact was convincingly demonstrated on Arizona's Kaibab Plateau.

The Kaibab Plateau disaster. In 1906, when deer populations were at an all-time low in the United States, foresighted people such as Teddy Roosevelt and others appreciated the need to

Normally arbovitae branches bear lush evergreen leaves on branches quite near ground level. Why not here?

> **Conservation**
>
> Theodore Roosevelt's chief forester, Gifford Pinchot, defined conservation this way: "Conservation is the use of natural resources for the greatest good for the greatest number for the longest time." And that definition still enjoys widespread political support, perhaps because it allows various interest groups to lobby on behalf of their constituencies, whether they be farmers, ranchers, loggers, hunters, real estate developers, foresters, ecologists, biologists, wildlife protectionists—or just homeowners and gardeners hoping to protect their plants. These interest groups are often at odds, with some forming powerful lobbies that outspend one another in winning the support of politicians who might otherwise have had no interest in their cause. Was this the political system the Founding Fathers and Mothers envisioned?

protect large tracts of land for wildlife and posterity. These were early glimmers of what eventually became today's national forests, national parks, and national wildlife refuges. Yet in those days, even high-minded conservationists had limited understandings of the complex workings of wild ecosystems.

At any rate, with a goal of reestablishing the mule deer population to northern Arizona's Kaibab Plateau, that area was set aside as the Grand Canyon National Game Preserve. *Note:* The mission was to preserve "game" such as mule deer, and not all native wildlife, for hunters.

In John Madson's words, "This was a unique area, 753,000 acres of forest and rugged canyon that held a herd of about 3,000 Rocky Mountain mule deer. It was virtually a biological island with the deep canyons to the south and west and open sagebrush plains to the north and northeast. . . . The area was closed to all deer hunting, and since human entry could be easily controlled, poaching was insignificant. Competition from livestock was reduced, and war was declared on predators. In the 17 years between 1906 and 1923, government hunters on the Kaibab killed 674 cougars, 11 wolves, 3,000 coyotes, and 120 bobcats."

By 1922, the Kaibab mule deer population had rebounded from 3,000 to 20,000. And by 1924, various estimates suggested the population had reached or exceeded 30,000 deer. However, by then the deer had so severely overbrowsed their habitat that it could no longer support numbers anywhere close to 30,000.

Shocked by the condition of the range, a commission recommended an immediate reduction of the herd by half. However, while this recommendation was being debated over the next 5 years, nature undertook herd management by presiding over massive winter starvation die-offs until the surviving deer represented only a fraction of their original, low number of 3,000.

Photos taken at Sowats Point on the Kaibab in 1931 and in 1954, 24 years later, show the area still struggling to recover from overbrowsing.

What lessons can we learn from Kaibab Plateau disaster?

In 1931, the badly overbrowsed Kaibab Plateau looked like this. (Photo by U.S. Forest Service)

1. Deer need natural predators to keep their populations within the carrying capacity of the land they inhabit.
2. When deer have too few natural predators, something needs to fulfill that role.

Winter Starvation

Overpopulation and overbrowsing allow northern deer too little food on which to fatten up for deep snow and cold winters, when they normally need to live mainly off body fat.

In the winter of 1926 to 1927, coincident with winter starvation of mule deer on Arizona's Kaibab Plateau, Pennsylvania's whitetails suffered a similar fate. Pennsylvania had begun importing livetrapped whitetails in the early 1900s in hopes of restoring the former population. However, those deer enjoyed protection from hunters in the absence of the long-gone natural predators. In badly overbrowsed range, they starved to death by the countless thousands.

Even so, winter starvation occurs in many regions, with or without overpopulations. In many cases, deer herds may "yard up" in traditional wintering areas, such as cedar swamps, that afford protection from wind. So ingrained is the yarding tradition in some herds that more than 100 deer may stay through winter even when better browse is available nearby.

Starving fawns, like this whitetail, stand in a hump-backed position, often too feeble to flee. (Photo by Lennie and Uschi Rue III)

HOME RANGES

Whitetails. In habitats with good cover and obstacles that hinder predators, whitetails tend to have smaller home ranges than otherwise. Like many other male mammals, whitetail bucks range more widely than does, usually by several times.

Even though whitetails may be drifters in the open plains of the Dakotas, they often establish small home ranges in farm country that has only narrow strips of shrubby cover that the farmers have left as windbreaks to reduce soil erosion. Farmers who've worked their own fields for years are often surprised when guest hunters take enormous bucks from those skimpy windbreaks. The farmers failed to spot those bucks because deer often lie motionless if they feel they aren't noticed.

Near country residences and even in suburbs, whitetails usually hide during the day and feed mostly at night, often avoiding notice by most residents except in car headlights or when motion lights switch on.

Even when pursued by dogs, deer that are well established in their home ranges rarely get caught when there's no deep snow. If they need to leave their home range to escape dogs, they soon return. However, when deep snow has a hard crust, deer break through and struggle to make progress, while packs of pursuing dogs can often travel atop the crust to catch up and mortally wound deer before heading

When pursued through snow, starving deer often break legs, which are made brittle by loss of fat in bone marrow. (Photo by Lennie & Uschi Rue III)

home to their pet chow. In such snow conditions, deer are often in weakened conditioned anyway and are more likely to break bones trying to escape.

Mule deer and blacktails. Habitat largely determines whether these animals stick to relatively restricted home ranges or feel the need to migrate. But in mountain and foothill regions, mule deer, especially, move to high country in summer for nutritious forage and cooler temperatures. In winter, they often retreat to lower elevations for milder temperatures as well as woodsy cover. Sometimes these migrations require swimming across lakes and reservoirs more than a half mile wide. In his *Encyclopedia of Deer,* Rue says, "Some mule deer travel as much as 100 miles in migration. Blacktails don't travel as far, but snow will force them down to the seacoast, where they often have to survive on seaweed and kelp."

SIGN

Feeding sign. Deer have no upper incisors, so they must press their lower incisors against the hard rough pad on the roof of their mouths before ripping vegetation away from stems. And this leaves ragged stem fibers. Rabbits and woodchucks clip stems off neatly. Rabbits and hares bite off stems at a 45-degree angle, leaving them looking as though they've been clipped by a bypass pruner.

Tracks. The front and back hooves of deer each leave a two-toed, "cloven" imprint much like that of cattle and pigs. Each hoof's toes have a hard, outer, keratinized shell and a softer, spongy center. Deer also have two dewclaws higher on each leg that may only register in tracks sunk deep into mud. Dewclaws are vestigial hooves from earlier evolutionary forms.

Front hooves on bucks tend to be larger than rear hooves. On bucks of average size, front hooves measure about 3¼ inches long. In his forthcoming book on whitetails, Rue says hoof prints longer than 4 inches belong to bucks weighing more than 250 pounds.

Trails. Whitetails and blacktails tend to travel the same beaten-down trails every day. These

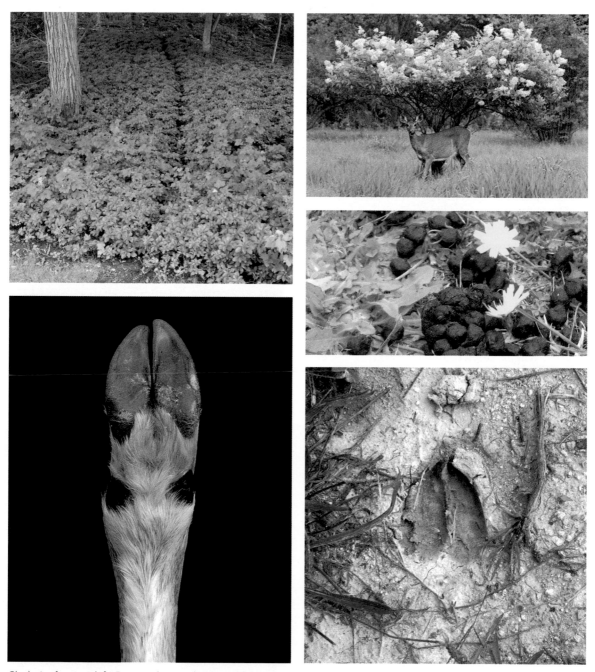

Clockwise from top left: *Deer tend to use the same safe trails every day, as seen going through these pachysandra. A peegee hydrangea reveals its faithful pruner. Deer droppings are often the shape and nearly the size of jelly beans by the dozens, compared to the relatively few pea-size droppings of rabbits. Deer hooves are two-toed; higher up, vestigial dewclaws seldom register except in snow or mud. (Top three photos by author; bottom two by Lennie and Uschi Rue III)*

usually show the deer's preference for easy walking and good visibility all around. The trail compulsion also allows deer to conserve energy, especially in snow, when exertion consumes precious stores of fat. Mule deer don't stick to trails as religiously as whitetails and blacktails do. Their movements tend to be more random, and this may serve them well in foiling predators, including human hunters, that watch game trails.

Feces. The jelly-bean-shaped pellets resemble those of rabbits but usually fall in the dozens, compared to just a half-dozen or so left by a rabbit. Rue develops this in more detail: "When deer are feeding on grasses, forbs, or fruits, their feces will often be a soft, unformed mass. Whereas the feces of deer feeding on corn, soybeans, or acorns will be more firm, perhaps segmented with bits of the undigested grain or nutmeat still noticeable. Feces in pellet form tell you that a deer has been feeding primarily upon browse, that is, leaves and tips of twigs. Feces of all shapes are usually dark brown when voided and bleach to a light brown in about 2 weeks, even without rain. Rain, according to its intensity, softens the feces and causes them to lose shape. By looking at the feces, you should have some idea what the deer is eating, and if you know the plants in your area, you might know where the deer has been feeding."

Scrapes. Whitetail bucks leave "calling cards" on the ground by scraping leaves and vegetation away in ellipses of 1 to 5 feet long. They then urinate directly onto the metatarsal glands inside their hind legs. Glandular secretions mix with urine that drips onto the soil. Simultaneously, whitetail bucks leave scent on overhead branches by biting them and rubbing their forehead glands on the branches. Thus bucks can leave calling cards to potential mates to investigate, as shown on page 26.

Mule deer don't make ground scrapes. Although mule deer does are attracted to tarsal-scented urine left by their bucks, they are usually more attracted to the musky smell of the buck itself.

Antler rubs. Bucks attempt to remove antler velvet in late summer by thrashing their antlers in the branches of trees and shrubs, often demolishing them. Bucks repeat this process in mock battle just before the fall rut. At this time, bucks also use small tree trunks as sparring partners, giving themselves a good workout while tearing off considerable bark in the process. Rue has found that rubs on the largest trunks in an area are made by the largest bucks. Antler rubs are shown on page 33.

ANTLERS

Male deer grow deciduous antlers of true bone that drop off annually, much like deciduous leaves on plants. Many people mistakenly refer to deer antlers as "horns." Horns that occur on animals such as sheep and bison continue growing throughout most of the animal's life. (When introducing my then 4-year-old nephew Grant Soderstrom to a set of plaque-mounted deer antlers, I mistakenly referred to the antlers as *deer horns*. Grant was quietly impressed and then inquired, "How does he blow them?")

Contrary to popular belief, antlers didn't evolve as weapons for dealing with predators. Although bucks will use their antlers against predators when cornered, they usually flee rather than fight. Instead, antlers evolved primarily as luxury ornaments that impress females and intimidate lesser bucks. As intimidators, large antlers minimize the likelihood of mortal combat between unequal opponents and thereby reduce injuries and deaths to lesser bucks.

Among whitetails, blacktails, and mule deer, the largest bucks tend to have the largest antlers through their seventh year or so, after which antler size may diminish. Interestingly, northern deer and deer that occupy higher elevations have larger antlers than southern deer and deer that occupy lower elevations and denser cover.

Antler growth and seasonally changing deer behaviors are based on a complex array of hormones that ebb and flow as the hours of daylight gradually increase and decrease through the year. This seasonally changing daylight is known as *photoperiod* and affects nearly all living organisms. It largely ensures that the young of all species are born at the best time for survival.

Each spring, antlers begin growing from two

pedicels on the male deer's forehead. The pedicels themselves actually begin forming on the skull plate of male fetuses but don't become evident on male fawns as little knobs until the fawns are about 3 months old. When fawns are about 5 to 6 months old, the pedicels are about ¾ inch tall.

Although antler conformation is based on genetic factors, protein in the diet greatly affects potential dimensions and mass. For example, research has shown that bucks whose feed has a low protein content of only 5 to 9 percent grow antlers with only half the mass of bucks whose feed is 16 percent protein.

Velvet. The antlers grow beneath a layer of soft, hairy skin known as velvet because it feels velvety to the touch. In spring, velvet antlers grow slowly, but during summer, growth rates may accelerate to nearly half an inch per day.

Like whiskers, the hair of velvet serves as sensory receptors, helping bucks feel branches that could damage the underlying maze of nerves and blood vessels. In fact, accidental whacks against wooden branches can cause profuse bleeding. Highly aware of their sensitive and fast-growing velvety antlers, bucks are reclusive in spring and summer. During this "velvet" period, bucks may seem to disappear from the landscape.

By late summer, the velvet begins drying up and losing sensitivity, except for feeling itchy to the buck as it eventually begins to slough off on its own. But bucks rub off most of the velvet on woody branches. The now "cleaned" antlers have a hard, bloodstained, bony shell and a spongy core.

Even though hard and insensitive to touch now, "memory" of each point was established during the velvet period.

Typical and nontypical antlers. Antlers of all deer tend to be symmetrical, each side a nearly mirror image of the other. Injury to the soft, growing antler during velvet can cause that side to grow abnormally. In addition, genetic abnormalities can result in classic nontypical antlers that take on bizarre shapes on each side.

Left: *In early summer, this blacktail buck's antlers in velvet may grow as much as ½ inch per day.* Right: *As on this whitetail, antler velvet dries and begins to slough off when underlying bone has nearly hardened, leaving a bloody residue. Bucks use branches to rub the velvet off. (Photos by Lennie and Uschi Rue III)*

Left: After the rut, huge whitetail bucks become pals again, shown here shortly before shedding their antlers, all cued by diminished day length. Right: Antlers on this Rocky Mountain mule deer buck are characteristically high and wide. Note the two "Y" branches on each side, also typical for Columbian blacktails. (Photos by Lennie and Uschi Rue III)

Whitetail antlers. On maturing bucks, antlers consist of a forward-sweeping main beam on each side with points projecting upward from that. Whitetail antler conformation tends to be more variable than that of mule deer and blacktails. Conformation and number of points may vary according to nutrition and genetics, as well as age.

It's unreliable to estimate a buck's age based on the number of points alone. Whitetail bucks 5 to 7 years old usually have at least three large tines and one smaller brow tine on each side. Instead, the standard field method of estimating age is based on presence and condition of teeth.

Blacktail and mule deer antlers. Mature bucks have antlers that divide on each side from the ascending main beam to form two Y-shaped branches. Each dichotomous antler normally features four prominent points, as well as a smaller brow tine near the base of each antler.

Antler casting (shedding) dates. These dates vary by deer species and region and are also cued by day length. Shortening day length in fall first triggers a rise in testosterone levels that stimulates hardening of antlers and the rut. Continued low levels of daylight decrease testosterone levels that cause the antlers to fall off singly after the rut.

Whitetails normally cast their antlers from late December into early February. Rocky Mountain mule deer usually cast their antlers from late January to early February.

SENSES

Sense of smell. Deer live in a world of scents largely unimaginable to us weak-nosed humans. Deer depend on their noses to catch wind of unseen predators and decide which plants might taste good. They also bond by sense of smell, which is affected by saliva during mutual grooming.

In addition, a deer's extraordinary sense of smell is crucial in communication, based strongly on glandular secretions. Between the hooves, interdigital glands leave a walking scent that deer use in recognizing territories and locating one another. At various times, bucks, does, and fawns also leave scent by urinating on the tarsal glands inside their hind legs and also rubbing their tarsals together. When any deer is stressed or excited, the tarsal muscles flare and send forth a burst of scent. And during the rut, the urine-stained tarsals of bucks emit a strong odor that conveys identity and is potent enough for people to notice 100 to 200 feet away.

After decades of observation, Rue concluded that forehead glands in rutting bucks are more significant communicators than the tarsals. In his

Left: *Reared on hind legs, this whitetail doe threatens to strike with front hooves to maintain her dominance. (Photo by Lennie and Uschi Rue III)* Right: *At Yellowstone National Park in early October, I photographed these California mule deer at close range. Accustomed to people, they paid little attention to me, instead keenly watching a forest edge 200 feet away that concealed a black bear dining on apples the deer probably felt they deserved.*

forthcoming book on whitetails, he says that during the rut, "when a buck walks through the woods, marking almost every projecting twig with his forehead scent gland, he isn't claiming a territory. Instead, he is, in effect, handing out business cards. His markings tell every other deer which buck passed by, when, and his status. A deer usually knows the status of every other deer it encounters. If it doesn't, that will soon be taught."

Vision. Deer are able to detect slight movements from goodly distances. Their large eyes also allow them to see well at night. Rue explains, "Deer have *dichromatic vision* and can see through the violet, blue, green, and yellow region of the light spectrum. They cannot see color in the orange and red range as we humans do. This is why the blaze-orange color that hunters are required to wear in most states has been so effective. The use of blaze orange has dramatically reduced hunting accidents but has not reduced hunting success because the deer don't see that color; they see it as a shade of gray."

Whitetails have poor depth perception, making it difficult for them to detect a motionless human against a busy background, especially if the person is wearing camouflage clothing. Deer compensate for visual deficiencies by being tremendously vigilant, constantly checking surroundings with their eyes, ears, and nose.

Rue has observed "that a deer almost always wags its tail before raising its head. The wagging tail is your clue to stop moving because as the head comes up the deer will look around for danger. However, if a deer is suspicious of danger, it may pretend to feed, and then raise its head without the tail wagging."

Hearing. Deer have keen hearing and are able to pivot each ear separately to help funnel sounds into their auditory canal and amplify them. In his book on whitetails, Rue writes, "A deer can be in a deep sleep, but its ears never stop moving, winnowing its surroundings for the slightest sound of danger. What is more remarkable is that even while a deer is sleeping, its brain is analyzing and filtering out sounds that don't represent danger. A deer's brain remembers a huge file of nonthreatening sounds, such as tree limbs rubbing gently against one another; dried leaves and nuts falling; mice, voles, and shrews scampering in the forest duff. Even the noisy sound of a squirrel scurrying in nearby leaves will not cause the deer to awaken. Yet the distant footfall of a human, a twig snapping, or hard-surfaced clothing scraping brush will waken that deer in an instant."

Top left: *This blacktail threesome performed the drama I recount in accompanying text. Top right: Whitetail bucks scrape leaves to reveal bare soil before urinating on the tarsal glands inside their back legs, which deposits gland-scented urine on the scrape. Later, receptive does visit buck scrapes and leave their own calling card. In the two bottom photos, whitetail bucks are rubbing their eye glands on branches to deposit scent warnings to rivals. (The four scent-marking photos are by Lennie and Uschi Rue III.)*

BREEDING AND REPRODUCTION

Courtship. In all deer, dominant bucks court females when they are in estrus and about to come into estrus, signaled by scent. The dominant buck attempts to isolate the female from other bucks and from her fawns. She typically rebuffs initial overtures by running away in a circular pattern.

Mule deer and blacktails usually court in small circles of 50 feet or less in diameter. Courting circles of whitetails are often more than a quarter mile in diameter. If a mule deer doe persists in avoiding the buck, the buck may bellow in frustration.

Early one October near Sonoma, California, I observed a state park's dominant blacktail buck beginning to pursue a reluctant female in small circles. When I returned the next day, that buck and doe seemed to have bonded, for they were resting side-by-side on a hill far from the rest of the herd. That second day, I photographed another doe keeping the park's second-ranking buck at a "safe distance" by circling the large pile of sawn logs shown in the top left photo. The doe's fawn was frightened by the buck's persistent pursuit. And the fawn occasionally ventured near its mother's nose, as if to ask, "What's that big guy doing? He scares me." Mom, on the other hand, had no time to explain the fall rut. Instead she continued circling the woodpile until I needed to depart for the afternoon. I imagine that second buck and doe were resting companionably the next day, too.

Bugling. Aside from snorting, whitetail bucks tend to vocalize little during the rut. However, dominant mule deer bucks may bugle somewhat like elk.

Rutting displays. Most bucks gathered near does in heat know one another well. That is, during most of the summer they have traveled in bachelor groups with companionable dominance hierarchies. In fact, before serious onset of the rut, many mule deer bucks form good-natured sparring partnerships. However, the flow of testosterone in fall increases aggressive, intolerant behaviors among bucks large enough to challenge one another. Even so, threat displays by the boss buck with ears back and rutting snorts are often sufficient to prevent serious battles. The boss buck's laid-back ears and lowered head are enough to make subordinates keep their distance, while still hoping for chances to breed.

I photographed these two California mule deer grooming one another like the pals shortly before the onset of the breeding season, known as the rut. However, skyrocketing testosterone levels would soon make them mortal enemies. In the Lennie and Uschi Rue photo at right, whitetails no longer feel like pals.

Fawn Rescuers

These blacktail orphans in California's Sonoma County enjoyed special fawn formula prior to release into sanctuaries in small bonded groups. Release occurs at about 4  months of age, after weaning. Also shown are legendary founder of Wildlife Fawn Rescue Marjorie Davis and former director Melania Mahoney, who shot the fawn photo.

Fawn Rescue receives many false alarms from people who assume fawns found alone have been abandoned. Mother deer routinely leave their fawns in hiding for extended periods before returning to nurse them. Mother deer don't abandon their fawns. And they will eagerly accept their fawns even after they've been handled. For more, visit fawnrescue.org.

Top to bottom: *A whitetail mother licks her newborn clean. Camouflage spots persist for about 4 months. (Photos by Lennie and Uschi Rue III)*

BIRTHING TIME

Come spring in the North and summer in the South, does that are pregnant for the first time separate from their family groups to find secluded birthing sites. Does that have given birth before often have yearlings accompanying them into spring. But as birthing time approaches, those mothers drive their yearlings and other group members away from the chosen birth territory.

Let's assume a single fawn is born, though twins are common with experienced mothers in good condition. Upon birth, the mother licks afterbirth from her fawn. This licking stimulates the fawn to struggle to its feet and begin nursing. The licking also deposits an ammonia-based saliva that scent-marks the fawn. During nursing sessions, the mother consumes her fawn's feces and urine, and this greatly reduces odors that could attract predators. After nursing, the mother either presses her fawn to the ground with her hoof or signals hiding posture with a hoof stomp, which the fawn obeys. Thereupon the mother may leave for several hours, first to feed and then to chew her cud. She returns only to nurse and lead the fawn to the next hiding place.

INTERPRETING DEER BEHAVIORS

Skulking. Whitetails are famous for sneaking away from danger if they think they are undetected. In this case, they may crawl away on their bellies like a commando. Mule deer may do this in social interactions, according to Valerius Geist, but probably not as an escape maneuver.

Snorts. Whitetail bucks and does may snort loudly when perturbed, as when offended by people. When I was attempting to approach a whitetail doe with her family near dusk, she spotted my movements before I froze. Then she approached 20 feet or more in my direction to get a better look, acting almost like a bull in a bull ring, snorting and expelling a long string of saliva that would have filled an espresso cup. Mule deer snort but more softly.

PREFERRED FOODS

Late one August, I arose before dawn on successive mornings in hopes of photographing three whitetails that were ravaging our hosta hillside. The three were a mother, her still-spotted daughter of the year, and a yearling doe that was probably a daughter of the previous year.

By then, our hosta leaves had begun drying up, signaling that photosynthesis had nourished the roots adequately to allow vigorous growth come spring. So I'd issued the "browse permit" in exchange for photo opportunities. Yet, like most whitetails, these three ate their fill in dim predawn light that didn't allow photography. Then they retreated into our woods to chew their cuds. Each night during the growing season, whitetails repeat this feeding/resting cycle several times.

Midmorning of the fourth day, while at my desk, I was surprised to see the fawn return alone. She waded resolutely down through the hosta stems, toward our last remaining hosta leaves. The mother certainly wouldn't have exposed herself so boldly in daylight.

As most gardeners know, hostas are a favorite food of deer; they are much favored also by slugs, snails, and voles. This may be in part because hostas aren't natives that evolved over millions of years to develop chemical or physical defenses against browsing by deer. On the other hand, my cousin Sharon Holbeck, in Minnesota, has a bed of three hosta cultivars that whitetails ignore even though they browse her other plants. Does each of Sharon's cultivars have unique chemistries that make it

Wading down our hill through bare hosta stalks, this fawn was eager to snack on the last remaining leaves.

smell or taste bad to deer? Or does Sharon's soil itself confer unique chemistries to her hostas? We're researching this.

Foods through the seasons. In late spring and early summer, many sprouting and young plants are tender, juicy, and palatable—if not downright tasty—to deer. During this vital period for deer, plants tend to be high in protein and other nutrients. And most grazing animals seem to switch selectively from one type of plant to another based on their nutritional needs at that moment.

Yet as summer progresses, most plants become tougher fibered and develop various toxins that deer sometimes avoid because of taste or odor. On the other hand, many toxins have no noticeable taste or odor and so aren't avoided until after a particular deer experiences what scientists like to call post-ingestive consequences in the form of nausea, vomiting, and other unpleasant symptoms. Deer also avoid plants at different growth stages because of physical defenses such as prickles, barbs, hairy leaves, and tough stems. Yet often more important, deer avoid many plants because of their chemistry at different growth stages. And this chemistry typically changes through the seasons, affecting scent, taste, and nutritional value—as well as toxicity.

Where whitetail and mule deer populations overlap, these deer tend to eat the same foods. So there's little reason to believe that whitetails and mule deer would have differing taste preferences in plants in the same garden. However, differing soil chemicals and moisture levels in different locales through the seasons can affect plant taste, odor, and toxicity. And this may in part explain why a mule deer in one region may avoid a plant favored by mule deer in another region.

Frost can increase or decrease plant toxins. After a hard frost, says Valerius Geist, mule deer eagerly consume otherwise toxic and repellent plants such as cow parsnip (*Heracleum mantegazzianum*) and false hellebore (*Veratrum album*). In effect, says Geist, frost converts these plants to the equivalent of fermented agricultural silage. Both of these plants are invasive aliens. When ingested

by humans, false hellebore has produced nausea and vomiting, along with abdominal pain, irregular heart rates, and sometimes death. In people, the leaves of cow parsnip cause oral ulcers and skin reddening and blistering. Geist says mule deer also avoid our native false Solomon's seal (*Smilacena racemosa*) until after it is frost-cured.

Edge and feeding schedules. Whitetails especially favor woodsy "edges" where they can emerge from cover to feed for an hour or two and then retreat to lie down and chew their cud before feeding again.

Deer are creatures of habit. They establish daily and nightly trails to food sources and tend to travel in matriarchal groups, with the dominant doe leading her young of the year and other deer. Once a lead doe has discovered delectables on your property, it's hard to discourage her.

Conveniently for deer, nocturnal feeding coincides with the hours when humans and most dogs are asleep.

How deer learn what's good to eat. Many factors affect a deer's food preferences. When fawns start accompanying Mom in early summer, they still depend mainly on nursing for nourishment. But between nursings, they begin nibbling halfheartedly at the same plants Mom is eating. This initial nibbling teaches fawns what's good to eat by

In reddish June coat, this gorgeous whitetail might have grown from the orphan fawn that approached Hannelore and me on our porch a few years earlier, as recounted on page 2.

implanting memories of appearance, taste, and aftereffects that will help guide independent choices in coming years. Fawns don't have much to worry about other than following Mom and feeling pleasantly full-bellied. Thus, a fawn's recognition and associations with specific plants are as clear and lasting as any child's would be after tasting his or her first apple, banana, or veggie burger—initial lasting memories.

■ *Conditioned aversions:* Like all grazing and browsing animals, deer develop aversions to specific plants and can be taught to avoid plants to which repellents are applied. For a brilliant scientific introduction to this range of subjects, search the Internet using keywords *conditioned aversions* and the names of pioneer researchers Frederick Provenza, PhD, professor of range science at Utah State University, and Michael Ralphs, PhD, USDA/ARS Poisonous Plant Laboratory. The following incorporates core concepts from their research as well as Provenza's many other writings.

■ *Change and learning:* Although most of Provenza's research has focused on how livestock learn which plants to select and which to avoid, his recent studies confirm that the same behavioral principles apply to elk, bison, and deer.

As summer progresses, fawns nurse less and browse more, continuing to learn from Mom, and by trial and error, how to recognize good nutritious plants as they change in appearance, taste, nutritional value, and toxic effects—or else pay the consequences.

■ *Perspectives on toxins:* "Most plants on pastures and rangelands produce toxins, often in high concentrations, that serve as chemical defenses against herbivores," explains Provenza. "Even garden vegetables—corn, tomatoes, potatoes, broccoli, spinach—contain toxins, but in low concentrations thanks to our efforts to select for low-toxin varieties of plants. There are tens of thousands of toxins, and they all vary in biochemical structures and activities. In animals, they interfere with metabolic processes or reduce digestibility of foods. They can also cause death."

The Walking Browser

Deer usually keep moving while browsing, all the while continuously listening for suspicious sounds and immediately looking up and around after biting off each mouthful. For several reasons, this walking-while-browsing trait may be an important key in the whitetail's 3-million-year survival story.

Back to Fred Provenza's credo, a walking browser tends to encounter a goodly variety of plants that help ensure balanced nutrition and reduce overindulgence in any single type of toxic plant. In addition, according to deer expert Leonard Lee Rue III, a walking browser reduces its vulnerability to predators in two ways: by keeping itself pointed into the wind to catch scents of approaching predators, and by forcing a predator stalking from behind to keep moving, thereby increasing the chances that the predator will betray itself with motion or noise.

■ *A mixed salad bar:* Deer, like people and livestock, prefer a variety of taste experiences, and this preference for variety helps ensure balanced nutrition, while also allowing the chemical compounds in one plant to reduce toxins—unrecognized by taste alone—in another otherwise palatable plant.

Digestion. Deer are ruminants—as are cattle, sheep, goats, and elk—which digest plants by passing them through a series of four different stomach chambers. While feeding, deer may need an hour or more to fill their rumen, the first chamber. With a full rumen, deer usually retreat to woodsy cover or to a hillside that will give them a good view of approaching predators all around. There they lie down to chew their cud. In this initial stage of digestion, the recently swallowed food is regurgitated along with digestive juices for finer chewing and mixing with saliva.

This cud-chewing stage can be critical in determining later food avoidances. That is, even if a plant may have tasted okay going down (and seemed initially palatable), it may have contained toxins that cause nausea, vomiting, and other side effects before or during cud chewing. These are

Provenza's "post-ingestive consequences" that teach avoidance of particular plants.

What about that cute fawn? Usually weaned by early fall, fawns following Mom have learned where to locate the same plants next year, whether on forest edges, in meadows, or in gardens.

Garden visits. The more we gardeners know about factors that affect the relative appeal of ornamental and food plants, the better our chances of selecting plants deer are likely to avoid and the better our chances of protecting plants deer relish.

When visiting a garden for the first time, "deer take a tasting bite of everything. And their evening feeding patterns target the same plants the deer liked during taste tests," assures Brad Roeller of the Institute of Ecosystems Studies in Millbrook, New York. For decades, Roeller has tested the deer-resistance of hundreds of plants. He adds, "I've observed deer movement at our gardens. As deer return, they know exactly where to go." (Plants that Roeller has found deer resistant are listed and profiled in Part 3 of this book. Those plants are also accompanied by reinforcing endorsements of many other experts on deer resistance from throughout the United States.)

Besides good-tasting plants, deer favor moist plants and seem to know which are the richest in nutrients needed on that day. Deer seem to find moist, nutritious plants in a well-watered and well-fertilized garden. During droughts and again in summer as wild plants dry up and become increasingly toxic, a garden can appeal to deer like an oasis in the Sahara. Unless discouraged in some way, garden raids continue until woody plants are badly damaged and herbaceous plants are mere stems.

In autumn, after decimating home gardens, deer may find renewed food abundance in woodsy areas in the form of soft and hard seeds and nuts, known as mast. East and West, deer especially favor acorns of white-oak species. And where oaks are plentiful, acorns can distract deer temporarily from garden plants. Such mast crops can largely determine the amount of fat deer can acquire before winter. In some regions, a good mast crop can exceed 500 pounds per acre, according to Lennie Rue.

Then, in winter, when evergreen leaves and dormant woody buds in home gardens are the only available food, starving deer may attempt to breach formidable fencing and other barriers by working themselves under, over, or through them—even pushing them down.

At left, deer avoided the variegated leaves of our bishop's weed (Aegopodium podagraria 'Variegata'), an invasive alien, while removing also alien hosta leaves. As Lennie Rue illustrates at right, deer also enjoy corncobs at all stages of growth.

From top left, clockwise: Native butterfly weed (Asclepias tuberosa) is deer resistant. Deer leave ripped-looking stems because they have no upper incisors. Bucks spar with tree trunks, initially to rub off antler velvet and later as imaginary foes when the breeding season approaches. This leaves "antler rubs" that often kill the tree. Fallen California white oak acorns (like eastern white oaks) are a favorite food of deer as well as of bears, rodents, turkeys, and waterfowl. (Buck photo by Lennie and Uschi Rue III)

OPTIONS FOR CONTROL

Removing food. As with all problem mammals, if people in your neighborhood feed deer or lure them close with large blocks of salt, it's wise to find means of persuading these neighbors to stop. It's often illegal to feed deer because feeding congregates them, increasing chances of the spread of disease and parasites.

Bird feeders often become unintended lures. For more on reducing access to spilled birdseed and to feeders themselves, see page 186.

Deer management and hunting seasons. Today, most authorities recognize that many regions are suffering from deer overpopulation. Game commissions attempt to manage deer populations by shortening or lengthening fall hunting seasons and increasing or decreasing bag limits. Most hunting seasons are designed to cull 20 to 30 percent of the deer population and so maintain herd size. However, in regions with severe overpopulation, culls of 40 to 50 percent of the herd may not be sufficient to return the land's carrying capacities to ideal levels. That's because badly overbrowsed land can't support a diversity of wildlife. And badly overbrowsed lands such as the Kaibab Plateau, described earlier, may never recover because alien plants can take over and prevent a normal succession of native plants.

Deer populations can be reduced most effectively by increasing the harvest of female deer, also called antlerless deer. But hunters tend to resist incentives to kill "mothers" and prefer to concentrate on getting a buck with a good set of antlers. Because one buck can breed with many does and because virtually all does become pregnant during the breeding season, even a drastic culling of adult bucks still allows the next year's deer population to grow.

Game commissions establish hunting-season lengths, bag limits, and deer gender harvests based on hoped-for results. Check local laws. A good resource for hunters is Rue's *Deer Hunting Tips and Techniques*, compiled from his column in *Deer and Deer Hunting* magazine.

Community action in residential areas. Public meetings on deer problems draw big crowds that often represent conflicting concerns. Some people may urge getting rid of deer, whatever the cost. Others may urge protecting them, whatever the cost.

Municipal and game officials are often caught in that crossfire. Hoping to please both extremes in the argument, some states have captured and relocated deer. However, relocation efforts in California, New Mexico, and Florida soon resulted in deer mortality rates of 53 to 85 percent. That's largely because deer relocated from overpopulated areas are often malnourished to start with and then have trouble adapting to new environments. Besides, such largely futile operations can cost upwards of $1,000 per deer.

So, at public meetings, when people ask whether relocation wouldn't be a good solution, a smart-aleck in the audience might suggest, "As long as you relocate far from here."

Lethal options: In suburban and town settings, concerns for public safety usually make standard hunting practices unfeasible. For this reason, some communities employ licensed wildlife-control professionals, including professional sharpshooters who sit with rifles in elevated blinds at night. The sharpshooters await deer lured to baits and then dispatch them instantaneously with a bullet to the brain. To allow night vision, the sharpshooters employ infrared equipment. And to muffle rifle muzzle blast, they use barrel-mounted noise suppressors. But this method often faces strong opposition, even if the venison is given to needy people.

My cousin Karen Spooner mailed me a news clipping describing annually sanctioned bow hunting of whitetails inside the city limits of Duluth, Minnesota (population 86,000). There, deer have routinely destroyed herbaceous plants during the growing season as well as trees and shrubs during winter. Based on public demand in 2005, the city council and the state's Department of Natural Resources (DNR) agreed to a test hunt they hoped would remove 150 to 200 deer per year.

Well, by 2008, the bow hunters had exceeded the DNR target. During the first three hunting seasons, they had taken a total of 1,375 whitetails, 85 percent of them antlerless. This suggests that Duluth bow hunters recognized their responsibility to harvest mainly female deer in order to help reduce the fawn crop the following spring. Come spring, residents were pleased to see their shrubs blooming for the first time in years.

Of course, the dangers in allowing citizen hunters within municipal limits are many. Not the least are the skill and judgment of hunters relative to public safety. It's key is that hunters shoot downward from elevated blinds. Inaccurate shooters cause suffering when wounding deer, not to mention causing trauma for people (especially children) who see wounded deer running around. And people that responsible hunters refer to as "slob hunters" might leave "gut piles," or even an intact buck's carcass missing only its head for someone else to clean up. Another concern is that some hunters would be tempted to focus mainly on trophy bucks, which tends to leave the next year's fawn crop as large as if no hunt had taken place.

Regarding sanctioned culls, there are no solutions that will please all residents all of the time.

Options other than hunting. As addressed on upcoming pages, many homeowners succeed in protecting plants by employing seasonally adjusted nonlethal measures, including:

- Deer-resistant plants
- Repellent substances
- Frighteners
- Deer birth control
- Deer fencing and other barriers

DEER-RESISTANT PLANTS

During the growing season, herbaceous plants that deer dislike can help screen other plants because deer have learned to avoid some plants on sight or smell. In fact, Hannelore has had good luck by using deer-resistant plants, such as cleome and zinnias, as "fronting borders" to screen the vulnerable plants.

Deer tend to avoid fuzzy and prickly leaved plants such as lamb's ear and cleome; toxic plants such as daffodils and monkshood; and strongly aromatic herbs—especially hyssop, lavender, mint, oregano, marjoram, rosemary, sage, and thyme. Deer also avoid strong-tasting plants, such as those in the Allium (Onion) family. And deer show little interest in ferns and ornamental grasses. Part 3 of this book presents "resistant plants" that deer tend to avoid unless starving. The bonus is that deer may avoid other plants that are growing in close proximity if they are not familiar with them. But there's no guarantee. Here's just a sampling from Part 3.

■ *Perennials:* amsonia, artemisia, asparagus, baptisia, bee balm, bergenia, bleeding heart, bugleweed, buttercup, candytuft, catmint, chrysanthemum, columbine, comfrey, coreopsis, corydalis, deadnettle, delphinium, dianthus, euphorbia, evening

Top: *We use bolted asparagus as a screen.* Bottom: *Designed by Kathleen Nolson, the rocky outcrop features columbine, prairie dropseed, hay-scented fern, agastache, and Russian sage.*

Proven deer resistant for us: rhubarb, zinnias, bolted asparagus, and currants. Elsewhere, surrounding our 4-foot fence, our zinnias and asparagus screen vulnerable plants.

wort, spirea, and viburnum. (However, in winter, starving deer may have no other option than evergreen leaves and the dormant buds of some of these woody plants.)

■ *Annuals:* ageratum, cleome, dusty miller, gaillardia, globe amaranth, lantana, lobelia, marigold, poppy, scented geranium, snapdragon, straw flower, sweet alyssum, verbena, and zinnia

Still, if you already have plants that deer favor or if you're determined to plant such delectables, it's wise to consider barrier options, which can include fencing as well as seasonally adjusted spray-on scent and taste repellents. Then, too, there are deer frighteners, which are less likely than old Rover to disturb the neighbors at night when deer are most active.

DEER REPELLENTS

Repellents originally designed to protect crops and forest seedlings are also available for home gardens. Many repellents work, initially at least, alone or in combination until deer become accustomed to them, until weather washes them away, or until starving deer are willing to swallow the worst we offer them.

Some repellents give plants a taste deer dislike. Others give plants a repulsive odor. Some products do both. Most are merely topical, doing their job by adhering to the surface of leaves and twigs. Others are systemic, transmitted throughout the plant by its leaves or through the soil.

primrose, foxglove, fritillaria, geranium, germander, globe thistle, goldenrod, groundseal, hellebore, iris, iron weed, Jacob's ladder, Joe Pye weed, knapweed, lady's mantle, lamb's ears, lavender, lemon balm, lily-of-the-valley, lilyturf, lobelia, lungwort, mayapple, milkweed, monkshoods, obedient plant, oriental poppy, ornamental onion, peony, plumbago, red-hot poker (a.k.a. torch flower), rhubarb, rose mallow, rudbeckia, Russian sage, salvia, turtle head, violet, Virginia bluebells, and yarrow

■ *Trees:* beech, birch, black locust, dogwood, eastern redbud, elm, false cypress, fir, hawthorn, honeylocust, horse chestnut, larch, locust, magnolia, maple, pine, plum, serviceberry, spruce, and sweetgum

■ *Shrubs:* abelia, andromeda, barberry, beautybush, boxwood, buckeye, butterfly bush, cinquefoil, currant, daphne, red osier dogwood, elderberry, forsythia, germander, heath, holly (some), lilac, Mexican orange, mountain laurel, oleander, Oregon grape, the pfitzer junipers, plum, St. John's

Repellent Cord

An innovative researcher in Tennessee protected test plots of soybeans and later his home garden with low-cost repellent "fencing." For his initial tests, he sprayed olfactory repellent on two kinds of "rope," one consisting of ½-inch electric polytape and the other a mere ⅛-inch nylon cord. He stretched his test ropes around different plots at a height of 2 feet and reapplied repellent monthly. Dramatic success! Deer browsing of protected plots with mere nylon cord was minimal and allowed bountiful harvests.

Spray-on repellent solutions may leave unsightly residues. Double-gloved fingers dipped into repellent allow precise application to buds and shoots––outer glove is absorbent cotton, while the inner glove is impermeable nitrile. A repurposed milk carton can serve as "paint pot."

Types of repellents. Available in powder or liquid concentrates, repellents need to be applied in prescribed mixtures when temperatures are above freezing and with no rain forecast. Other label directions may address season, type of plant, and plant parts.

Formulations vary widely among manufacturers, and many are not approved for use on food crops. Some are based on putrescent eggs with garlic, others on citrus extracts, hot peppers, bittering agents, or dried blood. Although manufacturer claims and customer testimonials can be impressive, independent researchers have found it helpful to change the type of repellent from time to time so deer don't get accustomed to any of them.

Before purchasing, try to consult with local gardeners who use repellents. Also, owners of nurseries and garden centers sometimes keep track of customer experiences with various repellents and so may have recommendations for specific situations. The Internet is also a good research tool.

Applying repellents. Manufacturers may suggest dipping an entire tree seedling before planting and then applying the solution to emerging shoots and later to dormant twigs. Because of blow-by,

spraying often wastes some costly repellent. So one manufacturer of an odor repellent suggests applying solution to shoots and twigs with a double-gloved hand—the outer cloth glove serving as the applicator, the inner impermeable glove protecting your hand. Because some people are allergic to latex, nitrile gloves are a safer impermeable choice.

Here are some homemade repellents.

■ *Hot pepper:* Repellents that contain high concentrations of hot sauce, containing capsaicin, can irritate a deer's nose and mouth enough to discourage browsing. At the Institute of Ecosystems Studies in Millbrook, New York, resistance authority Brad Roeller has developed this low-cost do-it-yourself recipe that's effective in fall through spring for protecting vulnerable woody plants. He advises applying every 10 days or so.

For every gallon of water, add:
1 egg
1 cup whole milk
1 tablespoon cooking oil
1 tablespoon lemon dishwashing liquid
1 tablespoon hot sauce
6 drops rosemary oil

■ *Baby formula:* Most commercial repellents rely on odor as well as taste for effectiveness. In their work at the USDA National Wildlife Research Center in Fort Collins, Colorado, Bruce A. Kimball and his colleagues discovered that several food-grade proteins were repellent to blacktail deer when applied to plants.

Manufacturers often suggest that odors from predator urine and scat, as well as from putrescent eggs and blood, make deer fear that predators are near. In addition, the rotten-egg sulfur odor is said to be as unpleasant to deer as it is to people. Instead, Kimball and colleagues hypothesized that herbivores avoid certain proteins, such as those found in urine, eggs, and blood, because they are distasteful. One common link among repellent proteins is that they all contain high levels of the amino acid methionine (although methionine is not itself repellent).

Encouraged by these findings, Kimball and his team began testing casein hydrolysate on plants exposed to blacktail deer. (This milk protein contains methionine and has been enzymatically broken down into smaller peptides.)

Repellent powders such as Deer Away, containing putrescent egg solids, won't stick unless sprinkled onto moist leaves. As discussed in accompanying text, powdered baby formula repels deer when sprinkled onto a "sticker" spray-on solution of nontoxic glue.

Casein hydrolysate proved as effective in repelling deer as odor-based commercial repellents. Some baby formulas are manufactured with casein hydrolysate but in weaker concentration than used in Kimball's tests. Even so, Kimball says, commercially available baby formulas with casein hydrolysate proved effective too. "From an evolutionary point of view," Kimball says, "protein hydrolysates may signal the presence of harmful microbes that could cause post-ingestive consequences. Strict herbivores cannot afford the microbial assault that may come from eating things with these protein cues."

Kimball says that it's possible to apply a baby formula repellent onto plants in its concentrated powder form. Application is a two-step process. To help the powder stick to foliage and flowers, Kimball creates a "sticker" solution by adding a tablespoon of Elmer's Glue-All to a gallon of water and dispensing that with a tank-type sprayer. (Glue-All is a latex formulation that Elmer's Web site says is nontoxic.)

Thereafter, it's a matter of poking a few holes in the lid of the can and lightly sprinkling the baby formula onto the wetted plant after.

After drying, the repellent is odorless and mostly invisible if not applied too liberally. Kimball suggests reapplying after extended heavy rain, to protect new growth, or after 30 days.

Note: Only those baby formulas with labels confirming that they are hypoallergenic may contain protein hydrolysates *(casein hydrolysate)* as indicated on the label of ingredients roughly as follows: "Ingredients—*Powder:* Corn syrup solids (46%), vegetable oils (25%), casein hydrolysate (from milk) (17%), modified corn starch (7%). . . ." as well as dozens more vitamins, minerals, and chemical compounds.

■ *Soaps and human hair:* Gardening magazines continually feature reader letters testifying to the efficacy of strongly scented soaps as well as odors of human hair and stinky clothes. Presented in net bags, all can be effective repellents at garden access points or near prized plants until their scents have dissipated or until deer have become accustomed to them. None look great, however.

Predator urine. The scent of predator urine can make deer nervous. But to be effective over time, such scents usually need to be reinforced by predators in the area—at least active dogs. Pour a small amount of urine into a vial containing absorbent fabric. Small holes near the top of the vial prevent rapid evaporation. *Caution:* Predator urine can contain disease organisms and parasites. Wear impermeable, disposable gloves when handling it.

FRIGHTENERS

Motion detectors. At night, standard motion detectors are most commonly used to switch on floodlights. However, the trigger motion might be heavy rain, a branch swaying in the breeze, or a deer approaching the branch. Motion detectors can also activate water sprays intended to surprise and insult deer.

Deer may become uneasy when caught in the beam of an overhead motion light but may soon adjust to it if it's not accompanied by an additional surprise. Battery-powered, motion-activated water sprays push deer beyond reach of the spray, if that's the only area you need to protect.

Noisemakers. The noisier the device, the less your neighbors will appreciate it.

■ *Radios:* In rural areas, beyond earshot of neighbors, nighttime talk radio can give deer the impression that you are up and about.

■ *Cannons:* Large farms employ propane gas exploders that fire throughout the night, though deer become accustomed even to loud sounds.

■ Also, lesser sounds and sudden movements can put deer on the run. These might come from homemade devices connected to trip wires of fish line in the deer's path that fire cap pistols, release jack-in-the-boxes, or set off mousetraps that break balloons. Lennie Rue says he uses a silent dog whistle to get a deer's attention when photographing. The inventor of a device that will blow such a whistle when a deer trips a wire near a garden won't likely need other income.

Dogs. The scent of a dog around a property perimeter can be enough to give deer pause, though sometimes not a long pause. In any case, the dog needs to be restricted to your property by means of a conventional fence or a shock collar that picks up electrical signals from an underground wire along your property line. Dog tethers are less effective because deer quickly determine how far the exasperated dog can reach.

Left: *Scent vials containing fabric soaked in predator urine make deer nervous, if reinforced by predators in the area.* Center: *The ScareCrow Motion-Activated Sprinkler sprays 2 cups garden-hose water per deterrence, powered by a 9-volt battery—also spraying you if you forget it's there.* Right: *An electric shock collar tells dogs, such as Joker here, how far they can go in scaring off deer and photographers.*

Virtually all plant nurseries employ dogs at night to ward off deer—as well as plant thieves.

Dogs allowed to range outdoors all night can keep deer away. But barking dogs wake neighbors. Of all dog breeds, border collies may naturally give chase without barking and waking the neighbors.

BIRTH CONTROL

Researchers are experimenting with birth-control darts and with deer feed laced with birth-control or abortion-causing agents. However, it's unclear how this could affect herd dynamics, the fertility or fetuses of deer, and scavengers and predators, including humans. Dangerous stuff!

DEER FENCING AND OTHER BARRIERS

Although fences are among the most effective options for protecting plants, they can kill and maim. Throughout North America, we're seeing increasing reliance on tall deer fences around large properties, some with razor wire along the top.

Yet how much fence do average homeowners need to protect their plants from deer? Based on personal experience and the experiences of researchers, it seems to me that many people need less fence than they think. Fencing and smaller "surrounds" can protect plants without becoming extensive roadside eyesores that also undermine native ecosystems.

A 9-foot impregnable fence is one of the surest means of keeping deer out, if you remember to close your gates. But local ordinances may prohibit tall fences and may also ban electric fences.

Before considering barrier options, consider a deer's jumping ability, as well as seasonal behaviors discussed on previous pages. From a standstill, healthy adult deer are usually capable of jumping 8-foot fences. Given a running start, whitetails have cleared 9-footers. Yet deer don't exert themselves more than they need to. With plenty of nutritious broad-leaved plants outside your property, deer might not bother to jump a 4-foot fence. Besides, lingering human scents from perspiration, soaps, deodorants, bug sprays, and dogs can make

Tall Fences

When Robert Frost suggested that "good fences make good neighbors," he was talking less about physical barriers than about personal relationships. Similarly, even though fences can keep deer out, they often undermine natural relationships by reducing travel and escape options for many kinds of wildlife, sometimes with tragic results.

This fact became disturbingly clear to Hannelore and me one spring morning. We were taking our "constitutional" up a nearby mountain road that passes a large deer farm. Its deer fence is woven wire about 9 feet tall.

"Look!" Hannelore gasped as she pointed toward the frantic movements of a whitetail doe near the fence. Suddenly, just out of our sight, the doe must have attempted to jump the fence to get away from us. In that effort, she must have caught a leg in the metal wire because we heard a reverberating *zinging* sound along the fence as the doe crashed backward onto rocky terrain.

Now we could see her on her belly, noisily churning up rocks and soil like a garden tiller. Unable to rise, she began pulling and pushing herself along the base of the fence to get away from us but soon gave up. When I moved closer for a better view, she lay on her side, momentarily raising her head in my direction before letting her head fall back to the ground. Her back was broken.

We hurried home and phoned the game manager,

who in turn requested a visit from the Department of Environmental Conservation (DEC). We later learned that the DEC official decided to leave the dead doe at the base of the fence, letting nature take its course. Sure enough, within a few days, the doe's body was being recycled by a variety of scavengers.

deer uneasy and therefore content with plants beyond your property.

However, if other plants become overbrowsed or toxic, deer will find your beautifully stocked salad bar hard to resist. And once a deer tastes something it likes, it will return for more.

Some questions to ask: How much browsing is tolerable? Could deer-favored plants somehow be protected without property-line fencing? Could taste and odor repellents be effective? Could you transplant vulnerable plants to protected areas?

Fence ordinances. If you live in a rural area, you might be free to erect fencing of any height or type. However, most municipalities have strict ordinances and codes that govern fence types, heights, and setbacks from property lines. For example, a front-yard fence might be limited to a 3- or 4-foot height, while a backyard fence of 5 or 6 feet might be allowed, even though deer can easily jump that.

Fence ordinances are intended to allow a measure of privacy while also establishing aesthetic standards that help property values. So before shopping for fencing, inquire with your local building officials. Also consult with adjacent neighbors because they might be willing to share costs for your mutual property line. Besides, if you wish to erect a fence at variance with ordinances, you'll likely need the written approvals of neighbors.

Surrounds. Young trees and shrubs are especially vulnerable to browsing until their lower branches are beyond reach of starving deer. In winter, starving deer rear up on their hind legs to reach browse. Rue measures or weighs just about everything personally before he writes about it. In his *Deer of North America,* he writes, "A 7-month-old fawn, standing on its hind legs, can reach up about 5 feet. An adult doe can reach up about 6 feet; an adult buck, about 7 feet. Naturally, the fawns get the least food. When all the available food is eaten up to the 7-foot height, a *browse line* is apparent. This is also called *high lining,* but it really means starvation."

On conifers, even a 5-foot wire-mesh surround can keep bucks from reaching the central leader. If deer nip a conifer's leader stem, multiple stems will emerge (looking like a bad-hair day) and begin competing for dominance, requiring that you prune all but a selected new leader.

The forest industry protects young hardwoods and conifers with corrugated polypropylene tubes. But, in the home garden, you can craft nearly invisible protective cylinders of wire mesh supported by stakes cut from electrical conduit or iron rebar, painted to blend with foliage.

Native-plant advocate Douglas Tallamy protects young trees with 5-foot mesh surrounds anchored by rebar (reinforcing bar) available at home centers and masonry suppliers. (Photo by Douglas W. Tallamy)

> **Caution:** Before driving posts, ensure that you won't breach buried utility lines, which utility companies gladly map for customers without charge. However, utility companies won't know locations of buried sprinkler pipes or low-voltage electrical wires.

Draped bird netting can protect fruit plants from deer, woodchucks, and birds—but not chipmunks that crawl underneath it.

In late summer, formerly reclusive bucks may rub their antlers on young trees to remove velvet. Then, prior to the rut in fall, bucks begin mock battles that may shred the smallest trees and create large scars on tree trunks of 4- to 6-inch diameter, badly wounding them. You can protect trees from rubbing by using commercial trunk wraps, a plastic drainpipe slit down one side to fit over the trunk, or 1/4-inch metal mesh. Fine 1/4-inch wire mesh also protects young trunks from voles that tunnel under the snow and from rabbits that pad over it. (For photos, see the chapter on rabbits and hares on page 124.)

Prior to winter, you can protect established trees and shrubs with home-crafted surrounds that keep the plant's dormant buds beyond reach of desperately hungry deer until spring. Thereafter deer favor emerging herbaceous plants. Position the surrounds just outside the drip line of low-branching hardwoods and just beyond the bottom spread of conifers. Deer don't like to jump into tight quarters. Traditional snow fences are also effective.

Wooden fences. As with hedge fences, if deer can't see inside, they are less likely to leap into the unknown. Although stockade fences of 6-foot height come in ready-made panels 8 feet long, they look far better on the face side than on the

backside. Unless the backside won't be visible to passersby or neighbors, stockade fences aren't the most neighborly option.

"Good-neighbor" fences look good on both sides. If you plan to install a fence on a property line, consider consulting with that neighbor on the design and perhaps sharing the cost. As shown in the top right photo on the opposite page, fancy wooden grillwork can largely conceal raw metal-mesh deer fencing that might extend beyond view.

Living fences. Hedges may be all you need to keep deer out and have the added benefit of usually allowing you to circumvent code restrictions on fence height. Many plants are suitable as hedges or screens. Among suitable evergreens, deer show least interest in firs, hemlocks, pines, spruces, junipers, Leyland cypress, and the hollies with the spikiest leaves. Yet, even if you choose plants that deer relish, such as arborvitae, code may allow you to protect the hedge with a 4- to 5-foot see-through fence and thereby somewhat mask the fence's presence on one side.

Bird-netting barriers. Bird netting, usually available at 7-foot heights, can provide almost invisible three-season protection to plants and

(continued on page 46)

Steel posts and 5-foot wire mesh hardly enhance a winter landscape but can protect prize trees, such as Camperdown elm.

Top: *Attractive grillwork can hide raw fencing, here shown receding in the distance at Shore Acres Garden, Coos Bay, Oregon.* Bottom left to right: *Stockade fences look good only on one side and thus can infuriate neighbors who see only the bad side. So-called "good-neighbor" fences looks equally attractive on both sides, such as this sandwiched bamboo fence at the home of California friends Dill and Cheryl Hunley. Raw gateposts can be dressed up with wooden cladding.*

Clockwise, from top left: Although 7-foot heights of flimsy ½-inch-mesh bird netting can deter deer during the growing season, the netting sags badly under wet snow, thereupon allowing deer to step over to browse shrubs and low tree branches. This whitetail doe was thwarted by 7½-foot plastic mesh surrounding the daylily nursery of our Connecticut friends Lee and Diana Bristol (bloomingfieldsfarm.com).
The bottom three photos suggest relative "invisibility" of thin 2-inch plastic mesh, which can be stapled to tree trunks or tied to metal posts.

Clockwise, from top left: *An 8-inch plastic UV-resistant tie holds plastic mesh snugly to the rebar post. Here, a 4-inch tie would have been less expensive and shown less tail.* Top right: *Here are whitetail rip-and-tear efforts near the crate-size opening in the accompanying photo.* Bottom right: *Vertical breaks here were caused by the chafing of a rebar post that had been experimentally woven through the mesh to support it.* Bottom left: *In this plastic mesh, I was surprised to find an opening large enough to insert this crate. Raggedly ripped to 53-inch height, the opening suggests the successful attempt of a whitetail mother to create access for her fawns.*

gardens. The netting isn't effective in snow regions because wet snow sticks to it and makes its top edges sag considerably, as shown in the photo at top left.

Plastic-mesh fences. Of the tall fences, plastic mesh is about the easiest and least expensive to install. In ideal settings, the 1- to 2-inch black mesh can look nearly invisible and can be attached to posts of metal, plastic, or wood. And it can be stapled to wooden posts and tree trunks.

Or you can craft your own fence posts, from conduit or rebar.

■ *Electrical conduit:* For economy and versatility, it's hard to beat galvanized electrical conduit in 10-foot lengths. I use it both for straight fence posts in ¾-inch diameter and for bending into arched fencing in either ¾-inch or ½-inch diameter. When spaced at 10- to 12-foot intervals, ¾-inch conduit is sturdy enough to support heavy-duty plastic-mesh deer fencing. Economical 10-foot lengths are available at home centers and allow you to drive each post 3 feet into soil.

Because the conduit's smooth silver-gray surface looks raw and unfinished in garden settings, I paint it. Even if you don't mind the silver-gray color, the metal will corrode underground slightly, but not badly, over 8 to 10 years unless you apply rust-proof paint to the underground portion. To do that, simply dip that end in rust-proofing paint, which also coats the hollow inside.

■ *Steel rebar:* For his fence posts, my friend Mel Bristol protects his daylily nursery (bloomingfieldsfarm.com) with repurposed 10-foot lengths of ½-inch diameter steel rebar. The term "rebar" is short for "reinforcing bar," which is actually designed to reinforce concrete prior to pouring. Conveniently for fencing, rebar has a raised surface pattern that

---

Installing Rebar

In soft or sandy soil, steel reinforcing bar (rebar) and electrical conduit can often be ridden, fire-pole fashion, a foot or two into soil by a person weighing upward of 160 pounds. This method is often sufficient for use with temporary bird netting.

> **Caution:** Before driving posts, ensure that you won't breach buried utility lines, which utility companies gladly map for customers without charge. However, utility companies won't know locations of buried sprinkler pipes or low-voltage electrical wires.

helps keep tie fasteners for the mesh from slipping down. Rebar is available at home centers and masonry suppliers.

Upon manufacture, rebar is dark gray but rusts upon exposure to humidity to a golden brown color that some people like in their gardens. But it's easy to paint rebar to match or complement dark plastic mesh.

■ *Painting options:* Whether you're using conduit or rebar, your painting options include brushing, rolling, or spraying. Brushing and rolling are probably the most economical options if you already own a brush or roller. But if you have fewer than a dozen posts to paint, spray cans are easiest—and maybe less expensive—because you'll have no brush or roller to clean later in solvent. However, if you use a spray can, you'll waste paint if you attempt to spray each post individually because of blow-by.

Whether spraying, rolling, or brushing, it's most efficient to lay a dozen or so posts tightly side by side. Paint the visible side and wait for that to dry. Then roll each post to expose its unpainted surface, and make another application. A single coat of paint,

The two capped plumbing pipes serve as post drivers for 10-foot lengths of repurposed electrical conduit (hollow steel) or rebar (solid steel reinforcing bar), per accompanying text and drawings.

How to Drive Tall, Slender Fence Posts

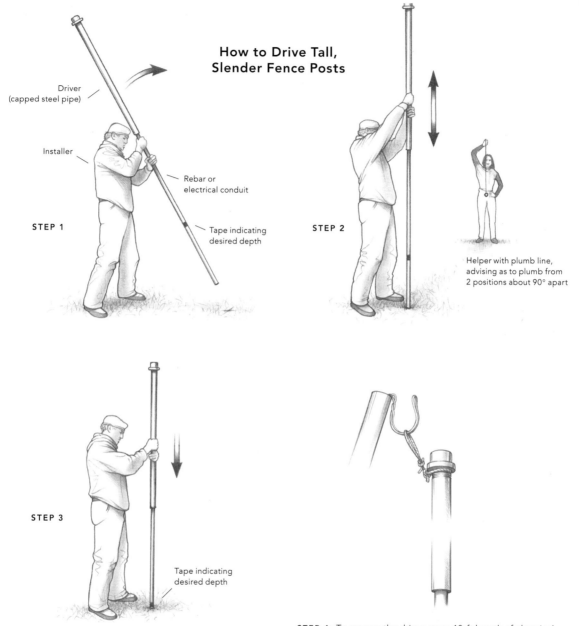

Driver (capped steel pipe)

Installer

Rebar or electrical conduit

Tape indicating desired depth

STEP 1

STEP 2

Helper with plumb line, advising as to plumb from 2 positions about 90° apart

STEP 3

Tape indicating desired depth

STEP 4: To remove the driver, use a 10-ft length of electrical conduit with coat hanger to "hook" a lift-loop of cord on the pipe.

Steel reinforcing bar (rebar) and electrical conduit of 10-foot lengths make excellent posts for plastic-mesh fencing. Rather than climbing a teetering stepladder to hammer posts into soil, you can drive posts more easily and safely while standing on the ground.

The secret is a homemade post driver about 5 feet long, which consists of heavy gauge plumbing pipe with threaded cap. To drive ½-inch and ⅝ inch rebar, as well as ½-inch conduit, the driver pipe should have a ⅞-inch interior diameter. To drive ¾-inch conduit, the driver should have a 1-inch interior diameter. That's because conduit is advertised and sold at nominal interior diameters, requiring that you compensate for its larger exterior diameter.

Before purchase of plumbing pipe for your driver, test-fit it over the rebar or conduit you decide to use. For examples of this hardware, see the photo on the opposite page.

with touch-ups of missed spots, is usually sufficient.

Illusional fences. Deer seem to be confident of jumping high fences that allow a view of the landing area. But they have poor depth perception and are far less confident in judging horizontal jumping distances. At the Institute of Ecosystems Studies, noted deer researcher Brad Roeller has had good results protecting shrubs in winter with three-strand cord stretched in two tiers a few feet apart and only about 3 feet tall; see page 50.

Low metal-mesh fences. We live in deer, rabbit, and woodchuck country. Yet the 4-foot metal-mesh fence around our 20 × 60-foot veg-etable garden has protected it on all but two occasions in more than 20 years. One fall, a whitetail leaped inside to sample Swiss chard we'd not yet harvested. And recently, several young rabbits managed to squeeze through its 2 × 4-inch mesh to sample our parsley, beans, and broccoli (as recounted in the chapter on rabbits and hares on page 124). However, to discourage deer while also keeping out tunneling voles, moles, and woodchucks as well as small rabbits, ¼-inch mesh should extend 2 feet belowground and 2 feet above. For more on that, see the illustrations below.

Easy Modifications for Wire-Mesh Animal Fencing

Whitetail deer can jump 9½-foot vertical mesh fencing, but they are smaller than most people believe. As illustrated below, a large whitetail doe stands only about 30 to 34 inches across to top of her back, known as the "shoulder." Large bucks are only a few inches taller. So deer can't really see over 4-foot-tall dense hedges, stone walls, or wooden fencing and won't jump barriers they can't see beyond.

Thus, standard 4-foot mesh fencing can discourage jumping if retrofitted with relatively opaque fabric along the upper half. Alternatively, a two-tier arrangement similar to that shown on page 50 can exploit a deer's poor depth perception. Deer are less confident in jumping two-tiered 3-foot depths than in jumping 8-foot heights. (In the top drawing on page 54, just imagine a white nylon cord for the outer tier, dabbed with deer repellent.)

Or you can temporarily increase fence height by clamping electrical conduit to each post and suspending low-cost "bird netting" from that, as shown.

Young rabbits can squeeze through 2 × 4-inch metal mesh. All rabbits will chew through plastic mesh, creating 2- to 3-foot openings that deer can also slip through. To keep woodchucks and rabbits from crawling under, install a horizontal wire mesh shelf concealed by woodchips. To turn shallow-tunneling moles and voles, you'll need ¼- to ½-inch wire mesh 12 inches above and below ground, although moles do tunnel deeper during the growing season and, in winter, tunnel below frost line to continue dining on worms. In our region of New York State, the frost line is 3½ feet deep.

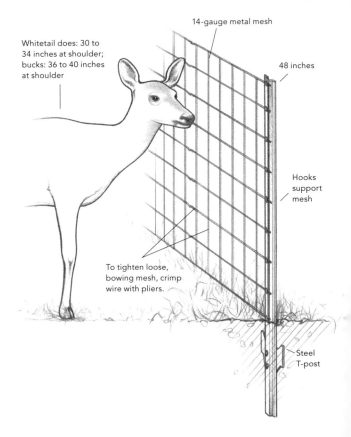

14-gauge metal mesh

Whitetail does: 30 to 34 inches at shoulder; bucks: 36 to 40 inches at shoulder

48 inches

Hooks support mesh

To tighten loose, bowing mesh, crimp wire with pliers.

Steel T-post

Tall metal-mesh fences. Tall chain-link and 6-inch-wire mesh fences can keep deer out but often look unfriendly to passersby. If jumping ability is the prime criterion, see-through fences for whitetails need to be about 9 feet tall, though some whitetails have cleared 9½ feet. For mule deer, such fences need to be about 8 feet tall, though some mule deer have cleared higher. And for blacktails, fences can probably be somewhat less than 8 feet. Most of the blacktail fences I've seen surrounding commercial vineyards in California's Sonoma Valley were only about 6 feet tall.

Cleome Screens

In rows along mesh fencing, *cleome* (Spider flower) can screen a deer's view of delectables inside. Stems growing into fence mesh prevent deer and other mammals from lifting it to sneak under.

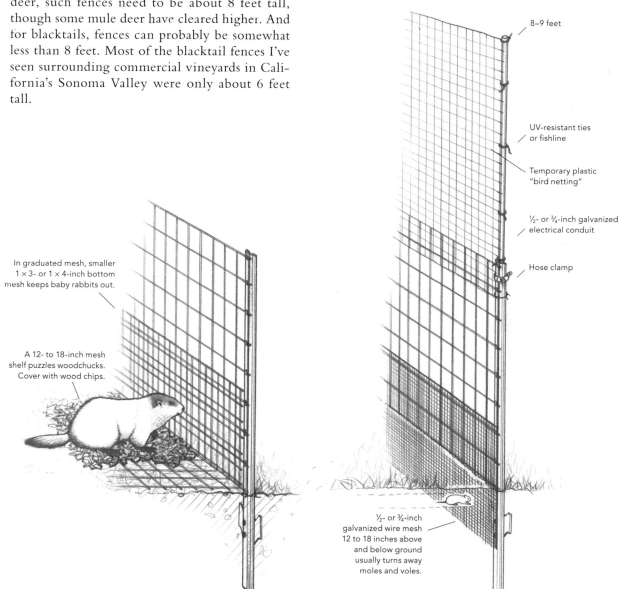

In graduated mesh, smaller 1 × 3- or 1 × 4-inch bottom mesh keeps baby rabbits out.

A 12- to 18-inch mesh shelf puzzles woodchucks. Cover with wood chips.

8–9 feet

UV-resistant ties or fishline

Temporary plastic "bird netting"

½- or ¾-inch galvanized electrical conduit

Hose clamp

½- or ¾-inch galvanized wire mesh 12 to 18 inches above and below ground usually turns away moles and voles.

Clockwise, from top left: *Tall deer-resistant annuals, such as zinnias, eventually create screens 4 feet tall that deer can't see through. Spider flower (Cleome) works, too.* Top right: *In summer, we protect plants in the cold frame with plastic mesh tied to electrical conduit. Deer-resistance expert Brad Roeller spaced these white cords in two tiers 3 feet apart, exploiting a deer's poor depth perception. The white flag may suggest a flagged white tail.* Bottom right: *Polytape electrical fencing can be energized by batteries, charged and recharged either by small solar panels or via house current. Test site: Johnny's Seeds, Winslow, Maine* Bottom left: *Instead of driveway gates, cattle guards that require a 14-foot horizontal entry leap keep deer from risking broken legs.*

Strand-wire fences. If horizontal wires are closely spaced between fence posts, deer may be discouraged. But deer often work their way through or under wires, unless electrified. *Caution:* The high tension on the wires requires strong and deeply installed corner posts.

Arched Soderstrom fencing. Most tall deer fencing looks ugly or unfriendly unless hidden behind trees and shrubs, and it can kill and maim deer that blunder into it or attempt to leap over it. Electric fences are often ineffective, pose shock hazards to children, and sometimes cause grass fires. So I've begun testing deer fencing that looks attractive, is inexpensive and easy to fashion and install, and employs electrical conduit as posts.

Electrical conduit described in the preceding section on fence posts is easy to bend into attractive arches as shown in the photos on page 52. Your bending template can be any solid round surface you might have available—whether that's a large tractor tire, a tank that contains furnace oil, or an old spool for high-power electrical cable available from cable companies. Or you can cut a 5-foot

Use 4-inch plastic ties to attach plastic mesh to hoop edges.

diameter semicircle from plywood sheeting. For smaller, tighter arches, I've used an oak barrel, a bicycle tire rim, and even a wheelchair wheel.

The ½-inch conduit is easier to bend than the ¾ inch. But because you are using the entire 10 feet, its long length provides tremendous leverage. Large and tight bends of ½-inch conduit can be accomplished by anyone with the strength of an average 12-year-old.

With bolted asparagus as a deer-resistant screen in the foreground, this shows my prototype hoop fencing supports prior to installation of full-height 2-inch plastic mesh. The support structure consists of ½-inch metal electrical conduit bent into semicircular arches that slip neatly over 4-foot-long iron rebar posts driven into the ground. For arch bending steps, see page 52.

Bending and Installing the Soderstrom Hoop Fence

To the best of my knowledge, this hoop-fence concept and bending method are new to the world. Here, a 5½-foot-diameter template allows easy bending of 10-foot lengths of ½-inch or ¾-inch electrical conduit into arches that extend 6 inches beyond true semicircles. The eventual straight 6-inch ends on each side slip snugly over ½-inch fence posts of any desired height. The posts can either be ½-inch electrical conduit or steel rebar. (The template is a discarded steel spool-end for high-power cable that I obtained from my cable company. It weighs enough to remain stable in spite of bending forces. Yet, plywood cut and assembled to 5½-foot diameter, plus about 6 inches beyond, would work just as well.)

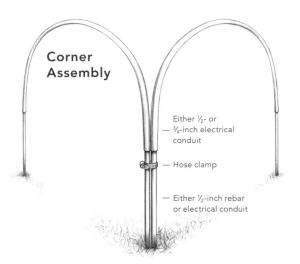

Corner Assembly

— Either ½- or ¾-inch electrical conduit

— Hose clamp

— Either ½-inch rebar or electrical conduit

STEP 1: *Insert one end of the conduit 6 inches into template edge and secure the conduit tightly with a hose clamp. If you use ½-inch conduit as posts, you'll need to bend ¾-inch arches to fit over them.*

STEP 2: *Exploiting leverage offered by the 10-foot length, bend the conduit around the template. Pull or push the unbent free end as far as you can against the template. (If you use a plywood template, you'll need someone to stand on it so it doesn't move.)*

STEP 3: *After pulling or pushing the unbent free end as far as you can against the template, you can gain tremendous final leverage by slipping your post driver (plumbing pipe shown on page 46) over just 6 inches of conduit.*

STEP 4: *Complete the bend to a semicircle. Upon release, the arch will spring open a foot or so. That's okay. You can wait to adjust diameter until slipping arches over posts. After spray-painting your arches, slip them snugly over posts, and attach plastic mesh with 4-inch UV-resistant plastic ties. A hose clamp secures post corners.*

From left to right: *One September at Johnny's Seeds research and production farm in Albion, Maine, John Young entertained Hannelore and me with praise for this a la carte solar-electric fence assembly. He laughingly recalled seeing deep scratch marks in the soil wherever raccoons had attempted to mount the fence. Far right: Deer-resistance authority Brad Roeller installed this high-tension setup each fall to protect plants at the Institute of Ecosystems Studies in Millbrook, New York. To attract deer for their initial correction, he attached tiny aluminum-foil "roofs" to the wire and dabbed foil undersides with peanut butter. Note the cautionary signage.*

Electric fences. These can be a single strand of tensioned metal wire or wire-embedded "rope," or a single strip of polytape with embedded wires. Polytape or rope with contrasting white and black fibers helps ensure that running deer spot it day or night.

Multistrand electric fences are more effective than single strand. Even so, deer can work their way through electric fences without feeling shock if their fur provides enough insulation. Then too, dry ground during droughts can prevent electrical flow through the deer into the ground. And, because vegetation touching lower wires can create ground faults, it must be mowed regularly. Also, you need to maintain a wide, clear swath in front of the fence so deer notice it. Otherwise, they may inadvertently hit it and break through.

Electric fences exploit a deer's preference for going under wires or through them, rather than jumping over. To teach fear of the fence, you can smear peanut butter onto the wires or under small aluminum-foil shelters attached to the wire, or use apple-scented caps, as shown in the illustration on page 54. A deer's wet nose or tongue touching the bait receives an unforgettable "correction." Thereafter, the deer tends to fear the entire fence. Thus, even though a savvy deer could easily jump the electric fence or slip through, the fence becomes a "psychological barrier."

For much in following paragraphs and in the drawings on page 54, I consulted Stephanie Sexton, marketing director for Premier 1, a leading fencing supplier (premier1supplies.com 800-282-6631). Stephanie explained that electric fences are powered by energizers that are either low or wide impedance (meaning low or wide amperages). Energized fences usually put out 3,000 to 9,000 volts at low amperage in pulses about every second. Low amperage ensures that the electricity merely stings. A pulse duration of less than 1/1,000 second helps ensure that the electrical flow doesn't "lock" people or animals to the fence when they touch the wire. A timer switch set for night operation can reduce the chances that children will be shocked. Low- and wide-impedance systems also pose lower risk of grass and weed fires.

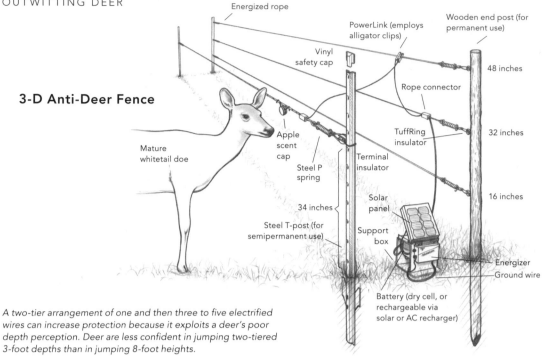

3-D Anti-Deer Fence

Energized rope

PowerLink (employs alligator clips)

Wooden end post (for permanent use)

Vinyl safety cap

48 inches

Rope connector

Apple scent cap

TuffRing insulator

32 inches

Mature whitetail doe

Steel P spring

Terminal insulator

16 inches

34 inches

Solar panel

Steel T-post (for semipermanent use)

Support box

Energizer

Ground wire

Battery (dry cell, or rechargeable via solar or AC recharger)

A two-tier arrangement of one and then three to five electrified wires can increase protection because it exploits a deer's poor depth perception. Deer are less confident in jumping two-tiered 3-foot depths than in jumping 8-foot heights.

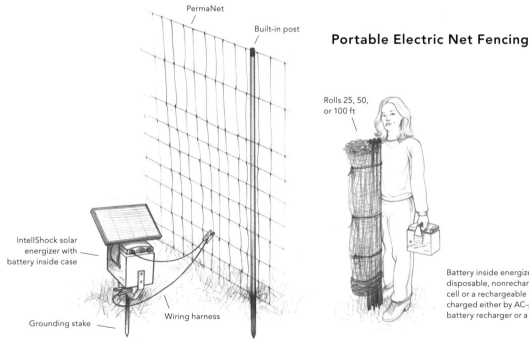

PermaNet

Built-in post

Portable Electric Net Fencing

Rolls 25, 50, or 100 ft

IntellShock solar energizer with battery inside case

Grounding stake

Wiring harness

Battery inside energizer may be a disposable, nonrechargeable 9v dry cell or a rechargeable 12v battery, charged either by AC-powered battery recharger or a solar panel.

For temporary or semipermanent protection of gardens or fruit trees, Premier 1 offers electric net fencing in roll lengths of 25, 50, and 100 feet, which can be set up easily without special tools in 15 minutes, after the reading the instructions. For more, contact premier1supplies.com in Washington, Iowa (800-282–6631).

Stephanie reminds, "All energizers need to be protected from the lightning damage with diverters from the fence side, as well as from the AC side if they are plugged into AC current. In addition, for the fence system to work effectively, all energizers need to be properly grounded. The rule of thumb is 3 feet of grounding per joule of energizer.

For the battery (energizer), you can use either a 9v disposable dry cell, which isn't rechargeable, or a rechargeable 12v battery, charged either by AC-powered battery recharger or a solar panel.

COMMUNICABLE DISEASES AND PARASITES

Deer are subject to a range of diseases normally confined to their own populations and those of other plant eaters, including livestock. However, deer have evolved with most of these diseases, suggesting that most populations will include resistant animals. Susceptibility increases among malnourished deer; malnourishment occurs during winter and whenever deer badly overpopulate and overbrowse their range. Diseases can spread rapidly when deer concentrate near supplemental feeding stations and salt or mineral licks. Transmission can also occur when infected deer are translocated, a practice now banned or closely monitored by game departments.

Diseases include bovine tuberculosis, blue tongue (BT), leptospirosis, and epizootic hemorrhagic disease (EHD).

Chronic wasting disease (CWD) has potential for drastically reducing deer, elk, and moose

Electrified Fencing

Before purchase, ensure that local building codes allow electrical fencing of the type you'd like to install and whether you need cautionary signage. Liability concerns: Electric fencing poses special hazards to young children and infirm adults, as well as pets—especially to the head and upper torso. Hazard increases if people or animals become entangled.

Electrified fences of 4-foot height can teach deer avoidance based on an initial stinging shock to the nose. To help ensure that initial shock, fencing supplier Premier 1 recommends using apple scent caps suspended at convenient sniffing heights. Upon contacting energized wire, the deer's wet nose receives as a memorable "correction." Thereafter, the fence serves more as a psychological barrier than an insurmountable physical barrier. Apple scent serves much like dab of peanut butter under a "roof" of aluminum foil along fence wiring, as mentioned in text.

Thanks to Premier 1 for allowing me to illustrate two of its many electrified fencing options. Premier 1 also offers nonelectric fencing.

populations throughout North America. CWD belongs to a group of spongiform diseases, one of which causes Mad Cow Disease. In this case, proteins make the deer's brain porous, like a sponge. Infected deer become wasted looking and disoriented, and they eventually die. The disease is especially dangerous for deer because they spread it in their saliva during compulsive mutual grooming. They also leave their saliva at salt licks and other artificial feeding locations, which is why many jurisdictions make deer feeding illegal.

CWD is thought to have been spread initially by the captive deer from a Colorado research facility.

Parasites. Deer arc host to roughly 100 internal and external parasites, including unsightly botfly larvae in their nostrils and various worms that affect deer and other herbivores but not humans. Of the external parasites, ticks pose the greatest health threat to people. Ticks can carry a range of very serious conditions, including Lyme disease and ehrlichiosis.

Deer Longevity

Tooth wear is a key factor in determining the longevity of deer, according to Leonard Lee Rue III. Rue has observed that captive deer with a diet richly supplemented with farm and home garden crops like grain and corn (rather than the gritty diet of wild deer) have far less tooth wear and so can continue to browse on grains, corn, and plants for 20 years or more. Teeth of wild deer tend to last fewer than 10 years.

PART 2

Outwitting Other Mammals

CHAPTER 2

Outwitting Other Mammals

HOW THIS PART IS ORGANIZED

There are 18 types of mammals addressed in this part of the book, some having many species and subspecies. In alphabetical order, these mammals are armadillos; bears; beavers and muskrats; chipmunks; gophers (pocket gophers); moles; opossums; peccaries (collared peccaries, or javelina); porcupines; rabbits (including cottontails, jackrabbits, snowshoe hares, and allies); raccoons; rats and mice; skunks; squirrels (ground and tree); voles; and woodchucks (groundhogs).

The final chapter, Communicable Diseases and Parasites, expands on the health issues in each mammal chapter. Most chapters include these sections:

- Problems for People
- Role in the Wild
- Origins, Species, and Distribution
- Identification
- Senses
- Preferred Foods
- Sign (scat, tracks, tunnels, nests, damage)
- Reproduction and Populations
- Behaviors and Seasonal Adaptations
- Options for Control
- Communicable Diseases and Parasites

Dear Reader: It's been my privilege to observe most mammals in these chapters and to interact with many. Some few—such as armadillos, gophers, and peccary—I've encountered so far only in scientific reports and books on wildlife control. So, it's as both wildlife enthusiast and garden gatekeeper that I blend the advice and experiments of professionals with my own, as well as those of garden-savvy friends and family. Our collective goal is to help you outwit mammals before they become problems, as well as after.—NS

All of these mammals are capable of causing us problems. Yet all play important roles in nature.

All of these mammals live fascinating lives. And all are marvels of evolution in the wild. Yet, many find it hard to survive on the shrinking wildlands we've left them. So they're forced to trespass onto the land we've tamed.

None of these mammals transforms native landscapes beyond recognition as we do. Nor do any of them claim and defend our transformations as we do. Still, when these mammals trespass, they often pay a dear price.

The better we understand each mammal's needs, abilities, and behaviors, the better our chances of protecting our plants, lawns, dwellings, bird feeders, garbage, and vehicles.

Mammal needs and concerns. The prime needs of all mammals are food and shelter. Thus, strategies that deny food and shelter often succeed in keeping these animals out. Yes, it's often that simple!

Wilber Woodchuck favored this apple core over the cherry tomato in my initial tests. But he liked the tomato, too.

Protect areas under porches with ¼-inch wire mesh that extends 18 inches belowground or forms an outward shelf, as shown.

Mice nest inside air-filter compartments of garden tractors and road vehicles. For resulting problems, see page 60.

Beyond food and shelter, mammals like to feel safe when foraging and resting. Thus, sensory surprises in the form of harmless frighteners and physical shocks can send mammals packing, reluctant to return.

Mammals also fear predators larger than they—particularly the large predators on hind legs who emit a disturbing range of odors and noises. All mammals in these chapters fear us far more than we fear them—or, let's say, far more than we *should* fear them.

Property rights. Here are the principal areas of contention:

■ *Vegetables, fruits, and ornamentals:* For the "Top Ravager Award," voles often compete with deer, woodchucks, rabbits, and gophers. Seldom earning top rank as garden ravagers, opossums and raccoons can sometimes offer stiff competition. Bears and squirrels tend to await ripening fruits, berries, and nuts. Unlike bears, squirrels don't break branches or topple young trees.

■ *Lawns:* Moles, skunks, opossums, and raccoons announce themselves initially on lawns. There they have no interest in the grass but relish life under it. Tunneling gophers raise unsightly mounds. In the South, armadillos leave significant excavations.

■ *Houses:* When rodents and raccoons take up residence, they create health and fire hazards, while also damaging structures, undermining foundations, and creating smelly messes. Mice and rats are particularly difficult to exclude from older homes with porous foundations and gaps in walls and trim. Still, mice and rats often find their way into new million-dollar homes, too.

■ *Bird feeders:* Although bird feeders allow us close looks at our feathered friends, they often attract mammals by day that associate bird activity with food. Even at night, with no bird activity, nocturnal mammals learn that pole-mounted and dangling little structures contain either seeds or nestlings. Of course, spilled seed is a surefire giveaway. Yet there are strategies that allow us to feed birds when they truly need help without attracting mammals.

■ *Garbage receptacles:* Bears and raccoons have good noses. And they learn to recognize garbage containers from a distance. Strong enough to dump receptacles, bears and raccoons are also smart enough to open all but bear-proof lids. Yet, even if you don't have a bear-proof receptacle, there are techniques for making standard containers less appealing and less accessible. Of course, containers dumped by bears and raccoons invite smaller

Big Lawns and Power Mowers

Modest amounts of lawn area can serve useful purposes. But chemical companies, mower manufacturers, and the landscape industry itself seem to have made monster lawns a fashion statement. These greenswards of alien grasses are sometimes planted with a few alien ornamentals that serve nature no better than lawn ornaments. Are these huge lawns designed to keep homes safely distant from native plants?

Herbicides and chemical fertilizers allow residential lawns to compete with golf courses and some botanical gardens as the most toxic real estate in their neighborhoods. Kids shouldn't go barefoot on such lawns, and pets shouldn't either—but they do and then track toxins onto carpeting. Then, too, lawn herbicides can't be good for little soil critters—the soil microbes and earthworms that aerate soil and release nutrients to plant roots.

And what about power mowers? We have gas mowers that belch pollutants and consume fossil fuel onsite. And we have electric mowers responsible for those same impacts elsewhere on the grid. Besides, the heavier the mower, the greater the soil compaction and the greater the need for soil-aerating machinery. These big machines help us avoid walking vigorously as doctors prescribe—in this case behind a good old-fashioned, leg-powered mower.

My drive-by surveys suggest that the larger the self-mowed lawn, the greater the operator's weight problem. For exercise, health spas charge more per month than an old-fashioned push mower costs per lifetime. Besides, a quiet, old-fashioned mower can give anyone with the strength of a 12-year-old as much exercise per hour as a spa can—and without requiring that we drive somewhere to access the exercise.

Let's not even consider the untold hours and dollars wasted in shopping for lawn chemicals and machinery, let alone in monster-mowing itself.

scavengers that are pleased to notice our offers of shelter as well.

■ *Vehicles:* Mice disable gas engines in mowers, lawn tractors, and road vehicles. They do this either by chewing through wiring or building nests inside air-filter casings. Clogged engine filters in mowers cause ragged operation and overheating that can crack engine blocks and start fires. Mouse urine corrodes engine parts. And airborne mouse "dust" circulated by air vents into a car's passenger compartment can carry the hantavirus, considered deadly by the US Centers for Disease Control and Prevention (CDC).

A CASE FOR TOLERANCE

A territorial mammal that causes only minor lawn or garden damage can help you exclude mammals that cause worse damage. For example, moles are fiercely territorial and drive off or kill their own kind. They also kill mice and voles encountered while tunneling. Besides, mole trapping often results in recolonization, and this can begin futile continuing efforts that yield only temporary relief from ridges and molehills. Instead, here are options that make tunnelings and turf turnings less noticeable, while also improving your environment and the world's.

Mowing higher. The simple act of setting your mower's blades to a 4-inch height can give you an attractive lawn, while improving lawn health. Taller grass can also conceal chipmunk holes and mole ridges, as well as the minor turf turnings of skunks, opossums, and raccoons. Meanwhile, higher mowing lets grass shade the soil, reducing the need for watering that results in shallowly rooted grass that can't tolerate drought. Taller grass can also compete better with emerging weeds. Even so, increased tolerance of lawn "weeds" can eliminate the need for herbicides and improve microbial health in the soil that releases nutrients to grass roots. Besides, many so-called lawn weeds, such as violet blooms and dandelion greens, can improve a spring salad.

Reducing lawn size. In his book *Bringing Nature Home: How Native Plants Sustain Wildlife in Our Gardens,* Douglas Tallamy, PhD, chairman of the department of entomology and wildlife ecology at the University of Delaware in Newark, reports that lawns in America occupy a land area equivalent to eight New Jerseys. Golly, if even half of that lawn area were planted with a variety of native plants, there'd be substantially less lawn susceptible to damage by moles, skunks, opossums, and raccoons. Besides, that would be the equivalent land area of four New Jerseys suddenly consuming no herbicides or fossil fuels and no longer causing air pollution or contaminating soil and water.

Planting for biodiversity. As Tallamy points out, plant diversity invites animal diversity. The caterpillars of native butterflies and moths (lepidopterans) represent half of all insects in North America, and they are especially important to birds feeding their young. Yet largely because of lawns, islands of native plants have become separated while shrinking in size. As a result, many native insects have too little food, causing some to recently become extinct, while others are threatened with extinction. In spite of his alarming message, Tallamy also offers hope, as described on page 223.

Fencing, repellents, and frighteners. Aside from mowing higher and shrinking our lawns, tolerance of mammals—within limits—can be expressed with judicious use of fences as well as barriers around prize plants. Tolerance can also be expressed in scent and taste repellents, commercial and homemade. Some electronic frighteners can help, as can dogs of the right temperament and training.

Aside from the options in the preceding paragraphs, our choices begin narrowing to livetrapping or resorting to lethal measures.

ISSUES OF CONTROL

Based solely on health and fire hazards, there's little reason to tolerate rodents inside the house or raccoons in the attic. Nor should we tolerate skunks, raccoons, or ground squirrels under our house foundation. Nor do we need to tolerate a black bear sleeping under the deck. One such bear in the Lake Tahoe region was discovered by a real estate agent whose car keys had fallen through

Use doubled plastic bags to pick up dead rodents. Then turn the bags inside out to enclose the rodent before sealing.

deck boards. I haven't heard if the agent changed professions.

All such mammals can be excluded before they show up. Or they can be driven out or livetrapped, and thereafter prevented from returning. You'll find options for dealing with specific mammals at the end of each of the following chapters.

Remember, before considering livetrapping or lethal measures, it's worth asking yourself this question: "Am I offering these critters food and shelter needlessly? If so, would removal of one or both solve or greatly reduce my problem?"

When options are limited to livetrapping and lethal measures, it's wise to evaluate your equipment and skills relative to those of professionals.

DO-IT-YOURSELF TRAPPING

As for trapping, do-it-yourselfers sometimes know the risks to themselves and their families—and sometimes not.

Lethal trapping. Most households have someone willing to set traps for mice and rats. Yet few households realize related disease risks, which include hantavirus, typhus, and plague. Discovered in 1993, hantavirus pulmonary syndrome is transmitted mainly by airborne (aerosolized) particles of mouse feces, urine, fur, and saliva. Typhus and plague are bacterial diseases transmitted mainly by rodents' fleas. After a flea's host dies, the flea eagerly

Treating Bites

Clean bites and scratches promptly with soap and water. All bites deserve prompt examination by a physician. Puncture wounds tend to be most dangerous.

jumps to the first warm mammal that comes along, be it rodent or human. Similar health issues arise when trapping other mammals. These concerns dictate that we protect our hands and lungs when handling dead animals.

Livetrapping. People who oppose lethal trapping tend to employ live traps and then release the mammals to the wild. However, state and provincial law may ban relocation because livetrapped mammals can transmit parasites and diseases to healthy populations and because released mammals can upset existing ecosystems.

Besides, studies show that released mammals often suffer more than they would if immediately euthanized. Here are common fates of released animals:

- Death from trap-and-transport stress
- Death from predators in unfamiliar habitat
- Death or severe wounding from territorial members of their own species
- Death from starvation in unfamiliar habitat
- Death from exposure to cold, heat, or drought
- Reinfestation of human dwellings elsewhere
- Return to your property, based on strong homing instincts. Even though a released mouse might not beat you home, released mice have returned home from more than a mile away. In this case, you would have little means of knowing that you were dealing with a returning customer.

Note: If you are determined to release rodents of any kind, check with your wildlife jurisdiction first. For example, the Arizona Fish and Game Department requests that livetrapped squirrels be released at designated sites, which may change from time to time. Never transport rodents inside your car's passenger compartment or trunk, which would increase your risk of breathing airborne pathogens, even if you've figured out how to sequester and dispose of urine and droppings.

Then, too, there's the question of contracting flea-borne diseases.

Licensed wildlife rehabilitators: Licensed individuals and organizations in your region might be willing to accept mammals that you live-trap. Some accept only particular species, such as squirrels, opossums, raccoons, skunks, deer fawns, or some combination. Thus, it's good to investigate options before setting live traps. Veterinary clinics often maintain a list of wildlife rehabilitators. For a listing of many state and provincial associations, visit the National Wildlife Rehabilitators Association at nwrawildlife.org. If that listing doesn't address your region, an Internet search using state/province name, municipality, and these key words should help you locate nearby rehabilitators: *wildlife, rehabilitator, rescue.*

Many rehabilitators are volunteers associated with veterinary clinics and/or large landowners who allow releases. Regarding nursing babies, rehabilitators caution against giving babies anything but water until the rehabilitator can provide milk formulated with protein and fat percentages appropriate for that species. For example, cow's milk and human baby formula can kill deer fawns. Cow's milk is only about one-third as rich as deer milk.

Nuisance wildlife control professionals: States, provinces, and even municipalities grant licenses to qualified nuisance wildlife controllers. The term *nuisance wildlife* generally excludes game animals such as deer and bear, as well as furbearers,

Latex gloves, bite-proof gauntlet gloves, lasso catchpole, and tong-style cat grasper (wildlifecontrolsupplies.com)

such as beavers and muskrats. For game animals and furbearers, there are usually official hunting or trapping seasons. Some wildlife controllers may agree to help you address mice and rats. Others may instead suggest using a pest-control firm.

In my state of New York, licensed wildlife controllers have passed a written test based on an impressive study manual developed by Cornell University and the Department of Environmental Conservation (DEC). The manual addresses topics such as laws, wildlife behavior, damage, animal tracks, diseases, and control options.

To find professional controllers in your town, contact your local police or look in the Yellow Pages directory. There's also a state-by-state listing at animalremovalpro.com, where you can search by zip code. If you browse the Internet, these search words should work: *state/province name* and then combinations of *wildlife, control, animal, nuisance, removal.*

Professional wildlife controllers often give free phone advice for minor problems. But they usually charge for a visit and assessment, as well as a written estimate. Services might include trapping as well as eviction and exclusion work, such as sealing house openings and installing chimney caps. There's often a surcharge for emergencies, defined as wildlife in your living quarters.

Livetrapping caveat: State and provincial law may forbid transport of some or all wildlife beyond the property on which it was trapped—this for multiple reasons listed in the previous section on livetrapping. Licensed pros know the laws and may honor your wishes to deliver animals to authorized release sites or to a licensed wildlife rehabilitator. However, law may require that specific mammals be euthanized onsite.

The pros I've interviewed have found that animal removal is usually only a temporary fix. The goal is to eliminate food, if that's the attractant, as well as shelter. After removal, the pros seal off access.

Following are excerpts from interviews with wildlife control operators in southern New York State:

■ For most mammals, Tony DeBonis, of Wildlife Control Services in Millbrook, New York, prefers

not to use bait because "baiting can attract all the skunks or raccoons in the neighborhood." Instead, he positions unbaited live traps so animals must pass through them when entering or exiting their burrows. As part of his preventive service, he also installs chimney caps with metal grills that exclude raccoons and squirrels while keeping out rain and snow that can damage flues during freeze-thaw cycles. DeBonis says lawsuits can result when people sell their houses without informing the buyer that critters are in the attic. So real-estate companies may now request wildlife inspections.

■ Colin Burgess, of Mid-Hudson Wildlife Management in Hyde Park, New York, says spring is his busy time for skunks, which complete their stinky mating period in early March and give birth in May. By June, mother skunks lead their babies over lawns, where they grub for earthworms and insect larvae, sometimes sending scent through open windows. If skunks nest under a porch, Burgess tries to livetrap entire families and release them together. His most interesting assignment began as a routine call to investigate "raccoon sounds" in a cellar, as recounted on page 138. Quite a story!

■ Besides knowledge of wildlife, Dermot O'Connor, of Critter Control in Beekman, New York, credits his earlier experience in house construction in helping him diagnose problems and propose solutions. These include animal removal as well as vital follow-up exclusion measures—sealing gaps, plugging holes, and installing flashing and mesh barriers around porches and decks.

Though his advice is outside the focus of this book, O'Connor cautions against feeding or handling stray cats, which aren't considered controllable wildlife and can't legally be handled by dog control officers. Stray cats, he says, are a prime vector of rabies, along with raccoons, skunks, and bats. In a recent case in his area, 20 people were required to get rabies vaccinations after handling a sick kitten that turned out to have rabies. Of course, if all people ensured that their cats and kittens were "fixed" and wormed and vaccinated—

and never dropped off to fend for themselves—the rabies problem would be far smaller.

LEAST INHUMANE DEATH

For mammals other than deer and bear, most jurisdictions allow lethal control of mammals that dam-age crops or property. The authorizing phrase for lethal control is often worded "by any legal means."

Regarding rodent control, the US Humane Society Web site implies that health concerns, fire hazards, and other risks justify lethal measures with this wording: "In considering the arsenal of lethal

---

Poison Baits

Each year, thousands of children and many thousands of dogs accidentally ingest rodent poison. As a result, some manufacturers have attempted to reduce appeal to children and pets by adding "bittering" agents. Although some poisons smell unpleasantly pungent to me, others don't. I haven't conducted taste tests.

Most states require a license for use of fast-acting pesticides, such as zinc phosphide. Without a license, the only options are slow-acting poisons available at supermarkets. These include either anticoagulants, which require multiple feedings, or compounds such as bromethalin that require only one feeding.

Anticoagulants thin the blood, resulting in internal bleeding. With safety of children and pets in mind, rodent anticoagulants are formulated in small enough doses to be slow acting. The assumption regarding safety is that symptoms in children and pets can be addressed by doses of vitamin K_1, if administered in time.

Bromethalin causes fluid buildups in the brain and spinal cord and is advertised to cause rodent death in 1 to 3 days, depending on dosage.

For use outdoors, manufacturers recommend par-affinized bait blocks, rather than pellets, because the bait blocks are relatively water- and heat-resistant and can be secured within bait stations that make removal and dissemination less likely than with small pellets.

Here are key reasons why I don't advocate poisons:

■ **Inhumane:** Poisons are slow acting, causing untold suffering over extended periods.

■ **Nontarget hazards:** The baits can be consumed by nontarget animals, including children and pets.

■ **Secondary poisoning:** The poisoned carcass itself can be consumed by other species, possibly resulting in secondary poisoning. At times, small rodents represent a major portion of some predators' diets. Defenders of anticoagulants suggest that predators and scavengers would need to consume a large number of poisoned rodents before suffering ill effects. I've not been able to locate reassuring, independent reports on the secondary hazards of any poison.

■ **Disease hazards:** The slow-acting poisons available to consumers give rodents time to go off and die in walls or in hidden places, distributing pathogens, fleas, and other parasites throughout your house—all before you notice the unmistakable odor of death. If you don't yet know what a dead rodent smells like, you will after it dies in your home!

■ **Handling hazards:** Poison manufacturers warn against breathing poisonous dust and getting poison on your clothes. If you accidentally touch bait with your bare fingers, one manufacturer of bromethalin advises, "Rinse skin immediately with plenty of water for 15 to 20 minutes . . . Call a Poison Control Center, doctor, or [the manufacturer]."

Caveat: If you are determined to resort to poisons in spite of the above concerns, here are tips that may help reduce hazards. Heed package warnings and instructions, which usually recommend placing bait blocks inside childproof and pet-proof bait stations, and otherwise keeping stored poisons safely locked away from children. Also, keep the packaging available, in the event a child or pet falls victim and needs to be rushed to a doctor or vet. (For more on these issues, see "Poisons" in the rats and mice chapter, on page 160.)

methods available for rodent control, the bottom line is that none are completely humane in their modes of action, but some inflict less suffering than others. Therefore if rodents must be killed in a given situation, it is far preferable that the least inhumane methods are used."

But what's least inhumane?

■ I oppose the use of toxic baits for reasons enumerated in "Poison Baits" on the opposite page. I've seen the effects of an anticoagulant on a mouse that had become pathetically disoriented and appeared to be in a world of hurt. The effects of bromethalin must be at least as inhumane.

■ For small rodents such as mice, voles, and rats, spring-activated snap traps cause sudden cervical dislocation (broken neck just behind the skull). This seems to provide the quickest and least inhumane mechanical dispatch of rodents. However, snap traps are less merciful when the rodent isn't struck precisely as designed. In addition, as snap traps increase beyond mouse size, they need greater force and thus pose threats to nontarget wildlife, as well as pets and children. For snap traps, protective housings called bait stations help prevent entry of nontarget animals, as shown on page 156.

■ Various lethal traps for moles, gophers, squirrels, and raccoons create chest-squeezing force that suffocates the animal—likely causing some pain and suffering—sometimes brief, sometimes prolonged.

■ Licensing jurisdictions for wildlife control officers may encourage livetrapping initially, followed with euthanasia by any of several means:

1. Injection of a lethal dose of barbiturate

2. Asphyxiation by release of CO_2 (carbon dioxide gas) into a container enclosing the live trap

3. Firing a small-caliber bullet or air-powered pellet into the animal's brain

4. Stunning and chest compression

However, if you are a determined do-it-yourselfer *with legal right and lethal intent,* none of the sanctioned lethal means above seems to me as humane as euthanasia by drowning. That is, our own best hospitals cannot guarantee our loved ones as painless or quick a death. As one who nearly drowned at age seven, I can assure you that the experience is physically painless. In this case, physical effort to reach air soon gives way to unconsciousness.

Animals don't connect confinement with euthanasia. Until being immersed, their great terror—with related stress—is trap confinement and fear of visible humans. Water immersion removes those fears. Instead, the animal gasps briefly for air as its lungs quickly fill with water, followed by painless unconsciousness.

When you compare gentle immersion and drowning with the stress and pain an animal experiences during a fight with a rival, pain isn't an issue. Nor is euthanasia by drowning nearly as stressful as being torn to bits by coonhounds or suffering several misplaced shots from a nervously held firearm. Drowning doesn't even inflict the painful prick of a needle that our pets feel when we ask our veterinarians to put them down.

Steps for Euthanasia by Drowning

1. After livetrapping or before, cover the trap with a dark plastic garbage bag so the mammal can't see you. Covering has a calming effect.

2. Immerse the trap completely into a plastic-lined trench filled with water deeper than the trap height.

3. Weight the trap down. In this situation, the mammal's lungs will fill with water almost immediately, followed quickly by unconsciousness. Because mammals, like people, can survive painlessly unconscious for many minutes underwater, it's wise to wait at least an hour before burying the remains or placing them in a sturdy garbage bag for removal.

4. Thereafter, soak the live trap in a disinfectant solution, followed by drying in full sunlight.

CHAPTER 3

Armadillos

(*officially* Nine-Banded Armadillos)

Distant relatives of anteaters and sloths, nine-banded armadillos have poor eyesight and need to rely largely on their noses to locate food. As a result, they may blunder upon and sniff the boots of motionless observers. Yet even though these curious-looking critters seem to wander aimlessly, they remain well oriented and know the exact direction of their nearest burrow.

"When highly alarmed, armadillos leap vertically into the air like a bucking horse before charging off to the burrow. This sudden upward leap may startle a predator enough to give the armadillo a head start in escaping," writes James Layne, PhD, research biologist emeritus at the Archbold Biological Station in Lake Placid, Florida. His armadillo chapter in Johns Hopkins University's monumental *Wild Mammals of North America* provided most of the background for this chapter.

Armadillos grub for small creatures and slurp them up with their long, sticky tongue. (Photo by Lennie and Uschi Rue III)

PROBLEMS FOR PEOPLE

In some states, armadillos generate about 10 percent of wildlife nuisance complaints. Why?

Using strong legs with formidable claws, armadillos forage for insects by digging soil pits to 6-inch depths in lawns and gardens. This also leaves heaps of excavated earth. On slopes, the excavations can promote erosion.

An armadillo may dig 10 or more separate burrows, some with multiple entrances. Burrows average 3 to 4 feet deep but may run more than 20 feet long. Thus, burrows can undermine houses and outbuildings, while posing hazards to livestock whose hooves could break through.

In addition to excavations, armadillos open cantaloupes and eat the fruit. They also rise on their hind legs to reach low-hanging fruit such as grapes. And they eat the eggs of sea turtles and ground-nesting birds, such as quail.

During a 7-year study of mammal roadkills in central Florida, armadillos were the most frequent mortalities. Armadillo roadkills peak during summer when the mating travel of males is highest. Ironically, many vehicles would pass over the armadillos without hitting them were it not for the armadillo's tendency to jump up when startled.

ROLE IN THE WILD

Armadillos use their long sticky tongues to slurp up insect adults and larvae, millipedes, snails, leeches, and earthworms, as well as small amphibians and reptiles. In the process, they also ingest large amounts of soil, leaf litter, and decaying wood. They relish termites and ants, and seem unfazed by the

Order: Cingulata (formerly Xenarthra) ■ **Family:** DASYPODIDAE ■ **Genus:** *Dasypus* ■ **Species:** *novemcinctus*

stings of fire ants. In an Alabama study, armadillos had disturbed every accessible fire-ant mound.

Armadillo burrows provide homes for insects, spiders, and centipedes and are sometimes used by cottontail rabbits, rodents, skunks, mink, snakes, and burrowing owls. Occasionally, researchers find an armadillo sharing its burrow with an opossum or a rabbit. Female armadillos sometimes share burrows with each other, too.

Yet, where drainage isn't good, or in captivity, armadillos build haystacklike surface nests of tall grasses that appear to have been dumped from a wheelbarrow. In Florida, armadillos are the principal fare of black bears. Other predators include cougars, coyotes, dogs, foxes, and raccoons. Youngsters fall prey to hawks, owls, and feral pigs. Interestingly, bobcats don't seem to favor armadillos and may give up stalking something that they only heard when they discover that an armadillo was the source of the noise.

SPECIES AND DISTRIBUTION

Among species of nine-banded armadillos in the Americas, only the subspecies *mexicanus* ranges northward into the United States. Unlike other species, the nine-banded cannot roll up in a ball but can curl somewhat to protect its soft underparts.

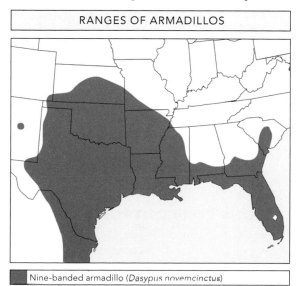

RANGES OF ARMADILLOS

Nine-banded armadillo (*Dasypus novemcinctus*)

What's in a Name?

The common name, *armadillo*, is Spanish, meaning "little armored one." The carapace, or shell, is segmented and consists of seven to ten, but usually nine, overlapping bandlike plates, thus the name "nine-banded armadillo." Latin roots in the species name include *novem*, meaning "nine," and *cinctus*, meaning "girdle," not far in meaning from "banded."

Although the nine-banded armadillo is established only in the Southeast, its range represents a tremendous expansion that began in south Texas in the late 1800s. From Texas, the population expanded eastward and northward and was eventually joined by an expanding population introduced to south Florida prior to 1922. Levees and raised roadbeds in the southern coastal states facilitated expansion.

Armadillos need the types of foods found in moist soils. And, in dry conditions, they can't conserve water well. So their westward expansion will probably continue to be limited by the aridity of west Texas and New Mexico. And because armadillos can't tolerate extended cold below 39°F, their northward expansion will likely await the pace of global warming.

IDENTIFICATION

An armadillo's head-and-body length is 15 to 22 inches, and its tail is 10 to 16 inches. Males weigh 12 to 17 pounds, females about 25 percent less.

The body-protecting carapace suggests a turtle with a highly arched back, although with coarsely hairy underarms. The narrow, funnel-shaped head has a piglike snout. Of the overlapping grayish brown bony plates, the shoulder plate and the rump plate are the largest. Many of the small scales are yellowish brown.

Carapace inner plates allow a degree of body flexing that only an intoxicated Olympic judge would describe as gymnastic. The tail's 12 to 15 overlapping rings gradually decrease in size toward the tip and appear about as delectable as armor-clad electrical cable.

SENSITIVITY TO WEATHER

Armadillos can't tolerate temperature extremes. Although burrows and nests provide protection from predators, they also insulate their maker from heat and cold. In fact, if exposed to extended temperatures in the 30s, armadillos can't survive. As to heat aversion, armadillos prefer not to leave their burrows when daytime temperatures exceed 85°F, and this partially explains their largely nocturnal foraging in warm months. In winter, armadillos forage more during the day, likely because they prefer the warmer temperatures and because warmed soil promotes more insect activity.

Although undeterred by rain, lightning, and thunder, armadillos are less willing to travel during windy conditions, which likely carry confusing scents and sounds. After snowfall, armadillos might not venture out for several days.

SENSES

An armadillo's small eyes can distinguish movements but aren't keen. So armadillos rely primarily on their noses to find food and follow scent marks. But they also have keen hearing. For example, pairs of armadillos can distinguish their own rustlings from intentional slight rustlings made by researchers—and thereupon either resume foraging, hide themselves partially, or dash off.

HOME RANGE AND SIGN

Home range. This averages about 10 acres, depending on habitat, and tends to be smaller in moist areas that offer better forage. Males travel more widely during the June through November breeding season and thereby become more vulnerable to vehicles.

Sign. Although armadillos have four front toes and five back ones, usually only two front claws and three back claws register birdlike tracks. Pits up to about 6 inches deep are usually found in moist soil. Droppings are the size and shape of marbles and are composed of partially digested insects and soil, as well as plant litter.

The carapace affords protection from some predators. Note the hairy "armpits." (Photo by Lennie and Uschi Rue III)

Burrow openings are semicircular, and you can often see the distinctive droppings and old nesting material that the animal has removed from its burrow. In flatter grasslands, armadillos may instead construct haystacklike surface nests of tall grass.

MATING AND REPRODUCTION

Breeding occurs June through November, but most is carried out in summer. The female lies on her back during these rites. First-time females come into estrus later than their mothers. Timing may also be delayed by drought.

Unique among mammals, armadillo females produce only one egg a year. When it is fertilized, it divides into four identical embryo quadruplets that are either female or male. That is, babies are clones based on division of the same inner cell mass. As a result, the babies are highly valued in medical research.

Gestation takes 8 to 9 months, and births occur from February through July. The young begin accompanying Mom after 2 or 3 months and are self-sufficient in 3 or 4 months.

OPTIONS FOR CONTROL

In some states, armadillos are considered invasive alien pests and so can be hunted and trapped year-

Researchers may lift youngsters as shown but turn adults onto their backs, wary of flailing claws. (Photo © Francois Savigny/ naturepl.com)

This youngster welcomes release. Live traps for adults should measure at least 10 × 10 × 36 inches. (Photo © Joyce and Frank Burek/Animals Animals Enterprises)

round. Many people consider the meat tasty. But check your state laws first.

Exclusion. In spite of their cumbersome appearance, armadillos can climb low livestock fences. Yet even low fencing of various types tends to guide these dim-sighted critters elsewhere.

Livetrapping. Researchers often stalk feeding armadillos from behind to capture them either by hand or with a long-handled net. Your state may discourage or prohibit transport and relocation, so check state law.

■ *Hand capture:* Although armadillos do not bite when handled, their flailing claws can inflict serious scratches. Researchers dexterously grab the base of the tail with one hand, overturning the animal, and support the carapace with the other.

■ *Long-handled net capture:* For most of us, this makes more sense than hand capture.

■ *Livetrapping:* Baits aren't usually effective, so researchers first locate an occupied den. They position the open end of the live trap at the den opening, requiring the armadillo to attempt to exit through the trap. If the trap can't be placed against the burrow opening, two wooden 2 × 6s positioned on the ground vertically can funnel the

armadillo into the trap. Traps should measure at least 10 × 10 × 36 inches.

Hunting and lethal trapping. Check your state laws.

COMMUNICABLE DISEASES AND PARASITES

Leprosy. Armadillos are susceptible to the bacilli *Mycobacterium leprae* that causes leprosy in humans, and this has led to alarmed misconceptions about armadillos and leprosy. Today, health authorities prefer to call leprosy Hansen's disease, perhaps to help dispel the stigmas of the traditional name. For more on Hansen's disease, see page 210.

Viruses. Virtually all mammals can contract rabies. With the incidence of rabies in armadillos exceedingly rare, further good news is that armadillos don't bite. Armadillos have been implicated in encephalitis outbreaks in Florida.

Parasites. Compared to raccoons, opossums, and skunks, armadillos have a relatively low incidence of parasites.

Fungal diseases. Because armadillos root around in moist soils, they ingest many soil fungi that can lead to yeast infections that also occur in other mammals, including humans.

CHAPTER 4

Bears (Black)

Black bears inhabit 39 states and 11 provinces. Along the California-Nevada border in the Lake Tahoe Basin, black bears routinely raid bird feeders, barbecues, garbage cans, berry bushes, and fruit trees. They sometimes also den under porches and break into houses after having first identified the refrigerator through the kitchen window. Although the Tahoe Basin's public officials and residents agree on most methods for reducing bear problems, they disagree on a few others, addressed later in this chapter.

Along the Tennessee-North Carolina border, in Great Smoky Mountains National Park, staff had trouble reducing bear-human conflicts until a veterinarian's examinations led to dental treatment that greatly reduced bear scavenging.

In northern Minnesota, black bears behave much like bears in the Tahoe Basin. In all parts of the United States and Canada, black bears respond to the same kinds of encouragement and the same kinds of discouragement, as we shall see. After all, black bears are black bears—not to be confused with grizzlies.

Brown and cinnamon-colored black bears are often mistaken for grizzlies. (Photo by Lennie and Uschi Rue III)

SPECIES, DISTRIBUTION, AND DISTINCTIONS

North America has three bear species: the black bear (*Ursus americanus*), the polar bear (*U. maritimus*), and the grizzly bear (*U. arctos*).

This chapter will focus almost entirely on black bears because they are far more likely to pose challenges for homeowners than their larger cousins. Polar bears live beyond the geographic scope of this book—and that is largely true for virtually all grizzlies, too. For the most part, grizzlies inhabit

Boars and Sows

Technically, male bears are called *boars* and female bears are called *sows*, which to me suggests an association with swine that isn't appropriate for these magnificent animals. So I'll stick with *males* and *females*—and sometimes *mothers*. Father bears are known for certain only in fairy tales.

Order: Carnivora ■ **Family:** URSIDAE ■ **Genus:** *Ursus* ■ **Species:** *americanus*

RANGES OF BEARS

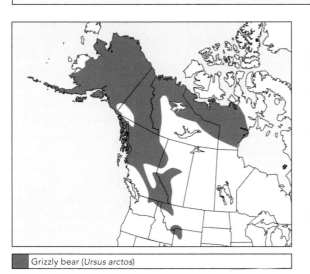

Grizzly bear (*Ursus arctos*)

Black bear (*Ursus americanus*)

undeveloped regions of the western provinces and Alaska. In the Lower 48 states, remnant populations occur mostly in western Montana and Wyoming, although some descend into northern Idaho and Washington State. Still, grizzlies will receive occasional mention to illustrate distinctions from black bears both in appearance and behaviors. And many of the same deterrents for black bears can be effective for grizzlies.

Distinguishing black bears from grizzlies. Color isn't always a reliable feature. In some parts of the West, only about half of the black bears are black. There black bears can instead be brown, to cinnamon, to blond. Although grizzly fur tends to be middle-brown, it can range from blond to dark brown to nearly black. Some grizzlies have silver-tipped guard hairs that looked "grizzled" to early explorers, thus the name *grizzly*. So physical shapes are more reliable distinguishers.

■ *Body shapes:* From the side, the grizzly has a prominent shoulder hump, whereas the black bear has a more prominent rump.

Grizzlies have a prominent shoulder hump. Black bears instead have a straight shoulder and prominent rump. The grizzly's face looks "dished-in" with prominent "eyebrows" and broad forehead, compared to the black bear's straighter face and conical head. With forepaw raised, 4-inch-long grizzly claws capture one's attention. (Drawings adapted by Anthony Serge from the Glacier National Park Web site)

■ *Head features:* The grizzly has a prominent broad forehead, and its facial profile is dished-in, usually with uniformly colored facial fur and cheeks. The black bear's head is more conical from ears to nose. And its usually beige snout contrasts sharply when the bear's other fur is black, brown, or cinnamon. Some black bears have white chest patches.

■ *Claws:* When a grizzly walks or rears up, its relatively straight front claws of up to 4 inches long show prominently. The black bear's shorter claws (up to 1¼ inches long) are more curved and less noticeable, but they are ideally adapted for climbing tree trunks as a means of escaping danger and for foraging. Although young grizzlies can climb vertical tree trunks, they gradually lose their climbing ability as their claw length and body weight increase.

■ *Weights:* In any given locale, polar, grizzly, and black bear males tend to weigh 20 to 50 percent more than females of the same age. Even though the black bear has the smallest bone structure of the continent's three bear species, it can reach weights exceeding those of adult grizzlies with less favorable diets.

Here are rough weight comparisons: Adult black bears from north to south normally weigh

Black-bear incurved 1-inch claws are ideally adapted for tree-climbing, escape, and foraging. (Photo by Lennie and Uschi Rue III)

100 to 400 pounds; whopper males exceed 600 pounds. Although male polar bears routinely weigh 1,000 pounds, whoppers exceed 1,500 pounds. Adult grizzlies vary more widely in weight, depending on regional diet. For example, along salmon-rich coastal Alaska, where grizzlies are commonly called brown bears, average adult males approach 800 pounds. Yet, inland male grizzlies of the same age must depend heavily on a plant diet and so tend to weigh less than half as much as their coastal brethren.

PROBLEMS FOR PEOPLE

Black bears are powerful, and some have maimed and even killed people. But black bears aren't naturally aggressive toward adult humans. In fact, they are considered the least predatory of all North American carnivores. Wilderness black bears tend to be shy of humans, usually retreating before we see them, and otherwise climbing trees when frightened. As Lynn Rogers, PhD, principal biologist at the Wildlife Research Institute in Ely, Minnesota, explains, the retreating instinct helped black bears survive the Ice Age when their enemies were huge "saber-toothed cats, dire wolves, American lions, and giant short-faced bears—none of which could climb trees." Today, black bears also escape larger grizzlies by climbing.

Although deep-woods black bears usually avoid people, bears learn quickly whether human foods come easily or accompanied by threats and pain. Many people feed bears unwittingly by attracting them to garbage, barbecues, birdseed, car-stored foods, and aromatic kitchens. To avoid us while enjoying our offerings, bears often switch from normal daytime foraging to nighttime foraging.

Bear-human confrontations usually involve bears that have grown accustomed to people—especially bears that have been intentionally fed, even hand-fed. Such bears begin to feel welcome and increasingly confident near people—a recipe for misunderstandings.

From great distances, a bear's keen sense of smell can direct the bear to whatever we unwit-

Bears can smell unsealed human foods from great distances, whether at campsites or around homes. (Photo by Lynn Rogers)

tingly offer. Black bears learn that bear-size vertical containers can be tipped over to offer a wide range of taste delights. Bears learn to spot unfinished bowls of pet food. And they learn that little hanging structures of varied shapes contain seeds of great variety. To reach some seed containers, bears climb stairs to large wooden platforms where they hear loud house noises sounding like, "He's on the DECK!"

From there, bears may investigate the garden. In summer, bears learn that vines, shrubs, and low-branching trees dangle sweet-tasting things. Bears learn to like apples, pears, peaches, cherries, plums, and grapes. And they relish seeing berries even more abundant than they've encountered in the wild. When black bears weighing 200 pounds or more climb young fruit trees, branches break and trees tip sideways.

Car owners sometimes find a door torn open and the unfinished doughnuts that were inside gone. Bears in the Tahoe Basin have shown an ability to open car doors using the handles, like humans. But when the door closes, trapping them inside, the bears don't bother to figure out indoor exit handles. Also, to investigate food smells emanating from car trunks, bears have broken into passenger compartments before tearing through backseats.

Beekeepers find their hives smashed and the honey gone. Livestock owners find barn doors open and sheep, goats, and calves gone.

All of this is exacerbated in years of natural food shortages, occasioned either by drought or a late frost that resulted in poor berry and nut crops.

ROLE IN THE WILD

In the wild, black bears need to survive principally as vegetarians, though not necessarily by choice. Although black bears are considered carnivores, they aren't nimble enough to catch most prey, other than stationary or slow-moving creatures, such as fawns in hiding, the young of ground-nesting birds, and the Southeast's dim-eyed armadillo. Male bears will sometimes kill and eat undefended bear cubs.

For protein, black bears eat carrion but depend more heavily on insect protein. They raid the nests of colonial insects, such as ants, bees, and hornets. In Minnesota, Lynn Rogers found that tent caterpillars become a favored food in years when they hatch in June. During one 24-hour walk with a small trusting mother bear, Rogers kept count as she ate 25,192 tent caterpillars—equivalent, he estimates, to roughly 7 gallons, or 31 pounds.

In Michigan, wildlife biologist Terry DeBruyn, PhD, found that meat protein, at one period, represented only 5 percent of one bear's diet, while ant protein made up 10 percent.

PERSONAL PERSPECTIVES

In 1948, along the north shore of Lake Superior, my hometown of Two Harbors experienced an unprecedented invasion of black bears (which Rogers tells me was repeated in 1985). Forest managers blamed the invasion on a dry summer that resulted in poor berry and nut crops. Scores of starving bruins assaulted the town's garbage cans, berry bushes, apple trees, and bird feeders.

I was just 5 years old then, but I vividly recall night sounds of garbage cans rolling thunderously down our alley. Although most bear activity occurred at night, daytime sightings were common.

■ Eight-year-old cousin Kathy had just descended from an apple tree with her T-shirt serving like an apple pouch when the sounds of men yelling in the alley preceded the sudden appearance of a black bear running toward Kathy. She didn't stop running until she'd reached our house, three blocks away, without her apples.

■ After kindergarten one day, I approached a crowd under a large silver maple on a street corner. Adults were gawking upward at a frightened bear cub. Under the maple, the distressed police chief was urging us to disperse. But at that moment, the little cub released the wet contents of its large intestine directly onto the chief. When we kids giggled, the chief's glare sent us packing.

■ But it was the kids with predawn paper routes who benefited most. They enjoyed the luxury of being driven around so they could toss rolled newspapers in the vicinity of front porches.

■ Neighbor Dickie Jenkins screamed when a bear dashed from under his back steps. Soon after, I watched with Dickie and his parents at the town outskirts as smiling town policemen fired .38 revolvers at long range, occasionally hitting that small bear. They didn't bother to walk out to determine if they'd finished him. That fall, town police felt they had to shoot other bears, too.

■ In the subsequent 1985 food shortage in northern Minnesota, starving bears headed southward along Lake Superior's shore toward Duluth at the lake's westernmost tip, perhaps somehow knowing of oak stands on the lake shore in northern Wisconsin. However, the large city of Duluth blocked their way. That fall outside Duluth, 90 bears were killed, according to Lynn Rogers, the Man Who Walks with Bears.

THE MAN WHO WALKS WITH BEARS

In 1969, near the town of Ely in northeastern Minnesota, Lynn Rogers began what would become the most extensive, longest-running black bear study ever conducted. Over the years, Rogers has published more than 100 widely cited scientific papers. He's written and been featured in countless

magazine articles and has been on radio and TV, most memorably perhaps on *Animal Planet*'s documentary "The Man Who Walks with Bears." At this writing, documentaries are in development with the BBC, the History Channel, and ESPN.

Rogers's work is often compared to that of Jane Goodall on chimpanzees and Dian Fossey on gorillas. Like Fossey, Rogers is no stranger to physical risks and local controversy. Rogers writes, "I'm continuing to study the bear-human interface to better understand how bears and people can coexist. Improving public understanding of bears is the key to coexistence and healthy bear populations." He's especially eager to point out misinformation in outdoors magazines that depict black bears as "savage beasts." At his Wildlife Research Institute museum, Rogers displays such magazine covers.

By phone years ago, Rogers told me he began his study with hopes of using radio telemetry to track bears from the air and on foot. But to do that, he first needed to fit bears with radio collars. He especially wanted to track mother bears with

As with other research bears, Dr. Lynn Rogers formed a trusting bond with 876-pound Duffy who allowed comradely travel for 24-hour periods––Duffy feasting, Rogers fasting. (Photo by Donna Rogers, wife of Lynn Rogers)

cubs, which he hoped would allow him to record family histories through generations.

Yet rather than using a rifle to "dart" bears with tranquilizers, Rogers pioneered a method that few mortals at that time would have attempted. Rogers snowshoed looking for den sites, which are often revealed by a small air hole in the snow. Upon finding a den, Rogers used a flashlight to confirm the presence of a mother bear with cubs. Then, fully aware that hibernating bears rouse easily, Rogers crawled inside headfirst with a tranquilizing syringe.

When I asked whether headfirst entry wasn't dangerous, Rogers explained that most mammals establish dominance by means of body language and threat display. So by crawling in headfirst, he showed dominance, causing the mother bear to cower. When I asked if he didn't worry that the mother would panic and tear his head off, Rogers said he always leaves room in the den opening for the mother to run out "if she gets scared."

With the mother cowering, Rogers would reach forward with the syringe and inject her. Thereafter, he removed the immobilized mother for collar fitting, also weighing and measuring her and taking a blood sample. Meanwhile, he kept the two or three cubs warm in his jacket, thereafter taking their measurements and blood samples before returning the family to their den.

Rogers has radio-collared more than 100 black bears. He's tracked them from the air and he's tracked them on foot. On foot, he needed to lug a radio receiver and cumbersome antenna. Even so, he was able to sneak up on a mother with cubs and surprise them by rushing at them, yelling and waving his arms. This sent a frightened mother and her cubs up separate trees, where they received tranquilizer injections, gentle rope-lowering, and ground-level health checks.

But Rogers wanted to learn more about bear behavior than he could gather from bears that feared him. So he began gaining the trust of individual bears, which allowed him to accompany them over a 24-hour period to record every behavior.

As a bonus, the trusting relationships eliminated the need to crawl into bear dens to apply initial radio collars. Rogers can now apply a collar to a trusting bear almost as easily as dog owners apply dog collars.

Although Minnesota allows hunting of its 20,000 black bears, most hunters in the Ely region appreciate the importance of radio-collared bears and usually pass up opportunities to shoot them.

Food Through the Seasons

In spring, after emerging from hibernation, bears are thin, often having lost 20 to 40 percent of their weight prior to denning. Having eaten nothing for months, they've lived entirely on fat reserves.

Rogers writes, "In spring, newly emerged vegetation is highly digestible and nutritious. Even so, mothers lose weight due to nursing, but other bears gain weight. Then during the mating season in June into July, males lose weight.

"In northeastern Minnesota, summer is the period of greatest weight gain," says Rogers, "especially in years with a good hazelnut crop. Farther south, in Tennessee, fall is more important because of plentiful acorns, including the favored white oak acorns, which are scarce in northeastern Minnesota. By late September into October, bears in northeastern Minnesota are already out of food and so enter their dens, while bears in Tennessee are starting to bulk up on nut crops. Tennessee and the eastern deciduous forest offers much better black bear habitat than northeastern Minnesota. Bears there benefit from a longer growing season, more food varieties, and richer food."

When the mast begins hitting the forest floor, bears need to compete with deer, raccoons, squirrels, waterfowl, and turkeys. Thus, autumn is literally and figuratively "crunch time" for bears. Across North America, oak acorns are everybody's favorite. In good years, oak mast can weigh more than 500 pounds per acre, says my friend Lennie Rue.

With a good mast crop, bears can gain more than 30 pounds per week. However, good oak mast crops tend to occur only every 2 to 4 years. Thus,

After spotting three unharvested pears atop this young tree on Carolyn Singer's California property, a black bear brought them down branch by branch. This shoe-shaped bear scat was nearly as large as a men's size 12 pottery shoe. The larger hind foot tracks here measure 5 × 7 inches. (Photo by Sue Mansfield)

years with poor mast followed by hard winters take a toll on bear populations and those of other denning mammals, as well as deer. Poor mast in fall may also force bears to abandon the wild for feeding opportunities among the humans they fear.

SIGN

Tracks of black bears may approach flapjack diameter and resemble those of a flat-footed human, with the claws sometimes leaving marks. In addition, bears leave scat on game trails and commonly defecate on scat of other mammals, as though leaving a calling card. In their search for insects, bears overturn large rocks and tear apart rotting logs and anthills. In berry patches, they leave matted trails.

When climbing, bears leave claw punctures that are easiest to see on smooth-barked trees such as apple, aspen, beech, and mountain ash. Larger bears often break branches.

The bark on so-called "bear trees" shows bite and claw marks, usually at heights of 4 to 7 feet. Wildlife professionals have long speculated about the significance of this bark damage. Some suggest that bear trees are invitations to mate. Others suggest that the marks are deliberate warning signs,

the height of the claw marks announcing the size of that bear to others who might challenge.

Rather than merely speculating based on bark damage alone, Rogers followed trusting male and female bears to observe how the marks are made. Of 29 trees he observed being marked in a single year, 25 were marked by mature males, mainly during the June-July breeding season in various female territories. Females marked their few trees after the breeding season in their own territory. Immature males and females made no such marks.

Rogers describes a large male's marking of three trees along a dirt road this way: " . . . he stood on his hind legs and rubbed his dorsal side, particularly his shoulders, neck, and head, on trunks of trees, frequently twisting his head around to bite the trunks. At one tree he also stood on all four feet and rubbed his hindquarters." Rogers notes that "Freshly marked trees had sufficient odor for human detection, and a dog showed intense interest in a bear tree more than a month after all radio-collared bears in the area had denned."

Such behavior suggests that scent marking in addition to the visual marking of tree trunks plays a role. Rogers found the case for scent marking reinforced at another location when that same large bear lay on his back on a fallen wooden signpost and "squirmed with all four feet in the air, twisting occasionally to bite it."

Later Rogers watched a 5-year-old male walk repeatedly over several 2- to 3-foot aspens: ". . . his chest and shoulder bent them to the ground and they rubbed along his underside until they sprang upright behind him."

Seems to me Rogers has shown that there's more to a bear's bark than its bite.

HIBERNATION, BIRTH, AND DEVELOPMENT

Before the onset of winter, north and south, black bears seek dens or create them. There they enter a period of dormancy called hibernation. In the North, Rogers says, pregnant bears begin entering dens as early as September; other bears wait until October. Dens tend to be just large enough for the bear to squeeze into and are within natural cavities or dug at ground level or under fallen trees where snow will hide them.

In the South, denning may not begin until December or January, if at all. In the Southeast, dens may be in dense thickets or in tree cavities as high as 100 feet off the ground.

Prior to hibernation, bears become less active, and their digestive systems slow down. Within the den, bears become drowsy and fall asleep, even though remaining easily roused. This "light sleep" leaves bears alert enough to react to threats. And it allows mothers to tend their cubs.

Snug in their winter dens, hibernating mother bears wake up regularly to nurse and care for their cubs. (Photo by Lynn Rogers)

"During the winter, a fecal plug gradually grows, made up of cells sloughed from the digestive tract and bits of vegetation the bear accidentally ingests while raking up bedding and rearranging it in the den periodically through the winter," according to Rogers. Thereafter, the bear lives almost entirely on fat reserves. Body temperature drops from 100°F to about 88°F, and heart rate drops from 40 or 50 beats per minute to 8 to 19 beats.

Hibernation serves several purposes. It allows bears to go without food when food is scarce. And it greatly reduces energy expenditure in the cold temperatures. But, as important, hibernation allows a mother to remain constantly with her two or three cubs, which are born chipmunk size and weigh only a pound—helpless, hairless, and with eyes closed.

Because mother black bears are still nursing in June and July, they don't come into estrus to breed that year. In fall, the cubs den with their mother again and so don't need to disperse until the following June or so, at 16 or 17 months old. That's when their mother enters her next breeding period. For youngsters, dispersal is a dangerous time that involves trespass issues with other bears, as well as humans. Dispersal-year mortality rates may exceed 35 percent.

Hibernation

In the recent past, some biologists contended that bears weren't "true hibernators" because their body temperatures drop only a little, allowing them to be easily wakened. By comparison, woodchucks become almost as cold as a stone. Yet the consensus now seems to be that drowsing through winter with various depths of sleep, heart rates, and body temperatures qualifies as hibernation.

This cub's mother would most likely protect it by retreating with it or sending it up a tree. (Photo by Lennie and Uschi Rue III)

BLACK BEAR ATTACKS

Rogers is eager to dispel myths about the likelihood of attacks by black bears. After the death of an infant that a black bear removed from her carriage in New York State in 2002, Rogers lamented the tragedy but put it in perspective this way:

> Only two people have been killed by black bears in the eastern United States in the last 100 years.
>
> There are about 750,000 black bears in North America with less than one killing per year—most in northern Canada and Alaska, where bears have little contact with people.
>
> According to the Departments of Justice in the United States and Canada, about one person in 16,000 commits murder each year. For grizzly bears, about one in 50,000 kills someone. For black bears, it is less than one black bear in a million.
>
> For each person killed by a black bear across North America, there are 13 people killed by snakes, 45 by dogs, 120 by bees, 250 by lightning, and 60,000 homicides.

Based on his Minnesota experiences, Rogers relays that hand-fed black bears usually "eat gently and timidly." But when the food source runs out, the bear suddenly realizes that the person seems

Dental Work at Great Smoky

In Great Smoky Mountains National Park, along the Tennessee–North Carolina border, park staff had trouble keeping their large population of black bears from scavenging garbage and panhandling in picnic areas. Such bears became increasingly confident near people, sometimes even swatting and biting.

Some problem bears were euthanized. Others were tranquilized and fitted with ear tags before being released more than 40 miles into National Forest. However, a high percentage of relocated bears found their way back, male bears especially, and resumed their bad habits.

Coincidentally, studies showed that bears with bad teeth can't crack the hard shells of acorns and hickory nuts. Such bears therefore feel compelled to seek soft foods, which in autumn are mainly human foods.

As a result, park staff began delivering tranquilized bears to veterinarians for dental checks, which revealed that many bears had tooth problems. Treatment included x-rays and root canals, followed by the strong aversive conditioning of rubber bullets. Bears that received dental care and aversive conditioning tended to stay away from people thereafter, much preferring natural foods.

"threateningly close. . . . At that point, some bears don't dare turn their backs to leave and may defensively slap the person before turning and running away. Slaps usually cause no more than welts where the claws scrape across the skin." Rogers continues, "Black bear claws are strong for climbing trees but aren't sharp like a cat's for holding prey. When bears get used to being hand-fed in a particular location, some may cautiously investigate people there. Finding no food to trigger familiar hand-feeding routines, some bears become nervous about the proximity and give a quick bite. These nips are not attacks and seldom break the skin, but they can hurt. The same bears will run from people they encounter elsewhere."

Grizzly versus black bear aggressiveness. "The idea that black bear mothers are likely to attack is one of the biggest misconceptions about black bears," says Rogers. "Grizzly cubs run to their mother for protection, while black bear cubs run for trees. . . . Attacks by defensive grizzly mothers account for 70 percent of human deaths from grizzly bears, but mother black bears are not known to have killed anyone in defense of cubs." Mother grizzlies, says Rogers, are more likely to attack partly because they evolved primarily in regions without trees.

Male black bears tend to be larger than females of the same age and, as a result, tend to become dominant and thus more aggressive with their own kind. Big male black bears drive smaller bears from the vicinity of females they want to mate with. Their mating ranges can be more than 100 square miles.

Bluff charges. While growing up in Minnesota's bear country, I never heard of injuries from bear attacks, even though black bears are notorious for bluff charging people to within 6 feet or so before veering away. When I asked Rogers whether it was true that black bears normally bluff-charge, he replied, "I've never seen them do anything but. In my more than 40 years of studying black bears, including catching cubs in front of wild mothers, I've never had a bear come after me and hurt me."

Rogers says: "When black bears are nervous, most of them either retreat or make one pounce, slam their front feet down, and blow loudly. Ferocious as that looks, experienced observers know that blustery black bears are not about to attack."

At his bearstudy.org Web site, Rogers elaborates in this way: "We thought gorillas were ferocious until close study showed them to be mostly gentle. We're learning the same thing about black bears. Both species have a blustering bluff charge that ends without contact." (Be it known that Rogers is a big, strapping fellow who knows the importance of conveying a confident demeanor to bears. As for the rest of us, there seems to be no data on the relationship of bluff charges to heart attacks.)

The National Park Service and others invariably suggest that during a black bear confrontation, it's important not to turn and run, which those authorities feel could trigger a chase impulse. Yet Rogers has found no reports of black-bear attacks that resulted when people turned and ran. Panicky people commonly do turn and run from black bears. But upon glancing back, they see the black bear running away, too.

Alas, there seems to be no reliable advice for every possible situation because each person is different in personality, preparedness, and physical strength—and because each bear is different in those ways, too.

DEFENSIVE ATTACKS VERSUS PREDATORY ATTACKS

Aside from black bear bluff charges that usually occur as blustery single pounces forward, Rogers makes a distinction between defensive attacks—with contact—and predatory attacks. Although attacks by mother grizzlies reflect a grizzly tendency to defend cubs, Rogers says that "attacks by mother black bears are very rare . . . In an attack by a mother black bear, her object is to neutralize an immediate threat. When the person stops fighting, the mother bear dares to gather her cubs and exit."

Rogers's research suggests that it's usually only about one in a million black bears that stalks and preys on people. Rogers likens such a bear to the rare, psychopathic serial killer among humans. Yet he agrees with most authorities that during a predatory attack it's important to use pepper spray and fight back. "In a predatory attack," Rogers says, "playing dead would be an invitation to dinner."

Bear confrontations and attacks. On this, the US National Park Service (NPS) at Glacier National Park offers visitors the same guidance regarding grizzlies and their far less aggressive black bear cousins. *Note:* The Glacier NPS Web site tends to assume grizzly behaviors because grizzlies are accustomed to dominating black bears in overlapping territories and because mother grizzlies with cubs are less likely to retreat when surprised than black bears are. Still, it's ill-advised to surprise a black bear.

To avoid surprising bears, Glacier NPS advises making plenty of noise in bear country by periodically clapping your hands and yelling, "Hey, Bear!" Little bells on backpacks may not be loud enough on windy days or when bears are making their own foraging noises. Glacier NPS also advises hiking in groups and avoiding early-morning, late-

> ### Pepper Spray Repels Bears
> Lynn Rogers says that in hundreds of tests, pepper spray has worked for him every time. This is the same spray that mail carriers use. The pepper is capsicum, used in human foods. "On black bears," Rogers says, "one squirt in the eye, and the bear doesn't go away mad, it just goes aways . . . I have never seen a bear become angry about being sprayed."

day, and nighttime hikes. Children should be kept close, preferably behind the lead adult.

What to do if you encounter a bear? *Do not run!* says Glacier. In a face-to-face encounter, says Glacier NPS, " . . . there is no easy answer. Like people, bears react differently to each situation . . . A bear's body language can help determine its mood. In general, bears show agitation by swaying their heads, huffing, and clacking their teeth. Lowered head and laid-back ears also indicate aggression. Bears may stand on their hind legs or approach to get a better view, but these actions are not necessarily signs of aggression. The bear may not have identified you as a person and is unable to smell or hear you from a distance."

Commenting on Glacier's characterizations of bear moods, Rogers stresses that in black bears, "huffing means the bear is getting over its fear and calming down. Clacking its teeth means it is afraid, the same clacking I heard when a large bear almost fell out of a tree and realized it had had a close call. Laid-back ears is a very defensive body language that I have seen precede a swat when someone was trying to pet a bear."

Note on predatory attack. The Glacier National Park Web site advises this on grizzlies and black bears, and Rogers agrees: "If you are attacked at night or if you feel you have been stalked and attacked as prey, try to escape. If you cannot escape or if the bear follows, use bear spray, or shout and try to intimidate the bear with a branch or rock. Do whatever it takes to let the bear know you are not easy prey."

NPS guidance at the Great Smoky Mountains Web site differs significantly from that offered by

Contrary to ferocious dental displays on bearskin rugs and on covers of hunting magazines, bears do not bare their teeth to threaten, as dogs and wolves do. This black bear is curious, not angry. (Photo by Lennie and Uschi Rue III)

Lake Tahoe's Black Bears

As in other parts of North America, housing development in the Lake Tahoe Basin has relentlessly encroached on black bear habitat. In addition, tourists and seasonal residents don't always use bear-proof garbage receptacles or good judgment. As a result, in the 1990s, law-enforcement and wildlife officials began receiving unprecedented numbers of complaints about bears, many of them about house break-ins.

When a tourist, in 1998, had the Department of Fish and Game kill a mother bear with cubs, rather than having them chased away, a self-described "shy wildlife rehabilitator" named Ann Bryant formed the BEAR League. Since then, public officials would describe Bryant as anything but shy. Bryant's goals are to engender respect for bears, while reducing bear deaths (killings) by teaching people how to remove attractants from their property and how to chase bears away by behaving territorially.

On the BEAR League's Web site (savebears.org), Bryant writes, "It is up to us to reestablish the bear's natural fear of humans so they will want to avoid us . . . In the thousands of phone conversations we have had with most of you, have we ever failed to tell you, 'Don't let the bear feel welcome in your territory, be mean to him, yell at him, throw a rock at him?'"

Now, in addition to throwing rocks, Bryant recommends shooting bears in the rump with a far more accurate paintball gun. She likens the impact of a paintball to the warning "swat" that bears give one another. The difference is that the paintball "swat" shows the bear that you can reach surprisingly far. In fact, teams of Tahoe Basin neighbors with paintball guns phone one another to warn when a "swatted" bear is heading in their direction—a citizen swat team.

Over time, Bryant has trained hundreds of volunteers to respond to bear questions and problems by phone and e-mail—and on-site. She and her volunteers often visit homes and even crawl under porches to scare bears out, spraying den areas with Original Pine-Sol cleaning liquid, which repels bears. (They're careful to use original scent, because Pine-Sol has other scents, such as lemon and orange, that attract bears. The active ingredient in Original Pine-Sol is real pine oil, according to the manufacturer.) Afterward, homeowners are obligated to seal the porch opening.

As demonstrated throughout this chapter, years of food shortage force black bears to scavenge near humans. Yet research shows that bears prefer to forage in the wild. In the Tahoe Basin, with hibernation time approaching during food shortage, anonymous citizens have engaged in a diversionary feeding program of giving bears apples and nuts, far from humans. And, so far, this seems to have greatly reduced the incidence of house break-ins prior to denning.

Wildlife defender Ann Bryant with Bogart, who'd overdosed on vodka but recovered with Ann's help (Photo by BEAR League)

Ann Bryant with Marvin, her pet porcupine (Photo by BEAR League)

parks that have grizzlies, because grizzlies tend to be more aggressive when surprised. For black bears, Great Smoky NPS suggests this (comments within brackets show my clarifications):

■ If the bear notices you and changes its behavior, you are too close. Back away slowly from the bear and make lots of noise.

■ Being too close to or threatening a black bear can cause the bear to make loud noises and exhibit aggressive behavior such as swatting the ground or rushing toward you [bluff charging].

■ Stand up large, slowly backing away from the bear. DO NOT RUN. If backing away does not work and [if the bear completes a charge by physically assaulting you], fight back using any weapons you can find, including rocks and branches.

On this NPS point, Rogers offers this qualification: "Maybe right and maybe wrong. If the black bear attacked defensively, like a mother defending cubs (happens rarely with black bears),

---

Surrounded by Black Bears

As an 18-year-old getting in shape for football, I decided to jog 2 miles to our town dump. As I huffed and puffed into the dump's loop drive, I needed to catch my wind before jogging home.

Walking well into the dump drive, I noticed one bear, and then several, and then at least a half-dozen bears of various sizes all around me. Each bear glanced up at me from its garbage foraging but seemed uninterested.

Unwittingly, I did the right thing. I nonchalantly backed out of the dump 50 yards or so, beyond sight of the bears. The next half-mile toward home was probably the fastest I've ever run, even though occasionally glancing back. Yet, as I learned from Lynn Rogers only recently, my fears that day were almost totally unfounded. He says that dump bears just want to concentrate on garbage. To test his view at a major International Bear Conference, Rogers asked the audience if anyone knew of a single bear attack at a dump. And no one did.

---

fighting back would prolong the attack. The idea that the bear charges makes me think it would be a defensive attack and fighting back would prolong it. Mother bears quit beating people up when they lie still. However, again, if a bear confidently and quietly sizes a person up and tries to take them down, I'd fight back. That's how predatory bears have been driven off in cases I investigated."

■ Playing dead is a last resort and may still result in serious injury. [Let your noisemaking include calls for help.]

OPTIONS FOR CONTROL

Around home, control options include denying bears access to unnatural foods, creating aversive stimuli, fencing, plant selection, livetrapping and relocation by authorities, and hunting.

Denying Food Access

As with most other nuisance mammals, denying access to unnatural foods is usually the most effective control. The first visit may simply be an exploratory stop of a bear passing through. If it finds nothing to snack on or is treated roughly, that bear might never return. *Note:* Rogers agrees that reducing attractants is generally good advice but cautions that "when wild food is extremely scarce, as in western towns afflicted by multi-year drought and unseasonable frosts, removing attractants, such as bird feeders and garbage, removes buffers, which can thereby increase the frequency of house break-ins."

Neighborhood bear feeding. If neighbors are feeding bears intentionally or unintentionally, find means to help them stop. If needed, wildlife and health officials may be willing to assist. The following are suggestions that reduce the appeal of household food.

■ *Kitchen prep:* Bag and freeze potentially smelly things, such as fish and meat scraps, until placing them in outdoor trash receptacles just before

Bear-proof garbage cans defy access to bears at the Wildlife Research Institute, headed by Lynn Rogers in Ely, Minnesota, at bearstudy.org. (Photo by Lynn Rogers)

roadside pickup. Wash and rinse food residues from cans and other containers before placing them in outdoor receptacles. Clean kitchen exhaust vents and ducts regularly, thereby also reducing fire hazard.

■ *Bear-proof garbage receptacles:* Bear-proof receptacles are available via the Internet by searching with the words *bear proof garbage.*

■ *Other garbage receptacles:* In the Tahoe Basin, Ann Bryant sprays original-scent Pine-Sol inside the garbage receptacle before closing the lid and trapping the scent. She says, "When bears open the can, Wham! They get a snout full of something that burns and disorients any critter that relies on its sense of smell."

In addition, use sealed plastic bags as liners, resealing them after each deposit. Keep garbage receptacles inside a closed garage or secure outbuilding until placing them outside, shortly before trash pickup. Otherwise, position receptacles in shade so the sun's heat doesn't generate fermentation. Avoid leaving receptacles along the roadside overnight.

■ *Barbecue:* Clean the unit after each use. Remove and clean grease traps. In charcoal grills, grease drippings can be caught in aluminum foil for removal. But with gas grills, adhere to the manufacturer's cleaning instructions, rather than introducing aluminum-foil retrofits that could overheat the gas lines.

Bird feeding. Feed birds only when bears are in hibernation. In most bear regions, hibernation often corresponds with snow cover. Birds don't generally need our help finding food, except after fresh snowfall or during extreme cold. Once snow cover is largely gone, birds can find plenty to eat. However, if you are determined to feed birds near your house throughout much of the year, take feeders in at dusk and find means of catching or removing fallen seed each night. This practice also helps to avoid attracting rodents.

Aversive Stimuli

Paintball shooting. Combined with territorial behavior, including yelling and arm waving from the safety of a porch or deck, well-placed paintballs have proven effective in the Tahoe Basin. The effect is similar to that achieved from rubber bullets fired by staff at Great Smoky Mountains National Park.

Critter Gitter. This scare device emits a startling high-pitched noise and flashing lights that scare animals away. A passive infrared sensor detects body heat within 40 feet. The noise pattern, with high/low volume settings, changes randomly so animals don't get used to it. It's powered by a 9-volt battery, which is not included. This is recommended by Cornell's Paul D. Curtis and Jill Shultz in *Best Practices for Wildlife Control Operators.*

Conditioned food aversion. Bears hate the smell of original-scent Pine-Sol. In addition, researchers commonly test effectiveness of foods treated with lithium chloride in making wild mammals and livestock feel nauseous and throw up. Thereafter test animals tend to avoid that food, anticipating post-ingestion consequences.

Dogs. To roust bears from dens under houses, Ann Bryant uses two intensively trained Russian-bred Karelian bear dogs—on and off leashes. However, she recommends Pyrenees mountain dogs as guard dogs. *Caution:* Even though a guard dog can discourage a bear from entering a fenced area, in a fight in a tightly restricted space, no dog is a match for an adult bear. After such a fight, the owner might find only the dog's collar.

Barrier Fencing

Bears can shred, pull down, or walk over plastic-mesh fencing used for deer. And they can climb almost all types of heavy-gauge wire-mesh fencing, even the so-called hurricane mesh that is well secured to sturdy, deeply embedded metal or wooden posts. Besides, most such fences tend to be eyesores better reserved for commercial growers who supplement their fencing with guard dogs.

Electric fencing. Fence manufacturers advise against simply installing an electric fence and hoping for the best. They say it's important to then attract bears (and deer) to the charged wire by means of peanut-butter bait protected from the elements by a flap of aluminum foil. One jolt is often enough to keep a bruin away—but not a guarantee. Thus, electric fencing is considered "psychological fencing," rather than barrier fencing. For more on electric fences, see page 53.

Plant Selection

If bears are a problem in your neighborhood and if you'd rather not invest in bear-proof fencing, it may be wise to refrain from planting fruit trees. As an alternative, bears don't bother nut trees, such as oaks. And nut trees aren't likely to produce significant mast crops for 30 years or more, and even when they do, they would attract bears and deer only in fall.

Livetrapping and Relocation

If a particular bear becomes a problem and can't be discouraged by the measures above, contact wildlife officials.

Relocation. Some jurisdictions prefer to relocate a problem bear, after ear-tagging, at least once rather than destroy it after an incident. This either requires livetrapping or "darting" with immobilizing drugs. However, some relocated bears find their way back home over great distances. Though rarely, bears have returned home after being transported more than 100 air miles away. Other relocated bears may quickly fall victim to territorial bears. And some continue to cause problems for homeowners in their new locations.

Euthanasia. Other jurisdictions may simply euthanize all problem bears. That policy may result from multiple factors: the financial costs for relocation, the homing instincts of bears, and the bear's potential for continuing to cause problems for people in the new location.

Hunting and Lethal Trapping

Depending on jurisdiction, the status of black bears ranges anywhere from pest, to game animal, to endangered species. So check applicable laws.

COMMUNICABLE DISEASES AND PARASITES

Bears are subject to a variety of diseases that don't seem to reduce bear populations or threaten humans. As to parasites, bears are less vulnerable than many other mammals. Cold temperatures in the North may help reduce external parasites. But in the Southeast, warm temperatures, high humidity, and brief hibernation periods offer conditions more favorable to parasites.

CHAPTER 5

Beavers and Muskrats

This chapter addresses beavers and muskrats together for these reasons:

■ Beavers and muskrats inhabit virtually the same parts of North America and share some behaviors.

■ In most jurisdictions, these rodents are protected furbearers, so trapping and hunting may require special permits.

■ Wildlife authorities may require rabies testing and assurances that nontarget species, such as otters and waterfowl, won't be trapped.

■ Plans to alter water flow or shorelines may require environmental impact statements. For example, destruction of a beaver dam can dramatically affect downstream ecosystems and properties, which may also create legal liabilities.

■ Unless you're dealing with muskrats in ponds with no outlets, it's best if you consult wildlife and environmental professionals before taking action.

PROBLEMS FOR PEOPLE

Beaver families create preferred habitat by building dams of woven branches in order to flood large areas. The resulting impoundments can greatly impact wildlife, homeowners, farmers, highway engineers, and the timber industry. On the other hand, single beavers sometimes attempt a shortcut by damming a roadside culvert. Because beavers and muskrats are mainly nocturnal, working through dawn and dusk, you may not notice activity until you have a problem.

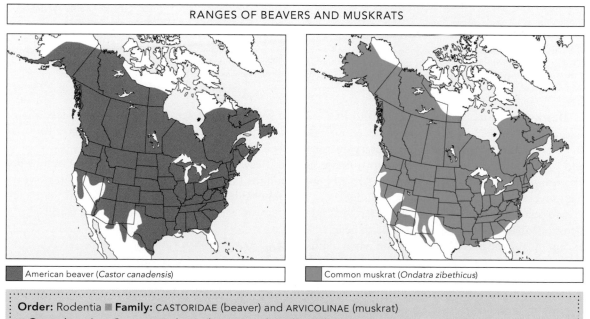

RANGES OF BEAVERS AND MUSKRATS

American beaver (*Castor canadensis*)

Common muskrat (*Ondatra zibethicus*)

Order: Rodentia ■ **Family:** CASTORIDAE (beaver) and ARVICOLINAE (muskrat)
■ **Genus/species:** *Castor canadensis* (beaver) and *Ondatra zibethicus* (muskrat)

Top left: *Swimming beavers alert family members to danger by slapping their tail on the water before diving.* Bottom left: *They use trails to drag wood into their pond. (Photos by Lennie and Uschi Rue III)* Right: *I photographed this unfinished work on a 14-inch cottonwood overlooking Connecticut's Housatonic River. The beaver had correctly assumed that tree lean would drop tree into the river for branch removal.*

Bankside dens. Both muskrats and beavers make bankside dens with underwater entrances. Beavers use these dens as initial temporary quarters and abandon them after the dam raises water level enough to allow construction of the first of perhaps several large, dome-shaped stick lodges.

Muskrats, on the other hand, prefer bankside dens to floating lodges. And they tend to be loners, except during the breeding season and when mothers are nursing. So bankside muskrat activity has comparatively mild implications, unless you live near an earthen dam or raised canal that muskrat burrowing could collapse. Beyond that, a key issue

is your relative tolerance for a muskrat's feeding on aquatic plants, such as cattails and water lilies, as well as nearby crops and clover.

Beavers run a family business—just Mom, Pop, and the kids, no outsiders. So if a dispersing 2-year-old decides to stake a claim, a potential mate may show up to share the claim and raise a family.

Bog Moats
Beavers can inhabit bogs with no flowing water by creating moatlike ponds and building floating lodges that rise and fall with the water level.

Riverside Restoration
In the West, where livestock overgrazing has caused severe erosion along creeks and rivers, officials have "stocked" beavers in successful efforts to restore habitat. If those areas lack sufficient woody material for dam construction, authorities have tree trimmings trucked in.

Food as construction material. During spring and summer, beavers favor highly nutritious greens and roots. But, throughout the year, they also dine on the less nutritious inner bark of trees. Beavers can fell a 5-inch-diameter willow in 3 minutes. And they can fell trees more than 2 feet in diameter with the intent to harvest the upper branches. After dragging saplings and branches into the water, beavers have two choices: They can eat the inner bark, corncob fashion, and then weave the debarked stick into the dam. Or they can add the material to a raft that becomes waterlogged and sinks to the bottom, where it will serve as a food cache under winter ice.

ROLE IN THE WILD

Beavers are considered a *keystone species* because they create their preferred ecosystem, while coincidentally providing habitat for many kinds of life. On the other hand, these ecosystems are often temporary because beaver families need to move on when they've consumed all food within reasonable distance from the water's edge. For a time, abandoned impoundments often continue to fill with sediment. But as the dams themselves deteriorate and allow drainage, the result is often a "beaver meadow," a brand-new ecosystem.

Factors that determine the environmental impacts of beavers and muskrats are enormously

Sewellel, or Mountain Beaver
Aplodontia rufa of the West Coast is not related to the American beaver; it is considered the most primitive living rodent. Average head and body length is 13 inches; the tail is 1 inch long.

complex. For example, although beaver impoundments attract and benefit many species, they also force other species to move on. And the effects are also felt downstream in reduced water flow after heavy rains.

Serving the food web, beavers and muskrats are prey to wolves, coyotes, bears, wolverines, river otters, lynx, bobcats, mink, alligators, and snapping turtles. Bears may tear into the lodges. Because muskrats are small, they are also prey to weasels, raccoons, owls, hawks, eastern cottonmouth snakes, large fish, and even big southern bullfrogs.

Lodges, feeding stations, and dams are often used as resting and nesting sites by an array of birds, reptiles, amphibians, woodland animals, and smaller critters.

SPECIES AND SIZES

American beaver (*Castor canadensis*): Head and body 2 to 3 feet long; tail 1 foot long and broad like a canoe paddle lying on the ground. Average weight: 35 to 70 pounds. Family: CASTORIDAE

Common muskrat (*Ondatra zibethicus*): Head and body 18 to 26 inches long; tail 10 to 12 inches long, narrow and laterally compressed, rather than round. Weight: 1½ to 4 pounds. Family: MURIDAE

Round-tailed muskrat (*Neofiber alleni*): Head and body 8 inches long; tail 5 inches long and rounded. Average weight: 10 ounces. This species is less aquatic than the common muskrat and is considered rare. Family: MURIDAE

REPRODUCTION AND POPULATIONS

Beavers breed once a year, beginning as early as December in the South, but northern beavers generally breed in January through March. Gestation is about 4 months. Litters in April through August average two to four kits that are ready to walk and swim in a few days. Youngsters work in the family business for 2 years before dispersing long distances.

Had he not paused for the photo, this beaver would have needed less than 2 minutes to chew through. (Photo by Lennie and Uschi Rue III)

Florida's round-tailed muskrats breed year-round. Litter size is one to four.

Common muskrats breed throughout the year in the South but only June through August in the Far North; breeding is usually initiated when northern waterways become ice free. Litters average only three in the South but may average ten in the North. Mothers provide care only through weaning.

SIGN

Swimmers. Beavers and muskrats look much alike when swimming except that adult beavers are much larger.

Tail slap. When frightened in the water, beavers loudly slap the surface with their tails, before diving, alerting all family members.

Bankside dens. Entrances are usually hidden below water level. More apparent for muskrats may be an airshaft above the den, concealed by twigs or vegetation.

Chewings. Beavers chew through saplings and tree trunks close to the water's edge, leaving a stump that resembles a roughly chewed pencil point before dragging the sapling into the water.

Tracks. Beavers have conspicuously webbed rear feet that are up to 8 inches long and much smaller front feet; the clawed front toes register like chubby fingers of a human hand. In muddy soil, the wide tail divides the tracks. Muskrat tracks are smaller and somewhat star-shaped; in wet soil, the narrow tail may score a line between the foot tracks.

Drag trails. Beavers tend to reuse trails to drag saplings and limbs into the water.

Scat. Beavers leave sawdust-packed cylinders that are the diameter of a golf ball. Muskrats leave clusters of ½-inch-diameter oval pellets in their trails and on rocks and logs.

Lodges and feeding stations. Beaver lodges are large domes of debarked saplings and tree limbs caulked with mud. Lodges of the common muskrat consist mainly of fibrous plant stems, sticks, and leaves. These muskrats also build smaller lodgelike feeding stations, where they tow food for dining safe from land predators. The lodges of round-tailed muskrats are grassier than those of the common muskrat.

To avoid predators, muskrats carry their food to natural feeding stations in open water or build their own. (Photo by Lennie and Uschi Rue III)

OPTIONS FOR CONTROL

For beavers, especially, authorities may want to visit and help you assess the situation.

Elimination of food sources. This means removal or protection of plants. Alas, mowed embankments may be as unappealing to beavers and muskrats as they are to people.

Wire-mesh exclusion. A sturdy wire-mesh fence following the shoreline will prevent beavers and muskrats from venturing farther ashore. Be sure fence height anticipates snow depth. If the rodents attempt to dig under, plug holes with concrete blocks wired together.

As an alternative, use mesh fencing to protect specific areas. In this case, fencing can protect just the shore side because beavers don't like to venture behind a fence that blocks escape to water.

Sturdy wire-mesh cylinders, staked at the bottom, can protect individual trees.

Electric fencing. Portable solar panels can electrify single-strand wire 4 to 6 inches off the ground. However, electric fencing requires regular mowing because vegetation can short out the wire. For more on this, see page 53.

Plant selection. Beavers are repelled by red maples, which are often the only tree species left standing around an old beaver impoundment. In one study, beavers avoided cutting their favored aspen trees after researchers painted the bark with red-maple extract. A Nevada study showed avoidance of Jeffrey pine. In the East, spruces seem of low interest.

Plants that get mad. After being cut down by beavers, aspens send forth juvenile shoots containing poisonous phenols that beavers avoid. Such chemical defenses are known as *secondary metabolic compounds,* and many plants send them forth after being browsed.

Repellent trunk paints. Researchers have repelled beavers from tree trunks by painting them with extracts of predator feces, red maple, or Jeffrey pine. The USDA National Wildlife Research Center suggests painting tree trunks with acrylic paint mixed with sand. So it seems logical that paint infused with both sand and odor repellent deserves a test. In winter, light-colored paint can also protect bark from sunscald. *Caution:* Avoid painting tender-barked saplings less than 6 feet tall.

Commercial repellents. Sulfur-based repellents and thiram-based Chew-Not have provided protection in field trials, according to the Web site beaversww.org.

Controlling water level. If you wish to allow beavers to build a dam but want to control its height and thus the size of the flooded area, you'll find good guidance on the Internet, using the search words *beaver* and *deceiver.*

Predators. Encouragement of some of the predators listed earlier in this chapter can help. For example, owl nesting boxes can attract owls. And minimal fencing around garden plots—rather than excessive property boundary fencing—encourages visits of foxes, coyotes, and bobcats.

Trap baits. Subject to local laws, apples and carrots are good muskrat baits. For beavers, professional trappers use castoreum from beaver scent glands.

COMMUNICABLE DISEASES AND PARASITES

Beavers and muskrats carry waterborne tularemia (Type B), which is not fatal to humans but accounts for 5 to 10 percent of human tularemia infections in North America. (Type A tularemia can be fatal but is carried by rabbits and ticks.)

All mammals can become infected with the rabies virus. The US Centers for Disease Control and Prevention (CDC) reports an increasing trend in rabies among all rodents, including beavers and muskrats. But the CDC says it has no record to date of rabies transmission from rodents to humans.

As for parasites, beavers and muskrats transmit the intestinal parasite *Giardia lamblia,* among others.

For more on these afflictions, see page 210.

CHAPTER 6

Chipmunks

For sheer enjoyment, chipmunk watching can rival bird-watching. These cute back-striped rodents dash about, drinking from basins, scooting under occupied deck chairs, and barely escaping dive-bombing birds that nest nearby. Generations of chipmunks have entertained our household, but only one little guy figured out how to pull mature seedpods from tall hosta stems.

In late summer, this chipmunk would climb each stem until his weight began swinging the stem downward. At that instant, he would let his hind legs dangle, like a trapeze artist, and would ride the stem to the ground. Next he'd pull off a banana-shaped seedpod that was as long as his front leg, allowing the hosta stem to spring upward again. Then, sitting upright with the seedpod between his front paws, he would use his incisors to peel the pod and stuff his cheek pouches with seed.

He'd repeat this circus act until both cheek pouches bulged and then dash off somewhere—but not always to his burrow. Throughout winter, under the woodpile roof, I'd find hosta seeds atop each newly exposed layer of firewood.

PROBLEMS FOR PEOPLE

Burrows sometimes undermine porches, stairs, concrete slabs, and house foundations. In spring, hungry chipmunks may dine on shallowly planted flower bulbs, such as crocuses, and their digging can uproot other plants. Chipmunks also raid bird feeders and eat bird eggs and nestlings. Unlike rats and mice, however, chipmunks that den under houses tend not to venture indoors.

This little guy or gal mastered the trapeze act with hosta stems described above, but I was always too late to capture the feat with camera. Chipmunks dominate smaller birds at feeders. If birds aren't getting their fair share, reduce chipmunk climbing options.

Order: Rodentia ■ **Family:** SCIURADAE ■ **Genus:** *Tamias* (Some authorities place the 21 western chipmunks in the *Neotamias* genus.) ■ Species north of Mexico: 22

ROLE IN THE WILD

Chipmunks are omnivores that forage mainly on the ground. They feed on seeds, insects, eggs, and nestlings, as well as fungi and green plant material. They favor habitats with some mature trees and shrubs. Chipmunks easily climb shrubs and small trees for berries and seeds, but most species prefer to remain near the ground for quick escapes.

IDENTIFICATION, SPECIES, AND DISTRIBUTION

Smaller than hot-dog buns, most chipmunks are light brown to orange-brown with alternating dark-and-light stripes on their backs. On some western species, the stripes continue across the face. Although the East has only one species, the West has 21. Why so many species in the West? As with other kinds of rodents, mountains and contrasting climates at different elevations may sometimes have created "island" ecosystems from which some species evolved because they lacked the option to travel.

The largest species is the eastern chipmunk, with an average head-and-body length of 5 to 6 inches, tail length of 3 to 4 inches, and weight of 3½ ounces. The smallest species, such as the least chipmunk, have average head-and-body lengths of 4 inches and weigh only 1¼ ounces, just a tad too heavy to mail with a first-class stamp.

Eastern chipmunk *(Tamias striatus):* The only chipmunk in the East. Its face is not striped; the rump is deep orange.

Western chipmunks are sometimes classed in the *Neotamias* genus. The distinguishing features listed below are paraphrased from *Mammals of North America,* a Peterson Field Guide by Fiona A. Reid.

Allen's chipmunk *(T. senex):* One of the larger chipmunks; fur is dark brown or grayish; pale stripes are gray

Alpine chipmunk *(T. alpinus):* Pale and grayish, with white fur on the tops of its feet

California chipmunk *(T. obscurus):* Large with faint stripes on its back

Chipmunk holes plunge straight down, unlike vole holes, and show no surface soil, unlike gopher holes. (Photo by Lennie and Uschi Rue III)

Cliff chipmunk *(T. dorsalis):* Grayish; dark stripes are very faint

Colorado chipmunk *(T. quadrivittatus):* Brownish; distinct markings

Gray-collared chipmunk *(T. cinereicollis):* Gray fur on its neck and shoulders; orange fur on its sides

Gray-footed chipmunk *(T. canipes):* Grayish fur on its rump and shoulders; ears long; feet usually light gray

Hopi chipmunk *(T. rufus):* Small; coloring is bright; sides bright orange

Least chipmunk *(T. minimus):* Longish tail; stripes usually bold

Lodgepole chipmunk *(T. speciosus):* Colorful; bright orange sides; white facial stripes

Long-eared chipmunk *(T. quadrimaculatus):* Large bicolored ears with white spots behind; stripes on face are prominently black and white

Merriam's chipmunk *(T. merriami):* Faint back stripes; pale stripes are gray

Palmer's chipmunk *(T. palmeri):* Gray fur on its upper neck and shoulders; cheeks grayish

Panamint chipmunk *(T. panamintinus):* Shoulders yellow-gray; no dark stripe below lower white stripe

Red-tailed chipmunk *(T. ruficaudus):* Colorful and long-tailed; cheeks usually pale orange

RANGES OF CHIPMUNKS

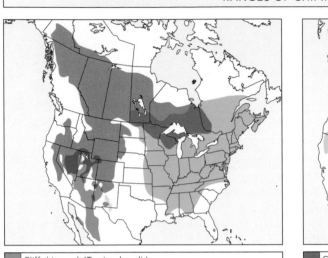

	Cliff chipmunk (*Tamias dorsalis*)
	Eastern chipmunk (*Tamias striatus*)
	Gray-footed chipmunk (*T. canipes*)
	Least chipmunk (*T. minimus*)

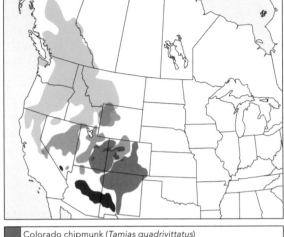

	Colorado chipmunk (*Tamias quadrivittatus*)
	Gray-collared chipmunk (*T. cinereicollis*)
	Hopi chipmunk (*T. rufus*)
	Palmer's chipmunk (*T. palmeri*)
	Uinta chipmunk (*T. umbrinus*)
	Yellow-pine chipmunk (*T. amoenus*)

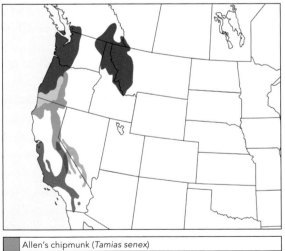

	Allen's chipmunk (*Tamias senex*)
	Merriam's chipmunk (*T. merriami*)
	Panamint chipmunk (*T. panamintinus*)
	Red-tailed chipmunk (*T. ruficaudus*)
	Siskiyou chipmunk (*T. siskiyou*)
	Townsend's chipmunk (*T. townsendii*)

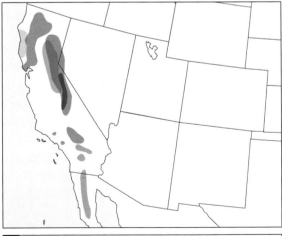

	Alpine chipmunk (*Tamias alpinus*)
	California chipmunk (*T. obscurus*)
	Lodgepole chipmunk (*T. speciosus*)
	Long-eared chipmunk (*T. quadrimaculatus*)
	Sonoma chipmunk (*T. sonomae*)
	Yellow-cheeked chipmunk (*T. ochregenys*)

Siskiyou chipmunk *(T. siskiyou):* Pale stripes are gray or brownish; cheeks grayish

Sonoma chipmunk *(T. sonomae):* Tail long and thick; prominent broad band of orange at center; mainly arboreal; nests in trees

Townsend's chipmunk *(T. townsendii):* Stripes not readily noticeable are gray or dull orange; coastal subspecies is reddish with orange and black stripes

Uinta chipmunk *(T. umbrinus):* Dark stripes are brown; doesn't usually hibernate; nests in tree holes often created by woodpeckers

Yellow-cheeked chipmunk *(T. ochregenys):* Upper pale stripe is brown; lower pale stripe is gray

Yellow-pine chipmunk *(T. amoenus):* Dark stripe below lower white stripe; may nest on tree branches

SIGN

Holes in soil are about 2 inches wide and usually go straight down (in contrast to vole holes), to no dirt mound (in contrast to pocket gophers). Gnawed nutshells are another sign. Chipmunks emit a sharp chirp followed by chatter when startled.

PREFERRED FOODS

Favorite foods are nuts, seeds, berries, and larger fruits. Chipmunks also eat insects, earthworms, mice, frogs, salamanders, carrion, and bird eggs and nestlings.

MATING AND BIRTH

The eastern chipmunk mates in early spring, soon after hibernation. In the South, it may breed again in late summer. Mating and birth of western species depend largely on climate and occur later in the South. Gestation is about 31 days, producing two to eight young, depending on the species. The young are weaned at 4 to 6 weeks and usually disperse within 2 weeks afterward.

HIBERNATION AND ESTIVATION

Chipmunks are considered true hibernators because their body temperature and heart rate drop during winter denning. But because they don't build up body fat prior to hibernation, they must rouse themselves from torpor now and then to eat from food caches. On warmer winter days, they may emerge and dash to food caches, underground or above.

Some western chipmunks in warmer states don't hibernate in winter. Instead, they may *estivate,* or become dormant during hot periods.

SENSES

All senses seem well developed. Chipmunks spot motion from goodly distances but may interpret

To attract chipmunks, sunflower seeds are hard to beat and don't attract ants and bears like peanut butter.

To protect your bulbs in spring, create a ¼-inch wire mesh box. Cover with larger mesh and remove when shoots pop through.

your stationary form as a landscape fixture before scooting over your foot.

OPTIONS FOR CONTROL

Eliminating food sources. Feed birds only during the winter months, when chipmunks and bears are hibernating. Also, use squirrel baffles to make bird feeders inaccessible from the ground or suspend feeders from rope that's run between pulleys, allowing you to position feeders away from the house foundation so fallen seed doesn't encourage nesting or food caching there. Bird feeders that close under a squirrel's weight of 1 pound won't close under a chipmunk's 1¼- to 3½-ounce weight unless they are also calibrated to close under the weight of birds of those sizes. (For comparison, blue jays weigh up to 3 ounces and Steller's jays up to 4½ ounces.) Store birdseed and pet food in chew-proof containers.

Exclusion. As cute as chipmunks can be outdoors, they can damage wiring and buildings.

■ *House seals:* Seal foundation and house openings larger than ¼ inch. This will also exclude mice as well as chipmunks. Use copper or galvanized ¼-inch mesh, supplemented by dollops of expanding foam or mortar. For more on sealing up, see the rats and mice chapter on page 145.

■ *Fencing:* Plant flower bulbs inside ¼-inch mesh boxes or surrounds, which will also exclude voles and moles. For chipmunks, cover the ground surface with 1-inch galvanized wire mesh that extends beyond the surround at least a few inches on all sides. Then conceal that with a thin layer of soil. You may need larger mesh to allow the stalks of tulips, hyacinths, and fritillaria to grow through it.

To protect planting beds from the tunneling of chipmunks as well as voles and moles, extend ¼-inch mesh 1 foot belowground with a foot-wide shelf extending from it. To discourage a wide range of mammals, use a fence like that shown on page 49.

Plant selection. Smaller types of bulbs, such as crocuses, are the most vulnerable to chipmunks because they usually require shallow planting with their bottoms no more than 4 inches deep. However, *Crocus tommasinanus* is one of the few crocuses that chipmunks and squirrels tend not to like, whether for scent or taste. The *Narcissus* genus (including daffodils and jonquils) contains toxic alkaloids and calcium-oxalate crystals that deter most mammals, including deer and chipmunks. Narcissus bulbs planted at bottom depths of 5 inches can provide a protective rooflike screen over bulbs that need to be planted at 8- to 10-inch depths, such as tulips and fritillaria.

Repellents. Connecticut gardening writer and lecturer Lorraine Ballato has had good success when overlaying bulbs with crushed oyster shells, seashells, and red-pepper flakes. She reapplies fresh flakes in spring just before her chipmunks rouse from hibernation.

Trapping. Rather than lethal trapping, 99 percent of people I've surveyed prefer to livetrap and release these cute and relatively harmless little guys. The best time for relocation is late summer in northern climes when young have dispersed and seeds are plentiful at the new location for caching. Use small cage traps or tip-up tube traps baited with peanut butter, seeds, nuts, or sliced apples. States such as Arizona request that residents inquire with their Fish and Game Department about authorized release sites before livetrapping. Rat-size snap traps will kill chipmunks. If used outdoors, place them inside covers that will keep birds, kids, and pets out.

Hunting and poisoning. Are you kidding? For more on hazards of poisons, see page 64.

COMMUNICABLE DISEASES AND PARASITES

Experts at Cornell University say disease risks are minimal, though chipmunks host parasites such as fleas, lice, worms, and botflies. Most rodents can host fleas that carry plague (see page 212).

CHAPTER 7

Gophers (Pocket)

The emergency call awakened the first responders of Fernley, Nevada, at 4:30 a.m. on January 5, 2008.

A roaring torrent of icy water was quickly flooding 590 homes and stranding 3,500 residents. In some areas, firefighters would find themselves wading in chest-deep water to rescue people. Even though Fernley was soon declared a federal disaster area, no one was injured and no one drowned, perhaps in part because the children had been safely asleep.

What caused this sudden flood? At the nearby Truckee Canal, a 50-foot section of earthen embankment had suddenly been breached. The canal is owned by the US Bureau of Reclamation, whose investigators concluded that the breach was caused primarily by "rodent activity." Near the breach, investigators found that some 3-inch-wide tunnels reached 25 feet into the embankment.

By phone, bureau spokesman Jeff McCracken told me that gophers had been the most prevalent rodents near the breach, confirmed by "the size of the holes." Also by phone, Fernley's director of parks and animal control, Keith Penner, agreed that tunnels nearest the collapse had probably been those of gophers and perhaps some ground squirrels.

PROBLEMS FOR PEOPLE

Besides undermining earthen embankments, gophers undermine house foundations, sidewalks, driveways, and even airport runways. The burrows pose break-through hazards to horses and other live-

Western Canals

Constructed from 1903 to 1906, the Truckee Canal is owned by the US Bureau of Reclamation, which also owns 7,911 miles of irrigation canals in 17 western states. However, maintenance is contracted to state water districts.

Like much of the bureau's canal system, Truckee was created by digging a wide ditch about 7 feet deep and using the excavated soil to create embankments that could contain canal flows higher than the surrounding landscape. The bureau is now working more closely with the states to ensure that its nearly 8,000 miles of embankments aren't threatened by gophers and other rodents.

stock. In addition, gophers chew into plastic water lines and underground electrical cables. Gopher mounds in lawns aren't merely unsightly; they also need to be knocked down to allow mowing.

In the backyard of my California friends, Dillard and Cheryl Hunley, gophers get rid of excess tunnel soil by filling the pit that houses the Hunleys' water meter. In Arizona, their daughter, Kelly, reports multiple gopher mounds in nearly all yards, as well as tunnels that collapse underfoot after rains.

If that's not enough, gophers earn heightened ire as voracious consumers of plants—vegetable and ornamental, including the roots and bark of costly trees and shrubs. Gophers favor deep roots of alfalfa and are often blamed for damage to 25 to 50 percent of the crop.

Order: Rodentia ■ **Family:** GEOMYIDAE ■ **Genera:** *Thomomys, Geomys,* and *Cratogeomys* ■ **Species:** Currently 19 north of Mexico, but the number is likely to increase as DNA testing continues.

Although gophers favor roots and bulbs, they sometimes emerge at "feed holes" to dine on woody bark and clip herbaceous plants including tomatoes, often pulling whole plants underground. Tunneling itself exposes plant roots to drying. Where there is significant snow cover, gophers may tunnel upward several feet to dine on bark.

ROLE IN THE WILD

Gophers are active day and night, year-round, though almost exclusively underground. Serving the food web, gophers are favored prey of badgers, which attempt to dig gophers out. Gophers also fall prey to weasels, bobcats, foxes, coyotes, owls, raptors, and snakes. When pursued by a snake through a tunnel, a gopher may create a soil plug to block the snake's advance.

Southeastern pocket gophers and most others are aggressive when handled. (Photo © Mendez, Raymond/Animals Animals Enterprises)

In the wild, gophers aerate and redistribute soils, contribute organic matter, and inoculate soil with beneficial soil microorganisms. The bare patches of mound soil invite plant succession and diversity.

ORIGINS, SPECIES, AND DISTRIBUTION

The "pocket" in the name pocket gopher refers to fur-lined external cheek pouches used for carrying food and bedding materials.

Of the 19 gopher species, all except two occur west of the Mississippi River. One of the two species of eastern gophers occurs in a narrow tongue of land into Indiana, and the other occurs in the extreme Southeast, as shown on accompanying maps. Within the three genera, species ranges tend not to overlap. (It's likely that continued DNA testing will increase the number of species.)

Gophers range in elevations from sea level to 12,000 feet. All but two species occur in arid climates, and species tend to have soil preferences.

IDENTIFICATION

Built powerfully for digging, gophers resemble bucktoothed, long-clawed lemmings on steroids. Their eyes and ears are small. The color of their short fur often closely matches associated soil color and thus may range through all brown shades to nearly white, sometimes with patches of white. Head-and-body length is 5 to 10 inches, with males averaging 10 percent larger than females of the same age and species. Larger size in a given species is often associated with lighter soils and better food availability.

The protruding front teeth aren't merely for beauty. Those incisors serve both as dining utensils and digging tools. When using their incisors for digging, gophers close their lips tightly behind the teeth to keep soil out of their mouths. Like the incisors of all rodents, those of gophers are ever-growing and must be kept short by gnawing.

The sparsely hairy tail serves two main purposes: It helps guide the gopher as it moves backward in its tunnel, and it helps dissipate body heat.

RANGES OF GOPHERS

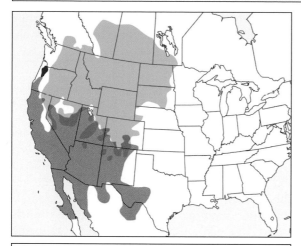

WESTERN POCKET GOPHERS

	Botta's pocket gopher (*Thomomys bottae*)
	Camas pocket gopher (*T. bulbivorus*)
	Northern pocket gopher (*T. talpoides*)

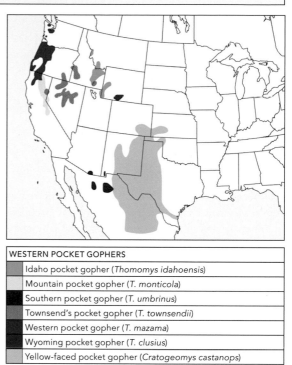

WESTERN POCKET GOPHERS

	Idaho pocket gopher (*Thomomys idahoensis*)
	Mountain pocket gopher (*T. monticola*)
	Southern pocket gopher (*T. umbrinus*)
	Townsend's pocket gopher (*T. townsendii*)
	Western pocket gopher (*T. mazama*)
	Wyoming pocket gopher (*T. clusius*)
	Yellow-faced pocket gopher (*Cratogeomys castanops*)

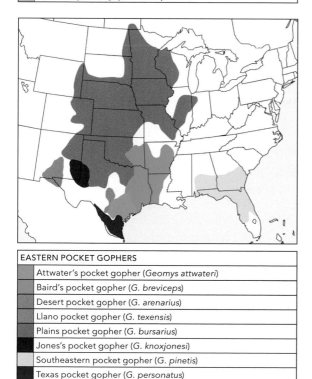

EASTERN POCKET GOPHERS

	Attwater's pocket gopher (*Geomys attwateri*)
	Baird's pocket gopher (*G. breviceps*)
	Desert pocket gopher (*G. arenarius*)
	Llano pocket gopher (*G. texensis*)
	Plains pocket gopher (*G. bursarius*)
	Jones's pocket gopher (*G. knoxjonesi*)
	Southeastern pocket gopher (*G. pinetis*)
	Texas pocket gopher (*G. personatus*)

Distinctions among genera. Field identifications of species are difficult even for specialists. So let's be content with distinctions among the three genera. For that, range maps, tooth grooves, and a few other traits allow basic identification:

■ **Western pocket gophers** (nine *Thomomys* species): No lengthwise groove in the top incisors; very prominent buckteeth; small forelegs and claws; usually attempts to bite when handled

■ **Eastern pocket gophers** (nine *Geomys* species): Two lengthwise grooves in both top incisors; large foreclaws; aggressive when captured

■ **Yellow-faced pocket gopher** (one *Cratogeomys* species): One lengthwise groove in both top incisors; incisors very large; largest of gophers, may have a head-and-body length of 8 or more inches and may weigh nearly 1 pound; surprisingly, most docile of all gophers when handled

Gopher Heat Stroke

Like humans, a gopher needs to maintain a fairly steady body temperature of about 98°F. While working in soil of 34° to 86°F, a gopher dissipates excess heat through its sparsely hairy tail. If exposed to temperatures around 100°F, even for a short period, a gopher overheats and dies quickly. This helps explain why gophers aren't seen on hot days. Instead, they are "cooling it" in their deeper burrows.

REPRODUCTION AND POPULATIONS

Gophers can breed at about a year old. The males apparently must entice females into their bachelor quarters to breed. In drier areas, breeding may occur only in late winter and early spring, but in irrigated and otherwise moist areas, it may occur several times a year. Litters average about five.

Except for females with young and during breeding season, gophers live solitary lives in a burrow system with a surface area from 200 to 2,000 square feet. The largest males tend to have the largest territories. In general, territories are smallest where food is most abundant during the growing season. Population densities range from 1 to 15 gophers per acre.

Mortality is highest when juveniles attempt to establish their own territories. Male mortality peaks during the breeding season, perhaps due to fighting.

SENSES

With little need for eyesight in their dark subterranean world, gophers use their sense of smell to locate food. And they depend on highly sensitive whiskers for tunnel navigation.

Why So Hungry?

When burrowing and maintaining their tunnels, gophers may expend several thousand times more energy than rodents such as squirrels that travel aboveground. Thus, they have a higher caloric need.

BURROWS

Most burrow systems have only one or two main tunnels and many lesser tunnels near the root zone for foraging. Special chambers serve for nesting, food caching, and fecal matter.

SIGN

Gopher sightings are uncommon because gophers seldom venture outside of their sealed burrow system. Unlike mole tunnels, gopher tunnels leave no telltale soil ridges because gophers tunnel deeper.

Mounds. The first sign is usually a mound of soil about 6 inches high, as shown in the photo on the opposite page. Gophers create these mounds through side tunnels to remove soil from tunnels below. In moist soils, as occur naturally in spring and after rains or irrigation, a gopher may create several mounds per day.

■ *Tunneling and mound building:* Gophers dig by passing the soil under themselves with their forepaws and pushing themselves forward with their hind paws. But they create mounds by pushing excavated soil with chin and front paws upward through sloping lateral tunnels. As a result, viewed from above, gopher mounds are fan-shaped to kidney-shaped, and the plugged hole itself is near the "handle" of the fan. By contrast, a mole mound is a symmetrical "volcano" that the mole pushes vertically upward, also headfirst.

■ *Soil plugs:* The plug in a gopher mound serves several purposes: It prevents easy access by snakes, weasels, and flamethrowers, and it helps assure humidity and temperature control below. In addition, if you or another predator disturbs a mound, letting light enter the hole, the gopher will instinctively seal up that tunnel, likely also burying your trap.

Feed holes. Gophers also create "feed holes" of 2½- to 3½-inch diameter at the soil surface, distinguished by clipped vegetation around them.

Tracks. Gophers have five toes on the hind feet and four toes on the slightly smaller front feet, both with long claws.

In good tunneling soil, gophers may create several mounds per day. Mounds conceal upward-sloping shafts that gophers use to push excavated soil out of the tunnel before plugging the shaft. As shown at right, the shaft opening is usually near one edge of the mound. This is unlike molehill shafts, which are centered under the molehill because moles push soil straight up.

Sign in snowmelt. With snow cover, gophers burrow in snowpack atop the soil, dining on plant life there. As spring melts the last remaining snow, it reveals networks for surface travel, called *cores,* which resemble the surface runways of voles, as shown on page 193. Snow protects gophers from most predators.

Soil Preferences

Gophers most prefer good nitrogen-rich garden soil because it can sustain a cornucopia of plant life, especially plants with fleshy roots. Gophers also like light-textured, well-drained soils because such soils preserve tunnel integrity while allowing gas exchanges with the atmosphere (incoming fresh air and outgoing soil gases, including methane and CO_2 produced by the gopher). By contrast, dry, sandy soil may force gophers to dig deeper for tunnel integrity. Clay soils and wet soils make tunneling difficult and also limit gas exchange. So it seems logical that a gopher's soil preferences could help inform strategies for deterrence, as discussed in the controls section near the end of this chapter.

OPTIONS FOR CONTROL

Most jurisdictions consider gophers to be nongame animals. In this case, landowners are usually allowed to prevent damage by any legal means, which may include lethal trapping and sometimes poisoning. Legal or not, poison baits can be terribly ill-advised for many reasons, as enumerated on page 64.

Exclusion. Experts at the University of California suggest that 1-inch galvanized wire mesh is the longest-lasting barrier. To prevent garden entry, the fencing needs to extend at least 1 foot aboveground and 2 to 3 feet deep. Yet a concrete foundation or a deep trench with packed 1-inch coarse gravel would serve as well. Alas, the occasional gopher may dig deeper than 3 feet. Gophers often create food caches 3 to 6 feet deep.

Among the most effective designs for small garden plots are variations based on the concept for a cold frame with a wire-mesh bottom. In fact, Gardens to Gro offers kits for constructing raised beds of redwood or plastic lumber, protected with wire-mesh bottoms. These "Gro" beds can be installed

Virtually gopher-proof—as well as rabbit-, vole- and mole-proof—kit "Gro" beds like the 6×6×12-foot model shown have wire-mesh bed floors attached to heart redwood or plastic lumber. For design options and more, visit gardenstogro.com. Why the owl? In one study, gophers made up 70 percent of barn owl diets. Large, elevated nest boxes attract barn owls. (Owl photo by Lennie & Uschi Rue III)

on top of the ground, as illustrated in the above photos. For design options and more information, visit gardenstogro.com.

My friend Dillard Hunley prefers chicken-wire cages to protect each of his tomato plants. As a fallback, his wife, Cheryl, has invested in hanging tomato planters, reasoning that gophers can't fly.

Plant selection. For farmers, the University of Montana Cooperative Extension recommends rotating crops annually, say, from alfalfa (which gophers love) to annual grains (which gophers can't survive on year-round). The Montana Extension therefore also suggests that buffer strips of grain can reduce gopher immigration.

Our sources suggest that there are no plants that gophers don't eat. Experts at the University of California mention the following plants as perhaps

repellent to gophers but don't substantiate the claims. I've added thoughts on toxins in these plants that might also occur in their root systems.

■ *Euphorbia lathyrus* (gopher purge): *Euphorbias* have a toxic milky sap, which might make these plants unpalatable. But there seems to be no evidence that the plant actually repels gophers from an area.

■ *Ricinus communis* (castor bean): The toxic seeds cause extreme digestive distress and diarrhea in many mammals. However, the leaf toxins, perhaps also in the roots, may profoundly affect the nervous system.

■ *Allium* species (garlic and onions): Members of the Onion family have particularly toxic effects on dogs and cats and can cause anemia in grazing animals that don't have food options. The strong smell and taste have deterred voles in our garden and thus might be worth testing on gophers.

Predators. Although various predators can keep rodent populations somewhat in check, most tend to hunt where populations are highest. In a Colorado study, gophers made up 7 percent of the red-tailed hawk diet and more than 70 percent of the barn-owl diet. Although barn owls are major gopher predators, especially at nesting time, they tend to hunt over a wide area, rather than where people have attracted them to nesting boxes. "Mouser" cats and "ratter" dogs often have luck. Alas, dachshunds are too large for 3-inch-diameter gopher tunnels.

Repellents. Because gophers feed mainly underground, there seems no practical means of delivering repellents like those applied to aboveground plant parts.

Frighteners. Whether ultrasonic noisemakers or underground vibrators, University of California researchers found none effective in keeping gophers away.

Tunnel flooding. Sudden deluges of water can sometimes force gophers to the surface, where they can be caught by a dog or dispatched with a shovel. But burrow systems are often so vast that a gopher can either plug that portion of the tunnel or find higher ground. And in arid regions, where water is precious, such extravagant water use might be expensive, if not illegal.

Mound surveillance. If you see movement on a mound, there's probably a gopher just below bringing soil to the surface. If you stand next to the mound with a shovel, awaiting the next soil movement, you might be able to scoop your friend into a large container or carrier, or determine another outcome.

Using coarse gravel. For a gopher barrier, researchers at the University of California suggest surrounding plastic water lines with coarse gravel. Hmm! Maybe there's more to this!

Indeed, the engineering report on the Truckee Canal failure noted that rodent burrows "were more

> **Trenching Machines for Rent**
> Gas-powered trenching machines can cut 3- to 6-inch-wide trenches 2 to 3 feet deep. Walking models resemble power tillers outfitted with a heavy-duty bar and rotating chain that functions much like chain-saw chain. There are also riding models. For a major project, consider getting estimates from installers of underground lawn sprinklers. (*Caution:* To avoid breaching underground utility lines, ask your major utility to visit and map out your underground lines. This service is usually free, with one utility often representing several. However, the utility company won't know where your underground sprinkler and low-voltage lines run.)

prevalent where the canal embankments were constructed of fine-grained soils, as was the case at the breach site, than where the canal was constructed of soils having a significant gravel content."

Surely, gravelly soil would be harder for gophers to chew and dig through. Speculating on this by phone with me, Fernley's director of parks and animal control, Keith Penner, suggested that gravelly soil might also deter gophers because it undermines tunnel integrity—therefore allowing cave-ins. This led us to speculate that a mix of soil and coarse 1-inch gravel to a 12-inch depth might be worth testing on gophers, as well as moles and voles. Plant roots would find it far easier to snake through coarse gravel than gophers would.

Although western gophers (*Thomomys* species) are often found in rocky and gravelly soils, eastern gophers (*Geomys* species) prefer sandy to loamy soils. Thus, eastern gophers, especially, might avoid soil infused with at least 50 percent coarse gravel. On the other hand, a 100 percent, hard-packed gravel trench 2 to 3 feet deep might serve well as a garden barrier against moles and other rodents. And a series of cross-hatched gravel trenches every 10 feet or so (like a tic-tac-toe grid) would surely make tunneling and general travel more challenging.

A high-gravel mix around the drip line of newly planted trees and shrubs might discourage tunneling, too, while still allowing roots to work through. The cost of gravel? If you have access to a dump truck, coarse gravel can be surprisingly inexpensive— around $15 per ton. It's the carting that's expensive.

Sweet chewing gum. University of California researchers dismiss chewing gum as a gopher killer. Yet some professional animal controllers swear by it, on the assumptions that sweetness attracts rodents and that gum plugs up their digestive systems. No one seems to have conducted postmortems to verify the plug-up theory.

Among chewing-gum advocates is Keith Penner of Fernley, Nevada. Based on his grandmother's advice, Penner has found Juicy Fruit highly successful. He says gopher problems stop in his parks and on his own property soon after he places a single dry stick of gum in all gopher holes he can locate. This method is most effective, he says, early

in the growing season before irrigation begins and then after irrigation ends.

Trapping. Although there's usually one gopher per burrow system, nature doesn't love a void. So if properties around yours also contain gophers, successful trapping will likely invite replacements unless the whole neighborhood traps diligently.

Gophers remain underground virtually all of the time, and their main tunnels run 8 to 18 inches below the surface, unlike the shallower tunnels of moles and voles. The strategies and techniques for livetrapping can closely approximate those for lethal trapping, which I'll address here.

Gopher mounds and feeding holes with clipped vegetation around them can help you locate travel tunnels, which will usually be within 18 inches of those holes. Experts use a metal rod to probe until feeling it punch through a few inches into the tun-

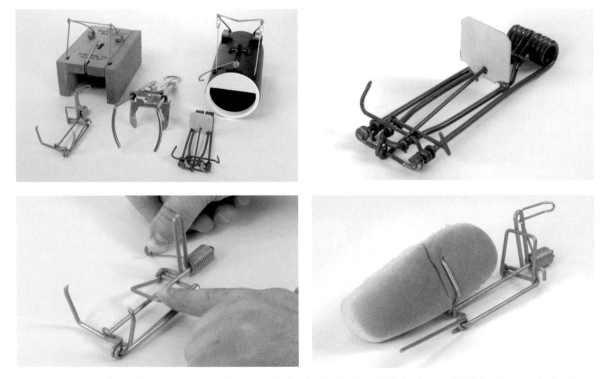

Clockwise from top left: *Gopher Getter Redwood Box Trap, Black Hole Gopher Trap, WCS Gophinator, Quick-Set Revenge Gopher Trap, and Macabee Gopher "Old Reliable,"* also featured top right. Bottom left: *Dan Bouchard sets the WCS Gophinator, which trapped my unsuspecting hot-dog bun.* For more on these and other traps and control equipment, visit wildifecontrolsupplies.com.

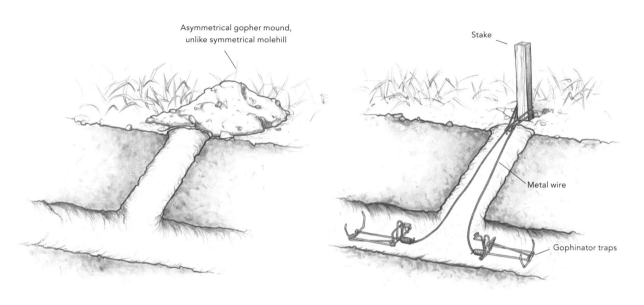

Gophers make asymmetrical mounds, with shaft plugs near the mound's edge. The shaft will slope downward to the tunnel. Place two traps in the tunnel in opposite directions, securing them with wire to an aboveground post. It's possible that Sherman live traps might also work in this situation, as shown in a photo on page 112. Be sure to secure them with wire cord, too.

nel. Thereafter, they use a spade or trowel to dig to the tunnel and place two traps end to end, facing in opposite directions, as shown in the drawing. Although the traps are designed to trigger without being baited, some experts place greens or apple slices just behind the trigger pan.

Relative Aggressiveness

When livetrapped, the three gopher genera vary in aggressiveness.

- **Most aggressive:** Eastern pocket gophers are fiercely aggressive, clicking their teeth and lunging toward almost anything moved towards them.

- **Least aggressive:** In 94 livetrappings of yellow-faced pocket gophers (in Texas and New Mexico), researchers could hold these large animals in their palms and even gently stroke them without being bitten.

- **Moderately aggressive:** Western pocket gophers generally try to bite when handled. Wear thick leather gloves.

As shown in the photos opposite, the principal types of traps employ either two-pronged pinchers or a choker. Be sure to attach the traps to a wire lead and a stake for ease of retrieval and to ensure that the gopher doesn't run off with the trap.

- *Light theories:* Professional trappers differ on light theory. Some recommend covering the hole with a board or turf, and then sealing the edges with soil to keep light out. This assumes that if light leaks in, the gopher may attempt to plug the hole and thereby cover the trap. Other pros leave the hole open on the assumption that air and light will force gopher efforts to seal them out and thereby trigger the trap.

Firearms. Even where legal, firearms would require that you see a gopher first—a fairly rare happening.

COMMUNICABLE DISEASES AND PARASITES

Gophers have fleas and lice.

CHAPTER 8

Moles

At the onset of a rainy week, our lawn displayed a meandering network of grassy ridges that sank underfoot like sponges. No doubt, we had a mole. Although I owned two big, fierce-looking mole traps, I hoped to avoid using them.

Coincidentally that week, Hannelore and I were awaiting arrival of plumbers with our new furnace. As their panel truck backed up our driveway, it veered errantly onto the wet lawn. Later, in the tire tracks, we were surprised to see a nearly flattened mole.

Rain continued for a few days, causing the soggy ridges to settle to ground level. When no more ridges emerged, we concluded that our mole had no accomplices. As I later learned, a single mole can tunnel up to 18 feet per hour, creating a crazy network of ridges that suggests a battalion of moles. It turns out that moles are territorial and

When an eastern mole took over our lawn, we were glad we had called a plumber, as described above. (Photo by Lennie and Uschi Rue III)

drive out other moles. So if you are lucky, removing just one mole may solve the tunneling problem—at least for a while.

I don't offer this anecdote to suggest that you attempt to solve a mole problem by inviting a plumber to back carelessly up your driveway. On the other hand, our plumber unwittingly demonstrated why savvy mole trappers position their traps along driveways and other lawn edges.

Such barriers often guide main mole runways in fairly straight lines. Ridges branching from main runways represent feeding tunnels that might be used only once. So the pros set their traps in main runways.

PROBLEMS FOR PEOPLE

Moles annoy people mainly because their tunneling creates raised soil in lawns and disturbs roots in gardens. Moles also push up symmetrical earth mounds known as molehills. And while tunneling at a routine pace of 15 to 18 feet per hour, moles dislodge plants and break roots or expose them to drying air that causes grass and other plants to struggle and sometimes die.

Unjustly, moles are often blamed for feeding on the roots and bulbs they rampage through. Moles do consume small amounts of plant matter in their haste, but they're really hunting earthworms, grubs, and insects. Blame for root-and-bulb consumption usually belongs with voles, mouselike rodents that feed mainly on roots, stems, seeds, and woody bark. Adding insult to the misplaced blame, voles (and mice) exploit mole tunnels as superhighways.

Order: Soricimorpha (formerly Insectivora) ■ **Family:** TALPIDAE ■ **Genera:** Various ■ **Species:** 7

Plant life often represents a tiny percentage of a mole's diet and often includes grass seed. I'd venture that moles inadvertently ingest some plant matter that clings to earthworms and insects.

In the western states, moles may receive misplaced blame for root damage caused by pocket gophers, rodents that are fond of plant roots, including those of costly trees and shrubs.

ROLE IN THE WILD

Moles are good little critters, although inconvenient in lawns and gardens. They're not rodents. They are insectivores that tunnel wherever the soil is warm enough to attract earthworms, soil-dwelling insects and their larvae (grubs), and centipedes, millipedes, and other small invertebrates.

Most mole species favor woodlands, where they play important ecological roles by consuming larvae that damage plants belowground. Many of these larvae would otherwise emerge as plant-damaging insects. Moles occasionally kill and eat mice. Their tunnels serve as thoroughfares for snakes, salamanders, shrews, and rodents as well as homes for ground wasps. In addition, moles are a principal food of foxes, coyotes, and bobcats. And, because the hairy-tailed mole ventures aboveground at night, it becomes prey to owls and bobcats.

At a California botanic garden, this Townsend's mole died in this climb-out position upon emerging. Garden staff suggested drowning was the cause, but I suspect fumigation.

Moles feed around the clock, day and night throughout the year, taking brief rests every few hours. Depending on circumstances, moles can consume the equivalent of their own body weight in 24 hours. They don't hibernate in winter. Instead, they follow earthworms below frozen soil (the frost line), which can be 3 feet deep or more in northern climes.

Early 20th-century moles had no choice but to work their way laboriously over, under, around, and through the tangled roots of forest and meadow. Those moles of long ago had no inkling of the grand scale on which we would ease the food-shopping efforts of their progeny. In the United States today, lawns occupy a land area more than eight times that of the state of New Jersey—providing moles the equivalent convenience of well-stocked supermarket aisles.

SPECIES AND DISTRIBUTION

Moles are members of the Talpidae family, which is represented by seven species in North America, a few of which have overlapping ranges. As the accompanying maps show, moles tend not to occupy drier regions where earthworms and most grubs would have trouble surviving.

Among the East's three mole species, the eastern and hairy-tailed moles cause the most problems in lawns and gardens. A third species, the star-nosed mole, tends to be less noticeable because it favors the very wet soils of marshes and shorelines. In fact, the star-nosed mole is semi-aquatic, often swimming underwater for its meals. When it makes tunnels near our homes, they are usually in overwatered or naturally wet soil.

The four western species range within 100 miles of the Pacific Coast, for the most part.

Among the seven North American species, adults vary significantly in size, from the tiny shrew mole of the West Coast, at ⅜ ounce, to about 4 ounces for California's Townsend's mole. Males tend to be larger than females. When a species' range is extensive from north to south, northern members tend to be larger, which is true of many

RANGES OF MOLES

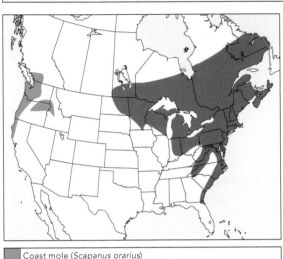

Coast mole (*Scapanus orarius*)
Star-nosed mole (*Condylura cristata*)

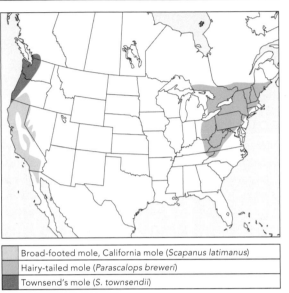

Broad-footed mole, California mole (*Scapanus latimanus*)
Hairy-tailed mole (*Parascalops breweri*)
Townsend's mole (*S. townsendii*)

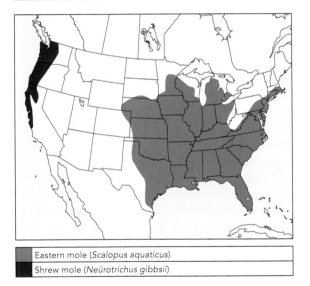

Eastern mole (*Scalopus aquaticus*)
Shrew mole (*Neürotrichus gibbsii*)

Moles must be able to survive in oxygen-deprived tunnels with high carbon dioxide levels. As a result, they have larger lungs than mammals of comparable size, as well as high levels of oxygen-storing blood hemoglobin and muscle myoglobin, which are also important to seals and manatees.

Eastern Moles

Eastern mole *(Scalopus aquaticus):* Average head-and-body length 5½ inches; nearly naked tail 1¼ inches long (The name "aquaticus" is a misnomer. The Swedish originator of the modern taxonomic system, Carolus Linnaeus, based his name for this species on the collector's label, which indicated the specimen had been found in water. Ironically, *S. aquaticus* is the least aquatic of our moles.)

Hairy-tailed mole *(Parascalops breweri):* Average head-and-body length 5 inches; hairy tail 1¼ inches long

Star-nosed mole *(Condylura cristata):* Average head-and-body length 4 inches; tail 3 inches long

mammals, in accord with Bergmann's Rule, which is explained on page 14. The tiny, barely noticeable eyes are thought to be useless except for light detection. All species have soft, velvety "hinged" fur, an adaptation that streamlines travel forward and backward. Average body temperature is roughly 98° to 100°F.

Star-nosed moles take their name from starlike appendages on their nose; they need soggy soil. (Photo by Dwight Kuhn) After being placed aboveground, as here, eastern moles like this quickly dig themselves below the surface. (Photo by Lennie and Uschi Rue III)

Western Moles

Broad-footed mole, California mole (*Scapanus latimanus*): Average head-and-body length 5½ inches; tail 1½ inches long

Townsend's mole (*S. townsendii*): Average head-and-body length 6 inches; tail 1¾ inches long

Coast mole (*S. orarius*): Average head-and-body length 5½ inches; tail 1½ inches long

Shrew mole (*Neürotrichus gibbsii*): Average head-and-body length 3 inches; tail 1⅝ inches long

REPRODUCTION

Mole breeding occurs once a year, in late winter to early spring, depending on species and geographic range. Gestation is 4 to 6 weeks and produces two to five naked pups, sometimes more. Known also as "The Mole Man," Cincinnati's Tom Schmidt says he begins receiving a dramatic increase in calls from anxious homeowners soon after the eastern mole pups disperse, which occurs in late April through mid-June. The young disperse somewhat earlier in southern climes and somewhat later farther north.

TUNNEL TYPES

There's usually only one highly territorial mole in modestly sized yards, although territories may slightly overlap at times. Because a single mole can create what looks like the work of an extended family, it's important to distinguish among several types of tunnels. This is true whether you plan to livetrap, lethal trap, drive-over, scoop a tunneling mole into a bucket with a well-timed shovel, or grab a tunneling mole with your heavily gloved hand, as Mole Man Tom Schmidt sometimes does when he has an audience.

Shallow tunnels. Lawns quickly acquire networks of ridges that may not be apparent immediately, unless you feel their sponginess underfoot. Ridges are usually more obvious when the sun is low, creating long shadows, so Schmidt checks for ridge locations by walking into the sun. If a mole is taking possession of your lawn and you haven't noticed ridges or felt them underfoot, dying grass will eventually reveal the network.

Shallow tunnels are of two types: main runways and feeder tunnels, sometimes called probes. Moles use their main runways repeatedly. These tend to run in fairly straight lines, often alongside features such as curbing, hedgerows, and driveways. Again, feeding tunnels branch haphazardly from main runways and may be used only once or twice, depending on the delights found there.

Moles versus Look-Alikes

Although they look somewhat alike as they dash out of sight, moles and their look-alikes leave distinctive evidence when they damage plants.

■ **Moles versus voles:** All moles except the shrew mole and the star-nosed mole have large, disk-shaped forepaws with stout, long claws for digging and fast travel belowground. Moles have no visible ears, and their tiny eyes are dysfunctional, except for light detection, whereas the small eyes and ears of voles are apparent. Moles have a pointed, naked snout rather than the relatively blunt, furry snout of a vole. An anomaly among moles, the star-nosed mole has a snout with 22 short pink, fleshy appendages that resemble the tentacles of a sea anemone. When they damage bulbs, moles leave shreds without tooth marks, whereas voles leave narrow incisor tooth marks on bulbs, roots, and bark.

■ **Western moles versus pocket gophers:** Pocket gophers, like voles, have visible eyes and ears. They are primarily western animals and dig by passing the soil under themselves, like dogs, rather than to the sides, as moles do. As a result, gopher mounds are somewhat asymmetrical in contrast to the symmetrical "volcano" that moles push upward headfirst. Gophers debark plants belowground and aboveground, leaving noticeable incisor tooth marks. They also clip stems, leaving an angular cut. Again, shredded underground plant parts tend to be mole leftovers.

■ **Moles versus shrews:** Shrews and moles are in the Soricimorpha order (formerly included in the Insectivore order) and have superficial resemblances. But unlike moles, shrews can't dig well in soil because their forepaws are far more delicate, somewhat like those of mice. Although shrews travel in soil tunnels dug by moles and voles, they forage mainly aboveground in soft humus and leaf litter.

Shrews are the smallest mammals in North America, best known for their high-strung behavior and enormous appetites. They tend to be nocturnal but are sometimes seen in daytime scuttling across paths and roadways, almost as if on tiny wheels.

Capable of consuming twice their body weight per day when stressed, shrews can die in just a few hours without food. Like moles, shrews feed mainly on earthworms, insect larvae, and adult insects. Among the many shrew species, only the northern short-tailed shrew, of eastern North America, has poisonous saliva that paralyzes larger insects and even mice. This unsung controller of mice sometimes also visits bird feeders for seeds.

Eastern mole's front foot

Eastern mole's back foot

Based on photographs, you might assume that moles "swim" through shallow soil with a motion resembling a swimmer's breaststroke. However, mole researchers suggest that moles use their powerful paws in a sideward pull stroke one at a time, forcing themselves zigzag through shallow soil like a projectile, or wedge, that heaves soil upward, causing the ridges.

Deep tunnels. Often running 18 to 24 inches belowground, deeper tunnels are used for nesting and when the soil's surface is too dry or cold to attract worms.

Molehills. During deep tunneling, moles push unwanted soil to the surface through chimneylike shafts that result in molehills, which tend to follow a line that reveals where their common tunnel lies. The relative positions of ridges and molehills inform the strategies of professional trappers.

OPTIONS FOR CONTROL

Independent research from Cornell University, Johns Hopkins University, and the University of California agrees with Mole Man Tom Schmidt that lethal trapping is the most effective means of controlling moles. Schmidt says catching the culprit will usually be only a temporary solution. That is, nature doesn't love a void, so tunnels leading to your property could result in recolonization. But, before addressing lethal trapping, let's consider other options.

Tolerance. In lawns mowed high (4-inch blade settings) with good soil, mole ridges may be hardly noticeable, except when the sun is low and when you step on the ridges. High mowing shades soil, reducing the need for watering and encouraging grass roots to plunge to depths of 18 inches or more, thereby helping grass plants survive the droughts that kill frequently watered grass, which tends to have shallow roots.

In fact, a mole can be good for a lawn. Besides aerating soil and consuming root-damaging grubs, the highly territorial resident will kill or drive off other moles as well as voles and mice, says control expert Ed Machowski, of Norfolk, Connecticut.

And, even if no mole comes to replace a mole you've removed, families of voles (with a "*v*") might infiltrate. Unlike moles, which are insectivores, voles have keen appetites for the roots and bark of ornamental plants, perhaps creating a new problem for you.

If mole impact is minor, Machowski suggests tolerance. Still, he usually recommends mole removal if ridges occur because underlying tunnels can cause erosion and washouts.

If your lawn has barely noticeable ridges that get flattened during lawn mowing or settle naturally after rains, consider mowing higher and tolerating the presence of a single mole. Otherwise, the territorial void created by its removal will invite another mole, beginning an endless cycle of mole trapping without permanently ridding the lawn of moles.

Deterrents. Various factors determine a soil's appeal to moles. Here are some options for reducing appeal.

■ *Watering and fertilizing less:* Compulsive watering and fertilizing improves soil attractiveness to earthworms and therefore to moles.

■ *Improving drainage:* If your soil is naturally wet, consider improving drainage and filling low areas that collect water at times.

■ *Altering soil type:* Moles dislike dry soil, sandy soil, heavy clay soil, and stony-gravelly soil. If you have such soil already, you might never have moles. Or, you could convert what you have to one of those soil types. For example, moles are less likely to visit raised rock gardens. Imagine the frustration of a mole trying to tunnel through coarse, gravelly soil mixed with just enough humus for plants that need little water. As an alternative, consider digging isolated humus-rich planting beds into otherwise gravelly soil.

■ *Converting to no-mow lawns:* Hoping to reduce their own environmental impacts, many people reduce or eliminate lawn mowing and trips to refill gas canisters by planting special no-mow

From left to right: *Capable of disguising mole ridges, no-mow grass is both attractive and a timesaver at the home of Duncan and Julia Brine, Pawling, New York (hortdesign@gardenlarge.com). Milky Spore kills lawn grubs but won't kill earthworms, a favorite mole food. Battery-powered soil vibrators cause a mole to avoid passing within about 5 feet but won't cause a mole to abandon your property.*

grass that results in flowing mounds of grass that can be quite attractive.

■ *Planting native-plant gardens:* Wildflowers or a mix of native annuals, perennials, and shrubs will invite butterflies and moths to lay eggs after supping on your flowers. The resulting caterpillars the next spring will feed songbirds. *Bonus:* This option tends to conceal mole tunneling.

■ *Installing mole "fencing":* Because moles are essentially blind, they often establish main runways along edges of barriers. So, if your lawn or garden border included either a barrier of ½-inch galvanized mesh sunk 2 feet deep or a narrow, 2-foot-deep trench filled with coarse gravel, moles would be likely to regard it as an impenetrable barrier and so would establish feeding tunnels outward from that. Bulbs can be protected in wire-mesh boxes, and cold frames can have wire-mesh floors.

Mesh fencing can also protect islands of ornamental and vegetable plants. To keep out moles, researchers at Cornell University recommend the fence be 2 feet high, but also buried a foot deep, with the bottom edge bent outward in an L-shaped shelf 1 foot wide. Thus, you'd be working with a 4-foot roll of mesh. Aboveground, this would discourage surfacing moles, as well as rabbits, but must be taller to exclude woodchucks.

■ *Selecting plants:* Because moles are insectivores, not herbivores, no plants seem to discourage mole infestations. Whatever attracts earthworms and grubs attracts moles.

Going into the tunnel. For success, all of the following options depend on your finding active main runways. Again, main runways tend to be longer and straighter than feeding tunnels, which usually meander haphazardly near the surface. It's wise to start your search by looking for the main tunnel leading to your property, often from nearby woodland. Then tamp suspected ridges down with your feet or flatten them with a water-filled lawn roller. If a ridge or two soon reemerge, you've located main tunnels.

■ *Repellents:* Folklore, home remedies, and commercial products suggest that moles can be driven away with repellent smells. But research by several universities says there's no evidence of effectiveness. Even if a repellent, such as mothballs, forces a mole to abandon a portion of a tunnel, the animal could easily dig a detour. Besides, mothball napthalene is a soil toxin.

■ *Grub killers:* Some people suggest that Milky Spore will kill enough lawn grubs to leave moles bereft of their favorite food. However, Milky Spore isn't thought to hurt earthworms—*the* favorite mole food—or other invertebrates, so it doesn't reduce the food supply much.

Developed by the US government in the 1920s to kill the white grubs of the Japanese beetle, Milky Spore is a naturally occurring bacterium (*Bacillus popillae-Dutky*) that is host-specific for Japanese beetle grubs. Manufacturers suggest placing a teaspoonful of Milky Spore at 2-foot intervals in a grid across your lawn and then wetting each pile of spore so it permeates the soil. Beetle grubs consume the spore, which kills them. As their bodies decompose, millions more spores are released into the soil. Other grubs eat these, and in so doing, exponentially "seed" your entire yard with more beneficial spores. Manufacturers claim effectiveness for up to 15 years from one application.

■ *Frighteners:* These tend to be noisemakers or soil vibrators of various types that are of questionable effect beyond a very short distance. Battery-powered soil vibrators may cause a mole to maintain about a 5-foot distance from the vibration, but they don't drive moles from the property, according to wildlife control operator Ed Machowski. He has observed mole ridges that simply detour about 5 feet away from vibrators.

■ *Predators:* These vary by region and behavior of mole species. Significant predators include weasels, foxes, coyotes, cats, opossums, hawks, and large snakes. Because the hairy-tailed mole ventures aboveground at night, it is often prey to owls. And the partially aquatic star-nosed mole is vulnerable to large fish.

■ *Toxic baits:* These seem the worst possible option because there's danger they could be ingested by children, pets, predators, or scavengers—and they could contaminate surface soil or be washed into ponds, streams, or drainage systems.

■ *Livetrapping:* Mole researchers often capture moles by digging a hole to accommodate a 1- or 2-gallon bucket with its lip at the base of a main runway. On both sides of the bucket lip, they plug the tunnel openings with just enough soil to make the mole believe the tunnel caved in there. So a mole hurrying down its main tunnel will often

Mole Live-Trap Bucket

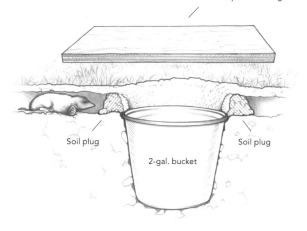

Board covers hole so no people fall in and helps seal out light.

Soil plug Soil plug 2-gal. bucket

Accustomed to fast travel in their main tunnels, moles assume that soil plugs represent routine tunnel collapse and so rampage through and fall into the bucket. If livetrapping is your goal, check the bucket every couple of hours because moles can die of starvation quickly. To prevent starvation overnight, place dozens of large earthworms, soil, and dead grass clippings in the bottom––the clippings feeding the earthworms.

barge straight through the soil block and fall into the bucket—with no means of climbing out. Be sure to completely cover the hole with a board to ensure that no one else falls in. This also keeps the tunnel looking naturally dark. The covering will also help protect the captured mole from the elements until you arrive.

Of course, any form of livetrapping poses conflicting concerns—some that may be addressed by state law. Most people prefer to treat captured animals humanely and avoid causing them unnecessary stress or pain. With this philosophy, there are basically two options: dispatching a livetrapped mole humanely onsite or releasing it in a distant wild setting, rather than near the property of the dentist who charged you too much. Most states discourage relocation of wild animals, and some make it illegal. A relocated animal can transmit diseases to its kind as well as to other animals while also becoming easy prey in an unfamiliar or unwelcoming environment.

If you plan to release a mole, be forewarned that they can starve to death in just a few hours—aside from the possibility that the bucket will have caught rainwater and that the air temperature may be cold enough to induce hypothermia.

Based in Maine, wildlife photographer Dwight Kuhn cautions that livetrapped moles need to be released in appropriate soil. Star-nosed moles need very wet or soggy soil. Other moles might not survive such soils.

When livetrapping, Kuhn leaves soil and a handful of worms in the bucket for the mole to feed on until the trap can be checked, which he

does every few hours. Of course, animal-rights purists in this case might also question whether this practice is fair to earthworms. If temperatures are chilly, it pays to include some grass and leaf litter in the bucket to serve as insulation.

When trapping star-nosed moles in soggy soil, Kuhn finds that Sherman traps work better than buckets because overly wet water tables often float the buckets upward. He places two traps in opposite directions in order to livetrap from either direction.

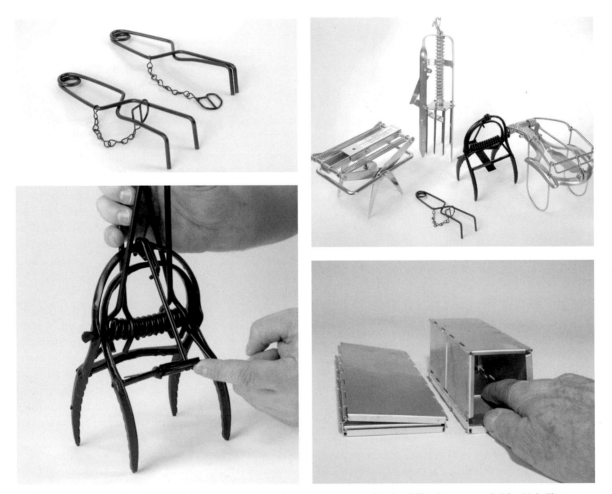

Clockwise, from top left: The WCS NoMol traps squeeze inward when the trigger is dislodged. This 5-trap array: E-Z Set Mole Eliminator, Victor Spear Mole Trap, Victor Out O' Sight Mole Trap (black), Nash Choker Loop, WCS NoMol (all from wildlifecontrolsupplies.com). WCS's Dan Bouchard points to the black trigger a mole pushes upward when crossing a soil "speed bump" you create in the tunnel. Used in quantity by researchers, Sherman live traps close at the near end when baited trigger is tipped inside, from shermantraps.com.

■ *Lethal trapping:* Most states allow landowners or tenants to control moles using any legal means. But one clearly illegal means would be using a firearm within municipal limits or near a residence.

Lethal traps are of several main types: vertical harpoon traps with multiple skewers, vertical scissors–squeeze traps, and the horizontal NoMol trap. Professional trappers rely on these three types and deploy a dozen or more traps on a single property.

The first two types are designed to be positioned only partially underground, just above the floor of a main runway. They are tripped by a trigger that the mole pushes upward while hurrying over a soil "speed bump."

Note: Harpoon and scissors traps tend to be heavy-duty mechanisms that require significant hand strength, and both types can hurt trappers who don't follow instructions—not to mention the hazards they can pose to children and pets that may lift them before they've fired.

NoMol traps are increasingly popular among professionals. Of German design, these slender traps are based on simple squeeze-tong principles. Used in

NoMol Sets

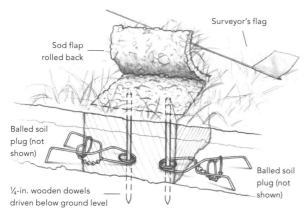

To place WCS NoMol traps, peel-back a flap of sod over a main tunnel and use a trowel to remove soil to the tunnel base. Plug each side of the tunnel with a ball of soil (not shown). Position traps back-to-back and secure with wooden stakes. Refill the hole, replace the soil flap, and mark the location with a surveyor's flag. Check traps every day or two.

> **De-Scenting Your Traps**
>
> Early in his mole-trapping experiences, wildlife control operator Ed Machowski, of Norfolk, Connecticut, was puzzled why moles avoided his traps either by covering them with soil or tunneling around them. Suspecting that the moles' keen sense of smell detected residual scent, he washed his traps in plain water and let them air-dry. The moles showed no aversion to the now scent-free traps.

pairs, they are positioned in opposite directions inside a main tunnel. NoMol traps seem less likely to injure a careless trapper than larger traps, which need to be powerful enough to force their way through soil before either impaling or squeezing a mole.

The NoMol trap is now the property of Wildlife Control Supplies (WCS). Owner Alan Huot has long relied on this trap for his mole trapping.

■ *Other "catching" options:* Some exasperated homeowners watch for moving earth along main tunnels and then attempt to drive over it with a vehicle, as our plumber did accidentally. A lawn tractor might serve this goal if the tunnel is shallow, but you might expend a lot of gas and tear up a lot of turf trying to drive over the mole. Other people have used axes to slice downward just an inch or two behind soil movement or blast it with a shotgun. Some dexterous people watch for ridge movement and use a shovel to scoop the mole into a large tub for release, or scoop first and then use the shovel to dispatch the mole. And then there's heavily gloved Mole Man Tom Schmidt, of Cincinnati, who's plucked moles out for awaiting cameras. His Web site provides an afternoon of informative, entertaining reading, particularly on the eastern mole: themoleman.com.

COMMUNICABLE DISEASES AND PARASITES

Aside from ticks, fleas, and mites, there's little evidence that moles can transmit to humans the wide range of serious health problems that rodents can. (For descriptions of health problems, prevention, and cures, see page 210.)

CHAPTER 9

Opossums (Virginia)

The Virginia opossum is the only native North American marsupial. Its newborns, like kangaroos, develop from the embryonic stage mostly after crawling inside their mother's external pouch. There they nurse for about 2 months. As the youngsters grow, not all can fit inside the pouch at the same time. So they take turns riding on Mom's back.

Uniquely, too, an opossum can hang by its prehensile tail and coil the tail to carry nest materials. Opossums are also virtually immune to the venom of

As possum youngsters grow, not all can fit inside Mom's pouch at the same time. Some ride on her back. (Photo by Lennie and Uschi Rue III)

American pit vipers, including rattlesnakes, copperheads, and cottonmouths. And 'possums are famous for "playing dead," which isn't play-acting at all.

PROBLEMS AND BENEFITS FOR PEOPLE

Because opossums are almost wholly nocturnal, they often elude notice except in the beams of car headlights and house motion lights. Opossums sometimes den and make messes in garages and attics—and under foundations. Yet because opossums change dens every night or two, except in winter, it's fairly easy to seal off access.

Opossums eat almost anything remotely edible, which is partly explained by their low taste sensitivity. Near homes, they forage in compost piles and eat garbage pulled from trash cans by raccoons, bears, and dogs. Opossums finish unfinished food in pet bowls, sometimes entering pet doors to find them. They also relish birdseed, nuts, grains, fruits, toads, frogs, and the eggs and young of nesting birds—as well as henhouse eggs and prize hens.

On the redeeming side, opossums feed heavily on insects and slurp up snails and slugs. They regularly prey on moles and voles as well as broods of young mice, rats, and rabbits. They also kill and eat snakes, venomous and nonvenomous. As scavengers, 'possums enjoy roadkill and natural carrion, including deceased opossums. Helping to keep the fly population down, they favor maggots over rotting flesh.

Order: Marsupialia ■ New-World **Order:** Didelphimorphia ■ **Family:** DIDELPHIDAE ■ **Genus:** *Didelphis* ■ **Species:** *virginiana*

ROLE IN THE WILD

In addition to the foods already mentioned, opossums eat grass and green vegetation. They tend to get along with competing mammals, often sharing multi-entrance dens with armadillos, rabbits, raccoons, and skunks.

They are important prey to coyotes, foxes, raccoons, bobcats, large snakes, and large raptors—especially horned owls. Domestic dogs take a heavy toll on them as well.

SPECIES AND DISTRIBUTION

When European settlers began arriving in the New World, the Virginia opossum *(Didelphis virginiana)* ranged only from what is now the southeastern United States into northern Ohio and northern West Virginia. Expansion from there resulted largely from land clearing and agriculture, as well as intentional introductions, particularly to the western states. Global warming will favor continued northward expansion. Opossums occur at elevations from sea level to 3,000 feet.

IDENTIFICATION

In 1612, Captain John Smith's description of Virginia animals included this: "An Opassum hath a head like a Swine, & a taile like a Rat, and is of the Bignes of a Cat. Under her belly shee hath a baggee, wherein she lodgeth, carrieth, and sucketh her young."

Actually, opossums have a pointed nose, more like a rat's. The head and the grayish, coarsely hairy body may reach 20 inches long, the tail 15 inches. In the Gulf Coast states and Texas into Mexico, the fur is darker.

After frostbite in the North, parts of an opossum's ear tips and the tail may drop off. The clawed feet resemble human hands. The hind foot has a long, clawless opposable "thumb."

SENSES

In daylight and lamplight, opossums often show uncertainty, as though visually impaired. Yet tests

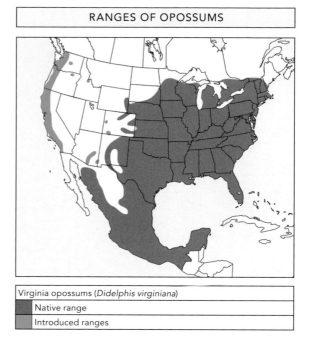

RANGES OF OPOSSUMS

Virginia opossums *(Didelphis virginiana)*
Native range
Introduced ranges

show they can perceive color and black-and-white patterns. When foraging, they often depend more on sound cues than vision, especially in locating critters under leaves. Again, their sense of taste is not highly developed.

HOME RANGE

Opossums are not territorial except near breeding time, but they have home ranges of dramatically varying sizes, depending on gender and availability of food. Most females stay close to their birth area. Males travel more widely. Although adult home ranges tend to be narrowly elliptical, juvenile ranges tend to be circular and smaller.

Preferred habitats include the edges of deciduous woods with access to water. Opossums often change dens every day or two, except during cold winter temperatures when they need to survive mainly on body fat.

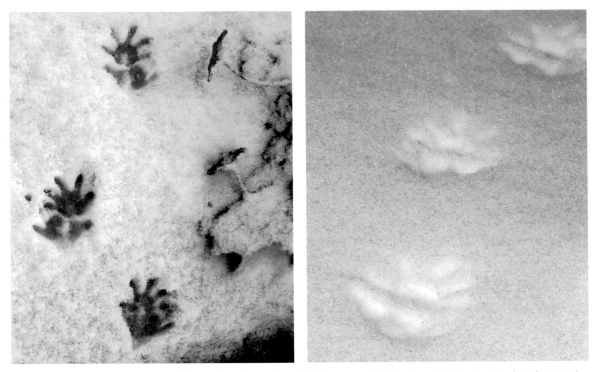

Left: *Possum tracks in wet snow show distinctive five-fingered handlike feet, the rear foot landing slightly behind the front foot, nearly overlapping it. (Photo by Lennie and Uschi Rue III)* Right: *One cold winter night our motion lights came on to reveal a slow-moving opossum making these tracks on crusted snow, again with rear foot registering barely behind the front.*

SIGN AND DENS

Tracks. Imprints resemble long-fingered human hands, especially the rear foot because its "thumb" extends exaggeratedly away from the "fingers" like a human thumb. At a walk, the rear foot lands close behind that of the forefoot, causing a slight overlap.

Chicken-coop mayhem. Opossums chew eggshells into small pieces and attack chickens from the rear end. By contrast, raccoons bite off egg ends and chicken heads.

Dens. Opossums do not dig their own burrows but will usually den in burrows dug by other mammals such as armadillos, skunks, and woodchucks. They also den in tree cavities, hollow logs, rock caves, and sheltered spaces under buildings. As mentioned earlier, except in winter, 'possums roam and often den in a different place every night or two.

MATING AND REPRODUCTION

In most regions, breeding begins in January or February and continues into fall, usually allowing two litters per year, rarely three. Within 13 days of their mother's breeding, 8 to 16 newborns emerge— $\frac{1}{2}$ inch long, blind, hairless, and helpless except for their instinctive ability to crawl into their mother's pouch. There they attach themselves to a nipple, which swells inside their mouth, helping them stay attached when jostled about. The nipple soon begins lengthening like a tether, allowing the babies to move within the pouch while nursing.

The babies stay inside the pouch for 7 to 8 weeks. Thereafter, youngsters do a little exploring

This youngster won't be weaned until about 3 months old. (Photo by Lennie and Uschi Rue III)

outside, often riding on Mom's back. But they continue returning to the pouch to nurse until weaned at about 3 months. In a few more weeks, they disperse.

OPTIONS FOR CONTROL

As with most mammals, elimination of food and shelter usually causes opossums to move on. Good baits for live traps include slightly spoiled fruit and cheese. For perspectives on control issues, see page 61. For guidance on exclusion, see pages 48 (fencing) and 59 (foundation barriers).

COMMUNICABLE DISEASES AND PARASITES

Many people mistakenly assume that a tooth-baring, hissing, and drooling opossum is rabid. Those are normal fright symptoms in healthy opossums, often accompanied by emission of foul-smelling green fluid from the anus. Opossums rarely contract rabies, although juveniles are more susceptible than adults.

However, opossums can be significant transmitters of leptospirosis to humans and wildlife and can spread various other afflictions, including tuberculosis and tularemia. *Leptospira* bacteria enter the body in contaminated drinking water but also through mucous membranes, as well as cuts and abrasions. So waters used for swimming and boating pose risks, especially after flooding. The bacteria begin their journey in urine of infected mammals, which often show no disease symptoms. In humans, symptoms are often mistaken for those of other tropical diseases. such as malaria.

'Possums host fleas, ticks, mites, and lice, especially dog and cat lice in residential environments. Carrion introduces internal parasites, including roundworms and pinworms.

For more on diseases and parasites, see page 210.

Playing 'Possum

When faced with an inescapable threat during a fight or in a trap, opossums often enter catatonic shock. This causes the animal to fall motionless on its side. Meanwhile, the eyes remain open, and the mouth is slightly open, revealing teeth, a lolling tongue, and a flow of saliva. From the anus, a foul-smelling greenish fluid may emerge.

Unresponsive to prodding, the stiff, motionless heap may puzzle a predator enough to abandon the prize. Through this trauma, the opossum's tiny brain remains conscious of surroundings. After the threat departs, the opossum cautiously rouses itself.

CHAPTER 10

Collared Peccaries
(Javelinas)

"Hey, Dad! Peccaries!" A quick U-turn brought us back to the peccary site, but too late. Our son, Nikolai, had taken a break from computer-game design to help me locate wildlife in Arizona's comparatively lush Sedona region, north of Phoenix.

My own first impression of peccaries came from a Disney wildlife film. In it, a ferocious herd of peccaries chased a bobcat up a large saguaro cactus and then maintained a squealing vigil below while the bobcat licked cactus spines in its paws.

ORIGIN AND DISTRIBUTION

Wild peccary populations occur in Arizona, New Mexico, and Texas. This represents a northward expansion from Mexico that appears to have begun less than a few hundred years ago. Peccaries are actually of South American origin, where they range all the way to Argentina.

These sparsely furred animals don't survive extended cold well. So their northward expansion may need to await the pace of global warming. When temperatures dip near freezing, peccaries huddle together to share warmth. In mountainous regions, snow and ice storms can wipe out whole herds.

PROBLEMS FOR PEOPLE

Human development continues to impose itself on peccary territories. So it's during drought especially that peccaries come searching for water and plants. During these residential raids, peccaries favor succulent plants, as well as bulbs, tubers, beans, fruits, nuts, and seeds, including birdseed. Powerful animals, peccaries can work their way through or under vulnerable fencing. They scavenge garbage, compost piles, unfinished pet food, and open campsite coolers. On hot days, they may

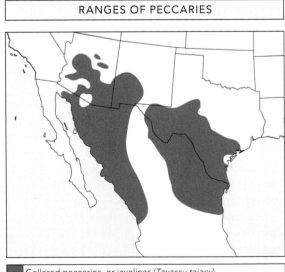

RANGES OF PECCARIES

Collared peccaries, or javelinas (*Tayassu tajacu*)

What's in the Names?
The official common name, "peccary," echoes the former genus name, *Pecari*. And "collared" refers to the band of light-colored collarlike hairs that are more evident in winter than in summer. Still, many people prefer the Spanish name, *javelina* (pronounced *ha-va-LEEN-a*), acknowledging javelin-pointed upper and lower canines measuring 1 to 1²/₅ inches long. Another common name, "musk hog," refers to the strong musk scent emitted by a gland on the animal's back, which allows you to smell peccaries before you see them.

Order: Artiodactyla ■ **Family:** TAYASSUIDAE ■ **Genus:** *Tayassu* ■ **Species:** *tajacu*

The "collar" in the name collared peccary refers to the light band of collar hairs. (Photo by Lennie and Uschi Rue III)

seek shade under porches and in crawl spaces. And peccary activity can attract mountain lions.

In hot weather, peccaries prefer to feed early or late in the day and at night, but in colder months, they forage more by day. In most seasons, peccaries depend heavily on prickly pear cactus as a water source. But they do favor and defend terrain with natural water. When plant moisture and open water become scarce, peccaries may chew into irrigation lines and visit home pools.

Herd sizes range from 2 to more than 20. Although peccaries prefer to avoid people and dogs, they can fight viciously if pressed or surprised. With long, sharp teeth, a single adult peccary is capable of killing or seriously wounding an aggressive dog. However, owing to poor eyesight, peccaries have sometimes been accused of charging people when they were actually trying to escape.

ROLE IN THE WILD

Depending on the availability of food and water, herd territories often range from 1 to 2 square miles. Although prickly pear isn't highly nutritious, peccaries depend on its high water content—sometimes as high as 90 percent. They eat other spiny cacti, too, along with agaves, yuccas, mesquite beans, grasses, forbs, insects, and snakes.

Larger predators include cougars and black bears. However, midsize predators such as bobcats, coyotes, and golden eagles need to consider the

defensive fury of peccary herds and often thus content themselves only with youngsters, which weigh only a pound at birth.

IDENTIFICATION

Adult peccaries weigh 28 to 68 pounds and stand 18 to 24 inches "at the shoulder" (top of their back). Males are about the same size as females, and look quite similar. Fur color varies from light brown to gray and nearly black, except for the light-colored "collar." Close up, the fur suggests a salt-and-pepper effect caused by bands of color on individual hairs.

Although peccaries are often called wild hogs or pigs, they are not closely related to the feral hogs of the United States. Those hogs are descended from escaped domestic pigs—animals that were originally bred from European wild boars. Today, feral pigs damage wild habitats in the South and spread fatal diseases to domestic pigs. Native peccary and alien pigs have some obvious differences: Peccaries have only three toes on their hind feet, rather than four; they have straight canines, rather than curved; and they have a mere 1-inch tail, rather than the longer tails of pigs. Also, peccaries weigh far less than feral pigs, which can reach 400 pounds.

SIGN

Tracks. Hoofs are two-toed, like deer hoofs, but rounder. Front hooves are about 1½ inches long; back hooves, 1 inch long. The third toe on the hind foot is a vestigial dewclaw on the leg that doesn't register.

Digging. Holes may be shallow or several inches deep and often show hoof marks.

Scat. Depending on forage, scat may be formless piles or sausage shaped.

MATING AND BIRTH

Like many mammals from South America, peccary females are capable of breeding year-round, some bearing two litters per year. Because herds are highly territorial, mating rights in small herds usually go to the dominant male, who may need to share those rights in larger herds.

Most breeding occurs from January through March, which ensures that most kits are born

Canine teeth may be 1²/₅ inches long. (Photo by Lennie and Uschi Rue III)

during the summer rainy season with its lush new plant growth. Litters usually consist of two 1-pound kits that can follow their mother soon after birth. Weaning takes about 6 weeks. The kits are sometimes called reds for their often reddish-brown fur that lasts several months.

SENSES

Researchers consider peccary eyesight poor and hearing only average. But peccaries have a keen sense of smell, often navigating as much by smell as by eyesight. In fact, a scent gland on their backs and preorbital glands in front of each eye are important in communication and bonding.

OPTIONS FOR CONTROL

Peccaries are protected big-game animals. So in residential areas, control requires visits by state wildlife authorities, as well as the cooperation of neighbors.

Eliminating food and water. If neighbors are intentionally or inadvertently feeding peccaries, find means of helping them stop. As peccaries become accustomed to people, they lose their fear. Attempts at hand-feeding, especially, can lead to serious bites.

Resistant plants. Peccaries often test-taste and dig up plants they don't actually eat. As with deer, peccary preferences may change through the seasons as plant chemistries and moisture levels change. So the safest precaution is a sturdy fence. However, based on 300 homeowner interviews, the University of Arizona Cooperative Extension developed a listing of 61 types of plants least favored by peccaries. You can obtain that list free on the Internet by using the search words *Arizona,*

javelina, resistant, and *plants.* Some of those plants are noted in Part 3 of this book.

Exclusion. Following are recommendations of experts at the University of Arizona. As to fencing, first ensure that the type you prefer is approved by local zoning authorities.

■ *Electric fencing:* Position one strand of solar-powered electric fencing 8 to 10 inches above the ground and another 6 to 8 inches above that.

■ *Masonry walls:* Besides being impregnable, masonry walls hide delectables.

■ *Metal-mesh fencing:* In addition to a heavy-duty mesh fence, preferably chain-link, university experts recommend a concrete footer buried 8 to 12 inches.

■ *House foundation seals:* If your property is unfenced, options beginning on page 58 may help.

Frighteners. Experts at Arizona Fish and Game advise driving peccaries away by noisemaking and gestures, as well as water sprays and rock throwing. Check local laws before using paintball guns, which have proven effective on bears, as described on page 83.

Repellents. Tucson Extension specialist Laurence Sullivan suggests spreading hot sauce in feeding areas and placing ammonia-soaked rags in resting areas.

Hunting and trapping. Peccaries are protected big-game animals. Aside from licensed hunting in designated areas, state game departments prefer to handle problem animals themselves.

COMMUNICABLE DISEASES AND PARASITES

Unlike feral hogs, peccaries aren't significant carriers of diseases to domestic pigs. And there has been only one reported case of rabies. The latest edition of *Wild Mammals of North America* mentions no transmission of peccary diseases to humans.

External parasites include ticks, lice, mites, chiggers, and fleas. Internal parasites include tapeworms, flukes, protozoans, and nematodes, which of course could infect water sources.

CHAPTER 11

Porcupines

One autumn long ago, at a rest stop along Wisconsin's I-94, I noticed a porcupine emerging from the woods and heading toward what appeared to be a suicidal highway crossing. I ran to intercept the slow-moving Porky and urged his return to the woods. At this, he paused 6 feet from me and attempted a detour, which I discouraged by stepping in that direction. Our dancelike standoff continued left and right until Porky turned in disgust and headed back toward the woods.

At this, I dashed to my car to retrieve a camera. But by then, Porky had changed his mind and was again heading toward the highway. When I again attempted to block his way, he charged—allowing only the blurry photo you see here.

Unwilling to watch the attempted crossing, I returned to my car and drove off, not knowing that the fall mating season had begun.

When Porky charged, this blurry photo was the best I got while backpedaling.

PROBLEMS FOR PEOPLE

Although porcupines favor coniferous forests, they thrive in a wide range of habitats. Porcupines damage trees and shrubs by eating the inner bark on the trunk and upper branches.

To satisfy their salt craving, porcupines visit roadsides to consume salt spread by snowplows. This often causes traffic jams and accidents. To obtain sodium, porcupines also chew on plywood, power cables, and the rubber fuel lines of vehicles. And they chew wood impregnated with human perspiration salts, including canoes, canoe paddles, and tool handles.

Dogs are vulnerable to the porcupine's prime defensive weaponry: Stiff, sharp quills project from virtually all exposed body parts. When assaulted by a dog, a porcupine turns its back to the commotion and whips its tail about. If the dog lunges into the quills or is struck by quills on the flailing tail, the porcupine's skin releases them. Poor dog!

Each quill point has reverse barbs that resist extraction. The quills ratchet themselves deeper into the skin when the dog paws at them and when the dog's facial muscles contract in response to the pain. This ratcheting action works the quills deeper into the victim until blocked finally by bone.

Fortunately, quills seldom cause infection because they are coated with an antibiotic fatty layer, which also protects porcupines during fights with other porcupines and when porcupines accidentally fall from a tree and "quill" themselves.

Veterinarians anesthetize the suffering dog, clip the exposed ends of the quills to reduce internal

Order: Rodentia ■ **Family:** ERETHIZONTIDAE ■ **Genus:** *Erethizon* ■ **Species:** *dorsatum*

pressure, and then pull them out. In the old days, dog owners and strong-handed friends blindfolded the dog and held it down during extraction. The blindfold helped ensure that the dog remained the owner's best friend.

ROLE IN THE WILD

Porcupines are primarily nocturnal in winter, but they do mix day and night feeding patterns most of the year. They often reside in rock dens and emerge to forage. In warmer months, they may spend most of their time in tree branches feeding and sleeping there. Among predators, fishers and mountain lions are the most adept at flipping porcupines over to expose their vulnerable underside.

DISTRIBUTION AND IDENTIFICATION

Hailing from South America, porcupines thrive everywhere in North America except in the Southeast and in the Midwest, though fossil records show that porcupines once lived in those regions, too.

The porcupine is the sole North American mammal armed with quills, and it is the largest rodent adept at climbing and living much of the time in trees. The 1- to 4-inch quills cover most of the animal's exposed parts but are disguised by long, soft guard hairs. In the East, porcupines are dark with white highlights. In the West, yellowish guard hairs predominate, except in winter. Average head-and-body length is 20 inches; the tail is 7 inches long.

PREFERRED FOODS

Active year-round, porcupines eat mainly woody buds in spring. In summer, they switch to the leaves of woody and herbaceous plants, which they supplement in fall with acorns and other nuts as well as apples. In winter, porcupines survive mainly on the inner bark of trees, along with conifer needles.

SIGN

Bark. Exposed patches of wood on the thinner bark of tree trunks and branches show paired incisor marks ¼ inch wide.

Tracks. The rear foot registers slightly ahead of the smaller front foot, and both look pigeon-toed (toed-in). The large, naked soles imprint with tiny depressions like pockmarks, as though each sole were covered with hundreds of tiny pebbles. In ideal tracking mud, only the four long toes and claws register for the front foot; all five of the long toes and claws register for the rear foot, giving an imprint up to 5 inches long.

Nipped twigs. In spring and summer, the ground beneath trees is often littered with fresh "nip twigs" from which the buds have been eaten.

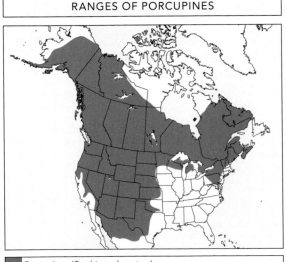

RANGES OF PORCUPINES

■ Porcupines (*Erethizon dorsatum*)

This hackberry trunk shows porcupine damage, says the biologist at Arizona's Montezuma Castle National Monument north of Phoenix.

Mushroom digs. Called "truffle digs" by biologists, these tend to be conical and 6 to 12 inches in diameter. Squirrel digs are smaller. Deer digs are flatter, more like hoof scrapes.

Scat. Droppings are bean shaped, 1 inch long, and often show undigested particles of bark pulp.

Salt chewings. These occur on tree trunks and any wood with salts deposited by snowplows or human perspiration. Porcupines also seek the salt in rubber vehicle hoses and tires.

MATING AND BIRTH

Mating occurs in fall. For this, males expand their range, as Porky was doing in this chapter's opening paragraphs. When a male spots a female in a tree, he climbs to a branch somewhat lower than hers to guard her from other males. He may also intermittently spray her with jets of urine. Breeding-season vocalizations include grunts, moans, and screams. Males often fight viciously over females, using teeth and quills.

A female signals her readiness to mate by descending to the ground and arching her tail over her back, which allows her champion to approach without being quilled. A gestation period of 7 months produces just one baby in summer. Weaning takes about 4 months.

OPTIONS FOR CONTROL

Porcupines tend to be solitary. Females are more territorial than males. Still, the size of home ranges depends on density. In a New York study, the average nonwinter home range of females was 56 acres, and the average male range was 180 acres. In Nevada, the nonwinter female range was 20 acres, and the male range was 37 acres. Winter ranges are smaller. From this, it's apparent that porcupines range widely. So if you want to protect just an acre or two of trees, your efforts can leave porcupines plenty to dine on elsewhere, without your need for firearms or traps.

Importing and protecting predators. Natural predators have proven highly effective in various states. In an Upper Michigan study, fishers introduced to a porcupine problem area reduced

If you find a littering of nipped twigs beneath a tree, the nipper may be overhead. (Photo by Lennie and Uschi Rue III)

the population by more than 95 percent. Thus, jurisdictions that allow fur trapping of fishers will be more vulnerable to tree damage from porcupines. Cougars are also effective predators.

Exclusion. Year-round wire-mesh guards at the bases of tree trunks can protect the area under them against bark damage from porcupines, as well as from voles and rabbits. Metal cylinders and flared baffles around trunks can discourage climbing.

Livetrapping. If porcupines are damaging your property, check with wildlife officials. For example, the Arizona Fish and Game Department requests that residents inquire about authorized traps, baits, and release sites before attempting livetrapping.

Hunting. Where hunting is legal, a treed porcupine is an easy target. But, as an alternative, consider harassing the animal down with a pole. Thereafter install a trunk guard.

COMMUNICABLE DISEASES AND PARASITES

Because porcupines tend to be solitary and often occupy trees, they are less often exposed to diseases and parasites that plague communal mammals and those that forage mainly on the ground. Porcupines suffer internal and skin parasites that don't cause much mortality among themselves or other animals. The latest edition of *Wild Mammals of North America* indicates no transmission of porcupine ailments to humans.

CHAPTER 12

Rabbits and Hares

For 19 years, cottontail rabbits were content to dine on clover *outside* our vegetable garden. We'd protected the garden with 4-foot-tall wire-mesh fencing. While Hannelore worked in the garden, baby cottontails approached outside, as though hoping to hear more sweet talk.

However, one June, Hannelore discovered that her parsley was being eaten by "something" that left neatly severed stems. We closely inspected the lower portion of the 2 × 4-inch mesh but found no breaks and no evidence of burrowing under it.

Hannelore hastily protected her parsley with 1 × 1-inch plastic mesh, as shown below. That halted further damage, while allowing the parsley to grow through. When "something" began eating the bush beans, Hannelore covered them with bird netting. This too proved reasonably successful, except at netting edges.

Finally, "something" began eating broccoli plants from ground level to heights of 15 inches. But the broccoli plants were spaced too widely for protection with bird netting.

About then, Hannelore saw a cottontail dash from the garden through the 2 × 4-inch wire mesh *at full speed,* as though the mesh weren't there. That puzzled me because young cottontails near our house looked too large to fit through mesh, let alone at full speed.

With camera in hand, I approached the garden. Sure enough, Peter Cottontail sat just outside the garden fence, watching me warily. As I drew near, Peter hopped toward the fence and carefully fit his head through the mesh before squinching his shoulders like a contortionist and lunging inside.

Lessons learned: (1) Rabbits squeeze through any opening wide enough for their heads. (2) Wire mesh for young rabbits needs to be 1 inch, rather than 2 inches.

Young Peter Cottontail showed no interest in our sage leaves in foreground or our tomato leaves behind. But he relished our parsley until Hannelore laid 1-inch plastic mesh over it. Peter feared the mesh because his feet slipped through.

Order: Lagomorpha ■ **Family:** LEPORIDAE ■ **Native Genera:** 3 ■ **Alien Genera:** 2 ■ **Species:** many

When I approached Peter Cottontail sitting outside our garden fence, I was surprised he could fit his head through the 2-inch-wide mesh and then squinch his shoulders and lunge through. As I stalked Peter with camera outside the fence, he enjoyed our broccoli, apparently aware the fence protected him. Lesson learned: Gardeners need 1-inch-wide mesh near ground level to exclude young rabbits.

Livetrap experiment: That week, I'd been noodling a concept for a homemade live trap. The quickly constructed trap worked beautifully. And Peter sat hunched dejectedly inside. However, I was astonished to see Peter's apparent sibling inside the garden. I dubbed her Pauline and baited a live-trap cage for her. (You'll find details on this episode and techniques later in this chapter.)

PROBLEMS FOR PEOPLE

Rabbits and hares can be major problems for gardeners, orchardists, farmers, and foresters whose plants aren't protected by some means. In late fall, when herbaceous plants are no longer available, the diet of rabbits and hares switches heavily to woody bark. In the North, increasing snow levels provide a rising platform on which to dine continually higher on tree trunks.

Although rabbits and hares are considered the most important game animal, based on hunter participation and harvests, they can transmit a variety of serious diseases and parasites to people who don't take precautions, as addressed at the end of this chapter.

ROLE IN THE WILD

Rabbits and hares are important in nature's food web. They feed foxes, coyotes, wolves, bobcats, lynxes, cougars, and members of the weasel family (including fishers), as well as owls, raptors, and snakes.

In some regions, the future of the golden eagle is linked strongly to the population of black-tailed jackrabbits. The four species of jackrabbits often represent more than half of the diet of bobcats and coyotes. When coyote populations fall as a result of predator control programs, jackrabbit populations rise. In the North, snowshoe hares are a principal food of lynx. There, too, red squirrels and arctic ground squirrels prey on newborn snowshoe hares.

RANGES OF RABBITS

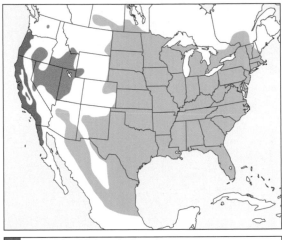

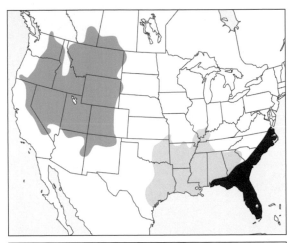

	Brush rabbit (*Sylvilagus bachmani*)
	Eastern cottontail (*S. floridanus*)
	Pygmy rabbit (*Brachylagus idahoensis*)

	Marsh rabbit (*Sylvilagus palustris*)
	Mountain cottontail, Nuttall's cottontail (*S. nuttallii*)
	Swamp rabbit, Cane cutter (*S. aquaticus*)

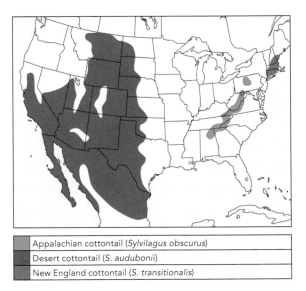

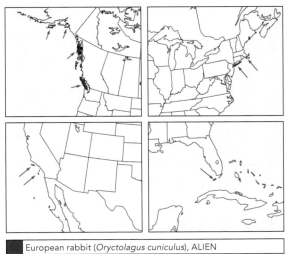

	Appalachian cottontail (*Sylvilagus obscurus*)
	Desert cottontail (*S. audubonii*)
	New England cottontail (*S. transitionalis*)

	European rabbit (*Oryctolagus cuniculus*), ALIEN

IDENTIFICATION, SPECIES, AND DISTRIBUTION

Rabbits and hares are not rodents. They are lagomorphs, distinguished from rodents in part by their two sets of upper incisors. One set consists of cutting teeth, like rodent teeth. The second set is a pair of "pegged" incisors right behind the cutting teeth. In further contrast, rabbits and hares have long ears, long hind feet, and a short tail.

To distinguish between rabbits and hares, we need to visit their birthing area. Mother rabbits make nests of vegetation and line them with their own fur; rabbit babies are born helpless and naked, with eyes closed. Mother hares don't make nests;

RANGES OF HARES

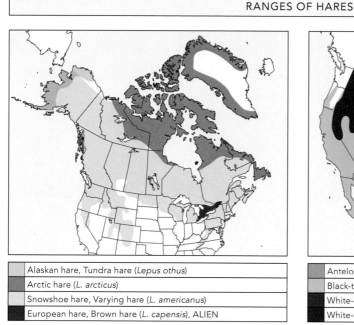

	Alaskan hare, Tundra hare (*Lepus othus*)
	Arctic hare (*L. arcticus*)
	Snowshoe hare, Varying hare (*L. americanus*)
	European hare, Brown hare (*L. capensis*), ALIEN

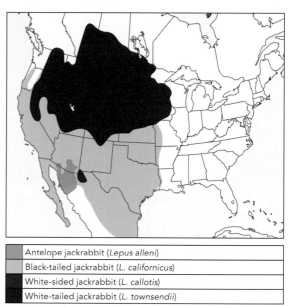

	Antelope jackrabbit (*Lepus alleni*)
	Black-tailed jackrabbit (*L. californicus*)
	White-sided jackrabbit (*L. callotis*)
	White-tailed jackrabbit (*L. townsendii*)

their newborns emerge with eyes open, have a full coat of fur, and can dash about soon after arrival.

Most hare species are larger than most cottontail species. However, the big marsh and swamp rabbits of the Southeast are larger than the snowshoe hare of the North. Nor is ear length a reliable distinguisher between rabbits and hares, except for the long 4- to 6-inch ears of the four species of jackrabbit.

Although cottontails sample zinnias in early summer, they don't seem to like mature zinnias much, preferring clover and plantain instead.

The name "jackrabbit" contributes to a common misconception. Jackrabbits aren't rabbits. They are hares.

Here are names and distinguishing features among rabbits and hares as presented in *Mammals of North America,* a Peterson Field Guide.

Rabbits (9 natives, 1 alien)

Pygmy rabbit *(Brachylagus idahoensis):* Average head-and-body length 9½ inches; ears 1¾ inches long

Brush rabbit *(Sylvilagus bachmani):* Head-and-body length 12 inches; ears 2½ inches long

Swamp rabbit, Cane cutter *(S. aquaticus):* Head-and-body length 17½ inches; ears 2¾ inches long

Marsh rabbit *(S. palustris):* Head-and-body length 15 inches; ears 2 inches long

Eastern cottontail *(S. floridanus):* Head-and-body length 14 inches; ears 3 inches long. Ears shorter in northern part of range. Orange-tinged fur on neck and back distinguishes this cottontail from New England and Appalachian cottontails. Sometimes has white blaze on forehead.

Jackrabbits aren't really rabbits. They are hares, like this snowshoe hare in winter coat. Unlike rabbits, hares don't make nests, and their newborns emerge with eyes open, have a full coat of fur, and can dash about soon after arrival. (Photos by Lennie and Uschi Rue III)

New England cottontail *(S. transitionalis):* Head-and-body length 15 inches; ear 2½ inches. Black spot on forehead and along front edge of ears

Appalachian cottontail *(S. obscurus):* Head-and-body length 14 inches. Externally same as New England species, distinguishable by range

Mountain cottontail, Nuttall's cottontail *(S. nuttallii):* Head-and-body length 13 inches; ears 2 inches long

Desert cottontail *(S. audubonii):* Head-and-body length 12 inches; ears 3 inches long

European rabbit *(Oryctolagus cuniculus):* Head-and-body length 16 inches; ears 2¾ inches long, ALIEN

Hares (7 natives, 1 alien)

Snowshoe hare, Varying hare *(Lepus americanus):* Head-and-body length 16 inches; ears 2¾ inches long. Fur turns white in winter, and exceptionally large hind foot (the snowshoe) facilitates travel in snow. This is the smallest hare, also smaller than swamp and brush rabbits.

Alaskan hare, Tundra hare *(L. othus):* Head-and-body length 22 inches; ears 3 inches long

Arctic hare *(L. arcticus):* Head-and-body length 21 inches; ears 3½ inches long

White-tailed jackrabbit *(L. townsendii):* Head-and-body length 21 inches; ears 4 inches long. Tail white. In northern part of range with snow, fur turns white in winter.

Black-tailed jackrabbit *(L. californicus):* Head-and-body length 18½ inches; ears 4⅓ inches long. Tail broad and black.

White-sided jackrabbit *(L. callotis):* Head-and-body length 18½ inches; ears 4¾ inches long

Antelope jackrabbit *(L. alleni):* Head-and-body length 22 inches; ears 6 inches long. Can run 45 mph and leap 23 feet. May sometimes hop like kangaroo

European hare, Brown hare *(L. capensis):* Head-and-body length 22 inches; ears 4 inches long, ALIEN

SIGN

Cottontails and brush rabbits tend to feed near escape cover. Although jackrabbits also prefer to have cover nearby, they often need to feed much farther into open areas.

Fecal pellets. The brown fecal pellets of cottontails are about ⅓-inch oblongs, as shown. Brown pellets of jackrabbits are closer to ½ inch. Actually, rabbits and hares excrete two kinds of pellets. The kind we don't see are soft green pellets called *cecotropes* that the animals re-ingest as the pellets emerge because they are high in partially digested nutrients. The brown pellets on the ground represent second-pass material, high in fiber and low in nutrients.

Cut stems and branches. Rabbits and hares bite off woody and herbaceous stems at a 45-degree angle as cleanly as a bypass pruner.

Tracks. Tracks for rabbits and hares occur in groups of four, the larger back feet registering ahead of the front feet, as the animals hop. Those of rabbits and jackrabbits tend to look pointy in soil. Those of snowshoe hares splay large and wide; the feet serve like snowshoes in winter and allow escape from predators whose paws often break through the snowpack, slowing them down.

Debarked trees and shrubs. Especially in winter, rabbits and hares gnaw on thin, smooth bark of shrubs and young trees, sometimes completely girdling them. Debarking tends to be heaviest near ground level but may extend 15 to 20 inches above snow level. You can distinguish rabbit gnawing by incisor marks and relatively clean edges between bark and raw wood. Deer have no upper teeth and so must tear bark off, leaving ragged edges.

Trails. Cottontails use preferred trails through vegetation, often clipping the stems to keep the trails open for fast escapes. Jackrabbit trails often appear as beaten paths in the soil.

Burrows. Only the pygmy rabbit is known to dig its own burrow. Rather than digging burrows,

> ### Hare Hair Color
>
> In northern snowy regions, "the hare is always camouflaged to suit the season, annually shedding its brown summer coat for a white winter garb," says Leonard Lee Rue III, author of *Game Animals of North America*. Diminished northern sunlight in autumn stimulates white hair growth. Increasing daylight after December stimulates a dark replacement coat.

cottontails and hares may seek refuge in abandoned burrows dug by badgers, woodchucks, or armadillos.

Forms. Cottontails and hares spend much of their time resting in "forms." These are usually hiding places beneath clumps of grass or in thickets that provide shade and cover. There the animal often excavates a saucerlike depression.

Birthing nests. Expectant cottontail mothers excavate saucerlike depressions in the soil and then build birdlike nests of grasses and other vegetation and line them with their own fur. After nursing her babies, the mother folds the sides of the nest over the babies like a blanket that serves as insulation, rain cover, and camouflage. The mother then moves away about 25 feet to watch the nest. She will often defend her babies from predators she thinks she can scare away, including rodents, cats, and dogs.

Antelope jackrabbit mothers also create nests lined with their own hair. They suckle their

Fecal pellets of cottontails are ⅓-inch oblongs; pellets of jackrabbits are about ½ inch long. In winter, rabbits feed on the smooth, thin bark of shrubs and young trees, often killing them. Rabbits and hares nip stems and branches as cleanly as a bypass pruner, usually at a 45-degree angle, as on this broccoli. Outside our garden fence, cottontails showed no interest in petunias or columbines.

young only at night, then cover them with soil and plant debris.

Rather than creating a nest, black-tailed jackrabbits create a mere shallow depression, also called a form, usually under protective cover.

BREEDING AND REPRODUCTION

All rabbits and hares have mating behaviors that involve boxing with forepaws and jumping over one another with frequent urination on each other, culminating in chases and mating.

Cottontails. Breeding occurs nearly year-round in the Far South but may not begin until late March in the North, continuing into fall. Increasing annual daylight hours and increasing temperatures bring females into heat in northern regions, triggering breeding about 28 days ahead of availability of succulent greens. Conveniently, 28 days is the average number of days for gestation. Babies begin "free living" in 10 to 14 days.

Litter sizes vary by species and latitude but tend to average four or five, usually fewer near the beginning and the end of the breeding season. Multiple litters provide a total of 15 to 30 babies per mother annually.

Jackrabbits. During the breeding season, female jackrabbits charge other females that approach. Competing male jackrabbits may head-butt, bite, jump, and run circles around one another. Antelope jackrabbit males tend to congregate around one female, whereas white-sided jackrabbits pair-bond during the breeding season.

The breeding season tends to be shorter in the North, running from January or February into May, but breeding continues longer in southern states. Gestation averages 43 days, which is about 2 weeks longer than that of cottontails. And this longer gestation seems to explain why jackrabbits emerge fully furred at birth and ready to move about. Litters average four *leverets* each, and multiple litters produce about 14 leverets per mother annually.

Snowshoe hares. Gestation is about 37 days. Litters range between two and five leverets, with total annual production per mother averaging only 5 to 13.

HOME RANGES AND FEEDING BEHAVIORS

Cottontails feed mainly between sunrise and sunset but also feed at night. Ranges depend on site and availability of food, but populations can grow to unusual highs of eight per acre.

Male black-tailed jackrabbits may range over hundreds of acres for food, but the females usually need to stay much closer to their babies. One study showed 50 percent of a black-tailed population occupying the best 7 percent of habitat. Although black-tails are able to digest many plants with compounds toxic to livestock, they tend to select younger, more succulent plants with high nutritive value. Black-tails feed mainly at night, beginning in the early evening and eating through early morning. They tend to avoid open areas, and feed near or under cover.

Snowshoe hares favor dense cover regardless of plant species and feed most at dawn and dusk. In winter, they dig craters to reach plant life below. Home ranges tend to be less than 16 acres.

SENSES

With large eyes protruding on each side of the head, rabbits and hares can see nearly full circle, but not directly ahead. To look at something, they need to turn their heads. Hearing is excellent, aided by the animal's ability to aim the ears independently to detect and then funnel sound. The constantly wiggling nose tests for danger and also serves in finding food.

OPTIONS FOR CONTROL

Rabbits and hares are prolific breeders, so elimination of one or more animals usually invites replacements. Thus, fencing and habitat modification are the best long-term solutions.

In many jurisdictions, rabbits and hares are considered game animals subject to official hunting seasons. However, landowners or tenants are often allowed to control crop destroyers by any legal means. Check with game officials.

Minimizing shelter. Unlike jackrabbits, cottontails prefer close proximity to vegetative cover with high stem densities associated with native,

Cottontails have routinely chewed through our plastic mesh fencing to reach bounty inside and to create escape routes. Prior to winter, ¼-inch wire mesh cylinders can eliminate rabbit and hare damage, while also minimizing vole damage. During winter, plastic drainpipe (slit to pry open on one side) protects young trees from chewing damage as well as winter sunscald, as described on the next page.

early-succession habitats, as advocated throughout this book. Although larger lawns discourage rabbits, they also discourage insects, birds, reptiles, and other small mammals that are suffering declining populations as a result of unrelenting habitat loss. So it seems more ecologically responsible to protect valuable plants with fencing and trunk guards than attempt to keep wildlife away by means of big lawns (additional reasons are enumerated on page 60).

Fencing. Rabbits and hares don't dig under fencing, but they will try to squeeze under if it isn't tight to the ground or embedded a bit. Cottontails and brush rabbits aren't known to jump 2-foot fences. Normally, most jackrabbits and hares won't either, except when frightened. However, antelope jackrabbits can clear 4-foot fences when frightened. So except in antelope-jackrabbit territory, not subject to snow cover, 2-foot fencing can serve well as barriers around individual plants wherever woodchucks, opossums, raccoons, armadillos, dogs, and small children aren't potential additional threats to plants. However, for a fenced garden, a height of 4 feet will serve better for the gamut of small to midsize mammals.

■ *Mesh fencing:* Rabbits commonly chew through plastic-mesh fencing, either to get at what's inside or to create escape holes for themselves. So wire mesh is needed. Because young rabbits and hares

can squeeze through 2 × 4-inch wire mesh, the mesh for them should be no larger than 1 inch wide. Farm and garden suppliers often stock fencing with mesh graduated in size from bottom to top, such as 1 × 6 inches at the bottom and 4 × 6 inches at the top. To locate mail-order suppliers on the Internet, use the search words *fencing, rabbit,* and *graduated.*

■ *Wooden fencing:* Ensure that spacing between lath or bamboo is no more than 1 inch. It's smart to extend 1-inch wire mesh into the soil, as well.

■ *Electric fencing:* For rabbits, hares, and similar size mammals, electric mesh fencing serves better than tape-type fencing.

Trunk guards. Various commercial and home-made guards can serve well. Most damage to woody plants occurs in winter because rabbits and hares prefer succulent green vegetation when available. For cottontails and snowshoe hares, winter guards should extend 20 inches above expected snowpack so the animals can't reach the bark on their hindquarters. For jackrabbits, winter guards should extend 30 inches above the snowpack.

■ *Wire mesh cylinders:* You can surround trunks with cylinders of ¼-inch mesh wire, first roller-painted to match trunk color so it is less conspicuous. The small mesh will also protect bark from voles.

■ *Flexible plastic drainpipe:* I first saw 6-inch drainpipe used at the Minnesota Landscape Arboretum, where it is applied mainly before snowfall to protect trees in two ways: to ward off gnawing rabbits and rodents, and to protect trunks from winter sunscald. Sunscald results in winter when sun on the trunk's south side thaws that bark. Thereafter plummeting nighttime temperatures refreeze the thawed tissue, causing cell damage in and under the bark.

■ *Plastic wraps:* Commercial trunk wraps of plastic or paper can protect trunks from rabbits, rodents, and deer.

Plant selection. Rabbits and hares tend to favor and avoid many of the same plants that deer favor and avoid. This is largely due to plant chemistry, especially to changing plant chemistry during growth stages that affect a plant's scent, taste, and toxicity. For example, young herbaceous plants and the buds and new shoots of woody plants are often favored because they are high in protein and taste good, because they haven't yet developed physical and chemical defenses against browsers. At this stage, especially, plants deserve extra protection, either with physical barriers or spray-on repellents.

In fall and winter in colder climates, rabbits and hares need to switch from herbaceous plants to less palatable and less nutritious bark, buds, and twigs of woody plants. Throughout the year, toxic *terpenes* in conifers discourage dining. Terpenes are essential oils used in the manufacture of solvents, such as turpentine.

You can appreciate the repellency of terpenes by breaking a single conifer needle and then tasting it. Terpenes are especially strong in spruces, which together with other hard-needled conifers can wisely serve as the "bones" in mammal-resistant landscaping.

In Part 3 of this book, you'll find hundreds of plants that rabbits, hares, and deer tend to avoid.

Repellents. For dissuading rabbits, researchers at the University of California have found that putrescent whole-egg solids work best on the bark of young trees and shrubs, as well as vines and her-baceous ornamentals. Many types of such commercial repellents need to be reapplied after rain and after plant growth. Because many are not food safe, be sure to read manufacturer labels before purchase and then follow application instructions.

Predators. Besides the variety of wild predators, house cats and dogs with a hunting disposition can take a toll on rabbits. "The rabbit is so familiar with its home territory that it runs in a large circle within that territory if pursued by a slow dog. A fast dog will force the rabbit to seek shelter as soon as it can. When the rabbit is flushed from its form, it bounds away in a zigzag pattern but as soon as it finds one of its well-used paths, it follows it," according to my friend Lennie Rue in his *Game Animals of North America.*

Frighteners. A dog's daily presence can make a garden area far less inviting to rabbits, especially if the dog has harassed the rabbit at least once. Even when a dog is snoozing in the house, its footprints, urine, and feces will have scent-marked a large area that says "Dog Territory: Beware!"

Livetrapping. In many jurisdictions, rabbits and hares are protected game animals but homeowners and tenants are often allowed to use legal means of control on their own property. However, transport and release may be illegal. If you are legally allowed to livetrap and release, check with local wildlife control officers or animal rehabilitators first. They may be able to suggest where releases are allowed.

Sliced apples and corn are good baits. Commercial baits may include apples, rabbit glands scented with

---

Livetrapping Downsides

In the confines of live traps, snowshoe hares often manifest a stress-related condition known as trap sickness. Symptoms resemble those of shock and prove fatal. Furthermore, one study showed that upon release in new habitat, snowshoe hares were challenged by resident hares and lost 90 percent of those battles. For more on related downsides of livetrapping, including communicable diseases and parasites, see page 62.

At left, Peter and Pauline await release. For bait, I place small apple slices outside like stepping-stones leading inside. I created the top live trap mostly from recyclables: The shell is a kitty-litter container, its mesh secured by an old bicycle inner tube. The bait treadle is a half section of the container lid, teetering on electrical conduit. At the far end, the door drops like a harmless guillotine within aluminum channel secured by machine bolts. The door consists of cutout container bottom shielded from chewing by aluminum flashing. The door descends when the near edge of the treadle pulls a length of dental floss running up and along the roof to a paperclip "wedge" supporting the door. The roof wards off sun and rain.

Regarding commercial metal traps, rabbits are reluctant to walk on wire floor grating because their feet can slip through. A wood floorboard removes that fear. (The wooden trap is by wildlifecontrolsupplies.com.)

rabbit urine, or Broccoli Essence, available from wildlifecontrolsupplies.com. Position the trap near rabbit activity and then place teaser bait like stepping-stones that lead to the trap's triggering mechanism.

Trap floors and covers: I've observed that rabbits hate to walk on 1-inch and larger plastic and wire mesh, likely because their feet will slip through. So if you are using a wire-mesh trap, place a board on the floor. For this reason, some pros prefer wooden traps. Pros may cover a wire-mesh live trap with canvas so the trap appears to be a safe shelter. Although canvas would also help protect a trapped animal from sun and rain, I've instead covered my wire-mesh trap with a wide board for that purpose. If you leave a trap out overnight, a canvas cover can ensure that an inadvertently caught skunk doesn't notice your approach.

Hunting and lethal trapping. Check local game laws.

Poisoning. Not recommended for reasons described on page 64.

COMMUNICABLE DISEASES AND PARASITES

■ Tularemia (rabbit fever) is always fatal to rabbits and hares and has proven fatal in humans in 7 percent of untreated cases. In early stages of the disease, rabbits look normal. In advanced stages, they appear sluggish. Tularemia can be transmitted to people who handle or skin rabbits bare handed or if they eat undercooked meat. (For more, see page 215.)

■ Bubonic plague can be transmitted to humans by rabbits' fleas, as well as unprotected skinning and cleaning of infected animals. (For more, see page 212.)

■ Eastern cottontails have been linked to the diseases *Staphylococcus aureas,* eastern encephalitis, and papillomavirus. Jackrabbits can be reservoirs for equine encephalitis as well as a range of tick-borne diseases.

■ Rabbits and hares are subject to a host of internal parasites, including various worms.

CHAPTER 13

Raccoons

On a sunny October morning, California garden designer Carolyn Singer gave me a tour of her own garden. Inside her deer-fenced vegetable garden, she pointed upward into a wooden grape arbor. The overhead leaves looked very healthy. But instead of large bunches of Concord grapes, only bare stems remained. The night before Carolyn's planned harvest, masked bandits climbed her 6-foot fence and sat atop the wooden arbor, lifting grape bunches, one by one, and picking them clean.

Carolyn says her raccoons also lift turf in search of earthworms, which isn't as vexing as when they remove her potted plants from containers to search through container soil.

In many urban areas, raccoons are more numerous per square mile than in wild areas. (Photo by Lennie and Uschi Rue III)

Carolyn's deer-resistant plants and floral arrangements are featured in Part 3 of this book. She is the author of a highly authoritative series of self-published books entitled *Deer in My Garden* and personally tested all recommended plants bearing her "CA.s" symbol (= California.singer) as noted in "Authorities on Deer Resistance" on page 234.

PROBLEMS FOR HUMANS

In addition to their grape and earthworm harvests, raccoons raid ripened patches of corn, berries, and melons. In August of the first year we planted corn, Hannelore headed to the field garden to pick the first ripened ears. Instead, she found a scene that resembled a tornado touchdown—broken stalks everywhere. Virtually every ear was partially eaten, often showing only a contaminating bite or two. In those years, raccoon rabies was new to the Northeast, so we didn't attempt to salvage any of those ears, not even for the compost pile.

Raccoons also spill and consume the contents of garbage cans. They den in outbuildings, under porches, and in woodpiles. And in houses, raccoons den in attics, chimney flues, and crawl spaces. Raccoons may also create fire hazards by chewing wiring and by blocking exhaust vents. Inside poultry coops, they dine on eggs, ducks, and chickens.

Wildlife control professionals tend to receive their peak number of raccoon complaints in spring, when raccoon females den in houses. Then, with nursing newborns, otherwise nocturnal mothers sometimes need to supplement nighttime foraging

Order: Carnivora ■ **Family:** PROCYONIDAE ■ **Genus:** *Procyon* ■ **Species:** *lotor*

during the day. As a result, many people mistakenly assume that daytime travel signifies rabid behavior.

Urban raccoons. Upon arriving at dusk at the home of friends in a classy old neighborhood in Dobbs Ferry, New York, I gazed in disbelief as a large raccoon emerged from a storm drain, glanced at me nonchalantly, and waddled off. My friends weren't surprised. They suggested that the raccoon might be the same one they'd seen on their patio, feeding at their cat's dish—together with their cat.

Indeed, raccoons by the tens of thousands have migrated into suburbs and cities. In urban areas, raccoons den in culverts, storm drains, abandoned vehicles, outbuildings, attics, and seasonally dormant fireplace flues. Scientists at Cornell University offer this surprising statistic: Although raccoon

Top: *Vulnerable garbage cans attract raccoons and bears. (Photo by Lennie and Uschi Rue III)* Bottom: *Uncapped chimney flues allow raccoons to den atop fireplace dampers. (Photo © Lockwood, C.C./Animals Animals Enterprises)*

population densities may average only 30 to 40 per square mile in rural areas, densities in urban areas commonly exceed 100 per square mile! One pest control professional pulled more than 10 raccoons from the Metropolitan Museum of Art in Manhattan. Although it faces onto 10- to 20-story buildings, the Museum's rear side adjoins Central Park.

Rabies. In the East, since the 1980s, raccoons have become the prime vector for rabies, "one of the most important wildlife diseases in the eastern United States," according to Johns Hopkins's monumental *Wild Mammals of North America*. Rabies

---

Rabid Attack

By the mid-1990s in Massachusetts, raccoon rabies had reached epidemic proportions. So much so that market gardeners were carrying firearms to protect themselves and co-workers. While working as a Community Supported Agriculture (CSA) manager at the New England Small Farm Institute, gardening author and friend Miranda Smith had this frightening encounter:

"On the way to water the greenhouses one morning, I was surprised by a raccoon that dropped from a nearby tree and charged me, making an unearthly sound somewhere between hissing and growling. I bolted towards a barn, calling for Brian, a nearby friend who was routinely carrying a shotgun. I was only inches ahead of the raccoon but managed to get into a barn office and slam a screen door shut, catching some of its whiskers. The maddened raccoon turned and charged Brian, who was in the barn by now and at such short range that he couldn't shoot. He swung the handle of the gun at the raccoon, hitting it squarely and stunning it for a brief moment. Seeing its confusion, as well as its proximity to Brian, I opened the screen door and called to it to draw its attention. The raccoon turned and ran toward me again, so Brian was able to shoot it in the chest moments before it reached the door I was once again safely behind."

Miranda further cautions, "If you want a state pathologist to test for the rabies, it's important not to destroy the raccoon's brains with a gunshot—aim for the chest so that you can have someone verify that it was, indeed, a rabid animal."

gradually kills infected coons but usually not before they infect their kind, other wildlife, feral cats, and unvaccinated pets—with a potential for infecting humans.

Until the 1970s, raccoon rabies was confined to Florida, Georgia, and South Carolina. However, in the late 1970s near Shenandoah National Park, a rabies outbreak began spreading throughout the northeastern United States and eventually into Canada. That Shenandoah epicenter represented a sudden jump northward of more than 300 miles from the historical endemic range. How did the disease suddenly jump so far northward into one small geographical pocket before spreading at a rate of about 25 miles per year up the Atlantic Coast?

Apparently, according to Johns Hopkins, a hunting club transported 3,500 raccoons from Florida to Virginia, legally, but without observing currently prescribed quarantine periods. The spread is thought to have been hastened "by trash trucks carrying infected raccoons." Alas, raccoon rabies is now also spreading westward.

Immunizing baits. Scientists are experimenting with oral baits laced with immunizing vaccines against rabies. Although effective, the eventual result is a potential increase in the raccoon population. A surer option for a problem raccoon is to livetrap it and have a licensed person inject it with immunizing vaccine before its release, which most states require be on your own property. Options for release are discussed later in this chapter.

Rabies in humans. Despite widespread association of raccoons with humans, and occasional bites, "there have been no documented cases of humans contracting rabies from raccoons," according to Johns Hopkins's *Wild Mammals of North America.* Key here is washing the bite followed by a doctor's visit. If the biting raccoon hasn't been quarantined and examined, a prescribed series of vaccinations has proven highly effective for people.

Other diseases and parasites. Raccoons transmit various maladies mentioned on page 144, including raccoon roundworm *(Bylisascaris procyonis).* Roundworm is relatively benign inside raccoons. But raccoons shed roundworm eggs in

their feces. The resulting larvae are pathogenic to more than 50 species, particularly rodents and birds that search for seeds in the feces. Roundworm eggs are also a hazard to children playing where raccoons have walked because children may inadvertently touch raccoon feces before putting their fingers in their mouths.

ROLE IN THE WILD

House, garden, and disease issues aside, raccoons should be appreciated for what they are—highly adaptable, beautifully evolved creatures that have a hard time resisting our offerings of food and shelter.

Mainly nocturnal, the raccoon is considered a carnivore, although it is not designed for fleet-footed chase. Instead, it is an opportunistic omnivore, much like a bear. It favors wetlands and damp woods, ambling along the ground, hunchbacked with head down. It climbs trees well, searching for food there, snoozing on limbs, and denning in tree hollows. Raccoons also den at ground level.

Depending on season and availability, plants often contribute a major portion of the raccoon's diet. Favorites include acorns and other nuts, corn, fruits, and berries. In seasons when plant foods are less available, raccoons increase their dependence on insects, earthworms, eggs, nestlings, turtles, snails, reptiles, and carrion. They use their dexterous front paws to turn rocks in search of small critters. At water's edge, raccoons snatch up clams, crayfish, and small fish. They also prey

Like bear cubs, raccoon cubs rely strongly on Mom's training. (Photo by Lennie and Uschi Rue III)

on muskrats and on waterfowl crippled during hunting seasons. On coastal islands, raccoons prey on seabirds, as well as their eggs and nestlings.

Adult raccoons are prey to wolves, coyotes, bobcats, alligators, and free-ranging dogs. Younger raccoons also succumb to foxes and owls. As to dogs, campfire tales suggest that a large raccoons chased into deep water by a hunting hound is capable of getting on top of the dog and drowning it.

IDENTIFICATION AND DISTRIBUTION

Thought to have originated in Central America, raccoons now range throughout the United States and southern Canada.

The closest North American relatives are the ringtail and the coati of the Southwest and Mexico (the other coons). Compared to them and other carnivores, the raccoon's distinctively masked head seems small for its large, broad body, especially when it's fattened up for winter. The bushy, banded tail may be 10 inches long.

In the North, raccoons can weigh upward of 30 pounds and measure 3½ feet in total length. In the South, raccoons tend to be smaller and have lighter-colored fur. On the Florida mainland, raccoons are longer legged, while in the Florida Keys,

> ### Raccoon Weights North to South
>
> The decided weight disparity in raccoons from the far North into the Florida Keys is consistent with Bergmann's Rule. Christian Bergmann, a 19th-century German biologist, noticed that northernmost members of a species with great north-south range tend to be larger than those at southern ends. He suggested that larger members of a species survive extreme cold better because they have greater body mass relative to surface area and therefore lose less heat per square inch than smaller individuals. Conversely, smaller members of the same species living in hot, dry regions can dissipate heat more quickly, helping them survive "heated situations" better than their larger brethren. However, Bergmann's Rule came into question in 1987, as explained on page 14.

raccoons weigh only 5 to 8 pounds. There they have lighter brown fur with less distinct markings, no doubt the result of evolutionary selection for beach terrain and light-colored, sandy soils.

The population density of raccoons throughout North America dramatically increased in the 1940s. One estimate suggests the population in the 1980s was 15 to 20 times greater than it was in the 1930s. Population fluctuations in some regions have reflected the price of pelts, but not always.

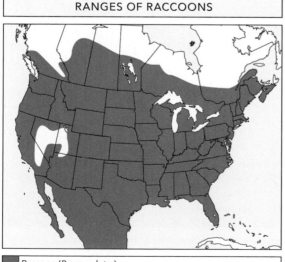

RANGES OF RACCOONS

Raccoon (*Procyon lotor*)

Upon emerging from winter dormancy, raccoons may weigh 50 percent less than in fall. (Photo by Lennie and Uschi Rue III)

SENSES

Like most nocturnal animals, raccoons have excellent hearing and pay attention to unusual noises. As to vision, raccoons—like deer—are color-blind but have good night vision. Although scientists rate a raccoon's sense of smell as only "adequate," raccoons seem able to smell ripening corn at a long distance.

But it's the tactile sense of the raccoon's forepaws that gives it a huge advantage over most mammals. Highly developed nerves in the footpads allow raccoons to distinguish prey in darkness and under dark water. Raccoons don't have the opposable thumb that rodents do, so they need to hold food "prayerfully" between both paws to manipulate it.

DISTINGUISHING SIGN

Raccoons can be identified before you see them.

Vocalization. Raccoons growl, hiss, grunt, and snarl at each other over food. They may screech when threatened. When traveling, mothers keep contact with cubs by chittering to them; the cubs respond with whistles. When nursing in the den, mothers purr, and babies make "churring" sounds.

Other sounds. An adult raccoon in your attic will lumber about noisily. There, the young make a chittering sound that some people mistake for young birds. When tearing their way through house siding and soffits, raccoons sound like demolition contractors. Raccoons also cause unmistakable sound effects upon dumping garbage cans.

Hyde Park, New York, wildlife controller Colin Burgess says his most interesting assignment began as a routine call to investigate what the caller thought were "raccoon sounds" in a cellar. But when he opened the cellar door, he instead saw a large bobcat bounding up toward him. He slammed the door and ran to his truck to retrieve a "catchpole," which is a short pole with a loop at the end that can be tightened like a collar over an animal's neck to control it. With his foot holding the cellar door partially shut, Burgess struggled for half an hour before collaring the now ferocious bobcat and removing it for eventual release. *Caution:* Adult bobcats may weigh 30 to 40 pounds and thus would probably be too much for most people to handle at the end of a catchpole. But Colin is 6 feet 8 and weighs 250 pounds. A raccoon of 30-plus pounds might have been even harder to deal with. (On the other hand, the 23-pound

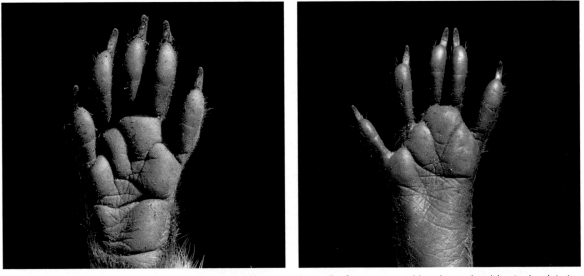

Sensitive footpads allow raccoons to distinguish prey in murky water. The smaller front paw resembles a human hand, but its thumb isn't opposable enough to grasp objects. Raccoons must hold their food "prayerfully" with both front paws. (Photo by Lennie and Uschi Rue III)

Upon discovering this 22-pounder, I covered the trap with a garbage sack to calm the animal and provide shade while I ran an errand. When I returned, most of the sack was inside the trap, parts of it lodged so forcefully into the mesh that I later had trouble pulling it out. At right, the wading raccoon is feeling with his sensitive front paws for underwater life. (Photo by Lennie and Uschi Rue III)

raccoon I livetrapped for the above photo felt far heavier; its movements made it impossible to balance the cage by the top handle alone.)

Tracks. Measuring 3¼ to 4¼ inches long, the rear paw resembles that of a flat-footed person but with five long toes and claws. The front paw makes an impression more like the ball of a human foot, also with five long toes and claws, and measures about 2 inches long. Tracks of adult males are almost always solitary. Tracks of females are often overlaid by those of cubs.

Scat. Near dens, raccoons often have a designated latrine area. Near eating sites, scat may be elongated cylinders or loose piles that reflect the diet. *Caution:* Scat also carries parasites, such as raccoon roundworm, a particular hazard to young children.

Garden damage. As mentioned, raccoons have an uncanny ability to pick fruit and corn the night before you intend to harvest. Melons will show holes with the pulp removed.

Garbage scatterings. Clever animals, raccoons soon learn how to dump garbage cans, usually dislodging the lids so they can pull out the plastic bags and tear them open. When a garbage can is secured upright, raccoons can often pull off the lid unless it's tied down.

Damage to buildings. You may see bent gutters where raccoons have climbed toward a roof entry. Raccoons also damage soffits under roof eaves. And they tear off siding.

Grease marks. A raccoon will intentionally scent mark by rubbing its rump, neck, and shoulders on building surfaces, leaving grease marks. Appreciating the irony, after a Vertebrate Pest Conference in Berkeley, California, Cornell University's Lynn Braband "noticed the telltale footprints and rub marks of a raccoon living in the canopy of the hotel's entrance."

Odors. Their dens can smell pungent and be dirty. Unpleasant odors emanating from confined spaces can also come from rodent carcasses if you've resorted to poisons.

Roadside litter. People who pick up roadside litter often find beer cans partially crushed and bitten through, reflecting a raccoon's disinterest in drinking from the "pop" opening. The raccoon leaves its saliva on these cans, which is a good reason to wear gloves when picking up litter.

MATING AND REPRODUCTION

In the North, most mating occurs from January through March, with young born in March through May, although some are born as late as August. In the South, mating and birth occur somewhat later. Courtship between a single male and female lasts 1 to 3 days, after which the male heads off. The female may then also mate with others.

Gestation is about 8 weeks. About a week prior to giving birth, females become intolerant of all other raccoons. Litter sizes are three to five, averaging four. But litters tend to be somewhat larger in the North than in the South. Newborns have little fur, and their eyes remain closed for about 3 weeks.

Cub raccoons begin accompanying Mom on foraging expeditions at 10 to 12 weeks. Weaning can occur at 2 to 4 months. Youngsters stay with the mother for 6 to 9 months, with the males usually dispersing in fall, and the females often overwintering with Mom before dispersing in spring.

DORMANCY, NOT HIBERNATION

Raccoons aren't true hibernators, as are woodchucks, whose body temperature dips close to that of its surroundings. A raccoon's at-rest body temperature of about 101°F in summer drops only about a degree in winter.

In winter in cold climates, raccoons enter a dormant period, sleeping much of the time. In the North, raccoons live almost entirely off fat reserves and may lose more than 50 percent of their body weight by spring. Mothers usually share their winter den and body heat with their offspring. First-year females, especially, benefit from shared heat because their fat reserves tend to be less than those of adult females and also because they aren't as fully furred.

OPTIONS FOR CONTROL

Near human habitation, raccoons are among the most commonly reported nuisance species. Options for control include elimination of food sources, exclusion measures, repellents, livetrapping, lethal trapping, firearms if legal on one's own property, and licensed hunting and trapping beyond one's own property.

Elimination of food sources. By far, most problems people have with raccoons can be prevented by common sense.

■ *Deliberate feeding:* If anyone in your neighborhood is feeding raccoons, find means of persuading them to stop. Presented well, the rabies and roundworm hazards alone may be persuasive.

■ *Pet food:* Don't leave unfinished bowls of pet food outdoors, a practice that can also reduce attraction to rodents, bears, and deer. Even empty bowls can emit odors that attract raccoons. The best practice is to feed pets only indoors. Portion the food so pets eat the entire serving at each feeding, Wash the bowl immediately afterward.

■ *Bird feed:* Empty or close bird feeders by dusk or otherwise prevent access. Baffle guards below feeders can thwart access by raccoons and squirrels. Raccoons are powerful and can bend weak support poles. The seasonally best practice for bird feeding is to wait until raccoons and bears have entered their dens for the winter and then discontinue feeding in spring when snow has melted enough for birds to find plenty of natural seed on their own—this before raccoons and bears have aroused themselves again. Find means of keeping spilled seed from reaching or staying on the ground, which also attracts rats, mice, and other rodents.

Exclusion from other food. Barriers of various types are vital.

■ *Garbage cans:* If you live in bear-country, consider bear-proof receptacles available via the Internet, using the search words *bear proof garbage*. Otherwise, store cans in closed garages out of reach of raccoons or in shaded areas so their contents don't ferment in warm weather. Coons have the most trouble with garbage cans secured upright to posts. Some of the better lid designs either snap securely in place or twist on. Lacking such lid-design features, you can hold lids down with heavy-duty straps or bungee cords attached to the can's handles. For this, recycled bicycle inner tubes can serve well and are usually available for free at bike repair shops.

■ *Pet doors:* Raccoons easily enter a two-way pet door unless the door prevents entry from the outside until released by a magnetic or infrared device in the pet's collar. For a wide selection of pet doors, visit moorepet-petdoors.com.

■ *Compost containers:* Composts should include only vegetable matter, never meat or fish. Even

Raccoons in the Kitchen

Connecticut attorney Stephanie Weaver describes herself as a "tree hugger," someone who loves all of nature. But that love was put to the test by a succession of raccoons that visited her kitchen.

It all began when Weaver arrived home and noticed that the kitchen food dish for her two cats was uncharacteristically empty and that their water bowl looked dirty. Puzzled, Weaver placed more food in the dish than she felt her cats would consume. The next morning, the dish was again empty and the water bowl again dirty.

Hmm! Weaver reasoned that a raccoon could have entered through her furnace-room "cat door" and then found the kitchen. She also recalled hearing that raccoons "wash" their food, explaining the murky water.

Weaver's handyman loaned her his Havahart trap, which Weaver baited with peanut butter and placed on the patio near the cat door.

That caught the raccoon, which Weaver's handyman delivered to a wild setting many miles away. Over the ensuing months, Weaver continued to bait the patio live trap—sometimes with peanut butter, sometimes with tuna fish—and caught 12 more raccoons.

Weaver's 14th and final raccoon proved harder to catch and otherwise far more interesting than the previous 13. It spurned the patio trap on its way through the cat door and into the kitchen, emptying the cat food dish and dirtying the water bowl.

Hoping to make the trap more inviting and denlike, Stephanie moved it onto her deck and laid a chaise-lounge cushion on top. That night around 1:00 a.m., Weaver heard commotion on the deck. The next morning, with coffee in hand, she ventured out and beheld "an amazing sight."

Virtually every hole in the trap was plugged from inside with cushion stuffing. That largest of all raccoons had torn the cushion apart to create a cozier "den" before going to sleep. And it must have been tired after the night's work, for it remained asleep when Weaver peeped in.

Weaver had experimented with a cat door with a magnetic catch. But the magnet caused resistance when Jams, her Blue-Point Himalayan, pushed his head on the door to pass through and so the cat gave up pushing. Weaver has since installed a cat door called Cat Mate Elite, which doesn't require that Jams push on the door to break a magnetic bond. Instead this door unlocks whenever his collar is within 5 inches. The secret is Radio Frequency Identification Technology (RFID). Door controls on this unit can be programmed for up to seven cats, based on each cat's unique collar code. As a bonus, the locking mechanism is raccoon-proof (available from moorepet.com).

so, many scraps, such as squash, melons, eggshells, and bread crumbs, appeal to raccoons, as well as rodents and bears. Thus, raccoon-proof commercial composters serve well. Or you can repurpose 55-gallon drums or galvanized garbage cans by aerating generously with a power drill. Otherwise, consider building boxlike frames from wood, plastic plumbing pipe, or galvanized electrical conduit of ¾-inch diameter or larger. Cover the frames with galvanized ¼ inch wire mesh so you have mesh-walled bins. The small mesh size also keeps out voles and mice.

Raccoon repellent. In the Tahoe Basin, animal-rehab expert Ann Bryant sprays or sprinkles full-strength Original Pine-Sol cleaning liquid inside garbage receptacles before closing the lids and trapping the scent. She says that when a critter opens the can, "Wham! It gets a snout full of something that burns and disorients." Bryant also sprays

Raccoons are agile climbers, able to surmount most mesh fencing unless electrified. (Photo by Dwight Kuhn) Raccoons often den inside unprotected chimney flues. As shown, grated chimney caps of stainless steel or copper can exclude raccoons as well as squirrels and chimney swallows. Such caps also eliminate damage caused by rain and snow during freeze-thaw cycles.

Original Pine-Sol in attics and under porches after evicting coons and other mammals so they won't attempt to return. (*Note:* The active ingredient in Original Pine-Sol is real pine oil, according to the manufacturer. Bryant uses only "Original," not any of various other Pine-Sol scents, such as lemon, orange, or wildflower. Bryant says such sweet scents could attract mammals, including bears!)

Garden fencing. Corn farmers often keep losses tolerable by planting far more than the local 'coons can handle over a short period. But home gardeners, after hearing commotion at night, are confronted with broken stalks and ears partially eaten.

Battery-powered electric fencing, where permitted by municipal ordinance, can serve well around corn patches, berry bushes, and fruit trees. Besides generating their own electricity, battery-powered fences are relatively portable, allowing you to move them to protect a succession of areas where fruits are coming ripe. (For photos and more information, see page 54.)

Fruit-tree trunk guards. Cylinders of roof flashing wrapped in bands around tree trunks can prevent raccoons from climbing higher. The flashing bottom should be at least 3 feet above the ground. Secure the top edge of the flashing to the nearest crotch. Allow about a half-inch of space between the flashing and the trunk. In this case, guards need to be in place for all trees whose branches connect with those of the fruit trees. Judicious pruning may be needed. (For a photo and more information, see page 185.)

Scare devices. Dogs with current rabies vaccinations can be good deterrents. Cornell University researchers suggest that motion-activated flashing lights with a siren are more effective than steady-on motion lights or steady sounds. One make is called the Critter Gitter, is shown on page 83.

Exclusion from chimneys. Raccoons are especially fond of fireplace flues because they are usually larger than furnace flues and aren't used much of the year. Raccoons den at the flue bottom, on the spacious shelf created by a fireplace damper. Licensed wildlife control pros have special tools for removing adult raccoons, as well as babies, without killing them. In this case, pros access the flue either through an exterior chimney cleanout door or reach up through the fireplace opening itself. Pros protect themselves with bite-proof gauntlet gloves and catchpoles, as shown on page 62.

Prevent raccoon denning in flues by installing metal chimney caps. These are rooflike structures for the chimney top with metal grills that exclude raccoons, as well as squirrels and chimney swallows. As a bonus, chimney caps also keep out rain and snow that can damage flues during freeze-thaw cycles.

Livetrapping. Because raccoons transmit a host of serious diseases and parasites, livetrapping deserves forethought and a review of state laws regarding release. For raccoons especially, it pays to consult a licensed wildlife control professional. These pros will know your state's laws regarding releasing wild animals. In some cases, the state may mandate euthanasia. For my thoughts on what the US Humane Society considers the "least inhumane" death for rodents and other health and fire threats, see page 64.

Relocating nuisance raccoons. Relocation is hotly debated and may be banned by state law. Based primarily on concern for disease transmission, departments of environmental conservation may forbid the release of raccoons or other wildlife except on the property where they were trapped. Such a law is often reinforced by a ban on transportation of wildlife.

Professional wildlife controllers are faced with the dilemma of euthanizing on the spot or finding legal (or extra-legal) places for release. Such decisions are troubling for most of us. We prefer not to kill needlessly, yet we wouldn't knowingly transmit diseases to healthy wildlife. We'd prefer to believe that a raccoon released in a wild setting will have a good chance of survival. That's not unreasonable because raccoons are highly adaptable, and a good percentage of them do survive after relocation.

However, relocations, which biologists call *translocations,* often have unintended impacts on other homeowners. That is, raccoons rarely stay anywhere near their release point. They usually wander widely, which brings them near human dwellings again. And dwellings may remind raccoons of the good life they once had in an attic or chimney, or under a porch. Such comfortable options may seem less risky to a homeless raccoon than attempting to push another adult from its den in the wild.

Lethal trapping. Standard options for lethal trapping include wire snares, head traps, foot traps, and powerful body squeezers that will cause suffocation.

However, all such traps could potentially injure nontarget animals, including pets and children. And if set inexpertly, some of these traps can injure the person attempting to set them. Most lethal traps for raccoons are better reserved for licensed wildlife control professionals.

Removal from buildings. Season is important to consider if you see raccoons in your attic or crawl space. In spring to early summer, your guest may have babies. Thus, if you block a mother raccoon's return after she departs, maternal devotion may compel her to force her way back inside somewhere else.

In spring to summer, after finding the entrance opening, wait till bedtime before blocking the opening with newspaper. By then, a mother raccoon will have departed for foraging. If the newspaper isn't torn open by morning or soon after, that probably indicates that the raccoon has no babies, and you can begin exclusion measures by permanently blocking the entrance.

If she does tear through the newspaper, however, you may need the help of a wildlife control officer to first capture mamma and then the babies. A one-way door is shown on page 141.

Mother and daughters may nap for days at a time, foiling tests that determine whether an animal is exiting and entering the building. So in winter, you may need to look for signs of denning raccoons. Your best option may be to wait for spring dispersal before blocking reentry.

Beginning in fall and during winter, a mother raccoon may still be accompanied by daughters from the previous spring.

Hunting. Some states allow licensed hunting and fur trapping during regulated seasons. Hunters are often allowed to use "coon hounds" to find a raccoon's scent and follow the animal's trail until treeing it and loudly baying while waiting for the huffing and puffing hunters. Check your state's game laws for details.

Population reduction. Although hunting and lethal trapping can reduce a local population briefly, nature doesn't love a void. If your neighborhood offers good raccoon habitat, especially if it provides water, food, and denning sites, raccoons will likely continue to be attracted until you remove attractions or exclude access.

COMMUNICABLE DISEASES AND PARASITES

All of the following raccoon-transmitted maladies are discussed in "Communicable Diseases and Parasites," beginning on page 210. However, as with many wild species, the list is long. Only the most common and concerning hazards are listed below. Measures to protect your family from these listed will also help protect you from the longer list of maladies.

Diseases

■ Raccoon rabies is a major concern for humans and wildlife. See page 212.

■ *Tularemia* (rabbit fever), a bacterium-caused disease in people, is considered a potential bioterrorist weapon in aerosolized (physically propelled into the air) form. See page 215.

■ *Canine distemper* occurs in raccoons in 4-year cycles. It kills raccoons and creates behaviors and symptoms often mistaken for rabies. See page 210.

■ *Leptospirosis* in humans is usually caused by bacteria-infected urine of the host animal being ingested or absorbed by people while in water, particularly during swimming, wading, or whitewater rafting. See page 212.

■ *Histoplasmosis* in people is caused by the fungus *Histoplasma capsulatum,* which normally affects the lungs in humans. See page 211.

Parasites

■ *Raccoon roundworm,* though relatively benign within raccoons, can debilitate and kill many other mammals, including humans. This roundworm is suspected of nearly eradicating native woodrats in some regions and can be a special hazard to small children playing where raccoons have defecated. See page 213.

■ *Ticks* carry a host of maladies. See page 214.

Children's play areas. A fenced play area or yard for small children can discourage raccoons and other mammals, including dogs and cats. (Of course, temperamental dogs can present more than disease hazards.) The play area should have self-closing two-way gates that children can easily operate and should be in view of parents. Cornell University and the US Centers for Disease Control and Prevention (CDC) urge that children wash their hands after outdoor activities and that toys possibly exposed to pathogens be washed in a 10 percent chlorine bleach solution, then rinsed. The immediate removal and washing of outdoor clothes also reduces chances that ticks on clothes will find bare skin—a wise practice for all adults as well.

Fecal matter is a special hazard for children. Even if the play area emits no food odors, sandboxes may appeal to pets and wildlife as possible litter boxes. With or without a fence around the area, it's best to cover a sandbox either with a tarp or with plastic mesh to prevent access by raccoons and cats.

If you're using a tarp, a "This Old House" cable-TV show recommends placing a large beach ball on the sand before draping the tarp over it and securing tarp edges to the box by means of Velcro tape. The beach ball creates a peaked roof that makes rainwater run off.

If using plastic mesh, you can adapt something like that shown over the cold frame on page 50. This cover is easy for adults and most children to roll back. Avoid bird netting for this purpose because it can entangle children and pick up lawn litter and leaves. Also avoid mesh with openings larger than 1 inch because it can trap children's hands and feet.

CHAPTER 14

Rats and Mice

Our appliance repairman slid the refrigerator away from the wall. After kneeling to look into the motor compartment, he smiled knowingly. He began removing trash that included aluminum foil, orange peels, soiled paper shreds, and fiberglass insulation. Next he produced two condenser wires, both chewed in half. The floor under the fridge showed dark urine stains and torpedo-shaped fecal pellets nearly ¾ inch long.

"A pack rat!" our repairman proclaimed. He contentedly announced that rats of various kinds give him a significant amount of business. He said, "I once received a call from a man who complained that his kitchen range wasn't working. When I suggested by phone that his problem might be rats, he scoffed. But when I arrived and lifted the range top, two rats were looking up at me."

Our repairman's perspectives prompted my mentioning our recently silent stereo amplifier and remote phone. "Check the wiring," he said. Sure enough, hidden from view, the wires to the amplifier and phone had been chewed apart by "something."

Although Hannelore is an excellent housekeeper, a succession of old houses throughout our long and otherwise happy marriage has forced us to wage continuing battles with rats and mice—first in apartments and then in our present home with porous stone foundation dating to 1850. Even though building codes require that new foundations be sealed against rodents, pest-control professionals say mice and rats often get into new homes as well.

Until the refrigerator episode, I'd been relying on an occasional baited rattrap in the basement.

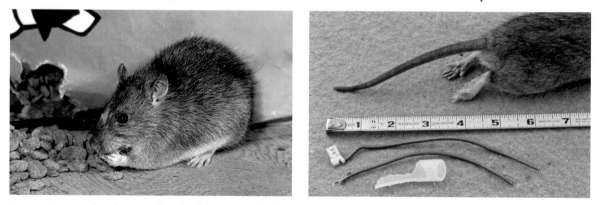

Norway rats enjoy dog chow as well as dog feces that aren't disposed of. (Photo by Lennie and Uschi Rue III) At right are the refrigerator condenser wires a rat severed in the episode above, along with the hind portion of the culprit, a Norway rat.

> **Order:** Rodentia ■ **Family (native):** MURIDAE (includes rats, mice, hamsters, voles, and gerbils)
> ■ **Family (alien):** MURINAE (includes Norway rat, roof rat, and house mouse—all of Asian origin)
> ■ **Genera:** many ■ **Species:** many

But I'd failed to keep up with advice on rodents from health authorities.

This chapter addresses the threats of rats and mice—both alien and domestic species—and suggests means of ridding them from homes, outbuildings, and vehicles and of preventing reentry.

PROBLEMS FOR HUMANS

Besides eating our foods, rats and mice can transmit dozens of diseases and parasites to us through our homes, outbuildings, and gardens—and through bites. If health threats weren't enough, rats and mice (like all rodents) have ever-growing incisor teeth, which they compulsively sharpen so they won't grow too long. Rodents sharpen their incisors by chewing on things. This includes wiring, which at best shuts down appliances and at worst burns down houses. Rats bite babies in their cribs and, when cornered, fight with people and pets.

Mice, especially, disable gas engines in mowers, tractors, and road vehicles. They do this either by chewing through wiring or by building nests inside engine air-filter casings. Clogged engine filters in garden mowers cause ragged operation at best, and, at worst, cause overheating that cracks engine blocks and causes fires. Mouse urine corrodes engine parts.

In cars and trucks parked for a few days, a new mouse nest can plug the engine air-filter compartment. In most cases, scheduled changing of air filters helps mechanics warn you that mice know your parking spot.

In addition, mice often nest in air vents leading to the passenger compartment. Here, the best-case scenario might be a trip to the repair shop to have the system vacuumed or blown out, followed by installation of new filters. Warning signs of nest blockage are weak streams of heated or cooled air.

My friend Girvan Milligan laughingly recounted switching on his hot-air blower for the first time one autumn and getting a blast of nest debris in his face. No laughing matter! Such dust can contain aerosolized, or airborne, droplets of mouse urine, saliva, feces, fur, and nest material

Rodent Teeth

All rodents have a pair of incisor teeth in the front of each jaw that grows continuously. These incisors have a thick enamel front layer that resists wear better than the tooth's backside. Thus, continual gnawing maintains a chisel-like front edge while preventing the teeth from growing beyond what the rodent considers acceptable lengths. Between the incisors and the molars, there's a gap in the gums where carnivorous mammals instead have canines (our eye teeth). A rodent's several molars on each side grind up foods the incisors deliver. To gnaw with the incisors, rodents push their lower jaw forward. And to grind with the molars, rodents pull their lower jaw backward. On that count, we have less to think about at mealtime, which—over thousands of years—allowed our ancestors to discuss strategies against rodents.

At left are normal front incisors of a white-footed mouse that kept its teeth trimmed down. At right are lower incisors that grew beyond control and would eventually have caused starvation or infection by growing into the roof of the mouth.

that may contain the deadly hantavirus and other pathogens mentioned later in this chapter.

ROLE IN THE WILD

In nature, native rats and mice are good. The majority live far from people. Native rats and mice are highly important in the food web, supplementing the diets of a host of predators, including owls, raptors, foxes, coyotes, skunks, and raccoons. They also consume a variety of plant-harming insects and help in nature's scheme for seed dispersal.

Sometimes called "packrats" for good cause, our native eastern woodrats are cuter than the aliens. (Photo © Rob and Ann Simpson/Visuals Unlimited, Inc.)

Our Kinship with Rodents

We share more than food and domicile with rodents. A recent rat genome sequencing consortium declared, "About 90 percent of rat genes have counterparts in the mouse and human genomes."

where they can forage in garbage and other foods. Living near us or sharing our homes, they enjoy a measure of protection from wild predators.

Most urban and suburban people have their first rat or mouse encounter with one of the three aliens—either the roof rat (black rat), the Norway rat (brown rat), or the house mouse.

ALIEN ORIGINS, IDENTIFICATION, AND DISTRIBUTION

In Asia, over many thousands of years, rats and mice evolved in close association with people because grains and other foods went largely unprotected and porous buildings invited domicile. Living closely with humans, those rats and mice enjoyed protection from natural predators. Little wonder alien rodents are attracted to our homes, where they are protected from predators as well as rain and snow. Near us, the aliens feel comfortably cool in summer and warm in winter. They tolerate our tastes in music and television during our waking hours and enjoy our foods while we sleep.

The roof rat, or black rat *(Rattus rattus),* originated in the Indo-Malayan region and arrived on our East Coast in the 1500s. That was at least 200 years ahead of the arrival of the roof rat's larger cousin, the Norway rat. The roof rat prefers to live in attics and treetops, which conveniently elevate it beyond reach of its more aggressive cousin. A dexterous climber and aerial artist, the roof rat often uses telephone wires and power cables to travel from house to house. It enters at roof level through structural gaps and broken vent screening.

Adult roof rats can measure 12 to 16 inches in total length, with an average weight of 7 ounces.

Distinguishing features: Naked tail longer than combined head-and-body length; large ears; black

Those that do live near dwellings may consume weed seeds that might otherwise find their way into our gardens. In addition, burrowing rats and mice aerate the soil. Alas, some native species of rats and mice are endangered due to habitat loss and to parasites, such as raccoon roundworm.

By contrast, two alien rat species and one alien mouse prefer living in close association with us,

Rat or Mouse?

The terms *rat* and *mouse* aren't scientific distinctions. They're simply common names that suggest size—mice usually being sparrow-size or smaller. Many of our native mouselike rodents with "mouse" in their names aren't closely related. The same is true for "rats." In fact, the two alien rats are more closely related to the alien house mouse than to our native rats and mice. In urban and suburban areas, the three most common house rodents are the three aliens—all distinguished by their nearly naked tail and smaller, beadier eyes (relative to head size) than the large, beautiful eyes of the natives that are more likely to share our homes only in suburban and rural areas.

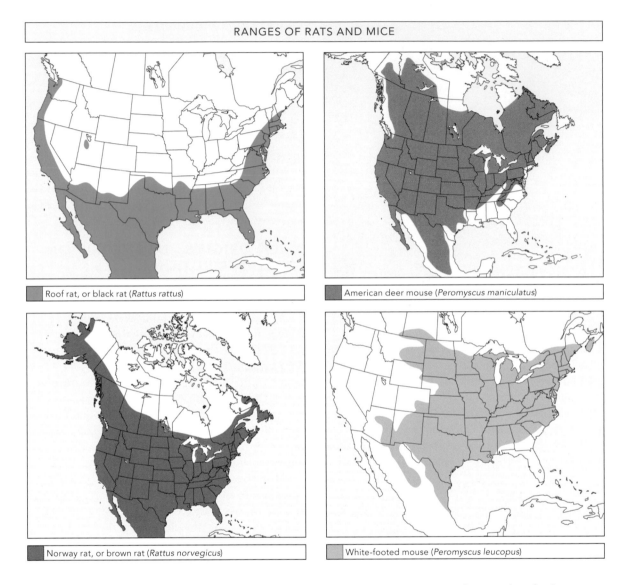

RANGES OF RATS AND MICE

Roof rat, or black rat (*Rattus rattus*)

American deer mouse (*Peromyscus maniculatus*)

Norway rat, or brown rat (*Rattus norvegicus*)

White-footed mouse (*Peromyscus leucopus*)

or dark brown fur, which explains its alternative name, black rat. May breed spring and fall or year-round. Litter size: 4 to 10. May carry plague and typhus.

As the map above shows, roof rats inhabit mainly coastal regions but are spreading inland in some areas. Although Norway rats often displace roof rats, especially in the North, California's San Diego County assesses its domestic rat popula-

tion as 95 percent roof rat and only 5 percent Norway rat.

The Norway rat, or brown rat (*Rattus norvegicus*), originated in southeastern Siberia and China, not in Norway. It didn't reach our East Coast until the 1700s. Yet it quickly spread throughout North America. This alien is "our most serious pest animal, causing enormous damage to stored grains, spreading disease, and damaging structures," according to the Peterson field guide, *Mammals of North America.*

Norway rats often live in extensive burrow systems in haremlike colonies, one male per several females. Yet they are notorious house crashers that make nightly raids or simply take up residence. Opportunistic omnivores, they kill and eat roof rats, smaller rodents, and bird eggs and nestlings, as well as poultry and young livestock.

This alien is big, averaging 16 inches in total head-and-body length and weighing 1 pound to occasionally 1¼ pounds. Thus, even housecats that are good "mousers" may prefer to attack their own food dishes instead.

Distinguishing features: Sparsely hairy, almost naked tail shorter than combined head-and-body length; small ears and eyes relative to head size; fur yellowish brown. Breeds year-round. Litter size: 2 to 22. Spreads various diseases.

Redeeming factors: Serves as prey to owls and nocturnal predators. Ancestors served as breeding stock for white laboratory rats and for fancy rats in the pet trade.

The house mouse *(Mus musculus)* originated in Asia and is found today throughout North America. In the wild and on farmlands, it feeds mainly on weed seeds and insects until locating stored or spilled grain. In homes, it can subsist on whatever crumbs we overlook, as well as birdseed.

This alien averages 6¼ inches in total head-and-body length, plus its semihairless tail at half that length. Its average weight is ½ ounce.

Distinguishing features relative to natives: Upper fur gray-brown to yellow-brown but not with sharply contrasting white belly of many natives. Has a musky, unpleasant odor.

May breed year-round. Litter size: 3 to 11, usually 6.

Redeeming factors: Serves as prey to owls and nocturnal predators. Not known to carry hantavirus often shed by native mice. Ancestors served as breeding stock for laboratory white mice.

Having evolved in close association with humans over thousands of years, these three aliens often survive better among us than in the wild. Top to bottom are the Norway rat; the roof, or black, rat; and the house mouse. (Top and bottom photos by Lennie and Uschi Rue III; middle photo © Stephen Dalton/ Photo Researchers, Inc.)

NATIVE IDENTIFICATION AND DISTRIBUTION

When our refrigerator repairman proclaimed "pack rat," he was referring to the collecting instincts of North America's native woodrat (genus *Neotoma*), with 10 species north of Mexico.

Woodrats (*Neotoma* species). Some of our 10 native species are considered endangered due to habitat loss or to parasites, such as roundworm. Most people would agree that woodrats are cuter than the two alien rats. In fact, woodrats often closely resemble our native deer mice, except for the woodrat's greater size. Like native mice, woodrats have large eyes and ears, and usually have a white belly and underside in sharp contrast to dark upper fur. The tail is furrier than that of alien rats and distinctly bicolored, like the body.

Depending on the species, woodrat total head-and-body lengths range from 12 to 18 inches; the tail is almost half of that length. Weights range from 7 to 15 ounces, with females weighing about 20 percent less than males except when pregnant.

> ### A Well-Deserved Nickname
> The "pack rat" moniker arose from the woodrat's compulsive caching tendency, which includes gathering nonperishable wild foods and nest materials as you might expect, as well as rusty nails, broken glass, empty shotgun shells, and jewelry left unguarded.

Distinguishing features relative to alien rats: Eyes larger relative to head size and cuter; belly usually white, in sharp contrast to fur above.

Woodrats are solitary and territorial. In rural areas, woodrats and native mice are sometimes the only rodents that invade homes, often entering in greater numbers for warmth and shelter as winter approaches and then departing in spring when natural foods and mild temperatures beckon.

Woodrats evolved in wooded or otherwise wild settings, where they depend heavily on seeds, fruits, and nuts. They climb trees and shrubs, sometimes nesting in them. But they usually live at ground level in protected dens or brush piles with stick nests that are separated from their food caches, called

These natives include a juvenile deer mouse and three white-footed mice, representing the two species most likely to share our homes and transmit hantavirus. These guys are hard to distinguish because of highly variable coloration within species and because their ranges largely overlap. Although both species feature contrasting white undersides, the white-footed mouse is said to have narrower, less hairy tail, among other slight differences. (Deer mouse photo by Dwight Kuhn; white-footed mouse photo by Lennie and Uschi Rue III)

middens, and separated from the lavatory. Given the option, woodrats prefer wild settings, away from human commotion. As with all rodents, if woodrats take up residence in buildings or vehicles, their chewing can lead to electrical failures and fires. And, they can foul whatever they walk on.

Woodrats are far less fecund than alien rats that invade their range, which perhaps partially explains their endangered status in some regions. The typical litter size is one to four. In colder regions, they might breed only in spring but tend to breed more often in warmer regions.

Deer mouse species (*Peromyscus* species). This section includes profiles of just 2 of the 16 quite similar-looking deer mouse species north of Mexico. Unlike the alien house mouse, these guys tend to be silent. When alarmed, they may drum with their front or hind feet. As the map on page 148 shows, the two profiled mice have combined ranges that occupy virtually all parts of North America. And they are often *commensal* (inclined to share our table). Unfortunately, the two profiled are considered the continent's prime vectors of the deadly hantavirus. The ranges of other listed species are indicated by region.

■ The American deer mouse (*Peromyscus maniculatus*) ranges throughout most of North America and vies with its also wide-ranging white-footed cousin as our "cutest" mouse. Total head-and-body length: 6¾ inches. Tail: 3¼ inches (prairie form tail: 2¼ inches). Back brown; belly and legs white. Large eyes and ears, though ears smaller than those of white-footed mouse. Litter size: one to eight, usually four. Range: everywhere but Southeast. What's not to like? Well, it's a vector of hantavirus, the Lyme disease tick, and plague. (Yes, the same plague once known as the Black Death. See "Communicable Diseases and Parasites" on page 210.)

■ The white-footed mouse (*P. leucopus*) has larger ears than the deer mouse. Total length: 6½ inches. Tail: 3 inches. Back paler brown than American deer mouse's, usually with orange-brown sides. Chin hair entirely white. Litter size: three to six.

Range: everywhere except West and extreme Southeast. Vector for hantavirus and nymph form of deer tick, known to transmit multiple tick-borne diseases. See page 214.

Following is an alphabetical listing of the other 14 deer mice species.

■ Brush mouse *(P. boylii)*: Southwestern United States

■ Cactus mouse *(P. eremicus)*: Southern Arizona, California, New Mexico, Nevada

■ California mouse *(P. californicus)*: Mainly coastal California

■ Canyon mouse *(P. crinitus)*: All of Nevada, spilling into surrounding states

■ Cotton mouse *(P. gossypinus)*: Southeastern United States

■ Keen's mouse, Northwestern deer mouse *(P. keeni)*: Coastal Washington and Canada's British Columbia and southern Yukon

■ Mesquite mouse *(P. merriami)*: Southern Arizona, into Mexico

■ Northern baja mouse *(P. fraterculus)*: Southern California

■ Northern rock mouse *(P. nasutus)*: Texas, northeastern Arizona, Colorado

■ Oldfield mouse *(P. polionotus)*: Alabama, Mississippi, South Carolina, Florida

■ Osgood's mouse *(P. gratus)*: Southwestern New Mexico

■ Piñon mouse *(P. truei)*: The Southwest

■ Texas mouse *(P. attwateri)*: Texas, Oklahoma, northwestern Arkansas, southwestern Missouri, southeastern Kansas

■ White-ankled mouse *(P. pectoralis)*: Texas and southeastern New Mexico

Cotton rat species (*Sigmodon* species). Of four species ranging in the southern half of the United States, only *S. hispidus* has delivered hantavirus to

Ranging throughout the South and Southwest, the cotton rat is also a vector of hantavirus. (Photo © Rick and Nora Bowers/Alamy)

humans, according to the US Centers for Disease Control and Prevention (CDC). The other three cotton rats occur in southern Arizona, southern New Mexico, Texas, and Mexico.

■ Cotton rat *(S. hispidus)*: Known vector of hantavirus. Total length 10 inches, tail 4 inches. Weight: 3½ ounces. Range: southeast and south-central United States, southern Arizona, and southeastern California

Rice rat species *(Oryzomys* species). Of the two species north of Mexico, only the marsh rice rat has been linked to hantavirus. But its range is huge. The Coues's rice rat *(O. couesi)* barely ranges northward into Texas from Mexico.

■ Marsh rice rat *(O. palustris)*: Southeastern United States and eastern portion of Mid-Atlantic Coast, to include eastern Pennsylvania and eastern Maryland.

Other Mice Genera and Lone Species

Grasshopper mouse species *(Onychomys* species). Of the three species north of Mexico, all live in the West and Southwest and prefer dry habitat and desert. Although these mice eat seeds and plant material, they are more carnivorous than most mice, favoring grasshoppers, as well as other insects, scorpions, smaller invertebrates, and other mice.

■ Northern grasshopper mouse *(O. leucogaster)*: Total length: 5¾ inches, tail only 1½ inches. Huge range: Plains and Rocky Mountain region into Canada

■ Southern grasshopper mouse *(O. torridus)*: Total length: 5½ inches, tail 2 inches. Southern Nevada and southern Arizona

■ Mearns's grasshopper mouse *(O. arenicola)*: Total length: 5½ inches, tail 2 inches. Arizona and western Texas

Harvest mouse species *(Reithrondontomys* species). These are tiny nocturnal mice with five species ranging north of Mexico. Head-and-body length averages only 2⅝ inches, tails usually longer. These mice feed on seeds, weeds, and grasses, as well as insects and sometimes invertebrates. Litter sizes: one to seven. Ranges are mostly southern, except for the Western harvest mouse, which occurs throughout the West and slightly into Canada

Golden mouse *(Ochrotomys nuttalli)*. Total length: 6 inches, tail 3 inches. Upper body rich orange-brown. Quite beautiful, this palomino climbs vines and shrubs using its prehensile tail for balance, feeding on nuts, berries, and invertebrates. Litter size: two to five, spring into fall. Southeastern United States

Florida mouse, gopher mouse *(Peromyscus floridanus)*. Total length 7½ inches, nearly naked tail 3½ inches. Back pale gray-brown, sides grading to orange, belly white. Threatened by habitat loss. Burrows more than most mice. Litter size: one to five born year-round. Florida

DISTINGUISHING SIGN

Rats and mice are primarily nocturnal, so you're likely to see their sign before you see them. Telltale evidence includes droppings, gnawings, runways, tracks, burrows, and mysteriously emptied nut bowls or mutilated loaves of bread. You may hear squeaking and rustling sounds in walls or light thumping sounds overhead. If you see rats, especially, during the day, overpopulation may have forced daytime scavenging.

Left: *Feces of Norway rats may be ¾ inch long.* Right: *Mice often nest in car trunks, favoring the spare tire's concealed well. Mice also nest in engine air-filter compartments and in ventilation ducts leading to the passenger compartment. Bored mice chew on wiring.*

Rat droppings can vary in shape depending on species and diet. Droppings of Norway rats tend to be dark, blunt cylinders up to ¾ inch long. Those of roof rats are smaller—less than ½ inch long—and tend to be curved. Mouse droppings resemble tiny, dark grains of rice, usually pointed.

Rat gnawings in wood show large teeth marks and entry holes of 1 inch or more in diameter. Mice gnawings look more like scratchings. Although mice are said to be capable of squeezing through dime-size holes, my recent measurement

of the head of an adult white-footed mouse showed a skull width closer to nickel width, or ¾ inch.

Rats and mice tend to reuse their runways night after night. Having poor eyesight, they rely greatly on their whiskers for guidance. Indoors, rats and mice tend to keep their whiskers in contact with vertical wall and beam surfaces. As a result, a rat's body often rubs along a wall, leaving greasy stains known as rub marks. Such stains are seldom evident along mouse runways.

In the dark, mice and rats rely on whiskers to guide them along floor edges—suggesting where traps should be placed. To determine whether your night visitor is a rat or a mouse, you can create a tracking medium from flour or unscented talc.

Our First Rat

Our first rat encounter began when we were newly-weds in Alexandria, Virginia, when we discovered rat droppings on the kitchen floor. What to do?

Earlier, while parking in our driveway, I watched dumbfounded as an enormous brown rat clumsily bounded from a nearby supermarket dumpster toward our house foundation and vanished. Perhaps shock-induced, memory reruns the approach of that blubbery rodent in slow motion. Though smaller than a rabbit, it was certainly larger than any squirrel I'd seen.

We did the time-honored thing. We bought one of those big wood-based, spring-activated Victor rat-traps and baited it with Swiss cheese, like I'd seen in *Tom and Jerry* cartoons. Before bedtime, I placed the baited trap near a chewed hole inside the kitchen broom closet. Next morning, I cautiously opened the broom-closet door. The trap had performed perfectly.

But instead of snapping on a rat, it had snapped onto a wad of steel wool, and the cheese was gone. I looked on the broom-closet shelves, but saw no steel-wool packaging that the pad could have fallen from. No other steel wool anywhere!

Hmmm! Still puzzled that night, I again cheese-baited and reset the trap. By the next morning, the trap had sprung onto a new wad of steel wool, and again the cheese was gone. We began to worry that we might be dealing with a genetically engineered smart rat, perhaps escaped from the nearby National Institute of Health (NIH).

On the third night, I placed the cheese-baited trap in the middle of the kitchen floor. The next morning, it had snapped across the neck of a rat, which I today know was a Norway rat. Thus began our trial-and-error, 4-decade battle with rats and mice.

If you are uncertain whether your night visitors are rats or mice, you can create a tracking medium. For this, sift a fine layer of flour or unscented talc onto construction paper or onto the floor where you anticipate traffic—or sprinkle around bait, such as peanut butter. Mouse tracks are tiny, compared to those of the Norway rat shown in the photo on page 153.

Although rats tend to be cautious about new things in their environment, such as traps, mice are curious about new things.

Rats eat heavily before seeking a drink and as a result leave obvious urine puddles. Mice seldom need supplemental water, and their urine is rarely apparent because mice urinate a fine mist as they travel, which also serves for scent marking. When inspecting for evidence of rodents, pest-control professionals often use a black-light (ultraviolet) lamp that makes rodent urine glow bluish white to yellowish white. However, before you sign a year's contract for rodent control, be forewarned that flu-orescence can also be a false-positive for chemicals in detergents and motor oil. *Hint:* Urine stains from mice, especially, will usually follow wall edges.

OPTIONS FOR CONTROL

Do-it-yourself options are essentially the same as those performed by pest-control professionals: livetrapping; lethal trapping; poisoning; elimination of food, water, and shelter; exclusion measures; and cleanup.

Although rodent-control professionals and animal-rights activists agree on the need to remove attractants and thereafter prevent house entry, they may strongly disagree on the options for trapping and on the use of poisons. Of course, poisons also introduce serious environmental concerns.

People who favor lethal options cite the over-riding human health concerns, as well as damage to property and potential for house fires. Those who favor the release of livetrapped animals sometimes know the risks to themselves and to other wildlife—sometimes not. For more, see page 61.

Acknowledging health concerns, the US Humane Society Web site states this: "In considering the arsenal of lethal methods available for rodent control, the bottom line is that none are completely humane in their modes of action, but some inflict less suffering than others. Therefore if rodents must be killed in a given situation, it is far preferable that the least inhumane methods are used."

Illustrating just one of many downsides of livetrapping, this physically uninjured white-footed mouse shows early symptoms of trap shock, which can lead to death prior to release. Such shock often kills other rodents, as well as rabbits and hares.

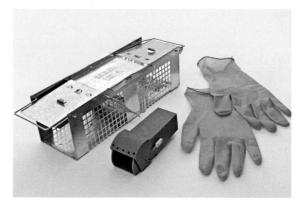

Metal-mesh live traps usually give rodents sufficient space and air circulation to survive until prompt release. However, small sealed live traps, as shown, cause severe stress, resulting in slathered, sweaty looking skin and fur that reduces chances of survival upon release. Protect your hands with disposable gloves or doubled plastic bags when touching things rodents have touched.

Livetrapping

People opposed to lethal trapping often employ live traps and then release rodents to the wild. Although some wildlife rehabilitators accept livetrapped native rodents, they spurn the three alien rodents, which—upon release—could become threats to native populations. On the other hand, state law may ban relocation because livetrapped animals can transmit diseases and parasites or introduce an alien that might out-compete natives; see page 61.

5-Gallon Bucket Traps: Two Ingenious Options

From a human-health standpoint, a bucket trap has advantages over snap traps. It works repeatedly without rebaiting. And you can either toss dead mice into the garbage or bury them without touching anything the mice have touched. A rinse in 10-percent bleach solution or other disinfectant should kill potential hantaviruses. Still, if you need to touch any bucket parts the mice have touched, use disposable gloves or repurposed plastic bags. Afterward, be sure to wash your hands with soap.

Option 1: Bucket with spinning coffee can. Wildlife control professional Ed Machowski, of

Norfolk, Connecticut, says that one of his clients caught 30 mice on his first efforts using Machowski's "repeating-capture device" shown here. For this, Machowski drills holes at the center of an empty coffee can, first emptied with the pointed end of a can opener so both lids remain firmly attached. He then runs cord through the holes and attaches the ends either to the bucket handle or through holes drilled into the bucket lip, making sure the can turns easily on the cord. Then he fills the bucket with a

Ed Machowski told me how to make his "repeating-capture device." My only innovations were the coat-hanger suspension wire and its stabilizing notches in the bucket lip.

few inches of water and applies peanut butter to the outside of the can. When mice reach for or jump to the can, it rotates and they fall into the water below.

Option 2: Open bucket. In Two Harbors, Minnesota, my cousin Kathy Goedel uses a 5-gallon bucket holding a few inches of water to catch multiple mice over a period of days. She first dabs peanut butter inside the bucket wall about 3 inches below the rim. Then she provides a ramp so mice can walk to the rim. Mice apparently attempt to reach downward so far that they lose their toehold and fall into the water and soon drown. In cold temperatures, frozen water or an empty bucket simply allows mice to freeze. Such a bucket can instead serve as a live trap, if checked regularly.

■ Is *drowning humane?* For a discussion of this issue, see page 64.

■ *Lethal trapping:* The better commercial traps work as effectively on rats as on mice, when sized accordingly. But it's vital to know which size trap to use. Otherwise, a rat duped into sampling bait in a measly mousetrap might suffer an unpleasant sting but would easily pull free, thereafter distrusting a

Top left: *This damaged bottom of a plastic garbage can first drew mice, like this poor white-footed fellow, but also attracted a Norway rat and ultimately the 22-pound raccoon shown on page 139. I thereupon switched to a galvanized can. Top right:* After baiting the Victor Quick Kill with peanut butter, raise the spring-loaded hammer. Bottom right: *To protect children and pets from injury, you can conceal lethal traps within a lockable Protecta Bait Station. (Commercial traps photographed at www.wildlifecontrolsupplies.com.)*

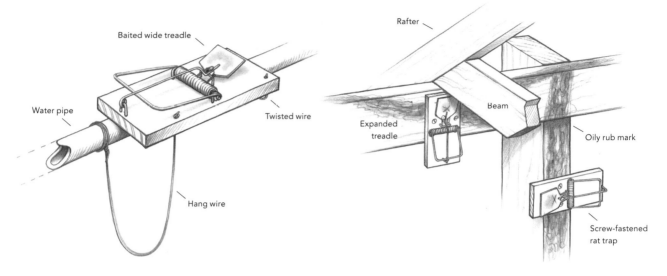

All rats and mice travel along water pipes. Fasten pipe-top traps with wire end inserted into the trap base securing it level. The force of the snapping trap and the rodent's weight itself will flip the trap off the pipe, leaving it suspended from the hang-wire. Roof rats favor attics and travel along beams, leaving oily rub marks that show where to screw-fasten traps. (Both concepts from Terrell P. Salmon, et al, Wildlife Pest Control Around Gardens and Home.*)*

Baits for Snap Traps

Virtually all snap traps depend on a rodent's attraction to bait, such as peanut butter, chocolate, cheese, seeds, grain, or fruit.

Rats and mice find peanut butter irresistible. Peanut butter is easy to apply to bait treadles. And even if it hardens and becomes moldy over time, it still attracts rodents. That's an advantage if you reuse traps because you don't need to rebait the treadle each time you release a rodent.

Yet peanut butter has failings: If left outdoors in the daytime, it might disappear without the trap's being sprung, perhaps leading you to blame the trap, when instead you should blame ants. Also, some trap designs require a significant nudge of the treadle before releasing and thus allow rodents to gently lick the peanut butter off.

Bait ratings. Victor, the brand name of a wide array of lethal traps, claims that rodents favor peanut butter over all other baits, and suggest that these rodents like chocolate second best, even better than cheese. (*Note:* All three baits are loaded with fat, and all are aromatic.) Roof rats especially like nutmeats and dried or fresh fruits.

■ **A cheesy solution:** To prevent rodents from licking the bait off, Rich Robbins, my county's public health sanitarian, cuts American cheese into 1-inch squares and microwaves them for a few seconds, just enough to make them gooey before molding them around trap treadles. I've tried Robbins's recipe and found it effective.

■ **Synthetic baits:** Snap traps are now available with a yellow plastic bait pedal that resembles Swiss cheese and smells good enough to rodents to tempt them. These fake-cheese treadles make trap setting and resetting easier and have the bonus of reducing the need to handle rodent-contaminated traps. However, when I left these cheesy-looking treadles in the open without setting the trap itself, rodents chewed them enough to render them useless.

Trap Placement and Fleas

Although rodent fleas prefer rodents, they will leave their rodent host when it dies and look for another warm-blooded host, sometimes human. Plague and typhus, especially, are spread to humans by rat fleas. The US Centers for Disease Control and Prevention (CDC) advises this: "If bubonic plague is a problem in your area, spray flea killer or spread flea powder in the area before setting traps."

similar-looking large trap. Conversely, mice are capable of licking bait delicately from rattraps and some mousetraps without triggering them.

■ *Snap traps:* Most commercial rattraps and mousetraps rely on spring tension to exert a crushing blow onto a rodent's spinal column, thereby causing nearly instant death. Known as snap traps, these devices come in various designs that borrow principles from the classic wood-based Victor model still popular today. All of these designs invite a rodent to disturb a baited treadle (trigger), which releases the spring-activated chopping blow of either a metal bow or an edged plastic plate.

To my mind, snap traps are the most humane of the commercial options because they dispatch rodents almost instantaneously—without the agonizing punishment of poisons or glue traps and without imposing the stresses of livetrapping that can send rodents into shock, killing them in spite of our best intentions.

Sticky glue traps are inhumane. When they don't cause intended suffocation, you are forced to deal with a live rodent.

It's usually best to position snap traps along walls or other vertical surfaces near suspect travel lanes so the treadle (trigger) end faces the wall. That way, rodents keeping one set of whiskers to the wall will be more likely to step onto the treadle than detour around the trap.

■ *Trap handling:* In past decades, trap manufacturers and enthusiasts touted the cost-effectiveness of reusable traps. But people then, as now, often handled contaminated traps unsafely. Today's trap packaging may or may not provide warnings on the hazards of handling dead rodents and contaminated traps. *These hazards are serious, owing to potential for communicable diseases and parasites.* In fact, the US Centers for Disease Control and Prevention (CDC) recommends disposing of both trap and rodent inside two sealed plastic bags, picking up rodents as shown on page 61. Or as a precaution, you can first place the baited trap inside an empty milk carton or on top of newspapers that you can fold over the "catch," thereby allowing you to simultaneously dispose of surrounding urine and feces. Lacking those options, disposable gloves are a wise precaution.

The classic old Victor design functions well but requires two-handed tensioning. *Caution:* Inept positioning of the locking bar can allow the wire bow to snap onto your fingers. A rat-size trap can snap with a force that seems to me powerful enough to break fingers, cut flesh, and blacken fingernails. Thus, be sure to keep set traps beyond the reach of children and pets. Various companies offer protective housings for traps, known generally as bait stations.

The classic old Victor model is also at a disadvantage when it's compared to the modern version, Victor Quick Sets, which can be opened with one hand, like a squeezeable clothespin, so you don't need to touch contaminated trap parts.

How many traps? Setting one or two traps tends to maintain rodent populations at a relatively constant level. Instead, researchers recommend buying enough traps to outnumber the rodents—thereby potentially driving the population way down in just a few days. Place traps throughout suspect areas,

Recipe for Surefire Bait

We unwittingly discovered bait better than peanut butter, first to a Norway rat and then to a white-footed mouse. An unknown critter ravaged both ends of a loaf of Hannelore's Christmas *Stollen*, a traditional German dessert bread.

Besides the savaged loaf ends, we saw no other sign. So to determine appropriate trap size, I created a large tracking pad by placing construction paper under several types of traps and baits and then sifting a thin layer of bread flour over the paper.

Next morning, when I entered the cold room, rodent tracks led inside the large Havahart trap, its door having slammed shut on somebody. But I saw no culprit inside. Tracks outside the trap showed that a rat had waltzed past peanut-butter baits, instead following the Stollen bread crumbs inside the trap. When the trap door slammed shut, the rat squeezed out through the 1- to 2-inch mesh designed for larger mammals.

The tracks shown in the accompanying photo matched those in Mark Elbroch's monumental *Mammal Tracks and Sign*. Clearly, the culprit was *Rattus norvegicus*.

I moved the bait buffet to the basement, placing Stollen bread crumbs on a board ramp leading to a length of horizontally suspended 4-inch plastic drainpipe with Stollen crumbs strewn all the way inside to the wire-mesh "bottom." I then balanced the drainpipe to be sensitive enough to tip vertically, as shown if even a mouse ventured more than halfway in. It worked! A refinement of this crude prototype appears on page 208.

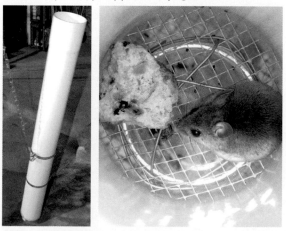

Stollen

Yield: Two loaves, each about 1 foot long

    2 cups raisins
    2 cups currants
    ½ cup candied lemon and orange peel, chopped
  2½ cups rum
    4 packets (¼ ounce each) yeast
    1 cup warm water
    ¾ cup plus 1 teaspoon sugar
    1 pound salted butter
    2 egg yolks
    8 cups unbleached white flour
    2 cups grated almonds
    ½ cup warm milk
       Grated peel of one lemon (organic if possible, otherwise wash under hot water)
    1 stick butter (4 ounces), melted
    ½ cup powdered sugar

1. Soak raisins, currants, and candied citrus peel in rum for at least 1 hour.
2. Combine the yeast, water, and 1 teaspoon of the sugar in a small bowl. Let stand in a warm place for 5 to 10 minutes, or until the mixture rises and bubbles.
3. Melt the butter. Allow it to cool slightly. Add the egg yolks to the butter.
4. In a large bowl, quickly knead the flour, almonds, milk, lemon peel, raisin mixture, yeast mixture, and butter mixture together.
5. Form two loaves and let rise overnight, covered with a clean kitchen towel.
6. Preheat the oven to 400°F. Bake for 1 hour or until the crust is light brown. (Bake the loaf you use for family consumption a little longer than the loaf you'll use for rodent bait. That is, a somewhat doughy consistency allows you to mold the bread around trap treadles, increasing the likelihood that the rodent will jostle the treadle enough to release it on lethal traps. Besides, those doughier morsels don't dry out as quickly and remain aromatic longer.)
7. While loaves are still hot, brush with melted butter and sprinkle with powdered sugar.
8. Store in a cool place, protected from critters.

especially along walls (again, with the business end facing the wall). Extra traps will help ensure that a rat or mouse passes near the pleasing aroma of at least one trap, and extra traps may help catch dispersing juvenile rodents.

If you decide to economize by reusing traps, a 1:10 solution of household bleach and water helps disinfect them. As an added precaution, the CDC says that direct sunlight can also kill viruses. Of course, wear disposable gloves or repurposed plastic bags when handling the traps.

Snap traps sometimes miss the vital spinal cord and don't deliver a killing blow, perhaps catching only a leg and allowing a rat, especially, to drag the trap away and chew its way out. Thus, it's smart to anchor rattraps with wire or metal chain. To catch roof rats, fasten traps high in trees or in structural wood, as illustrated on page 157.

Glue traps work much like flypaper. They also tend to be lethal, whether from stress, starvation, or the temperatures that trapped rodents may experience. *Downsides:* Glue traps seem less humane than sudden death, imposing a lengthy period of stress. Their stickiness can be undermined by dust, dirt, and temperature extremes. And, glue traps may occasionally force you to deal with a frightened rodent.

Poisons

Each year, thousands of children and many thousands of dogs accidentally ingest rat poison. As a result, some manufacturers have attempted to reduce its appeal to children and pets by adding

I advise against poisons. But if you are determined to use them, avoid pellets and flakes because rodents cache them. House bait blocks in tamperproof stations. Alternatively, the hollow core allows anchoring with wire. Follow manufacturer precautions.

"bittering" agents. Although some poisons smell unpleasantly pungent to me, others don't.

From the 1950s into the 1990s, a rat poison called warfarin was highly popular. An anticoagulant, warfarin caused internal bleeding that killed rodents after multiple feedings. Warfarin was hailed as safer than quick-kill poisons if consumed by children and pets because it had an antidote of medically administered doses of vitamin K_1. However, genetically resistant rats and mice soon created offspring that were also resistant to warfarin. Today some manufacturers employ anticoagulants with other names, such as defathialone and diphacinone. Others may employ a poison called bromethalin.

For more arguments against such poisons, see page 64.

Poison Confession

Long ago, I ignorantly succumbed to the assurances of a friend who recommended anticoagulant poison. She enthused, "Mice are supposed to eat it for a while and then go outside looking for water, where they die and dry up."

With more writing deadlines than time for poison research, I bought a package containing wallet-size cardboard bait boxes, each filled with greenish blue pellets. Following manufacturer instructions, I opened the bait boxes and placed them in our basement.

I watched with satisfaction as the pellets disappeared. But, some weeks later, while beginning to slip my foot into a hiking boot, my toes were blocked from entry by a pile of poison pellets. Where else had those provident little mice stashed pellets?

A short time later, while watching television in the living room, I noticed movement along a baseboard. There, a white-footed mouse was attempting to travel. But it kept bumping its head into the baseboard, looking pathetically disoriented. The effects of anticoagulants aren't pretty.

Eventually we smelled decomposing corpses behind walls. That same poison manufacturer later offered 1-inch blocks of paraffinized anticoagulant that mice couldn't readily drag into storage. Manufacturers now recommend placing these blocks inside tamper-proof housings called bait stations. The aroma of the bait entices rodents to enter and feed without removing much poison for storage.

Eliminating Food, Water, and Shelter

All pest-control authorities emphasize the importance of denying rodents the slightest crumb of food, except when trapping. Indoors, keep your eating and cooking areas spotless. Daily vacuuming or sweeping of floors reduces food availability there, while also making trap baits the only food option for rodents.

Protect packaged grains, cereals, and the like inside sealed glass or metal containers. Never leave dirty dishes overnight for rodents to lick clean.

As to pets, our county's public health sanitarian Rich Robbins says that the most fastidious people often overlook the obvious. They allow bowls of half-eaten pet food to remain outdoors or indoors. Instead, Robbins advises, "Condition pets to eat an entire meal at one time and then take the bowls

Half-inch wire mesh can protect open freezer and refrigerator bottoms from rats and mice.

away." Pet food, including feed for sheep, chickens, and goats, should be kept in steel containers with tight-fitting lids. If bears live in your area, you can shop for bear-proof garbage cans on the Internet using the search words *bear proof garbage.*

Our county bans feeding wild birds directly on the ground, which of course can provide seed to rodents. Even bird feeders themselves attract mice and rats, as well as squirrels and bears. To prevent rodent raids, baffles known as squirrel guards can serve well. If bears travel your locale, it's wise to postpone bird feeding until the bears have gone into hibernation, which in northern Minnesota usually occurs by October but in the South may not occur until January, if at all. Anyway, except immediately after snow or sleet storms, birds tend to do fine without us.

As for household garbage, Robbins recommends steel cans, rather than plastic, which rats can chew through. He advises placing garbage cans outdoors just before scheduled pickup, rather than allowing critters to tip them overnight and scatter the contents. If left outdoors, garbage cans should be shaded to prevent odor-generating fermentation.

Also, rats will dine on pet feces, so it's wise to observe pooper-scooper ordinances and ask your neighbors to observe them too. In addition, pick up and dispose of fruit fallen from trees.

As for vehicles, cars often have vent flaps that allow mice to enter and build nests. Rust holes in vehicles permit even easier access. Thus, near vehicles, traps baited with cotton batting will attract rodents interested in nesting material.

Water. Rats need a water supply, especially after gorging on dry foods such as grains. So indoors, it's important to eliminate water sources: leaky water pipes and faucets, water bowls, open toilet lids. Also insulate cold-water pipes that cause drip condensation in summer. Outdoors, some of the same practices that deny water to rodents will deny mosquitoes a chance to breed. Eliminate causes of standing surface water. Keep drain troughs running freely and seal rain barrels.

Shelter. Rats and mice seek protected places for nesting. They like concealed voids in house

How Disinfectant Viricides Work

The lipid (fatty) envelope surrounding hantaviruses is somewhat fragile. It can be destroyed by solvents such as a 10-percent bleach solution or ordinary disinfectants, including alcohol, according to the US Centers for Disease Control and Prevention (CDC). Wet solvents kill the virus while also reducing the chances of stirring up dust containing aerosolized contaminated droplets.

structures where you can't get at them. Although Norway rats often prefer outdoor underground burrows, from which they make nightly house raids, they'll also nest indoors. Roof rats prefer attics and upper-story walls. Mice like any place they feel safe. (I once found a mouse nest behind a bookshelf near my desk.) You can discourage nests in air conditioners and under freezers and refrigerators by protecting them with quarter-inch wire mesh. Outdoors, rodents like to nest in woodpiles, under brush piles, and behind rock walls. It's wise to store firewood 100 feet from the house and elevated off the ground on masonry tiers. (This also reduces the chance that wood-eating insects will enter the house while still active before departing or going dormant in cold temperatures.)

To avoid airborne pathogens, Alan Huot wears the Survivair Half Face Mask (wildlifecontrolsupplies.com).

Indoors, whether in garages or basements, use racks to elevate boxes and crates off the floor, spaced away from the wall, thereby reducing the temptation for baseboard nesting. This also creates accessible avenues for your snap traps.

Exclusion Measures

Timing of exclusion efforts will depend on whether you have an infestation. While removing rodents, you can begin checking for possible points of entry.

■ Rodents often enter houses through open doorways, such as those leading to attached garages. The remedy in this case is an automatic door closer and tight weather stripping at door bottoms.

■ Two-way pet doors allow access to rodents. (Low-tech pet doors can also admit raccoons. For more on pet doors, see that section in the raccoons chapter, on page 134.)

■ Mice enter through louvered vents and air spaces around entrance holes of plumbing and power cables. They squeeze through dilapidated weather stripping. As mentioned, they work their way through small holes and infiltrate narrow cracks that open as a new foundation settles.

■ A careful indoor and outdoor inspection can reveal points of entry. Talc or fine sand sprinkled around suspected points of entry outdoors can reveal tracks. Look for potential entry points at all house levels, including the roof.

In his book *Over the Mountain and Home Again*, author-naturalist Ed Kanze includes a hilarious chapter called "Rodents of Mass Destruction." In it, he recounts how he succeeded in blocking every mouse entrance to his old house. To locate points of entry, Kanze livetrapped mice indoors and dropped them into a bag of orange DayGlo powder. Upon release, the powdered mice headed for house egress/access holes, leaving a powder trail as well as telltale powder on hole edges. In the dark, Kanze's black light caused the powder to glow. Kanze then blocked holes and gaps with various devices, including metal flashing and wire mesh that he sealed with spray-in expanding foam. After publishing his book, Kanze says, he used the same technique to determine how mice were entering his car trunk and passenger compartment. Detected by black light, points of entry proved to be under the rear fenders.

■ Try to plug openings in masonry with mortar, with a combination of mortar preceded by copper mesh manufactured for this purpose, or with ¼-inch galvanized mesh. To plug holes in moist areas, rolls of copper mesh serve better than steel wool because the copper won't rust. Copper mesh in 100-foot rolls is available from firms such as wildlifecontrolsupplies.com. Spray-in expanding foam can fill tiny voids that other materials can't.

■ Ensure that floor drains have tight, screw-down covers with grate spacing of no more than ¼ inch.

■ Use spray foam or silicone caulk to seal small openings around incoming pipes and power cables and around vents.

■ Check the integrity of door and window screening and the condition of its framing. Ensure that weather stripping doesn't leave more than a ¼-inch space, even at door bottoms.

■ Use ¼-inch metal mesh to prevent entry through porch grillwork, as shown on page 59.

■ Trim trees and shrubs so they don't reach within 6 feet of the roof for rats or within 10 feet of the roof for squirrels.

■ Trim shrubs and plants used as ground cover so they're 18 inches from the foundation, allowing you to inspect regularly for evidence of burrows and tracks. Coarse 1-inch gravel in that space discourages digging while revealing efforts at digging.

■ If vines climb on the house, roof rats and other rodents will use them like ladders to the attic. If possible, remove house vines, perhaps transplanting them under an arbor or pergola.

Cleanup

For major cleanup operations, you'll probably be safer hiring a licensed pest-control professional with the knowledge and equipment to minimize health risks to everybody. Professionals don full Tyvek suits and wear special respirators. Some pros may suggest that vacuums with HEPA (high-efficiency particulate air) filters are adequate. But even though HEPA filters are capable of removing 99.97 percent of particles 0.3 microns and larger, they probably won't capture tiny viruses, such as hantavirus.

For do-it-yourselfers, Robbins advises against attempting to clean up rodent droppings when they're dry. Out of concern about airborne pathogens in stirred-up dust, he advises "wetting droppings and dust with a dilute bleach solution, which is a viricide, and removing the moist material with a dustpan or shovel before bagging it for disposal." In any case, wear a protective hat, plastic goggles, disposable stretch gloves, tight-fitting protective clothing, and disposable boot covers or rubber boots. After cleanup of rodent materials, either discard protective clothing or wash and disinfect it.

Avoid operating a wet/dry shop vac indoors because it can stir up general dust, while exhausting its fine particles. Again, filters in consumer vacuums can't contain the finest particles. However, you will be safer working indoors if you can position the vacuum outdoors and use extension vacuum hoses to reach the wetted dust.

Disposable construction-grade dust masks rated in the 90s aren't adequate against aerosolized pathogens. You instead need a high-efficiency dust-mist respirator mask, rated at least P-100. Follow manufacturer guidelines to test the fit. For example, for a proper seal, a man needs to be clean-shaven. (For more on cleanup precautions, visit cdc.gov.com and search *hantavirus*.)

COMMUNICABLE DISEASES AND PARASITES

These threats include rat-bite fever, hantavirus, flea-transmitted typhus and plague (once known as the Black Death), worms, ticks, various protozoa, and more, but so far, not rabies. That is, the CDC says it has no evidence that rats or other rodents have transmitted rabies to humans, even though tiny percentages of rats sometimes test positive for the virus. *Reminder:* Rodents bite humans mainly when being handled. For more on these hazards, see "Communicable Diseases and Parasites" on page 210.

CHAPTER 15

Skunks

Dogs learn about skunks the hard way. Some of us do, too.

I'd once baited a live trap near our dining porch, hoping to catch a woodchuck I'd seen there. However, that night I forgot to bring the trap in. Woodchucks don't forage at night. Skunks do, as do opossums and raccoons. Of those mammals, only the skunk has a weapon that can reach well beyond a trap.

The next morning, a striped skunk paced inside the trap. My initial challenges seemed to be three-fold: moving the caged skunk away from the house, protecting the house from spray, and avoiding getting sprayed myself. For this, I was less than certain about how to proceed.

I decided to try to approach close enough to drape a large plastic garbage bag over the trap. I hoped that might help keep the skunk calm. Conveniently, the garbage bag disguised me as I approached, while shielding me from potential spray. With bag draped over the cage, leaving trap uncovered, I used several squeeze clothespins to secure the bag to the cage. Next, I tied a 100-foot nylon cord to the cage and backed away, unrolling the cord to full length before pulling the cage over the lawn toward me, like a sled.

With the cage a safe distance from the house, I had two options. I could release the skunk there, where it could run back under our porch or head for our neighbor's porch. Or I could attempt to load the plastic-wrapped cage onto my car rack and drive to a nearby hiking trail for release—which seemed the wiser option.

Using old bicycle inner tubes, I tied the trap to a wide plank. Then with car windows closed, I

Striped skunks have a narrow white stripe on their face, but body striping can be highly variable, as shown on page 167.

tied the cage-mounted plank to the top of the car rack. After parking near the hiking trail, I grasped the cage's top handle through the garbage bag and carried the trap like a suitcase. At this point, one-handed control of the cage became a challenge because the skunk paced forward and backward, continually shifting the balance point.

In a sunny woods opening, I placed the trap on the ground, opened its door, and stepped back. For perhaps a minute, the skunk stayed inside. Then it calmly walked out without looking back and disappeared into the woods, as though this were its daily routine.

Covering live traps. I've since learned that wildlife-control pros cover baited live traps for most animals, not just skunks. The cover makes the trap appear to be a secure place initially. After the trap's door closes, a cover can protect animals from sun and rain. And a cover allows your

Order: Carnivora ■ **Newly created family:** MEPHITIDAE ■ **Genera:** 3 ■ **Species:** 5 north of Mexico

Upon baiting, Lennie Rue covers live traps to help ensure unalarmed release. (Photo by Lennie and Uschi Rue III)

approach without dramatically increasing the animal's stress.

Caveat: While writing this chapter, I live-trapped a raccoon and covered the cage with a large plastic garbage bag before running an errand. By the time I returned, the raccoon had pulled nearly the entire bag inside the cage, as if in an attempt to create a protective cover inside. So, for compulsive raccoons, a tarp seems a better cover than a garbage bag.

PROBLEMS FOR PEOPLE

When perturbed, skunks spray musk that is pungent, penetrating, and nauseating. Besides the odor, droplets in the eyes can cause a severe burning sensation and temporary blindness. Adult skunks can spray up to six times without a recharge. Much spraying occurs during the mating season and later on, when mothers defend their kits from male skunks, including the kits' own father. While romping around, young skunks often spray inadvertently. And when threatened, young skunks are usually more trigger happy than adults.

In suburban areas, striped skunks often reach densities of more than 50 per square mile. There, they sometimes fall into window wells and can't get out without help. Skunks den under buildings, woodpiles, and brush piles, and in culverts,

sometimes communally. They dine on garbage and unfinished pet food. In gardens, they enjoy berries, fallen fruits, some vegetables, and unprotected compost piles. In rural areas, they raid beehives and chicken coops, sometimes eating only eggs, sometimes a chicken or two.

On lawns, skunks dig shallow holes while searching for insect larvae and earthworms. With this same goal, they also roll back newly laid sod. In fact, golf courses are principal clients of skunk-control professionals, who may patrol fairways in electric golf carts at night—scope-mounted air rifles at the ready.

A skunk's spray can temporarily blind a dog or, at best, cause the dog's banishment to the doghouse until being bathed in odor remover. Some dogs will repeat their mistakes and so shouldn't be trusted out alone at night.

Along with raccoons and bats, skunks are the primary vectors of the rabies virus. They also carry other transmissible diseases and parasites.

ROLE IN THE WILD

Officially considered carnivores, skunks are opportunistic omnivores. Mostly nocturnal, skunks feed on available insects. They also like earthworms, snails, crayfish, frogs, small rodents, moles, carrion, and the eggs and young of ground-nesting birds. In winter, with fewer insects available, skunks hunt for rodents, including voles and rats. Yet skunks also relish wild fruits, berries, nuts, corn, and grain.

Of our five North American species, only the spotted skunk climbs well enough to den high in trees.

Predators such as coyotes, foxes, bobcats, cougars, and wolverines kill skunks, though I wonder if

---

What's in a Name?

The name *skunk* originated with Algonquin Indians. From Latin, the genus name *Mephitis* means bad odor, and the species name *putorius* means bad stink. As to the Worst Stink Award, skunk researcher R. F. Patton conferred that honor on the white-backed, hog-nosed skunk.

the first meal doesn't reduce interest in a second. However, skunks are favored prey of large owls, which lack a sense of smell. Owl researchers often locate owl nests by following skunk odor to the base of nest trees, where skunk fur and bones have fallen.

SPECIES AND DISTRIBUTION

Skunks are members of the newly created Mephitidae family. Until DNA testing, skunks were thought to be members of the Weasel family (Mustelidae) that includes badgers and wolverines, which skunks somewhat resemble.

Skunks occur only in the New World, including the Philippines and Java. Of the 9 to 13 species in the Americas, depending on which taxonomist is counting, only 5 species live north of Mexico.

Because the striped and spotted skunks range throughout most of North America, this chapter will focus mainly on them—although control options for all species are relatively similar.

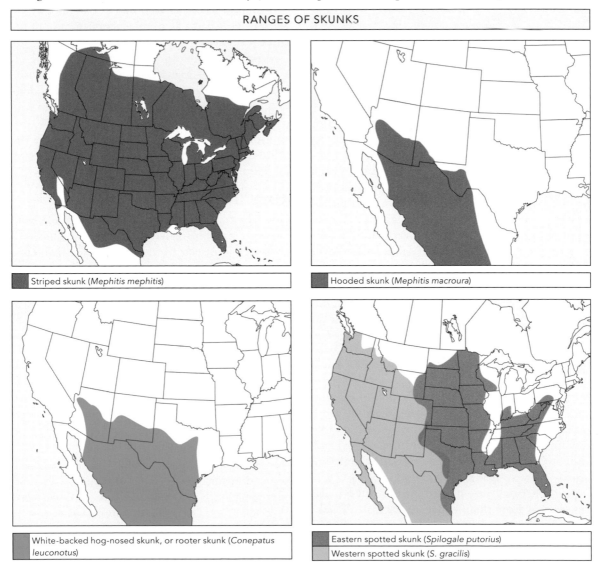

RANGES OF SKUNKS

Striped skunk (*Mephitis mephitis*)

Hooded skunk (*Mephitis macroura*)

White-backed hog-nosed skunk, or rooter skunk (*Conepatus leuconotus*)

Eastern spotted skunk (*Spilogale putorius*)
Western spotted skunk (*S. gracilis*)

IDENTIFICATION AND CHARACTERISTICS

Skunks are roughly the size of house cats, some small, some large. They have black-and-white spots and stripes that can be quite variable within a single species. Adult males tend to be larger than females, a phenomenon known as *sexual dimorphism*. In colder climates, skunks fatten up for winter and doze much of the time until warmer weather makes food available. In warmer climates, skunks remain active year-round.

Spraying behaviors. Skunks tend to be easygoing creatures that prefer to walk away from trouble or dash short distances for cover. However, their poor eyesight often allows predators and bumbling humans to violate the skunk's "fight-or-flight" distance. Spray behaviors differ by species but involve a raised tail that reveals anal spray nozzles. For example, striped skunks and hooded skunks, being in the same genus, raise rump and tail, often stamping their front feet while shuffling backward before spraying.

In spectacular contrast, the two species of spotted skunks often run toward the threat before stopping to do a handstand and then either hosing the threat from that position or, more often, dropping to all fours and bending into a horseshoe shape to keep the target in sight. The white-backed hog-nosed skunk may first stand on its hind legs before hissing and assuming a horseshoe

> ### Childhood Memories
> As a lad of 12 in northern Minnesota, I used an 8-foot pole to carry a dead skunk away from our family's cabin, all the while trying to keep the stinky fellow downwind. Even so, my clothes and nostrils absorbed the pungent odor. Dad kept the car windows open as we drove home. Mom washed my clothes a time or two before throwing them away. Odor molecules remained in my nostrils for days, still vivid in memory.

shape that signals spraying; it sometimes also charges and bites.

Species profiles. Following are the five skunk species ranging north of Mexico, in order roughly by largest distributions.

Striped skunk *(Mephitis mephitis):* Head and body up to 20 inches long; tail up to 14 inches long. Larger in the North than in the South. Occasionally weighs 12 pounds. Has a white stripe down the center of its face. Although body striping is variable, there are usually two broad stripes from head through tail. Thrives in varied climates and habitats, but not in deserts.

Western spotted skunk *(Spilogale gracilis):* Head and body up to 11 inches long; tail up to 6½ inches long. This smallest and quickest skunk climbs trees and rough walls well. Has a large white triangle between the eyes and rows of white spots and stripes on the back and rump. Tail tip is bushy

Left: *This striped skunk has only small patches of white on its back. (Photo by Lennie and Uschi Rue III)* Right: *To spray, western spotted skunks may run toward you before doing a handstand. (Photo © Stephen J. Krasemann/Photo Researchers, Inc.)*

With tail raised, this eastern spotted skunk isn't preparing to spray. It's taking a dust bath. (Photo by Lennie and Uschi Rue III)

white. Vocalizations include grunts and a scream like a blue jay's.

Eastern spotted skunk *(S. putorius):* Head and body up to 17 inches long; tail up to 11 inches long. Has a smaller white triangle between the eyes than its Western cousin's, but spraying and other behaviors are similar to those of the Western species.

White-backed hog-nosed skunk, or rooter skunk *(Conepatus leuconotus):* Head and body up to 21 inches long; tail up to 16 inches long. This largest North American skunk also has the proportionately longest tail. Not as agile a climber as the spotted skunk. As for "hog" in its name, its long, bare snout has wide nostrils and is three times wider than the striped skunk's. More insectivorous than other species, this one roots like a hog (thus the nickname "rooter"), also digging deeper than the hooded skunk that shares its range.

Hooded skunk *(M. macroura):* Head and body up to 14 inches long; tail up to 17 inches long. Has a white stripe from head to rump. Uncommon and secretive, this skunk is little studied. It doesn't dig deep like the "rooter" skunk that shares its range.

REPRODUCTION AND POPULATIONS

The following mating and dispersal dates may help in determining the best times for exclusion measures or livetrapping. The humane approach is to avoid separating kits from their mother.

Striped skunks. These guys breed once per year in mid-February through mid-April, later at higher altitudes. Rutting males are polygamous and will defend their harem from other males. Male fights may involve shoulder hits and leg bites. After kits are born, the mother sometimes needs to defend them from their father. Most litters are born in mid-May to early June; average size is six. Newborns are naked and remain blind for about a month. Thereafter, they begin following their mother on her nightly foraging trips. Youngsters disperse in fall at about 3 months old. Birthing dens are in ground burrows.

Spotted skunks. Unlike striped skunks, rutting males tend not to be territorial. There are dramatic differences between the eastern and western species of spotted skunks as well. Easterners breed in March through April, and kits are born from May through June. In contrast, western species breed from September to October, except in southern states, where breeding may begin as early as July; even so, delayed implantation of the embryo allows births in May to early June. Litter sizes average nearly five to six in the East but three to four in the West. Birthing dens may be in ground burrows or in tree hollows more than 20 feet off the ground.

Hog-nosed skunks. Breeding occurs in February, and kits are born from April to early May. Litter size is usually fewer than four. The young disperse in August.

Hooded skunks. Breeding occurs from late February to early March. Litter size is three to six.

SENSES

Hearing and an excellent sense of smell help skunks locate food under leaves and in soil. However, distance eyesight is poor. I once approached a striped skunk within 15 feet in daylight without seeming to be noticed.

BURROWS

Skunks can dig their own burrows. Yet they often occupy unused burrows of woodchucks, badgers, foxes, muskrats, and ground squirrels. Especially in winter, denning may be communal. Striped skunks tend to den on warmer, south-facing slopes in winter and on cooler, north-facing slopes in summer.

SIGN

Lawn damage. In his self-published book *Innovative Skunk Control,* wildlife-control expert Rob Erickson shows comparative photos of lawn damage made by skunks and raccoons. Skunks dig shallow, funnel-shaped holes closely together, each about the diameter of a 50-cent piece, much like those I've seen chipmunks dig. By contrast, raccoons peel back sod in ragged patches. Hog-nosed skunks leave rooting trails.

Tracks. Skunks have five toes on their front and hind feet. In soft soil, all five claws on each foot show, with the front ones projecting significantly.

Burrow entrances. If dug by skunks, the opening can be 4 to 14 inches wide, says Erickson. He says that inactive den openings will have cobwebs in them. Active den openings will have white and black hair in them. Dens with active kits may show small tracks and smaller claw marks.

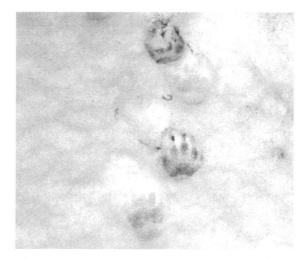

When a skunk walks in soft snow or mud, all five toes and claws register. (Photo by Lennie and Uschi Rue III)

Eggs in chicken coops. Eggs left by striped skunks are usually crushed at one end, with the shell fragments pushed aside. If spotted skunks can't crush an egg with their teeth, they may shove the egg backward in order to give it a kick with a hind paw. In captivity, hog-nosed skunks did not

Getting the Stink Out

When perturbed, skunks spray an oily, yellow sulfur-alcohol compound called butylmercaptan. Veterinarians often sell odor removers. Your veterinarian might also approve one or both of the following two home brews, described in *Best Practices for Wildlife Control Operators,* by Cornell University professors Paul D. Curtis and Jill Shultz. Keep these shampoos out of your pet's eyes.

■ **Vinegar-enhanced tomato juice:** To remove the stink from dogs or clothing, mix tomato juice with equal parts vinegar, and use a bathtub to shampoo and soak *for at least an hour.* Baths of shorter duration don't work as well. Thereafter, wash with soap and then rinse. Curtis and Shultz offer no cautions regarding potential skin allergies in humans. Thus, a good precaution would be to test this formula on a small skin area well before jumping into a full tub. Still, stinky Old Rover might feel more willing to reuse your

blood-red "bathwater" if he has seen you enjoying it, however briefly.

■ **Alternative recipe:** The Cornell professors also recommend this alternative recipe developed by chemist Dr. Paul Krebaum.

    1 quart 3-percent hydrogen peroxide
    ¼ cup baking soda
    1 teaspoon liquid soap

1. Mix immediately. While the solution is bubbling, use protective gloves to "shampoo" dog or clothing.
2. Then rinse. *Caution:* If you try to bottle the bubbling solution, the expanding oxygen could very well cause the bottle to explode later on.

■ **Commercial odor removers:** University of California researchers recommend products that contain neutroleum-alpha. For Internet sources, use the keywords *skunk, odor, and remover.* However, by then you may want overnight delivery.

recognize eggs as food. In contrast, raccoons usually remove one end of the egg without crushing it. Weasels and mink crush the entire shell. Foxes run off with the egg.

HOME RANGES

When food and denning sites are plentiful, as in some urban settings, home ranges tend to be less than half a square mile. In rural areas, striped skunks usually have ranges of 1 to 3 square miles. The females have far smaller ranges than males.

Hibernation. Northern skunks retire to winter dens. During this time, they may lose nearly 40 percent of their fall body weight. However, on warm winter days, skunks often rouse to forage.

OPTIONS FOR CONTROL

Many jurisdictions consider skunks nongame animals and allow landowners and tenants to control them by any legal means. Due to disease concerns, relocation may be banned or may require a permit.

Elimination of food sources. General guidelines apply to skunks, as well as to raccoons, bears, and rodents, as described on page 82.

Exclusion. Use wire-mesh fencing around building foundations and gardens as suggested for mammals of various sizes on page 59. If a skunk is denned under a foundation, a one-way door can prevent reentry through the same opening. But if a mother has kits inside, she may dig a fresh entry. Before installing a one-way door, ensure that the skunk or family has left to forage. You can make sure by sifting a shallow layer of flour in front of the opening to create a tracking patch.

Predators. Although large owls can help keep a skunk population somewhat in check, most owls hunt where prey populations are highest. Horned owls like to hunt from tall conifers.

Repellents. No authorities recommend repellents. Some caution against using mothballs, which are toxic to soil and groundwater.

Frighteners. There seem to be none.

Livetrapping. If you have skunks denning under your house foundation, consider hiring a pro who's experienced in skunk removal as well as follow-up exclusion measures. Rob Erickson is so confident of his skunk-trapping abilities that he assures prospective customers, "If they spray, no pay." Pros know all options for removal without causing spraying under a dwelling. They sometimes use muskrat colony traps to catch an entire family.

In open areas, the method I described at the beginning of this chapter should work. Place the baited trap in the early evening. As bait, sliced apples with dabs of peanut butter are irresistible to most mammals. Pros often use fish or special bait pastes. Place bait stepping-stone fashion outside the trap and leading onto the trap treadle. Erickson has found that young skunks are apprehensive about the smell of traps that have held raccoons or opossums, so he either uses skunk-exclusive traps or washes others well before using them for skunks.

Removal from window wells. It's mostly young skunks that fall into window wells and can't climb out. If window wells are long enough, a board can be placed at an angle less than 45 degrees to provide an exit ramp. Wooden cleats or the flat heads of roofing nails driven into the plank will provide helpful traction. As an alternative for young skunks, a baited live trap sometimes works.

Pros may guide a skunk inside a trap or cardboard box using a broom. Instead, Erickson often uses a water hose or a squirt gun to harass young skunks into a trap. Or he may use a nooselike cat grabber on a pole.

To prevent future episodes, install a wire-mesh barrier around the window well or install a commercial cover that resembles a clear plastic bubble.

Lethal trapping. Skunks are large enough to require lethal traps that could also injure or kill pets and other nontarget animals. To me, livetrapping seems the smarter option; it allows you to ensure that you've caught the intended mammal before reconsidering lethal intent, relative to legality. For thoughts on euthanasia options, see page 64.

Poisoning and chemical fumigant. I don't recommend poisons, for multiple reasons explained on page 64. However, if a skunk has shown aggressive or listless daytime behavior, that might suggest late-stage rabies. Or if a skunk can't otherwise be

The great horned owl favors skunks partly because it has no sense of smell. (Photo by Lennie and Uschi Rue III) Top right: WCS Spray-proof Skunk Trap. Right: This one-way door, called the "Coontroller," has rear flanges that screw-fasten to wood surfaces surrounding den openings. Actually, this unit contains two, angled top-hinged door panels, like the visible one, that easly swing open when pushed from inside but remain cam-locked against lifting efforts from the outside. (Both units from wildlifecontrolsupplies.com)

excluded or removed, a fumigant (where legal) inside a burrow poses low risk to nontarget species and low risk of secondary poisoning. However, it may pose a fire hazard as described at the end of the woodchucks and marmots chapter; see page 201. (*Caveat:* Elimination of a skunk usually invites a new skunk to take up residence unless the old burrow is effectively sealed.)

Firearms. Even where legal, a bullet to the head usually causes spraying, whereas a shot to the heart and lungs might not, say Cornell University authorities. Professional skunk controllers may instead give lethal injections through the lungs.

COMMUNICABLE DISEASES AND PARASITES

Diseases. Skunks are a principal vector of the rabies virus and are routinely involved in 20 to 30 percent of reported cases in wildlife. In skunks, advanced symptoms range from dumb-and-docile to furious. Because rabies is generally transmitted through saliva, have all skunk bites treated by a physician. Many people assume that normally nocturnal skunks that feed by day are likely to be rabid. Mother skunks with nursing young may need to supplement their own feeding by day. During daylight, listless tame behavior and furious or aggressive behavior may be symptomatic.

At times, 15 to 60 percent of skunks have carried the *Leptospira* bacteria, which they transmit through infected water. Skunks sometimes also have tularemia, pulmonary fungal diseases, canine distemper, and canine hepatitis, among other diseases.

Parasites. Externally, skunks endure fleas, lice, ticks, and mites. Internally, skunk roundworm eggs and larvae can be transmitted to humans.

For more information, see page 210.

CHAPTER 16

Squirrels (Ground)

Although true ground squirrels resemble tree squirrels, they are more closely related to prairie dogs and marmots—all ground dwellers. When frightened, ground squirrels retreat to burrows. Tree squirrels retreat to trees.

Broadly speaking, there are four ground squirrel genera.

■ **True ground squirrels** (*Spermophilus,* 21 species) are the focus of this chapter. In colder regions, they hibernate in winter. In hotter regions, they may become dormant for periods in summer. The smallest species weigh only 4 to 5 ounces; the largest may exceed 1½ pounds. The genus name *Spermophilus* means "seed lover."

■ **Antelope squirrels** (*Ammospermophilus,* 4 species) are tinier than virtually all ground squirrels. They weigh only 3 to 4 ounces and are active year-round.

Cheeks bulging with hackberries, this rock squirrel made frequent trips to its burrow under a large rock shelf.

■ **Prairie dogs** (*Cynomys,* 5 species) are larger than ground squirrels, with some species weighing up to 4 pounds.

■ **Woodchucks and marmots** (*Marmota,* 6 species) are addressed in their own chapter, beginning on page 201.

This chapter addresses only true ground squirrels because many live in close association with people and cause significant problems. Still, the control measures for them often apply to all four ground squirrel genera.

PROBLEMS FOR PEOPLE

Although adults live in belowground colonies, each has its own separate burrow system and feeding area, which it defends from other colony members. Adult populations tend to be fewer than 10 per acre, often increasing to more than 25 after the pups are weaned. But when food is plentiful, say, near alfalfa fields, populations can exceed 100 per acre.

Besides gnawing on sprinkler heads and plastic irrigation pipe, ground squirrels eat many plants at seedling stage. They also dig bulb plants and eat ornamental annuals and perennials. They like lettuce, tomatoes, and fruits such as strawberries, apples, peaches, and oranges. They love seeds and cultivated nuts such as almonds, walnuts, and pistachios. In fact, ground-squirrel colonies are capable of carrying off an entire backyard nut crop.

Ground squirrels damage trees and shrubs by eating buds, leaves, and twigs and by gnawing on bark. They also burrow under young trees and

Order: Rodentia ■ **Family:** SCURIDAE ■ **Genus:** Spermophilus ■ **Species:** many

shrubs, which can dry the roots enough to kill them. If enough roots are destroyed, the whole plant will die.

Populations increase where wildlands are converted to agriculture. There, ground squirrels compete with farmers and livestock for grains and alfalfa.

Burrows can undermine porches, stairs, concrete slabs, and house foundations and can interfere with surface irrigation. Burrows can also cause erosion and the collapse of hillsides and the earthen embankments of dams and canals. In fact, ground squirrels may be partly the cause of the 2008 collapse of a section of the Truckee Canal in Nevada that flooded 590 homes. For more on that, see the gophers chapter on page 95.

Burrow entrances pose injury risks to people and livestock—as well as damage to garden machines.

ROLE IN THE WILD

Ground squirrels are good. In fact, they are considered *keystone species* in their ecosystems because so many other species depend on them for food and shelter. Their avian predators include hawks, prairie falcons, golden eagles, and ravens. Gopher snakes and western diamondback rattlers can swallow ground squirrels whole and readily pursue them inside burrows. Mammalian predators include badgers, weasels, coyotes, and foxes. Interestingly, before excavating the main entrance of a ground squirrel burrow, badgers seal secondary burrow entrances to prevent escape. Rabbits, toads, and snakes shelter in squirrel burrows. And burrowing owls nest there.

Tunneling improves soil in several ways. It aerates soil and allows deeper penetration of rainwater. It also brings deep soil nutrients to the surface, which is especially valuable in arid areas where earthworms are rare. Some squirrel populations literally kick tons of soil to the surface—tonnage no doubt increases when badgers join the party. Ground squirrels are mainly herbivores but also eat insects, bird eggs, baby mice, and carrion. In spring, newly weaned pups learn which grasses and forbs to eat by observing their mother. By

---

Warning Cries

Some species of ground squirrel have different warning cries for different types of predators. For example, when the Belding's ground squirrel sees a hawk, it issues a single-note warning. But when it spots a ground predator, it utters a trill. Snakes get added attention by having dirt thrown in their faces.

---

summer, though, most species favor seeds, fruits, and berries. As exceptions to the norm, the forest-dwelling Cascade ground squirrel feeds heavily on fungi. And the Mexican ground squirrel feeds mainly on leaves and mesquite beans.

IDENTIFICATION AND VARIATIONS

Active aboveground only by day, true ground squirrels vary widely in size, color, and habitat. Adults of the smallest species may weigh only 4 to 5 ounces; larger species may weigh up to 1¾ pounds. Ground squirrels have short, strong forelimbs with sharp claws for digging. They have four toes on their front feet and five on their hind feet. Some species, such as the rock squirrel, are large and have long, bushy tails like the tails of some tree squirrels, giving them better balance when climbing trees. Others, such as the Mohave and the round-tailed, have short, thin tails. Desert species often have tails with white undersides that the animals carry over themselves like a reflective awning. Ears vary in size and shape.

The teeth, like those of all rodents, grow continuously and so must be filed down with use. Some ground squirrels have internal cheek pouches in which they carry food and nest materials.

SPECIES AND DISTRIBUTION

Mountains and contrasting climates at different elevations have sometimes created "island" ecosystems from which some species evolved without option to travel beyond. Where ranges overlap, species of smaller body size are usually pushed into poorer habitat by larger species. Thus, the maps on page 175 often show broad-brush ranges of species whose habitat fragmentation could better be represented by isolated dots. Some species move in and out of endangered and threatened status from time to time, especially in isolated locales.

- **Townsend's ground squirrel** *(Spermophilus townsendii)*
- **Great Basin ground squirrel** *(S. mollis)*
- **Columbia Plateau ground squirrel** *(S. canus):* Up to 1¾ pounds, the largest ground squirrel
- **Washington ground squirrel** *(S. washingtoni)*
- **Idaho ground squirrel** *(S. brunneus):* Status: Endangered
- **Richardson's ground squirrel, picket pin, prairie gopher** *(S. richardsonii)*
- **Wyoming ground squirrel** *(S. elegans)*
- **Uinta ground squirrel** *(S. armatus)*
- **Belding's ground squirrel** *(S. beldingi)*
- **Columbian ground squirrel, called red digger in Oregon** *(S. columbianus)*
- **Arctic ground squirrel, sik–sik** *(S. parryii)*
- **Thirteen-lined ground squirrel, striped gopher** *(S. tridecemlineatus):* Status: Populations declining
- **Mexican ground squirrel** *(S. mexicanus)*
- **Spotted ground squirrel** *(S. spilosoma)*
- **Franklin's ground squirrel** *(S. franklinii)*
- **California ground squirrel** *(S. beecheyi):* Large with bushy tail, resembles tree squirrels
- **Rock squirrel** *(S. variegatus):* Large with bushy tail, resembles tree squirrels
- **Mohave ground squirrel** *(S. mohavensis)*
- **Round-tailed ground squirrel** *(S. tereticaudus)*
- **Golden-mantled ground squirrel** *(S. lateralis)*
- **Cascade ground squirrel** *(S. saturatus)*

POPULATION DYNAMICS

Depending on the availability of food prior to hibernation, long, cold winters can reduce populations by more than half. In addition, predation and infectious diseases, such as plague, take significant tolls. Some species, such as the Arctic ground squirrel, experience population crashes every 10 to

From top to bottom: *California ground squirrels have large ears and a whitish shoulder mantle. Uinta ground squirrels are medium size and grayish. Mexican ground squirrels resemble thirteen-lined ground squirrels but don't have their stripes. (Photos by Lennie and Uschi Rue III)*

RANGES OF GROUND SQUIRRELS

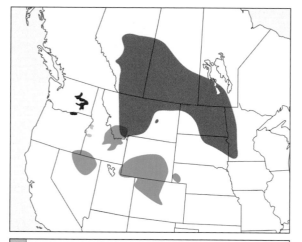

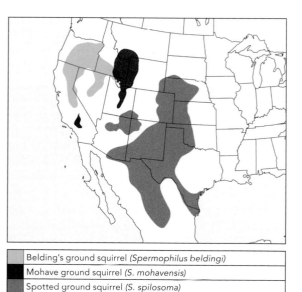

	Idaho ground squirrel (*Spermophilus brunneus*): Endangered
	Richardson's ground squirrel, picket pin, prairie gopher (*S. richardsonii*)
	Washington ground squirrel (*S. washingtoni*)
	Wyoming ground squirrel (*S. elegans*)

	California ground squirrel (*Spermophilus beecheyi*)
	Columbian ground squirrel, called red digger in Oregon (*S. columbianus*)
	Franklin's ground squirrel (*S. franklinii*)
	Rock squirrel (*S. variegatus*)

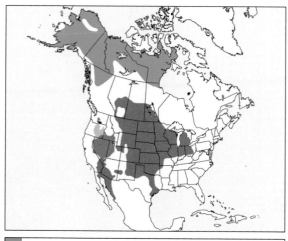

	Arctic ground squirrel, sik-sik (*Spermophilus parryii*)
	Columbia Plateau ground squirrel (*S. canus*)
	Great Basin ground squirrel (*S. mollis*)
	Round-tailed ground squirrel (*S. tereticaudus*)
	Thirteen-lined ground squirrel, striped gopher (*S. tridecemlineatus*)
	Townsend's ground squirrel (*S. townsendii*)

	Belding's ground squirrel (*Spermophilus beldingi*)
	Mohave ground squirrel (*S. mohavensis*)
	Spotted ground squirrel (*S. spilosoma*)
	Uinta ground squirrel (*S. armatus*)

(maps continue on next page)

RANGES OF GROUND SQUIRRELS

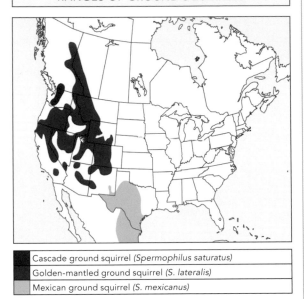

■	Cascade ground squirrel (*Spermophilus saturatus*)
■	Golden-mantled ground squirrel (*S. lateralis*)
■	Mexican ground squirrel (*S. mexicanus*)

11 years, following the population crashes of snowshoe hares, perhaps partly because predators must then concentrate on ground squirrels.

HIBERNATION

In cold climates, hibernation begins after ground squirrels have laid on sufficient fat reserves. To fatten up, ground squirrels need to be selective with seeds and nuts, often limiting their intake. For example, seeds with high levels of polyunsaturated acids can produce toxic lipid peroxides in squirrel tissue that can kill them. To maintain a safe body chemistry, the golden-mantled ground squirrel switches back and forth from pine seeds to herbaceous plants.

Even with a good fat reserve, a ground squirrel's hibernation survival can be threatened by long, cold winters and deep snow. During hibernation, loss of body mass may range from 31 to 51 percent. However, in a few species, the males store seeds for winter snacks and so can emerge from hibernation weighing

The Burrow System

Burrows are usually located on slopes that allow visibility of approaching predators. Preferred soil is soft with good drainage.

Even though burrows usually occur in colonies, each adult maintains and defends his or her own burrow system, usually with multiple entrances. Burrows dug by males are simpler and shorter than those needed by females to rear pups. Nursery burrows of smaller species may be only 8 to 30 feet long. However, nursery burrows of California ground-squirrel mothers may have total lengths of 100 to 200 feet. To protect their nurseries from predators, mothers often plug entrances with soil for several days at a time. Hibernation burrows are difficult to locate because the owners plug them from inside. These burrows are only about 6 feet long and have two chambers, one for the nest, and the other for the lavatory. To ensure drainage, hillside nest chambers are positioned above the main entrance. In flatter terrain, drainage is encouraged by means of a dip in the tunnel, serving much like the J-shaped trap pipe under a kitchen sink.

Ground squirrels often den under trees for the shade but also because the roots reinforce tunnels.

almost as much as when they entered. That's important because the competitive breeding season begins immediately upon emergence from hibernation.

SIGN

Plant damage. Plant stems are severed cleanly. Hard nutshells are chewed open. Bark is chewed from tree trunks.

Burrows. The main entrance is often under a protective feature, such as a tree, shrub, or large rock. Trees and shrubs offer shelter from direct rain and snow as well as a root system that reinforces tunnels. Depending on the species, entrances may be a few inches or more wide, and they're usually wider than they are tall. Some species surround entrances with excavated soil.

Runways. These run through grass and are usually about 3 inches wide.

MATING AND BIRTH

Upon emerging from hibernation in late winter to early spring, a male begins looking for females, which usually emerge shortly after males do. Most species mate underground, presumably for safety and privacy. But females normally mate with more than one male, which results in multiple fathers for the litter. Females raise only one litter per year. Litter sizes average four to six pups, depending on species.

Gestation is 3 to 4 weeks for smaller species and longer for larger species. Young are usually weaned within another 3 to 4 weeks. But larger litters require more nursing time because the pups are smaller at birth than those in small litters. Juveniles usually disperse before their first winter. Although juvenile females tend to burrow close to Mom, upward of 85 percent of young males head to distant territories by fall, and the remaining males depart the following spring.

OPTIONS FOR CONTROL

Endangered and threatened species. As noted in the earlier section on distribution, some species may be at risk for extinction and therefore are protected by law.

Eliminating food sources. Bird feeders attract ground squirrels as well as other wildlife. For options, see page 82.

Exclusion. Ground squirrels can climb over or tunnel under most kinds of fencing. Some dig to depths greater than 6 feet. Still, all rodents can usually be excluded from buildings by the methods suggested on page 59.

Frighteners and repellents. Pet dogs can discourage burrowing on a small property. Cats with hunting prowess can help keep squirrel populations within reason but not eliminate them. University of California researchers have found no other frighteners effective and no repellents effective.

Trapping. Researchers place live or lethal traps near main entrances of burrows. For quickest results, they walk toward an individual and follow it to its burrow entrance. There, they block all auxiliary exits with rocks or boards before placing four open-ended traps at the main entrance, inviting the squirrel to use one of them. On warm, sunny days, be sure to place boards or fabric on top of live traps to provide shade so captives won't overheat. As to baits, chopped apples, peanut butter, and nuts are effective. Various lethal and live traps are available from wildlifecontrolsupplies.com.

Lethal traps for squirrels have powerful springs that could injure children and kill nontarget animals, including pets. Avoid tragedy by enclosing them in secured containers.

Live traps help ensure that you don't kill or injure animals other than ground squirrels. Options for euthanasia are discussed on page 64.

> ## Watch Out for the Neighbors
> In some ground squirrel species, rival females sometimes kill newly weaned pups, perhaps to protect territory for their own daughters. When yearling males kill newly weaned pups, they eat them.

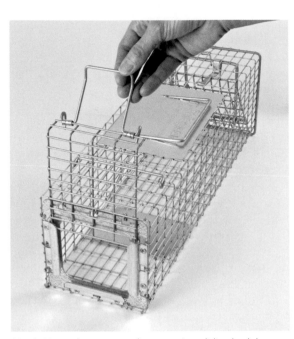

Mandy Nurge demonstrates the convenient sliding backdoor release on Safeguard traps, available in various sizes from wildlifecontrolsupplies.com.

Livetrapping and release. Many jurisdictions forbid transportation and release of wild mammals. However, some states, such as Arizona, request that residents inquire at their Fish and Game Department about authorized release sites before livetrapping. For more on the downsides of translocating animals, see page 62.

Hunting. Where legal, small-caliber firearms and air rifles can be effective in skilled hands. But in unskilled hands, they often merely wound and create prolonged, agonizing deaths.

Poisoning. Toxic baits can have life-threatening effects on children, pets, and nontarget wildlife, as discussed on page 64.

Fumigation. When used according to the manufacturer's instructions, smoke/gas cartridges can be far safer to nontarget wildlife than toxic baits, as discussed on page 209.

Destruction of burrows. Researchers at the University of California suggest tilling to depths of 20 inches with a tractor and ripping bars. If you simply fill burrow entrances with soil, ground squirrels can usually reopen them.

COMMUNICABLE DISEASES AND PARASITES

Ground squirrels are host to lice, worms, ticks, and fleas. When ground squirrels are infected with plague, their fleas can transmit the disease to people. Plague doesn't always wipe out ground-squirrel populations but often kills many. Interestingly, juvenile males prior to dispersal are more likely to be infested with plague than females, which seldom disperse far. If you notice numbers of dead ground squirrels, notify your public health officials. Avoid touching dead animals. For more information on plague, see page 212.

CHAPTER 17

Squirrels (Tree)

Although some species of tree squirrels resemble some species of ground squirrels, tree squirrels are tree dwellers. When frightened, tree squirrels retreat to trees. Ground squirrels retreat to burrows.

Most natural history in this chapter is from the monumental *Wild Mammals of North America,* second edition, by George A. Feldhamer, et al, 2003. Much in the section on options for control is from *Best Practices for Wildlife Control Operators* by Paul D. Curtis and Jill Shultz. The following names and measurements are based on *Mammals of North America,* a Peterson Field Guide, by Fiona A. Reid.

SPECIES AND IDENTIFICATION

Scientific names and newly recognized subspecies continue to change as DNA research provides additional information.

Fox squirrels and gray squirrels (*Sciurus* species). These squirrels favor deciduous woodlands, especially those with oaks. Both squirrels' tails are longer and bushier than those of pine squirrel species. Females usually have two litters per year. Unlike gray squirrels, fox squirrels favor upland woodlands with sparse undergrowth rather than lowland woodlands with dense undergrowth. Fox squirrels are more likely than grays to venture far beyond forest edge.

■ Eastern fox squirrel *(S. niger):* Average head and body 14½ inches long, tail 13 inches long; weight 3 pounds

■ Mexican fox squirrel *(S. nayaritensis):* Average head and body 11 inches long, tail 10½ inches long; weight 1½ pounds

■ Eastern gray squirrel *(S. carolinensis):* Average head and body 11 inches long, tail 10 inches long; weight 1½ pounds

■ Western gray squirrel *(S. griseus):* Average head and body 11½ inches long, tail 11½ inches long; weight 1¾ pounds

■ Arizona gray squirrel *(S. arizonensis):* Average head and body 11 inches long, tail 10 inches long; weight 1½ pounds

Largest of eastern squirrels, the eastern fox squirrel can weigh up to 3 pounds. (Photo by Lennie and Uschi Rue III)

Order: Rodentia ■ **Family:** SCURIDAE ■ **Genera:** *Sciurus, Tamiasciurus, Glaucomys* ■ **Species:** many

RANGES OF TREE SQUIRRELS

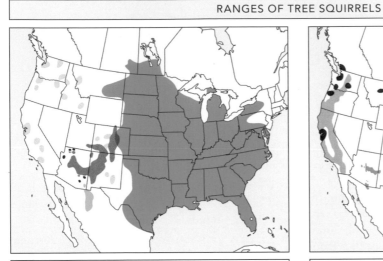

FOX SQUIRRELS (*Sciurus* species)

	Eastern fox squirrel (*S. niger*)
	Mexican fox squirrel (*S. nayaritensis*)
	Tassel-eared squirrel (*S. aberti*)
	Fox squirrel introductions
	Tassel-eared squirrel introductions

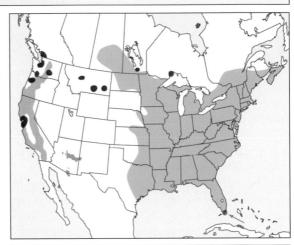

GRAY SQUIRRELS (*Sciurus* species)

	Arizona gray squirrel (*S. arizonensis*)
	Eastern gray squirrel (*S. carolinensis*)
	Red-bellied squirrel (*S. aureogaster*), ALIEN
	Western gray squirrel (*S. griseus*)
	Gray squirrel introductions

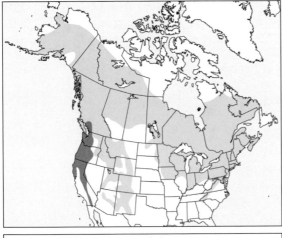

PINE SQUIRRELS (*Tamiasciurus* species)

	Douglas squirrel, Chickaree (*T. douglasii*)
	Red squirrel, Pine squirrel (*T. hudsonicus*)

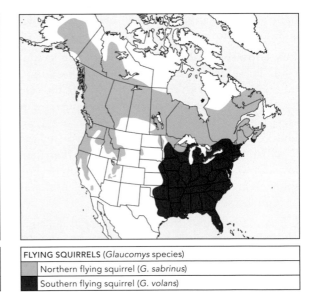

FLYING SQUIRRELS (*Glaucomys* species)

	Northern flying squirrel (*G. sabrinus*)
	Southern flying squirrel (*G. volans*)

Fox squirrels and gray squirrels may share feed. At right, strictly nocturnal flying squirrels make graceful floating descents. Their glider "wings" consist of furry membranes stretched tightly between "wrist" and "ankle." (Photos by Lennie and Uschi Rue III)

Tassel-eared squirrel *(S. aberti):* Average head and body 10 inches long, tail 8½ inches long; weight 1½ pounds

Pine squirrels (*Tamiasciurus* species). These squirrels favor mature coniferous woodlands with closed canopies that allow tree-to-tree travel. Their tails are shorter and flatter than those of fox and gray squirrels. Females usually have only one litter per year. Unlike other tree squirrels, they shelter under snow or in the ground in winter.

■ Red squirrel, Pine squirrel *(T. hudsonicus):* Average head and body 7 inches long, tail 5 inches long; weight 6 ounces; color, reddish brown

■ Douglas squirrel, Chickaree *(T. douglasii):* Average head and body 7 inches long, tail 5 inches long; weight 8 ounces; color, olive brown to grayish brown

Flying squirrels (*Glaucomys* species). North America's only gliding mammals, these squirrels are more closely related to Asian flying squirrels than to the tree squirrels listed in the preceding paragraphs. These nocturnal hang gliders are far more common in deciduous woodlands than most people believe. To glide in graceful floating descents from tall trees, they rely on furry membranes, which they stretch tightly between their "wrists" and "ankles." Glides

average 65 feet. Using their tail as a rudder, these squirrels can make in-flight turns and even create a brief uplift before landing on tree trunks a few feet above the ground.

■ Northern flying squirrel *(G. sabrinus):* Average head and body 6½ inches long, tail 5½ inches long; weight 4 ounces

■ Southern flying squirrel *(G. volans):* Average head and body 5 inches long, tail 4 inches long; weight 2½ ounces

PROBLEMS FOR PEOPLE

Nature watchers rank squirrels second in popularity only to songbirds. But squirrels annoy some bird-watchers by taking over bird feeders and eating bird eggs and nestlings.

Most nesting problems in homes occur in spring. Squirrels nest in house attics, roof eaves, deserted buildings, and chimney flues. In fireplace flues, the nests may not be discovered until the annual chimney cleaning, which is better for all concerned if you wait until youngsters have dispersed. In furnace flues, blockages can create fire hazards.

Like all rodents, squirrels keep their ever-growing teeth filed down by chewing on things, including electrical wires and house structures. Squirrels

For tips on protecting bird feeders from overindulgent squirrels, see page 186. (Photo by Lennie and Uschi Rue III)

can also cause neighborhood power outages when they nest inside transformers, though they usually get fried in the process. Other problems may apply more to specific squirrel genera, as follows.

Fox squirrels and gray squirrels. Favoring deciduous woodlands, both of these squirrels depend mainly on cached nuts, which they store in shallow depressions in the ground, often in lawns. Thus, they can be significant threats to backyard nut crops. But in spring they need to concentrate on what's available, including succulent plants and the buds and flowers of trees and shrubs. In summer, they switch to ripening berries and fruits. I've often watched gray squirrels taste and toss away immature crabapples, moving impatiently to another and another in search of a sweeter one.

Squirrels damage tree bark when scent marking. In this case, they chew bark away without eating it and then deposit scent by rubbing their checks and chin on the exposed wood; they sometimes also urinate on it, which leaves a dark stain. They also strip bark for nests.

Pine squirrels. Besides favoring seeds of conifers, pine squirrels also consume buds, flowers, and shoots of fruit trees. They strip bark from limbs and trunks in order to eat the soft, nutritious underlayers. Stands of lodgepole pine and paper birch can be seriously damaged when the open wounds allow

Nut and Cone Caching

Fox and gray squirrels cache nuts in soil and leaf litter with the intent of returning for them within days or months. Although these squirrels may forget a small percentage of locations or die before returning, they remember most locations. In a Michigan study, fox squirrels were able to relocate 83 to 99 percent of their cached nuts based on memory and scent. So it appears that germination of hardwood trees may depend as much on squirrel mortality as it does on memory lapses.

■ **Storing acorns:** In late summer and fall, gray squirrels cache whole acorns of the red oak group, which won't germinate until the following spring. But before caching acorns of the white oak group, which would otherwise germinate that same fall, the squirrels cut the seed embryo. This minimizes transfer of food energy into the taproot before the squirrels have returned to consume the remaining nutmeat. Of

course, it's unlikely that squirrels realize the potential for imminent fall germination of white oak acorns, yet their instinctive cutting of the white oak seed embryo often determines their food store through fall and winter into spring.

■ **Storing conifer cones:** Pine squirrels store mainly conifer cones within middens in the ground. Their warning scolds alert other wildlife of approaching predators. This scolding may last for many minutes, as I found out one October in Oregon while photographing plants beneath a Sitka spruce. From 40 feet overhead, a Douglas pine squirrel had been tossing spruce cones near me for eventual retrieval. When scolding didn't make me depart, that squirrel seemed to escalate the conflict by attempting to bomb me with spruce cones. And when the little bombs failed to scare me away, an 18-inch spruce branch soon followed, not as a peace offering.

Leonard Lee Rue's Flying Squirrels

Wildlife author-photographer Leonard Lee Rue III pioneered photography of flying squirrels in flight. Although few people see these "little woodland sprites," as Rue says in his forthcoming autobiography, "flying squirrels are common in almost every forested part of our country. Their peak periods of activity are about 1 hour after dark and another ending an hour before sunrise."

Rue first saw flying squirrels one night while standing near one of his bird feeders. He recalls, "I felt a light touch, like a gentle pat, on my back. Before I had a chance to be startled, the little squirrel scampered up to my left shoulder, launched itself into the air, and landed on an oak trunk. I could see the squirrel in the light spilling forth from the living room window.

"A few years later, large numbers of flying squirrels came to my feeder and landed on me. On several occasions, I sat on the ground beneath a feeder I'd hung under a big Norway spruce. There, I'd sprinkle handfuls of sunflower seeds over my legs and on top of my broad-brimmed hat. I often had as many as a dozen of these elfin squirrels feeding, scrambling, and sitting on me at one time. I soon discovered that they were all launching themselves from the same limb of the same tree, one in a row of trees that bordered the lawn. When I got my electronic flash unit, it was a simple matter to chart the squirrels' flight plan. What I didn't know, until I sold the first batch of photos, was that I'd gotten the first photos ever taken of a flying squirrel in flight."

entry of fungi and bacteria. Pine squirrels also drink sap after biting holes in maple bark.

Flying squirrels. Wildlife author-photographer Lennie Rue tells me that many people encounter their first flying squirrel after it has nested in their attic and drowned in their toilet bowl after trying to take a drink. Dozens of flying squirrels may nest together.

One cold February long ago, I heard thumping sounds in the attic. My flashlight revealed an odd-looking rodent of some sort that hopped clumsily from view. I thereupon baited a live trap with nuts and peanut butter, which proved irresistible to the mysterious attic dweller. A field guide provided the ID: a northern flying squirrel. Alas, I ignorantly released that little guy in a snowy wild area without considering the difficulties it would have finding shelter and food. Instead, I should have checked the Yellow Pages for a wildlife rehabilitator willing to lodge one more critter till spring.

Near residences, flying squirrels sometimes nest in birdhouses, which most people wouldn't mind if the squirrels waited for the nestlings to fledge. But these cute little squirrels tend to be more carnivorous than their far larger cousins. They may take their evening's first flight to a bird feeder, wondering perhaps why pole-mounted feeders have squirrel guards *below* the feeder.

ROLE IN THE WILD

The various species of tree squirrels tend to have different habits and preferences that help reduce competition among them, even though their ranges overlap.

Serving the food web, squirrel nestlings elevated in high tree cavities are vulnerable to opossums, raccoons, martens, and large tree-climbing constrictor snakes, such as rat snakes and pine snakes. Martens are especially adept at catching adult squirrels in trees. In dim light, owls also grab squirrels that are out too late or up too early. At ground level, squirrels fall victim to hawks, bobcats, foxes, coyotes, wolves, weasels, mink, dogs, cats, and rattlesnakes. As predators themselves, squirrels prey on nestling birds, rabbits, and rodents, including baby squirrels.

Flying squirrels often den in abandoned woodpecker holes. These nocturnal feeders like insects and meat. They relish large silk moths as well as nestling birds and rodents. They also enjoy bird eggs, nuts, fruits, and seeds. Their main predators are owls—especially screech and horned owls—cats, foxes, and raccoons.

POPULATION DYNAMICS

From birth, the average life expectancy of tree squirrels (with the exception of pine squirrels) is just 1 year. Squirrels die from many causes—predation, injury, disease, hunting, and starvation. In years following poor fall mast crops, survival of juveniles in unhunted populations may be only 5 percent. But in years following good mast, juvenile survival may improve to 30 percent. After the first year, a squirrel's prospects of surviving another year may exceed 50 percent. Yet, in the wild, some tree squirrels have lived more than 8 years.

Pine squirrels. Average life expectancy is slightly less than 1 year, though some pine squirrels have lived more than 7 years. However, average life expectancy increases or decreases by several months following years of good or poor conifer seed crops.

NESTING IN THE WILD

Fox squirrels and gray squirrels both nest in tree cavities but also construct leaf nests in tree crotches and in grapevines. Usually preferring the security of tree cavities in winter and spring, tree squirrels begin building leaf nests in summer and fall to be near favored food trees. In one study, 59 percent of gray-squirrel leaf nests connected with grapevines, which researchers speculated might telegraph warning vibrations of approaching predators. Gray squirrels

and fox squirrels sometimes nest communally, more often in cold months, perhaps to share body heat.

Pine squirrels in winter often den under snow or in the ground. This allows them quicker access to middens of stored cones.

WINTER DORMANCY

Fox squirrels and gray squirrels. Survival through winter largely depends on fat reserves laid on in autumn as well as food stores. Yet even in coldest winter, tree squirrels can maintain a fairly constant body temperature of 98° to 104°F because of a phenomenon known as *nonshivering thermogenesis*. They improve insulation by wrapping themselves within their bushy tails. In freezing temperatures, these squirrels can survive several days without food.

Pine squirrels. In bad weather and in winter, these squirrels shelter underground or under snow, where they become inactive but don't hibernate. At these times, they rely on underground middens, each containing 2,000 to 3,000 conifer cones.

SIGN

Squirrels leave sign that's easy to overlook or to mistake for that of other wildlife.

House exterior. Entrance holes are often chewed under roof eaves. Claw marks and muddy tracks may appear on siding.

Attic and eave noises. If squirrels are present, daytime thumping and scratching noises will be those of fox, gray, and pine squirrels. At night, such sounds are more likely to be those of flying squirrels, rats, or mice. Raccoons may be noisy around the clock, with the babies chirping like little birds.

Scat. Most squirrels leave ¼-inch smooth ovals. Flying squirrels leave distinctive little piles.

Tracks. Front feet register four toes (the vestigial thumb doesn't register). Rear feet register all five toes.

Leaf nests. Mainly in summer and fall, squirrels make leaf nests in the crotches of deciduous trees. Nests of flying squirrels are only about

These hopping tracks show all five back toes and the four front toes that register. (Photo by Lennie and Uschi Rue III)

8 inches in diameter. Those of larger squirrels are usually at least 10 inches in diameter.

Bark stripping. Pine squirrels strip 1- to 3-inch strips of bark from limbs and trunks in order to eat the soft, nutritious underlayers of the bark. Evidence is strips of bark at the base of trees. The exposed wood itself doesn't show teeth marks, as it does when porcupines debark a limb.

Nuts versus cones. Fox, gray, and flying squirrels leave piles of gnawed nutshells. Pine squirrels are more likely to leave piles of conifer cones, mixed with nutshells.

BREEDING AND BIRTH

If you know the approximate dates of breeding, birth, and dispersal in your region, you may be able to anticipate problems. Local wildlife-control professionals are often willing to share such information.

Fox squirrels and gray squirrels. Adult females breed twice a year; the exact times are affected by latitude and local conditions. For example, squirrels in the Midwest normally breed in January to February and then again in May to June. But in the South, breeding may begin in December and span a longer period and resume in summer, again spanning a longer period, though usually not

during May or September. Gestation takes about 6 weeks. Litter size is two to four.

As with deer, the dominant male asserts his right to travel closest to the female until she indicates readiness to mate, after which both cleanse themselves. The female then usually decides to mate with additional suitors.

Pine squirrels. Although females normally breed only once each year, the exact time depends on the availability of food from territory to territory. Gestation takes nearly 5 weeks. Litter sizes vary from one to seven.

Flying squirrels. Northern flying squirrels breed in late winter. Litters are two to four in late spring; youngsters sometimes stay with Mom through the next winter. Southern flying squirrels breed once or twice a year, first usually in late spring, and litters are usually two to four, sometimes up to six.

OPTIONS FOR PROTECTION AND EXCLUSION

Protecting trees. Fruit and nut trees can be protected with loose-fitting smooth metal cylinders around their trunks. Stovepipes can be repurposed for smaller trees. However, because most squirrels can leap vertically, cylinders need to be at least

To protect fruit and nut trees from squirrels, metal cylinders need to be at least 7 feet tall and 2 feet deep.

7 feet tall. In addition, if any one tree allows access to its branches, squirrels can jump from tree to tree unless canopies are separated by several feet.

Protecting bird feeders and birdhouses. Some feeders are designed to close off access to seed when the weight of a squirrel rests on the perches. However, to block out little flying squirrels, the closing mechanism needs to be sensitive enough to close under a weight of only 3 to 4 ounces. These are roughly the weights of blue jays and Steller's jays respectively, birds that many people want to block out anyway.

Metal baffles below pole-mounted bird feeders and birdhouses can prevent access by all squirrels except flying squirrels. Stovepipes of 4-inch diameter and a minimum length of 2 feet can be repurposed as squirrel baffles. Inverted metal cones above and below feeders can work well too. Baffles mounted below on support poles need to be at least 6 feet above the nearest leaping surface and should extend outward at least a foot from the pole. Baffles above should serve like slippery, tipping roofs.

Eliminating food sources. If anyone in the neighborhood is feeding squirrels, and your goal is to discourage squirrel visits to your property, you might try to persuade neighbors to stop. Bird feeders and unfinished pet-food dishes attract ground squirrels as well as other wildlife. For related considerations, see page 82.

Some birdfeeders have doors that close under weights exceeding a few ounces. (Photo by Lennie and Uschi Rue III)

Garden exclusion. Tree squirrels are acrobatic climbers and so can scale most types of fencing. Protect bulbs within galvanized wire-mesh surrounds or boxes as shown on page 93. All rodents can usually be excluded from buildings by the methods suggested on page 59.

Removal and exclusion from buildings and chimneys. Wildlife-control professionals know how to reduce the chances of orphaning young squirrels. For example, one-way doors allow squirrels to exit but not return. So it's important to postpone installation until youngsters are able to depart with their mother; if they can't, the mother may chew her way back inside. Wildlife control professionals usually have multiple-catch cage traps capable of livetrapping entire families for release together.

Frighteners and repellents. Dogs can discourage visits to small properties. Cats with hunting prowess can help keep squirrel populations within reasonable numbers but not eliminate them. People who feed birds often use seed flavored with hot peppers, which has the active ingredient *capsaicin*. Although squirrels reject hot-flavored seed, birds supposedly don't taste it. However, I once suffered hot-pepper burns on the roof of my mouth that caused my mouth skin to peel. So I'd be reluctant to offer that same stuff to birds, whether they can taste it or not.

TRAPPING AND HUNTING

Check local laws. Tree squirrels are considered game animals in some places and so may be protected except when causing damage. California, for example, requires that you show proof of damage before being issued a permit to control squirrels according to strict guidelines.

Trapping. Lethal traps for squirrels have powerful springs that could injure children and kill nontarget animals, including pets. Enclose them in tamperproof containers. A live trap helps you avoid tragic accidents by ensuring that you don't kill or injure animals other than tree squirrels. Various lethal and live traps are available from

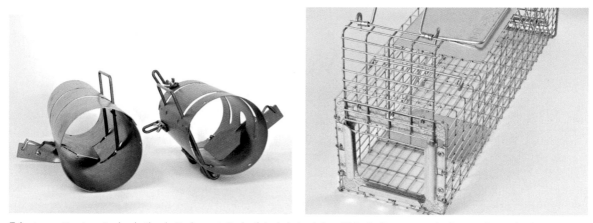

Tube traps attract squirrels whether baited or not. Each of the lethal pair has 4½-inch-diameter steel tubing and a crusher bow activated by a powerful spring. The live trap is by Safeguard. (All from www.wildlifecontrolsupplies.com)

wildlifecontrolsupplies.com. (Options for eutha-nasia are discussed on page 64.)

For fox and gray squirrels, researchers place live or lethal traps at building entrances used by squir-rels as well as at the bases of trees squirrels use for feeding and nesting. As to baits, chopped apples, peanut butter, and nuts are effective.

For pine squirrels, researchers place traps near feeding sites and near entrances to the squirrel's underground cone middens.

Livetrapping and release. Pine squirrels are especially susceptible to fatal shock from trapping and handling. Many jurisdictions forbid transporta-tion and release of wild mammals. Some states, such as Arizona, request that residents inquire with their Fish and Game Department about authorized release sites before livetrapping. It's inhumane to release squirrels in cold months when no food is available. Flying squirrels should be released at night. For more on translocating animals, see page 61.

Hunting. Prior to the decline in the popularity of hunting in recent decades, annual harvests of gray squirrels alone were estimated at 40 million. Yet, even where squirrels are hunted seriously, hunting mortalities often represent less than 15 percent of total mortalities. In areas where high squirrel populations were a problem, researchers found that hunting didn't diminish the next year's population unless the harvest was greater than 40 percent, except in relatively isolated habitats.

Poisoning. Toxic baits may be illegal in some jurisdictions. They can also have life-threatening effects on nontarget wildlife, as well as children and pets, as discussed on page 64.

Unintentional poisoning. People who use cocoa hulls as garden mulch can inadvertently poi-son their own dogs. Chocolate can be toxic to dogs, as can cocoa-hull leftovers from the chocolate trade. The toxins are caffeine and *theobromine*. One garden writer reported that squirrels that broke into one of her bags of cocoa-hull mulch began acting like wild drunks. She wasn't able to verify whether the effects became more serious. For example, symptoms in dogs can include hyperactivity, vomiting, arrhyth-mia, seizures, coma, and death.

COMMUNICABLE DISEASES AND PARASITES

Rabies is rare in tree squirrels, but squirrels are sometimes infected with encephalitis, leptospirosis, tularemia, tetanus, typhus, and more. Any squirrel bite should be treated by a physician. Squirrels are parasitized by lice, mites, ticks, fleas, worms, and a host of others. So avoid handling dead squirrels without protective gloves or plastic bagging as shown on page 61.

CHAPTER 18

Voles

One spring, while inspecting her garden in north-western Connecticut, Mary Ann McGourty noticed a few blank spots here and there and thought, "Oh well, so-and-so didn't make it through the winter."

Next she came upon a wilting dianthus. "When I gave it a tug," she said, "I was holding what felt like a toupee in my hand. And other of my established plants with fleshy roots were disappearing too—iris, alliums, hostas, ornamental grasses—as well as newly planted things."

McGourty suspected that she had either moles or voles. For advice, she phoned Ed Machowski, a licensed wildlife-control officer living in her town of Norfolk. Machowski was certain that McGourty had voles, rather than moles, offering her this easy means of remembering their food preferences:

The "v" in vole stands for vegetable.
The "m" in mole stands for meat.

Machowski explained that northwestern Connecticut has three vole species, and he suspected that McGourty had meadow voles, based on his trapping experiences near her property. He added that voles that year were creating a population explosion, perhaps because snow had come the previous winter before the soil had frozen. This, he said, provided voles with an insulating blanket while also concealing them from predators. Because voles breed year-round, they tend to produce more babies during favorable winters.

Machowski advised that McGourty buy at least 15 snap-type mousetraps and bait them with peanut butter near vole holes, covering them with 1-gallon plastic plant pots weighted down with rocks. The plastic

The woodland (pine) vole is distinguished by its snub nose and short tail, as well as its range shown on the map on page 191. Place vole traps near holes and cover with plastic plant pots, as Mary Ann McGourty did with stunning success in the accompanying anecdote.

Order: Rodentia ■ **Family:** MURIDAE ■ **Subfamily:** ARVICOLINAE ■ **Genera:** 5 (*Arborimus, Clethrionomys, Lemmiscus, Microtus, Phenacomys*) ■ **Species:** many

pots would make voles feel safer out of their holes day or night, while also keeping birds from harm.

The goal, he said, should be to trap heavily, all at once, rather than in steady small numbers. Heavy trapping drops the population quickly and slows the rate at which it can climb again.

McGourty and her husband acquired snap traps of the type shown in the accompanying photo. They then checked the traps each morning. On best days, they caught a dozen voles. By year's end, they had caught 290!

"The whole experience amazed me," McGourty says. "The next year, we didn't have a vole problem and so didn't continue to trap. But, without trapping over the next 5 years, the vole population became large again."

As in the McGourtys case, Machowski often explains how people can handle their own wildlife problems, rather than doing the trapping or exclusion measures himself. He's begun specializing in removal and exclusion of bats.

PROBLEMS FOR GARDENERS

Voles are rodents that feed mainly on roots, stems, and seeds—and on tree bark. They annoy us mainly by injuring and killing ornamental and crop plants. Damage is especially great during years of population explosions, which biologists call *irruptions*.

Because voles tunnel near the surface and exploit mole tunnels as well, voles are sometimes confused with moles, which are insectivores. Moles feed mainly on earthworms and grubs, but they often receive misplaced blame for eating bulbs and fleshy roots. Though committed plant eaters, voles also give gardeners occasional help by eating slugs, insects, carrion, and one another's babies.

ROLE IN THE WILD

Voles are good. Besides aerating soil and improving its drainage, voles are a crucial link in the food chain between carnivores and plants. Because voles feed around the clock, they are breakfast, lunch, dinner, and midnight snack for a great variety of predators, including snakes and birds of prey. At

From top to bottom: *A California vole (photo by Will Elder); a prairie vole (photo © Gary Meszaros/Visuals Unlimited); and a woodland (pine) vole (photo © Rob and Ann Simpson/Visual Unlimited)*

Many people feel uneasy when red foxes den nearby. Yet if the chicken coop is tight and housecats are safe, foxes can help you put a four-season damper on vole populations. Prairie falcons and hawks patrol for voles that forage by day.

times, voles represent 85 percent of the barn owl's diet. Even herons snack on voles now and then.

Mammals that prey on voles include weasels, foxes, coyotes, wolves, badgers, bobcats, skunks, and shrews (which travel in vole tunnels and are ferocious carnivores for their size). Foxes, coyotes, and wolves often subsist largely on voles and—in winter—depend on keen hearing to track vole movement under the snow before plunging head-first after them.

During cyclic vole population irruptions, seagulls forsake shorelines and landfills. And when voles take to the water, fish and large bullfrogs swallow them whole.

Domestic cats also prey on voles. But my friend and gardening mentor Kathy Nelson laments, "People who don't have a serious vole problem always tell me confidently, and often smugly, 'You need a cat.' But the worst vole problem I ever saw was on a property with 14 barn cats that got fed only on weekends." (More on house cats later.)

SPECIES AND DISTRIBUTION

Voles are members of the Muridae family, which includes rats and mice, and the subfamily Arvico-

linae, which includes lemmings and muskrats. Taxonomists continue their debate on the total number of distinct vole species north of Mexico—somewhere between 17 and 24 species.

It's little wonder there's debate on the number of species. Several species have more than a dozen subspecies. The comparatively greater number of species and subspecies in the West is thought to reflect the isolating influences of mountain ranges that serve like "island" ecosystems and climates. The range of the meadow vole is by far the largest—more than twice that of the also wide-ranging woodland (pine) vole in the East and more than three times that of the long-tailed vole in the West.

IDENTIFICATION

Vole adults are usually larger than mice and smaller than rats. Unlike most rats and mice, their tails are shorter than their bodies, some just 1 inch or so. With map ranges shown on page 191, the two largest voles—the Taiga vole of the far North and the water vole—measure about 7 inches, including tail, and weigh about 4.2 ounces, roughly the weight of the larger species of moles. The smallest vole, with four subspecies, is the Oregon vole, also

RANGES OF VOLES

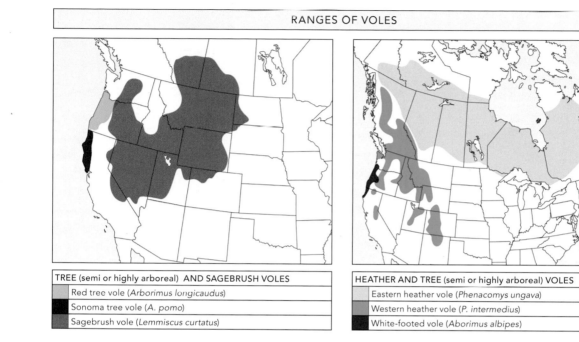

TREE (semi or highly arboreal) AND SAGEBRUSH VOLES

	Red tree vole (*Arborimus longicaudus*)
	Sonoma tree vole (*A. pomo*)
	Sagebrush vole (*Lemmiscus curtatus*)

HEATHER AND TREE (semi or highly arboreal) VOLES

	Eastern heather vole (*Phenacomys ungava*)
	Western heather vole (*P. intermedius*)
	White-footed vole (*Aborimus albipes*)

known as creeping vole. This smallest of voles weighs less than an ounce and so could be mailed with a first-class stamp.

Voles tend to have rounder bodies than those of mice and rats. Also, voles tend to have cuter, stubbier noses than rats and mice—making voles adorable to aesthetes who don't garden. Vole whiskers are less evident and thus less useful than those of rats and mice.

Now to the "business" end—the teeth—which can put farmers, orchardists, and nursery growers out of business and cause home gardeners to toss in the trowel. As with all rodents, vole teeth are "ever growing." This is crucial for vole survival because tough cellulose and silica cells in plants would otherwise rapidly grind their teeth down to their gums. The wear patterns keep the incisors sharp for cutting and the molars raspy for grinding.

Sign: Runways, tunnel openings, and nests. Although woodland voles (pine voles) are industrious tunnelers and remain mostly underground, meadow voles and prairie voles tend to

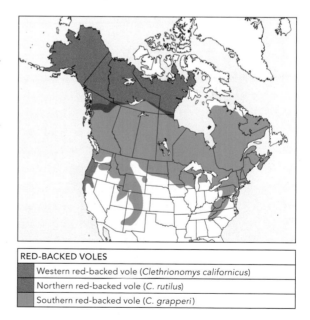

RED-BACKED VOLES

	Western red-backed vole (*Clethrionomys californicus*)
	Northern red-backed vole (*C. rutilus*)
	Southern red-backed vole (*C. grapperi*)

RANGES OF VOLES

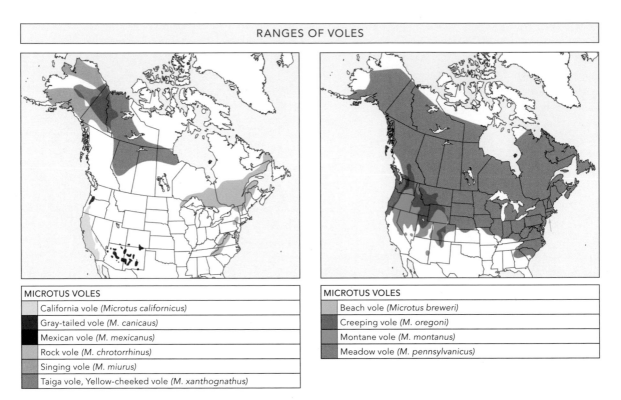

MICROTUS VOLES

	California vole (*Microtus californicus*)
	Gray-tailed vole (*M. canicaus*)
	Mexican vole (*M. mexicanus*)
	Rock vole (*M. chrotorrhinus*)
	Singing vole (*M. miurus*)
	Taiga vole, Yellow-cheeked vole (*M. xanthognathus*)

MICROTUS VOLES

	Beach vole (*Microtus breweri*)
	Creeping vole (*M. oregoni*)
	Montane vole (*M. montanus*)
	Meadow vole (*M. pennsylvanicus*)

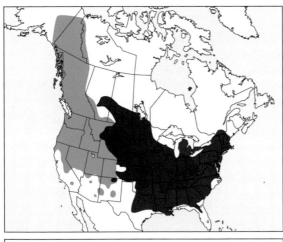

MICROTUS VOLES

	Long-tailed vole (*Microtus longicaudus*)
	Prairie vole (*M. ochrogaster*)
	Woodland vole, Pine vole (*M. pinetorum*)

MICROTUS VOLES

	Water vole (*Microtus richardsoni*)
	Insular vole (*M. abbreviatus*)
	Townsend's vole (*M. townsendii*)
	Tundra vole (*M. oeconomus*)

rely on aboveground runways through leaves and vegetation. These runways become especially apparent on lawns in late winter when snow has largely melted away.

Another sure sign is tree and shrub bark near the ground or at snow line with tooth marks in tiny crosshatch patterns about ⅛ inch wide and ⅜ inch long. These tiny tooth marks can partially or completely girdle a tree, killing it.

Depending on the species, vole nests may be aboveground or belowground. They are often under or against protective cover such as rocks, logs, and brush piles. Meadow voles tend to be territorial during most of the year. But they become more tolerant of their kind in winter, even living in communal groups like raccoons often do.

> **Moles versus Look-Alikes**
> Although voles, moles, shrews, and mice look much alike when they dash from view, they leave distinctive plant damage. For comparisons among these look-alikes and their damage, see the mole chapter under this heading, beginning on page 104.

A sure sign of the mainly surface-traveling meadow voles is many tunnel-like, crisscrossing runways that are roofed-over by high grass and weeds. Upon close mowing, you'll see open runways with stem cuttings ¼ to ½ inch long. These runways become obvious as snow melts away.

Soil-dwelling woodland voles create multiple holes of 1 to 2 inches in diameter near the surface. The burrows are shallow, just 3 to 4 inches deep—

Top left: *Most vole species build their nests aboveground.* Right: *In* Audubon *magazine, the late, great John Madson described this very snow scene as an example of "the oldest writing," here with phrasing begun by a vole and end punctuated by a kestrel.* Bottom left: *Melting snow in spring often reveals vole-runway traceries. (Nest photo by Lennie and Uschi Rue III; vole/kestrel meeting by Tom Murphy/National Geographic Stock).*

this compared to chipmunk holes that descend straight down. Where woodland-vole infestation is heavy, the ground will feel spongy. By contrast, moles leave noticeably raised soil ridges and don't leave their holes exposed as woodland voles do. Instead, a mole covers its vertical "mine shaft" under a large symmetrical molehill of soil. The mole creates molehills by pushing soil upward from deep tunnels.

WINTER ADAPTATIONS

Different types of rodents deal differently with below-freezing temperatures. As winter approaches, woodchucks, or groundhogs, retreat into burrows to hibernate, becoming nearly cold as a stone. But voles—like mice and rats—need to maintain a fairly constant body temperature. They do this by continuing to forage. They don't rely as much on food stores as mice and other rodents, such as chipmunks and squirrels. Rather than shivering like humans when cold, voles are capable of *nonshivering thermogenesis*, which increases metabolism and heat production.

Beneath snow cover, where temperatures are often warmer than above, voles continue to forage where most predators can't see them. Foxes and coyote listen for vole activity before diving headfirst into the snow. When voles do surface onto snow and dash toward cover, they leave hopping tracks that sometimes end abruptly under the imprint of large wings.

REPRODUCTION AND POPULATION IRRUPTIONS

Voles are prolific breeders. Population irruptions occur from time to time, devastatingly for farmers and gardeners. A team of biologists with a mathematical bent suggested that "100 pairs of voles in April could potentially create a population of 8,900 by September."

Unlike female moles (with an "m"), which breed only once a year and produce an average of four babies, female voles breed many times per year. In fact, a female may ovulate and become pregnant at just 3 weeks of age. Gestation takes just 3 more weeks, and usually results in three to six babies. So the female in this example would have given birth just 6 weeks after her own birth. (Interestingly, her male siblings wouldn't have produced mature sperm until 6 to 8 weeks of age, an important developmental difference that helps prevent inbreeding.)

One captive meadow-vole female produced 17 litters in a single year, resulting in 83 babies. So it appears that if half of her offspring had been female (41+), each of her daughters could then have produced more than 70 babies apiece before their mother produced her 83rd. And each of Grandma's many hundreds of granddaughters could each have produced more than 50 great-grandchildren by the time Grandma set her record. Of course, none of these calculations addresses the toll of infant mortality, predators, disease, population-control efforts by farmers and gardeners, and the relative fecundity of other vole species. For example, woodland voles aren't as fecund as meadow voles.

Populations can fluctuate several times a year with no human intervention, or there can be full-scale cyclical irruptions every 4 to 5 years, suddenly skyrocketing to more than 200 voles per acre and then crashing near zero. Regarding these irruptions and crashes, biologists argue about the relative importance of food supply, predation, snow cover, dispersal of young, preferences regarding spacing—and more recently, cannibalism and toxic plants.

Seems to me that overcrowding and the resulting food shortages would encourage higher-than-normal aggression and cannibalism and perhaps force dependence on less-appealing food plants that may prove toxic to voles. This very theory has gained credence regarding population crashes in Arctic lemmings, closely related to voles.

Historical records of irruptions can be staggering. In one count in the early 20th century, California agricultural fields were honeycombed with up to 24,000 "mouse holes" per acre, encouraging perhaps exaggerated estimates of more than 20,000 voles per acre. That irruption decimated 75 percent of the potato and 30 percent of the alfalfa crop. Yet, the following summer, that irruption showed a dramatic abatement. And crashes should hearten anyone suffering a vole plague. Populations may fall of their own accord as suddenly as they arose, no matter what we do.

MATING

Some species, such as the woodland vole and the prairie vole, tend to be monogamous, though not reliably so. Other species are highly promiscuous. This variation seems linked to whether the males or the females are strongly territorial and, therefore, which gender is freer to go a-courtin'. Mating success often depends on the receptivity of the female. That is, she may reject some suitors by severely wounding them and then hotly pursue others. Sexual arousal and courting rituals are based heavily on scent.

SENSES

The sense of smell is normally more important to voles than hearing and sight. In fact, voles don't see well. They live in a world of scents produced by glands in their hips and flanks and consciously deposit these scents by rubbing and scratching, much as deer do. Voles use "odors to mediate individual identity, including age, sex, reproductive condition, diet, social status, and degree of relatedness," according to Johns Hopkins University Press's *Wild Mammals of North America*.

In that case, I wonder if scientists couldn't come up with nontoxic bait that simply reduces a vole's sense of smell for short periods after consuming the bait, thus reducing mating ardor. Key would be bait that temporarily affects only the vole's sense of smell and not that of other mammals. Birds of prey don't have much of a sense of smell anyway and so wouldn't be affected secondarily.

PREFERRED FOODS

Voles seem to know which plants and plant parts provide more nutrition at given times. They normally favor protein-rich foods. Although researchers know much about food preferences, there seems little research on vole dislikes. Thus there's little information on potentially vole-resistant plants for gardeners, except for a few. Indeed, preferences among the species and regions may vary, especially

for home gardeners. Much of what follows in this section is based on findings in *Wild Mammals of North America*.

Vole preferences for given plants and plant parts seem to differ depending on species, seasonal availability, and quality at that time. For example, one study showed that the California vole feeds mainly on seeds and fruits in summer and switches to leaves, stems, and roots in winter. A study in the Midwest suggested that meadow voles in Indiana ate mainly monocots (grasses), while meadow voles in Indiana prairie habitats ate mainly dicots (flowering plants with netlike leaf veins). The voles in both states also consumed significant amounts of lichen and fungi. The prairie vole preferred grasses in winter but switched heavily to flowering plants in summer, along with large amounts of seeds. There seems to be no seasonally preferred list of foods for all vole species in North America. Here's my distillation of findings by the contributors M. L. and Sherry Johnson:

Preferred crops
- Root vegetables: Carrots, beets, turnips, sweet potatoes
- Tubers: Potatoes, yams
- Leaf and leafstalk vegetables: Cabbage, lettuce, celery, spinach
- Bark and roots of woody plants, especially in winter—fruit trees a favorite, tree bark being particularly vulnerable under snow cover
- Grain, pasture, grassland, and hay crops (especially during vole population irruptions)

Less-preferred crops
- Stem vegetables, such as asparagus and kohlrabi
- Immature artichoke, broccoli, cauliflower
- Immature beans, okra, sweet corn
- Mature melons, pumpkins, tomatoes

Tree damage. Although voles may damage the roots and bark of trees and shrubs throughout the year, girdling damage is greatest during long winters. That stands to reason wherever soil is frozen, because frozen soil prevents voles from tunneling and dining on fleshier roots, which they prefer. And snow cover allows voles to travel unseen by most predators and subsist on what must seem to them meager rations, much in the way tree bark served as starvation rations for Native Americans.

A yellowing or wilting perennial here and there due to voles makes gardeners angry. But trees and shrubs dying from vole damage drastically alter the landscape—not to mention the impact on the pocketbook if purchased as balled-and-burlapped plants. Such trees and shrubs can cost $1,000 or more. Woe unto voles that dine on costlier temptations!

During vole irruptions, tree damage tends to be the worst. And snow cover can be critical. A study in Washington State showed a dramatic increase in damage to fruit trees wherever the ground had snow cover and little damage where there had been little to no snow cover. Voles tend to favor fruit trees and berry shrubs, yet woody plants of all types are vulnerable, especially when young bark is thin. Studies of vole damage to conifers vital to the lumber industry showed lowest vole damage to the white spruce, which is native throughout most of Canada and the northern United States. Aha! Spruce needles tend to be of low interest to deer as well. If you live in a northern region, white spruce might be worth a try.

In the same studies, several larch species also proved of low appeal to voles. Coincidentally, larches are also of low interest to deer.

OPTIONS FOR CONTROL

By "control," no authority would suggest the feasibility or desirability of extermination of entire vole populations. But combined measures can significantly reduce vole populations without eliminating them. Such measures include:

- Selecting resistant plants
- Encouraging natural predators
- Tilling before planting
- Minimizing groundcover, especially during fall cleanup
- Using metal-mesh fencing belowground
- Lethal trapping
- Cautious use of poisons to ensure they aren't

consumed by nontarget species and otherwise don't enter the food chain via vole carcasses. I don't personally advocate poisons.

Plant selection. Vole species show differing food preferences in different seasons. It's wise to consult neighboring gardeners and local authorities on plants that do well in your climate while also "seeming" of low interest to vole species.

For example, my friend Kathy Nelson has maintained a thriving perennials nursery in western Connecticut, despite a relentless population of woodland voles (pine voles). This species is hard to trap because it stays mostly underground, unlike meadow voles.

Kathy finds it helpful to conduct a thorough fall cleanup and shave her perennial beds down to an inch or two, reducing the cover that voles prefer.

Regarding pine voles, Kathy says, "There are probably a few plants they won't eat. But the best you can say about a plant is that 'it hasn't been eaten—*yet!*'" A few plants seem to contain a chemical that keeps them safe. Kathy has found that plants with dense root systems seem to have a better chance than plants with loose, running root systems. She's found that voles have little interest in a wide variety of ferns. As to perennials, in her most recent *Fine Gardening* article, Kathy mentioned the following native plants as pine-vole resistant in her garden. But she says she feels confident in recommending only *Amsonia, Pycnanthemum,* and *Solidago.*

- *Amsonia hubrichtii* and *A. tabernae-montana,* blue star (Zones 3–9)
- *Asarum canadense,* Canadian wild ginger (Zones 2–8)
- *Chelone lyonii,* turtlehead (Zones 3–8)
- *Eupatorium perfoliatum,* boneset (Zones 3–8)
- *Eupatorium fistulosum,* Joe Pye weed (Zones 3–8)
- *Monarda didyma* and cultivars, bee balm (Zones 4–9)
- *Phlox glaberrima,* smooth phlox (Zones 3–9)
- *Pycnanthemum* species, mountain mint (Zones 4–8)
- *Solidago* species, goldenrod (Zones 5–9)
- *Waldsteinia fragarioides,* barren-ground strawberry (Zones 3–8)

Gardeners often assume that yellowing plants, such as these hostas, are merely suffering from nitrogen deficiency and so top-dress the plants with fertilizer. However, if a slight tug on the stem brings the plant up easily, fertilizers won't have roots to nourish. This root pruning of a woodland vole occurred at the home of Kathleen Nelson. Her comments enliven the previous page and much of this book.

Regarding hostas, Kathy speculates, "My blue-flowered hostas seem less vulnerable than the white-flowered ones. And my hostas with yellow leaves or yellow variegation on the leaves are less likely to be eaten, except when they have white flowers. Based on hosta root damage, I wonder if there might be chemicals associated with flower and leaf color also found in the roots of those plants."

Kathy has found voles particularly fond of alliums. She says voles seem to like some kinds more than others. "*Allium cernuum* is their favorite," she assures. "I can't keep this more than a few days. I plant a lot of the beautiful but inexpensive 'Purple Sensation', also because at least a few won't be eaten over the winter." Regarding deer, Kathy observes, "Deer aren't supposed to eat alliums. But deer have sometimes lopped the heads off alliums in one of my client's gardens. Perhaps just that one deer has developed a taste for them."

Alien plants that may suffer little to no woodland-vole damage include lady's mantle (*Alchemilla* species), corydalis (*Corydalis* species), bleeding heart (*Dicentra* species), and catnip (*Nepeta* species), except for the cultivar 'Souvenir d'André Chaudron'.

Cats and other predators. Although determined mousers can catch a goodly number of voles and other rodents, cats often get help from wild predators.

On page 189, "Role in the Wild," many predators are named. Ironically, the fences we erect to keep rodents and deer out can also keep predators out and limit attack routes.

Altering soil type. I asked Kathy Nelson if she thought it worthwhile to till coarse gravel into garden soil, making it more difficult for voles to dig through. Her response: "You name it, I've tried it. I've tried the commercial brand of sharp gravel called Vole-bloc, which may have helped a little bit, but I'm not sure.

"In the past," Kathy says, "I always 'improved' the soil—digging deeply to loosen it, adding lots of compost. Now I'm experimenting with planting into unimproved hard-packed dirt. I planted one vole favorite, butterfly weed, last fall, and so won't know the results for a while."

Overplanting. Rodale's senior editor for this book, Karen Bolesta, plants twice as many beets as she hopes to harvest, assuming voles will damage about half of them. Karen says that she has very cunning voles that outsmart whatever barrier she's tried, from sinking wire around the entire bed, to building a $75 wood-and-wire cage, to nailing hardware cloth under and over her new raised beds. "The beets look great right up until harvest time. Then I'm always amazed at how many are devoured or chewed below the soil line. So now I oversow and crowd in double the beets—just so I have enough in the end for meals and for preserving," says Karen.

Modifying lawns. Lawn-cutting strategies for voles differ dramatically from those for moles. Voles tend to avoid open lawn or to dash across it for cover rather than feeding in the open. Thus, authorities at Cornell University, Johns Hopkins University, and the University of California suggest that mowing in swaths at least 15 feet wide tends to discourage vole travel. On the other hand, lawns tend to invite moles in search of earthworms and grubs, such as Japanese beetle larvae that feed on grass roots. The conflict: Lower mowing makes lawns less inviting to voles, and higher mowing shades the soil, keeping it moist and thus more attractive to earthworms and therefore to moles.

Reducing lawn size by planting a diversity of native plants can often allow both voles and moles to survive there relatively unnoticed. As a bonus, such plantings attract many native insects that attract birds. Leaf-eating caterpillars, often dependent on a single native plant species, come back the following year as flower-visiting butterflies and moths.

Installing fencing. Regarding trees and shrubs, first ensure that "vole cover," such as mulch and leaf litter, is removed from the base of the trunk. Authorities at Cornell University then advise installing cylindrical ¼-inch wire-mesh "tree guards" around the base 3 to 6 inches deep, if possible without damaging existing roots. These cylinders should allow for 5 years of growth and be removed before bark grows into the mesh. Cylinders should be taller than anticipated snow cover. And for your safety, point the cut, ragged edge into the soil. Virtually all rolls of wire mesh have "safety" edges.

To protect small garden areas, experts at the University of California suggest fencing, as voles are poor or reluctant fence climbers. Experts recommend a mesh barrier only 1 foot aboveground

or above anticipated snow cover. And because voles tend not to be deep tunnelers, the experts suggest burying the mesh only 6 to 10 inches deep.

However, if the fencing is also intended to keep out rabbits, you should extend it to 2 feet aboveground and above snow cover. For woodchucks and raccoons, the aboveground fencing needs to be taller and equipped with either electric or mechanical deterrents, as discussed in the woodchucks and marmots and raccoons chapters.

To discourage moles and woodchucks from burrowing under it, bury the mesh 2 feet deep. To especially deter woodchucks, bend the mesh 1 foot from the end into a right angle and bury this "shelf" pointing outward from your garden.

Metal mesh can also protect plants inside cold frames. For this, fashion a mesh box that fits just inside the base of the cold frame. Use stainless-steel staples to fasten the edges. To protect your hands from accidental contact with the ragged mesh edges, fasten a thin protective wood strip there.

Using repellents. Connecticut gardening writer and lecturer Lorraine Ballato discourages voles and other rodents by scattering crushed oyster shells and hot red-pepper flakes onto the soil over her bulbs and around perennial roots and annual plantings. On Ballato's recommendation, mail-order garden supplier Wildflower Farm (wildflowerfarm.com) tested oyster shells and pepper flakes over tulip bulbs with such success that it now sells 10-pound bags of oyster shells. Ballato also likes the red-pepper flakes because they blend into the landscape, while being inexpensive, nontoxic, and available at most supermarkets and health-food stores.

Using scare devices. University research hasn't found ultrasonic devices or soil vibrators effective for voles. Even if these devices deter voles for short distances initially, causing them to take detours soon after installation, most mammals eventually become accustomed to steady noises.

Livetrapping. Most states discourage livetrapping of wildlife and often prohibit the transport and release of wildlife beyond one's own property.

This for good justification: No matter your best intentions, livetrapped animals can die of stress inside traps or soon after release. In addition, released wildlife is more vulnerable to the elements and to predators in unfamiliar habitat. Besides, released animals are often killed or wounded by territorial members of their own kind. More importantly, released voles can transfer a host of parasites and diseases to other wildlife, while also sparking vole population growth in their new locale.

Wildlife rehabilitators sometimes accept voles and other rodents as food for raptors and owls but may need assurances that the rodents come from areas that haven't been contaminated by rodenticides. Rather than driving some miles to contribute each newly trapped rodent to a rehabilitator, wildlife-control officers might save them in a freezer. (I once had a friend who did just that with her poultry that died in winter and frozen ground prevented burial till spring. Still, I was relieved to learn that she never served her own poultry.)

Lethal trapping. Classic old-style snap traps require two-handed setting and removal of rodents. This can expose bare fingers to vole parasites and diseases rodents can transmit, as addressed at the end of this chapter. Newer snap traps open and close like spring clothespins, allowing one-hand operation. They can reduce the chances that your

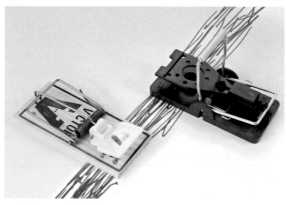

Wildlife Control Supplies owner Alan Huot used this simulation to show how he places unbaited wide-treadle mousetraps in vole runways.

fingers will contact the rodent, or its blood, fur, or feces.

In any case, health authorities strongly urge that you avoid skin contact. You can do this either by donning single-use latex or nitrile gloves or by grasping a thin plastic bag so it serves like a protective mitten that allows you to "bag" the vole or other rodent for burial or for disposal in the trash. Carefully avoid touching the vole or any part of the trap it has contacted. Also avoid breathing airborne fur or dust from vole urine or feces. For a photo demonstrating plastic-bag pickup, see page 61.

Check traps daily. Forceful snap-type traps can kill voles effectively. But the gentler-snapping mousetraps don't snap powerfully enough on larger voles. For them, it's better to use mousetraps that pack a wallop. Mice have very fragile neck vertebrae to which even the gentler-snapping traps can cause the desired cervical dislocation, resulting (assumedly) in a painless, if not instant, death.

Unbaited snap traps (sometimes called professional traps) have large treadles with a scent that attracts rodents. So even without bait, they will catch voles if placed in vole runways and wiggled into the soil a bit so the treadle aligns with the soil surface.

When baiting these traps, place the bait deep into the treadle near its hinge, requiring that the vole insert its entire head to taste the bait. As for baits, voles find apples, oatmeal, and peanut butter irresistible, but so do mice and larger rodents such as squirrels and chipmunks, as well as raccoons, opossums, and even passing bears. The larger mammals may announce their annoyance with the trap's mild sting before flinging the trap into the next county.

So when baiting near a vole hole, cover the trap with an inverted 1-gallon plastic flowerpot and weight it down.

Resorting to toxic baits. Most states require a license for use of fast-acting pesticides, such as zinc phosphide. Without a license, the only options are slow-acting poisons. These include either anticoagulants, which require multiple feedings, or compounds such as bromethalin that require only one feeding. For perspectives on use of poisons, see page 64.

COMMUNICABLE DISEASES AND PARASITES

The good news is that compared to other small mammals, voles have far fewer fleas on themselves and in their nests. Biologists often find voles that have no fleas at all. Thus, relative to other small mammals, the chances that voles will transmit flea-borne diseases to humans tend to be much lower.

The bad news: Voles, like other small rodents and their canid, or dog-family, predators, serve as hosts to parasites, bacteria, and viruses that can be transmitted to us, making us gravely ill and worse. Here's just a sampling. (For more on these woes, see "Communicable Diseases and Parasites" on page 210.)

Parasites. Larval cestodes, or flatworms, cause enlargement of the liver in mammals. Humans can be infected by inhaling vole feces, just as they can from inhaling infected dog feces. Untreated, the larval parasite can lead to 75 percent mortality in humans. Fortunately, voles tend to avoid habitation in our homes.

Tularemia. Voles (like more than 100 other mammals) can transmit tularemia. For more, see page 215.

Plague. Once known as the Black Death, the plague is not merely a nightmare tucked safely away in European history. For more, see page 212.

Tick-borne diseases. For the basics on tick-borne diseases, see page 214.

Intestinal parasites. *Giardia* species are flagellated protozoans dispersed in vole feces. For more, see page 210.

The Case of the Disappearing Peanut Butter

I once mistakenly blamed the engineering of the classic, wood-based Victor trap for the disappearance of peanut butter from the bait treadle. It happened after most of our potato plants had wilted, and we had discovered the tubers were badly chewed.

Hoping to catch the suspected vole, I baited a Victor snap trap with peanut butter near a surviving potato plant and then returned to the house for a few hours. Upon returning, I was surprised to see the trap still set, except that all of the peanut butter was gone. Hmm! At that point, I mistakenly assumed that the trap either had a faulty "trigger" mechanism or that we were dealing with a vole that knew how to lick the off bait.

Determined, I slathered peanut butter more generously onto the treadle, both top and bottom, this time vowing to check the trap within the hour in hopes of seeing our clever vole in the act. But to my surprise, the culprit was instead many culprits—a battalion of ants.

So, if you also have garden ants, you can instead skewer apple slices onto trap treadles. Apples take longer for ants to make off with.

Viral diseases. Although voles can carry strains of various serious viruses—such as rabies, hantavirus, and equine encephalitis—"no viral diseases have been associated with North American *Microtus* [voles] with certainty," according to Johns Hopkins University's *Wild Mammals of North America*. Still, most of the same precautions for protecting your hands, mouth, and lungs from other vole-transmitted woes can help ensure that you don't become Case No. 1 in the virus category. Health officials usually suggest that viruses can be killed by a 1:10 bleach:water solution and by direct sunlight. For more on viral diseases, see page 210.

CHAPTER 19

Woodchucks and Marmots

Author-naturalist John Burroughs (1837–1921) loved nearly all wildlife. Yet it's unlikely that *love* is the primary emotion the elderly Burroughs recalled when naming his final Catskill summer home "Woodchuck Lodge." In his vegetable gardens, Burroughs often fought losing battles with woodchucks.

In *Wake-Robin,* Burroughs describes the woodchuck this way: "In form and movement the woodchuck is not captivating. His body is heavy and flabby. Indeed, such a flaccid, fluid, pouchy carcass I have never before seen. It has absolutely no muscular tension or rigidity, but is as baggy and shaky as a skin filled with water. . . . The legs of the woodchuck are short and stout, and made for digging rather than running. The latter operation he performs by short leaps, his belly scarcely clearing the ground. For a short distance he can make very

In taste tests, Wilber Woodchuck relished an apple core and a cherry tomato but had no interest in this carrot root.

good time, but he seldom trusts himself far from his hole . . ."

PROBLEMS FOR PEOPLE

Woodchucks (groundhogs) pose far more problems than their Western cousins, the marmots. That's mainly because marmots usually occupy higher and remoter terrains with low human populations. Because woodchucks range so widely and affect so many people, this chapter focuses mainly on them. Even so, many of the behaviors of woodchucks and marmots are similar, as are options for control.

Woodchucks inhabit varied terrain in lower elevations north to south. They also inhabit towns, suburbs, and major cities such as Atlanta, where Georgia's Department of Natural Resources receives calls from residents complaining that their gardens look as though mowing machines have passed through.

Crop and garden damage. Farmers consider woodchucks and marmots costly nuisances and so invite visits of hunters with scope-mounted rifles accurate to distances exceeding 200 yards. When hunters can't keep the varmint population in check, farmers often resort to burrow fumigants or other poisons.

Woodchucks relish field crops, such as alfalfa and soybeans. But they also like most homegrown vegetables—including lettuce, broccoli, spinach, peas, beans, and squash. They love berries and fruit as well as many herbaceous ornamentals.

Tree damage and climbing. Woodchucks may scent-mark tree trunks while stripping bark.

Order: Rodentia ■ **Family:** SCURIDAE ■ **Genus:** *Marmota* ■ **Species:** 6

This gnawing occurs very near burrows and usually in spring. Woody plants more than 40 feet away seldom suffer gnawing damage.

When we moved into our present New York farmhouse, I mistakenly assumed that woodchucks were ground huggers. So I was astonished to see a medium-size 'chuck descending our hackberry tree—headfirst. I've since learned that woodchucks will climb more than 20 feet into trees to dine on leaves and fruit, but they usually feel safer in lower branches that allow quicker descent and escape. My friend and wildlife author Leonard Rue says, "Chucks will often climb saplings if they can't outrun dogs."

Compulsive chewing. Like all rodents, woodchucks need to chew on hard and gritty things in order to keep their ever-growing incisors filed to proper length. This compulsion sometimes leads to chewing on structural wood and lawn furniture as well as underground electrical cables and water lines.

Burrowing hazards and catastrophes. Powerful diggers, woodchucks and marmots create extensive burrow systems that can erode hillsides and undermine sidewalks, driveways, and building foundations. Camouflaged emergency

For dens, woodchucks may use rock openings but favor slopes with good drainage and forage. (Photo by Lennie and Uschi Rue III)

entrances pose hazards to livestock and people that blunder in.

The Department of Homeland Security, through its Federal Emergency Management Agency (FEMA) branch, worries about woodchucks and, to some extent, marmots, because their burrowing can create catastrophe for people living downslope from earthen dams or raised canals; burrowing can weaken embankments, causing collapse and flooding. For example, the US Bureau of Reclamation owns more than 8,000 miles of raised canals in the West. In 2008, rodent tunneling was blamed for the collapse of a canal embankment in Nevada that flooded 590 homes (more on that event on page 95).

ROLE IN THE WILD

Woodchucks and marmots are important in nature's food web. Woodchuck predators include coyotes, badgers, bobcats, black bears, wolves, lynxes, and foxes. Eagles and large hawks prey on smaller 'chucks. And unused burrows often shelter rabbits, raccoons, opossums, skunks, weasels, and even the occasional ring-necked pheasant.

In the West, marmots have several additional predators to worry about: wolverines, mountain lions, and grizzly bears. Grizzlies attempt to dig marmots from the talus slopes created by rockslides. And at times, young marmots make up more than 70 percent of the golden eagle's diet.

Woodchucks create "vegetational mosaics" of plant diversity near their burrows, writes University of Kansas marmot authority Kenneth B. Armitage in *Wild Mammals of North America*. He suggests that the lush growth commonly found near main entrances is stimulated by the higher soil nitrogen levels there because of woodchuck urine and feces.

IDENTIFICATION, SPECIES, AND DISTRIBUTION

Woodchucks and marmots are the largest members of the squirrel family. Of the six species in North

RANGES OF WOODCHUCKS AND MARMOTS

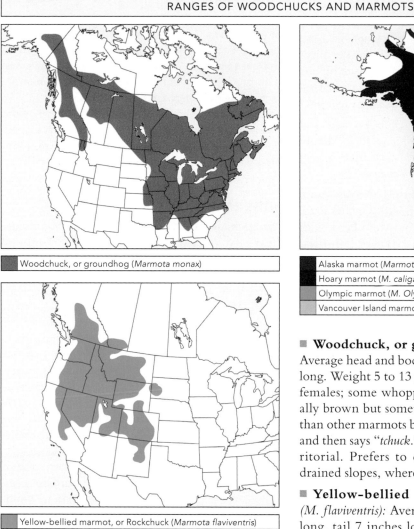

Woodchuck, or groundhog (*Marmota monax*)

Yellow-bellied marmot, or Rockchuck (*Marmota flaviventris*)

Alaska marmot (*Marmota broweri*)

Hoary marmot (*M. caligata*)

Olympic marmot (*M. Olympus*)

Vancouver Island marmot (*M. vancouverensis*)

America, only woodchucks (groundhogs) range throughout eastern North America and across Canada. The five Western cousins all have "marmot" in their common name.

Unlike woodchucks, marmots tend to live in family groups. Armitage speculates that marmots evolved family social structures because their longer hibernation periods delay maturity of youngsters until their second year.

■ **Woodchuck, or groundhog** (*Marmota monax*): Average head and body 18 inches long, tail 6 inches long. Weight 5 to 13 pounds. Males are larger than females; some whoppers exceed 25 pounds. Usually brown but sometimes nearly black. Less vocal than other marmots but does whistle when alarmed and then says "*tchuck*." Tends to be solitary and territorial. Prefers to dig main burrows on well-drained slopes, where available.

■ **Yellow-bellied marmot, or rockchuck** (*M. flaviventris*): Average head and body 16 inches long, tail 7 inches long. Weight 5 to 10 pounds. Lower parts pale to orange. Makes loud, "*sirk, sirk*" whistles and undulating screams. Lives in mother-daughter-sister kin groups, usually above 2,000 feet and often on steep rocky slopes above timberline, sometimes to 12,000 feet.

■ **Hoary marmot** (*M. caligata*): Average head and body 22 inches long, tail 9 inches long. Weight 8 to 20 pounds. Grizzled gray fur, often whitish. A noisy communicator with high-pitched whistles as well as barks and yells. Lives in male-female families; young males disperse.

■ **Alaska marmot** *(M. broweri):* Average head and body 18 inches long, tail 6 inches long. Vocalizes much like the hoary marmot. Family based on one adult breeding pair, subordinate nonbreeding adults, and youngsters—all hibernating together.

■ **Olympic marmot** *(M. olympus):* Average head and body 20 inches long, tail 9 inches long. Weight 11 to 15 pounds. Lives in male-female families, young males disperse. *Population restricted and protected.*

■ **Vancouver Island marmot** *(M. vancouverensis):* Head and body 18 inches long, tail 9 inches long. Weight 6 to 14 pounds. Dark brown or black with white muzzle. Lives in male-female families, young males disperse. *Population endangered.*

An earthmover inadvertently removed part of this chuck's hibernation den. With body temperature having dropped from 96°–99°F to near 39°F, the chuck didn't waken. (Photo by Lennie and Uschi Rue III)

> **Groundhog Day**
>
> Folklore suggests that groundhogs (woodchucks) emerge from their burrows each February 2nd to decide whether they should continue hibernating. Supposedly, if the groundhog sees his shadow upon emerging, he retires for 6 more weeks of winter. In fact, both woodchucks and marmots do arouse themselves at least several times during hibernation before dropping back into deep torpor. Woodchucks of the Far North and northern marmots often may not emerge through snowpack until May.

HIBERNATION

Woodchucks and marmots need to accumulate heavy fat reserves to survive many months of hibernation without food. All species begin hibernation soon after the first frost, when succulent plants have dried up, which may occur by September 1 in colder regions. Woodchucks hibernate longer in the North than in southern latitudes (5½ months in Canada, compared to 3½ months in Maryland). However, marmots often hibernate for 7 to 8 months. So marmot survival through hibernation depends strongly on the length of hibernation, which drains fat reserves. Survival rates increase when the previous growing season was longer than usual and when spring snowmelt comes earlier than usual.

Both woodchucks and marmots arouse themselves periodically in warmer temperatures to access prospects for browsing. During hibernation, woodchucks lose about 30 percent of their prehibernation weight. The longer-hibernating hoary marmot loses nearly 50 percent of its body weight.

Within the burrow, the woodchuck enters a special hibernation chamber and seals it with soil before curling up for winter. Gradually, body temperature drops from its normal temperature of 96 to 99°F to just a few degrees above ambient temperature. During this process, heart rate slows from 80 to 95 beats a minute to just a few beats. Respiration slows from 12 breaths a minute to just a few. Even so, woodchucks can be aroused by sounds.

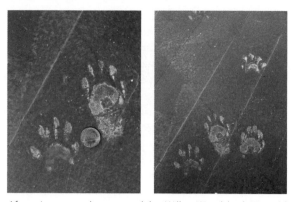

After rain, our porch suggested that Wilber Woodchuck IV would den on our hosta hillside. Proof appears on page 208.

SIGN

In the North, wildlife-control professionals receive their peak number of woodchuck complaints in mid-June to early July. That's when young woodchucks disperse from their mother's burrow.

Sightings. Woodchucks are considered a forest-edge species, and they prefer well-drained hillside burrows near open feeding areas. They feed most heavily during the early morning and near nightfall, but often feed throughout the day. With belly full on cooler days, they enjoy basking in the sun but avoid overheating on hot, sunny days.

Cut stems. Woodchucks cut herbaceous stems off cleanly. However, a 'chuck isn't as neat when devouring cabbage. Our neighbor showed me the remains of a savoy cabbage that looked as though it had been gouged with a posthole digger. Raspberry bushes may show broken branches to 20 inches or more because a 'chuck rises on its haunches and uses its forepaws to pull branches toward its mouth.

Woodchuck burrow entrances. Both males and females occupy multiple burrow systems, often using more than one burrow daily. Each burrow usually has a main entrance with a broad opening 8 to 16 or more inches wide (depending on 'chuck size) and some smaller emergency entrances, known as plunge holes. The main entrance has a large amount of excavated soil in front of it. Dug from inside, the plunge holes tend to be well hidden. Older burrow systems may have more than 10 entrances.

Soil mounded at the main entrance allows the woodchuck to peek above, revealing only its eyes and small ears. The mound also provides a raised platform for seeing over vegetation. After emerging from hibernation and periodically through the year, woodchucks usually houseclean by sending a fresh layer of excavated soil out the main entrance.

Trails. These radiate from the main entrance to regular feeding areas.

Scat. It's uncommon to find much scat near the burrow because woodchucks use a special lavatory chamber inside.

Tracks. Although all woodchucks and marmots have five toes on front and back feet, the vestigial "thumb" on the front foot may register. When walking, the hind foot overlaps the back portion of the front track.

Whistles. Woodchucks often give an alarm whistle when frightened, causing nearby 'chucks to issue echoing alarms. But the dozen or so woodchucks I've stalked and dealt with remained silent, both when dashing from me and when attempting to sneak away in slow motion.

BREEDING AND REPRODUCTION

Woodchuck and marmot reproductive activity differs in several respects.

Woodchuck youngsters stay with Mom until she chases them away in summer. (Photo by Lennie and Uschi Rue III)

Woodchucks. Male woodchucks seek a mate as soon as they emerge from hibernation, often breeding with the same female or females on successive years. If a female accepts the male, mating occurs inside the den.

Gestation is about 30 days. The young are born without fur and with eyes closed. Litter sizes among lab animals average four, and young are weaned at about 6 weeks. The mother raises her playful youngsters alone and chases them from her burrow by July. Thereafter, woodchucks tend not to socialize much.

Marmots. Pair bonding and mating behaviors differ among the species. Gestation is about 30 days. Average litter size is about four among lab animals. The young usually stay with the mother in family groups into their second year, when the males disperse. Some young females may stay with the family.

HOME RANGES

Home ranges are largely determined by food availability. Female woodchucks tend to be content with a range of half an acre. Male territories generally average about 2 acres, often overlapping with the ranges of females but not those of other males. Both males and females occupy and maintain multiple burrow systems, sometimes using more than one daily.

Marmots may need to travel long distances from hibernation to dens nearer feeding areas. They too have multiple dens often shared by family groups. Smaller dens serve primarily for escapes.

SENSES

Sight. Like deer, woodchucks can spot movement at great distances and may race for their dens if the stalker dips from sight. However, unlike deer and rabbits, the eyes of a woodchuck are forward in their face, which leaves a significant blind area behind the head. This makes 'chucks more vulnerable than rabbits when feeding. I've been able to stalk woodchucks to within 30 feet by waiting for them to turn their heads toward food before I slowly continued my approach. I would freeze whenever the 'chuck looked up. Like deer, woodchucks seem to have difficulty distinguishing a motionless person from a vegetative background.

Hearing. Slight sounds can put a vigilant woodchuck on high alert. However, the noise of chewing food seems to partially drown sounds they might otherwise notice.

Smell. Although woodchucks and marmots undoubtedly have a better sense of smell than humans, hunters report that 'chucks often pay little attention to human scent carried to them by the wind.

OPTIONS FOR CONTROL

Principal options include habitat alteration, exclusion, frightening, removal, and killing. Yet, because nature does not love a void, empty burrows often receive replacement tenants.

Questionable habitat alteration. Large, closely trimmed lawns offer little food for woodchucks. However, lawns offer little for the whole range of native insects, birds, and mammals whose ancestors depended on the same land. If one's goal is total elimination of wildlife, paving is more effective than lawn, while providing more parking spaces for gas-guzzling SUVs. For additional concerns about large lawns, see page 60.

Removal from house foundations. To force woodchucks and marmots to abandon a den under a foundation, professionals determine if and when the den is occupied. They do this by securing a sheet of newspaper over the opening. If the den is occupied, the animal easily breaks through the newspaper. However, before livetrapping, if a female is denned with young, it's more humane to wait until the young can emerge on their own, when the whole family can disperse elsewhere.

The options at that time include livetrapping of each animal or installation of a one-way door. A one-way door resembles a live trap but has a pair of cam-activated drop-down door that allows exit but not reentry. For a photo example, see page 187.

Fence exclusion. Options include wire-mesh or electric fencing—or a combination—or wood.

■ *Wire-mesh fencing:* For woodchucks and marmots, university research suggests that wire mesh needs to extend at least 3 feet aboveground, because these animals climb well. Yet mesh should also extend outward as a shelf to prevent burrowing under. Fencing that extends above- and belowground is often called rat-wall fencing because small mesh near the bottom can also exclude smaller rodents and moles. For options, see page 49.

Mesh also serves well in preventing 'chucks from denning under decks and porches. In this case, you need to fasten wire mesh to the back of decorative grillwork under a porch or deck and extend it into the soil as shown on page 59.

■ *Wooden fencing:* Fasten wire mesh to the bottom and extend it into the soil, as described for mesh fencing on page 48.

■ *Electric fencing:* For woodchucks and other small mammals, electric-mesh fencing serves better than single-wire or tape-type electric fencing. Single-wire serves best if strung horizontally either near the top of a mesh fence or strung about 5 inches from the ground and about the same distance outward. However, such low positioning makes weed control challenging unless the area is mulched well enough to prevent weed or grass growth. If vegetation touches electric wires, it can cause electric shorts. Besides, any low electric wire poses shock hazards for small children. For examples, see page 54.

Trunk guards. Because woodchucks and marmots hibernate in winter, they don't pose a winter threat to bark and low branches, as voles, mice, rabbits, and hares do. However, especially in spring, woodchucks will strip bark near their burrows as part of scent marking. Thus, wire-mesh or plastic guards around potentially vulnerable trees and shrubs can be a worthwhile year-round precaution.

Plant selection. I've not been able to locate studies that suggest plants that woodchucks and marmots don't like. Yet it seems reasonable to assume that most plants of low appeal to deer, rabbits, and hares might be of low appeal to woodchucks and marmots, too, whether for their chemical or physical defenses. On the other hand, deer and rabbits sometimes show differences in taste. Our cottontails haven't bothered our tomatoes or tomato leaves even though deer surely would if given the chance. 'Chucks like tomatoes.

Repellents. Cornell University testing found no commercial deer or rabbit repellent effective in warding off woodchucks. However, bobcat urine sprayed on lower portions of tree trunks greatly reduced trunk damage, according to the University of Kansas's Kenneth Armitage.

Predators. Landscaping that allows free travel of foxes, coyotes, and bobcats (rather than fencing them out) and free flight of raptors can invite an around-the-clock rodent patrol. Roosting trees and raised nest boxes can help encourage the presence of large owls, but their main contribution is typically the dispatch of the occasional 'chuck that timidly ventures out at night.

A red fox can help keep populations of many rodents in check. (Photo by Lennie and Uschi Rue III)

Organic fumigant. In the *New York Times,* writer Cass Peterson recounted a series of unsuccessful attempts to drive a "groundhog" from its burrow until dumping cat-fouled litter into it. Peterson speculated that ammonia fumes did the trick. To read that entertaining article, use Internet search words *groundhog, Cass, Peterson, New York Times.*

Frighteners. Woodchuck-chasing dogs and their daytime presence and scent around a garden can make a garden area a scary place for a woodchuck. Over the years, my friend Kathy Nelson has depended on a succession of large, otherwise-friendly poodles to chase away woodchucks that have attempted to enter her deer-fenced nursery.

Market gardeners sometimes report scarecrows resembling gardeners can be effective if those garden areas normally have human activity and if the scarecrows are moved regularly.

Livetrapping. Although many jurisdictions allow property owners and tenants to control 'chucks and marmots, trap-and-release measures are often forbidden for reasons explained on page 61. Yet, if local law allows release of woodchucks, check with officials or control professionals for authorized release areas.

■ *When to livetrap:* The best times to trap are in early spring, before young are born, and then in midsummer, after youngsters have dispersed.

■ *Trap sizes:* Single-door cage traps should be at least 24 inches long. Double-door traps should be at least 30 inches long because the extra door consumes space when it swings down.

■ *Where to place traps:* Professional wildlife controller Cricket Creary feels it's a waste of time to place live traps in any garden that a woodchuck is ravaging. She reasons that woodchucks usually have plenty else in gardens to distract them from traps. Instead, Creary scouts for an active main entry to the burrow. Then she waits till dark to be sure the 'chuck has retired for the night before returning with a double-door cage trap—open at both ends. She places the trap so it will prevent exit except through the trap.

When the 'chuck emerges for breakfast, it finds added incentive to enter the trap—pieces of cooked chicken! (However, Creary advises against using meat bait for 'chucks overnight in a garden or yard because it could attract night-foraging skunks, opossums, raccoons, and bears.)

Left: *The bottom opening in this Safeguard Universal Den Trap fits over a burrow opening (wildlifecontrolsupplies.com).* Right: *This homemade live trap swung to vertical when young Wilber Woodchuck IV entered for apple slices. At the near end of the 6-inch plastic drainpipe, I drilled holes to receive crisscrossed lengths of coat-hanger wire, secured by a bicycle inner tube. Machine bolts on each side are suspended from coat-hanger wire hose-clamped to ¾-inch electrical conduit, which I bent around an oak barrel before fitting over ½-inch conduit posts. Wire-suspended license plates can keep rain off captives till you arrive.*

■ *Baits:* If you position a cage trap at the entrance of the main burrow, bait isn't usually needed. Elsewhere, you'll need bait. In hopes of photographing Wilber Woodchuck on our stone wall, I tested apple slices, a cherry tomato, and a carrot without its greens. Wilber let me photograph him enjoying apple slices and then the tomato, but he showed no interest in the carrot. No doubt he'd never seen a carrot before. Various authorities recommend sliced apples, peanut butter, cantaloupe, cabbage, fresh peas, and lettuce.

■ *Trap covers:* Pros often cover live traps for several reasons: They make the space look secure from above; they shield a trapped animal from direct sun and rain; and the animal doesn't see your approach, which can cause stress. And that's especially helpful if you inadvertently catch a skunk, which I did once.

■ *Livetrapping downsides:* For more, see page 61.

Lethal trapping. Woodchucks and marmots are large enough to require lethal traps that could also kill pets and other nontarget animals. To me, livetrapping seems the smarter option because it allows you to ensure that you've caught the intended mammal before considering lethal controls, relative to legality. For thoughts on euthanasia options, see page 64.

Hunting. Check local hunting and firearms laws. Many jurisdictions consider woodchucks and selected marmots game animals, often with no prescribed hunting seasons or bag limits.

I once investigated the violent shaking of one of our raspberry bushes. The shaker, it turned out, was a big 'chuck raised on his hind legs and using his front paws to pull berry-laden branches toward his mouth. In his orgiastic delight, he failed to notice my approach with a small 4-10 shotgun, which I maintained as a precaution against rabid raccoons. Although rabid raccoons were prevalent in those years, they weren't nearly as prevalent as woodchucks in our inaugural garden. That year was the last I used a firearm to outwit competing mammals, a lesson not yet learned by most world leaders.

Poisoning and chemical fumigant. I don't recommend poisons, for multiple reasons described on page 64. However, if a woodchuck has shown aggressive behavior, suggesting late-stage rabies, or if it can't otherwise be excluded or removed, a fumigant inside a burrow poses low risk to nontarget species and low risk of secondary poisoning. (*Reminder:* Elimination of one burrow occupant usually invites a new one unless the old burrow is effectively sealed.)

The standard fumigant is discharged from slow-burning chemicals inside a cardboard cartridge. Instructions usually suggest sealing all entrances except the main entrance with large sections of sod before lighting the cartridge fuse and placing the cartridge deep into the main entrance.

The resulting slow burn produces carbon monoxide and other toxins. Because carbon monoxide is heavier than air, it tends to descend through passageways without readily escaping through burrow entrances. Still, instructions will advise watching for smoke arising from openings and sealing off any that you see.

Caution: Any burning process poses fire risks near combustible materials, including wooden buildings. If you are interested in fumigation, check local laws before acquiring a fumigant and then follow the package instructions carefully—this also will help you to avoid breathing toxic fumes or causing an explosion.

COMMUNICABLE DISEASES AND PARASITES

Woodchucks are subject to an array of diseases and parasites transmissible to people and other animals. But experts say transmissions are relatively low. The diseases include rabies and flea-borne plague. Parasites include raccoon roundworm and ticks. If woodchucks contract rabies, they "may become very aggressive in the final stages of the disease," according to the Georgia Department of Natural Resources.

For more on these hazards, see the next chapter.

CHAPTER 20

Communicable Diseases and Parasites

Wild mammals transmit many diseases and parasites to people and pets. This chapter addresses, alphabetically, some of the most common and serious health risks. How serious? Two of the bacteria are considered to be potential bioweapons.

Anticipating bites and scratches, people who work with wild mammals often get rabies vaccinations in addition to routine tetanus boosters. Serious afflictions can also arise from mammal urine and feces, and from fleas and ticks. So it's even unsafe to handle dead mammals without protective gear. And airborne dust from rodent urine, feces, and saliva can deliver the deadly hantavirus.

Most of the information in this chapter is based on Internet guidance from the US Centers for Disease Control and Prevention (CDC). Supplemental information is from webmd.com and diagnose-me.com.

To obtain expanded information and updates, simply use those Internet search words and the name of the hazard or mammal.

Babesiosis. See "Tick-borne diseases," page 214.

Canine distemper virus (CDV). Although CDV is not transmissible to humans, unvaccinated

Cats, Dogs, and Ferrets

As a minimum, these pets deserve rabies vaccinations. In addition, spayed or neutered pets are less likely to roam and become infected by bites, feces, ticks, and fleas of other mammals. As a bonus, "fixed" pets can't contribute unwanted new offspring to the millions upon millions of stray animals harboring afflictions transmissible to other mammals, including people.

dogs are susceptible, especially puppies. Fortunately, vaccinations are very effective.

CDV creates behaviors and symptoms that are often mistaken for rabies. The CDV virus invades through mucous membranes, killing raccoons, foxes, skunks, and other carnivores. Symptoms include coughing and shivering, nasal discharge, pneumonia, diarrhea, and vomiting. Then come seizures, tremors, and more.

Ehrlichiosis. See "Tick-borne diseases," page 214.

Giardiasis. *Giardia* species are flagellated protozoans dispersed in rodent feces. Often known as backpacker's diarrhea, giardiasis is one of many serious afflictions by protozoans throughout the world. I've known people who've survived "giardia," as the affliction is popularly called, usually ingested from outdoor water that hasn't been purified. One spokesperson for a major brand of water-purification tablets confided to me that the only sure way to purify wilderness water is to boil it for 10 minutes and then serve it in containers and with utensils that haven't been contaminated.

Hansen's disease (leprosy). "If left untreated, Hansen's disease can result in crippling of the hands and feet and blindness," says the CDC. Because the disease always involves peripheral nerves, early symptoms may include loss of feeling in the hands and feet. Other possible symptoms include pale or red skin areas on the extremities, or a rash on them, perhaps followed by symmetrical skin lesions, skin nodules, and congested eye and nasal glands.

Armadillos are susceptible to the bacillus *Mycobacterium leprae* that causes leprosy in humans, and this has led to the alarmed misconception that armadillos are a principal cause of leprosy. However, even though armadillos range only in the South and Southeast, the disease has been reported in many states outside that region. Within the armadillo's range, only two states have reported infection in their armadillos. Louisiana infection rates have sometimes been as high as 10 percent. Texas rates have approached 5 percent. Because the leprosy bacillus was endemic in humans in those states long before armadillos arrived, researchers suggest that the soil and climate there may be conducive to its survival and spread.

The CDC feels that the disease is most frequently spread from person to person through respiratory droplets. But there's good news: The disease is not highly contagious. In fact, about 95 percent of people are naturally immune. Those most vulnerable in households are blood relatives, such as children and siblings, rather than spouses who may not share the genetic vulnerability. Hansen's disease is readily treatable with antibiotics, and patients become noninfectious after only a few treatments and so can soon return to family and work. Even so, treatments may continue for several years.

Hantavirus. The CDC characterizes Hantavirus Pulmonary Syndrome (HPS) as "a deadly disease from rodents." First identified in 1993 in the Southwest, "hantavirus is transmitted to humans primarily by aerosolized droplets of fresh urine, saliva, and feces of native rodents." Thus, there's extreme danger in stirring up infected dust by sweeping and vacuuming. Also, your contaminated fingers can transmit the virus via your nose, mouth, or eyes. Mouse fur and nest materials should also be suspect. Ironically, virus-infected rodents don't become ill themselves, even though they continuously shed the virus.

Early symptoms of HPS in humans begin somewhat like a cold or influenza, with fever and muscle ache. About half of all victims also experience headache, dizziness, chills, and abdominal problems. Then 4 to 10 days after the initial symptoms come coughing and extreme shortness of breath that may rapidly become fatal. There is no vaccine and there is no cure, other than respiratory therapy in intensive-care wards.

In the United States, scores of new cases are reported each year. Most have occurred in the West—that is, westward from an imaginary north/south line between Texas Bayou country and the Dakotas. But scattered cases have occurred in the Midwest and the Northeast.

Of the four native mouse species, the one whose range overlaps most with reported cases is the deer mouse. But cases are also associated with three other mouse species described on page 151. However, other native mice have tested positive for other strains of hantavirus.

On a somewhat reassuring note, the CDC observes that our three alien rodents haven't been associated with HPS. So that's finally something positive to say about the house mouse, the Norway rat, and the roof rat.

For precautions against contracting hantavirus, see the "Cleanup" section of the rats and mice chapter, beginning on page 145; that chapter also suggests means to prevent rodents from becoming pests and eliminating those that do.

Histoplasmosis. This is caused by the fungus *Histoplasma capsulatum,* which normally affects a person's lungs. Symptoms, including fever, chest pain, and dry cough, may begin 3 to 17 days after exposure. Chest x-rays may reveal patterns like those of tuberculosis. Severe cases are treated with antifungal medication.

The disease is transmitted by spores, usually breathed from contaminated soil or droppings from birds and bats. Somewhat reassuringly, the CDC suggests that 80 percent of people in infected areas may test positive in skin tests without showing ill effects. Mild cases usually resolve themselves and may confer partial resistance to reinfection.

Leprosy. See "Hansen's Disease," on the opposite page.

Leptospirosis. *Leptospira* bacteria enter the body in contaminated drinking water but also through mucous membranes, as well as cuts and abrasions. So waters used for swimming and boating pose risks, especially after flooding. The bacteria begin their journey in the urine of infected mammals, which often show no disease symptoms.

In humans, symptoms are often mistaken for those of other tropical diseases such as malaria. Symptoms include "high fever, severe headache, chills, muscle aches, and vomiting, and may include jaundice (yellow skin and eyes), red eyes, abdominal pain, diarrhea, or rash. If the disease is not treated, the patient could develop kidney damage, meningitis (inflammation of the membrane around the brain and spinal cord), liver failure, and respiratory distress. In rare cases, death occurs," says the CDC.

Illness may begin abruptly anytime from 2 days to 4 weeks after exposure. Although patients may recover from the first phase of leptospirosis, they may become ill again, this time more severely. This second phase is also called Weil's disease.

Diagnosis is confirmed via blood tests or urine samples. Treatment is with antibiotics. Even though there is no vaccine, malaria antibiotics can help resist *Leptospira* bacteria as they enter the body.

Lyme disease. See "Tick-borne diseases," on page 214.

Plague. In Europe, from 1330 to 1352, a pandemic plague known as the Black Death killed many millions of people. The infecting bacillus, *Yersinia pestis,* first killed roof rats, whose fleas then needed a temporary host—humans. Although known today simply as plague, the disease is hardly tucked safely away in history books. Yet it is usually curable with antibiotics if addressed in time.

The US Department of Defense says the number of US cases usually numbers 10 to 15 annually. Most occur in rural areas of the Southwest, with "14 percent" fatalities. Although fleas of the roof rat (black rat) were the main cause of the Black Death pandemic in Europe, plague can be transmitted by fleas of most rodents, including those of other rats, as well as mice, voles, and ground squirrels.

Besides flea transmission, humans can be infected by contact with an infected animal's body fluids or by inhaling aerosolized sneeze droplets from infected mammals, including humans. The aerosol infection (pneumonic plague) is so deadly that it's considered a potential bioweapon. However, the most common form of the disease is bubonic plague, which begins with painful swelling of a lymph gland, known as a *bubo*, in the neck, groin, or armpit. That swelling is accompanied by fever, chills, headache, and extreme exhaustion before symptoms worsen; these can include the blackened, gangrenous flesh that, in part, gave rise to the more frightening old name for the disease—the Black Death.

Rabies. All unvaccinated mammals, including humans, can die from the classic rabies virus. Once symptoms occur in humans, coma and death follow within 10 to 14 days. However, if a person receives a series of inoculations soon after being bitten or scratched by an infected mammal, protection is virtually assured.

In the United States, confirmed cases of rabies in wildlife and pets have increased since the 1970s. Most cases occur in the East, but infections are increasing westward, as discussed in the raccoons chapter on page 134.

More than 90 percent of the 7,000 to 8,000 confirmed cases of mammal rabies are in wild mammals. Less than 10 percent are in unvaccinated domestic animals, including dogs, cats, and livestock. Among wild mammals, the most commonly infected are raccoons, skunks, insect-eating bats, and foxes, in that order. Opossums are rarely infected.

In the United States in some years, up to 40,000 people have received the rabies vaccine after being exposed to or bitten by a suspected rabid mammal. Many veterinary workers and wildlife handlers receive the vaccine as a precaution. There are usually fewer than five human deaths in the United States annually, most occurring because victims don't receive inoculations promptly following bites from bats.

■ *How is rabies transmitted?* Transmission occurs through infected saliva or mucus that enters a new host's bloodstream. Virtually all transmissions result from bites or from scratches by claws recently licked by an infected mammal. Fortunately, the virus is not hardy outside its host and is quickly "inactivated" by drying, sunlight, and detergents, says webmd.com.

■ *Virus incubation.* The rabies virus enters a mammal cell, where it multiplies and travels along peripheral nerve cells to the brain and spinal cord (the central nervous system). This incubation process usually takes 20 to 90 days in humans, depending on the amount of virus absorbed and its proximity to the central nervous system. So, it's important to consult a physician immediately after being bitten by a mammal, even if the mammal shows no symptoms. (If the pet or other mammal can be safely captured, authorities may want to observe it for 10 days to see if it remains healthy, reducing concern of infection. If the animal is killed, authorities may want to examine its brain for evidence of infection.)

■ *Mammal symptoms.* Sick mammals tend to act either "furious" or—more commonly—"dumb." With dumb symptoms, the mammal may appear tame or apathetic. Pets may even appear uncharacteristically timid. With furious symptoms, the animal may be aggressive, perhaps biting at things. In most cases, excess saliva causes drooling.

■ *Human symptoms.* After the onset of symptoms, there is little hope for recovery. Symptoms usually appear 20 to 90 days after the incident and may include pain or tingling at the bite or scratch site, as well as flulike manifestations. Subsequently, humans also show either "dumb" or "furious" symptoms, in the latter case cycling between furiousness and calm. Confusion, hallucinations, and even biting may occur.

■ *If you get bitten.* The CDC recommends washing bites and scratches with soap and water for at least 5 minutes and then seeing a physician. As a precaution, six immunization shots are given over a period of 1 month—the first shot near the wound and the rest in the arm. There's no longer need for 23 painful shots in the stomach. A tetanus shot often accompanies treatment.

■ *If your pet gets bitten.* If a vaccinated pet is bitten by a suspected rabid animal, vets often administer a booster shot to help fight off the virus.

■ *Inoculating neighborhood wildlife.* In areas with rabies outbreaks, health and wildlife officials can distribute baits containing oral vaccines that protect predator and prey species prior to infection.

Raccoon roundworm. Although this disease is relatively benign within raccoons, it can debilitate and kill many other mammals, including humans. This roundworm is suspected of nearly eradicating native wood rats in some regions and can be a special hazard to small children playing where raccoons have defecated. For precautions, see page 144.

Rat-bite fever. This is of concern after a bite from any rodent, not just rats. The disease is often transmitted by saliva but also by rodent urine, feces, and secretions from a rodent's eyes and nose. In the United States, rat-bite fever is usually caused by *Streptobacillus moniliformis,* a nasal and oral flora that occurs naturally in most rodents, including our native and alien rats, as well as white lab rats and "fancy rats" sold in the pet trade. Owners of fancy rats sometimes contract the disease after kissing their pets. Human symptoms usually include fever, chills, headache, and muscle pain within 2 to 10 days of exposure, followed by a diffuse rash, and sometimes red, painfully swollen joints. Symptoms may subside and then recur, leading to more serious problems. This disease is treatable with antibiotics.

Rodent bites, generally. In the United States, rodent bites number in the hundreds of thousands annually, many resulting from inept handling attempts. Still, rat bites include unprovoked attacks on babies and the frail elderly. Although rats and mice aren't known to transmit rabies, their bites can transmit hantavirus, rat-bite fever, tetanus, and other woes. If bitten, consult a physician, who will, at a minimum, ensure that your tetanus booster is up to date.

Tapeworms. These parasitic cestodes can occupy the liver and intestines of all mammals. Dogs often infect owners and children with larvae when licking on the mouth. Owners can infect their fingers when crushing fleas. Pets can also be infected by eating rodents. Routine deworming of pets causes tapeworms, larvae, and eggs to dissolve. For more, visit diagnose-me.com.

Tetanus (lockjaw). This disease is caused by a neurotoxin that develops in people after receiving wounds involving the bacillus *Clostridium tetani,* which is almost everywhere in the environment. With the most common form of infection, symptoms begin with muscle stiffness and pain in the jaw, neck, and abdomen. Spasms and seizures follow, causing death in 10 to 20 percent of cases.

Tetanus bacilli grow in anaerobic environments (without air). So bites and other puncture wounds are of special concern because they make cleansing difficult. Yet tetanus infection can also result from cleansed superficial wounds, insect bites, and even dental infections.

To be safe, the CDC recommends booster shots periodically after receiving an initial series of inoculations.

Tick-borne diseases. Although Lyme disease gets the most press, ticks can transmit other serious bacterial diseases, including tularemia, ehrlichiosis, babesiosis, and Colorado tick fever. The white-footed mouse is the most common host in the deer tick's tiny, hard-to-see nymph stage. But many mammals have tested positive for bacteria that cause Lyme disease and ehrlichiosis as well as the malaria-like parasites that cause babesiosis. Many mammals, not just deer and mice, host deer ticks and other types of ticks.

From left to right: *Tweezers don't remove ticks as efficiently as Pro-Tick Remedy II, which employs thin spring steel to exploit the nail-pulling principle of a claw hammer. In many tests, our tool has never failed to remove tick mouthparts (commonly called the "head"). We incinerate the tick with a match before capturing the cinder in toilet paper for flushing. We strike a second match to sterilize the claw before dipping in Lysol or a 1:10 bleach solution. At right, Kathleen Nelson protects herself with latex gloves and shirtsleeves sealed with rubber bands. Light-colored clothing makes ticks easier to spot before tossing the clothes into the washer. (Photo by Liz Accas)*

Disease symptoms usually appear within 5 to 10 days of the bite. Yet symptoms may vary and so may puzzle physicians even after blood tests. Symptoms may include swelling or reddening at the site of the bite but may otherwise be very mild. More severe symptoms may include fever, chills, fatigue, headache, nausea, rash, joint swelling, and confusion. If you experience any of these symptoms after a tick bite, see your physician.

The standard guidance for tick bites is to remove the tick as promptly as possible and immediately save it in a plastic bag for storage in a freezer, with date noted. Should symptoms arise, the tick type and vector can be determined in lab tests. Avoid touching the tick with bare fingers, but if you make that mistake, wash your hands and then the bite site with antiseptic soap.

The most effective tick-pulling tool I've encountered is Pro-Tick Remedy II, shown in the photos on the opposite page. It pulls ticks based on the principle of a nail-pulling claw hammer and almost always removes the tick's mouthparts (commonly called the head) intact, unlike the results with mere tweezers.

As to bite prevention, if you expect to brush against vegetation, light-colored clothing without a pattern will help you spot the little critters. Also, long sleeves with buttoned cuffs and long socks pulled up over pant legs help keep ticks from reaching flesh. All such clothing should first be sprayed with tick repellent. Immediately upon completion of your outdoor activity, toss the clothing into the washing machine for immediate washing. Then conduct a skin check.

Tularemia (rabbit fever). Rodents, rabbits, and hares—like most other mammals—can transmit tularemia. And so can ticks. In the United States, about 200 people are diagnosed annually. These cases occur primarily in south-central and western states.

Tularemia can be fatal if not treated with antibiotics. In fact, the bacterium *Francisella tularensis* is so infectious when airborne that it is considered a potential bioweapon. The bacterium can survive for weeks in soil and water. Although a vaccine has been used to protect vulnerable lab workers, it wasn't available to the public at this writing.

Symptoms usually develop 3 to 5 days after exposure but depend on the means of exposure. For example, inhaled bacteria may cause sudden fever and flulike symptoms, as well as dry cough and progressive weakness, perhaps also pneumonia. Other symptoms may include skin ulcers, swollen and painful lymph glands, inflamed eyes, sore throat, mouth sores, and diarrhea.

Hunters and trappers are especially vulnerable when skinning infected animals and eating meat that isn't thoroughly cooked. But tularemia is also transmitted by insects, such as ticks and deer flies, that have feasted on the infected animal. You can also fall ill after drinking infected water or inhaling the bacterium. Preventive measures include insect repellent and the use of protective gloves or plastic sacks when handling animal carcasses.

Scientists suspect that some mammals may contract tularemia through cannibalism. The name of the disease acknowledges Tulare County, California, where it was first diagnosed.

PART 3

Deer-Resistant Plants

CHAPTER 21

Research on Deer Resistance

What plants don't deer eat? And why? What plants don't bears, gophers, rabbits, voles, and other garden mammals eat?

The answers to these questions aren't easy because they are complex. And most answers are undermined by exceptions. Yet when we consider the following three factors together, the answers— and the exceptions—make better sense:

- Field tests of plants in deer-browse areas
- Chemical analyses of plants
- Research by animal behaviorists

Many books provide lists of so-called deer-resistant plants—lists compiled from various authorities living in widely scattered growing regions. Other books focus on toxic properties in plants that can repel, sicken, and kill browsing animals, as well as people. But there appears to be no book that attempts to link deer resistance and plant toxins with the browsing behaviors of deer. Research on browsing behaviors so far seems to occur only in scientific studies. And these studies are crucial to understanding what deer don't eat and why. Continuing field tests may well show

Dolly returns with fawns each August to finish off our hosta hillside after photosynthesis has nourished the roots adequately.

that some plants chemically repellent to deer may also repel other garden mammals.

Besides suggesting deer-resistant plants, field tests and behavioral studies can inform strategies for garden design. For example, deer-resistant plants can visually screen other plants from notice. And a mix of deer-resistant plants with others can emit a confusing mishmash of repellent scents, odors, and tastes.

However, many plants that are deer resistant are also highly invasive aliens that jump garden fences and threaten native ecosystems.

All of the more than 1,000 plants in this part of the book are considered "deer-resistant" by a consensus of regional authorities—people who have tested these plants where deer browse.

Yet comparatively few of these "deer-resistant" plants should be considered "deer-proof" in all stages of growth or all growing conditions. This is

Deer Dislikes

Deer tend to dislike strong-scented plants, such as most culinary and medicinal herbs. They also dislike strong-tasting plants, as those in the Onion family. Deer often prefer mild-tasting plants, the same plants whose original toxins were bred out of them, such as lettuce and parsley. On the other hand, deer enjoy the strongly scented leaves of tomatoes, which are toxic to humans. Go figure.

especially true of tender, nutrient-rich shoots in spring that may soon acquire chemical or physical defenses that make them far less appealing. So, most young shoots probably need protection, whether by fencing or spray-on repellents.

Then, too, the plants that authorities recommend in the upcoming pages have normally proven of low interest to deer only when other plants are available, and this suggests mainly that they rank low on deer-preference lists. This is best illustrated in winter when starving deer will often taste, and sometimes severely browse, plants they would reject in seasons of plenty. In winter, when evergreen leaves and dormant woody buds are the only food available, starving deer may attempt to breach formidable fences by working themselves under, over, or through them—even pushing weaker fencing down. Such determined efforts may also occur during extreme drought.

As you browse the listing of deer-resistant plants by category (page 235) and then read about selected plants in the plant profiles (page 260), please consider the credentials of the recommending experts in "Authorities on Deer Resistance" and "Authorities on Rabbit Resistance" on page 234. The profile of each deer-resistant plant concludes with symbols representing specific authorities and their home regions. If you live in that authority's region, you might share many significant growing conditions, as discussed in the next section. Also consider the cautions about a plant's potential invasiveness where you live (can differ by region).

CHEMICAL ANALYSES

Plants that seem deer-resistant in one region may not be in another. Relative differences in deer resistance can be due to differing soil chemicals, soil moisture,

Deer-Resistant Flower Arrangement

Early one October in the foothills of the California's Sierra Nevadas, garden designer Carolyn Singer created this deer-resistant arrangement. Most here are also featured in Carolyn's excellent book series, *Deer in My Garden*, where she profiles plants she's found deer resistant over more than 2 decades. The plants in the bouquet are: *Rudbeckia triloba* (Brown-eyed Susan); *Chrysopsis mariana* (Maryland golden aster); *Perovskia atriplicifolia* (Russian sage); *Calamagrostis brachytricha* (Feather reed grass); *Calamagrostis acutiflora* 'Karl Foerster' (Feather reed grass); *Miscanthus sinsensis* 'Gracillimus' (Eulalia grass); *Origanum laevigatum* 'Hopley's' (Oregano); *Helianthus maximillianii* (Maximillian sunflower); *Solidago* sp. (Goldenrod); *Chasmanthium latifolium* (Northern seas oats); *Caryopteris incana* (Bluebeard); *Tanecetum parthenium* (Feverfew); *Penstemon* 'Garnet' (Beardtongue); *Gaillardia grandiflora* 'Burgundy' (Blanket flower); *Verbena rigida* (Vervain); *Lychnis coronaria* (Rose campion); *Bouteloua gracilis* (Blue grama grass); and *Schizachyrium scoparium* (Little bluestem).

and growing conditions. Combined with differing growth stages, growing conditions can affect a plant's odor, taste, and general toxicity, as well as relative toxicities of various parts of that plant.

We need only taste the increasing bitterness of bolted lettuce to appreciate chemical changes that occur in plants as they mature. In addition, that same lettuce could taste somewhat different in another soil and climate.

FEEDING BEHAVIORS

The following perspectives are based largely on the work of Frederick Provenza, PhD, professor of range science at Utah State University, and that of his coauthors on various studies. Provenza pioneered behavioral research on livestock browsing. Based on those findings, Provenza discovered corresponding browsing behaviors of deer, elk, and bison—all cud-chewing herbivores, after all.

I discussed Provenza's perspectives more broadly in Part 1 of this book, beginning on page 2. Yet you'll probably find the following distilled considerations on plant deer resistance quite useful here as well.

■ Young cud-chewing herbivores, such as deer fawns, greatly depend on Mom and older sisters to show them what's good and what isn't through the seasons. And those early lessons form lasting impressions. In fact, in trusting Mom's choices, the fawn may not bother to taste plants it might otherwise like. In this case, Mom may be avoiding some plants—in gardens especially—simply because they look unfamiliar.

■ Plants change in physical and chemical makeup through the seasons. Plants that were tender, tasty, and nutritious in spring may quickly acquire physical and chemical defenses against browsing.

Authorities on Toxins

Each of the upcoming plant profiles lists toxins if known. The Burrows and Tyrl book focuses primarily on plant toxins as they affect livestock, particularly ruminant livestock, with occasional mention of effects on deer (which are also ruminants) and humans.

The books by Dr. James Duke and Dr. Lewis Nelson focus primarily on toxic effects on humans, which don't always correlate closely with effects on ruminants. For example, toxins such as deadly cyanide don't develop until plant compounds subjected to rumen microorganisms and high pH generate cyanide in a process known as *cyanogenesis*. Oh, so much to learn!

Burrows and Tyrl = *Toxic Plants of North America* by George E. Burrows and Ronald J. Tyrl (Iowa State Press/A Blackwell Publishing Company, 2001). A favorite book of veterinarians and emergency room physicians, this is arranged by plant family and includes drawings of representative plants, range maps, cultural

information, descriptions of toxic properties, clinical symptoms in animals and humans, and recommended treatments.

James Duke = books by retired USDA ethnobotanist Dr. James A. Duke, including *Handbook of Medicinal Herbs*, second edition (CRC Press, 2002) and *The Green Pharmacy* (Rodale Books, 1997) by Dr. James A Duke, retired USDA ethnobotanist. Addressing 800 plants, the *Handbook* compares Dr. Duke's medicinal versus toxic ratings with those of other authorities.

Nelson *et al* = *Handbook of Poisonous and Injurious Plants*, second edition, by Lewis S. Nelson, MD; Richard D. Shih, MD; and Michael J. Balick, PhD (Springer Science+Business, 2007). This New York Botanical Garden replacement of the *AMA Handbook of Poisonous and Injurious Plants* (1985) addresses plant poisons, intoxication symptoms in humans, and clinical management.

Physical defenses include prickles, thorns, hairy leaves, toughened leaves, and even airy insubstantial leaves. Yet, as important—often more important—chemical changes within a plant may affect odor, taste, nutritional value, and toxicity.

■ Sometimes deer can detect toxins based on odor or taste, sometimes not. For example, the leaves of native skunk cabbage *(Symplocarpus foetidus)* smell skunklike when crushed. Also, oxalates in the leaves burn the mouth and throat. As another example, deer that happen upon blooming narcissus (daffodils) for the first time may bite off a flower but immediately spit it out, never to sample such alkaloid-loaded plants again.

■ While browsing, deer and other ruminants learn to balance palatability and nutrition along with the effects of toxins by switching from one type of plant to another. Regarding toxins, deer sometimes switch almost like humans do when reaching for antacids. However, many toxins are odorless

An Airy Physical Defense

In our garden, Hannelore lets our rows of asparagus *(Asparagus officinalis)* bolt in mid-June. This serves several purposes. It allows photosynthesis to fully nourish the roots for next year's growth. And it creates gorgeous, 5-foot-tall screens that hide vulnerable parts of her vegetable garden. Deer don't seem interested in the airy, threadlike leaves of asparagus, perhaps because the leaves don't yield a mouthful per bite and so may seem more work than they're worth. Deer haven't discovered our young asparagus shoots yet—rich in healthful antioxidant glutathiones. And the plant's berries, bright red in fall, may contain enough sapogenins to cause mild digestive distress in deer and people.

and tasteless going down. So they may make themselves known to deer only in what scientists call post-ingestive consequences. These unpleasant consequences teach deer to avoid that plant, at least at that growth stage. On the other hand, livestock will often continue to browse some plants until

Narcissus 'Mon Cherie' (Daffodil)

Symplocarpus foetidus (Skunk cabbage)

beginning to suffer severe nerve, organ, or digestive tract damage—resulting in agonizing death. Such fatal attractions may also be true of deer, rabbits, and rodents, but research in this field is in its infancy.

■ Toxic compounds often differ in various plant parts but usually strengthen as plants mature. As summer wears on and wild plants toughen and dry, they usually lose nutrients while becoming increasingly toxic. So in summer and into early fall, where should deer go to find moist, tender, highly palatable, and nutritious plants? In our well-watered and well-fertilized gardens, of course. Besides, our vegetable gardens contain mostly plants that were developed for our palates to be low in toxins.

■ Soil pH, soil chemicals, and soil moisture levels can determine which minerals and compounds a plant absorbs. In many cases, a plant drinks up harmless minerals and compounds and converts them to toxins.

On the other hand, plants can directly absorb soil toxins such as lead and selenium. In fact, at chemical waste sites, scientists have found some plants especially effective in removing specific toxins from the soil. For example, ragweed can remove significant amounts of lead. Such plants are called *hyperaccumulators*.

Potatoes and tomatoes readily absorb cadmium, suggesting it's smart to have your vegetable-garden soil tested for heavy metals.

Deer-Resistant Veggies and Berries

Virtually all authorities on deer resistance focus entirely on ornamental plants and culinary herbs, rarely mentioning vegetables that also serve wonderfully as ornamentals, such as asparagus, gooseberries, and rhubarb.

Little wonder that deer and other mammals relish most vegetables. Virtually all were bred to taste good and be nontoxic.

Following is a listing of veggies rated as "Rarely Damaged" or "Occasionally Damaged'" by Cooperative Extensions at Michigan State (MI.s) and Oklahoma State (OK.s), which look suspiciously copied by one of them. The symbol NY.s indicates veggies and berry plants deer haven't bothered outside *our* fenced vegetable garden.

■ Asparagus (*Asparagus officinalis*), NY.s, MI.s and OK.s occasionally damaged SEE PAGE 268

■ Cantaloupe (*Cucumis melo cantalupensis*), MI.s, OK.s Warning: Our rodents seem to have loved the fruits—NY.s

■ Flowering currants (*Ribes sanguinium*), NY.s SEE PAGE 314

■ Eggplant (*Solanum melongena*), NY.s, MI.s, OK.s

■ Gooseberries (*Ribes uva-crispa*), NY.s SEE PAGE 314

■ Hot peppers (*Capsicum annuum*), MI.s, OK.s

■ Okra (*Abelmoschus esculentus*), MI.s and OK.s occasionally damaged

■ Onion species (*Allium*), MI.s, NY.s, OK.s SEE PAGE 264

■ Potatoes, Irish (*Solanum tuberosum*), MI.s and OK.s occasionally damaged

■ Radish (*Raphanus sativus*), MI.s and OK.s occasionally damaged

■ Rhubarb (*Rheum rhabarbarum = × cultorum*). Deer never touch our rhubarb, perhaps because oxalates and glycosides in the leaves cause nausea and worse in ruminants and humans. However, Anne Cleary (northcreeknurseries.com) says deer have eaten her rhubarb leaves down to the stalks, leaving just the edible stalks. She found no dead deer. SEE PAGE 314

■ Squash (*Cucurbita pepo*), MI.s and OK.s occasionally damaged. *Note:* In spring deer have halfheartedly browsed leaves of our butternut squash but relented as those leaves toughened and other plants became available—NY.s

■ Watermelon (*Citrulus lanatus*), MI.s, OK.s

CHAPTER 22

Deer-Resistant Plants

This section lists plants that deer tend to avoid or tend to browse only lightly when other options are available. However, authorities often differ in their ratings of deer resistance for given plants. Differing experiences of authorities can be due to climate, soil, season, competition among deer for food, and the taste preferences of individual deer, which can differ as much as in people.

Many of the so-called deer-resistant plants depend on physical defenses, such as spines, prickles, or hairy leaves. Other plants may rely on chemical defenses, such as repellent scent or taste. Still others may rely on toxic chemicals that announce themselves quickly in the deer's mouth or later during digestion. Many toxic plants may seem palatable to deer and other mammals and don't cause distress until their compounds react with stomach acids and mircroorganisms. Some toxic plants cause only temporary "post-ingestive consequences" that create feeding aversions. Others may cause sudden or slow, agonizing death. Well-armed plants often rely on combinations of chemical and physical defenses in differing degrees that change through the seasons.

On deer resistance, I've occasionally relied on single endorsements, such as those from Carolyn Singer and Brad Roeller, who have been testing deer resistance for decades. When they agree on a given plant, their combined endorsements suggest continent-wide deer resistance because Singer designs gardens that resist California blacktails and Roeller tests plants on New York whitetails.

BENEFITS OF NATIVE PLANTS

Douglas Tallamy, PhD, is chairman of the department of entomology and wildlife ecology at the University of Delaware in Newark. He makes a persuasive case for "the liberal use of native plants in the landscape" in his book *Bringing Nature Home: How Native Plants Sustain Wildlife in Our Gardens.*

Like most of us, Tallamy hates bulldozer landscaping that removes native plants along with their topsoil and replaces them with vast lawns that feature alien ornamental plants. This, he says, has decimated "plant diversity that historically supported our favorite birds and mammals."

■ *Why attract caterpillars?* Our overdependence on alien plants often results in gardens that are nearly devoid of native insects on which 96 percent of native birds depend to feed their young, according to Tallamy. Without palatable leaves for caterpillars to consume, fewer survive to become butterflies the next year, and so on throughout the food web toward extinction in some regions. (How

Aster 'Woods Pink' (Aster) and *Danaus plexippus* (Monarch butterfly)

important are these caterpillars of butterflies and moths? Lepidopterans, Tallamy points out, represent more than 50 percent of insect herbivores in the United States.)

But why plant things whose leaves caterpillars will dine on? Studies show that richly diverse native habitats seldom suffer more than 10 percent leaf damage. And 10 percent damage from even a moderate distance is hardly noticeable to most people.

■ *Lawn-based ecosystems.* Tallamy says that lawns in the United States now occupy an area equivalent to eight times that of the state of New Jersey. Much of that lawn area is doused with herbicides and pesticides that destroy microbial soil life essential to soil health. Virtually all of that land is mowed with heavy, air-polluting machines that compact the soil while cutting the grass shorter than 4 inches, which then allows weeds to compete, requiring more herbicides. Then, too, grass cut too short exposes soil to drying sunlight, which then requires more watering. Ain't that a counterproductive cycle!

■ *Creating biodiversity.* Tallamy explains, "We simply have not left enough intact habitat for most of our species to avoid extinction."

In this case, "islands" of native habitat are shrinking and even disappearing, leaving remaining islands farther and farther apart. Yet Tallamy assures us that it's not too late to create new islands of native plant diversity on our own properties, so they connect with native plantings on neighboring properties. Cooperating neighbors can thereby create interconnected native habitat, neighborhood by neighborhood and community by community. Even though such connections can resemble gerrymandered voting districts, they can function much like original, intact native ecosystems. Besides, Tallamy reminds us, natives are "well adapted to their particular ecological niche and so are often far less difficult to grow than species from other altitudes, latitudes, and habitats."

■ *Alien invasions.* For centuries now, the quest for pest-free alien plants has allowed many of them to

> ### *Homo horticulturalis confusus* 'Obscurus'
>
> George Guthrie likes to belittle his enormous facility with scientific names by referring to himself as *Homo horticulturalis confusus* 'Obscurus.' In truth, George has a tremendous recall of thousands of scientific names at Shore Acres Garden on the Oregon coast, where he is landscape maintenance superintendent. While giving me an early October tour of the 30 or so plants he'd found to be deer resistant outside the garden fence, Guthrie admitted, "I don't know any plant that's deer resistant all the time." He confides that during his apprentice days, he eagerly accepted the claim of a western gardening publisher that tulips were deer resistant. He planted a huge number—with tragic results.

spread catastrophic diseases to native plants. For example, the fungus that caused the destruction of the American chestnut throughout the East in the early 20th century arrived here in 1876 on Japanese chestnuts. In addition, many aliens prove invasive by jumping the garden fence and threatening wild habitats. The so-called pest-free aliens are pest-free because they've left their natural pests on distant continents, pests that evolved with those plants over thousands of years and thereby kept those plant populations in balance within their original ecosystems. Again, consider the cautions regarding species that have proven invasive in some regions or continentwide.

■ *What's alien?* Tallamy reminds us that an "alien" plant could be from North America if it's not native to one's own region. That is, a Douglas fir *(Pseudotsuga menziesii),* native only in the Pacific Northwest, is an alien in the East and so can be just as unpalatable to eastern insects as related species from China. Yet instead of suggesting that we ban all North American plants that aren't native to our own region, Tallamy cautiously admits that plants of the same genus, native to nearby regions, may share enough genes with our natives to be considered "congeners." Therefore, native insects may find such congeners palatable. (*Note:* Douglas fir is not a member of the Fir genus *(Abies),* which has nine species native to North America, mostly in the West.)

■ *How aliens attract mammal pests.* Ironically, wildlands that can no longer support a diversity of wildlife may force deer and other mammals into our gardens. Our lawns are seeded with alien grasses whose roots attract alien grubs and earthworms, which thereupon invite native moles that pay a dear price (when trapped) for accepting our alien invitation. And by planting a wide-ranging buffet of expensive aliens, people invite deer and voles to treat themselves to our international cuisine: hostas, crocuses, tulips, and daylilies.

Most alien garden plants can not contribute to our native ecosystems. Of course, we're all entitled to indulge a bit in attractive, relatively pest-free alien plants. Still, when selecting plants from the upcoming lists and profiles, I've tried to favor natives instead that regional authorities have found deer resistant.

■ *Natives needing initial protection.* Native trees and shrubs support a phenomenally wide range of native wildlife. Tallamy especially advocates planting oak acorns, a gesture that costs not a dime. With 58 native species of oaks north of Mexico, you can easily find acorns from regional natives for immediate planting in fall. All the while, oaks feed and shelter more than 500 species of native moth and butterfly caterpillars, not to mention providing roosts and nesting sites, as well as mast crops of acorns that can weigh up to 500 pounds per acre, helping many mammals and larger birds fatten up for winter. However, oaks and some other native trees aren't particularly deer resistant in their early years and so need to be protected within woven-wire surrounds until growing beyond the reach of deer.

THE ALIEN INVASION

Many of the plants most widely hailed as being deer resistant are invasive aliens, sometimes invasive only regionally, sometimes continent-wide.

Yet, just as some plants won't be deer resistant in all regions and growing conditions, some might never become invasive in a region, especially plants that are vulnerable to extremes in temperature and precipitation. As to invasiveness of plants both alien and native, I've relied on warnings from the Plant Conservation Alliance (PCA) at nps.gov/plants/alien/list/WeedUS.xls and anti-invasive-plant activist Connecticut-based Kathleen Nelson, credited as CT.n in the lists. Nelson's silence on any given alien does not imply her endorsement of it. She's instead noted those she's found invasive herself.

Invasive aliens are hard to control in most gardens, while also posing threats to native ecosystems. Their spread often goes unnoticed because birds may carry seeds far from the garden, often to forest edge. An invasion often takes years. Aliens that show only spotty invasiveness are likely to be "discovered" only gradually, state by state and province by province. After all, a plant that merely doubles in number each year (second year 2 plants, third year 4 plants) will by the 20th year number 524,288. The worst invasives crowd out native plants on which entire ecosystems depend. They accomplish this either by seed dispersal or "by bulldozing their way across the land," says Kathy Nelson. She advises avoiding the temptation to use any plants she's warned about on upcoming lists, adding that "if you plant them, you may either inadvertently damage a native ecosystem or find yourself overrun with something you have grown to hate."

On the other hand, I'm not yet ready to suggest a ban on aliens that aren't highly invasive, especially those that occupy our orchards, fill our salad bowls, and flavor our cooking. After all, *Malus pumila* (Common apple) and *Prunus persica* (Peach) are invasive in some states. Nor am I ready to suggest banning *Mentha spicata* (Spearmint), whose leaves flavor my tea. Although spearmint is considered invasive in California and Tennessee, it's never done more than crowd other plants in our New York garden. Frankly, it's hard to be an absolute purist in anything, let alone going totally native in the garden.

Some aliens are well behaved in most places so far, such as our *Asparagus officinalis*. In fact, asparagus was already well established in 1900 along the Rio Grande in New Mexico when, as a boy, renowned foraging author Euell Gibbons harvested young spears. So far, asparagus has made the invasive lists only in Arizona, South Dakota, and Tennessee. I've seldom encountered "wild" asparagus in New York except near foundations of long-gone farmhouses, where the roots were originally planted.

By contrast, while many alien plants serve only as ornaments, their invasive progeny may threaten native ecosystems. Alien garden plants are often advertised as pest-free because their natural predators, parasites, and diseases remain on other continents. Some invasives may also thrive because they repel or poison deer and other herbivores, including caterpillars. Aliens that are toxic also sicken and kill livestock. The scent or taste of some others may simply repel livestock, and thereby still allow those plants to take over rangeland. And, yep, many of these same aliens are toxic to pets and people.

While Miranda Smith and I were cowriting the plant profiles in Chapter 23, Miranda focused on cultural information and her experiences as a market grower, and I focused on deer resistance and toxicity. But we hadn't yet studied recent research on invasive aliens and natives. So we wound up writing profiles on some plants we later decided not to include in the plant profiles (many of our deletions were also based on Kathy Nelson's warnings). Among them were *Cortaderia selloana* (Pampas grass), *Aegopodium podagraria* (bishop's weed, goutweed), and *Lysimachia nummularia* (creeping Jenny), though all are flagged in the accompanying lists. Invasive others, such as *Foeniculum vulgare* (fennel), remain among profiles with the cautionary note, "Invasive as ornamental if allowed to reseed. If growing it as a culinary herb, remove flowerheads before seeds mature."

As for notoriously invasive vincas (periwinkles), they don't seem to travel by seed, instead spreading across the ground. So they need to be contained by barriers and mowing. For vincas, I'm told that the

---

Low-Growth Defense

Deer may avoid some ornamental plants and vegetables simply because they look unfamiliar. In addition, the low growth of some ground covers and vegetables makes them less convenient—or less safe—to browse because deer prefer to see clearly in all directions when feeding, especially in home gardens where tall plants, buildings, and other barriers limit visibility and escape routes.

'La Grave' cultivar (synonym 'Bowles') tends to be clump-forming, rather than spreading.

As for cultivars, Kathy Nelson explains, "In the past, cultivars of some plants turned out to be sterile. As a result, some breeders are searching for this quality among invasives." Still, only time will tell whether "tamer" cultivars and sterile cultivars stay home.

GOOD, BAD, AND POTENTIALLY UGLY

Rather than listing only plants that are both deer resistant and *non*invasive, we decided to list all plants that have multiple authority endorsements on deer resistance, while also cautioning about invasiveness. That way, when you shop for plants, you'll know the Good, the Bad, and the Potentially Ugly.

As to invasiveness, state and regional reporting often lags behind the fact. In addition, some aliens remain well-behaved for decades before becoming invasive, whether by evolutionary adaptation or hybridizing, or simply gaining critical mass for exponential expansion. Only time and scientific research will tell which of the so-called well-behaved aliens prove invasive—and where.

So, for the environment's sake, it's wise to grow mainly plants native to your region and their cultivars. For a periodically updated listing of invasive plants, visit nps.gov/plants/alien/list/WeedUS.xls, created by the Plant Conservation Alliance. For options to popular alien invasives, you'll find many in *Native Alternatives to Invasive Plants* by C. Colston Burrell, published by the Brooklyn Botanic Garden.

LEARNING ABOUT PLANT NAMES

Most of us feel more confident using a plant's common name than its scientific name. As to deer-resistant plants, most of us say bleeding heart, rather than *Dicentra*. Peony, rather than *Paeonea*. And mayapple, rather than *Podophyllum peltatum*, for goodness' sakes!

On the other hand, we're often relieved to learn that the names of many plants we knew as kids have matching scientific names: Irises remain *Iris*. Phloxes remain *Phlox*. And yuccas remain *Yucca*. So why aren't plant scientists satisfied with simple direct translations and with simple spellings like *Iris, Phlox,* and *Yucca?*

Clockwise, from top left: Podophyllum peltatum (Mayapple); *Dicentra spectabilis* (Bleeding heart); *Paeonia* 'Bev' (early double hybrid herbaceous peony); *Iris* 'Raspberry Blush' (Bearded iris); *Phlox stolonifera* (Creeping phlox)

First, there are pitfalls in relying on common names. Many plants are known by more than one common name, often differing by region. In addition, some common names are used for more than one plant.

Common names may describe a plant part, such as the torchlike flower clusters of "red-hot poker," also known appropriately as "torch flower." Then, too, a common name for one highly toxic plant might describe flower shape, as in "monkshood," while that plant's other common name, "wolfsbane,"

refers to its historical use as wolf poison. Adding to everybody's confusion, "dusty miller" is the common name of four plant species in two plant families that exhibit "dusty," silvery gray leaves.

Like red-hot poker (torch flower), many plants have common names that suggest flower shape. "Bleeding heart" is an apt description of each flower. And "Jack-in-the-pulpit" has multiple parts atop its long stem that are humorously analogous to a preacher in a canopied pulpit. However, the tiny flowers themselves are hidden inside.

Clockwise, from top left: Kniphofia 'Alcazar' (Red-hot poker); Arisaema triphyllum (Jack-in-the-Pulpit); Aconitum carmichaelii 'Ardensii' (Monkshood) and Heterotheca = Chrysopsis villosa (Hairy golden aster)

Scientific names. Plant experts throughout the world use the same naming system devised by a Swede named Carolus (common name "Carl") Linnaeus. In *Systema Naturae* (1735), he classified and grouped plants based on similarities and differences in the sexual parts of their flowers. These distinctive *taxa* (or "categories," from Greek) gave rise to the science of *taxonomy*, groupings of living things by family relationships. Linnaeus decided to rely on Latin rules and pronunciations, both because they were widely known and because Latin was a "dead language" and therefore not subject to continually evolving vocabularies.

■ *Genus* and *species* names. To help everybody recognize relationships of related plants, Linnaeus adopted a two-name (binomial) system. He used the Latin word *genus* to suggest close kinship of a group of related things—rendered in plural as *genera*. The second word is the *species* name for plants that are almost identical and can readily fertilize one another or themselves to reproduce. The *genus* name is always spelled with an initial capital letter and shown in italics. The *species* name follows in lowercase, also in italics, as here: *Genus species*.

Digitalis purpurea (Common foxglove)

> ### Name Changes
> Adding some confusion and frustration of late, DNA testing has shown that plants and animals long thought to be part of one family are descended within another family. So name changes will continue to occur until the DNA of all plants (as well as animals) has been definitively analyzed. These name changes are driving garden writers and publishers nuts. To help readers, publishers often follow the new name with the former name preceded by an equals (=) sign or the abbreviation for synonym (syn.), like this: Shasta daisy *(Leucanthumum × superbum = Chrysanthemum maximum).*

A goodly percentage of scientific names describe a plant feature. When Latinizing the genus name of the deer-resistant plant most people know as foxglove, the 16th-century German herbalist Leonhart Fuchs might have felt that the flowers resembled human fingers, or digits—thus, *Digitalis.* (Similarly, the common name for foxglove may derive from the Old English *foxes glofa,* perhaps suggesting that the flower could serve a fox paw like a glove. Who knows?)

To be certain of the identity of plants you purchase, it's wise to verify the scientific name. Easier scientific names have root words recognizable in English, such as *aromaticus* (aromatic), *minor* (small), and *grandiflora* (big flowered). Other times, the species name will include a Latinized version of a plant's discoverer or early chronicler, as in *Fuchsia* (named after the abovementioned Leonhart Fuchs).

■ *Family names.* Latinized family names always end in "EAE," and are usually spelled in all capital letters and not italicized. Further illustrating the pitfalls of common names while showing the utility of family names, the above-mentioned "dusty miller" is the common name for four different plant species, including *Centaurea cineraria* (a perennial), *Senecio cineraria* (an annual), and *Senecio viravira*—all in the ASTERACEAE (Aster) family, and *Lychnis coronaria* (a biennial or short-lived perennial known as rose campion) in the CARYOPHYLLACEAE (Pink) family.

■ *Cultivars.* The term *cultivar* is short for *cultivated variety,* which is abbreviated as *cv.* Older references often use the term *variety.* Cultivars are mutations or strains of an original species, whether occurring naturally or produced by breeding. Cultivars have distinctive features, such as leaf or flower color or plant size. Some cultivars are propagated from leaf or stem cuttings and are therefore clones of their parent plant. But you can also buy seed of many cultivars. If you later allow these cultivars to be propagated the natural way, by flower pollination, the resulting seeds usually develop as plants that revert in appearance closer to one of the parent plants rather than the cultivar. Cultivar names are written within single quotes following the genus name, as in *Iris* 'Aachen Elf' (suggesting small size), or the species name, as in *Myosotis scorpioides* 'Sapphire' (suggesting the jewel-blue flowers). Other cultivar names may be followed by a trademark symbol (™) or a registration symbol (®) or an acronym such as PFAF. In these cases, the name is not usually shown within single quotes.

Myosotis sylvatica 'Bluesylva' (Forget-me-not). Caution: Although *M. sylvatica* (Woodland forget-me-not) and *M. scorpioides* (Water forget-me-not) are considered deer resistant, both are highly invasive. We have no reports on invasiveness of cultivars.

From left: *Senecio cineraria* 'Silver Dust' (Dusty miller) and *Salvia farinacea* 'Strata'; *Centaurea cineraria* (Dusty miller); *Lychnis coronaria* (Rose campion)

■ *Hybrids.* Hybrids can occur naturally when different species interbreed and may show attributes of both parents. Plant hybridizers also fertilize the ovaries of one species with pollen from another, hoping to create a hybrid with appealing features. Hybrids are sometimes written with a multiplication symbol to indicate that they are "crosses," like this: *Genus × species*, and many have a F1 or F2 after their name, designating their generation.

■ *Worldwide adoption.* The Linnaean system was promptly adopted by botanists worldwide. Today, most plants and seed packets you purchase show the scientific name as well as the common name. Incidentally, the Linnaean binomial system was soon adopted for animal taxonomy as well. And this makes each of us vulnerable to pranksters who ask if we've heard of the carefree and self-planting *Scalopus aquaticus,* referring of course to the Eastern mole. Fortunately, family names for animals end in −AE, rather than the −EAE used for plants, no doubt helping botanists and mammalogists show up at the right conferences.

Pronouncing scientific names. It's fairly easy to use scientific names when ordering by mail or e-mailing fellow gardeners. But few of us feel comfortable pronouncing scientific names we have never heard pronounced by people schooled in scientific Latin. Besides, some of us have been embarrassed by Latin-literate *cognoscenti* (common name: know-it-alls) who either snicker at our pronunciations or grow bug-eyed. Thank goodness for the considerate cognoscenti who wait a tactful amount of time before working the correct pronunciation into the conversation.

For a few years, it was my privilege to photograph for Petronella Collins, president and curator

PRONOUNCING SCIENTIFIC NAMES

I had hoped to offer you universally sanctioned phonetic pronunciations in each plant profile. But, alas, pronunciations offered by the magazines *Fine Gardening* and *Horticulture* often differ. And both often differ from British pronunciations in the Allen J. Coombes *Dictionary of Plant Names,* further reminding us of George Bernard Shaw's observation that "England and America are two countries divided by a common language."

Perhaps worth a chuckle, here's a sampling of pronunciation differences among the three main sources:

Genus Name	*Fine Gardening*	*Horticulture*	British
(*American Horticultural Society A–Z Encyclopedia of Garden Plants*)	(the Editors)	(Thomas Fischer)	(Allen J. Coombes)
Aconitum (Monkshood)	a-cone-EYE-tum	ack-oh-NYE-tum	a-coe-NEE-tum
Ageratum (Floss Flower)	ah-jer-AY-tum	a-JUR-a-tum	a-GE-ra-tum
Anemone (Windflower)	ah-NEM-oh-nee	an-eh-MONE-ee	a-NEM-o-nee
Dicetra (Dicentra)	die-SEN-trah	dye-SEN-truh	di-KEN-tra
Echinops (Globe Thistle)	EH-kin-ops	eh-KINE-ops	eh-KEE-nops
Erica (Heath, Heather)	None listed	eh-RIKE-a	e-REE-ka
Penstemon (Penstemon)	PEN-sta-men	pen-STEE-mun	pen-STAY-men
Polygonatum (Solomon's Seal)	pol-ig-on-AY-tum	pol-ee-GON-a-tum	po-li-go-NAH-tum
Viola (Violet)	vy-OH-la	VYE-o-la	VEE-o-la

of the world-famous Innisfree Garden in Millbrook, New York. Of British heritage, Mrs. Collins was then in her mid-eighties. On our first walking tour of Innisfree, she recounted scientific plant names with an exactitude, demeanor, and voice uncannily like that of actress Katharine Hepburn. Then, during our first review of the photos I shot, she listened politely as I attempted with occasional success to recall her pronunciations. She didn't laugh, nor did she attempt to correct me.

But at our next meeting, she met me with a gift: *Dictionary of Plant Names* (with pronunciations) by Allen J. Coombes, the renowned British botanist and horticultural author. In fact, the Coombes *Dictionary* was then the only pronunciation guide distributed by the leading US horticultural publisher, Timber Press.

None of us wants to put the *in-COR-ect ak-CENT* on the wrong *syl-AB-le.* In fact, pronunciations are so important that *Fine Gardening* and

Clockwise, from top left: Dicentra eximia (Fringed bleeding heart), native to eastern North America; Viola tricolor 'Helen Mount' (Johnny jump-up); Erica carnea 'Springwood Pink' (Heath) ; Echinops ritro 'Veitch's Blue' (Small globe thistle)

Horticulture magazines both devote multiple pages to phonetic spellings in each issue. In addition, *Fine Gardening* provides phonetic and audio pronunciations on its Web site: www.finegardening.com.

Who's right? And who's wrong? If those three authorities can't agree, why should we be afraid to make our mistakes with enthusiastic fluency?

Incidentally, pronunciations in *Horticulture* magazine were provided through July 2008 by its former editor-in-chief, Thomas Fischer, who is now editorial director of Timber Press. The pronunciations in *Fine Gardening* magazine and on its Web site have been provided by various of its editors over the years. Taking the matter of pronunciation lightly, as perhaps we all should, the *Fine Gardening* Web site admits to options by offering Ira Gershwin's song lyric, "You say tow-MAY-tow, and I say tow-MAH-tow."

As for classical Latin, we can feel reasonably assured that our pronunciations won't give a single additional falling-down fit to an eavesdropping Julius Caesar. Come to think of it, could it have been Caesar's corrections of plant pronunciations during garden walks with Cassius and Brutus that forced them to do him in?

Sedum kamptschaticum, Pycnanthum tenuifolium (American mountain mint), *Perovskia atriplicifolia* (Russian sage). Design: Kathleen Nelson, Gaylordsville, CT

Left: Native *Panicum capillare* (Ornamental witch grass) and *Pennisetum glaucum* 'Jester'. Site credit: Johnnysseed.com
Right: Rudbeckia 'Indian Summer', red and blue salvias. Site credit: Hollandia Nursery & Garden Center, Bethel, CT

Authorities on Deer Resistance

Each plant profile lists the following symbols representing specific authorities and their home regions to guide you to plants that may offer deer resistance in your home garden or landscape.

■ AZ.u = University of Arizona College of Agriculture and Life Sciences Web site

■ CA.s = Carolyn Singer, garden designer and longtime deer-resistance tester in USDA Hardiness Zone 6 (Sierra Nevada foothills). Also author of award-winning multivolume full-color series *Deer in My Garden* (self-published), which includes plant descriptions, cultural requirements, uses, seasonal interest, companions, propagation, maintenance, and more. Pertinent in most regions and hardiness zones. From www.gardenwisdom.com.

■ CA.u = University of California Cooperative Extension

■ CO.u = Colorado State Cooperative Extension

■ CT.n = Kathleen Nelson, Connecticut nursery owner, gardening writer, lecturer, and advocate of native plants

■ GA.a = Allan M. Armitage, author of *Native Plants for North American Gardens* (Timber Press) and professor of horticulture at the University of Georgia, Athens

■ GA.u = University of Georgia Cooperative Extension

■ IL = Morton Arboretum, Illinois (list in *Deer-Proofing* by Rhonda Massingham Hart) (Storey Publishing)

■ MA = William Cullina, author of *Native Trees, Shrubs, and Vines* (Houghton Mifflin Co.)

■ MO = Missouri Department of Conservation

■ MT = Montana State University, R.E. Gough, extension horticulture specialist

■ NC = North Carolina State University Cooperative Extension

■ NY.d = Vincent Drzewucki Jr., USDA Zone 6, author of *Gardening in Deer Country* (Brick Tower Press) and horticulturist and director of the Long Island Nurseryman's Association

■ NY.l = Norbert Lazar, USDA Zone 5, owner of the Phantom Gardener in Rhinebeck, New York (thephantomgardener.com)

■ NY.r = Brad Roeller, USDA Zone 5, manager of grounds and display garden at the Institute of Ecosystems Studies in Millbrook, New York (20+ years testing and observation); www.ecostudies.org/welcome/perennial2.htm

■ NY.rug = Mike Ruggiero, gardening author and retired senior curator, New York Botanical Garden

■ NY.s = Neil Soderstrom, yours truly

■ NY.v = John Van Etten, USDA Zone 5, former grounds superintendent at Mohonk Mountain House in New York

■ OR = George Guthrie, USDA Zone 9, landscape maintenance superintendent at Shore Acres Gardens in Coos Bay, Oregon

■ PA = Larry Weaner Landscape Design in Glenside, Pennsylvania, USDA Zone 6 (www.lweanerdesign.com)

■ TX.a = Forrest Appleton, USDA Zone 8, retired nursery professional (list in *Deer-Proofing* by Rhonda Massingham Hart)

■ TX.m = Janis Merritt, USDA Zone 9, native plant specialist at the San Antonio Botanic Gardens

■ WA = Russell Link, USDA Zone 8, urban wildlife ecologist (list in *Deer-Proofing* by Rhonda Massingham Hart)

■ WV = West Virginia University Extension Service, USDA Zones 4–7

Authorities on Rabbit Resistance

■ AZ.d = Desert Botanic Garden, Phoenix, Arizona

■ AZ.u = University of Arizona College of Agriculture and Life Sciences Web site

■ CO.p = Craig Miller, forester/horticulturist, the town of Parker, Colorado

■ IA.b = *Better Homes and Gardens* magazine

■ LEW = LewisGardens.com

■ MN.g = Gertens Greenhouses, Inver Grove Heights, Minnesota; www.gertens.com

■ WA.f = Washington State Department of Fish and Wildlife

List of 1,000+ Deer-Resistant Plants

Trees, shrubs, and woody plants are most susceptible to browsing when they are small, so it's smart to protect leader branches, especially, by means of surrounds, fencing, or repellents until the plants grow beyond a deer's reach. In winter, starving deer may have no other food options than evergreens and dormant buds.

During other seasons, deer are selective browsers. And many factors may affect their preferences, including a plant's smell, taste, growth stage, and moisture content—as well as the availability of alternatives, distance from dwellings, nutritional needs, and conditioning by Mom.

The following listing of "Deer-Resistant Plants by Category" groups plants alphabetically by type and use: Annuals, Ferns, Grasses (ornamental), Groundcovers, Herbs, Perennials, Shrubs, Trees (large), Trees (small), and Vines. Plants that qualify in multiple categories such as Ground Cover, Herb, and Perennial recur in appropriate lists.

For profiles of select plants, go to the pages cited.

Annuals and Biennials

Ageratum houstonianum (Ageratum, Floss flower), CA.u, GA.a, IL, NY.d, NY.r, WA SEE PAGE 263.

Amaryllis species (Amaryllis), CA.u, GA.a, OR SEE PAGE 264.

Angelonia angustifolia cvs (Angelonia), NY.v

Antirrhinum majus (Snapdragon), GA.a, IL, NY.d, WV. Rabbits: LEW, WA.f SEE PAGE 266.

Argyranthemum frutescens (Marguerite daisy), CA.u Note: A subshrub, usually grown as annual in pots, except in Zones 10–11.

Begonia semperflorens (Wax begonia), AZ.u, GA.a; B. tuberhybrida (Tuberous begonia), CA.u Note: "Tuberous begonia is a tender bulb, grown as an annual in most places, but is sometimes eaten by deer on Long Island,"—Gardening author/ designer Anne Halpin.

Borago officinalis (Borage), IL

Brachyscome = Brachyscome iberidifolia (Swan River daisy), AZ.u

Bracteantha bracteata = Helichrysum (Strawflower, Golden everlasting), AZ.u, CA.u Note: Grown as annual north of Zones 10–11.

Calendula officinalis (Pot marigold), gardening author Anne Halpin. "However, deer pulled netting away to eat our flowers, but not the leaves."—NY.s

Calibrachoa (Million bells), Relatively new in commerce, this resembles a miniature, cascading petunia. In containers, it's proven deer-resistant and noninvasive for gardening author Anne Halpin.

Catharanthus alba rosea (Annual periwinkle), GA.a

Catharanthus roseus (Madagascar periwinkle), TX.a Note: Invasive in FL

Centauria cyanus (Bachelor's button, Cornflower), GA.a, WA *Note:* Invasive in MD, TN. Many other Centaureas (Knapweeds) are highly invasive. SEE PAGE 275.

Clarkia species (Clarkia, Godetta), WA

Cleome hassleriana (Spider flower, Cleome), GA.a, NY.s, NY.v. *Rabbits:* NY.s SEE PAGE 278.

Consolida ajacis = *C. ambigua* (Larkspur), IL, MO, TX.a, WA, WV SEE PAGE 278.

Coreopsis tinctoria (Calliopis), AZ.u, GA.a, GA.u, IL, MT, NC, NY.d, NY.r, WA, WV *Note:* Most in genus are perennials SEE PAGE 279.

Cosmos bipinnatus (Cosmos), WA

Eschscholzia californica (California poppy), AZ.u, GA.u, WA SEE PAGE 285.

Gaillardia pulchella (Gaillardia, Blanket flower), GA.a, GA.u *Note:* Other species are perennials.

Gerbera jamesonii (Gerbera daisy, Transvaal daisy), GA.u

Gomphrenia globosa (Globe amaranth), NY.v

Helianthus annuus (Sunflowers), GA.a, IL, MT, WA *Note:* "Ate our young plants."—NY.s

Heliotropium arborescens (Heliotrope), IL, NY.d *Note:* Shrub grown as annual

Ipomoea alba (Moonflower), IL, MO, NY.d *See next entry.*

Ipomoea purpurea (Morning glory), IL, MO, NY.d *Note:* Invasive AZ, KY, TN, VA. Avoid confusing with *Convolvulus arvensis* (Wild morning glory), a noxious weed. SEE PAGE 292.

Lantana species (Lantana), AZ.u, MO, NC, NY.v, TX.a; *L. camara,* GA.u *Note:* Invasive in southern states. Grown as annual in the North SEE PAGE 296.

Lobelia species (Lobelia), GA.u, IL; *L. erinus,* NY.d *Note:* Grown as annual SEE PAGE 299.

Lobularia maritima (Sweet alyssum), GA.u, IL, MO, WA, WV SEE PAGE 299.

Matthiola species (Stocks), IL

Melampodium (Melampodium)*,* GA.u

TAGETES TENUIFOLIA 'LEMON GEM' (MARIGOLD) at the home of friend and garden author Barbara W. Ellis

Mimulus species (Mimulus), IL; *M. cupreus,* NY.d SEE PAGE 302.

Mirabilis jalapa (Four o'clocks), NY.d

Papaver species (Poppies), AZ.u, CA.s, CA.u, GA.u, IL, NY.l, WA; *P. orientale,* NY.r SEE PAGE 308.

Petunia species (Petunia), IL, NY.d (occasionally browsed), "Deer/rabbits haven't bothered our petunias grown from collected seed."—NY.s

Salvia species grown as annuals, GA.u, IL; *S. splendens* (Scarlet sage), NY.d SEE PAGE 316.

Senecio cineraria (Dusty miller), CA.u, GA.a, GA.u, OR, TX.a *Note:* Shrub grown as annual. *S. jacobea* invasive to Zone 5 SEE PAGE 318.

Tagetes species (Marigolds), GA.u, IL, WV; *T. lemonii* (Tangerine-scented marigold), *T. lucida* (Mexican tarragon, Sweet mace), TX.a; *Tagetes patula* (French marigold), NY.d SEE PAGE 320.

Tithonia rotundifolia (Mexican hat), IL

Tropaeolum species (Nasturtium), MO, NY.d, NY.s, WV *Note:* "Deer avoid ours until September."—NY.s SEE PAGE 322.

Verbascum species (Mulleins), GA.a, IL, NY.l, NY.r *Note: V. blatteria* invasive NJ, OR, WA; "These mostly biennials may be hard to control."—CT.n. SEE PAGE 323.

Verbena × *hybrida* (Verbena), AZ.u, GA.u *Note:* Often grown as annuals SEE PAGE 323.

Zinnia species (Zinnias), GA.a; *Z. elegans,* GA.u, NY.s, TX.a, WA SEE PAGE 326.

Ferns and Allies

Adiantum pedatum (Northern maidenhair fern), PA
SEE PAGE 262.

Athyrium filix-femina 'Lady in Red' (Lady fern), PA
SEE PAGE 269.

Blechnum spicant (Deer fern), *Fine Gardening*
magazine, Northwest

Dennstaedtia punctilola (Hay-scented fern), PA SEE
PAGE 282.

Dryopteris × *australis* (Dixi wood fern), PA

Dryopteris goldiana (Goldies wood fern), PA

Dryopteris marginalis (Marginal wood fern), PA, WV

Matteuccia struthiopteris (Ostrich fern), NY.l, PA, WV
SEE PAGE 301.

ONOCLEA SENSIBILIS
(SENSITIVE FERN, BEAD FERN)
scorches in sun, wilts when
picked, and dies with frost.
Thus, *sensitive!*

Consultant Kathleen Nelson (CT.n) comments, "We have
a great selection of native ferns. I understand that people
like Japanese painted, which does 'seed' a bit and cross
with Lady fern. Other than that, I'd stay with natives. I
especially like *Dryopteris australis* (Dixi wood fern), an
apparently natural hybrid of native ferns. It's a great
plant—handsome, tall, vigorous, clump forming. The
other tall ferns are either slow growing (Goldies), travel
too much (Ostrich), or need water (Cinnamon)."

Onoclea sensibilis (Sensitive fern), NY.l, PA SEE PAGE
305.

Osmunda cinnamomea (Cinnamon fern), GA.u, NC,
NY.l, PA SEE PAGE 306.

Osmunda claytoniana (Interrupted fern), NY.l, PA
SEE PAGE 306.

Osmunda regalis (Royal fern), NC, NY.l, PA SEE
PAGE 306.

Polystichum acrostichoides (Christmas fern), GA.u,
NY.l, PA SEE PAGE 312.

Thelypteris noveboracensis (New York fern), PA
SEE PAGE 321.

Thelypteris palustris (Marsh fern), PA

Grasses and Allies

Andropogon (Beard grass, Bluestem), GA.a

Andropogon gerardii (Big bluestem), PA

Arundo donax (Giant reed) *Note:* Invasive MD, KS, CA to FL, AZ, and in HI, PR

Bambusa species (Bamboo), AZ.u, CA.u *Note:* Not recommended unless roots are confined by formidable barriers, such as buildings or deeply embedded steel plates. "Even the advertised 'clump formers' outgrow their spots quickly. Better to resist these"—CT.n.

Bouteloua gracilis (Blue grama grass), GA.a, PA

Bouteloua species, GA.a; *B. curtipendula* (Sideoats grama), PA

Calamagrostis (Feather reed grass), NY.rug SEE PAGE 272.

Chasmanthium latifolium (Northern sea oats, River oats, Wild oats), GA.a, PA, TX.a SEE PAGE 277.

Cortaderia jubata, selloana (Pampas grass) *Note:* Invasive VA, TN south to GA, LA, TX; also OR, UT

Deschampsia flexuosa (Common hairgrass), PA

Elymus hystrix (Wild rye, Bottlebrush grass), PA *Note:* Invasive *E. repens* (Quackgrass) will find you, no shopping necessary.

Eragrostis spectabilis (Purple lovegrass), PA

Festuca (Fescue grass), NY.rug

Festuca arundinacea (Tall fescue) *Note:* Invasive N.A.

University of Minnesota *Miscanthus* expert Dr. Mary Hockenberry Meyer advises against using the self-seeding grass species *M. sinensis*. Some cultivars don't set viable seed, she says, but all should be watched for signs of self-seeding. A safer bet with existing plants would be to prune all flower stems before seeds ripen. For more information, visit http://horticulture.cfans.umn.edu/miscanthus/recommendations.htm.—NY.s

"Grasses are tricky to recognize as invasive because the invaders look pretty much like all the other grasses." —CT.n

Festuca ovina (Blue fescue), AZ.u, CA.u *Note:* Invasive NY

Juncus effusus (Common rush), PA

Miscanthus sinensis (Eulalia grass, Chinese silver grass) *Note:* Considered deer resistant, but invasive in many states. Although CT.n says some late-blooming cultivars may not always have time to set seed in northern climates, the entire genus worries her. "We planted the variegated *M. s.* 'Cabaret'. It's not yet sent up flower heads, but we'll remove them as soon as they appear."—NY.s

Muhlenbergia species (Muhley), TX.a

Ophiopogon japonicus (Mondo grass), NY.r

Panicum species, NY.rug; *P. amarum* 'Dewey Blue' (Atlantic Coastal panic grass), *P. virgatum* 'North Wind', 'Heavy Metal', and 'Shenandoah' (Switchgrass), PA *Note:* CT.n highly recommends native *P. virgatum* and cultivars, also because some stand well through winter snows. But *P. repens* (Torpedo grass) is invasive FL, GA, TX SEE PAGE 307.

Pennisetum species, NY.rug; *P. setaceum* (Purple fountain grass), TX.a *Note:* Invasive FL to CA. Other Pennisetums appear on invasive lists. SEE PAGE 308.

Phalarus arundinacaea (Ribbon grass, Reed canary grass) *Note:* "Though widely grown, highly invasive."—Gardening author Anne Halpin

Schizachyrium scoparium 'The Blues' and 'Blaze' (Little bluestem), PA *Note:* "Highly recommended native."–CT.n

Sorghastrum nutans 'Sioux Blue' and 'Indian Steel' (Indian grass), PA *Note:* "Highly recommended native."–CT.n

Sporobolus heterolepis (Northern dropseed), PA *Note:* "Highly recommended native."—CT.n

Stipa species (Feather grass), AZ.u

Groundcovers
(also Rock Garden Plants)

Achillea species, WV; *A. ageratifolia* (Greek yarrow), *A.* × 'King Edward' (Creeping yarrow), *A. clavennae* = *A. argentea* (Silvery yarrow), *A. millefolium* (Common yarrow), CA.s *Note:* Mowed as groundcover. *A. tomentosa*, *A. tomentosa* 'Maynard's Gold' and 'Moonlight' (Woolly yarrow), CA.s SEE PAGE 261.

Aegopodium podagraria (Bishop's weed, Goutweed) *Note:* Too invasive to recommend; spreads by rhizomes and seeds

Ajuga reptans (Carpet bugleweed), *A.* 'Caitlin's Giant' and 'Burgundy Lace' = 'Tricolor', CA.s *Note:* Invasive in MD, TN, VA SEE PAGE 263.

Ajuga species (Bugleweed), AZ.u, CA.s, GA.u, IL, MT, NY.d, NY.r See previous entry.

Alchemilla mollis (Lady's mantle), CA.s, NY.d SEE PAGE 263.

Alyssum montanum (Mountain alyssum), 'Berggold' = 'Mountain Gold', CA.s SEE PAGE 264.

Antennaria dioica 'Rosea' (Pussy-toes, Cat's ears), CA.s

Arabis caucasica and *A. c.* 'Variegata' (Wall rockcress), *A. procurrens* and *A. p.* 'Variegata' = *Arabis Ferdinandi-Coburgi* 'Variegata' (Rockcress), CA.s

Arctostaphylos uva-ursi (Bearberry, Kinnikinick, Creeping manzanita), NY.d, WA, WV; *A. u-u* 'Radiant' and 'Point Reyes' *Note:* CA.s says blacktails have always eaten her *A.* 'Emerald Carpet'. SEE PAGE 266.

CONVALLARIA MAJALIS (LILY-OF-THE-VALLEY) is a highly toxic alien. Cats and dogs are frequent victims.

Artemisia species, *A. alba* = *canescens* 'Sea Foam', CA.s; *A.* 'Powis Castle' (Wormwood), *A. schmidtiana* (Angel's hair), CA.s *Note:* Many species in this genus are invasive in the garden and in the wild, including but not limited to *A. absynthium* (Wormwood), OR, ND, WA; *A. stelleriana* (Oldwoman), NJ; *A. vulgaris* (Mugwort, Wormwood), MD, NJ, NY, PA, TN, VA

Asarum species (Wild ginger), NY.r; *A. canadense* (Canadian wild ginger), CA.s, IL; *A. caudatum* (Western wild ginger), CA.s *Note:* "Deer have eaten native ginger when raised on my nursery tables, but never touched them on the ground." —CT.n SEE PAGE 268.

Aubrieta × *cultorum* = *A. deltoidea*, CA.s

Aubrieta gracilis, CA.s

Campanula poscharskyana (Serbian bellflower), CA.s

Cerastium tomentosum (Snow-in-summer) *Note:* Although considered deer resistant, this is invasive, like other *Cerastiums* (Chickweeds).

Ceratostigma plumbaginoides (Dwarf plumbago), AZ.u, CA.s *Chamaemelum nobile* (Lawn chamomile, Roman c., Russian c.), CA.s *Note:* Not the same chamomile used for tea SEE PAGE 276.

Convallaria majalis (Lily of the valley), CA.s, IL, NY.r, MO, MT, NY.d, NY.v, WV *Note:* Invasive WI. SEE PAGE 279.

Coreopsis verticillata 'Moonbeam' (Threadleaf tickseed), CA.s

Cotoneaster apiculatus 'Tom Thumb' (Cranberry cotoneaster)

Cymbalaria muralis (Kenilworth ivy), CA.s *Note:* "Although this alien doesn't appear on invasive lists I've unearthed, it self-seeds on our patio and rock wall. As to deer resistance, small leaves and low or hanging growth may make this inconvenient for deer to browse."—NY.s

Delosperma nubigenum 'Lesotho' (Ice plant), CA.s

Dianthus species (Pinks) *Note:* Deer tend to avoid these with low, tight growth habit: *D. erinaceus, gratianopolitanus, microlepis, petraeus* subsp. *noeanus, simulans, squarrosus.*—CA.s.

"I find that deer really go for large mouth-height flowers, especially those that almost glow in the dark. For that reason, one might want to avoid plants that produce just a single flower or clump of flowers once in the season. For example, chomped irises are gone for the season, whereas a deer's pruning of *Rudbeckia* 'Goldsturm' stimulates more flower growth. Even though deer may not usually eat ornamental alliums, they often chomp a flower head or two of my *Allium* 'Purple Sensation'. Planting large quantities might help—I doubt deer would eat them all."—*Kathleen Nelson (CT.n)*

Epimedium species (Barrenworts), CA.u, IL, MT, NY.r, WV; *E. grandiflorum* (Bishop's hat, Longspur barrenwort), NY.d SEE PAGE 284.

Erigeron karvinskianus (Santa Barbara daisy), CA.s SEE PAGE 285.

Euphorbia amygdaloides var. *robbiae* (Mrs. Robb's bonnet, Wood spurge) *Note:* Invasive SEE EUPHORBIA CAUTIONS ON PAGE 246.

Euphorbia cyparissias (Cypress spurge) *Note:* A serious weed

Fragaria species (Wild strawberry), IL

Galium odoratum (Sweet woodruff), CA.s, IL

Gaultheria procumbens (Wintergreen), NY.r, WA

Geranium macrorrhizum (Scented geranium) *Note:* "A very handy ground cover. Dense, weedproof, long season of good foliage. I've sometimes had decent plants to show people in December. I hope it doesn't turn out to be invasive."—CT.n

Geranium sanguineum and *G.* × *cantabrigiense* (Geranium species), CA.s

Gypsophila repens (Creeping baby's breath), CA.s *Note: G. paniculata* (Baby's breath) invasive in CO, MI, OR, WA, WI

Helianthemum species (Rock rose, Sun rose), WA

Herniaria glabra (Rupturewort), CA.s

Iris unguicularis (Winter iris), CA.s *Note:* Blooms late winter, early spring on short stems

Juniperus species (Creeping junipers), IL; *J. horizontalis*, MT

Lamium galeobdolon = *Lamiastrum g.* (Yellow archangel, Dead nettle) SEE NEXT ENTRY.

Lamium maculatum, CA.s ('Album' and other cultivars) *Note:* Species itself invasive in MD SEE PAGE 295.

Lavandula angustifolia nana 'Alba' (Dwarf white English lavender), CA.s

Lysimachia nummularia (Creeping Jenny, Moneywort) *Note:* Invasive in many states

Mahonia repens (Creeping holly grape), CA.s *Note:* Native West Coast SEE PAGE 301.

Maianthemum canadense (Canada mayflower), PA

Myosotis species (Forget-me-nots), *M. scorpioides* (Water forget-me-not), *M. sylvatica* (Woodland forget-me-not) *Note:* Both seed heavily and are highly invasive.

THYMUS VULGARIS 'ARGENTEUS' (THYME), like most thymes, contains volatile oils that discourage browsers.

Nepeta × *faassenii* cultivars: 'Blue Wonder', 'Select Blue', 'Snowflake,' and 'Walker's Low'; *N. reichenbachiana* (Catmint), CA.s *Note: N. catara* invasive in MD SEE PAGE 304.

Oenothera fruticosa subsp. *glauca* (Sundrops, Evening primrose), CA.s *Note:* Native eastern US SEE PAGE 305.

Origanum species (Oregano), AZ.u, CA.s, IL, MO, NC, NY.l, NY.r, WA; *O.* 'Betty Rollins', *O. laevigatum, O. libanoticum, O. pulchellum* (Pretty oregano), *O. sipyleum* (Showy pink oregano), *O. vulgare* (Common oregano), *O. vulgare* 'Aureum' (Gold common oregano),

O. vulgare nanum (Dwarf common oregano), CA.s SEE PAGE 306.

Pachysandra procumbens (Pachysandra), AZ.u, GA.a, IL, NY.r, WV; *P. terminalis,* MT, NY.d *Note: P. terminalis* invasive VA, DC SEE PAGE 307.

Penstemon hirsutus (native E. NA) and *P. pinifolius* (native southern US), CA.s SEE PAGE 309.

Phlox subulata (Creeping phlox, Moss pink), AZ.u, CA.s, PA SEE PAGE 309.

Potentilla canadensis (Creeping cinquefoil), CA.s SEE PAGE 312.

Pratia pedunculata (Blue star creeper), CA.s

Prunella vulgaris (Selfheal), CA.s *Note:* On *P. grandiflora,* CA.s says, "Deer may browse these larger flowers but rarely eat the foliage."

Pulmonaria species (Lungworts), IL, MT, NY.l, NY.r, WA SEE PAGE 313.

Rosmarinus officinalis 'Lockwood de Forest' (Trailing rosemary), *R.* 'Prostratus', CA.s SEE PAGE 315.

Rubus pentalobus = *R. calycinoides* (Creeping raspberry), CA.s

Salvia officinalis (Common sage) 'Nana', 'Berggarten', 'Purpurascens', CA.s SEE PAGE 316.

Sanguinaria canadensis (Bloodroot), NY.r, NY.s

Santolina chamaecyparissus and cultivars (Lavender cotton), AZ.u, CA.s, CA.u, MO, NC, NY.d, NY.r, OR, TX.a, WA, WV *Note:* Also used as shrub SEE PAGE 317.

Sarcococca hookerana humilis (Sweet box, Christmas box, Creeping sweet vanilla plant), CA.s

Scleranthus uniflorus, CA.s

Sedum species (Sedum), IL *Note:* Low growers such as *S. kamptshaticum* may be a less convenient browse.

Solidago 'Golden Baby' (Dwarf goldenrod), CA.s SEE ALSO PERENNIALS ON PAGE 250.

Spiraea japonica 'Alpina' (Alpine spirea), CA.s *Note:* Leaves likely generate cyanide upon digestion. SEE PAGE 319.

"Deer may avoid many groundcovers because they are low growing and not at convenient mouth height." —CT.n

Stachys byzantina (Lamb's ears), AZ.u, CA.s, CA.u, IL, NC, NY.l, NY.r, NY.s *Note:* "*S.* 'Silver Carpet' was bred not to bloom but sometimes does. Also, it's annoyingly rot-prone in CT. The new version is *S. b.* 'Big Ears' = 'Helene von Stein', less rot-prone and seldom blooms."—CT.n SEE PAGE 319.

Tanacetum densum subsp. *amani* (Dwarf tansy), CA.s

Teucrium × *chamaedrys* 'Compactum' (Prostrate germander, Trailing germander), *T. cossonii* subsp. *majoricum* (*T. cussonii majoricum, T. majoricum*), *T. polium,* CA.s SEE PAGE 320.

Thymus species (Thyme), AZ.u, CA.s, IL, NY.d, NY.r, NY.rug, TX.a, WA, WV; *T. cherlerioides* (Silver needle thyme), CA.s SEE PAGE 321.

Tropaeolum species (Nasturtiums), MO, NY.d, WV *Note:* "Deer ate ours in September."—NY.s SEE PAGE 322.

Verbena rigida (Vervain), CA.s SEE PAGE 323.

Veronica peduncularis 'Georgia Blue', *Veronica* 'Waterperry', *V. repens* (Speedwell) *Note:* CA.s says good between stepping-stones because slow spreading

Vinca species, AZ.u; *V. major* (Greater periwinkle), MT, NY.l; *V. minor* (Creeping myrtle, Lesser periwinkle), GA.u, IL, NY.d, NY.r *Note:* Species invasive unless contained. Cultivar *V.* 'La Grave' = 'Bowles' is reportedly less aggressive. SEE PAGE 324.

Viola species (Violets), IL; *V. labradorica* (Labrador violet), *V. odorata* (Sweet violet), CA.s SEE PAGE 325.

Waldsteinia fragarioides (Barren strawberry), IL

Zauschneria californica (California fuchsia, Hummingbird trumpet), AZ.u, CA.s, OR, WA; *Z.* subsp. *cana* 'Etteri' is mat-forming to 6 in. tall. SEE PAGE 326.

Herbs

Allium species (Onions), CA.u, GA.u, WV;
A. schoenoprasum (Chives), NY.d, WA; *A.tuberosum*
(Garlic chives*)*, WA SEE PAGE 264.

Anethum graveolens (Dill), IL, WV

Angelica archangelica (Angelica), NY.d

ALLIUM SCHOENOPRASUM
(CHIVES), like most alliums,
contains sulfur compounds
that repel mammals and
insects.

Artemisia absinthium (Artemisia), CA.u, IL, NY.l,
TX.a *Note:* Invasive OR, ND, WA SEE PAGE 267.

Artemisia dracunculus (Tarragon), NY.rug SEE PAGE
267.

Foeniculum vulgare (Fennel), IL, MO, NY.r *Note:* "If
growing as culinary herb, remove flower heads to
avoid invasive reseeding. Too invasive to grow as
flowering ornamental."—NY.s SEE PAGE 287.

Hyssopus officinalis (Hyssop), IL, NY.d, WA

Lavandula species (Lavenders), AZ.u, CA.u, IL, MO,
MT, NY.d; *L. angustifolia, L. × intermedia,* and
L. dentata, CA.s; *L. officinalis,* NY.l, NY.r, WA,
WV; *L. stoechas* (French lavender), NC, WV SEE
PAGE 296.

Marrubium vulgare (Horehound), NY.r

Matricaria species (Chamomile), IL

Melissa officinalis (Lemon balm), IL, MO, NY.d,
NY.r, NY.s *Note:* Can be invasive SEE PAGE 301.

Mentha species (Mints), CA.u, IL, MO, NY.l, NY.r,
NY.rug, WA; *M. × piperita* (Peppermint), NY.d;
M. pulegium (Pennyroyal), NY.d SEE PAGE 302.

Nepeta species (Catmints), AZ.u, CA.u, MO, NC,
NY.r, WA; *N. × faassenii* cultivars, CA.s, IL;
N. cataria, GA.u, NY.d; *N. reichenbachiana,* CA.s
Note: N. cataria invasive in MD SEE PAGE 304.

Ocimum basilicum (Basil), IL, NY.d, NY.rug *Note:*
Others say deer do eat basil.

Origanum species (Oregano, Marjoram), AZ.u, CA.s,
IL, MO, NC, NY.l, NY.r, WA SEE PAGE 306.

Petroselinum species (Parsley), GA.u, IL

Pimpinella anisum (Anise), NY.d

Rosmarinus officinalis (Rosemary*)* species, AZ.u,
CA.u, IL, MO, NC, NY.l, NY.r, OR, TX.a, WA
SEE PAGE 315.

Ruta graveolens (Rue), IL, NY.d, WA

Salvia species (Sage), AZ.u, CA.u, GA.a (most
species), IL, MO, NY.r, WV SEE PAGE 316.

Satureja montana (Savory), CA.u, IL, NY.d SEE PAGE
317.

Symphytum species (Comfrey), IL, NY.r *Note:*
Invasive and difficult to kill

Tanacetum coccineum (Pyrethrum), *T. parthenium*
(Feverfew), IL *Note:* Avoid invasive *T. vulgare*
(Tansy). SEE PAGE 320.

Thymus species (Thyme), AZ.u, CA.s, IL, NY.d,
NY.r, NY.rug, TX.a, WA, WV SEE PAGE 321.

ORIGANUM × MAJORICUM
(HARDY MARJORAM,
OREGANO) is grown
primarily for its fragrant,
flavorful leaves.

Perennials (including Bulbs; excluding Ferns and Grasses)

Acaena species (New Zealand burs), NY.r

Acanthus species (Bear's breeches), NY.r

Achillea species (Yarrow), AZ.u, CA.s, GA.u, IL, MT, NY.d, NY.r, NY.s, TX.a, WA. *Rabbits: AZ.* u, CO.p, IA.b, LEW, MN.g, WA.f SEE PAGE 261.

Aconitum species (Monkshoods), CA.u, GA.a, IL, MO, NY.r, WV; *A. carmichaelii,* NY.d. *Rabbits:* LEW, WA.f SEE PAGE 261.

Actaea racemosa = Cimicifuga racemosa (Black snakeroot, Bugbane), CA.u, GA.a, NY.l, PA, WV SEE PAGE 261.

Adenophora species (Ladybells), *A. confus,* CA.s; *A. lilifolia* , NY.r

Agastache species (Giant hyssop), NY.r

Agave species (Agave), AZ.u, CA.u SEE PAGE 262.

Ajuga reptans (Bugleweed), AZ.u, CA.s, GA.u, IL, MT, NY.d, NY.r; *A.* 'Caitlin's Giant' and 'Burgundy Lace' = 'Tricolor', CA.s *Note:* *A. reptans* invasive MD, TN, VA SEE PAGE 263.

Alcea rosea (Hollyhock), NY.r

Alchemilla mollis (Lady's mantle), CA.s, NY.d SEE PAGE 263.

Allium species (Onions), CA.u (some), GA.u, WV; *A. cernuum* (Nodding pink onion), PA; *A. giganteum* (Ornamental onion), IL, NY.d, NY.r, NY.v; *A. schoenoprasum* (Chives), NY.d, WA; *A. tuberosum* (Garlic chives), TX.a, WA *Note: A. vineale* (Field garlic, Wild garlic) invasive in CT, MD, NC, NJ, PA, TN, VA, WV

Aloe species (Aloe), CA.u

Alyssum species (Madworts), MO, NY.r; *A. montanum* (Mountain alyssum) 'Berggold' = 'Mountain Gold', CA.s SEE PAGE 264.

Amaryllis belladonna (Amaryllis), AZ.u, CA.u, GA.u, OR SEE PAGE 264.

Amsonia species (Blue star, Willow blue star), *A. cilata* (Blue star), CA.s; *A. hubrichtii* (Amsonia, Arkansas blue star flower), GA.a, PA; *A. tabernaemontana* (Willow blue star), GA.a, NY.r, PA SEE PAGE 265.

Anaphalis margaritacea (Pearly everlasting), PA

Anemone species (Anemone), IL, NY.r; *A. canadensis* (Canada anemone), PA; *A.* × *hybrida,* WV SEE PAGE 265.

Anemonella thalictroides (Rue anemone), WV

Angelica species (Archangel), NY.r

Anisacanthus wrightii (Hummingbird bush), TX.a *Note:* A subshrub

Anthemis tinctoria (Golden marguerite), CA.s, NY.r

Aquilegia species (Columbines), AZ.u, GA.a, IL, MT, NY.r, WV; *A. canadensis,* PA. *Rabbits:* NY.s SEE PAGE 266.

Arabis species (Rockcress), IL, NY.d, NY.r, WA, WV

Arenaria montana (Sandwort), NY.r

Argyranthemum frutescens (Marguerite daisy), CA.u *Note:* A subshrub, usually grown as annual, except in Zones 10–11

Arisaema species (Jack-in-the-pulpit), NY.l, NY.r; *A. triphyllum,* PA SEE PAGE 267.

Armeria maritima (Sea thrift), AZ.u, NY.r, WA

Artemisia species (Wormwoods, Mugworts), AZ.u, CA.s, CA.u, GA.u, IL, NY.l, NY.r, WV; *A. absinthium,* CA.u, IL, NY.l, TX.a; *A. ludoviciana,* TX.a; *A.* 'Powis Castle', CA.s; *A. schmidtiana,* NY.d; *A. alba* (= *A. canscens*) 'Sea Foam', CA.s *Note:* Invasives include *A. absinthium* (Wormwood), OR, ND, WA; *A. stelleriana* (Oldwoman), NJ; *A. vulgaris* (Mugwort, Wormwood), MD, NJ, NY, PA, TN, VA SEE PAGE 267.

Arum italicum (Arum, Lords and ladies), CA.u, NY.r SEE PAGE 267.

Aruncus species (Goatsbeard), NY.r

Asarum species (Gingers), NY.r; *A. canadense* (Wild ginger), CA.s, IL; *A. caudatum* (Wild ginger), CA.s SEE PAGE 268.

Asclepias species (Milkweeds), NC, NY.r; *A. incarnata* 'Ice Ballet', PA; *A. tuberosa* (Butterfly weed), GA.a, IL, NY.d; *A. tuberosa* 'Hello Yellow', PA SEE PAGE 268.

Asparagus officinales (Asparagus) 'Martha Washington', NY.s *Note:* Invasive AZ, SD, TN SEE PAGE 268.

Aster species (Asters), AZ.u, GA.a, NY.d; *A. novi-belgi, A. oblongifolius* (Fragrant aster) 'October Skies', 'Raydons Favorite', PA SEE PAGE 269.

Astilbe species (Astilbe), AZ.u, IL, MT, NY.d, NY.r, NY.s SEE PAGE 269.

Astrantia major (Masterwort), NY.r

Atennaria species (Pussy-toes), NY.r

Aubreta × cultorum = A. deltoidea (Purple rockcress), NY.d, WV

Aurinia saxatilis (Basket of gold), NY.d, NY.v, WV

Baptisia species (False indigo, Wild indigo), GA.u, NC, NY.l, NY.r; *B. alba* (White false indigo), *B. australis,* CA.s, GA.a; *B. australis* 'Purple Smoke', PA; *B. sphaerocarpa* (Yellow false indigo), 'Screaming Yellow Zonker', PA SEE PAGE 270.

Begonia species (Begonia), AZ.u. GA.a; *B. tuberhybrida* (Tuberous begonia), CA.u *Note:* "Tuberous begonia is a tender bulb, grown as an annual in most places, but is sometimes eaten by deer on Long Island," —Garden author Anne Halpin.

Belamcanda chinesis (Blackberry lily, Leopard lily), CA.s

Bergenia (Bergenia), IL, NY.l, NY.r, WV SEE PAGE 271.

Berlandiera (Green eyes), GA.a *Note:* Native US/Mexico

Blephilia ciliata (Downy wood mint), PA

Boltonia asteroides (Boltonia), GA.a, GA.u, NY.r SEE PAGE 271.

White flowers of deer-resistant BOLTONIA ASTEROIDS (BOLTONIA) backdrop *Bouvaridia ternifolia*, which none of our sources consider deer resistant.

Bracteantha bracteata = Helichrysum (Strawflower, Golden everlasting), AZ.u, CA.u *Note:* Grown as annual north of Zones 10–11

Brodiaea species (Brodiaea), CA.u *Note:* Native

Brunnera macrophylla (Siberian bugloss), NY.r

Buphthalmum = Telekia species SEE PAGE 251.

Caltha palustris (Marsh marigold), IL, PA SEE PAGE 273.

Camassia species (Quamash), NY.r SEE PAGE 273.

Campanula species (Bellflower), AZ.u, CA.s; *C. carpatica, C. rotundifolia,* NY.r; *C. posharskyana,* CA.s SEE PAGE 274.

Carex species (Sedges), CA.u; *C. appalachica* (Appalachian sedge), *C. flaccosperma* (Wood sedge), *C. grayi* (Common bur sedge), *C. laxiculmis* (Spreading sedge 'Bunny Blue'), *C. pensylvanica* (Pennsylvania sedge), *C. platyphylla* (Blue satin sedge), PA *Note: C. kobomugi* (Asiatic sand sedge, Jap. sedge) is invasive in MD, NJ, VA SEE PAGE 274.

Catanache caerulea (Cupid's dart), CA.s

Catharanthus rosea (Madagascar periwinkle), CA.u

Centaurea species (Knapweeds), AZ.u, NY.r; *C. montana* (Mountain bluet), CA.s *Note:* Many Centaureas are invasive, including the annual, *C. cyanus* (Bachelor's button). SEE PAGE 275.

Centranthus ruber (Jupiter's beard), NY.r

Cerastium tomentosum (Snow-in-summer) *Note:* Although considered deer resistant, this is invasive, like other *Cerastiums* (Chickweeds).

Ceratostigma plumbaginoides (Leadwort, Plumbago), AZ.u, CA.s, NC, NY.r, WV SEE PAGE 276.

Ceratostigma wilmottianum (Chinese plumbago), CA.s SEE PAGE 276.

Chelone species (Turtleheads), GA.a, NY.r; *C. glabra*, PA; *C. lyonii* 'Hot Lips', PA SEE PAGE 277.

Chionodoxa luciliae (Glory-of-the-snow), IL

Chrysanthemum Note: See *Leucanthemum* PAGE 297.

Chrysogonum virginianum 'Allen Bush' (Goldenstar flower), PA

Chrysopsis mariana (Maryland goldenaster), CA.s, PA

Cimicifuga racemosa = *Actaea r.* (Black snakeroot, Black cohosh), CA.u, GA.a, NY.l, PA, WV SEE PAGE 261.

Clivia miniata (Clivia), CA.u

Colchicum autumnale (Autumn crocus, Meadow saffron), IL, WV; *C. speciosum*, WV

Convallaria majalis (Lily of the valley), CA.s, IL, MO, MT, NY.d, NY.r, NY.v, *WV Note:* Spreads aggressively unless confined. SEE PAGE 279.

Coreopsis species (Tickseed), AZ.u, GA.a, GA.u, IL, NC, NY.d, NY.r, MT, WA, WV; *C. grandiflora*, CA.s; *C. lanceolata*, CA.s; *C. auriculata* (Mouse-eared tickseed) 'Nana', *C. verticillata* (Whorled tickseed) 'Zagreb', PA; *C. verticillata* 'Moonbeam', CA.s. *Rabbits:* AZ.u, CO.p, WA.f SEE PAGE 279.

Corydalis lutea (Corydalis, Gold bleeding heart), NY.r SEE PAGE 280.

Crinum americanum (Southern swamp lily), CA.u, GA.u

Crocosmia × *crocosmiiflora* (Montbretia), CA.s, CA.u SEE PAGE 281.

Crocus species (Crocus), AZ.u, WA; *C. tomassinianus* (Dalmatian crocus), NY.r

Cyclamen species (Cyclamen), CA.u; *C. hederifolium*, WV

Cymbalaria muralis (Kenilworth ivy, Coliseum ivy), CA.u *Note:* Invasive in some states

Cyperus species (Cyperus), CA.u

Dahlia species (Dahlias), AZ.u, GA.u *Note:* Not generally deer resistant in North, where grown as annual or tender bulb that must be dug and stored in winter

Datura species (Angel's trumpet), TX.a

Delosperma species (Ice plant), *D. cooperi,* NY.r, OR

Delphinium (Delphinium), *D. elatum,* GA.a, NY.d; native *D. exaltatum,* PA SEE PAGE 282.

Dianella tasmanica (Flax lily), OR

Dianthus species (Pinks), GA.u, IL, MO, MT, NY.r; *D. barbatus* (Sweet William), IL

Dicentra species (Bleeding hearts), AZ.u, CA.s, CA.u, GA.a, MO, MT, NY.l, NY.r, WA; native *D. exima* (Fringed bleeding heart), PA; *D. spectabilis,* WV SEE PAGE 283.

Dictamnus albus (Gas plant), NY.r

*Dierama pulcherrimum (*Fairy's wand, Angel's fishing wand), CA.s

Digitalis species (Foxgloves), CA.s, CA.u, IL, MT, NY.r, WV; *D. ferruginea* (Rusty foxglove), *D. lutea* (Yellow foxglove), *Digitalis* × *mertonensis* (Strawberry foxglove), CA.s. *Rabbits:* CO.p, IA.b, LEW SEE PAGE 283.

Dodecatheon meadia (Shooting star), NY.r, PA

Doronicum species (Leopard's bane), NY.r

DICENTRA SPECTABILIS (BLEEDING HEART) forms delicately handsome mounds spurned by deer and cottontails.

Echinacea species (Coneflowers), GA.a, GA.u; *E. purpurea* (Purple coneflower), CA.s, IL, MT, NY.d, NY.r, WA, WV *Note:* Native MI, VA, LA, GA, Zones 3–9. SEE PAGE 283.

Echinops species (Globe thistle), NY.l, NY.r, WA; *E. exaltatus,* CA.s SEE PAGE 284.

Epimedium species (Barrenworts), CA.u, IL, MT, NY.r, WV; *E. grandiflorum* (Bishop's hat, Longspur barrenwort), NY.d SEE PAGE 284.

Equisetum species (Horsetail), GA.a

Eranthis hyemalis (Winter aconite), IL, MO, NY.r SEE PAGE 284.

Eremurus species (Foxtail lily), NY.r

Erigeron species (Fleabane), AZ.u, NY.r, WA; *E. × hybridus,* IL; *E. karvinkianus* (Santa Barbara daisy), CA.s SEE PAGE 285.

Eriogonum species (Wild buckwheat), WA

Eryngium species (Sea hollies), GA.a, NY.r, WA

Erysimum asperum (Siberian wallflower), NY.r

Erysimum species (Wallflowers), WA

Erythronium americanum (Trout lily), NY.r

Eupatorium species (Joe Pye weeds and more), GA.a, MT, NY.l, NY.r; *E. coelestinum* (Mistflower), PA, TX.a; *E. rugosum* (Snakeroot), IL SEE PAGE 286.

Euphorbia species (Spurges), AZ.u, CA.s, CA.u, NY.l, NY.r, WV; *E. × martini* (Spurge), *E. amygdaloides* var. *robbiae* (Mrs. Robb's bonnet), CA.s *Note:* Avoid invasive aliens *E. cyparissias* (Cypress spurge) and *E. esula* (Leafy spurge). SEE PAGE 286.

"I was once in love with Euphorbias and tried many species and cultivars. Alas, I'm still trying to get rid of one species that has seeded all over my greenhouse and is hiding under other plants in my garden. I've gradually removed the more commonly grown Euphorbias from my clients' gardens too because they seed all over everything. They include *E. myrsinites* and *E. dulcis chameleon.* Luckily, I've never planted any of the ground runners in anybody's garden."—CT.n

Filipendula species (Queen of the prairie), CA.u, IL, NY.l, NY.r; *F. ulmaria* (Meadowsweet), NY.d

Foeniculum vulgare (Fennel), NY.r *Note:* Invasive as ornamental if allowed to reseed SEE PAGE 287.

Fritillaria species (Fritillaries), WA, WV; *F. imperialis* (Crown imperial), IL, MO, NY.d, NY.l, NY.r SEE PAGE 288.

Gaillardia species (Blanket flower), GA.a; *G. aristata,* NY.r, WA; *G. × grandiflora,* AZ.u, CA.s, NY.r *Note: G. puchella* is an annual. SEE PAGE 288.

Galanthus nivalis (Snowdrop), IL, NY.d, NY.r

Galium odoratum (Sweet woodruff), CA.s, CA.u, NY.r, WV *Note:* Invading CT's woodlands; other species invasive in MD, NJ

Gaultheria procumbens (Wintergreen), NY.r, WA, WV SEE PAGE 288.

Gaura lindheimeri (White gaura), NY.r

Gentiana species (Gentians), IL

Geranium (Cranesbill), AZ.u, GA.a, IL, MO, MT, NY.d; *G. × cantabrigiense,* CA.s; *G. macrorrhizum* (Scented geranium), CT.n; *G. maculatum* (Wild geranium) 'Espresso' and 'Alba', PA; *G. sanguineum* (Bloody cransebill) 'Cedric Morris', CA.s *Note:* CA.s says blacktails eat some geraniums. SEE PAGE 289.

Gerbera jamesonii (Gerbera daisy, Transvaal daisy), GA.u *Note:* Usually grown as annual north of Zone 11

Geum species (Avens), IL, NY.r

Glaucium flavum (Horned poppy), NY.r

Gloriosa superba (Gloriosa lily), GA.u, WV

Gonilimon tataricum (German statice), NY.r

Gunnera tinctoria (Gunnera) CA.u, OR

Gypsophila (Baby's breath), *G. repens,* CA.s, NY.r, WA; *G. paniculata,* NY.r, WA *Note: G. paniculata* invasive in CO, MI, OR, WA, WI SEE PAGE 290.

Helenium autumnale (Sneezeweed), CA.s, IL, NY.d, NY.r *Note:* Native Canada and eastern US SEE PAGE 290.

"*Geranium macrorrhizum* (Scented geranium) is a good deer-resistant groundcover, almost evergreen in CT. Fragrant, dense, weed resistant. *G.* × *cantabrigiense* is a hybrid of this, slightly less fragrant, shorter, but also a good plant. *G. sanguineum* is, too."—NY.s

Helianthus species (Perennial sunflower), GA.u, NY.r; *H. angustifolius* (Swamp sunflower), *H. maximilianii* (Maximillian sunflower), CA.s

Helichrysum bracteatum (Strawflower) = *Bracteantha bracteata*, AZ.u, CA.u *Note:* Grown as annual north of Zones 10–11

Helleborus species (Hellebores), GA.u, IL, MO, MT, NY.r, WA; *H. argutifolius* (Corsican hellebore), *H. foetidus* (Stinking hellebore), CA.s; *H. orientalis* (Lenten rose), CA.s, GA.u SEE PAGE 290.

Hemerocallis species (Daylilies) *Note:* Although mentioned as deer resistant on some lists, daylilies are usually favored whitetail food along with hostas.

Hepatica species (Hepatica), NY.r

Hesperis matronalis (Dame's rocket), NY.r, WV *Note:* Invasive alien in many states

Heuchera species (Coralbells, Coral flower), NY.r

Hibiscus mosheutos (Rose mallow), GA.a, IL, NY.d, NY.r, PA, TX.a SEE PAGE 291.

Hippeastrum × *johnsonii* (Amaryllis), TX.a SEE PAGE 291.

Hosta (Hosta), CA.u *Note:* "Deer love hostas in every garden I know in the East," says Anne Halpin. "Planting them is like putting out the salad bar."

Hyacinthus orientalis (Hyacinth), WV

Hydrastis canadensis (Goldenseal, Orange root), NY.r

Hypericum species (St. John's wort), CA.u, TX.a; *H. androsaemum, H.* × *moserianum,* CA.s; *H. calycinum* (Aaron's beard), NY.r; *H. ascyron* (Great St. John's wort), PA SEE PAGE 291.

Iberis sempervirens (Perennial, or Evergreen, Candytuft), AZ.u, IL, MT, NY.d, NY.r, TX.a *Note:* "Mixed resistance ratings suggest that low growth may simply make this less convenient to browse."—NY.s SEE PAGE 292.

Impatiens species (Impatiens), AZ.u; *I. walleriana,* CA.u

Inula species (Inula), NY.r

Ipheion uniflorum (Ipheion), NY.r

Iris species (Bearded irises), AZ.u, CA.u, GA.u, IL, MO, MT, TX.a, WA, plus *I. cristata* 'Alba' and 'Powder Blue Giant', *I. cristata, I. versicolor,* PA; *I. germanica, I. sibirica, I. ensata, I. tectorum.* NY.r; *I. sibirica, I. unguicularis, I. spuria,* CA.s *Note:* "Avoid invasive *I. pseudocorus* (Yellow flag), a serious pest of wetlands and waterways."—CT.r SEE PAGE 293.

Ixia species (Corn lily), WA

Jeffersonia diphylla (Twinleaf), PA

Kirengeshoma palmata (Yellow waxbell), NY.r

Knautia macedonia (Field scabiosa), NY.r

Kniphofia uvaria and hybrids (Red-hot poker), AZ.u, CA.u, NC, NY.r, OR, WA SEE PAGE 295.

Lamium = Lamiastrum species (Deadnettle), AZ.u, CA.u, IL, MO, MT, NY.r, WV; *L. galeobdolon* (Yellow archangel) *Note:* Invasive OR; *L. maculatum* (Spotted deadnettle), CA.s, NY.d *Note:* Invasive in MD SEE PAGE 295.

Lantana species (Lantana), AZ.u, MO, NC, NY.v, TX.a; *L. camara,* GA.u *Note:* Invasive in southern states; grown as annual in North SEE PAGE 296.

Lavandula (Lavender) SEE PAGE 296.

Leucanthemum × *superbum = Chrysanthemum maximum* (Shasta daisy), CA.u, GA.u, IL, NY.l, NY.r, OR, TX.a, WA; 'Silver Princess', 'Snow Lady', 'Little Miss Muffet', CA.s *Note: L. vulgare* (Ox-eye daisy) invasive in many states SEE PAGE 297.

Leucojum aestivum (Summer snowflake), CA.u, GA.u, MO, NC, NY.r

Liatris species (Blazing stars), CA.s, GA.a, NY.r; *L. spicata* (Spike grayfeather), MT, NY.l, PA, WA; *L.s.* 'Kobold', CA.s

Ligularia species (Golden groundsell), NY.r

Lilium lancifolium (Tiger lily), NY.l

Oenothera speciosa 'Siskiyou' (Evening primrose) offers welcome relief from the strident yellows of most evening primroses.

Limonium latifolium (Statice), GA.u, NY.r

Linaria species (Toadflax), IL, NY.r; *L. purpurea*, CA. s; *L. vulgaris* (Butter and eggs), WV *Note: L. vulgaris* is invasive in many states. SEE PAGE 297.

Linum perenne (Perennial blue flax), CA.s, NY.r

Liriope species (Lilyturf), CA.s, CA.u, IL; *L. spicata*, NY.r SEE PAGE 298.

Lobelia species (Lobelias), GA.a, GA.u, MO, NY.r; *L. cardinalis* (Cardinal flower), PA, WA; *L. laxiflora*, GA.u, IL, NY.d; *L. siphilitica* (Blue cardinal flower), GA.a, PA SEE PAGE 299.

Lupinus species (Lupines), AZ.u, NY.l, NY.r, PA; *L. perennis* (Wild lupine), WA SEE PAGE 300.

Lychnis coronaria (Rose campion, Crown-Pink), AZ.u, CA.s, CA.u, IL, MT, NY.d, NY.r, WV *Note:* CA.s says deer have eaten her *L. chalcedonica* (Maltese cross). SEE PAGE 300.

Lysimachia species (Loosestrifes) *Note:* Including *L. nummularia* (Creeping Jenny), all in this genus seem to be invasive in most places. Avoid confusing the common name with that of also invasive Purple Loosestrife (*Lythrum salicaria*), a major thug in wetlands.

Maianthemum canadense (Canada mayflower), PA

Malva alcea (Hollyhock mallow), NY.r

Marrubium vulgare (Horehound), NY.r *Note:* Invasive AZ, CA, NV, TX, UT

Meehania cordata (Creeping mint), PA

Melampodium leucanthum (Blackfoot daisy), AZ.u

Melissa officinalis (Lemon balm), IL, MO, NY.d, NY.r, NY.s *Note:* Invasive OR SEE PAGE 301.

Mentha species (Mints), CA.u, IL, MO, NY.l, NY.r, NY.rug, WA; *M. × piperita* (Peppermint), NY.d; *M. pulegium* (Pennyroyal), NY.d *Note: M. pulegium* invasive in CA and OR; *M. spicata* (Spearmint) invasive in CA, TN SEE PAGE 302.

Mertensia species (Mertensia), GA.a; *M. pulmonarioides* = *virginica* (Virginia bluebells), GA. a, NY.r, PA SEE PAGE 302.

Mirabilis jalapa (Four o'clocks), CA.u, IL

Mitchella repens (Partidgeberry), NC, NY.l, NY.r, PA SEE PAGE 303.

Monarda species (Bee balms), AZ.u, GA.a, GA.u, IL, MO, NC, NY.r. PA, WA SEE PAGE 303.

Muscari species (Grape hyacinth), IL, MO, NC (occasionally browsed), NY.d *Note:* Invasive MD, TN, WV SEE PAGE 303.

Myosotis scorpioides (Forget-me-not), AZ.u, CA.s, CA.u, GA.u, IL, MO, NY.l *Note:* Invasive CT, NJ, OR, WI; *M. sylvatica* (Woodland forget-me-not) invasive WI

Myrrhis odorata (Sweet cicely), NY.r SEE PAGE 304.

Narcissus species (Daffodils), AZ.u, CA.u, GA.u, IL, MO, MT, NC, NY.d, NY.l, NY.r, WV SEE PAGE 304.

Nepeta species (Catmints), AZ.u, CA.u, MO, NC, NY.r, WA; *N. × faassenii* cultivars, CA.s, IL; *N. cataria*, GA.u, NY.d; *N. reichenbachiana*, CA.s *Note: N. cataria* invasive MD SEE PAGE 304.

Nicotiana alata (Flowering tobacco), GA.u, WV

Oenothera species (Evening primroses), GA.a, NY.l, NY.r, NY.s; *O. fruticosa* (Sundrops) 'Fireworks', PA; *O. f.* subsp. *glauca*, CA.s SEE PAGE 305.

Opuntia compressa = *O. humifusa* (Prickly pear cactus), NC, NY.r, PA, TX.a SEE PAGE 306.

Origanum vulgare (Oregano), AZ.u, CA.s, IL, MO, NC, NY.l, NY.r, WA SEE PAGE 306.

Pachysandra species (Pachysandras), AZ.u, GA.a, IL, MO, MT, NY.d; *P. terminalis* (Japanese spurge), NY.r, WV *Note: P. terminalis* invasive in DC, VA SEE PAGE 307.

Paeonia (Peonies), CA.s, CA.u, IL, MO, NY.d, NY.r, NY.rug SEE PAGE 307.

Papaver species (Oriental poppy), AZ.u, CA.s, CA.u, GA.u, IL, NY.l, NY.r, WA; *P. orientale* (Oriental poppy), CA.s, GA.u, IL, MO, NY.l, WA, WV SEE PAGE 308.

Parthenium integrifolium (Wild quinine), PA

Pavonia lasiopetala (Texas swamp mallow), TX.a

Pelargonium species (Scented geranium), WV

Penstemon species (Beardtongue), AZ.u, CA.s, GA.a; *P. digitalis* 'Huskers Red', PA; *P. hirsutus*, PA; *P. pinifolius*, CA.s; *P. campanulatus* 'Evelyn' and 'Garnet', CA.s SEE PAGE 309.

Pentas species (Pentas), GA.u

Perovskia atriplicifolia (Russian sage), CA.s, IL, NC, NY.d, NY.r, NY.v, WA, WV SEE PAGE 309.

Philodendron selloum (Philodendron), TX.a *Note:* This Z14–15 tropical is grown mainly as a houseplant.

Phlomis species (Sticky Jerusalem sage), NY.r; *P. russeliana* (Jerusalem sage), CA.s; *P. fruticosa*, CA.u, TX.a

Phlox divaricata (Blue phlox, Woodland phlox), IL, NY.r; *P. glabberima* (Smooth phlox), NY.s

Phlox subulata (Creeping phlox, Moss phlox), AZ.u, CA.s, NY.r; *P. s.* 'Moss Pink', 'Millstream Daphne', 'Emerald Cushon', PA; *P. stolonifera* (Creeping phlox), NY.r SEE PAGE 309.

Phormium tenax (New Zealand flax), CA.u

Physostegia virginiana (Obedient plant), NY.r, PA SEE PAGE 310.

Platycodon grandiflorus (Balloon flower), NY.l, NY.r

Plectranthus species (Plectranthus), GA.u

Plumbago auriculata (Blue plumbago), CA.u, TX.a

Podophyllum peltatum (Mayapple), NY.r, NY.s SEE PAGE 311.

Polemonium caeruleum (Jacob's ladder), GA.a, IL, NY.d, NY.l SEE PAGE 311.

Poliomintha maderensis (Mexican oregano), TX.a

Polygonatum species (Solomon's seal), WA

Potentilla species (Cinquefoils), IL, NY.l, NY.r; *P. canadensis*, CA.s; *P. fruticosa* (Shrubby cinquefoil), AZ.u, CA.s, NY.r, NY.rug, PA, WA; *P. tridentata* (Three-tooth cinquefoil), PA *Note: P. recta* (Sulfur cinquefoil) invasive CO, ID, MD, MT, OR, WA, WY SEE PAGE 312.

Primula species (Primroses), NY.l, NY.r *Note: P. japonica* invasive

Pulmonaria species (Lungworts), IL, MT, NY.l, NY.r, WA SEE PAGE 313.

Pycnanthemum species (Mountain mints), CT.n, NY.r; *P. muticum* (Big leaf mountain mint), *P. tenuifolium* (Slender mountain mint), PA SEE PAGE 313.

Ranunculus species (Buttercups), NY.l, NY.r, WV SEE PAGE 313.

Ratibida columnifera (Prairie coneflower, Mexican hat), GA.a, NY.r, TX.a

Rheum species (Rhubarbs), NY.l, NY.r, NY.s, WV SEE PAGE 314.

Rhexia mariana (Meadow beauty), PA

Rodgersia species (Rodgerflower), NY.r

Romneya coulteri (Matilija poppy, Tree poppy, Fried egg plant), CA.s, CA.u SEE PAGE 315.

Rudbeckia species (Coneflowers, Black-eyed Susans), GA.a, MT, NY.d; *R. fulgida* 'Goldsturm', CA.s; *R. hirta*, AZ.u, IL; *R. maxima*, NY.r, WA, WV *Note:* CA.s says blacktail deer eat her *R. nitida* and *R. triloba* (Brown-eyed Susan) but not her 'Goldsturm'. SEE PAGE 316.

PAPAVER ORIENTALE (ORIENTAL POPPY) and other poppies contain alkaloids that disturb the digestive tract and nervous system.

Ruellia humilis (Wild petunia), PA

Ruta graveolens (Rue), CA.s, NY.r

Saccharum arundinaceum (Hardy sugarcane), *Fine Gardening*

Salvia lyrata 'Purple Knockout' (Lyre-leaved sage), PA SEE ALSO NEXT ENTRY.

Salvia species (Salvias), AZ.u, CA.u, GA.a (most species), IL, MO, NY.r, WV *Note: S. aethiopsis* (Mediterranean sage) invasive AZ, OR, UT, WA; *S. minima* (Water spangles) invasive GA, TX; *S. molesta* (Giant salvinia) invasive CA, GA, III, TX. SEE PAGE 316.

Sanguinaria canadensis (Bloodroot), NY.r, NY.s

Santolina chamaecyparissus (Lavender cotton), AZ.u, CA.s, CA.u, MO, NC, NY.d, NY.r, OR, TX.a, WA, WV; *S. rosmarinifolia,* TX.a *Note:* Also used as shrub SEE PAGE 317.

Saponaria species (Soapwort), NY.l, NY.r; *S. officinales* (Bouncing bet), TX.a

Saxifraga species (Saxifrages), AZ,u

Scabiosa species (Scabiosas), AZ.u, CA.u; *S. caucasica* (Pincushion flower), NY.r

Scilla species (Scillas, Squill), AZ.u, CA.u, NC; *S. peruviana* (Cuban lily, Peruvian jacinth), IL, NY.d; *S. siberica* (Siberian squill), MO, NY.l, NY.r, WV SEE PAGE 317.

Scutellaria species (Skullcaps), *S. incana* (Skullcap), NY.r; *S. ovata* (Heart-leaf skullcap), *S. serrata* (Showy skullcap), PA

Sedum species (Stonecrops), GA.a, IL; *S. kamtschaticum, S. spurium* (Stonecrop), NY.r; *S. spectabile* (Showy stonecrop, Everlasting stonecrop), WA; *S. ternatum* 'Larinem Park' (Wild stonecrop), PA *Note:* Avoid invasive *S. acre* (Gold moss sedum); still, deer seem to favor taller Sedums over low growers.

Sempervivum tectorum (Hens-and-chickens), IL, NY.d, NY.r

Senecio species (Groundseal), CA.u, GA.a, GA.u, NY.r; *S. aureus* (Golden groundsell), PA; *S. cineraria* (Dusty miller), CA.u, GA.a, GA.u, MO, NC, OR, TX.a *Note:* Shrub often grown as annual SEE PAGE 318.

Senna = Cassia species, *S. hebecarpa* (Wild senna), PA; *S. marilandica Note:* Both natives, the latter may spread less aggressively.

Sidalcea malviflora (Miniature hollyhock), NY.r

Silene species (Campions, Catchflies), GA.a; *S. regia* (Royal catchfly), PA; *S. virginica* (Fire pink), PA

Silphium species (Rosinweed), NY.r, WA *Note:* "Native to OK–GA–Ont., but *S. perfoliatum* seeds so profusely, it can be invasive,"—CT.n.

Sisyrinchium angustifolium 'Grass Lucerne' (Stout blue-eyed), PA

Sisyrinchiumgraminoides = S. angustifolium (Blue-eyed grass), NY.r, PA

Smilacina species (False Solomon's seal, Starflower), GA.a

Solidago species (Goldenrods), CA.s, GA.a, GA.u, IL, MT, NY.d; *S.* 'Golden Baby', CA.s; *S.* hybrids, NY.l, NY.r; *S. rugosa* 'Fireworks' and *S. sphacelata* 'Golden Fleece', PA *Note:* "Although some species of goldenrod spread too quickly to use in gardens, others are well behaved."—CT.n. SEE PAGE 318.

Spigelia species (Pink root, Worm grass), GA.a; *S. marylandica* (Indian Pink), PA

Stachys byzantina (Lamb's ears), AZ.u, CA.s, CA.u, IL, NC, NY.l, NY.r, NY.s; *S. coccinea* (Texas betony), *S. palustris* (Marsh hedgenettle), PA *Note:* "*S.* 'Silver Carpet' was bred not to bloom, but sometimes does. Also, it's annoyingly rot-prone in CT. The new version is *S. b.* 'Big Ears' = 'Helene von Stein', that's less rot-prone and seldom blooms."—CT.n SEE PAGE 319.

SENECIO CINERARIA 'SILVER QUEEN' (DUSTY MILLER) and *ZINNIA ELEGANS* 'PROFUSION ORANGE' (ZINNIA) make attractive low borders.

Strelitzia reginae (Bird of paradise), CA.u *Note:* A Zones 13–15 greenhouse plant throughout most of North America

Stylophorum diphyllum (Celandine poppy, Wood poppy), GA.a, NY.r, PA *Note:* Native, not to be confused with invasive aliens *Chelidonium majus* (Celandine) or *Ranunculus ficaria* (Lesser celandine)

Symphytum species (Comfrey), IL, NY.r *Note:* "Invasive and difficult to get rid of."—CT.n

Tanacetum species (Feverfew), IL; *T. coccineum* (Pyrethrum), *T. densum* ssp. *amani* (Dwarf tansy), *T. parthenium* and *T. p.* 'Aureum' (Golden feverfew), CA.s *Note: T. vulgare* (Tansy) highly invasive SEE PAGE 320.

Telekia salicifolium = *Buphthalmum* (Willowleaf oxeye), CA.s; *T. speciosa* (Heartleaf oxeye), NY.r

Teucrium species (Germanders), *T. canadense* (American germander), NY.r; *T. chamaedrys* (Wall germander), IL, NY.r; *T. chamaedrys* 'Compactum', *T. cossonii* ssp. *majoricum, T. polium,* CA.s; *T. fruticans* (Bush germander), CA.u, TX.a SEE PAGE 320.

Thalictrum species (Meadow rue), IL, NY.r

Thymus species (Thyme), AZ.u, CA.s, IL, NY.d, NY.r, NY.rug, TX.a, WA, WV; *T. cherlerioides,* CA.s SEE PAGE 321.

Tiarella species (Foamflower), CT.n, GA.a, NY.r; *T. cordifolia,* NY.d, WV *Note:* "A great native, all the rage in breeding circles."—CT.n SEE PAGE 321.

Tradescantia virginiana (Spiderwort), NY.r

Trillium species (Wake-robin), CA.u, NY.r, WA *Note:* "Deer ate one I'd protected under a tripod overnight before I could return to photograph the next morning."—NY.s

Trollius europaeus (Common European globeflower), NY.r

Tulbaghia violacea (Society garlic), GA.u, NC, OR SEE PAGE 322.

Valeriana species (Valerian), NY.r; *V. officinales,* IL *Note:* Invasive CT, IL, WI

Verbascum species (Mulleins), GA.a, IL, NY.l, NY.r *Note:* "*V. blatteria* is invasive in NJ, OR, WA; others, mostly biennials, may be hard to control."—CT.n. SEE PAGE 323.

Verbena species (Vervain), AZ.u, CA.s, CA.u, GA.u, NY.r; *V. bonariensis, V. rigida* (Vervain), CA.s *Note: V. bonariensis* invasive GA, OR SEE PAGE 323.

Vernonia noveboracensis (Ironweed), NY.r SEE PAGE 323.

Veronica species (Speedwells), AZ.u, IL; *V. austriaca,* NY.r; *V. latifolia* (Speedwell), NY.l; *V. officinales,* MT ; *V. spicata* (Spike speedwell), NY.r *Note:* Invasive speedwells: *V. anagallis-aquatica* (Water speedwell), CA, UT; *V. arvesis,* HI, SD; *V. beccabunga* (European speedwell), CT, NJ; *V. biloba* (Two-lobed speedwell), WY; *V. hederifolia* (Ivy-leaved speedwell), MD, NJ, TN, VA, WV; *V. serpyllifolia* (Thymeleaf speedwell), MD, TN

Veronicastrum virginicum (Culver's root), NY.r

Vinca species (Vincas), AZ.u; *V. major* (Greater periwinkle), MT, NY.l; *V. minor* (Creeping myrtle, Lesser periwinkle), GA.u, IL, NY.d, NY.r *Note:* The species are invasive unless contained by barriers or mowing. Cultivars such as *V.* 'La Grave' (= 'Bowles') may be less aggressive. SEE PAGE 324.

Viola species (Violets), GA.a, IL; *V. odorata* (English violet), AZ.u, CA.s; *V. labradorica* (Labrador violet), CA.s, NY.l, NY.r, PA SEE PAGE 325.

Yucca species (Yuccas), MT, NY.d, NY.l, NY.r; *Y. filamentosa,* TX.a, WV SEE PAGE 326.

Zantedeschia species (Calla lily), OR (Zones 8 or 9 max.)

Zauschneria californica (California fuchsia), AZ.u, CA.s, OR, WA SEE PAGE 326.

Zizia aurea (Golden Alexander), PA

Shrubs

Abelia × *grandiflora* (Glossy abelia) AR, AZ.u, CA.s, OR SEE PAGE 260.

Aesculus parviflora (Bottlebrush buckeye), GA.u, PA, WV SEE PAGE 262.

Amorpha candens (Lead plant), MT

Arctostaphylos species (Manzanita, Bearberry), AZ.u, WA, WV; *A. uva-ursi,* PA; *A.* 'Massachusetts' SEE PAGE 266.

Asimina triloba (Pawpaw), WV

Aucuba japonica (Japanese laurel), NY.d *Note:* Female, 'Gold Dust'; male, 'Mr. Goldstrike'

Bambusa species (Bamboo), AZ.u, CA.u *Note:* Actually a grass, *B. vulgaris* invasive DC; not recommended unless roots are confined by barriers: "Even the advertised 'clump formers' outgrow their spots quickly."—CT.n

Berberis (Barberry), AZ.u, CA.u, GA.u, MT, NY.l, NY.r, WV; *B.* × *gladwynensis* 'William Penn', NY.r; *B. darwinii,* OR *Note: B. japonica* (Japanese barberry) terribly invasive SEE PAGE 270.

Buddleia davidii (Butterfly bush), AZ.u, GA.u, NY.d, NY *Note:* Invasives: *B. davidii* (Orange-eye butterfly bush), CA, KY, NC, NJ, OR, PA, WA, WV; *B. lindleyana* (Lindley's butterfly bush), FL, GA, NC, TX SEE PAGE 272.

Buxus species (Boxwoods), AZ.u, CA.u, IL, MT, NY.r, TX.a, WV; *B. sempervirons,* NY.l SEE PAGE 272.

Calliandra species (Powderpuff tree), AZ.u

Callicarpa americana (American beautyberry), PA

Calycanthus species (Allspices, Sweetshrubs), *C. floridus* (Carolina allspice)*,* GA.u, IL, NY.d; *C. floridas* 'Athens' and 'Michael Lindsey', PA; *C. occidentalis* (California allspice)*,* CA.u SEE PAGE 273.

Caranga arborecens (Siberian pea shrub), MT *Note:* Invasive WI

Caryopteris × *clandonensis* (Blue mist), CA.s, WV; *C. incana* (Bluebeard), CA.s

Ceanothus species (California lilacs)*, C. americanus* (New Jersey tea), PA; *C. gloriosus* (Point Reyes creeper), CA.u (not deer resistant for CA.s); *C. velutinus* (Tobacco brush), MT SEE PAGE 275.

Celastrus scandens (American bittersweet), WV *Note:* "Avoid confusing this with *C. orbiculatus* (Oriental bittersweet, Staff vine), which is destroying native forests."—CT.n

Cephalanthus occidentalis (Common buttonbush), PA

Cephalotaxus species (Plum yew), GA.u; *C. harringtonia* var. *koreana,* WV

Chaenomeles species (Flowering quince), AZ.u

Choisya species (Mexican orange blossom), WA; *C. ternata* (Mexican orange), CA.s, OR

Chrysothamnus species (Rabbitbush), WA

Clethra alnifolia (Summersweet), NY.r

Comptonia peregina (Sweetfern), PA

Cornus stolonifera = *C. sericea* (Red osier dogwood), MT, NY.d, NY.s, WA, WV SEE PAGE 279.

Corokia cotoneaster (Wire netting bush), CA.u

Corylus species (Hazel), WA; *C. cornuta* var. *californica* (Beaked filbert), CA.u

Cotinus species (Smoke bush), IL

Cotoneaster species (Cotoneaster), AZ.u, GA.u, WA; *C. apiculatus* (Cranberry cotoneaster) 'Tom Thumb', CA.s; *C. buxifolius,* CA.s, CA.u; *C. glaucophyllus* (Gray cotoneaster), TX.a; *C. integrifolius* (Rockspray cotoneaster), CA.s *Note:* Invasive in CA: *C. fanchetii* (Orange cotoneaster), *C. lacteus* (Milk-flower cotoneaster), *C. pannosus* (Silver-leaf cotoneaster) SEE PAGE 280.

Cytisus scoparius (Scotch broom), CA.u *Note:* Invasive in many states

Dalea species (Indigo bush), AZ.u

Daphne species (Daphne), AZ.u; *D. odora* (Winter daphne), CA.s, GA.u; *Daphne* × *burkwoodii,* NY.d, NY.v SEE PAGE 281.

Dasylirion species (Sotol), TX.a

Diervilla lonicera (Dwarf bush honeysuckle) 'Copper', PA

Native *Cornus florida* (Flowering dogwood) can be grown either as a shrub or a tree.

Dirca palustris (Leatherwood), PA

Dodonaea viscosa (Hop bush), CA.u

Elaeagnus angustifolia (Russian olive, Oleaster) *Note:* Far too invasive

Elaeagnus commutatus (Silverberry), WA

Elaeagnus × ebbingei, CA.s

Elaeagnus pungens (Thorny eleagnus) *Note:* Invasive TN, VA

Empetrum nigrum (Black crowberry), OR

Encelia farinosa (Brittlebush), AZ.u

Enkianthus campanulatus (Red-vein enkianthus), NY.d

Ericarmeria laricifolia (Turpentine bush), AZ.u

Erica species (Heaths, Heathers), CA.u, NY.l, OR, WA; *E. × darleyensis* (Heath), CA.s SEE PAGE 285.

Eriogonum species (Buckwheat), AZ.u

Euonymus japonica 'Microphyllus' (Box-leaf euonymus), TX.a

Feijoa sellowiana (Pineapple guava), TX.a

Forsythia (Forsythia), GA.u, IL, MO; *F. × intermedia*, NY.d SEE PAGE 287.

Gardenia species (Gardenias), GA.u

Gaultheria species, *G. procumbens* (Wintergreen), NY.r, WA, WV; *G. shallon* (Salal), CA.u, OR, WA SEE PAGE 288.

Hamamelis species (Witch hazel), IL, NY.d (occasionally eaten)

Hamelia patens (Firebush), TX.a

Heliotropium arborescens (Heliotrope), IL, NY.d *Note:* Shrub grown as annual

Hibiscus syriacus (Rose of Sharon), NY.d, WV *Note:* Officially invasive KY, PA, VA but also elsewhere SEE PAGE 291.

Hypericum species (St. John's worts), CA.u, TX.a; *H. androsaemum* (Purple St. John's wort), CA.s; *H. frondosum* (Golden St. John's wort) 'Sunburst', *H. kalmianum* (Kalms St. John's wort) 'Ames', PA; *H. × moserianum*, CA.s SEE PAGE 291.

Ilex species (Hollies), AZ.u, CA.u (except thornless), *I. opaca* (American holly), MO, NY.l; *I. verticillata* (Winterberry holly) 'Winter Red', 'Red Sprite', 'Winter Gold', PA; *I. vomitoria* (Yaupon holly), TX.a, TX.m; *Ilex vomitoria* 'Nana' or 'Stokes' (Dwarf Yaupon holly), CA.s SEE PAGE 292.

Jasminum mesnyi (Primrose jasmine), TX.a

Jasminum nudiflorum (Winter jasmine), WA

Jasminum species (Jasmine), CA.u

Juniperus species (Junipers), AZ.u, CA.u, GA, IL, MT, WA; *J. chinensis*, MO, NC, NY.d; *J. pfitzeriana* (Pfitzer juniper), NY.r SEE PAGE 293.

Justicia californica (Chuparosa), AZ.u

Justicia spicigera (Mexican honeysuckle), TX.a

Kalmia latifolia (Mountain laurel), NY.d, TX.m, WA SEE PAGE 294.

Kerria japonica (Kerria, Japanese rose), AZ, GA, IL, NY.d SEE PAGE 294.

Kolkwitzia amabilis (Beautybush), MO, MT, NY.d, NY.v *Note:* Invasive, says CT.n SEE PAGE 295.

Lagerstroemia indica (Crape myrtle), GA.u

Lantana species (Lantanas, Shrub verbenas), AZ.u, MO, NC, NY.v, TX.a; *L. camara*, GA.u *Note:* *L. camara* invasive in FL; grown as annual in the North SEE PAGE 296.

Lavandula species (Lavender), AZ.u, CA.u, IL, MO, MT, NY.d; *L. angustifolia*, *L. × intermedia*, *L. dentata*, CA.s; *L. officinalis*, NY.l, NY.r, WA, WV; *L. stoechas* (French lavender), NC, WV SEE PAGE 296.

Leucophyllum species (Leucophyllum, Texas sage), AZ.u, TX.a

Leucothoe fontanesiana (Drooping leucothoe), MO, NY.l, NY.d

Leucothoe species (Leucothoe), WV; *L. axillaris* (Coast leucothoe), PA; *L. fontanesiana* (Dog hobble), PA; *L. racemosa* (Fetterbush), PA

Ligustrum vulgare (European privet), WV

Lindera benzoin (Spice bush), CT.n, IL, PA SEE PAGE 298.

Lonicera species (Honeysuckles), *L. nitida* (Boxleaf honeysuckle) 'Maigruen' and 'Baggesen's Gold', CA.s; *L. sempervirens* (native Trumpet honeysuckle), GA.u, MO, MT, NC, PA *Note:* Avoid confusion with terribly invasive *L. japonica* (Japanese honeysuckles), still sold in nurseries. SEE PAGE 299.

Mahonia species, AZ.u, IL; *M. aquifolium* (Oregon grape holly), AZ.u, IL, MO, NY.d, OR, WA; *M. japonica* (Leatherleaf mahonia), GA.u; *M. repens* (Creeping mahonia), CA.s, CO.u; *M. trifoliata* (Agarita), TX.a SEE PAGE 301.

Melianthus major (Honey bush), CA.u

Michella figo = *fuscata* (Banana shrub), GA.u

Microbiota decussata (Siberian arborvitae), NY.rug

Mitchella repens (Partridgeberry), NC, NY.l, NY.r, PA SEE PAGE 303.

Myrica species, *M. californica* (Wax myrtle, native coastal western US), OR, WA; *M. cerifera* (native southeastern US), *M. pensylvanica* (Northern bayberry), NY.r, PA

Nandina species (Heavenly bamboos), AZ.u, CA.u, GA.u; *N. filamentosa*, CA.s

Nerium oleander (Oleander, Rose bay), CA.u, GA.u, NY.r, NY.rug, TX.a, WV *Note:* Invasive CA, FL, GA, NV, TX SEE PAGE 305.

Pachystima myrsinites (Oregon boxwood), WA

Perovskia atriplicifolia and cvs. (Russian sage), CA.s, IL, NC, NY.d, NY.r, NY.v, WA, WV

Petasites palmatus (Western coltsfoot), OR

Phlomis fruticosa (Jerusalem sage), CA.u, TX.a

Pieris species, *P. floribunda* (Mountain andromeda, Fetterbush), NY.r; *P. japonica* (Andromeda), MO, NY.d, NY.l SEE PAGE 310.

Pinus mugo (Mugo pine), NY.d, WA

Podocarpus species (Podocarps), CA.u; *P. macrophyllus* (Bhuddist pine, Southern yew), TX.a

Potentilla species (Cinquefoils), NY.l; *P. fruticosa* (Shrubby cinquefoil), AZ.u, NY.r, NY.rug, PA, WA; *P. tridentata* (Three tooth cinquefoil), PA *Note: P. recta* (Sulfur cinquefoil) invasive CO, ID, MD, MT, OR, WA, WY SEE PAGE 312.

Prunus species (Cherries, Cherry laurels, Plums), *P. americana* (American plum), PA; *P. caroliniana* (Carolina cherry laurel), CA.u, GA.u, MT, NC; *P. fruticosa* (Steppe cherry), *P. laurocerasus* (English laurel), OR; *P. maritima* (Beach plum), PA; *P. virginiana* (Choke cherry), PA, WA SEE PAGE 312.

Punica granatum (Pomegranate), TX.a

Pyracantha species (Firethorn), AZ.u, GA.u; *P. coccinia*, NY.d

Retama monosperma = *Genista* (Broom), CA.u

Deer-Resistant Roses

Deer browse new growth on virtually all roses. The safest bet is fencing or a regimen of repellent sprays. To confirm that advice, I phoned Dr. John Dickman, longtime "Q&A" columnist for *American Rose* magazine, published by the American Rose Society. He agreed, saying he knows of no roses that deer dislike and knows of no scientific studies on the subject. "Considering the prickles on some roses," he said, "I'm amazed deer can eat them with their tender noses." Dr. Dickman has heard that low-growing roses receive less damage. And this is consistent with reports that other low, mat-forming plants, such as phloxes, receive less damage than taller cousins, mainly because they grow at a less convenient browsing height. This may be especially true near homes, where deer tend to be nervous and prefer clear lines of sight. Incidentally, an admirer of Dr. Dickman's column, who is also a breeder of miniflora roses, has named a mauve mini *Rosa* 'Dr. John Dickman'.

Rhamnus species, *R. californica* (Coffeeberry), WA *Note:* Avoid invasive *R. cathartica* (Buckthorn), MT, WV. "You can't imagine how much time and money is being spent trying to rid the alien buckthorn."—CT.n

Rhododendron species (Rhododendrons), CA.s, CA.u, NY.h, NY.s *Note:* Large-leaved evergreens, not the Azalea group. SEE PAGE 314.

Rhus species (Sumacs), AZ.u, WA; *R. aromatica* (Fragrant sumac), *R.* 'Gro-Low', PA; *R. virens* (Evergreen sumac), TX.a; *R. ovata*, CA.u; *R. tilobata*, MT; *Rhus typhina* 'Laciniata' (Staghorn sumac), PA

Ribes species (Currants and Gooseberries), AZ.u, CA.u; *R. aureum = odoratum* (Buffalo currant, Clove currant), WA; *R. sanguineum* (Red-flowered currant), WA; *R. viburnifolium, Fine Gardening* magazine SEE PAGE 314.

Ricinus communus (Castor bean), CA.u

Rosa species. See "Deer-Resistant Roses" on opposite page.

Rosmarinus species (Rosemary), AZ.u, CA.u, GA.u, IL, MO, NC, NY.l, NY.r, OR, TX.a, WA; *R.* 'Arp', 'Prostratus', 'Lockwood de Forest', CA.s SEE PAGE 315.

Salvia species (Sages), AZ.u, CA.u, GA.a (most species), IL, MO, NY.r, WV. SEE PAGE 316.

Sambucus species (Elderberry), WA, WV; *S. canadensis* (American elder) 'Laciniata', PA; *S. racemosa* subspecies *pubens,* PA SEE PAGE 316.

Santolina species, *S. chamaecyparissus* (Lavender cotton), AZ.u, CA.s, CA.u, MO, NC, NY.d, NY.r, OR, TX.a, WA, WV; *S. rosmarinifolia = S. virens* (Green santolina), OR, TX.a, WA SEE PAGE 317.

Sarcococca confusa and *S. ruscifolia* (sweet vanilla plant), CA.s; *S. humilis* (Dwarf sweet Christmas box), WV

Senecio cineraria (Dusty miller), CA.u, GA.a, GA.u, MO, NC, OR, TX.a SEE PAGE 318.

Seriphidium tridentatum = Artemisia (Sagebrush), WA

Simmondsia chinensis (Jojoba), AZ.u

Skimmia japonica (Japanese skimmia), NY.d, OR SEE PAGE 318.

Sophora secundiflora (Texas mountain laurel), TX.a

Spiraea species (Spirea), IL, NY.v, WA; *S. japonica* 'Alpina', CA.s; *S. prunifolia* (Bridalwreath), MT; *S. × bumalda* cultivars, *S. japonica, S. nipponica* cultivars, *S. × vanhouttei, S. dolchica, S. prunifolia,* NY.r; *S. cantoniensis* (Reeve's spirea), TX.a SEE PAGE 319.

Symphoricarpos species (Snowberry), IL, NY.d, PA; *S. orbiculatus* (Coralberry), WA

Syringa species (Lilacs), AZ.u, IL; *S. × persica* (Persian lilac), NY.d, WA; *S. reticulata* (Japanese tree lilac), IL SEE PAGE 319.

Tecoma stans (Espanza), TX.a

Teucrium species (Germander), *T. canadense* (American germander), NY.r; *T. chamaedrys* (Wall germander), IL, NY.r; *T. chamaedrys* 'Compactum', *T. cossonii* ssp. *majoricum, T. polium,* CA.s; *T. fruticans* (Bush germander), CA.u, TX.a SEE PAGE 320.

Vaccinium species (Blueberries, Cranberries), *V. corymosum* (Highbush blueberry), NY.s; *V. macrocarpon* 'Pilgrim' (Cranberry), PA; *V. ovatum* (Box blueberry, California huckleberry), WA SEE PAGE 322.

Viburnum species (Viburnums), AZ.u, GA.u, NY.r; *V. davidii,* CA.s; *V. opulus,* MT; *V. acerifolium* (Mapleleaf), *V. × burkwoodii* and cvs., *V. lantanoides* (Hobblebush), *V. plicatum* var. *tomentosum* (Doublefile viburnum), *V. × sargentii* and cvs, NY.r *Note:* Beware of these alien species invasives: *V. dilatatum* (Linden viburnum), *V. lantana* (Wayfaring-tree), *V. opulus* (Guelder rose, Cranberry bush viburnum), European cranberrybush, *V. plicatum, V. sieboldii* (Siebold viburnum). "Double-file *V. p. forma tomentosmum* 'Marliessii' is seeding all over my property. I'll find it painful to cut down the mama plant, though I wish I hadn't planted it. Yet I doubt that plant is going anywhere soon, invasive or not. I confess, I'm subject to the usual gardener temptations and should have a clause in my will with a list of plants to be destroyed when I'm gone."—CT.n SEE PAGE 324.

Vitex species (Chaste tree), NY.v

Xanthorhiza simplicissima (Yellowroot), PA

Yucca species (Yuccas), MT, NY.d, NY.l, NY.r; *Y. filamentosa,* TX.a, WV SEE PAGE 326.

Trees, Small
(usually less than 30 feet tall)

Acer species (Maples), *M. circinatum* (Vine maple) AZ.u, CA.u (native Zones 6–9); *A. griseum* (Paperbark maple), CA.s; *A. negundo* 'Variegatum' (Variegated boxelder), CA.s; *A. palmatum* (Japanese maple), CA.s, CA.u SEE PAGE 260.

Albizia species (Mimosa, Albizia), AZ.u *Note:* Considered deer resistant, but too invasive Zones 6–9

Amelanchier species (Shadbush, Serviceberry, Juneberry), NY.r, NY.v; *A. arborea* (Downy serviceberry), WV SEE PAGE 265.

Asimina triloba (Pawpaw), PA

Beaucarnea recurvata (Ponytail palm), CA.u

Berberis darwinii (Darwin barberry), OR SEE PAGE 270.

Betula species (Birches), GA.u; *B. nigra* 'Heritage', IL, MA, MT, NY.d, PA, WV; *B.papyrifera,* NY.r, PA, WA, WV SEE PAGE 271.

Carpinus caroliniana (Ironwood), PA

Carya illinoensis (Pecan), PA

Cercis canadensis (Eastern redbud), AZ.u, IL, MA; *C.c.* 'Alba', 'Forest Pansy', 'Pauline Lily', PA SEE PAGE 276.

Chionanthus species (Fringe trees), *C. retusa* (Chinese fringe tree), CA.s; *C. virginicus* (Fringe tree), PA

Cornus alternifolia (Pagoda dogwood), MA, PA SEE PAGE 279.

Cornus florida (Flowering dogwood), MA; *C.f.* 'Pink', 'Appalachian Spring', 'Cherokee Princess', PA SEE PAGE 279.

Cornus kousa (Siberian dogwood), CA.s, NY.d SEE PAGE 279.

Cotinus obovatus (American smoketree), IL, MA, PA

Crataegus species (Hawthorns), AZ.u, MA, MO, MT; *C. laevigata = oxycantha*, NY.d SEE PAGE 280.

Cupressocyparis = × Cupressocyparis leylandii (Leyland cypress), GA.u, MA

Cycas species (Sago palm, False palm), CA.u

Diospyros virginiana (Persimmon), PA

Ficus carica (Fig), WA

Halesia carolina = H. tetraptera (Caroline silver bell), CA.s, PA

Hovenia dulcis (Japanese raisin tree), CA.s

Ilex (Holly), 'Lydia Morris' and 'John T. Morris', WV SEE PAGE 292.

Illicium species (Anises), GA

Lithocarpus densiflorus (Tanbark oak), WA

Magnolia species (Magnolias), MA, NY.r (most); *M. stellata* (Star magnolia), CA.s SEE PAGE 300.

Oxydendrum arboreum (Sourwood), MA, IL, NY.d, PA

Pinus mugo (Mugo pine), MT, NY.d, WA SEE PAGE 311.

Prunus species, *P. virginiana* (Choke cherry), *P. americana* (American plum), P

Rhus species (Sumacs), AZ.u, WA; *R. aromatica* (Fragrant sumac), *R.* 'Gro-Low', PA; *R. virens* (Evergreen sumac), TX.a; *R. ovata,* CA.u; *R. tilobata,* MT; *R. typhina* 'Laciniata' (Staghorn sumac), PA

Salix (Coyote willow), MA

Sophora secundiflora (Mescal bean, Texas mountain laurel), AZ.u

Styrax japonicus (Japanese snowdrop), CA.s

Syringa reticulata (Tree lilac), IL SEE PAGE 319.

Trees, Tall
(growing more than 30 feet tall)

Abies (Firs), AZ.u, GA.u, MA, WA SEE PAGE 260.

Acer (Maples), AZ.u, GA.u, MA, NY.r; *A. rubrum* 'October glory' (Red maple), PA; *A. saccharinum* (Silver maple, Soft maple), MT; *A. saccharum* 'Legend' (Sugar maple, Hard maple), PA *Note: A. platanoides* (Norway maple) invasive SEE PAGE 260.

Aesculus species (Buckeyes), MA; *A. flava* (Yellow buckeye), PA; *A. parviflora* (Bottlebrush buckeye), GA.u, WV; *A. pavia* (Red buckeye), PA, NY.r *Note: A. hippocastanum* (Horse chestnut) invasive GA, ME, OR, PA, WI SEE PAGE 262.

Betula (Birches), GA.u; *B. nigra* 'Heritage', IL, MA, MT, NY.d, PA, WV; *B. papyrifera,* NY.r, PA, WA, WV SEE PAGE 271.

Calocedrus decurrens (California incense cedar), NY.r *Note:* Beware starving deer.

Carpinus betulus (European hornbeam), NY.d

Carya species (Hickories), *C. cordiformis* (Bitternut hickory), NY.d; *C. ovata* (Shagbark hickory), PA

Castanea species (Chestnuts), IL, MA; *C. molissima* (Chinese chestnut), NY.d

Catalpa species (Catalpas), IL, MA; *C. speciosa* (Northern catalpa), NY.d *Note:* Native to a small region from southwestern IN, southwestern IL to TN and AR, *C. speciosa* is considered invasive in FL, MD, NJ, TN, VA. Southeastern native *C. bognonioides* (Southern catalpa) is invasive in CA. SEE PAGE 275.

Cedrus species (Cedars), AZ.u; *C. atlantica,* NY.d; *C. deodara* (Deodar cedar), GA.u

Celtis species (Hackberries), AZ.u; *C. occidentalis* (Common hackberry), PA

Cercocarpus montanus (Mountain mahogany), CO

Chamaecyparis (False cypresses), GA.u, MA, WA, WV; *C. obtusa* (Hinoki cypress), NY.d; *C. pisifera* 'Filifera' (False cypress, Thread cypress), OR SEE PAGE 276.

Cladrastis lutea = *C. kentukea* (Yellowwood), PA, WV SEE PAGE 278.

Crataegus species (Hawthorns), AZ.u, MA, MO, MT; *C. laevigata* = *oxycantha,* NY.d SEE PAGE 280.

Cryptomeria japonica (Japanese cedar), OR, WV

Cupressus species (Cypress), AZ.u; *C. macrocarpa* (Monterey cypress), OR

Fagus species (Beeches), IL, MO, NY.r; *F. grandifolia* (American beech), *F. sylvatica* (European beech), NY.d

Fallugia paradoxa (Apache plume), CO

Fraxinus (Ashes), AZ.u, IL, MA; *F. americana* (White ash), PA; *F. latifolia* (Oregon ash), WA; *F. pennsylvanica* (Green ash), NY.d, PA

Native *CLADASTRIS LUTEA* (*YELLOWWOOD*) has mid-green foliage in summer, turning bright yellow to orange in fall.

Ginkgo biloba (Ginkgo, Maidenhair tree), AZ.u, GA.u, IL, NY.d, PA

Gleditsia triacanthos (Honeylocust), IL, MA, MT, NY.d, NY.r; *G. triacanthos* var. *inermis* (Thornless honeylocust), NY.r SEE PAGE 289.

Gordonia lasianthus (Loblolly bay), GA.u, MA

Gymnocladus dioicus (Kentucky coffeetree), PA

Ilex opaca (American holly), CA.u (except thornless), MO, NY.d

Laburnum anagroides (Golden-chain tree), NY.d

Larix (Larches), IL, MA SEE PAGE 296.

Liquidambar styraciflua (Sweet gum), GA.u, IL, MA, MO, NY.d; *L.s.* 'Rotundiloba', PA SEE PAGE 298.

Liriodendron tulipifera (Tulip poplar), IL, MA, PA

Magnolia species (Magnolia), AZ.u, CA.s, GA.u, NC; *M. acuminata* (Cucumber tree), PA; *M. grandiflora* (Southern magnolia) 'Edith Bogue', 'Brackens Brown Beauty', PA; *M.* × *soulangiana* (Saucer magnolia), most authorities; *M. stellata* (Star magnolia), MA, NY.d, (most) NY.r; *M. tripetala* (Umbrella tree), *M. virginiana* (Swamp magnolia, Sweet bay magnolia), NC, PA SEE PAGE 300.

Metasequoia glyptostroboides (Dawn redwood), IL

Nyssa sylvatica (Blackgum), PA

Ostrya virginiana (Hop hornbeam), IL, MA, PA

Picea species (Spruces), AZ.u, GA.u, IL, MA, MO, MT, NY.r; *P. glauca,* NY.d, NY.rug, WA; *P. pungens* (Colorado spruce), NY.d, NY.l; *P. pungens glauca* (Colorado blue spruce), WV

Pinus species (Pines), AZ.u, GA.u, MA, NC, WA; *P. edulis* (Pinyon pine), CO.u; *P. mugo* (Mugo pine), MO, MT, NY.d, WA; *P. resinosa* (Red pine), MO; *P. strobus* (White pine), PA; *P. sylvestris* (Scots pine), MO, MT, WV *Note: P. sylvestris* invasive IA, MA, ME, NJ, NY, OH, PA, VT, WI SEE PAGE 311.

Platanus species (Sycamores), IL, MA, NY.d *Note:* Natives *P. occidentalis* (Sycamore, Buttonwood) endorsed by PA (native in eastern N.A.) and *P. racemosa* (California sycamore)

Pseudotsuga menziensii (Douglas fir), AZ.u, CO.u, MA, WA, WV

Quercus (Oaks), AZ.u, MA, NY.r

Robinia pseudoacacia (Black locust), IL, MO, NY.d, NY.r *Note:* Considered invasive outside its two native ranges in eastern U.S. SEE PAGE 315.

Salix pseudoacacia (Corkscrew willow), NY.d

Sassafras albidum (Sassafras), IL, NY.d, PA

Taxodium distichum (Bald cypress), GA.u, IL, MA

Thuja species, *T. orientalis* (Oriental arborvitae), NY.r; *T. plicata* (Western arborvitae), NY.r *Note:* Both need protection from deer when starving in winter.

Tilia americana (Americal linden), PA

Tsuga species (Hemlocks), MA, WA *Note:* Need protection from deer when starving in winter. However, meanwhile, many are succumbing to the woolly adelgid, which makes planting either risky or optimistic of near-term cure.

Ulmus americana (American Elm) 'Princeton', PA

Umbellularia californica (California laurel, Oregon myrtle), WA

Native *PINUS STROBES* (WHITE PINE) leaves and buds contain resins that cause digestive disturbance.

Vines

Akebia quinata (Five-leaf akebia, Chocolate vine)
  Note: "Too invasive."—CT.n

Aristolochia macrophylla = A. durior (Dutchmans pipe),
  PA

Bignonia capreolata (Trumpet vine), GA.u. Native

Campsis radicans (Trumpet creeper), NY.d, PA *Note:*
  Can be invasive outside its native range in
  southeastern US SEE PAGE 274.

Celastrus scandens (American bittersweet), IL, MT,
  NY.d, PA *Note:* "Avoid confusing this with
  C. orbiculatus (Oriental bittersweet, Staff vine),
  which is destroying native forests."—CT.n

Clematis species (Clematis), IL, MT; *C. virginiana*
  (Virgin's bower), PA *Note:* Avoid invasive
  C. terniflora (Sweet autumn clematis)

CAMPSIS RADICANS (*TRUMPET CREEPER*) attracts humming-birds, rather than deer.

"Vines and aquatic plants are probably the hardest groups in which to find noninvasive plants. Actually, in the vine category, even the natives can be real annoyances. For example, I hear people complaining about native *Bignonia capreolata* (Trumpet vine)."—CT.n

Gelsemium sempervirens (Carolina jessamine), GA.u

Hedera helix (English ivy), AZ.u; *H.h.* 'Baltica', MT
  Note: The species is invasive in many states.

Lonicera species (Honeysuckles), native
  L. sempervirens (Trumpet honeysuckle),
  GA.u, MO, MT, NC, PA; *L. nitida* (Boxleaf
  honeysuckle) 'Maigruen' and 'Baggesen's Gold',
  CA.s *Note:* Virtually all alien *Lonicera* species are
  invasive, some widely so. SEE PAGE 299.

Parthenocissus species (Virginia creeper, Boston ivy),
  AZ.u, IL SEE PAGE 308.

Passiflora lutea (Yellow passionflower), PA

Rosa laevigata (Cherokee rose), GA.u

Vitis coignetiae (Grape), IL

Vitis labrusca (Fox grape vine), NY.d

Wisteria species (Wisterias), AZ.u, GA, IL, NY.d;
  W. frutescens 'Amethyst Falls' (American wisteria),
  PA; *Wisteria macrostachya* (Kentucky wisteria)
  'Clara Mack', 'Aunt Dee', PA *Note:* Alas,
  W. floribunda (Japanese wisteria) and *W. sinensis*
  (Chinese wisteria) are invasive in many states
  northward into Zone 6. SEE PAGE 325.

CHAPTER 23

Profiles of Deer-Resistant Plants

Abelia × *grandiflora* 'Francis Mason' (Glossy abelia)

Abies fraseri (Fraser fir)

Acer griseum (Paperbark maple)

Abelia × *grandiflora*

Glossy abelia

Honeysuckle family (CAPRIFOLIACEAE)

Appearance: Evergreen or semi-evergreen shrubs that can grow 10 ft high by 12 ft wide, glossy abelias are known for their fragrant, white, bell-shaped flowers touched with pink that open at the ends of the branches from midsummer to fall.

Nativity: Himalayas, E. Asia, Mexico

Uses: Hedgerows, buffers, mixed borders, and focal points

Toxicity: Our sources offer no toxins.

Propagation/Care: Root softwood cuttings in early summer; semiripe cuttings in late summer

Preferences/Hardiness: Thrives in full sun to partial shade in a location sheltered from wind. Plant in deep, well-drained, fertile soil with a high humus content. Zones 6–9.

Authorities: AZ.u, CA.s, OR

Abies species

Firs

Pine family (PINACEAE)

Appearance: The species are highly diverse, ranging from 6 to 200 ft tall.

Nativity: N. America, Europe, N. Africa, Asia

Uses: Hedgerows, buffers, focal points

Toxicity/Repellency: Resins and terpenes in this family discourage browsing.

Propagation/Care: Plant seeds as soon as they are ripe and feel dry to the touch. Hold them in a cold frame over winter to stratify for at least a month. Graft cultivars in early spring.

Preferences/Hardiness: Plant in a slightly sheltered area to protect from drying winds. Firs grow well in well-drained soil with moderate to high fertility, good moisture retention, and a slightly acid to neutral pH. Zones 3–9.

Authorities: AZ.u, GA.u, MA, WA

Acer species

Maples

Maple family (ACERACEAE)

Appearance: The 150 maple species vary in size, leaf shape, and color.

Nativity: N. and C. America, Europe, N. Africa, Asia

Uses: Hedgerows, borders, specimens

Toxicity: Tannins in dry leaves of red maple *(A. rubrum)* cause severe anemia in horses and other herbivores.

Propagation/Care: Plant seeds when ripe in fall, shown by hardened seed coats, and hold in a cold frame over the winter. Graft in early spring; bud in late summer.

Preferences/Hardiness: Plant in fertile, well-drained soil in full sun to partial shade. Zones 3–9.

Authorities: AZ.u, CA.s, CA.u, GA.u; MA, MT; PA, NY.r. For details,, see pages 256 and 257.

Achillea 'Summer Mix' (Yarrow)

Aconitum sp. (Monkshood)

Actaea racemosa = Cimicifuga racemosa
(Black cohosh, Black snakeroot, Bugbane)

Achillea species

Yarrows

Aster family (ASTERACEAE)

Appearance: Herbaceous perennials, most yarrows are either clump-forming or mat-forming and produce tiny daisylike flowers in dome-shaped clusters 3 to 5 in. across from midsummer to fall. Colors vary. Leaves are finely divided and featherlike.

Nativity: Europe, W. Asia

Uses: Mixed and herbaceous borders; 'King Edward', a creeping yarrow, is used as a ground cover.

Toxicity: Contains the irritant thujone, which is considered toxic. The medicinal scent and taste likely repel most mammals. In the leaves, bitter astringent from monoterpenes, including camphor, cause digestive disturbance. Guanianolides cause contact dermatitis in humans.

Propagation/Care: Plant seeds or divide in spring. Many produce runners.

Preferences/Hardiness: Grow in full sun and moist, well-drained soil; most yarrows tolerate a range of conditions. Zones 3–9.

Authorities: Deer—AZ.u, CA.s, GA.u, IL, MT, NY.d, NY.r, NY.s, TX.a, WA; Rabbits—AZ.u, CO.p, LEW, MN.g, WA.f

Aconitum species

Monkshoods

Buttercup family (RANUNCULACEAE)

Appearance: This tall perennial with striking foliage blooms in midsummer to fall. The name "monkshood" suggests the hooded flower shape. Most are deep blue-purple, but cultivars may be pink, yellow, or white.

Nativity: N. Hemisphere; 5 US species

Uses: Middle to back of borders

Toxicity: All parts contain toxic alkaloids that profoundly affect heart rate and the nervous system. Mammals may be initially repelled by a tingling tongue and burning mouth. Avoid planting near root crops, such as parsnips. Sap causes skin irritation.

Propagation/Care: Plant seeds in spring. Divide every few years in fall or early spring without disturbing central roots.

Preferences/Hardiness: Tolerates sun, but prefers partial shade and night temperatures below 70°F. Plant in cool, rich, moist soil. Some, Zones 3–8; others, Zones 5–8.

Authorities: Deer—CA.u, GA.a, IL, MO, NY.r, WV; *A. carmichaelii,* NY.d; Rabbits—LEW, WA.f

> Abbreviations for **Authorities** can be found on page 234.

Actaea racemosa (= *Cimicifuga racemosa*)

Black cohosh, Black snakeroot, Bugbane

Buttercup family (RANUNCULACEAE)

Appearance: Perennial 4 to 7 ft tall, with graceful spikes of tiny white flowers, sometimes with a pink cast. Shiny white, red, maroon, or black berries follow and stand until winter.

Nativity: E. North America

Uses: Mixed borders

Toxicity: Ethnobotanist James Duke mentions hazards of black cohosh, including nausea, headache, and organ damage. In *Toxic Plants of North America,* Burrows and Tyrl say the leaves and berries of related native white baneberry (*A. pachypoda*) and red baneberry (*A. rubra*) have a bitter taste and nauseating aftertaste; the berries cause a burning sensation in the stomach.

Propagation/Care: Plant seeds in fall and stratify their containers in a cold frame all winter. Divide mature plants in early spring.

Preferences/Hardiness: Thrives in partial shade and in cool, moist, moderately fertile soil mulched with leaf mold. Zones 4–9.

Authorities: CA.u, GA.a, NY.l, PA, WV

Adiantum pedatum
(Northern maidenhair fern)

Aesculus × *carnea*
(Red-flowering horsechestnut)

Agave parryi var. *huachucensis* (Agave)

Adiantum pedatum

Northern maidenhair fern

Maidenhair Fern family (PTERIDACEAE)

Appearance: This delicate-looking deciduous fern features leaf segments radiating from an elevated horseshoe-shaped stalk. Plants generally grow 12 to 16 in. high and wide.

Nativity: Eastern N. America

Uses: As part of a shady border, around woodland creeks or shaded water features

Toxicity: Most ferns are toxic. Some members of the Maidenhair Fern family cause violent trembling seizures in sheep, as well as lung hemorrhages and foam in air passages, although our sources offer no assay on toxins for this species.

Propagation/Care: Divide the creeping rhizomes in early spring, just as the plant is breaking dormancy, and plant to the same depth in a similar location as the parent.

Preferences/Hardiness: Northern maidenhair ferns thrive in partially shaded locations and well-drained but moist soil of moderate fertility with high humus levels. Zones 3–8.

Authorities: PA

Aesculus species

Buckeyes, Horse chestnuts

Horse Chestnut family (HIPPOCASTANACEAE)

Appearance: In midsummer, these trees have brushlike, generally fragrant, white, pink, or red blooms rising in 6- to 10-in. panicles above the umbrella-like leaflets that turn yellow, orange, or red in fall. Clusters of large, often spiky, hulls enclose the seed.

Nativity: N. America, S.E. Europe, Himalayas, E. Asia

Uses: Specimen, hedgerow, border

Toxicity: Saponins in young spring leaves and in fallen seed cause lack of coordination and seizures in deer and other ruminants. Seeds, especially those of horse chestnut *(A. hippocastanum),* have killed children.

Propagation/Care: As soon as they drop, immediately plant seeds and hold in a cold frame to stratify all winter. Graft in late winter; bud in summer.

Preferences/Hardiness: Grow in full sun or partial shade in well-drained, moist, fertile soil. Zones 3–8.

Authorities: MA; *A. flava* (Yellow buckeye), PA; *A. parviflora* (Bottlebrush buckeye), GA.u, WV; *A. pavia* (Red buckeye), NY.r PA, *Note: A. hippocastanum* (Horse chestnut) invasive GA, ME, OR, PA, WI.

Agave species

Agaves

Agave family (AGAVACEAE)

Appearance: These succulent perennials have upright, often thick, pointed leaves growing in rosette form. Various species have blue-green, gray, mid-green, and dark-green leaves, some with lighter borders and spines on leaf margins. Groups of flower clusters, followed by fruits, form in the center of the rosettes.

Nativity: N., S., and C. America

Uses: Specimen plants, mixed borders, xeriscapes

Toxicity: *Agave americana* has oxalates that burn the mouth. *Agave lecheguilla* has saponins that cause liver and kidney damage in sheep and goats, followed by swelling and discharges from the eyes and nose. Yet mule deer can subsist on this plant from winter through spring without apparent ill effects.

Propagation/Care: Remove offsets as soon as they form roots.

Preferences/Hardiness: Agaves thrive in full sun and sandy, moderately fertile, slightly acid soil. Zones 9–11.

Authorities: AZ.u, CA.u

Ageratum houstonianum 'Blue Horizon' (Floss flower)

Ajuga reptans (Bugleweed)

Alchemilla mollis (Lady's mantle)

Ageratum species

Ageratum, Floss flower

Aster family (ASTERACEAE)

Appearance: Normally grown as an annual, the species and cultivars range from 6-in. dwarf mounds to 2½-ft-tall spreading cultivars such as 'Blue Horizon'. Clusters of brushlike flowers in blue, blue-gray, pink, or white bloom midsummer until first frost.

Nativity: Extreme S. US and in Mexico

Uses: Bedding, edging, and containers. Tall types are good cut flowers.

Toxicity: Precocenes in ageratum can alter insect growth and cause extensive liver damage in rats. But low concentrations in ageratum aren't thought to pose health risks to livestock, according to Burrows and Tyrl in *Toxic Plants of North America*.

Propagation/Care: Plant indoors in early spring. It transplants easily, even when in bloom.

Preferences/Hardiness: Grow in full sun to partial shade in fertile, moist, well-drained soil. Zones 10–13.

Authorities: CA.u, GA.a, IL, NY.d, NY.r, WA

Ajuga species

Bugleweeds

Mint family (LAMIACEAE)

Appearance: Most ajuga species have mid-green leaves, although some, such as *A. reptans* 'Multicolor', have variegated leaves showing pink, cream, and bronze. Others have bronze-red, purple, or wine-red leaves. Ajugas bloom in spring to early summer, sending up spikes of blue, white, or pink flowers.

Nativity: Europe, Asia

Uses: Bugleweed makes an excellent groundcover.

Toxicity: Heavily studied for their medicinal properties, ajugas have bitter derpinoids that repel insects and perhaps also browsing mammals.

Propagation/Care: Divide in early spring or root cuttings in late spring.

Preferences/Hardiness: Grow in partial shade or filtered light in moist soil. They tolerate low fertility and somewhat acid conditions. In good soils, can become somewhat invasive and may grow into lawns. Zones 3–9.

Authorities: AZ.u, CA.s, GA.u, IL, MT, NY.d, NY.r

Alchemilla mollis

Lady's mantle

Rose family (ROSACEAE)

Appearance: The clear lime green leaves, mounded habit, and frothy flowers make Lady's mantle a garden favorite. The tiny blooms are held above the leaves and, from a distance, can look like a yellow-green mist. They make excellent cut flowers.

Nativity: N. temperate and arctic zones, mountainous areas in Africa, India, Sri Lanka, and Indonesia

Uses: Mixed borders, edgings, rock gardens, groundcovers

Toxicity: Tannins are the likely repellents.

Propagation/Care: Start seeds early inside or in a cold frame. Divide plants in early spring or autumn.

Preferences/Hardiness: Thrives in partial shade or full sun in moist, fertile, and humus-filled soil with a slightly acid pH. Zones 3–7.

Authorities: CA.s, NY.d

Abbreviations for **Authorities** can be found on page 234.

Allium schoenoprasum (Chives)

Alyssum (Madworts)

Amaryllis belladonna (Belladonna lily, Naked lady, Resurrection lily)

Allium species

Onions, Chives

Lily family (LILIACEAE)

Appearance: Upright, strap-shaped leaves have a strong, pungent odor and flavor. Blooms consist of ball- or dome-shaped clusters of tiny florets.

Nativity: N. Hemisphere

Uses: In vegetable gardens and around roses and other perennials to repel insect attack

Toxicity: Sulfur compounds create the strong odor and flavor that repels mammals and insects. These plants can cause severe anemia in dogs, cats, and cattle.

Propagation/Care: Plant seeds indoors in early spring or plant bulbs outside in spring. Divide clump-forming ornamental species in spring.

Preferences/Hardiness: Grow in full sun in fertile, humus-filled, well-drained soil. Zones 3–9.

Authorities: CA.u (some), GA.u, WV; *A. cernuum,* (Nodding pink onion), PA; *A. giganteum* (Ornamental onion), IL, NY.d, NY.r, NY.v; *A. schoenoprasum* (Chives), NY.d, WA; *A. tuberosum* (Garlic chives), TX.a, WA *Note: A. vineale* (field garlic, wild garlic) invasive in CT, MD, NC, NJ, PA, TN, VA, WV

Alyssum species

Madworts

Mustard family (BRASSICACEAE)

Appearance: Whether annual or perennial, herbaceous or woody, *Alyssum* species are grown for their clusters of usually fragrant, small, cross-shaped, magenta or white flowers that rise above the leaves.

Nativity: C. and S. Europe, N. Africa, SW. and C. Asia

Uses: Grow them in rock gardens, tucked into crevices in stone walls, or as the edging for a mixed border.

Toxicity/Repellency: Although alyssums hyper-accumulate toxic soil nickel, our references suggest no other toxic or repellent properties. Low growth habit and flower fragrance discourage browsing.

Propagation/Care: Plant seeds in flats as soon as they are ripe in the fall (shown by hardened seed coats), and hold the container in a cold frame over the winter months. Take softwood or greenwood cuttings in early summer.

Preferences/Hardiness: Plant in full sun in soil that drains freely and contains moderate levels of organic matter and nutrients. Zones 4–9.

Authorities: MO, NY.r; *A. montanum* (Mountain alyssum) 'Berggold' = 'Mountain Gold', CA.s

Amaryllis belladonna and cultivars

Belladonna lily, Naked lady, Resurrection lily

Amaryllis family (AMARYLLIOACEAE)

Appearance: This S. African bulb's scientific name, *Amaryllis,* often causes confusion with its also deer-resistant C. and S. American cousins sold as "amaryllis" houseplants, which are actually Dutch hybrid *Hippeastrums. A. belladonna* is far hardier. It produces one or two 2–ft bare stalks with 4 to 12 large, trumpet-shaped flowers that last 4 to 6 weeks, followed by the appearance of straplike leaves.

Nativity: S. Africa

Uses: Mixed borders, containers

Toxicity: Phenanthridine alkaloids, like those in fellow family members *Narcissus* and *Hippeastrum,* can cause nausea, vomiting, and diarrhea in mammals.

Propagation/Care: Plant bulbs and offsets with their necks at soil level. From seed, this plant may take several years to flower.

Preferences/Hardiness: Full sun to partial shade. Zones 7–10.

Authorities: AZ.u, CA.u, GA.u, OR

Amelanchier sp. (Serviceberry)

Amsonia hubrichtii (Thread-leaf blue star)

Anemone blanda 'White Splendor' (Anemone)

Amelanchier species

Shadbush, Serviceberry, Juneberry

Rose family (ROSACEAE)

Appearance: These deciduous shrubs are grown for their usually fragrant white flowers that appear in spring and blue-black or red-purple fruit that ripens in autumn. Many cultivars, such as 'Regent', and all of the *A. x grandiflora* series produce fruit sweet enough to use in jams and jellies.

Nativity: N. America, Europe, and Asia

Uses: Plant as a specimen shrub or part of a border or hedgerow.

Toxicity: All parts of Saskatoon serviceberry *(A. alnifolia)* and shadbush/eastern serviceberry *(A. canadensis)* contain prunasin, a cyanide-generating toxicant that occurs in high, 4-percent concentrations early in the growing season.

Propagation/Care: Take greenwood or softwood cuttings and root over heat; remove rooted suckers and transplant to a new location.

Preferences/Hardiness: Plant in full sun or partial shade in slightly acid, well-drained, moist, and fertile soil. Zones 4–9.

Authorities: NY.r, NY.v; *A. arborea* (Downy serviceberry), WV

Amsonia species

Blue-star, Willow blue-star

Dogbane family (APOCYNACEAE)

Appearance: These graceful perennials supply panicles of long-lasting blue flowers in late spring or early summer. The lance-shaped leaves provide interest when the plant isn't in bloom. Leaves of many species turn golden yellow in fall.

Nativity: S.E. Europe, Turkey, Japan, N.E. and C. United States

Uses: Mixed borders, wildflower gardens

Toxicity: The Dogbane family contains plants with deadly toxins as well as plants widely used medicinally. Our sources provide no toxin assays.

Propagation/Care: Start seeds inside in early spring or in containers in fall to overwinter in a cold frame. Divide in spring or take softwood cuttings.

Preferences/Hardiness: Plant in full sun to partial shade in moist, fertile, well-drained soil. Tolerates brief droughts. *A. tabernaemontana,* Zones 3–9; most species 5 or 6–9.

Authorities: *A. cilata,* CA.s; *A. hubrichtii,* GA.a, PA; *A. tabernaemontana,* GA.a, NY.r, PA

Anemone species

Anemones, Windflowers

Buttercup family (RANUNCULACEAE)

Appearance: All species of these perennials have open, single blooms with distinctive centers and long petioles that hold them above the attractive leaves. Various species bloom in spring, summer, or fall. The flowers are white, pink, blue, purple, or coral.

Nativity: N. and S. Hemispheres

Uses: Mixed borders, woodland edges

Toxicity: The foliage has an acrid taste, and most species irritate the digestive tract.

Propagation/Care: Plant tubers in summer or early fall; divide rhizomes in spring; plant seeds as soon as they ripen and feel dry to the touch, and hold in a cold frame over winter.

Preferences/Hardiness: Various species have different needs, whether light, sandy soil or moist, humus-rich soil. Grow in full sun in the North, partial shade in the South. Most species, Zones 5–9; some 8–11.

Authorities: IL, NY.r; *A. canadensis,* PA; *A. × hybrida,* WV

Abbreviations for **Authorities** can be found on page 234.

Antirrhinum majus 'Rocket Mix'
(Snapdragon)

Aquilegia canadensis (Canada columbine)

Arctostaphylos uva-ursi (Bearberry)

Antirrhinum majus

Snapdragons

Figwort family (SCROPHULARIACEAE)

Appearance: This short-lived perennial is often grown as an annual. Flowers in a host of colors rise in dramatic spikes.

Nativity: S.W. Europe, Mediterranean

Uses: Tall cultivars, to 3 ft, make good cut flowers; 2-ft-tall intermediates are good bedding plants, and 1-ft dwarfs are used for edging and containers.

Toxicity: Snapdragon species are closely related to *Linaria* species (toadflaxes), which contain alkaloids and glycosides that affect respiration, heart rate, and blood pressure in dogs, cats, and rabbits. Other deer-resistant family members include *Digitalis, Verbascum,* and *Penstemen.*

Propagation/Care: Plant seed indoors 8 to 12 weeks before last frost in northern areas, in late summer or fall in the South.

Preferences/Hardiness: Grow in full sun to partial shade in well-drained, fertile soil. Zones 7–10. First-year plants might survive Zones 5–7 winters if mulched deeply.

Authorities: Deer—GA.a, IL, NY.d, WV; Rabbits—LEW, WA.f

Aquilegia species

Columbines

Buttercup family (RANUNCULACEAE)

Appearance: This genus of perennials offers bell-shaped flowers, many with brightly colored tepals and long spurs. Colors range from the red of Canada columbine to white, pink, rose, blue, purple, yellow, and bicolors.

Nativity: N. America and mountainous areas of the N. Hemisphere

Uses: Borders, containers, cut flowers

Toxicity: Many plants of this family cause pain and burning in the mouth.

Propagation/Care: Plant seeds indoors 8 weeks before frost or in containers in fall to overwinter in a cold frame. Carefully divide in early spring.

Preferences/Hardiness: Grow in full sun in northern areas, partial shade in the South. All but alpine species thrive in moist, well-drained soil. Alpine species like a gritty, fast-draining soil.

Authorities: Deer—*Aquilegia* species, AZ.u, GA.a, IL, MT, NY.r, WV; *A. canadensis* & cvs, PA; Cottontail rabbits—*A.* species, NY.s

> Abbreviations for **Authorities** can be found on page 234.

Arctostaphylos species

Bearberry, Manzanitas

Heath family (ERICACEAE)

Appearance: All but *A. alpina* in this genus of shrubs and small trees are evergreen, and many are prostrate. Common bearberry *(A. uva-ursi)* is a low-lying shrub with an attractive, branched form; white, pink, or red summer flowers; and bright red fall berries. Manzanita trees *(A. manzanita)* have ornamental, reddish brown bark, racemes of white or pink blooms, and berries that turn from white to red.

Nativity: W. North America

Uses: Focal points, understory plants, rock gardens

Toxicity: Medicinal uses of *Arctostaphylos* are associated with nausea, convulsions, and worse. Deer avoid many members of the Heath family.

Propagation/Care: Root semiripe cuttings in summer; layer in autumn; dig rooted stems in early spring.

Preferences/Hardiness: Grow in full sun in moist but well-drained, acid soil with moderate fertility. Zones 2–10.

Authorities: AZ.u, WA, WV; *A. uva-ursi* 'Massachusetts', PA

Arisaema triphyllum (Jack-in-the-pulpit)

Artemisia 'Powis Castle' (Mugwort, Wormwood)

Arum italicum (Italian arum, Lords and ladies)

Arisaema triphyllum

Jack-in-the-pulpit
Arum family (ARACEAE)

Appearance: This perennial has three broad, arrow-shaped leaves that partially hide a flaplike green or purplish striped spathe shaped like a canopied preacher's pulpit that curves over the club-shaped spadix—Jack, the preacher. The flowers hide around Jack's ankles and aren't seen without close inspection. The spathe dies to the ground in late summer, exposing a cluster of brilliant red berries.

Nativity: E. North America

Uses: Woodland gardens

Toxicity: Characteristic of the entire Arum family, calcium oxalate crystals in all plant parts cause intense though temporarily burning and irritation in the mouth, mucous membranes, and digestive tract.

Propagation/Care: Plant seed in spring or autumn; divide offset tubers in autumn.

Preferences/Hardiness: Partial shade and well-drained neutral to acid, humus-rich soil. Native *A. triphyllum* (sometimes suggested as three different varieties) is more cold hardy than most Asians. Zones 4–9.

Authorities: NY.l, NY.r; *A. triphyllum*, PA

Artemisia species

Wormwoods, Mugwort, Sagebrush
Aster family (ASTERACEAE)

Appearance: Annuals, perennials, evergreen or deciduous shrubs, most have soft gray-green to silver leaves.

Nativity: N. America and N. Hemisphere, some S. America, S. Africa

Uses: Borders, rock or herb gardens

Toxicity: Artemisias contain volatile oils called monoterpenes, including camphor and thujone, that undermine bacterial digestion in the rumen and irritate the digestive tract. Thujones cause nerve and brain damage.

Propagation/Care: Start seeds early indoors. Divide in spring or fall; take softwood in spring or heel in cuttings of semiripe wood in summer.

Preferences/Hardiness: Grow in full sun in well-drained, fertile soil. Prune woodies to maintain vigor. Zones 3–9.

Authorities: AZ.u, CA.s, CA.u, GA.u, IL, NY.l, NY.r, WV; *A. absinthium*, CA.u, IL, NY.l, TX.a; *A. ludoviciana*, TX.a; *A. 'Powis Castle'*, CA.s; *A. schmidtiana*, NY.d; *A. alba* (= *A. canscens*) 'Sea Foam', CA.s *Note:* Invasives include *A. absinthium* (Wormwood), OR, ND, WA; *A. stelleriana* (Oldwoman), NJ; and *A. vulgaris* (Mugwort, Wormwood), MD, NJ, NY, PA, TN, VA

Arum italicum

Arum, Lords and ladies
Arum family (ARACEAE)

Appearance: The arrow- or spear-shaped leaves of this tuberous perennial are marked in patterns of lighter and darker green and often have white veins. They appear in late winter and persist until summer, when they wither away and the plant sends up tall, hooded flower spathes from which orange-red berries develop. Berries may persist until the leaves reappear in late winter.

Nativity: S. Europe, N. Africa, W. Asia, W. Himalayas

Uses: Understory plants in a shrub border, containers

Toxicity: Calcium oxalate crystals in most arums cause burning and swelling in mouth tissues.

Propagation/Care: Divide clumps of tubers after bloom. Remove seeds from fruit in autumn and plant in containers in a cold frame.

Preferences/Hardiness: Plant in full sun or partial shade in humus-rich, well-drained soil with moderate fertility. Shelter from harsh winds. Zones 8–10.

Authorities: CA.u, NY.r

Asarum europaeum (European wild ginger)

Asclepias tuberosa (Butterfly weed)

Asparagus 'Jersey Knight' (Asparagus)

Asarum species

Wild gingers

Birthwort family (ARISTOLOCHIACEAE)

Appearance: The lush leaves of these woodland perennials are sometimes marbled with white veins and sometimes as shiny as if they were waxed. Flowers are often hidden under the leaves.

Nativity: N. America, Europe, E. Asia

Uses: As shady-garden edging or as an understory plant in a grouping of trees

Toxicity: Although our resources suggest no toxins, the ginger flavor may repel browsers.

Propagation/Care: Plant seeds in a container as soon as they ripen, shown by hardened seed coats, and hold them in a cold frame over the winter months. Divide carefully in early spring, taking care not to injure the roots.

Preferences/Hardiness: Wild ginger thrives in partially shaded locations but will tolerate full shade. Soil should be well-drained but moist, fertile, and humus-rich. Zones 4–9.

Authorities: *A. canadense,* CA.s, IL, NY.r, PA; *A. caudatum,* CA.s, CA.u

Asclepias species

Milkweeds, Butterfly weed

Milkweed family (ASCLEPIADACEAE)

Appearance: These perennials have milky sap. Clusters of waxy florets in shades of white, pink, orange, and salmon open in midsummer, followed by seedpods. Each seed has a silky windsail.

Nativity: N. and S. America, S. Africa

Uses: Mixed borders, cutting gardens, herb gardens

Toxicity: Most milkweed species contain toxic cardenolides that taste bad enough to teach avoidance. If swallowed, cardenolides usually cause vomiting. If digested, they can cause digestive and heart issues, sometimes death. Some other milkweeds defend themselves with more palatable neurotoxins.

Propagation/Care: Plant seeds in early spring; take basal cuttings in spring; divide in spring.

Preferences/Hardiness: Grow in full sun in fertile, well-drained, friable soil. *A. incarnata* and *A. speciosa* thrive in very wet soils. Zones 3–9.

Authorities: NC, NY.r; *A. incarnata* 'Ice Ballet', PA; *A. tuberosa* (Butterfly weed), GA.a, IL, NY.d; *A. tuberosa* 'Hello Yellow', PA

Asparagus officinalis

Asparagus

Lily family (LILIACEAE)

Appearance: This perennial sends up edible shoots from May into June; allow them to bolt to 5-ft high, billowing ferns that nourish the roots.

Nativity: Europe, Asia, Africa

Uses: Border plant or in dedicated patches

Toxicity: Although berries in houseplant species contain sapogenins, Burrows and Tyrl indicate no other plant toxins. Deer possibly ignore the light, feathery leaves because they are insubstantial. Deer and rabbits disregard shoots.

Propagation/Care: In early spring, plant spiderlike crowns horizontally in 12-in.-deep trenches enriched with compost. Plants may need 2 to 3 years to become established. As the spears grow through the first season, gradually fill in the trench with a mixture of compost and good topsoil.

Preferences/Hardiness: Grow in full sun in the North, partial shade in the South, in deep, friable, well-drained soil with good moisture-holding capacity. Zones 4–8.

Authorities: *A. officinalis* 'Martha Washington', NY.s

Aster laevis 'Bluebird' (Smooth aster)

Astilbe 'Red Sentinel' (Astilbe)

Athyrium filix-femina (Lady fern)

Aster species

Asters

Aster family (ASTERACEAE)

Appearance: This genus includes annuals, perennials, biennials, and subshrubs. Most species have composite, daisylike flowers, borne singly or in groups at stem tops in pink, blue, purple, rose, white, or yellow with distinctive yellow centers.

Nativity: N. America, S. Africa

Uses: Mixed borders, rock gardens, wildflower patches

Toxicity: Relative appeal to deer may be affected by the garden buffet. Our resources suggest no toxins or reasons for repellency beyond taste.

Propagation/Care: Plant seeds in containers in spring or fall; if fall, hold over winter in a cold frame. Divide runners or root softwood or basal cuttings.

Preferences/Hardiness: Most thrive in full sun in the North, partial shade in the South. Plant in well-drained, moderately fertile soil. Zones 3–9.

Authorities: AZ.u, GA.a, NY.d; *A. novi-belgi, A. oblongifolius* (Fragrant aster) 'October Skies', 'Raydons Favorite', PA

Astilbe species

Astilbes

Saxifraga family (SAXIFRAGACEAE)

Appearance: Plumes of brightly colored florets wave above the delicate, finely cut leaves of this perennial. Depending on cultivar, flowers may be yellow, orange, red, pink, or white. Leaf colors include purplish green, mid-green, and rich brown.

Nativity: N. America, S.E. Asia

Uses: Mixed borders, woodland gardens, stream banks

Toxicity: Our sources offer no toxin assays. But deer and rabbits seem to ignore astilbes.

Propagation/Care: Start seed very early in spring; these take a long time to reach planting size. Every 3 years, divide plants in early spring while still dormant—they emerge late, so don't assume they have been winter-killed.

Preferences/Hardiness: Plant in a spot with filtered light or partial shade in rich, moist soil. Zones 3–8.

Authorities: AZ.u, IL, MT, NY.d, NY.r, NY.s

Athyrium filix-femina

Lady fern

Wood Fern family (DRYOPTERIDACEAE)

Appearance: This highly variable native fern has feathery, lacy fronds that grow to 3 ft long. The genus includes about 180 species and numerous cultivars, many of which are equally mammal-resistant.

Nativity: United States and N. Hemisphere. The cultivar *A. angustum* 'Lady Red' is redder than red-stemmed lady ferns native to N.E. United States woodlands.

Uses: Shady borders to woodland gardens

Toxicity: European members of this family are associated with livestock poisoning that includes severe digestive disturbance and blindness.

Propagation/Care: Sow ripe spores at 59° to 61°F. Divide in spring.

Preferences/Hardiness: Grow in moist, fertile, compost- or leaf-mold-enriched, neutral to acid soil. Zones 4–9.

Authorities: Most

Abbreviations for **Authorities** can be found on page 234.

Athyrium niponicum var. *pictum*
(Japanese painted fern)

Baptisia australis
(False indigo, Wild indigo)

Berberis thunbergii var. *autropurpurea*
'Crimson Pigmy' (Barberry)

Athyrium niponicum var. *pictum*

Japanese painted fern
Wood Fern family (DRYOPTERIDACEAE)

Appearance: This low-growing fern is celebrated for bicolored fronds that may vary from silver-gray to green. *Cautions:* May hybridize with other *Athyriums,* and the color of spore-grown plants may vary from those of the purchased parent. Spreads slowly.

Nativity: Japan

Uses: Shady borders to woodland gardens. Texture looks especially good against large-leaved hostas.

Toxicity: European members of this family are associated with livestock poisoning that includes severe digestive disturbance and blindness.

Propagation/Care: Sow ripe spores at 59° to 61°F. Divide in spring.

Preferences/Hardiness: Grow in moist, fertile, compost- or leaf-mold-enriched, neutral to acid soil. Zones 5–8.

Authorities: Most

> Abbreviations for **Authorities** can be found on page 234.

Baptisia species

False indigo, Wild indigo
Pea family (FABACEAE)

Appearance: Spikes of white or blue, pea-shaped flowers form on this perennial plant in mid- to late summer. Mid-green, divided leaves are decorative all through the season. Seedpods look almost black.

Nativity: E. and S. United States

Uses: Mixed borders, wildflower gardens

Toxicity: In livestock, quinolizidine alkaloids cause excess salivation, lack of coordination, and tremors. Horses and cattle often reject baptisia in hay.

Propagation/Care: Divide in early spring; plant seed as soon as it is ripe and feels dry to the touch. Hold in a cold frame over the winter months.

Preferences/Hardiness: Grow in full sun in extremely well-drained, preferably sandy soil with moderate fertility levels. Deadhead after bloom to retain plant vigor, and mulch well over winter. Zones 3–9.

Authorities: GA.u, NC, NY.l, NY.r; *B. alba* (White false indigo), *B. australis,* CA.s, GA.a; *B. australis,* 'Purple Smoke', PA; *B. sphaerocarpa* (Yellow false indigo), 'Screaming Yellow Zonker', PA

Berberis species

Barberries
Barberry family (BERBERIDACEAE)

Appearance: This genus includes more than 450 species of evergreen and deciduous shrubs. All have berries. Flowers are yellow or orange; berries can be red, orange, or dusty blue. Leaves are often ornamental and most turn vivid colors in autumn. Avoid Japanese barberry *(B. vulgaris),* an invasive weed.

Nativity: N. Hemisphere, Africa, N. and S. America

Uses: Mixed borders, specimen plants, hedges, hedgerows

Toxicity: Most species have bitter, unpalatable leaves. Alkaloids in some cause nausea, vomiting, and diarrhea.

Propagation/Care: Take softwood cuttings from deciduous species in early summer, semiripe cuttings from deciduous and evergreen species in mid- to late summer.

Preferences/Hardiness: Grow in full sun to partial shade in well-drained, moderately fertile soil. Prune to supplier instructions. Zones 6–9.

Authorities: *Berberis* species, AZ.u, CA.u, GA.u, MT, NY.l, NY.r, WV; *B. × gladwynensis* 'William Penn', NY.r; *B. darwinii,* OR

Bergenia 'Bressingham Ruby' (Bergenia)

Betula nigra 'Heritage' (River birch)

Boltonia asteroides (Boltonia), white flowers, and *Bouvardia ternifolia*

Bergenia species

Bergenia

Saxifrage family (SAXIFRAGACEAE)

Appearance: The leaves on this low-lying perennial add a note of lushness to any garden. Thick and leathery, some are glossy and some are hairy, some are a bronze-green color, some are reddish green, and others are a sharp lime-green. Plants are evergreen in mild climates but lose leaves in cold climates. Spikes with clusters of small, pink or white blooms rise above the leaves in spring.

Nativity: C. and E. Asia

Uses: Woodland gardens, mixed borders, edging plants

Toxicity: Our resources offer no toxin assays.

Propagation/Care: Divide clumps in spring or root rhizomes with one or more leaves in autumn; hold these in cold frames over the winter months.

Preferences/Hardiness: Plant in full sun in the North, partial shade in the South. Bergenias thrive in well-drained, moist, humus-rich soil.

Authorities: IL, NY.l, NY.r, WV

Betula species

Birches

Birch family (BETULACEAE)

Appearance: The more than 60 birch species range from trees to shrubs. All are deciduous and all produce male and female catkins in early spring. The most popular landscaping species have attractive, peeling bark. Leaves are toothed and turn yellow or orange in autumn.

Nativity: N. Hemisphere

Uses: As specimens or shade trees, and in hedgerows

Toxicity: Leaves and stems of some species have a wonderful wintergreen scent that might not appeal to deer. Our resources offer no toxin assays.

Propagation/Care: Root softwood cuttings in summer or graft in very early spring.

Preferences/Hardiness: Plant in full sun or dappled shade in well-drained, moist, and moderately fertile soil.

Authorities: *Betula* species, GA.u; *B. nigra* 'Heritage', IL, MA, MT, NY.d, PA, WV; *B.papyrifera,* NY.r, PA, WA, WV

Boltonia asteroides

Boltonia

Aster family (ASTERACEAE)

Appearance: This perennial with delicate-looking, daisylike flowers has an open habit that gives an airy feeling to any location. Despite this feeling and the delicacy of its flowers, it can grow 6 ft tall and 3 ft wide.

Nativity: N. America

Uses: At the back of the border, in wildflower gardens, in cutting gardens

Toxicity: Our resources offer no toxin assays.

Propagation/Care: Plant seeds in early spring inside or in containers destined for the winter cold frame in autumn. Divide plants in early spring. Zones 4–8.

Preferences/Hardiness: Plant in full sun or partial shade in well-drained, fertile, moist soil. Divide every 3 years to maintain plant health.

Authorities: GA.a, GA.u, NY.r

Buddleia davidii 'Harlequin'
(Butterfly bush, Summer lilac)

Buxus microphylla 'Winter Gem'
(Boxwood)

Calamagrostis × *acutiflora* 'Karl Foerster'
(Feather reed grass) & Marigold

Buddleia davidii

Butterfly bush

Logania family (LOGANIACEAE)

Appearance: Arching panicles of brightly colored florets droop gracefully from the branch ends of this perennial shrub. The blooms are usually fragrant and may be blue, violet, pink, or white. Even when not in bloom, the graceful habit of this shrub lends elegance to the garden.

Nativity: Americas, Asia, Africa

Uses: Mixed borders, specimen plants, butterfly or wildflower gardens

Toxicity: Although members of this family are known for powerfully neurotoxic alkaloids, our resources offer no toxin assays on this plant.

Propagation/Care: Start seeds early inside in spring; transplant after last frost. Take semiripe cuttings in mid- to later summer and hardwood cuttings in fall. Root over heat.

Preferences/Hardiness: Plant in full sun in well-drained, moderately fertile, moist soil. Prune after flowering, cutting stems back by about a third. Zones 4–8.

Authorities: AZ.u, GA.u, NY.d, NY.l
Note: Invasives: *B. davidii* (Orange-eye bb), CA, KY, NC, NJ, OR, PA, WA, WV; *B. lindleyana* (Lindley's bb), FL, GA, NC, TX

Buxus species

Boxwoods, Boxes

Boxwood family (BUXACEAE)

Appearance: Responding well to pruning, these profusely branched evergreen shrubs are ideal for hedges and a favorite for formal designs. Leaves of some cultivars are variegated, although most boxwoods have deep green, somewhat glossy leaves.

Nativity: Europe, Asia, Africa, C. America

Uses: Hedges, topiary, herb gardens, specimen plants

Toxicity: Bitter alkaloids in the leaves cause diarrhea, colic, excessive salivation, and dehydration in livestock. Symptoms may include tremors, seizures, and breathing problems.

Propagation/Care: Take semiripe cuttings in summer and root over heat. Graft in very early spring.

Preferences/Hardiness: Plant in partial shade or filtered light whenever possible. Plants will tolerate full sun if soil is consistently moist. Soil must be well-drained and fertile. Zones 6–9.

Authorities: AZ.u, CA.u, IL, MT, NY.r, TX.a, WV; *B. sempervirens,* NY.l

Calamagrostis species

Reed grass, Smallweed

Grass family (POACEAE)

Appearance: These perennial grasses can grow anywhere from 2 to 6 ft tall. The tall spikes of tiny flowers, or inflorescences, are light enough to move gracefully in every passing breeze. Leaves are flat, sometimes with channels that give them the appearance of being almost striped.

Nativity: N. Hemisphere

Uses: Mixed borders, in woodland gardens, as specimen plants

Toxicity: Many grasses have mechanical defenses in their stiff, tough, or sharp-edged leaves. Others may concentrate nitrates, cyanide, oxalates, or fungal endophytes. Our resources offer no toxin assays on this grass.

Propagation/Care: Divide in spring, once growth has begun.

Preferences/Hardiness: Grow in partial shade unless soil is consistently moist. In moist soils, plants tolerate full sun. Soil should be humus-rich and fertile. Cut back to 3 in. in late winter. Zones 5–9.

Authorities: NY.rug

Caltha palustris (Marsh marigold)

© WILDLIFE GmbH / Alamy

Calycanthus species (Carolina and California allspices, Sweet shrub)

Camassia leichtlinii 'Blue Shades' (Quamash)

Caltha palustris

Marsh marigold

Buttercup family (RANUNCULACEAE)

Appearance: These post-emergent aquatics prefer wet locations. Each of the 10 species produces glossy green leaves and scores of beautiful yellow or white flowers. But the kidney- or heart-shaped leaves are dramatic enough by themselves.

Nativity: All temperate and cool regions in N. America and elsewhere

Uses: Bog gardens, water's edge

Toxicity: Plant parts irritate skin and mucous membranes, and sniffing broken stems can induce sneezing, says ethnobotanist James Duke. Even so, Burrows and Tyrl say toxin concentrations are much lower in *Caltha* species than in other family members, such as hellebores and buttercups.

Propagation/Care: Plant seed as soon as it ripens, shown by a hardened seed coat, and keep it consistently cool and moist through the winter months. Divide plants in late summer or early spring.

Preferences/Hardiness: Plant in a boggy soil in full sun. Soil should be nutrient-rich. Zones 3–7.

Authorities: IL, PA

Calycanthus species

Carolina and California allspices, Sweetshrub

Strawberry-Shrub family (CALYCANTHACEAE)

Appearance: These deciduous shrubs, which grow up to 12 ft tall, have highly fragrant, long-lasting burgundy or brown blooms, except 'Athens' with yellow blooms. The leathery leaves are dark green and fragrant if crushed.

Nativity: United States

Uses: Shrub borders, specimen plants

Toxicity: Alkaloids in the fruits cause sudden symptoms like those of strychnine poisoning, including muscular spasms, sensitivity to touch and stimuli, loss of coordination, inability to stand, and sudden or slow death.

Propagation/Care: Remove suckers in spring; layer in autumn; take softwood cuttings in summer; plant seed as soon as it ripens (shown by a hardened seed coat) in containers in a cold frame.

Preferences/Hardiness: Grow in full sun or partial shade in moist, humus-rich soil with high to moderate fertility. Zones 6–9.

Authorities: *C. floridus* (Carolina allspice), GA.u, IL, NY.d; *C. floridas* 'Athens' and 'Michael Lindsey', PA; *C. occidentalis* (California allspice), CA.u

Camassia species

Quamash

Lily family (LILIACEAE)

Appearance: These bulbous perennials are grown for their tall spikes of white, blue, or purple flowers that rise above the highly decorative, gray-green, narrow leaves. The flowers are often multicolored, with lighter blue stripes running through the center of the petals and bright yellow centers. The flowers have a long vase-life; after the blooms fade, they leave decorative capsules.

Nativity: N. America

Uses: Mixed borders, wildflower gardens, containers

Toxicity: Sources suggest no toxins.

Propagation/Care: Remove rooted offsets in late summer and replant immediately. Plant just-ripened seed (shown by hardened seed coats) in containers and hold in the cold frame over winter.

Preferences/Hardiness: Grow in full sun or partial shade in well-drained but moist soil of moderate to high fertility. Zones 3–11.

Authorities: *Camassia* species, NY.r

Abbreviations for **Authorities** can be found on page 234.

Campanula 'Cherry Bell' (Bellflower)

Campsis radicans (Trumpet creeper, Trumpet vine)

Carex elata 'Aurea' (Bowles' golden sedge)

Campanula species

Bellflowers

Bluebell family (CAMPANULACEAE)

Appearance: The 300 species in this genus include annuals, biennials, and perennials. Some are low and spreading, some trailing, some clump-forming, some tall and airy. The blue, pink, and white flowers in most species are bell-shaped—some narrow and tubular, others open and star-shaped.

Nativity: S. Europe, Turkey particularly

Uses: Mixed borders, edging plants, hanging baskets, rock gardens, woodland plantings

Toxicity: Our sources offer no toxin assays. But family member *Lobelia* species have paridine alkaloids that produce serious toxic effects similar to those of ingested nicotine.

Propagation/Care: Plant seeds early in spring or in containers in a cold frame in autumn. Divide in spring or fall; take basal cuttings or softwood cuttings in spring.

Preferences/Hardiness: Species vary; Check with your supplier on exposure, soil pH, and fertility levels. Zones 5–9.

Authorities: *Campanula* species, AZ.u, CA.s; *C. carpatica, C. rotundifolia,* NY.r; *C. poscharskyana,* CA.s

Campsis radicans

Trumpet creeper, Trumpet vine

Bignonia family (BIGNONIACEAE)

Appearance: These woody climbers produce masses of vividly colored, trumpet-shaped flowers in shades of orange and red that attract hummingbirds. Using aerial roots, the vines climb up trees, trelliswork, and fences. Leaves are glossy green.

Nativity: N. America, China

Uses: Over trellises, to provide screening

Toxicity: Burrows and Tyrl report no ingestion issues. But some people suffer contact dermatitis.

Propagation/Care: Root semiripe cuttings in summer; graft in winter; take root cuttings in early winter. Plant ripe seeds (shown by hardened seed coats) in containers held in a cold frame over winter or stratify seeds and plant inside in early spring.

Preferences/Hardiness: Plant in full sun to partial shade in moist but well-drained soil of moderate to low fertility. This plant tolerates less than ideal conditions and can grow large enough to overwhelm a small support or tree. Zones 5–9.

Authorities: *C. radicans,* NY.d, PA

Carex species

Sedges

Sedge family (CYPERACEAE)

Appearance: These perennials suggest fancy grasses. Many are striped or have an olive green, reddish brown, or rich yellow hue. Flowers in some colors contrast with the leaves.

Nativity: Temperate and arctic regions

Uses: Mixed borders, woodland gardens, boggy areas

Toxicity: Sedges are poor forage, better reserved for basketry. However, family-member bulrushes (*Scripis* species) can cause severe respiratory and organ problems in cattle.

Propagation/Care: Divide in midspring, after plants have broken dormancy.

Preferences/Hardiness: Most sedges grow best in well-drained soils that are consistently moist. Sun and moisture requirements vary. Zones 5–9.

Authorities: CA.u; *C. appalachica* (Appalachian sedge), *C. flaccosperma* (Wood sedge), *C. grayi* (Common bur sedge), *C. laxiculmis* (Spreading sedge 'Bunny Blue'), *C. pensylvanica* (Pennsylvania sedge), *C. platyphylla* (Blue satin sedge), PA *Note:* *C. kobomugi* (Asiatic sand sedge, Jap. sedge) is invasive in MD, NJ, VA.

Catalpa species (Indian bean tree, Northern catalpa)

Ceanothus americanus (New Jersey tea)

Centaurea montana (Mountain bluet)

Catalpa species

Indian bean tree, Northern catalpa

Bignonia family (BIGNONIACEAE)

Appearance: Large leaves and thick canopies make catalpas good shade trees. A few cultivars have yellow leaves, but most are dark green. Catalpas are often grown for their clusters of white, bell-shaped flowers in spring and the long, brown, cylindrical seedpods, which can be a nuisance if they drop onto sidewalks or driveways so site these trees over grassy areas.

Nativity: E. Asia, N. America

Uses: Specimen trees

Toxicity: Our references offer no toxin assays.

Propagation/Care: Root softwood cuttings in late spring or summer; graft in late winter.

Preferences/Hardiness: Plant in full sun in well-drained soil with moderate fertility that consistently maintains good moisture levels. Zones 4–8.

Authorities: IL, MA; *C. speciosa* (Northern catalpa), NY.d *Note:* Native to a small region from S.W. IN, S.W. IL to TN and AR, *C. speciosa* is considered invasive in FL, MD, NJ, TN, VA. Southeastern native *C. bognonioides* (Southern catalpa) is invasive in CA.

Ceanothus species

California lilacs

Buckthorn family (RHAMNACEAE)

Appearance: The *Ceanothus* genus contains about 55 species of shrubs, some evergreen and some deciduous. They produce panicles or racemes of small white, pink, or blue flowers. Some cultivars, such as 'Cascade', grow only a ft or so tall and make good ground covers, but most are 6- to 15-ft-tall shrubs.

Nativity: United States and Mexico

Uses: Shrub borders, specimen plants, groundcovers, rock gardens

Toxicity: Our sources offer no toxin assays.

Propagation/Care: Root greenwood cuttings of deciduous cultivars in early summer; root semiripe cuttings of evergreens in mid- to late summer.

Preferences/Hardiness: Plant in full sun in medium to low fertility soil. Do not water or fertilize during the summer months. Zones 4–10.

Authorities: *C. americanus* (New Jersey tea), PA; *C. gloriosus* (Point Reyes creeper), CA.u (not deer resistant for CA.s); *C. velutinus* (Tobacco brush), MT

Abbreviations for **Authorities** can be found on page 234.

Centaurea species

Knapweeds

Aster family (ASTERACEAE)

Appearance: These annuals and perennials are grown for their blooms. Some, such as the annual bachelor's buttons *(C. cyanus),* are long-lasting cut flowers, and others, such as the perennial mountain bluet *(C. montana),* have a long bloom season. Most species have blue, white, or pink flowers. Those of perennial giant knapweed *(C. macrocephala)* are a bright, clear yellow.

Nativity: N. America, Europe, Asia, Australia

Uses: Mixed borders, cutting gardens, rock gardens

Toxicity: Our sources offer no toxin assay on cultivated *Centaurea.* Weedier species are relatively unpalatable to livestock. However, prolonged eating can cause brain damage with initial Parkinson-like symptoms in horses.

Propagation/Care: Plants self-seed easily. Divide in spring and take root cuttings in early winter.

Preferences/Hardiness: Plant in full sun in moist, well-drained soil with moderate fertility. *C. montana* also does well in partial shade. Zones 3–9.

Authorities: *C.* species, AZ.u, NY.r; *C. montana,* CA.s

Ceratostigma plumbaginoides
(Plumbago, Dwarf plumbago)

Cercis canadensis (Eastern redbud)

Chamaecyparis pisifera 'Filifera'
(Thread cypress, Sawara cypress)

Ceratostigma species

Plumbago

Leadwort family (PLUMBAGINACEAE)

Appearance: The clear blue, single, open flowers of plumbago bloom for at least 2 to 3 months in frost-free climates and a minimum of 6 weeks in areas with frost. Depending on the species, plumbago can grow to 3 or 4 ft high. In cold regions, in fall, its leaves turn vivid orange or red.

Nativity: Africa, Himalayas, China, S.E. Asia

Uses: Mixed border, specimen plants

Toxicity: Our sources offer no toxin assay on this genus. However, in this family, leadworts (*Plumbago* species) cause digestive disturbance, including vomiting.

Propagation/Care: Take softwood cuttings in spring, semiripe cuttings in winter. Layer in autumn and divide suckers in spring.

Preferences/Hardiness: Plant in full sun in very well-drained soil with moderate fertility. Can tolerate periods of drought. Zones 5–9.

Authorities: AZ.u, CA.s, NC, NY.r, WV

Site credit: Duncan Brine/Horticultural Design, Pawling, NY

Cercis canadensis

Eastern redbud

Pea family (FABACEAE)

Appearance: A harbinger of spring, redbud trees open their pink or white flowers just as the first crocus are blooming. The branches of this tree are literally coated with blooms because they grow on very short stalks, right out of the old wood of the tree. Leaves are often heart shaped, and the cultivar 'Forest Pansy' has deep red-purple leaves that make the tree stand out even in summer.

Nativity: N. America, S. Europe, C. and E. Asia

Uses: Specimen plants, hedgerows

Toxicity: Our sources offer no toxin assay.

Propagation/Care: Root semiripe cuttings or bud in summer.

Preferences/Hardiness: Plant in full sun or dappled shade in deep, friable, well-drained, moist, and fertile soil. Transplant into its final position when only a year or two old. Prune only lightly to shape the tree. Zones 6–9.

Authorities: AZ.u, IL, MA; *C. canadensis* 'Alba', 'Forest Pansy', 'Pauline Lily', PA

Chamaecyparis species

Cypresses

Cypress family (CUPRESSACEAE)

Appearance: The seven species and hundreds of cultivars of evergreen trees in this genus are remarkably variable in appearance. Some have golden yellow needles. Others have branches that seem to droop under imagined weights. Some are tall and skinny. And many are naturally rounded.

Nativity: N. America, Taiwan, Japan

Uses: Specimen plants, hedges, hedgerows

Toxicity: Our sources provide no toxin assay.

Propagation/Care: Root semiripe cuttings in summer.

Preferences/Hardiness: Plant in full sun in well-drained but moist soil with average fertility. When pruning, leave some of the current year's growth because plants do not regrow from old wood. Zones 4–9.

Authorities: *C.* species, GA.u, MA, NY.d; *C. obtusa* (Hinoki cypress), WA, WV

Site credit: Shore Acres Garden, Coos Bay, OR

Chasmanthium latifolium (Northern sea oats, Wild oats, Spangle grass)

Chelone lyonii 'Hot Lips' (Turtlehead)

Chionanthus virginicus (Fringe tree)

Chasmanthium latifolium

Northern sea oats, Wild oats, Spangle grass

Grass family (POACEAE)

Appearance: This perennial grass has broad, lance-shaped leaves 4 to 10 in. long. In late summer, spikes form that carry flat, almost oatlike panicles of seeds. In fall, the leaves turn yellow and the seeds turn bronze.

Nativity: E. and C. United States, Mexico, C. America

Uses: In mixed borders, woodland gardens, wildlife gardens

Toxicity: Although many grasses have glucosides that metabolize as cyanide, our sources provide no toxin assay on this one. Deer might simply avoid the dry, grassy appearance.

Propagation/Care: Plant seeds in early spring and transplant after frost. Divide naturally spreading plants.

Preferences/Hardiness: Tolerant of many conditions, from full sun to partial shade and moderately fertile to rich soil, but they require good drainage. Cut back to a few inches tall in winter. Zones 5–9.

Authorities: GA.a, PA, TX.a

Chelone species

Turtleheads

Figwort family (SCROPHULARIACEAE)

Appearance: Each of the six species in this genus of perennials has opposite, toothed leaves that are decorative with or without bloom. Pink, white, or purple flowers form on short spikes above the leaves and are hooded in such a way that they resemble turtles' heads. Sometimes the yellow beard on the bottom lip is visible, but usually, it is not.

Nativity: United States

Uses: Mixed borders, near water features, woodland gardens

Toxicity: Although our sources provide no toxin assay on turtleheads, family members with significant toxin issues include foxgloves *(Digitalis)* and toadflaxes *(Linaria).*

Propagation/Care: Plant seeds early inside; divide plants in early spring; root softwood cuttings in midspring.

Preferences/Hardiness: Grow in full sun or partial shade in moist, deep, fertile soil. Zones 3–9.

Authorities: *C.* species, GA.a, NY.r; *C. glabra,* PA; *C. lyonii* 'Hot Lips', PA

> Abbreviations for **Authorities** can be found on page 234.

Chionanthus species

Fringe trees

Olive family (OLEACEAE)

Appearance: These trees are grown for their fragrant white flower panicles—pendent in native *C. virginicus* (Fringe tree) and erect in *C. retusus* (Chinese fringe tree). Blue-black berries ripen in autumn. These trees grow only about 10 ft tall and can look shrubby unless you prune off bottom branches.

Nativity: E. United States, E. Asia, Korea, Japan

Uses: Specimen trees, mixed woodland plantings

Toxicity: *C. virginicus* liquid root-bark extract has caused frontal headache, slow pulse, and vomiting in people, says ethnobotanist James Duke.

Propagation/Care: Plant seed as soon as it ripens, shown by a hardened seed coat, and keep it in a protected spot. You may need to wait 18 months or more for germination.

Preferences/Hardiness: Grow in full sun in well-drained, fertile, humus-rich soil. Plants flower and fruit best in southern areas with long, warm summers. Zones 4–9.

Authorities: *C. retusus,* CA.s; *C. virginicus,* PA

Cladrastis lutea = C. kentukea
(Yellowwood)

Cleome hassleriana (Spider flower,
Cleome)

Consolida ajacis = C. ambigua (Larkspur)

Cladrastis lutea
(= *C. kentukea*)

Yellowwood

Pea family (FABACEAE)

Appearance: The native yellowwood
is grown for its attractive mid-green
foliage in summer and bright yellow
to orange fall foliage, as well as long
racemes of fragrant white, yellow-
marked flowers that reveal the family
relationship with wisteria and sweet
peas. *C. l.* 'Rosea' has pink-tinged
flowers. Both grow 40 ft tall. The
Asian *C. sinensis* can reach 70 ft tall.

Nativity: S.E. United States

Uses: Specimen trees, shade trees

Toxicity: Our sources offer no assay on
toxins.

Propagation/Care: Plant scarified
seeds in a nursery bed in autumn or
take root cuttings in winter.

Preferences/Hardiness: Grow in full
sun in well-drained, fertile soil. Plant
it in a sheltered area because the wood
is brittle and can snap in strong winds.
Zones 4–9.

Authorities: PA, WV

Abbreviations for **Authorities** can
be found on page 234.

Cleome hassleriana

Spider flower, Cleome

Caper family (CAPPARIDACEAE)

Appearance: Flower clusters of this
annual wave gracefully at heights of
4 to 6 ft from late summer till frost.
Cultivars are pink, rose, purple, and
white.

Nativity: S. America. *C. serrulata* is
native to C. and S.W. United States

Uses: Cleome looks good massed and
at backs of borders where its spindly
stems are concealed by smaller plants.
Caution: Cut arrangements look better
than they smell; wear gloves for the
prickly stems.

Toxicity: Repellency is likely due to
unpleasant odor, stem hairs, and the
sharp thorn at the base of each leaf
stem. Although cleomes accumulate
toxic nitrates and selenium, this
probably doesn't determine repellency.

Propagation/Care: Readily self-sows.
Start seed inside at 65°F, a month
before last frost.

Preferences/Hardiness: Grow in full
sun to partial shade in well-drained,
preferably sandy, soil.

Authorities: Deer—GA.a, NY.s,
NY.v; Rabbits—NY.s

Consolida ajacis
(= *C. ambigua*)

Larkspur

Buttercup family (RANUNCULACEAE)

Appearance: Once known as
Delphinium consolida, this annual is
grown for its white, blue, purple, rose,
and pink flower spikes and its delicate,
feathery leaves. Larkspur is often
called annual delphinium because its
flower spikes resemble delphinium
blooms, but lack the contrasting eye.

Nativity: S.E. Europe, W. Mediterranean, C. Asia

Uses: Mixed annual borders, cutting
gardens

Toxicity: Larkspurs and closely related
N. American delphiniums contain
alkaloids toxic to cattle, which can
develop aversions based on unpleasant
aftereffects. However, overeating can
result in tremors, lack of coordination,
and death from respiratory failure.

Propagation/Care: Plant seeds in peat
pots indoors in very early spring or
plant in situ. The taproot resents
disturbance. Self-seeds readily.

Preferences/Hardiness: Grow in full
sun in well-drained, moderately fertile
soil. Keep flower spikes cut to prolong
the bloom season; once they set seed,
these annuals die.

Authorities: IL, MO, TX.a, WA, WV

Convallaria majalis (Lily-of-the-valley)

Coreopsis lanceolata 'Baby Gold' (Dwarf lance-leafed tickseed)

Cornus florida (Flowering dogwood)

Convallaria majalis

Lily of the valley

Lily family (LILIACEAE)

Appearance: These perennials are grown for their arching, broad leaves and spikes of fragrant, waxy, bell-shaped flowers. Gardeners prize the long life span and ability to gradually spread without becoming invasive.

Nativity: N. temperate regions

Uses: Mixed borders, woodland gardens, groundcover

Toxicity: Presence of more than 20 cardenolides makes lily of the valley one of the most potent cardiotoxic plants. Salivation and vomiting precede heart issues and seizures. Most poisoning cases involve dogs and cats.

Propagation/Care: Plant rhizomes in spring or fall; separate rhizomes and replant in fall. If planting seeds, remove the flesh and plant in containers kept in a cold frame over winter.

Preferences/Hardiness: Grow in full sun to full shade in moist, fertile, humus-rich soil. Apply leaf mold or composted yard waste in autumn. Zones 2–7.

Authorities: CA.s, IL, MO, MT, NY.d, NY.r, NY.v, WV *Note:* Invasive WI

Coreopsis species

Tickseed

Aster family (ASTERACEAE)

Appearance: Most species are perennials; two are annuals. Most have clear, bright yellow flowers with distinct centers and toothed petals, although pink cultivars exist. Flowers are long-lasting in both the garden and the vase.

Nativity: N. and C. America, Mexico

Uses: Mixed borders, woodland gardens, wildflower gardens

Toxicity: Deer avoid this native, even though Burrows and Tyrl's monumental *Toxic Plants of North America* suggests no toxins.

Propagation/Care: For continuous bloom, sow annual seed in ground at 3-week intervals beginning in spring or start early inside. Often self-seeds. Start perennials early inside and plant out after danger of frost has passed. Divide perennials in early spring.

Preferences/Hardiness: Grow in full sun to partial shade in fertile, well-drained soil. Zones 4–9.

Authorities: Deer—AZ.u, CA.s, GA.a, IL, MT, NY.r, PA, WA, WV; Rabbits—AZ.u, CO.p, WA.f

Cornus species

Dogwood

Dogwood family (CORNACEAE)

Appearance: Most of the 45 species are deciduous trees and shrubs that bear cross-shaped white or pink flowers in spring; the ostensible "petals" are actually enlarged bracts. The berries are a favorite food for birds. Fall brings brightly colored leaves.

Nativity: N. temperate regions

Uses: As specimens or in mixed woodland plantings

Toxicity: In humans, the bark can affect the heart and cause nausea, headache, vomiting, abdominal pain, and diarrhea. Perhaps deer feel similar effects after browsing the twigs and maybe the leaves.

Propagation/Care: Graft cultivars in spring; root greenwood cuttings in summer; plant seeds in fall.

Preferences/Hardiness: Preferences vary by species. Zones 3–7.

Authorities: *C. alternifolia* (Pagoda dogwood), MA, PA; *C. florida* (Flowering dogwood), MA, MO, PA; *C. kousa* (Kousa dogwood), CA.s, NY.d; *C. stolonifera* (Red-osier dogwood), MO, MT, NY.d, WA, WV

Corydalis lutea (Corydalis, Gold bleeding heart)

Cotoneaster apiculatus (Cranberry cotoneaster)

Crataegus arnoldiana (Arnold hawthorn)

Corydalis lutea

Corydalis, Gold bleeding heart

Poppy family (PAPAVERACEAE)

Appearance: This little perennial grows about 16 to 18 in. tall and has attractive drooping leaflets. The plant flowers freely from early summer to early autumn, its blooms clear yellow with spurs.

Nativity: S. Alps; other species native to N. America

Uses: Mixed borders, rock gardens

Toxicity: All species contain toxic alkaloids, including protuberines, that quickly cause depression and rapid respiration followed by disorientation, muscle twitching (especially in the face), and then staggering and collapse with seizures.

Propagation/Care: Plant seed in a protected spot as soon as it's ripe, shown by a hardened seed coat; divide plants in early spring.

Preferences/Hardiness: Plant in full sun to partial shade. Thrives in moderately fertile soil with good drainage and high humus levels. Zones 5–8.

Authorities: NY.r

Cotoneaster species

Cotoneaster

Rose family (ROSACEAE)

Appearance: These shrubs and trees may be deciduous or evergreen, most grown for white, pink, or reddish flowers and their red, yellow, or orange berries. Deciduous leaves color vividly in fall.

Nativity: N. temperate regions of Europe, N. Africa, and Asia

Uses: Foundation plantings, shrub borders, hedges, groundcovers

Toxicity: Many cotoneasters contain glycosides that metabolize as toxic cyanide.

Propagation/Care: Take semiripe cuttings of evergreens in mid- to late summer; greenwood cuttings of deciduous plants in early summer.

Preferences/Hardiness: Deciduous plants prefer sun; evergreens, sun or partial shade. Grow in well-drained soil with moderate fertility. Zones 4–9.

Authorities: AZ.u, GA.u, WA; *C. apiculatus* (Cranberry cotoneaster) 'Tom Thumb', CA.s; *C. buxifolius*, CA.s, CA.u; *C. glaucophyllus* (Gray cotoneaster), TX. a; *C. integrifolius* (Rockspray cotoneaster), CA.s *Note:* Invasive in CA: *C. fanchetii* (Orange c.), *C. lacteus* (Milkflower c.), *C. pannosus* (Silver-leaf c.)

Site credit: Forestfarm Nursery, Williams, OR

Crataegus species

Hawthorn

Rose family (ROSACEAE)

Appearance: Most of the 200-plus species of hawthorn trees are thorny and deciduous, and bear red, purplish, blue-green, or black fruit. The white or pink to red spring-blooming flowers of some species are quite showy. Some hawthorns grow 50 ft tall.

Nativity: N. temperate regions

Uses: Specimen trees and hedging

Toxicity: Like other Rose family members, many hawthorns contain glycosides that generate cyanide in the leaves and seeds, which in mammals can cause weakness, rapid respiration, incoordination, collapse, seizures, and death. Ruminants are especially susceptible.

Propagation/Care: Graft in late winter; bud in summer. If planting seeds, place containers in a sheltered spot. Germination can take 18 months.

Preferences/Hardiness: Plant in full sun or partial shade in any well-drained, moderately fertile soil. Zones 3–8.

Authorities: AZ.u, MA, MO, MT; *C. laevigata = oxycantha*, NY.d

Crocosmia 'Lucifer' (Montbretia)

Cryptomeria japonica 'Monstrosa Nana' (Japanese cedar)

Daphne × *burkwoodii* 'Carol Mackie' (Daphne)

Crocosmia × *crocosmiiflora*

Montbretia

Iris family (IRIDACEAE)

Appearance: Standouts in the mixed border or vase, these perennials are grown for both their slender lance-shaped leaves and for their orange, pink, white, and red flowers, which form in midsummer on spikes above the leaves.

Nativity: S. Africa

Uses: Mixed borders and as focal points

Toxicity: Our sources offer no toxin assay.

Propagation/Care: Plants form seeds and also reproduce by making more corms. Plant seeds as soon as they are ripe, shown by hardened seed coats, and hold the containers in a cold frame over the winter. Divide plants in spring, just before growth resumes.

Preferences/Hardiness: Plant in full sun or partial shade in spring, setting the corms 3 to 4 in. deep. Plants thrive in well-drained, moderately fertile, humus-rich soils. Zones 6–9.

Authorities: CA.s, CA.u

Cryptomeria japonica

Japanese cedar

Yew family (TAXODIACEAE)

Appearance: The many cultivars of Japanese cedars are grown as much for their graceful habits as for the way their leaves, or needles, grow in tight spirals around the shoots. Female cones have individual scales shaped like shields with pointed teeth along the apex. Some cultivars are conical, some columnar, and others so small they fit nicely in a rock garden.

Nativity: China, Japan

Uses: Specimen trees, windbreaks, rock gardens

Toxicity: Our sources offer no toxin assay.

Propagation/Care: Take hardwood cuttings in early autumn and root over heat during the winter.

Preferences/Hardiness: Grow in full sun or partial shade in well-drained soil that is deep, fertile, and moist. Shelter from strong winds. Zones 6–9.

Authorities: OR, WV

> Abbreviations for **Authorities** can be found on page 234.

Daphne species

Daphne

Mezereum family (THYMELAEACEAE)

Appearance: The more than 50 species of daphne shrubs are decidu-ous, semi-evergreen, or evergreen and range from 4 in. to 12 ft tall. Most have fragrant clusters of tubular, waxy-looking flowers in white, pink, red-purple, lavender, or yellow.

Nativity: Europe, N. Africa, Asia

Uses: Groundcovers, rock gardens, mixed borders

Toxicity: Bitter, highly irritating diterpenes in berries and plant parts cause blistering and swelling in the mouth. Ingestion leads to nausea, vomiting, diarrhea, and sometimes death in children.

Propagation/Care: Graft or layer in early spring; take softwood cuttings in early summer and semiripe and evergreen cuttings in mid- to late summer.

Preferences/Hardiness: Full sun to partial shade. Moist, well-drained, moderately fertile, humus-rich soil. Dislike transplanting, so move from starting containers into final growing locations. Zones 6–9.

Authorities: AZ.u; *D. odora* (Winter daphne), CA.s, GA.u; *Daphne* × *burkwoodii*, NY.d, NY.v

Delphinium 'Galahad' (Delphinium)

Dennstaedtia punctiloba (Hay-scented fern)

Dianthus 'Princess Pink' (Pinks, Carnation, Sweet William)

Delphinium species

Delphiniums

Buttercup family (RANUNCULACEAE)

Appearance: *Delphinium* annuals (larkspurs), biennials, and perennials have tall flower spikes. Flowers are either tightly massed along the stalk (Elatum group) or loose (Belladonna group). Colors include white, pink, blue, purple, red, and yellow. The usually lobed leaves form a mound.

Nativity: Mountainous areas worldwide

Uses: Mixed borders, rock gardens

Toxicity: Delphiniums and closely related larkspur contain alkaloids toxic to cattle, which may develop aversions based on digestive consequences. Overeating can cause tremors, incoordination, and respiratory failure.

Propagation/Care: Plant seeds early indoors at 55°F. In early spring, just as growth resumes, take basal cuttings with a "heel" by including a bit of bark and its underlying cambium layer.

Preferences/Hardiness: Sheltered location in full sun. Fertile, well-drained soil. Stake the flower stalk when taller than the leaves. Cut back to 2 to 3 in. in autumn. Zones 3–7.

Authorities: *D. elatum,* GA.a, NY.d; native *D. exaltatum,* PA

Dennstaedtia punctiloba

Hay-scented fern

Bracken Fern family (DENNSTAEDTIACEAE)

Appearance: This deciduous fern's fronds emerge from a steadily branching rhizome. The arching fronds are yellow-green and grow up to 18 in. tall. When dried, they have the fresh scent of hay.

Nativity: N. America

Uses: Shaded borders

Toxicity: Family member *Pteridium aquilinum* (Bracken) is highly toxic and a carcinogen to ruminants and horses over time, but our sources offer no assay on hay-scented fern. Deer that have suffered unpleasant aftereffects from one fern might begin avoiding all.

Propagation/Care: Divide in spring by cutting and transplanting rooted pieces of the rhizome. Spreads easily.

Preferences/Hardiness: Grow in partial or full shade in moist soil with moderate fertility, high humus levels, and an acid pH. Zones 3–8.

Authorities: PA

Abbreviations for **Authorities** can be found on page 234.

Dianthus species

Pinks, Carnation, Sweet William

Pink family (CARYOPHYLLACEAE)

Appearance: The hundreds of species include annuals, biennials, perennials, and small shrubs. Most are grown for their white, pink, red, or yellow blooms—many double with toothed petals, some with picoteed edges and colorful centers.

Nativity: One Alaskan native, mat-forming *D. repens;* S., C., and E. Europe; Japan, N. Asia

Uses: In mixed borders, cutting gardens, rock gardens

Toxicity: Species contain steroidal saponins known in other genera to reduce appetite in ruminants, while causing digestive distress, muscle spasms, and paralysis.

Propagation/Care: Start seed early indoors; plant biennials in place in early summer. Take cuttings from nonflowering shoots in early to midsummer.

Preferences/Hardiness: Plant in full sun in well-drained soil with moderate fertility. Deadhead to prolong flowering. Zones often 3–9, sometimes 9–11.

Authorities: GA.u, IL, MO, MT, NY.r; *D. barbatus* (Sweet William), IL

Dicentra spectabilis (Bleeding heart)

Digitalis purpurea (Common foxglove)

Echinacea purpurea (Purple coneflower)

Dicentra species

Bleeding hearts

Fumitory family (FUMARIACEAE)

Appearance: Forming delicately handsome mounds, these plants feature racemes of pendent heart-shaped pink, red, yellow, or white flowers. Leaves are lobed and highly decorative in themselves. *Dicentra* (from Greek) refers to each flower's two (*di-*) spurs (*kentron*).

Nativity: N. America (the fringed species), Asia

Uses: In shade gardens or mixed borders with other deer-resistant plants, such as ferns, columbine *(Aquilegia),* barrenworts *(Epimedium),* sweet alyssum *(Lobularia maritima),* and foamflowers *(Tiarella)*

Toxicity: Isoquinoline alkaloids vary by species but can cause trembling, staggering, and seizures in livestock.

Propagation/Care: From seedlings or root division. However, roots are very brittle.

Preferences/Hardiness: Grow in partial to full shade and moist, fertile, humus-rich, well-drained soil. Zones 3–9.

Authorities: AZ.u, CA.s, CA.u, GA.a, MO, MT, NY.l, NY.r, WA; native *D. exima* (Fringed bleeding heart), PA; *D. spectabilis,* WV

Digitalis species

Foxgloves

Figwort family (SCROPHULARIACEAE)

Appearance: Many foxgloves grow 3 to 5 ft tall. Most are biennials, creating a rosette of basal leaves the first year and sending up flower spikes the second.

Nativity: Europe, N.W. Africa, and Asia (naturalized in parts of the United States)

Uses: Mixed borders, shade gardens

Toxicity: Digitalis and its extracted cardenolides have long been used to treat heart disease in humans. But concentrations in the seeds, flowers, and immature leaves can be highly toxic to humans, other mammals, and birds.

Propagation/Care: Sow indoors in early spring or outside in late spring. Divide in spring or fall. Many self-seed prolifically; deadhead to avoid this.

Preferences/Hardiness: Grow in full sun to partial shade in well-drained, fertile soil. Zones 3–9.

Authorities: Deer—CA.s, CA.u, IL, MT, NY.r, WV; *D. ferruginea* (Rusty foxglove), *D. lutea* (Yellow foxglove), *Digitalis* × *mertonensis* (Strawberry foxglove), CA.s. Rabbits—CO.p, IA.b, LEW

Echinacea species

Coneflower, Purple coneflower

Aster family (ASTERACEAE)

Appearance: Purple coneflower (*E. purpurea*) is the best-known member of this genus composed of perennials with open blooms with prominent golden to brown, cone-shaped centers that steadily extend upward as the flower ages. Flowers may be purple, white, pink, or red, depending on species, and leaves are often thick and deeply veined.

Nativity: C. and N. America

Uses: Mixed borders, open woodland

Toxicity: Our sources offer no toxin assay.

Propagation/Care: Plant seeds in early spring indoors and transplant after frost-free date. Divide clumps in early spring every 3 to 4 years.

Preferences/Hardiness: Plants thrive in full sun but will tolerate partial shade in warm climates. Grow in deep, moderately fertile, humus-rich, and well-drained soil. Deadhead to prolong blooming season. Zones 3–9.

Authorities: GA.a, GA.u; *E. purpurea,* CA.s, IL, MT, NY.d, NY.r, WA, WV

Echinops bannaticus 'Veitch's Blue' (Blue globe thistle)

Epimedium (Barrenwort)

Eranthis hyemalis (Winter aconite)

Echinops species

Globe thistle
Aster family (ASTERACEAE)

Appearance: Blue, white, or silver-gray florets form spherical, prickly looking balls that rise above foliage in this genus of more than 120 annuals, biennials, and perennials. Many species have spined, deeply lobed leaves that are grayish white or silvery thanks to a coating of fine hairs.

Nativity: C. and S. Europe, C. Asia, India, mountains in Africa

Uses: Mixed borders, cutting gardens, wildflower gardens

Toxicity: Although our sources offer no toxin assay, the spines everywhere must give browsers pause.

Propagation/Care: Start seeds in an outdoor seedbed with deep soil in midspring. Divide in fall or early spring. Take root cuttings in fall. Self-seed prolifically; deadhead to prevent unauthorized seed spread.

Preferences/Hardiness: Globe thistles thrive in full sun and extremely well-drained, moderate to low fertility soil but will tolerate a range of soils. Zones 3–9.

Authorities: NY.l, NY.r, WA; *E. exaltatus*, CA.s

Epimedium species

Barrenwort
Barberry family (BERBERIDACEAE)

Appearance: These perennials are characterized by panicles or racemes of spurred yellow, pink, white, red, or purple flowers that rise above the leathery leaves with spines at their margins. Some species are deciduous, while others retain their leaves all winter. Leaves often turn a bronzy color in spring and autumn.

Nativity: Mediterranean, E. Asia

Uses: Groundcover, mixed border, rock garden

Toxicity: Our sources offer no toxin assay.

Propagation/Care: Start seed as soon as it is ripe and feels dry to the touch; hold in a cold frame over winter. Transplant to the open after danger of frost has passed. Divide in autumn or after flowering.

Preferences/Hardiness: Barrenworts thrive in partial shade. Protect from winter winds and plant in well-drained, fertile, humus-rich, and moist soil.

Authorities: CA.u, IL, MT, NY.r, WV; *E. grandiflorum* (Bishop's hat, Longspur barrenwort), NY.d

Eranthis hyemalis

Winter aconite
Buttercup family (RANUNCULACEAE)

Appearance: One of the earliest of all bulbs to bloom, winter aconite embodies cheerfulness. The cup-shaped blooms are a clear, bright yellow and can be more than an inch across. Each bloom is surrounded by a collar of green, softly pointed leaves. They easily naturalize, so it doesn't take long for a small patch to become a broad swath.

Nativity: Eurasia

Uses: Plant under and around deciduous trees and shrubs, in bulb gardens, or in rock gardens.

Toxicity: Ingestion causes mild stomach upset, and sap may irritate skin, says the American Horticultural Society.

Propagation/Care: Dig, separate, and replant the tubers immediately after they flower. Tubers do not survive being dried out. If you buy them in autumn, buy only plump, moist tubers.

Preferences/Hardiness: Grow in full sun or light shade in well-drained soil that remains moist over the summer. Zones 4–9.

Authorities: IL, MO, NY.r

Erica carnea 'Springwood Pink' (Alpine heath)

Erigeron glaucus 'Olga' (Beech aster)

Eschscholzia californica (California poppy)

Erica species

Heaths, Heathers

Heath family (ERICACEAE)

Appearance: The huge *Erica* genus includes almost 700 species of perennial evergreen subshrubs and shrubs. The flowers are often bell-shaped and liberally coat the branch ends. Some species are tall shrubs, but others grow only about 6 in. tall and make excellent ground covers.

Nativity: Europe, Africa, W. and C. Asia

Uses: Specimen plants, groundcovers, mixed borders, mixed shrub plantings

Toxicity: Deer find other genera in this family unpalatable, often toxic, but our sources offer no comment on *Erica* specifically.

Propagation/Care: Layer in spring; take semiripe cuttings in summer.

Preferences/Hardiness: These plants thrive in full sun in well-drained soils with moderate to good fertility. Additionally, the majority of *Erica* species requires acid soil; check with your supplier about requirements.

Authorities: CA.u, NY.l, OR, WA; *E.* × *darleyensis,* CA.s

> Abbreviations for **Authorities** can be found on page 234.

Erigeron species

Fleabane, Sea holly

Aster family (ASTERACEAE)

Appearance: This genus includes annuals, biennials, and perennials, some low growing and some erect. All species have composite blooms with yellow centers and narrow, pointed petals. Colors include shades of white, pink, yellow, blue, and purple. The leaves are mid-green and lance-shaped.

Nativity: N. America; dry, temperate areas in Europe

Uses: Mixed borders, rock gardens, cutting gardens

Toxicity: Our sources offer no toxin assay.

Propagation/Care: Plant seeds indoors in early spring; divide perennials in spring; take basal cuttings in spring.

Preferences/Hardiness: Grow in full sun in northern regions, in dappled sun in the South; and in well-drained soil of moderate fertility, high humus content, and with consistent moisture. Zones 2–8.

Authorities: AZ.u, NY.r, WA; *E.* × *hybridus,* IL; *E. karvinkianus* (Santa Barbara daisy), CA.s

Eschscholzia californica

California poppy

Poppy family (PAPAVERACEAE)

Appearance: Satiny, cup-shaped flowers bob among the finely divided, almost fernlike, gray-green leaves of this lovely little annual. Most cultivars have single yellow flowers, but you can also find doubles and cultivars with orange, red, apricot, and creamy white blooms. The leaves are decorative on their own, but the plant has such a long flowering season that it's easy to ignore them.

Nativity: W. North America

Uses: Mixed borders, containers, rock gardens

Toxicity: Various toxic alkaloids likely cause bad taste.

Propagation/Care: Plant seeds where they are to grow. For blooms throughout the season, plant them from just before last frost until midsummer.

Preferences/Hardiness: California poppies thrive in full sun. They grow best in well-drained soil with average to low fertility levels.

Authorities: AZ.u, GA.u, WA

Eupatorium fistulosum 'Gateway'
(Joe Pye weed)

Euphorbia amygdaloides var. *robbiae*
(Mrs. Robb's bonnet)

Fagus sylvatica forma *pendula*
(Weeping beech)

Eupatorium species

Joe Pye weeds, Snakeroot,
    and more

Aster family (ASTERACEAE)

Appearance: This genus includes
annuals, herbaceous perennials,
subshrubs, and evergreen shrubs.
Favored by bees and butterflies, the
flower clusters are usually pink,
purple, or white.

Nativity: N. and S. America, Europe,
Africa, Asia

Uses: Back borders or mixed,
depending on height

Toxicity: Lactones in various *Eupatori-
ums* cause cell damage in mammals.
But tremetol in white snakeroot causes
milk-sickness deaths in people and
cows. Producing initial symptoms
known as the trembles, this plant also
kills horses and goats.

Propagation/Care: Take softwood
cuttings in spring; divide hardy
perennials; plant seeds in containers in
a cold frame to stratify over winter.

Preferences/Hardiness: Plant in full
sun. Most species do well in slightly
alkaline (pH of 7.5) soil that is well
drained and moderately fertile.

Authorities: GA.a, MT, NY.l, NY.r;
E. coelestinum (Mistflower), PA, TX.a;
E. rugosum (Snakeroot), IL

Euphorbia species

Spurge

Spurge family (EUPHORBIACEAE)

Appearance: The nearly 2,000 species
include annuals, perennials, biennials,
succulents, subshrubs, shrubs, and trees.
Some resemble cacti, some herbaceous
perennials, some aliens from another
planet. Avoid invasive aliens *E.
cyparissias* (Cypress spurge) and *E. esula*
(Leafy spurge).

Nativity: Temperate, subtropical, and
tropical regions

Uses: Xeriscapes, mixed borders,
specimens

Toxicity: The sap contains esters that
irritate the mouth, skin, and digestive
tract—even potentially through bee honey
and cow milk. Symptoms may include
salivation, vomiting, diarrhea, and
worse. Diterpenes from some cactuslike
species taste like hot peppers on steroids.

Propagation/Care: Depends on
species. Plant annual seeds in the
ground in spring. Divide perennials in
early spring; root stems of succulents;
root cuttings of shrubs and trees.

Preferences/Hardiness: Follow
supplier's guidance. Zones 5–15.

Authorities: AZ.u, CA.s, CA.u, NY.l,
NY.r, WV; *E. × martini* (Spurge), *E.
amygdaloides* var. *robbiae* (Mrs. Robb's
bonnet), CA.s

*Fagus grandifolia,
F. sylvatica*

American beech,
    European beech

Beech family (FAGACEAE)

Appearance: When grown in the
open, these woodland and forest trees
become magnificent specimens with
broad, dense crowns to 80 ft tall.
Yet there are small cultivars, such as
the 10-ft-tall purple-leaved weeping
F. sylvatica 'Purpurea Pendula'. A few
cultivars have yellowish leaves, but
most have deep green leaves that turn
brilliant yellow in fall.

Nativity: N. Hemisphere

Uses: Woodland gardens, specimen
trees

Toxicity: Saponin-like substances in the
nuts of European beeches have caused
digestive tract "derangement" and
seizures in horses and people. But our
sources are silent on leaf palatability.

Propagation/Care: Stratify (chill) seed
over winter and plant in spring; graft
cultivars in late winter.

Preferences/Hardiness: Grow in full
sun or partial shade in well-drained
soil of average fertility. Zones 3–9.

Authorities: IL, MA, MO, NY.r;
F. sylvatica (European beech), NY.d

Foeniculum vulgare (Fennel)

Forsythia × *intermedia* 'Lynwood'
(Forsythia)

Fraxinus (Ashes)

Foeniculum vulgare

Fennel

Carrot family (APIACEAE)

Appearance: Fennel, a perennial in warm climates, is a favorite seasoning and vegetable. The leaves and seeds are used in Italian sausage and tomato sauces, and the bulblike stem of the biennial *F. vulgare* var. *azoricum* is used raw in salads or cooked as a vegetable. Invasive as ornamental if allowed to reseed. If growing it as a culinary herb, remove flowerheads before seeds mature.

Nativity: Mediterranean

Uses: Herb garden, vegetable garden, cutting garden

Toxicity: Fortunately, our sources suggest no toxin issues. Perhaps the airy leaves appear insubstantial to browsers with other choices.

Propagation/Care: Direct-seed into the garden location or start seed early in peat pots or soil blocks; taproots resent transplanting. Plants self-seed in warm climates.

Preferences/Hardiness: Plant in full sun in well-drained, humus-rich, moist soil with moderate to high fertility.

Authorities: IL, MO, NY.r

Forsythia species

Forsythia

Olive family (OLEACEAE)

Appearance: These spreading shrubs are cloaked in cheery bright yellow flowers in very early spring. Because the flowers open before the leaves, they can be forced indoors; for that, cut branches when buds swell and place in water in a cool to warm room. The leaves are a dark green.

Nativity: E. Asia, one species from S.E. Europe

Uses: Shrub borders, hedges, specimen plants

Toxicity: In our tests, young tender leaves on new shoots tasted slightly bitter and left an unpleasant aftertaste. Leaves on old wood are tough chewing. Our sources offer no toxin assay.

Propagation/Care: Layer in spring; take greenwood cuttings in late spring and semiripe cuttings in summer. Forsythia sucker freely, enlarging their footprint every season unless cut back.

Preferences/Hardiness: Grow in full sun or lightly dappled shade in well-drained, moderately fertile, moist soil. Zones 4–9.

Authorities: GA.u, IL, MO; *F.* × *intermedia*, NY.d

Fraxinus species

Ashes

Olive family (OLEACEAE)

Appearance: Most of the trees are deciduous, grown for their brilliant fall foliage and graceful habits. Blooms of species such as *F. ornus* (Flowering ash) and *F. sieboldiana* are fragrant and form large, showy panicles, but flowers of most ashes are inconspicuous.

Nativity: N. America, Europe, Asia

Uses: Specimens, woodland gardens

Toxicity: Leaves of some species have caused digestive problems in cattle, perhaps owing to various glycosides.

Propagation/Care: Stratify seeds for 4 months before planting or plant them in containers and hold them in a cold frame over the winter months. Graft in late winter.

Preferences/Hardiness: Grow in full sun in well-drained, fertile soil with steady moisture levels and a neutral to alkaline pH. Zones 3–8.

Authorities: AZ.u, IL, MA; *F. americana* (White ash), PA; *F. latifolia* (Oregon ash), WA; *F. pennsylvanica* (Green ash), NY.d, PA

Abbreviations for **Authorities** can be found on page 234.

Fritillaria imperialis (Crown imperial)

Gaillardia × grandiflora 'Portola Giants'
(Blanket flower)

Gaultheria shallon (Salal, Shallon)

Fritillaria species

Crown imperial, Fritillary

Lily family (LILIACEAE)

Appearance: These perennials have striking, cup- or tube-shaped flowers in pendent clusters on top of tall spikes. Flowers may be green, yellow, pink, purple, orange, white, red, or checkerboard reds and browns. Some species grow only 8 in. tall; others, 4 ft.

Nativity: W. North America, Mediterranean, S.W. Asia

Uses: Woodland gardens, rock gardens, bulb gardens

Toxicity: Most contain alkaloids like those in family member hellebores, which cause nausea, vomiting, abdominal pain, and decreased blood pressure and heart rate—sometimes blurred vision.

Propagation/Care: In autumn, plant bulbs in several inches of sharp sand to ensure good drainage. In soggy soils, they often rot. Dig and separate bulbs in crowded plantings. If plants form offsets, divide these in early spring.

Preferences/Hardiness: Follow distinct supplier guidance for each of the four groups.

Authorities: WA, WV; *F. imperialis*, IL, MO, NY.d, NY.l, NY.r

Gaillardia species

Blanket flower

Aster family (ASTERACEAE)

Appearance: The *Gaillardia* genus includes annuals, such as *G. pulchella*, as well as biennials and perennials, grown for their vivid red, yellow, and orange blooms with colored centers. What resemble toothed petals around the centers are actually bracts. In some cultivars, such as *G. × grandiflora* 'Dazzler', these bracts are tipped with another color.

Nativity: W., C., and S. North America, S. America

Uses: Mixed borders, cutting gardens

Toxicity: Bitter sesquiterpene lactones, like those in most members of the Aster family, deter livestock and insects.

Propagation/Care: Plant seed early inside; divide perennials in spring.

Preferences/Hardiness: Grow in full sun in well-drained soil with average to poor fertility. Deadhead and cut perennials back to a few inches in fall. Zones 3–8.

Authorities: GA.a; *G. aristata*, NY.r, WA; *G. × grandiflora*, AZ.u, CA.s, NY.r

Gaultheria procumbens, G. shallon

Creeping wintergreen, Salal, Shallon

Heath family (ERICACEAE)

Appearance: Shrubs to 5 ft and shrublets to 6 in. have fragrant, bell-shaped spring flowers, generally white, pink, or pink-beige. Berries are red, purple, yellow, or white and mature in fall.

Nativity: N., S., and C. America; Himalayas; E. Asia

Uses: Groundcovers, rock gardens, woodland gardens

Toxicity: Wintergreen aroma in crushed leaves arises from methyl salicylate, which can cause headache, nausea, fever, dizziness, ear ringing, reduced hearing, dim vision, confusion, fatigue, drowsiness, seizures, and coma.

Propagation/Care: Plant ripe seeds, shown by hardened seed coats, in containers and overwinter in a cold frame. Take semiripe cuttings in summer; remove rooted suckers.

Preferences/Hardiness: Grow in partial shade in moist, rich soil. Plants tolerate pH levels of 5.0 or so. Zones 4–8.

Authorities: NY.r, WA, WV; *G. shallon* (Salal), CA.u, OR, WA

Geranium maculatum (Wild geranium)

Ginkgo biloba 'Princeton Sentry' (Ginkgo, Maidenhair tree)

Gleditsia triacanthos (Honeylocust)

Geranium species

Cranesbill

Geranium family (GERANIACEAE)

Appearance: With delicate, cup-shaped, flat, or star-shaped flowers in various colors and deeply cut leaves, these dainty perennials can be show-stoppers in partial shade.

Nativity: All temperate regions

Uses: Rock gardens, groundcovers, under shrubs, mixed borders

Toxicity: Not all species are deer-resistant, but those with the family's characteristic aromatic oils tend to be.

Propagation/Care: Plant seeds early indoors or when ripe (shown by hardened seed coats) in containers held for winter in a cold frame. Divide plants in spring. Take softwood or basal cuttings in spring.

Preferences/Hardiness: Plant in partial shade or full sun in the North in well-drained soil with moderate fertility. Remove spent flower stems and trim to keep tidy. Zones 5–8.

Authorities: AZ.u, GA.a, IL, MO, MT, NY.d; *G.* × *cantabrigiense,* CA.s; *G. macrorrhizum* (Scented geranium), CT.n; *G. maculatum* (Wild geranium) 'Espresso' and 'Alba', PA; *G. san-guineum* (Bloody cranesbill), 'Cedric Morris', CA.s *Note:* CA.s says blacktails eat some geraniums.

Ginkgo biloba

Ginkgo, Maidenhair tree

Ginkgo family (GINKGOACEAE)

Appearance: This ancient genus has a single surviving species with either male or female trees. Their youthful columnar forms become graceful, wide-spreading trees to 120 ft tall. Fan-shaped green leaves turn butter-yellow in fall. Male cultivars include conical 'Autumn Gold' (50 ft) and twirly hairbrush-shaped 'Princeton Sentry' (65 ft). Female trees drop foul-smelling grape-size fruits in fall.

Nativity: S. China

Uses: Specimen tree, shade tree

Toxicity: Seeds contain methylpyridox-ine that in quantity causes vomiting, diarrhea, seizures, and sometimes death. Ginkgolic acid in fruit flesh causes contact dermatitis like that from poison ivy. Medicinal leaf extracts may cause headache, gastric upset, and diminished blood clotting.

Propagation/Care: Plant seed in a nursery bed in autumn; take semiripe cuttings in summer; graft in late winter.

Preferences/Hardiness: Plant in full sun in well-drained, fertile soil. Zones 5–9.

Authorities: AZ.u, GA.u, IL, MO, NY.d, PA

Gleditsia triacanthos

Honeylocust

Pea family (FABACEAE)

Appearance: These large trees are grown for their elegant forms and lovely leaves that grow opposite one another on long stems. With the exception of cultivars of native *G. triacanthos,* most honeylocusts have long, sharp thorns on their branches and sometimes their trunks. Many develop long seedpods that hang from the branches in fall and early winter. Some species have red leaves; the leaves of others are yellow-green.

Nativity: N. and S. America, Asia, Africa

Uses: Specimen trees

Toxicity: Our sources offer no toxin assay.

Propagation/Care: Graft in early spring or bud in summer.

Preferences/Hardiness: Place in a location with deep, fertile, well-drained soil and full sun. Zones 7–10.

Authorities: *G. triacanthos,* IL, MA, MO, MT, NY.d, NY.r; *G. tiacanthos* var. *inermis,* NY.r

Abbreviations for **Authorities** can be found on page 234.

Gypsophila paniculata (Baby's breath)

Helenium autumnale (Sneezeweed)

Helleborus orientalis (Lenten-rose)

Gypsophila species

Baby's breath
Pink family (CARYOPHYLLACEAE)

Appearance: These mound-forming perennials have a liberal sprinkling of dainty white flowers and sparse foliage, attributes that serve beautifully in flower arrangements and rose bouquets. Baby's breath also dries well. Annuals in this genus also make good cut flowers.

Nativity: C., S., and E. Europe

Uses: Cutting gardens, rock gardens, mixed borders

Toxicity: Steroidal saponins occurring in Pink family members can reduce appetite in ruminants and cause digestive distress, muscle spasms, and paralysis.

Propagation/Care: Plant seeds inside in early spring and transplant after all danger of frost has passed. Take root cuttings in winter.

Preferences/Hardiness: Grow in full sun in extremely well-drained, moderately fertile soil that has a pH close to neutral or on the alkaline side. Zones 4–9.

Authorities: *G. repens,* CA.s, NY.r, WA; *G. paniculata,* NY.r, WA *Note: G. paniculta* invasive in CO, MI, OR, WA, WI

Helenium autumnale

Sneezeweed
Aster family (ASTERACEAE)

Appearance: This native perennial's yellow flowers with brown centers suggest miniature sunflowers. The genus also includes many native annuals and biennials, some of them weedy. Attractive to bees and beneficial insects, *Helenium* species have a long flowering period and long vase-life.

Nativity: N. America

Uses: Mixed borders, cutting gardens, near beehives

Toxicity: All species contain bittering sesquiterpene lactones that discourage browsing. Some species cause regurgitation and vomiting in sheep. Fed to research dogs in 1915, *A. autumnale* caused diarrhea, vomiting, and death due to heart paralysis. The lactones also impart bitter taste to milk, butter, and meat.

Propagation/Care: Plant seeds indoors in early spring and transplant after all danger of frost has passed. Divide in spring every third year.

Preferences/Hardiness: Grow in full sun in well-drained soil of moderate to high fertility. Deadhead to prolong bloom. Zones 3–8.

Authorities: CA.s, IL, NY.d, NY.r

Helleborus species

Hellebores
Buttercup family (RANUNCULACEAE)

Appearance: These perennials bloom early, often through snow, and have long-lasting blooms that may be light green, purple, pink, yellow, or white, some with contrasting spots. The leaves remain decorative through summer. *H. veridis* may become invasive.

Nativity: Europe, W. Asia

Uses: Mixed borders, woodland gardens, rock gardens

Toxicity: Cardenolides cause mouth pain after ingestion and painful digestive distress, followed by heart failure. Dry plants remain toxic.

Propagation/Care: Divide all species except *H. foetidus* and *H. argutifolius.* They must be started from seed, planted as soon as ripe (shown by hardened seed coats), and overwintered in a cold frame.

Preferences/Hardiness: Some hellebores require alkaline soil and some acid soil. Follow supplier guidance. All like dappled shade and good drainage. Zones 5–9.

Authorities: GA.u, IL, MO, MT, NY.r, WA; *H. argutifolius* (Corsican hellebore), *H. foetidus* (Stinking hellebore), CA.s; *Helleborus orientalis* (Lenten rose), CA.s, GA.u

Hibiscus moscheutos (Rose mallow, Swamp mallow)

Hippeastrum 'Scarlet Leader' (Amaryllis)

Hypericum densiflorum (Dense-flowered St. John's wort)

Hibiscus species

Rose mallow, Rose of Sharon
Mallow family (MALVACEAE)

Appearance: This genus has more than 200 species of annuals, perennials, shrubs, and trees. Some are deciduous and some evergreen, but all produce large, brightly colored blooms with prominent stamens.

Nativity: Temperate, subtropical, and tropical regions

Uses: Mixed borders, shrub borders, greenhouses, sun spaces

Toxicity: Our sources offer no toxin assays. Various leaf acids may discourage browsing.

Propagation/Care: Divide perennials in spring. Root greenwood cuttings in spring, semiripe cuttings in summer. Layer in spring. Start seed inside for annuals and fast-growing perennials grown as annuals in early spring.

Preferences/Hardiness: Give plants full sun and well-drained, moist soil. They require long summers to bloom well.

Authorities: GA.a, IL, MO, NY.d, NY.r, PA, TX.a; *H. syriacus* (Rose of Sharon), NY.d, WV

> Abbreviations for **Authorities** can be found on page 234.

Hippeastrum species

Amaryllis
Amaryllis family (AMARYLLIDACEAE)

Appearance: The common name "amaryllis" for these Dutch hybrids causes confusion with their hardier S. African cousin, *Amaryllis belladonna.* Hardy only in frost-free areas, *Hippeastrums* are sold mainly as winter-blooming houseplants that can thereafter be grown outdoors only in warmer months. In Zones 10–12, they bloom outdoors in January.

Nativity: C. and S. America

Uses: Mixed borders, under deciduous shrubs and trees, houseplants

Toxicity: Phenanthridine alkaloids can cause nausea, vomiting, and diarrhea.

Propagation/Care: Plant bulbs in autumn, leaving neck and shoulders exposed. Keep on the dry side until the leaves and flower stem begin to elongate. Fertilize after bloom and remove offsets in late fall, every 2 or 3 years, when you divide or repot.

Preferences/Hardiness: Grow in bright light in the North, partial shade in the South, in well-drained, moderately fertile soil. Remove flower stalk after bloom. Zones 9–12.

Authorities: *H. × johnsonii,* TX.a

Hypericum species

St. John's wort, Aaron's beard, Goldcup
St. John's-Wort family (CLUSIACEAE)

Appearance: This genus includes more than 400 species of annuals, perennials, shrubs, and trees. Flowers come in various shades of yellow, sometimes tinged with red, sometimes pale. Stamens are prominent.

Nativity: Worldwide in many habitats

Uses: Depends on species

Toxicity: As they mature, most *Hypericums* become less palatable to livestock. Glandular black dots on sepals and leaves of alien species contain hypericin, which makes skin especially susceptible to sunburn.

Propagation/Care: Plant seeds in early spring indoors or in autumn in containers to overwinter in a cold frame. Divide perennials in spring; take softwood cuttings in late spring and semiripe cuttings in summer.

Preferences/Hardiness: Full sun or partial shade in moderately fertile, well-drained, moist soil. Check supplier guidance.

Authorities: CA.u, TX.a; *H. androsaemum, H. × moserianum,* CA.s; *H. calycinum* (Aaron's beard), NY.r; *H. ascyron* (Great St. John's wort), PA

Iberis sempervirens (Candytuft)

Ilex opaca (American holly)

Ipomoea purpurea 'Kniola's Black' volunteer (Morning glory)

Iberis species

Candytuft

Mustard family (BRASSICACEAE)

Appearance: Clusters of tiny, fragrant flowers characterize the 40 species of annuals, perennials, and evergreen subshrubs in this genus. Flowers of most *Iberis* are white, but some species also have red, pink, or purple blooms. The plants may be short-lived, but annual cultivars self-seed readily in most situations.

Nativity: Alkaline soils in S. Europe, the Middle East, N. Iraq, N. Africa

Uses: Mixed borders, rock gardens

Toxicity: Many members of the Mustard family contain sulfur toxins that irritate the digestive tract. But our sources offer no comments on candytuft itself. Low growth may provide some protection from browsers.

Propagation/Care: Plant annual seeds in the ground in spring or autumn; root softwood cuttings in late spring.

Preferences/Hardiness: Plant in full sun in well-drained, neutral to alkaline soil with moderate to low fertility. Zones 5–9.

Authorities: AZ.u, IL, MT, NY.d, NY.r, TX.a (*Caution:* Mixed resistance ratings suggest that low growth may simply make this less convenient to browse.)

Ilex species

Holly

Holly family (AQUIFOLIACEAE)

Appearance: The 400 holly species include deciduous and evergreen shrubs and climbers. The leaves of many are glossy and spiny; some are variegated. Plants are usually male or female. In fall, females produce red, black, orange, or yellow berries if pollinated from nearby male.

Nativity: Temperate in tropical regions

Uses: Shrub borders, foundation plantings, hedges, woodland gardens

Toxicity: Glucosidic saponins in leaves and berries cause vomiting and diarrhea. Other toxins vary by species.

Propagation/Care: Take semiripe cuttings in late summer.

Preferences/Hardiness: Plant variegated cultivars in full sun. Green cultivars prefer sun but tolerate partial shade. Provide well-drained, moist, high-humus soil. Except for *I. vomitoria*, hollies thrive in acid conditions.

Authorities: AZ.u, CA.u (except thornless), *I. opaca* (American holly), MO, NY.l; *I. verticillata* (Winterberry holly) 'Winter Red', 'Red Sprite', 'Winter Gold', PA; *I. vomitoria* (Yaupon holly), TX.a, TX.m; *Ilex vomitoria* 'Nana' or 'Stokes' (Dwarf Yaupon holly), CA.s

Ipomoea species

Morning glories

Morning Glory family (CONVOLVULACEAE)

Appearance: Grown mainly as climbing vines with beautiful flowers, common morning glories are annuals that bloom in solid colors and tricolor. Moonflower is perennial only in Zones 10–12; its white blooms open late in the day and seem to glow in the dark.

Nativity: Warm regions worldwide

Uses: Screening plants, focal points

Toxicity: Old World *Ipomoea* foliage has calystegins that cause crazy-cow disease. Australian *I. muelleri* and African *I. carnea* foliage cause incoordination, tremors, and worse. Mold-damaged sweet potatoes (*I. balatas*) can kill livestock. Seed alkaloids in many species and cultivars induce intense vomiting and are hallucinogens.

Propagation/Care: Plant seeds inside in early spring in large peat pots or 4-in. plastic pots; transplant after all danger of frost has passed. Plants often self-seed and may become weeds.

Preferences/Hardiness: Grow in full sun in fertile, well-drained soil with good moisture levels in summer.

Authorities: *I. alba* (Moonflower) and *I. purpurea* (Common morning glory), IL, MO, NY.d

Iris (Bearded irises)

Iris douglasiana (Pacific Coast iris)

Juniperus chinensis 'Saybrook Gold'
(Juniper)

Iris species

Bearded irises
Iris family (IRIDACEAE)

Appearance: Stiff green leaves, growing in a "fan" from a rhizome, keep bearded irises looking good all season. In midspring, flowers form on tall stalks. These have three upright petals, called standards, and three hanging petals, called falls. The color range is huge, and often falls and standards are different colors.

Nativity: N. Hemisphere

Uses: Mixed borders

Toxicity: Rhizomes and leaves have a strong purgative effect. The leaves have been associated with depression and respiratory problems.

Propagation/Care: Lift and divide rhizomes after blooming and immediately replant where they are to grow. Most irises require dividing every 3 years.

Preferences/Hardiness: Plant in full sun to very light shade in fertile, well-drained, slightly acid soil. Stake tall cultivars; deadhead when flowers fade.

Authorities: AZ.u, CA.u, GA.u, IL, MO, MT, TX.a, WA

Abbreviations for **Authorities** can be found on page 234.

Iris species

Beardless, Crested, and Bulbous iris
Iris family (IRIDACEAE)

Appearance: These huge groups of iris vary in flower forms, although all have the characteristic six petals— three standards and three falls. They also have straplike leaves, but some, such as Siberian irises, are tall and slender with dainty blooms. Others, such as reticulatas, are short.

Nativity: N. Hemisphere

Uses: Vary by type. Blue flag irises grow well in bog gardens, *reticulatas* in rock gardens, and *Laevigatae*, particularly the Japanese irises, highlight mixed borders. Avoid invasive alien *I. pseudoacorus* (Yellow flag).

Toxicity: See bearded irises.

Propagation/Care: Divide rhizomes after plants bloom and replant immediately. Lift bulbous cultivars after bloom and separate nearly full grown bulbs to replant with wider spacing.

Preferences/Hardiness: Vary by species.

Authorities: See bearded irises, plus *I. cristata* 'Alba' and 'Powder Blue Giant', *I. cristata, I. versicolor,* PA; *I. germanica, sibirica, ensata, pseudoacorus, tectorum,* NY.r; *I. sibirica, I. unguicularis, I. spuria,* CA.s

Juniperus species

Junipers
Cypress family (CUPRESSACEAE)

Appearance: These more than 50 evergreen conifers vary widely in shape, texture, color, and fragrance. Shapes include prostrate, spreading, and columnar. Colors range from a blue-green to golden in spring, to multicolored in 'Blue and Gold'.

Nativity: 13 N. American; others N. Hemisphere

Uses: Hedges, specimens, foundations, rock gardens, groundcovers

Toxicity: Terpene-based volatile oils repel deer, except when starving, and cause abortions and fetal deformities in mammals. Seeds are important food for mammals and birds.

Propagation/Care: Take hardwood cuttings in autumn through early winter or softwood cuttings in early summer.

Preferences/Hardiness: Plant in full sun or dappled light in well-drained, moderately fertile soil. Junipers tolerate relatively dry or sandy soils but don't fare well in soggy ones. Zones 3–9.

Authorities: AZ.u, CA.u, GA.u, IL, MO, MT, NY.d, WA; *J. chinensis* (Chinese j.), MO, NC, NY.d; *J. pfitzeriana* (Pfitzer j.), NY.r

Kalmia latifolia (Mountain laurel)

Kerria japonica 'Pleniflora' (Double-flowering kerria)

Kalmia latifolia

Mountain laurel
Heath family (ERICACEAE)

Appearance: This evergreen shrub grows to about 10 ft tall and wide. Large, showy clusters of cup-shaped white, pink, or red flowers appear in summer.

Nativity: E. United States

Uses: Mixed shrub borders, woodland gardens

Toxicity: All parts contain toxins, including terpenoids. Deer are reluctant to eat mountain laurel when other plants are available but may feel forced to sample it in winter and spring, when toxins are more potent. Flower nectar makes bee honey toxic to humans. Symptoms in livestock include vomiting, foaming nose and mouth, abdominal pain, irregular pulse and breathing, and paralysis. In humans, grayanotoxins cause burning in the mouth, followed by vomiting, diarrhea, skin tingling, headache, dim vision, heart irregularities, seizures, and death.

Propagation/Care: Layer in late summer.

Preferences/Hardiness: Grow in partial shade in moist, humus-rich, slightly acid soil. Water when the soil is dry. Zones 3–8.

Authorities: NY.d, TX.m, WA

Kerria japonica

Kerria, Japanese rose
Rose family (ROSACEAE)

Appearance: This deciduous shrub has single or double yellow flowers. Toothed leaves may be 4 in. long. *K.* 'Picta' has variegated leaves, and double-flowered 'Pleniflora' can reach 10 ft tall.

Nativity: China, Japan

Uses: Shrub borders, foundation plantings, specimen plants

Toxicity: As in other Rose family members, glycosides in the leaves metabolize as cyanide. Ruminants are especially susceptible because microbes and high pH in the rumen hydrolyze the glycosides. Symptoms occur soon after ingestion and may include weakness, rapid respiration, incoordination, collapse, seizures, and death. The prognosis improves if the animal survives the first hour.

Propagation/Care: Take greenwood cuttings in summer; divide in autumn.

Preferences/Hardiness: Grow in full sun or partial shade in well-drained soil with moderate fertility. Because this shrub is prone to fungal diseases, site where air circulation is high. Zones 4–9.

Authorities: AZ.u, GA.u, IL, MO, NC, NY.d

Cyanide Poisoning

Humans and other mammals can detoxify small amounts of cyanide through respiration and urination. Members of the Rose family, especially, contain glycosides in the leaves, seeds, and fruits that metabolize as cyanide. Deer and other ruminants are especially susceptible because rumen fluids have a high pH and microbes in the rumen hydrolyze the glycosides. Symptoms usually occur within 20 minutes of significant ingestion and include weakness, rapid respiration, incoordination, collapse, seizures, and death. Prognosis for recovery improves if the animal survives the first hour, sometimes the first 15 minutes.

Kniphofia uvaria 'Wayside Flame' (Red-hot poker) & *Perovskia* 'Blue Spire' (Russian sage)

Kolkwitzia amabilis 'Pink Cloud' (Beautybush)

Lamium maculatum forma *album* (Deadnettle)

Kniphofia species

Red-hot poker, Torch lily

Lily family (LILIACEAE)

Appearance: This genus of perennials includes about 70 species, some evergreen, as well as countless cultivars, ranging from 2 ft to 6 ft. Most form dense clumps of tall grasslike leaves and fiery, torchlike spikes composed of hundreds of tiny tubular flowers attractive to bees. Flowers open from bottom to top along the spike, some beginning red or orange before turning yellow, resulting in a two-tone hot-poker effect. Cultivars may be pink, yellow, orange, and various combinations.

Nativity: Southern Africa

Uses: Mixed borders, containers

Toxicity: Aside from personal allergies, the California Poison Control Center and the University of California consider this plant safe if accidentally ingested in small amounts.

Propagation/Care: Start seeds early indoors; remove offsets in early spring.

Preferences/Hardiness: Grow in full sun or partial shade in well-drained, moderately fertile soil, preferably sandy. Zones 5–9.

Authorities: AZ.u, CA.u, NC, NY.r, OR, WA

Kolkwitzia amabilis

Beautybush

Honeysuckle family (CAPRIFOLIACEAE)

Appearance: These lovely shrubs are known for their showy, bell-shaped flowers in various shades of pink that liberally coat the branches in late spring through early summer. The bushes naturally form a pleasing, mounded shape and need very little pruning.

Nativity: China

Uses: Specimen plants, hedges, shrub borders

Toxicity: Our sources offer no toxin assay.

Propagation/Care: Plants sucker readily; remove suckers in early spring and replant. Take greenwood cuttings in late spring or early summer.

Preferences/Hardiness: Plant in a site with full sun in well-drained soil of moderate fertility. Plants tolerate dappled shade in warm climates. Zones 5–9.

Authorities: MO, MT, NY.d, NY.v
Note: Invasive, says CT.n

> Abbreviations for **Authorities** can be found on page 234.

Lamium species

Deadnettles

Mint family (LAMIACEAE)

Appearance: These annuals and usually rhizomatous perennials form attractive ground covers in shaded areas. The variegated leaves of species and cultivars are striking. In summer, tiny hooded blooms appear that are not as impressive as the leaves.

Nativity: Europe, Asia, N. Africa

Uses: Groundcovers

Toxicity: Our sources suggest no toxin issue, though the noxious weed *L. amplexicaule* (Henbit) has given digestive distress to sheep and cattle in Australia.

Propagation/Care: Like other mints, some Lamiums, such as *L. galeobdolon* (Yellow archangel) are very invasive. Cut back the rhizomes to prevent spreading and separate the new plants.

Preferences/Hardiness: Plant in partial to full shade and moist, well-drained soil of average fertility.

Authorities: AZ.u, CA.u, IL, MO, MT, NY.r, WV; *L. maculatum* (Spotted deadnettle), CA.s, NY.d

Lantana camara 'Patriot Honeylove' (Lantana)

Larix deciduas 'Pendula' (Weeping larch)

Lavandula angustifolia 'Munsted' seedlings (English lavender)

Lantana species

Lantana, Shrub verbena

Verbena family (VERBENACEAE)

Appearance: This genus of 150 shrubs and perennials is often evergreen in warm regions. The flowers are usually bicolored and form showy domes.

Nativity: N., C., and S. America, S. Africa

Uses: Mixed borders, groundcovers

Toxicity: Ruminants, horses, and dogs are highly susceptible to lantadene in the leaves. Concentrations vary but are usually most potent in plants with red flowers. Ingestion symptoms include a severely irritated digestive tract, constipation, increased photosensitivity, diarrhea, and then liver and kidney failure. Green fruits are more toxic than ripe ones. Leaves may irritate human skin.

Propagation/Care: Root semiripe cuttings in summer or plant seeds early indoors, keeping the soil mix at 62°–65°F.

Preferences/Hardiness: Grow in full sun in well-drained soil with moderate fertility and moderate to high summer moisture levels. Lantanas tolerate a dry winter. Zones 9–12.

Authorities: AZ.u, MO, NC, NY.v, TX.a; *L. camara*, GA.u

Larix

Larches

Pine family (PINACEAE)

Appearance: This genus of 10 to 14 conifers is deciduous rather than evergreen. In autumn, the needles turn bright, beautiful yellows to reds before dropping. Larches are best known for graceful, downward-arching branches and upright forms to 100 ft tall in *L. occidental* (Western larch) and *L. decidua* (European larch). Yet some cultivars weep, such as *L. decidua* 'Pendula'. And *L. d.* 'Corley' is just 3 ft tall and wide.

Nativity: W. N. America, Europe, Asia

Uses: Specimen trees, hedgerows

Toxicity: Bare branches in winter help discourage browsing. And plant oils may afford larches some protection because they cause contact dermatitis in humans and, when inhaled, can inflame the respiratory tract.

Propagation/Care: Root semiripe cuttings in summer under mist; these are difficult unless you control their environment. Graft in winter.

Preferences/Hardiness: Plant in full sun in a site with deep, moderately fertile, well-drained soil. Most are hardy in Zones 4–8.

Authorities: IL, MA, NY.s

Lavandula species

Lavender

Mint family (LAMIACEAE)

Appearance: These shrubs and subshrubs have fragrant leaves and flowers on tall spikes that in summer bloom in shades of blue, pink, and purple. Leaf colors range from yellow-green to gray-green. Plant sizes range from 1-ft cultivars of *L. angustifolia* (English lavender) and *L.* × *intermedia* (Lavandin) to 3-ft species such as *L. pinnata*.

Nativity: Rocky, warm areas in the Mediterranean, N.E. Africa, S.W. Asia, India

Uses: Mixed borders, herb gardens, low hedges

Toxicity: Aromatic oils, rather than toxins, likely repel mammals.

Propagation/Care: Start seed indoors in early spring; layer in spring; take semiripe cuttings in summer.

Preferences/Hardiness: Plant in full sun in soils with moderate fertility and excellent drainage. Lavenders tolerate sandy soil conditions. Zones 5–9.

Authorities: AZ.u, CA.u, IL, MO, MT, NY.d; *L. angustifolia, L.* × *intermedia,* and *L. dentate,* CA.s; *L. officinalis,* NY.l, NY.r, WA, WV; *L. stoechas* (French lavender), NC, WV

Leucanthumum × superbum = Chrysanthemum maximum (Shasta daisy)

Leucojum aestivum (Summer snowflake)

Linaria (Toadflax)

Leucanthumum × superbum (= *Chrysanthemum maximum*)

Shasta daisy

Aster family (ASTERACEAE)

Appearance: With some people, the latest scientific name hasn't caught up with the long-established former name, *Chrysanthemum,* which now officially applies only to mums. Some *Leucanthumum* cultivars, such as 'Horace Read', 'T.E. Killin', and 'Cobham Gold' have double flowers, but most bear single white flowers with golden centers—the archetypal "daisy."

Nativity: Europe and Asia

Uses: Mixed borders, wildflower gardens

Toxicity: The aromatic oils that cause contact dermatitis in humans may also discourage browsing.

Propagation/Care: Plant seeds indoors in early spring or in containers in a cold frame in autumn. Divide plants every 3 years to keep them healthy.

Preferences/Hardiness: Plant in full sun in well-drained soil of average fertility. Keep moisture as consistent as possible.

Authorities: CA.u, GA.u, IL, NY.l, NY.r, OR, TX.a, WA; 'Silver Princess', 'Snow Lady', 'Little Miss Muffet', CA.s *Note: L. vulgare* (Oxeye daisy) invasive in many states.

Leucojum aestivum

Summer snowflake

Amaryllis family (AMARYLLIDACEAE)

Appearance: Growing from bulbs, summer snowflakes bear nodding little cup-shaped flowers that hang from spikes growing amid the straplike foliage. The white flowers have a green tip on each petal and resemble Snowdrops *(Galanthus).* Their subtle fragrance reminds people of chocolate.

Nativity: W. Europe, the Middle East, N. Africa

Uses: Mixed borders, rock gardens, edging for shrub borders

Toxicity: Phenanthridine alkaloids cause nausea, excess salivation, vomiting, and diarrhea. These same alkaloids discourage browsing of *Narcissus* and *Amaryllis.*

Propagation/Care: Plant bulbs in autumn, where they are to grow. Divide offsets every 2 to 3 years to keep them from becoming too crowded.

Preferences/Hardiness: Plant in a brightly lit area but protect from direct sunlight, particularly in warm climates. The plants require moist soil with good drainage and moderate fertility and high organic matter.

Authorities: CA.u, GA.u, MO, NC, NY.r

Linaria species

Toadflaxes

Figwort family (SCROPHULARIACEAE)

Appearance: Closely related to snapdragons *(Antirrhinum),* this genus includes annuals, biennials, and perennials whose blooms resemble miniature snapdragons with especially long spurs. Rising on spikes above the leaves, the flowers may be white, pink, red, purple, orange, yellow, or bicolor.

Nativity: N. Hemisphere, particularly the Mediterranean

Uses: Borders, rock gardens, edges

Toxicity: Some species contain alkaloids and glycosides that conspire to decrease heart rate and blood pressure, while increasing respiration rate.

Propagation/Care: Plant seeds in spring. Divide perennials then too.

Preferences/Hardiness: Plant in full sun and in very fast-draining soil of moderate fertility. All *Linaria* self-seed easily and can become weeds.

Authorities: IL, NY.r; *L. purpurea,* CA.s; *L. vulgaris,* WV. *Note: L. vulgaris* (Butter and eggs) is invasive in many states.

Abbreviations for **Authorities** can be found on page 234.

Lindera benzoin (Spice bush)

Liquidambar styraciflua (Sweetgum)

Liriope 'Silvery Sunproof' (Lilyturf)

Lindera benzoin

Spice bush
Laurel family (LAURACEAE)

Appearance: Grown mainly for their butter-yellow fall color, spice bushes are either male or female and so must be planted together to have fruits. *Lindera benzoin* grows 10 ft tall and wide. It has clusters of tiny star-shaped greenish-yellow flowers that appear along the branches ahead of the scented pale green leaves. The berries become shiny red.

Nativity: N. America

Uses: Mixed shrub borders, specimens, woodland gardens

Toxicity: The piquantly scented leaves are likely repellent to deer. Also, the stems contain the laurotetanine alkaloid, a potential cell toxin, says ethnobotanist James Duke.

Propagation/Care: Take greenwood cuttings in early summer; plant seeds in autumn and overwinter their containers in a cold frame.

Preferences/Hardiness: Grow in partial shade in well-drained soil that has high humus levels and is moist and fertile. Zones 4–9.

Authorities: CT.n, IL, PA

Liquidambar styraciflua

Sweetgum
Witchhazel family (HAMAMELIDACEAE)

Appearance: These popular street trees are known for their brightly colored autumn leaves and naturally elegant habit. The female flowers of most cultivars develop relatively large, spiked seedpods that drop in autumn. If you want to plant sweetgum near a driveway or walkway, choose 'Roundiloba' because it does not bear fruit.

Nativity: N. America, Asia, Mexico

Uses: Specimen trees, shade trees

Toxicity: Our sources offer no toxin assay.

Propagation/Care: New plants will grow from greenwood cuttings taken in summer and from seeds planted as soon as pods turn brown and the seeds have a firm seed coat.

Preferences/Hardiness: Tolerates alkaline soil and partial shade but thrives in full sun and neutral to acid soils. Plant in full sun where possible, in well-drained soil of moderate fertility.

Authorities: GA.u, IL, MA, MO, NY.d, PA

> Abbreviations for **Authorities** can be found on page 234.

Liriope species

Lilyturf
Lily family (LILIACEAE)

Appearance: These perennials form tufts of grasslike leaves that are evergreen in most regions. In summer, spikes of white, purple, violet, or pink flowers rise above the leaves. Blooms are followed by black berries that drop in autumn. Some cultivars, such as 'John Burch', 'Silver Dragon', and 'Variegata' have variegated leaves, generally with yellow or silver stripes or edging.

Nativity: Southeast Asia

Uses: Groundcover, particularly under trees that give dense shade and promote soil acidity; also mixed borders.

Toxicity: Aside from personal allergies, the California Poison Control Center and the University of California consider this plant safe if accidentally ingested in small amounts.

Propagation/Care: Plant seed as soon as it has a firm seed coat and overwinter in containers in a cold frame. Divide plants in spring.

Preferences/Hardiness: Plant in partial shade in a moist, acid, well-drained, and light soil. *Liriope* tolerates full shade or sun in consistently moist soil.

Authorities: CA.s, CA.u, IL; *L. spicata*, NY.r

Lobelia 'Wildwood Splendor' (Lobelia)

Lobularia maritima 'Snow Crystal' (Sweet alyssum)

Lonicera × *brownii* 'Dropmore Scarlet' (Scarlet trumpet honeysuckle)

Lobelia species

Lobelias

Bluebell family (CAMPANULACEAE)

Appearance: This genus includes annuals, perennials, and shrubs with tubular flowers in a wide color range.

Nativity: N., C., and S. America

Uses: Mixed borders, hanging baskets

Toxicity: *L. berlandieri* in South Texas kills livestock. In many lobelias, pyridine alkaloids, including lobalines, can cause nausea, vomiting, dizziness, diarrhea, tremors, coma, and death in humans. Considered a poison commercially, *L. inflata* (Indian tobacco) has effects like nicotine and affects heart rate.

Propagation/Care: Plant seeds indoors in early spring; divide perennials in spring.

Preferences/Hardiness: Vary by species. All thrive in moist soil, but *L. paludosa* (Swamp lobelia) is a marginal aquatic plant. *L. erinus* cultivars thrive in hanging baskets. Most tolerate full sun but grow best in partial shade.

Authorities: GA.a, GA.u, MO, NY.r; *L. cardinalis* (Cardinal flower), PA, WA; *L. laxiflora,* GA.u, IL, NY.d; *L. siphilitica* (Blue cardinal flower), GA.a, PA

Lobularia maritima

Sweet alyssum

Mustard family (BRASSICACEAE)

Appearance: This annual is grown for its low mounds with clusters of fragrant blooms in shades of white, pink, and red. Sweet alyssums brighten the edges of spring and early summer flower beds and make excellent container plants. Their nectar nourishes beneficial wasps that prey on many pests, so these plants promote biological control.

Nativity: Mediterranean, Canary Islands

Uses: Bedding plants, containers

Toxicity: Some Mustard family members cause serious digestive, respiratory, and neurological problems, but our sources don't comment on *Lobularia.*

Propagation/Care: Start seeds early inside for the first bloom, and seed directly in the garden at 2-week intervals for continuous bloom. Alyssum reseeds in good conditions.

Preferences/Hardiness: Full sun in well-drained, moderately fertile soil. Cut back after first bloom for a second flush of flowers.

Authorities: GA.u, IL, MO, WA, WV

Lonicera species

Honeysuckles

Honeysuckle family (CAPRIFOLIACEAE)

Appearance: The 180 or so honeysuckle species are either climbers or shrubs with highly fragrant flower clusters. Flowers are white, pink, yellow, orange, red, or bicolor.

Nativity: N. America, N. Hemisphere

Uses: Shrub borders, hedges, trellises, groundcovers

Toxicity: Terpenoids and glucosides are thought to irritate digestive tracts of horses but seldom cattle. Berries have caused nausea, vomiting, and diarrhea in children.

Propagation/Care: Layer in spring; take semiripe cuttings of evergreen species in late summer and greenwood cuttings of deciduous species in early summer. Plant seeds of hardy species in containers as soon as they are ripe, shown by hardened seed coats, and then overwinter in a cold frame.

Preferences/Hardiness: Plant in full sun or partial shade in well-drained soil of average fertility with high humus content. Zones 4–9.

Authorities: Native *L. sempervirons* (Trumpet honeysuckle), GA.u, MO, MT, NC, PA; *L. nitida* (Boxleaf honeysuckle) 'Maigruen' and 'Baggesen's Gold', CA.s

Lupinus sp. (Lupines) naturalized along roadside

Lychnis coronaria (Rose campion)

Magnolia stellata (Star magnolia)

Lupinus species

Lupines
Pea family (FABACEAE)

Appearance: Lupines include more than 200 native and alien annuals, perennials, and shrubs. Flowers of garden annuals and perennials have a wide color range and grow on tall spikes rising above the leaves. The leaves are usually lobed.

Nativity: N., C., and S. America, Mediterranean, N. Africa

Uses: Mixed borders, wild gardens

Toxicity: The foliage and seeds vary widely in toxic alkaloid levels by species and locality.

Propagation/Care: Plant seeds for transplants in peat pots because roots resent disturbance. Plants self-seed easily.

Preferences/Hardiness: Lupines thrive in full sun to partial shade as long as their soil is moist, well-drained, slightly acid, and moderately fertile and they have cool summer conditions. Zones 5–8.

Authorities: AZ.u, NY.l, NY.r, PA; *L. perennis* (Wild lupine), WA

Lychnis coronaria

Rose campion
Pink family (CARYOPHYLLACEAE)

Appearance: This biennial or short-lived perennial has purple-red flowers and woolly, silver gray leaves.

Nativity: S.E. Europe

Uses: Mixed borders

Toxicity: Woolly leaves may help deter browsers. Other Pink family members, such as dianthus, contain toxic saponins, but our sources are silent on this plant.

Propagation/Care: Plant seed as soon as the seed coat is tough and the seed looks dry in containers destined for the cold frame or indoors in early spring. Divide in early spring. Take basal cuttings in early spring.

Preferences/Hardiness: Plant in full sun or partial shade in well-drained, fertile soil. Rose campion prefers somewhat dry conditions. Deadhead to prolong bloom. Zones 3–8.

Authorities: AZ.u, CA.s, CA.u, IL, MT, NY.d, NY.r, WV

> Abbreviations for **Authorities** can be found on page 234.

Magnolia species

Magnolias
Magnolia family (MAGNOLIACEAE)

Appearance: These 125 species of trees may be evergreen or deciduous and range from 8 to 60 ft tall. Most have large, often fragrant, creamy or pink flowers followed by reddish brown, cone-shaped fruits.

Nativity: Eastern N. America, tropical N. and S. America, Asia, Himalayas

Uses: Specimen trees, woodland plantings

Toxicity: Our sources suggest no toxins.

Propagation/Care: Graft in late winter; take semiripe cuttings in late summer; plant seeds in containers as soon as they are ripe, shown by a hardened seed coat, and overwinter in a cold frame.

Preferences/Hardiness: Most require well-drained soil of average fertility. Choose trees grown in your cold-hardiness zone.

Authorities: AZ.u, CA.s, GA.u, NC; *M. acuminata* (Cucumber tree), PA; *M. grandiflora* (Southern m.) 'Edith Bogue', 'Brackens Brown Beauty', PA; *M.×soulangiana* (Saucer m.), most authorities; *M. stellata* (Star m.), MA, NY.d, (most) NY.r; *M. tripetala* (Umbrella tree), *M. virginiana* (Swamp m., Sweet bay m.), NC, PA

Mahonia aquifolium (Oregon grapeholly)

Matteuccia struthiopteris (Ostrich fern)

Melissa officinalis (Lemon balm)

Mahonia species

Mahonias and Oregon grape

Barberry family (BERBERIDACEAE)

Appearance: These evergreen shrubs to 12 ft tall have beautiful, often pointy, leaves. Low growers make good ground covers. Fragrant flower clusters precede berries. Bark on taller species is deeply fissured.

Nativity: Western N. America, S. and C. America, Himalayas, E. Asia

Uses: Specimens, woodland plantings, seaside gardens

Toxicity: Like its cousins, the barberries, mahonias contain berberine alkaloid, which can reduce blood pressure and cause seizures.

Propagation/Care: Take semiripe cuttings in late summer; start seed outdoors as soon as it ripens, shown by a hardened seed coat.

Preferences/Hardiness: Plant in partial shade. These plants tolerate full shade or, if the soil is consistently moist, full sun. Soil should be well drained, even if moist, humus-rich, and fertile. Zones 5–10.

Authorities: AZ.u, IL; *M. aquifolium* (Oregon grape holly), AZ.u, IL, MO, NY.d, OR, WA; *M. japonica* (Leatherleaf mahonia), GA.u; *M. repens* (Creeping mahonia), CA.s, CO.u; *M. trifoliata* (Agarita), TX.a

Matteuccia struthiopteris

Ostrich fern

Wood fern family (DRYOPTERIDACEAE)

Appearance: This fern's fronds grow 5 or more ft tall. In mid- to late summer, it sends up tightly curled, relatively short, dark-colored fronds in the center of the plant that bear spores capable of reproduction.

Nativity: E. North America, Europe, and E. Asia

Uses: Good in mixed borders and by water features, streams, and ponds. Spring fiddleheads (rosiers) to 8 in. long are sold for human consumption, after steaming or boiling.

Toxicity: Even though most livestock poisonings are associated with family member bracken ferns, ostrich ferns are capable of causing thiamin deficiencies. Symptoms may include digestive disturbance, incoordination, and blindness.

Propagation/Care: Spreads vigorously by rhizomes; divide these in early spring. Plant divisions 2 to 3 ft apart.

Preferences/Hardiness: Plant in partial shade in moist, neutral to acidic soil. Tolerates deep shade. Zones 2–8.

Authorities: Many

Melissa officinalis

Lemon balm

Mint family (LAMIACEAE)

Appearance: The highly fragrant leaves of this perennial look almost quilted because they are puckered between every vein. They are also regularly toothed and grow opposite each other on the stem. In mid- to late summer, spikes of tubular, fragrant, yellow or white flowers rise above the leaves, attracting bees and other beneficial insects. Some cultivars are variegated, and all can be used as a mint, in tea, as a garnish, and as a flavoring for peas and many cold salads and cooked dishes.

Nativity: Europe, C. Asia

Uses: Mixed borders, herb gardens, containers, tea gardens

Toxicity: Fragrance likely deters browsers.

Propagation/Care: Start seed indoors in early spring; divide in spring or fall.

Preferences/Hardiness: Grow in full sun in well-drained soil with low to barely moderate fertility. Plants die with excess moisture or nutrients.

Authorities: IL, MO, NY.d, NY.r, NY.s

Mentha spicata (Spearmint)

Mertensia virginica (Virginia bluebells)

Mimulus guttatus
(Common large monkey flower)

Mentha species

Mints

Mint family (LAMIACEAE)

Appearance: All members of the Mint family have toothed leaves opposite each other on square stems. True mints, those in the *Mentha* species, have a characteristic "minty" fragrance. Some are variegated and some have dark green, almost brownish, leaves. Fragrance and flavor vary, depending on the species, but all make good teas and seasonings.

Nativity: Europe, Africa, Asia

Uses: Sunken pots or confined areas to prevent their taking over the garden; near water features

Toxicity: Minty fragrance and taste likely deter browsers.

Propagation/Care: Plants spread rapidly by rhizomes that can be cut apart and separated to make new plantings. Seeds rarely come true because plants interbreed easily.

Preferences/Hardiness: Plant in full sun or partial shade in fertile, humus-rich, moist soil. Zones 3–11.

Authorities: CA.u, IL, MO, NY.l, NY.r, NY.rug, WA; *M.* × *piperita* (Peppermint)*,* NY.d; *M. pulegium* (Pennyroyal), NY.d

Mertensia species

Mertensias, Virginia bluebell

Forget-me-not family (BORAGINACEAE)

Appearance: The 50 mertensia perennials range in height from 4-in.-tall *M. maritime* (Oyster plant) to the highly popular 18-in.-tall *M. virginica* (Virginia bluebells) and taller. Most of the 20+ natives occur in the West. Flowers are blue and bell-shaped. Foliage may be heart-shaped, rounded, or lance-shaped, some bluish green, some grayish, and some pale green.

Nativity: N. America, Europe, Asia, Greenland

Uses: Mixed borders, rock gardens, alpine plantings, woodland gardens

Toxicity: Comparatively low levels of pyrrolizidine alkaloids are not considered health risks to livestock.

Propagation/Care: Plant seeds in containers and overwinter in a cold frame; divide clumps in early spring.

Preferences/Hardiness: Plant in partial or dappled shade in well-drained but moist soil with high humus content. Alpine species, such as *M. echioides,* tolerate full sun and require gritty soils. Zones 3–9.

Authorities: GA.a, NY.r, PA

Mimulus species

Monkey flowers

Figwort family (SCROPHULARIACEAE)

Appearance: The annuals, perennials, and shrubs in this genus have flowers with a funnel shape with two upward-facing petals and three petals that point downwards. Many have spotted throats. Flower colors include pinks, yellows, oranges, and reds.

Nativity: N., C., and S. America, S. Africa, Asia, and Australia

Uses: Mixed borders, containers, rock gardens, woodland gardens

Toxicity: Our sources suggest no toxin issues.

Propagation/Care: Divide perennials in spring or root softwood cuttings in early summer and semiripe cuttings in summer. Start seeds of annuals indoors in early spring and plant out when the weather is warm.

Preferences/Hardiness: Grow in full sun or light shade in well-drained but moist, fertile soil. Zones 6–11.

Authorities: IL; *M. cupreus* (= *M.* 'Whitecroft Scarlet'), NY.d

> Abbreviations for **Authorities** can be found on page 234.

Mitchella repens (Partridge berry)

Monarda didyma 'Scorpion' (Bee balm)

Muscari armeniacum
(Armenian grape hyacinth)

Mitchella repens

Partridge berry

Madder family (RUBIACEAE)

Appearance: Native partridge berry is a mat-forming 2-in. perennial with small white to pink fragrant flowers. Heart-shaped leaves have a white central vein. Red berries appear in fall. *M. f. leucocarpa* has white berries.

Nativity: N. America

Uses: Shrub borders, woodland gardens, rock gardens

Toxicity: Our sources offer no toxin assay.

Propagation/Care: Dig and transplant rooted stems.

Preferences/Hardiness: Grow in light or dappled shade in well-drained but moist, humus-rich soil with moderate to good fertility. Zones 4–9.

Authorities: NC, NY.l, NY.r, PA

Monarda species

Bee balms

Mint family (LAMIACEAE)

Appearance: Although the perennial bee balms are better known, annual forms, such as *M. punctata* (Spotted bee balm), deserve consideration. Bee balms are grown for both their showy red, pink, or purple flowers that rise above the leaves as well as their fragrant leaves that make excellent mint tea. These plants are a favorite food of bees, hummingbirds, and many beneficial insects.

Nativity: N. America

Uses: Mixed borders, herb gardens, containers

Toxicity: Aromatic oils likely deter browsers. When applied to skin, *M. punctata* (Spotted bee balm = Horsemint) can cause blistering unless diluted with olive oil, says ethnobotanist James Duke.

Propagation/Care: Plant seed indoors in early spring or directly in the garden. Divide in early spring; root basal cuttings in spring.

Preferences/Hardiness: Plant in full sun or dappled shade in moist, well-drained soil of average fertility but with good humus levels.

Authorities: AZ.u, GA.a, GA.u, IL, MO, NC, NY.r, PA, WA

Muscari species

Grape hyacinth

Lily family (LILIACEAE)

Appearance: These perennial harbingers of spring grow from bulbs that multiply each year. But it's difficult to imagine having too many of these dainty plants that look like miniature hyacinths and have a much more subtle fragrance. Bloom colors include blue, purple, white, pink, and pale yellow. The narrow straplike leaves are bright green.

Nativity: Mediterranean, S.W. Asia

Uses: As companions to other early bulbs, in rock gardens, under deciduous shrubs

Toxicity: Although our North American sources suggest no toxin issues, maltawildplants.com says the bulbs contain comisic acid, which acts like saponins, which are bittering agents.

Propagation/Care: Bulbs multiply easily. Lift, separate, and replant in autumn, every 2 to 3 years.

Preferences/Hardiness: Plant in full sun in moist, well-drained soil of average fertility. Zones 4–8.

Authorities: IL, MO, NC (occasionally browsed), NY.d

Myrrhis odorata (Sweet cicely)

Narcissus 'Mon Cherie'
(Large-cupped daffodil)

Nepeta 'Six Hills Giant' (Catmint)

Myrrhis odorata

Sweet cicely

Carrot family (APIACEAE)

Appearance: This 6-ft perennial forms a lacy-looking screen. The large umbels of tiny white flowers look fresh and clean in vase and garden. And the edible shoots, leaves, and seeds give a sweet, aniselike flavor to fruit dishes, salads, and sauces.

Nativity: S. Europe

Uses: Herb gardens, screens for utility areas

Toxicity: Our sources suggest no toxin issues, even though family members *Conium maculatum* (Poison hemlock) and *Circuta* species (Water hemlocks) contain powerful neurotoxins.

Propagation/Care: Plant seed in a peat pot or soil block as soon as the seed coat darkens and dries so you won't disturb the roots when transplanting, or direct-seed in the ground. Plants self-seed easily, so deadhead to keep the planting manageable.

Preferences/Hardiness: Grow in partial shade in well-drained, moist, moderately fertile soil. Zones 3–7.

Authorities: NY.r

> Abbreviations for **Authorities** can be found on page 234.

Narcissus species

Daffodils, Narcissus

Amaryllis family (AMARYLLIDACEAE)

Appearance: This family of about 50 species of bulbous spring-blooming perennials has hundreds of cultivars. There are 13 narcissus divisions based on flower shape, though all daffodils have a central corona surrounded by at least six petals. Colors: yellow, white, pink, orange, and bicolor.

Nativity: Europe, N. Africa

Uses: Mixed borders, bulb gardens, under deciduous shrubs

Toxicity: Phenanthridine alkaloids produce nausea, vomiting, excess salivation, and diarrhea, though usually of a transient nature. Calcium oxalate crystals cause watery swelling of the mouth and contact dermatitis.

Propagation/Care: Plant purchased bulbs in autumn; they will multiply. Divide and replant offsets every few years in autumn.

Preferences/Hardiness: Grow in full sun in well-drained soil of average fertility; keep moist during active growth. Plants go dormant in summer and can tolerate somewhat dry, but never soggy, soils then. Zones 4–9.

Authorities: AZ.u, CA.u, GA.u, IL, MO, MT, NC, NY.d, NY.l, NY.r, WV

Nepeta species

Catmints

Mint family (LAMIACEAE)

Appearance: Most catmints are perennial, and the annuals self-seed readily. Although most catmints grow less than 18 in. tall, traditional catnip (*N. cataria*) can grow 3 ft tall. Blooms are white, blue, pink, or purple. The aromatic leaves grow opposite each other on the stem and vary in edge pattern.

Nativity: N. Hemisphere

Uses: Mixed borders, herb gardens, tea gardens

Toxicity: Our sources suggest no toxin issues.

Propagation/Care: Plant seed directly in the ground in spring or in containers and overwinter in a cold frame. Divide clumps in early spring. Take softwood cuttings in late spring or early summer.

Preferences/Hardiness: Plant in full sun or partial shade in well-drained soil of average fertility. After trimming, *N.* × *faassenii* will send up a second set of flower spikes.

Authorities: AZ.u, CA.u, MO, NC, NY.r, WA; *N.* × *faassenii* cultivars, CA.s, IL; *N. cataria*, GA.u, NY.d; *N. reichenbachiana*, CA.s

Nerium oleander (Oleander, Rose bay)

Oenothera speciosa 'Siskiyou'
(Evening primrose)

Onoclea sensibilis
(Sensitive fern, Bead fern)

Nerium oleander

Oleander, Rose bay

Dogbane family (APOCYNACEAE)

Appearance: In summer, these evergreen shrubs to 20 ft tall produce large, beautiful clusters of blooms in white, yellow, pink, salmon, red, purple, or lavender. The beanlike seedpods are showy.

Nativity: Mediterranean to China

Uses: Shrub borders, hedges, specimens

Toxicity: Glycosidic cardenoloids cause digestive distress with bloody diarrhea, followed by heart, lung, and vision problems based on dosage. Terpenoid acids aggravate digestive disturbance. Livestock tend to reject the apparently bad-tasting green leaves but suffer after eating dried leaves. For humans, skin contact and wood/leaf smoke are also hazards.

Propagation/Care: Air layer in spring. Root semiripe cuttings in late summer. Plant seed in spring and hold over moderate (60°–63°F) heat until germination.

Preferences/Hardiness: Plant in full sun in well-drained but moist, fertile soil. Decrease watering in winter when the plant slows growth. Zones 8–15.

Authorities: CA.u, GA.u, NY.r, NY. rug, TX.a, WV *Note:* Invasive CA, FL, GA, NV, TX.

Oenothera species

Sundrops, Evening primrose

Evening Primrose family (ONAGRACEAE)

Appearance: This genus includes annuals, biennials, and perennials, most with cup-shaped flowers in yellow, pink, white, and orange-red. Leaves and stems of many species have a red blush.

Nativity: N. and S. America

Uses: Mixed borders, edging, rock gardens, containers

Toxicity: Our sources offer no cautions regarding livestock. Used medicinally, *Oenothera* has caused headache and nausea in some people.

Propagation/Care: Plant seeds indoors in early spring or in garden beds in autumn. Divide plants in spring. Take softwood cuttings in spring. Start plants in peat pots to avoid disturbing roots when transplanting.

Preferences/Hardiness: Plant all species except *O. fruticosa* (Sundrop) in full sun in well-drained soil of average to low fertility. Sundrops require higher fertility and more organic matter. Zones 4–9.

Authorities: GA.a, NY.l, NY.r, NY.s; *O. fruticosa* (Sundrops) 'Fireworks', PA; *O. f.* subsp. *glauca*, CA.s

Onoclea sensibilis

Sensitive fern, Bead fern

Wood Fern family (DRYOPTERIDACEAE)

Appearance: The broadly toothed, pale green leaves don't look sensitive, but wilt soon after being picked and die with first frost. Fronds easily scorch in direct sun. This plant's alternate name, Bead fern, refers to beadlike fertile fronds in the plant's center.

Nativity: Eastern N. America, E. Asia

Uses: Damp, shady border or at shady water's edge

Toxicity: When this fern makes up 10 to 20 percent of horse feed, its enzymes break down body thiamin, causing unsteadiness and incoordination, followed by "blind" walking, lying down, paddling seizures, and death. The effects may not be as apparent in ruminants.

Propagation/Care: Divide in spring. If you know how to propagate with spores, plant spores at 60°F when ripe.

Preferences/Hardiness: Plant in dappled shade and avoid direct sunlight. These ferns require moist, nutrient-rich, acid soil. Zones 4–9.

Authorities: NY.l, PA

Opuntia sp. (Prickly pear cactus)

Origanum × majoricum (Hardy marjoram)

Osmunda sp. (Cinnamon fern)

Opuntia compressa = *O. humifusa*

Prickly pear cactus

Cactus family (CACTACEAE)

Appearance: One of 200 species in the greatly varied *Opuntia* genus, prickly pears have lightly spined, padlike segments that in late spring and summer produce yellow flowers up to 2½ in. across. The red or purple fruit is considered edible.

Nativity: E. and C. United States

Uses: Xeriscape gardens, foundation plantings, mixed cactus gardens

Toxicity: Besides having low nutritional value, prickly pear contains calcium oxalates that irritate the mouth and throat and often cause kidney disease in collared peccaries (javelinas) that are forced to depend mainly on this plant for water.

Propagation/Care: Soak seed for 12 hours before planting in early spring. Stem segments will also root.

Preferences/Hardiness: Plant in full sun and well-drained, moderately fertile soil. Water during the growing season. In winter, decrease watering, allowing plants to rest.

Authorities: NC, NY.r, PA, TX.a

Origanum species

Oregano, Marjoram

Mint family (LAMIACEAE)

Appearance: Grown primarily for their fragrant, flavorful leaves, the perennial oreganos and annual marjorams are quite varied. Culinary oreganos *(O. vulgare)* grow 12 to 18 in. tall and bear spikes with whorls of pink or white flowers in midsummer to fall. In contrast, species such as the rock garden favorite *O. dictamnus* (Dittany of Crete) are only about 6 in. tall.

Nativity: Mediterranean, S.W. Asia

Uses: Herb gardens, rock gardens, mixed borders

Toxicity: Fragrant, flavorful leaves are the likely deterrents.

Propagation/Care: Plant seeds indoors in early spring or in a cold frame in autumn. Divide in spring; take basal cuttings in spring.

Preferences/Hardiness: Grow in full sun in well-drained soil with low to moderate fertility. These plants thrive in alkaline soils but will tolerate slight acidity.

Authorities: AZ.u, CA.s, IL, MO, NC, NY.l, NY.r, WA

:::
Abbreviations for **Authorities** can be found on page 234.
:::

Osmunda species

Cinnamon, Royal, and Interrupted ferns

Royal Fern family (OSMUNDACEAE)

Appearance: *O. cinnamomea* (Cinnamon fern) is an elegant 3-footer that derives common and scientific names from fertile sporangia growing from the center of the plant that turn cinnamon colored in fall. *O. regalis* (Royal fern) is much larger and produces fertile fronds that can grow 6 ft long.

Nativity: Eastern N. America

Uses: Damp borders, pond edges

Toxicity: Our sources don't comment on this genus, though other ferns can be very toxic. Bad taste may be key here. Deer having suffered toxic effects from one fern may avoid all.

Propagation/Care: Sow ripe spores at 59° to 61°F. Divide clumps in fall or early spring.

Preferences/Hardiness: Grow in light, dappled shade in fertile, humus-rich, acid soil. With good soil moisture, these ferns tolerate sunny conditions. Zones 4–8.

Authorities: *O. cinnamomea,* GA.u, NC, NY.l, PA; *O. claytoniana* (Interrupted fern), NY.l, PA; *O. regalis,* NC, NY.l, PA

Pachysandra procumbens
(Allegheny spurge)

Paeonia 'Bev' (herbaceous Peony)

Panicum virgatum 'Cloud Nine'
(Switch grass)

Pachysandra species

Pachysandras

Boxwood family (BUXACEAE)

Appearance: These perennials are best known as ground covers that form attractive green or variegated mats in shady spots, often where little else could thrive. The small, white spring flowers of native *P. procumbens* (Allegheny spurge) are fragrant.

Nativity: S.E. United States, China, Japan

Uses: Groundcovers, woodland gardens

Toxicity: Our sources suggest no toxin issues.

Propagation/Care: These plants spread rapidly by rhizomes. Divide or take root softwood cuttings in spring.

Preferences/Hardiness: Grow in full shade to full sun in soil with average to low fertility. Pachysandra tolerates somewhat wet conditions but thrives in moist, well-drained soils.

Authorities: AZ.u, GA.a, IL, MO, MT, NY.d; *P. terminalis* (Japanese spurge), NY.r, WV

Paeonia

Peonies

Peony family (PAEONIACEAE)

Appearance: These perennials, shrubs, and subshrubs produce showy flowers in late spring and early summer. Most perennials derive from *P. lactiflora* (Garden peony) and grow in mounded forms to about 3 ft tall. *P. suffruticosa* (Tree peony) is deciduous and grows to 7 ft. Flower colors include white, rose, salmon, red, pink, and yellow—no blues or purples. In the right conditions, peonies are extremely long-lived, producing blooms and healthy new growth for nearly 100 years.

Nativity: Western N. America, Europe, E. Asia

Uses: Shrub borders, mixed borders

Toxicity: Leaves taste slightly bitter. Taken medicinally, root peoniflorin and peonol can cause vomiting, colic, and diarrhea, says James Duke.

Propagation/Care: Take root cuttings of herbaceous plants in winter. Divide carefully in spring because these plants often die after root disturbance.

Preferences/Hardiness: Grow in full sun or partial shade in deep, rich, moist, but well-drained soil. Mulch with compost to supply nutrients. Zones 3–8.

Authorities: CA.s, CA.u, IL, MO, NY.d, NY.r, NY.rug

Panicum (native species)

Switch grasses, Panic grass

Grass family (POACEAE)

Appearance: Leaves of the clump-forming native perennial grasses arch to 3–4 ft tall, midgreen to bluish green in summer, yellow in autumn, and brown in winter. Many cultivars need support. *Panicum virgatum* 'Heavy Metal' stands well even after snow.

Nativity: S. Canada and US into Mexico

Uses: Open areas, shrub borders

Toxicity: In lambs, goats, and horses, saponin calcium salts crystalize in the liver. Saponins also cause UV sensitivity of thinly furred facial skin.

Propagation/Care: Plant cultivars in early spring. Divide plants midspring to early summer.

Preferences/Hardiness: Full sun and fertile, well-drained soil. Zones 5–9.

Authorities: NY.rug; also *Panicum amarum* 'Dewey Blue' (Atlantic Coastal panic grass), PA; *P. virgatum* 'North Wind' and 'Shenandoah', PA; *P.v.* 'Heavy Metal', CT.n, PA. *Note:* Invasives: *P. repens* (Torpedo grass), FL, GA, TX, and *P. capillare* (Witch grass), AZ

Papaver orientale (Oriental poppy)

Parthenocissus quinquefolia
(Virginia creeper)

Pennisetum alopecuroides 'Cassian'
(Fountain grass, Feathertop)

Papaver species

Poppies

Poppy family (PAPAVERACEAE)

Appearance: Grown for their short-lived, usually bowl-shaped, often bicolored flowers, poppies develop "pepperpot" seedpods from which you can shake hundreds of tiny black seeds like those that decorate bagels. Stems and leaves are hairy, often coarsely attractive, but fade soon after bloom.

Nativity: Europe, Asia, N. Africa, Middle East, subarctic regions

Uses: Massed; mixed borders. Near tomatoes, also outside the garden fence, poppies discourage deer.

Toxicity: All poppies contain alkaloids that disturb the digestive tract and nervous system. Livestock and deer reject green plants but may eat trimmings that cause either excitation or depression depending on species.

Propagation/Care: These self-seeders germinate well from seed broadcast in fall.

Preferences/Hardiness: Full sun for maximum number of blooms and well-drained, deeply fertile soil (for the long taproot). Zones 2–9.

Authorities: AZ.u, CA.s, CA.u, GA.u, IL, NY.l, NY.r, WA; *P. orientale* (Oriental p.), CA.s, GA.u, IL, MO, NY.l, WA, WV

Parthenocissus species

Virginia creeper, Boston ivy

Grape family (VITACEAE)

Appearance: These climbers are deciduous, and most cling to surfaces with suction cup–like disks at the ends of their tendrils. Unlike many climbers, these are grown for their foliage rather than flowers. The large, handsome leaves are lobed or divided and turn vivid colors in autumn. Berries are a favorite food for birds.

Nativity: N. America, Himalayas, E. Asia

Uses: Wall covers, screen covers

Toxicity: Burrows and Tyrl say leaves have caused vomiting, diarrhea, sweating, and deep sleep in children. Berries cause stomach upset. The University of Arkansas Cooperative Extension says soluble salts in leaves can cause organ damage.

Propagation/Care: Take softwood cuttings in late spring, greenwood cuttings in early summer, and hardwood cuttings in winter.

Preferences/Hardiness: Plant in full sun or partial shade in well-drained soil with good fertility. Trim overgrown branches in late winter or early spring.

Authorities: AZ.u, IL, NC (occasionally damaged)

Pennisetum species

Pennisetum, Fountain grass, Feathertop

Grass family (POACEAE)

Appearance: This genus includes annual and perennial grasses, many grown for their long, arching seed heads. Cultivars such as 'Burgundy Giant' are a deep burgundy color. 'Atropurpureum' is burgundy purple.

Nativity: Worldwide in woodlands and grasslands

Uses: Mixed borders, woodlands, rock gardens

Toxicity: Oxalates in some species cause calcium deficiencies leading to lameness and face swelling in horses. Nitrate accumulations in *P. glaucum* (Pearl millet) forage cause respiratory failure.

Propagation/Care: Weed self-seeding species. Divide others in late spring or plant seeds in autumn in the ground or in containers indoors in early spring.

Preferences/Hardiness: Plant in full sun in well-drained, light soil with moderate fertility. Cut back and remove old stems in mid- to late winter to allow new growth enough space to grow. Zones 6–9.

Authorities: NY.rug, TX.a; *P. alopecuroides* (Fountain grass) and *P. orientale,* NC

Penstemon 'Evelyn' (Penstemon, Beardtongue)

Perovskia atriplicifolia (Russian sage)

Phlox subulata (Creeping phlox, Moss phlox)

Penstemon species

Beardtongue

Figwort family (SCROPHULARIACEAE)

Appearance: These perennials and subshrubs have tubular blooms on spikes. Colors include white, red, pink, purple, salmon, and bicolor. The stems of the cultivar 'Husker Red' are deep purple-red.

Nativity: N. and C. America

Uses: Mixed borders, rock gardens

Toxicity: Some species, including *P. whippleanus* (Whipple's penstemon), native Idaho to N. Mexico, contain monoterpene alkaloids that should discourage browsing. Perhaps other species do, too.

Propagation/Care: Plant seeds indoors in early spring and keep the container on a heating mat set to 55°–60°F. Divide in spring. Take softwood cuttings in early summer. Take semiripe cuttings in midsummer.

Preferences/Hardiness: Plant in full sun or partial shade in very well-drained soil with average to moderate fertility. Mulch over winter in cool climates.

Authorities: AZ.u, CA.s, GA.a; *P. digitalis* 'Huskers Red', PA; *P. hirsutus*, PA; *P. pinifolius*, CA.s; *P. campanulatus* 'Evelyn' and 'Garnet', CA.s

Perovskia atriplicifolia

Russian sage

Mint family (LAMIACEAE)

Appearance: The deciduous perennials in this genus are considered subshrubs. They have finely cut, silver- or gray-green foliage. The shoots are striking even when plants are not in bloom. Flowers form on tall panicles. From a distance, the tiny, purple-blue blooms look like a fine haze or fog.

Nativity: C. Asia, Himalayas

Uses: Mixed borders, complementing hot-colored blooms

Toxicity: Our sources offer no toxin assay.

Propagation/Care: Take softwood cuttings in late spring; take semiripe cuttings in summer.

Preferences/Hardiness: Grow in full sun in well-drained soil with moderate fertility levels. Russian sage tolerates alkaline soil and periods of slight drought.

Authorities: CA.s, IL, NC, NY.d, NY.r, NY.v, WA, WV

> Abbreviations for **Authorities** can be found on page 234.

Phlox subulata

Creeping phlox, Moss phlox

Phlox family (POLEMONIACEAE)

Appearance: This creeping perennial forms mats of oval-shaped, bright green leaves. In late spring and early summer, plants are literally covered with brightly colored flowers in various shades of pink, purple, lavender, blue, and white. Flowers of many cultivars have a colored eye, often of a different color than the petals.

Nativity: E. to C. United States

Uses: Rock gardens, edging

Toxicity: Our sources suggest no toxin issues. Low-growth habit may make browsing less convenient. The University of Arkansas Cooperative Extension considers this plant nontoxic to humans.

Propagation/Care: Divide plants in early spring; layer stems in spring.

Preferences/Hardiness: Plant in full sun or dappled shade in well-drained soil with good fertility. Zones 3–8.

Authorities: AZ.u, CA.s, NY.r; *P. s.* 'Moss Pink', 'Millstream Daphne', 'Emerald Cushon', PA; *P. stolonifera* (Creeping phlox), NY.r

Physostegia virginiana 'Pink Bouquet'
(Obedient plant)

Picea pungens 'Hoopsii'
(Hoopsi blue spruce)

Pieris japonica (Japanese andromeda,
Lily-of-the-valley bush)

Physostegia virginiana

Obedient plant

Mint family (LAMIACEAE)

Appearance: This perennial is named
for the uncanny habit of its flower
stalks to stay where you move them.
Children delight in this, so if you have
children, don't be surprised to see the
flower spikes pointing in odd directions. The tubular flower colors include
purple, pink, and white, and the leaves
are usually toothed and dark green.

Nativity: Eastern N. America

Uses: Mixed borders, cutting gardens;
long-lasting in vases

Toxicity: Our sources suggest no toxin
issues.

Propagation/Care: Start seed indoors
in early spring in individual containers
or plant them in autumn and
overwinter in a cold frame. Divide in
early spring.

Preferences/Hardiness: Plant in full
sun or partial shade in moist soil of
high fertility that is rich in humus.
Zones 2–8.

Authorities: NY.r, PA

Abbreviations for **Authorities** can
be found on page 234.

Picea species

Spruces

Pine family (PINACEAE)

Appearance: The 40 or so species of
spruce trees have hundreds of cultivars
in a wide range of sizes, habits, and
colors. Native *P. breweriana* (Brewer
spruce) has weeping branches.
P. omorika (Serbian) 'Nana' is a dwarf.
Native *P. pungens* f. *glauca* (White)
cultivars have blue-green needles.
P. abies (Norway) 'Aurea' has
yellowish needles.

Nativity: Cool areas of N. Hemisphere

Uses: Specimens, woodland plantings,
hedgerows, foundation plants

Toxicity: Resins contain volatile
terpenes that taste and smell much like
their toxic commercial distillation,
turpentine, putting spruces near the
bottom of the herbivore menu.

Propagation/Care: Graft in late
winter. Take hardwood cuttings in
late summer. Plant seed in containers
to overwinter in a cold frame.

Preferences/Hardiness: Plant in full
sun in well-drained, moist, deep soil
with good fertility. Zones 3–9.

Authorities: AZ.u, GA.u, IL, MA,
MO, MT, NY.r; *P. glauca*, NY.d,
NY.rug, WA; *P. pungens* (Colorado s.),
NY.d, NY.l; *P. pungens glauca*
(Colorado blue s.), WV

Pieris species

Pieris

Heath family (ERICACEAE)

Appearance: Two species and
cultivars of these evergreen shrubs
dominate commercially. Flowers are
bell-shaped and pendent. The glossy
leaves are green when mature, reddish
when young, giving a two-tone effect.
P. floribunda (Fetterbush, Mountain
pieris) is native to the Southeast.
P. japonica (Andromeda, Lily-of-the-
valley bush) hails from E. China.

Nativity: S.E. United States, E. Asia,
Himalayas, W. Indies

Uses: Specimen borders, woodlands

Toxicity: Ingestion by humans causes
mouth burning, salivation, vomiting,
diarrhea, headache, and tingling skin.
Dim vision, heart stress, severe blood
pressure change, coma, and death may
follow. The honey is also toxic.

Propagation/Care: Take greenwood
cuttings in early summer; semiripe
cuttings in late summer. Plant seeds in
containers in a cold frame in spring or
autumn.

Preferences/Hardiness: Plant in full
sun or light shade in well-drained,
acid soil with high humus levels and
moderate fertility. Zones 5–9.

Authorities: *P. floribunda*, NY.r;
P. japonica, MO, NY.d, NY.l

Pinus strobus 'Pendula'
(Weeping white pine)

Podophyllum peltatum
(Mayapple, American mandrake)

Polemonium reptans 'Stairway to Heaven'
(Jacob's ladder)

Pinus species

Pines

Pine family (PINACEAE)

Appearance: This genus of evergreen conifers contains 120 species. Needles generally grow in bundles of 2 to 5 and persist for 2 to 3 years. Species grow 6 to 100 ft tall.

Nativity: In N. America from the Arctic Circle to C. America but throughout N. Hemisphere

Uses: Specimens, hedgerows, windbreaks

Toxicity: Resin acids in pine needles and budding branch tips affect microorganisms in the rumen, causing digestive consequences as well as late-stage abortions in cattle, bison, and sheep.

Propagation/Care: Graft cultivars in late winter. Plant seeds as soon as ripe, shown by a hardened seed coat, in containers in a cold frame.

Preferences/Hardiness: Plant in full sun in well-drained soil. Choose species native to your climate, or their cultivars. Zones 3–9.

Authorities: AZ.u, GA.u, MA, NC, WA; *P. edulis* (Pinyon pine), CO.u; *P. mugo* (Mugo), MO, MT, NY.d, WA; *P. resinosa* (Red), MO; *P. strobus* (White), PA; *P. sylvestris* (Scots), MO, MT, WV *Note: P. sylvestris* invasive IA, MA, ME, NJ, NY, OH, PA, VT, WI

Podophyllum peltatum

Mayapple, American mandrake

Barberry family (BERBERIDACEAE)

Appearance: Young spring shoots of this native perennial resemble folded umbrellas that gradually open into large, rooflike green leaves that conceal a single cup-shaped white flower with yellow stamens and pistil. The mature yellow fruit resembles a small lemon.

Nativity: Eastern N. America

Uses: Woodland gardens, shade gardens

Toxicity: Podophyllotoxins cause profuse salivation, loss of appetite, colic, and diarrhea in animals, sometimes accompanied by facial swelling. In humans, symptoms include nausea, vomiting, and diarrhea, sometimes worse depending on dosage. Extracts are used in wart removal. The pulp of the ripe yellow fruit is considered edible, tasting in our test somewhat like that of a fibrous ripe peach.

Propagation/Care: Divide in spring or summer. Plant seeds as soon as they are ripe, shown by a hardened seed coat, in containers left open to the elements.

Preferences/Hardiness: Plant in full or partial shade in moist, humus-filled soil with good fertility levels.

Authorities: N Y.r, NY.s

Polemonium caeruleum

Jacob's ladder

Phlox family (POLEMONIACEAE)

Appearance: This perennial takes its common name from ladderlike leaves that don't quite climb to heaven as in biblical Jacob's dream. The scientific name *caeruleum* means "sky blue" in Latin, describing the open cup- or bell-shaped flowers in early summer. *P. caeruleum* var. *lacteum* has white flowers.

Nativity: W. North America, N. and C. Europe, N. Asia

Uses: Mixed borders, woodland gardens

Toxicity: Our sources suggest no toxin issues.

Propagation/Care: Plant seeds indoors in early spring or in autumn in a cold frame. Divide in spring.

Preferences/Hardiness: Plant in full sun or partial shade in well-drained, fertile soil with good organic matter content. Zones 4–9.

Authorities: GA.a, IL, NY.d, NY.l

Polystichum acrostichoides
(Christmas fern)

Potentilla fruticosa 'Primrose Beauty'
(Shrubby cinquefoil)

Prunus 'Snow Fountain' (Cherry) and
Narcissus 'Mon Cherie' (Daffodil)

Polystichum acrostichoides

Christmas fern

Wood Fern family (DRYOPTERIDACEAE)

Appearance: This evergreen perennial is one of nearly 200 usually evergreen species of *Polystichums*. Often low spreading, Christmas ferns have dark green fronds that grow about 18 in. tall and spread 36 in. in diameter.

Nativity: N.E. North America

Uses: Woodland gardens, near water features, rock gardens

Toxicity: Deer don't browse this evergreen, even in winter. Although many members of this family are toxic, our sources offer no assay on this one.

Propagation/Care: In good conditions, spores of these ferns germinate well. Carefully transplant seedlings to give them adequate space to develop. Divide in spring.

Preferences/Hardiness: Plant in deep or partial shade in well-drained, moist, fertile soil with high humus content. Trim off dead fronds as you notice them and in late winter.

Authorities: GA.u, NC, NY.l, PA

Potentilla species

Cinquefoils

Rose family (ROSACEAE)

Appearance: This genus includes perennials, shrubs, annuals, and biennials. Most gardeners are most familiar with cultivars of native *P. fruticosa* (Shrubby cinquefoil), which grows about 3 ft tall. Cultivars bloom in red, white, yellow, pink, or salmon. Many have gray- or silver-green, finely cut foliage. *P. tridentate,* also native, grows just 6 to 12 in. tall.

Nativity: N. Hemisphere

Uses: Mixed borders, woodland gardens, groundcovers, rock gardens

Toxicity: Our sources suggest no toxins.

Propagation/Care: Divide perennials in spring. Take greenwood cuttings in early summer. Plant ripe seeds (shown by a hardened seed coat) in containers overwintered in a cold frame.

Preferences/Hardiness: Plant in full sun in well-drained, moderately fertile soil. The plants tolerate dry spells. Zones 3–10.

Authorities: IL, NY.l, NY.r; *P. canadensis,* CA.s; *P. fruticosa* (Shrubby cinquefoil), AZ.u, CA.s, NY.r, NY. rug, PA, WA; *P. tridentata* (Three-tooth cinquefoil)*,* PA *Note: P. recta* (Sulfur cinquefoil) invasive CO, ID, MD, MT, OR, WA, WY

Prunus species

Almonds, Cherries, Cherry laurels, Nectarines, Peaches, Plums

Rose family (ROSACEAE)

Appearance: This diverse genus is grown mainly for the fruits and nuts that follow beautiful, fragrant pink or white spring-blooming flowers. Ornamentals are grown for their flowers.

Nativity: N. temperate regions, Asia, S. America

Uses: Specimens, orchards

Toxicity: Leaves and seeds contain glycosides that generate cyanide during digestion, causing weakness, rapid respiration, incoordination, collapse, seizures, and death. Ruminants are especially susceptible. See page 274.

Propagation/Care: Graft in early spring or bud in summer. Take semiripe cuttings in late summer. Take hardwood cuttings in winter.

Preferences/Hardiness: Plant in full sun in well-drained, moderately fertile, humus-rich soil. Pruning instructions vary by species. Zones 4–10.

Authorities: *P. americana* (American plum), PA; *P. caroliniana* (Carolina cherry laurel), CA.u, GA.u, MT, NC; *P. fruticosa* (Steppe cherry), *P. laurocerasus* (English laurel), OR; *P. maritima* (Beach plum), PA; *P. virginiana* (Choke cherry), PA, WA

Pulmonaria longifolia 'Bertram Anderson' (Lungwort)

Pycnanthemum virginianum (American mountain mint)

Ranunculus repens 'Buttered Popcorn' (Buttercups, Crowfoot)

Pulmonaria species

Lungworts

Forget-me-not family (BORAGINACEAE)

Appearance: Harbingers of spring, lungworts send up stems topped with blue, white, red, or pink flowers. Once blooms fade in many cultivars, the spotted or streaked summer leaves appear. Bees and other beneficial insects relish the flower nectar.

Nativity: Europe, Asia

Uses: Groundcovers, woodland gardens, wildflower gardens, orchards

Toxicity: Our sources are silent on toxins, except James Duke's mention of a study showing the plant's tendency to accumulate copper, iron, manganese, and phosphorus, which perhaps affect taste.

Propagation/Care: Plant seed as soon as it is ripe, shown by a hardened seed coat, and place containers in a cold frame. Divide every 3 years after flowering or in fall. Take root cuttings in winter. Saved seed rarely comes true, so buy it.

Preferences/Hardiness: Plant in full or partial shade in moist, fertile, humus-rich soil. Zones 3–8.

Authorities: IL, MT, NY.l, NY.r, WA

Pycnanthemum species

Mountain mints

Mint family (LAMIACEAE)

Appearance: These 2- to 4-ft tall perennials are often grown near beehives. White or light pink flowers bloom late in the season. Prior to blooming, the slightly hairy, clear green leaves form opposite each other on square, sometimes brownish stems. The minty tea is tasty.

Nativity: E. United States

Uses: Herb gardens, orchards, tea gardens

Toxicity: The leaves are aromatic when browsed, a Mint family defense that deters browsing.

Propagation/Care: Plant seeds in place in spring or autumn. Divide in early summer.

Preferences/Hardiness: Plant in full sun to partial shade in well-drained, somewhat moist soil with high humus levels and moderate fertility. Zones 3–8.

Authorities: CT.n, NY.r; *P. muticum* (Big Leaf mountain mint), *P. tenuifolium* (Slender mountain mint), PA

Abbreviations for **Authorities** can be found on page 234.

Ranunculus species

Buttercups, Crowfoot

Buttercup family (RANUNCULACEAE)

Appearance: The 400 species in this genus include annuals, biennials, and perennials—some evergreen, some deciduous. Many are much showier than the roadside buttercup *(R. acris)* and deserve greater popularity.

Nativity: Temperate regions world-wide

Uses: Mixed borders, wildflower gardens

Toxicity: During flowering, some *Ranunculus* species develop heightened levels of ranunculin glycoside, which causes nausea, vomiting, diarrhea, and blistering of the mouth and digestive system. Alkaloids may also be present, along with low amounts of cyanide-generating glycosides.

Propagation/Care: Plant seeds in open frames and allow to germinate over several years. Divide perennials in spring.

Preferences/Hardiness: Vary according to species. Some grow well in aquatic or marginal situations and some in sandy soil, some in full sun, and some in shade. So check with supplier. Zones 4–8.

Authorities: NY.l, NY.r, WV

Rheum rhabarbarum 'Victoria' (Rhubarb)

Rhododendron catawbiense (Catawba rhododendron, Mountain rosebay)

Ribes sativum (Red currant)

Rheum species

Rhubarbs

Buckwheat family (POLYGONACEAE)

Appearance: Like *Rheum rhabarbaraum* = × *cultorum* (the plant used in pies), ornamental rhubarbs have large, spreading leaves and tall clusters of tiny flowers that rise stiffly above the leaves. Blooms are red or white. Although mature leaves of most cultivars are green, some are red, and young buds and leaves may be red or red-brown.

Nativity: E. Europe, C. Asia, Himalayas, China

Uses: Woodland gardens, near streams or ponds

Toxicity: Leaves contain tart-tasting oxalates and anthraquinone glycosides that if eaten in quantity can cause nausea, vomiting, abdominal cramps, diarrhea, and kidney damage in livestock and humans.

Propagation/Care: Plants self-seed easily. Transplant seedlings when young. Plant ripe seeds (shown by a hardened seed coat) in a cold frame in autumn. Divide mature plants.

Preferences/Hardiness: Plant in full sun or partial shade in deep, very moist soil with high humus content. Zones 3–9.

Authorities: NY.l, NY.r, NY.s, WV

Rhododendron species

Rhododendrons

Erica family (ERICACEAE)

Appearance: Deer tend to avoid large-leaved evergreens called rhododendrons, but relish the often deciduous rhododendron subgenera called azaleas. Bloom times vary by region. Large-leaved natives include *R. catawbiense* (Catawba rhododendron), *R. minus* (Carolina rododendron), *R. macrophyllum* (Pacific rhododendron), *R. maximum* (Rosebay rhododendron).

Nativity: N. America

Uses: Shrub borders, focal points

Toxicity: As with some other Ericas, deer reluctantly eat rhododendron leaves. In humans, the leaves cause mouth burning, salivation, vomiting, diarrhea, and skin tingling—sometimes also convulsions, coma, and cardiac arrest. Flower nectar can poison honey, and leaf toxins affect deer more strongly in winter.

Propagation/Care: Because plants commonly hybridize, collected seed can produce surprises. Place young plants shallowly in moist, humus-rich, acid soil (pH 4.5–5.5).

Preferences/Hardiness: Dappled shade and woodlands. Depending on cultivar, Zones 4–9.

Authorities: CA.s, CA.u, NY.s, OR

Ribes species

Currants, Gooseberries

Currant family (GROSSULARIACEAE)

Appearance: These shrubs are grown both for their flowers and, in the case of gooseberries and currants, their fruit. They bloom early in the year, in shades of yellow, pink, and greenish white, and some are sweetly fragrant. Leaves turn brilliant colors before dropping in fall.

Nativity: North temperate zones, S. America

Uses: Borders, hedges, woodlands

Toxicity: Sources suggest no toxins.

Propagation/Care: Root hardwood cuttings in winter; take semiripe cuttings in late summer.

Preferences/Hardiness: Grow most species in full sun; *R. laurifolium* and *R. sanguineum* (Flowering currant) do better in partial shade. All species require well-drained, moderately fertile soil. Zones 5–9.

Authorities: AZ.u, CA.u, WA; *R. aureum* (Buffalo currant, Clove currant), WA; *R. sanguineum,* WA (Zones 9–10)

Abbreviations for **Authorities** can be found on page 234.

Robinia pseudoacacia 'Frisia'
(Black locust)

Romneya coulteri
(Matilija poppy, Tree poppy)

Rosmarinus officinalis 'Prostratus'
(Dwarf rosemary)

Robinia pseudoacacia

Black locust

Pea family (FABACEAE)

Appearance: This native grows to 80 ft with columnar habit, tortuously upright limbs, deeply fissured bark, dark green pealike foliage, and fragrant clusters of pendent white flowers. Cultivars are smaller and vary in leaf color. 'Umbraceulifera', to 20 ft, has a rounded crown. 'Frisia' (shown), to 50 ft, features yellow-green foliage turning orange-yellow in fall. 'Tortuosa', to 50 ft, produces twisted shoots.

Nativity: Eastern N. America

Uses: Specimens, woodland gardens

Toxicity: Although leaves pose low risk, ingested branch bark causes nausea, weakness, vomiting, diarrhea, and dilated pupils in cattle, horses, and humans. Breathing difficulty, weakened pulse, and paralysis may follow. Horses also suffer inflamed hooves. Seeds cause vomiting in children.

Propagation/Care: Graft in late winter. Remove suckers in autumn. Take root cuttings in autumn.

Preferences/Hardiness: Grow in full sun in moderately fertile, well-drained soil. These trees tolerate dry periods and low-fertility soils. Zones 5–9.

Authorities: IL, MO, NY.d, NY.r

Romneya coulteri

Matilija poppy, Tree poppy

Poppy family (PAPAVERACEAE)

Appearance: This stunning woody perennial grows 3–8 ft tall and at least as wide, unless restrained. The fragrant summer flowers are up to 5 in. across, with ruffled "crepe-papery" white petals and prominent bright yellow centers. They bloom May to July, into fall if watered. Leaves are gray-green.

Nativity: S.W. United States

Uses: Hillside soil binder, back of garden, wall accent, screen

Toxicity: Namesake "poppy" family members contain alkaloids that disturb digestive and nervous systems of livestock. But our sources offer no toxin assay on this species.

Propagation/Care: Established plants sucker; remove and transplant rooted suckers. Plant seeds in spring in containers kept about 60°F. Root basal cuttings in spring. Take root cuttings in winter.

Preferences/Hardiness: Grow in full sun in well-drained, fertile soil. Cut nearly to ground in fall, and mulch over winter. Protect from cold winds. Zones 8–10.

Authorities: CA.s, CA.u

Rosmarinus officinalis

Rosemary

Mint family (LAMIACEAE)

Appearance: This is the aromatic evergreen rosemary used in cooking. It's also grown for its attractive foliage and flowers. It grows 5 ft tall and wide. 'Arp' is the most hardy cultivar, and 6-in.-tall 'Prostratus' makes an excellent ground cover. Flowers in most cultivars are blue or purple. 'Roseus' has pink flowers.

Nativity: Mediterranean region

Uses: Herb gardens, rock gardens, edging plants

Toxicity: Camphor-fragranced oils likely discourage browsing. Used medicinally, large doses of essential oils can irritate skin and digestive tract, says ethnobotanist James Duke.

Propagation/Care: Root semiripe cuttings in spring; plant seeds indoors in early spring.

Preferences/Hardiness: Plant in full sun in well-drained soil of low to moderate fertility. Let dry between waterings, especially in winter when the plant rests. Zones 8–11.

Authorities: AZ.u, CA.u, GA.u, IL, MO, NC, NY.l, NY.r, OR, TX.a, WA; *R.* 'Arp', 'Prostratus', 'Lockwood de Forest', CA.s

Rudbeckia fulgida var. *sullivantii* 'Goldsturm' (Black-eyed Susan)

Salvia elegans (Pineapple-scented sage)

Sambucus canadensis 'John's American Elder' (Elderberry)

Rudbeckia species

Coneflower, Black-eyed Susan, Gloriosa daisy

Aster family (ASTERACEAE)

Appearance: This genus includes 18 native annuals, biennials, and perennials with showy, daisylike flowers. Petals are yellow, orange, or red-brown, often with dark centers as in *R. fulgida* var. *sullivantii* 'Goldsturm'. *R. hirta* 'Irish Eyes' has a green center.

Nativity: N. America

Uses: Mixed borders, bedding plants

Toxicity: Bad odor and taste likely repel most mammals. Yet plant lactones have caused incoordination, rapid breathing, loss of appetite, and death in sheep and pigs.

Propagation/Care: Start seed indoors in early spring or in garden after last frost. Divide in early spring.

Preferences/Hardiness: Plant in full sun in moist but well-drained soil of moderate fertility. Deadhead to prolong bloom. Zones 4–9.

Authorities: GA.a, MT, NY.d; *R. fulgida* 'Goldsturm', CA.s; *R. hirta*, AZ.u, IL; *R. maxima*, NY.r, WA, WV. CA.s says blacktail deer eat her *R. nitida* and *R. triloba* but not her 'Goldsturm'.

Salvia species

Sages

Mint family (LAMIACEAE)

Appearance: These 900 species include annuals, biennials, perennials, subshrubs, and shrubs. Although a few are grown for culinary or medicinal uses, most are grown as ornamentals with flower spikes in blues, purples, reds, pinks, and whites. Foliage may be yellow, gray-green, blue-green, clear green, or variegated.

Nativity: Temperate and tropical regions

Uses: Herb gardens, orchards, mixed borders

Toxicity: Scent and taste likely deter browsers. Nitrates in some species have poisoned goats.

Propagation/Care: Start seeds indoors in early spring. Divide perennials in spring. Take softwood cuttings in spring. Take semihardwood cuttings in late summer.

Preferences/Hardiness: Plant in full sun or partial shade in well-drained soil with moderate fertility and high humus levels. Avoid overwatering, particularly in winter. Zones 4–9.

Authorities: AZ.u, CA.u, GA.a (most species), IL, MO, NY.r, WV.

Sambucus species

Elderberries

Honeysuckle family (CAPRIFOLIACEAE)

Appearance: This genus includes 6- to 12-ft shrubs and trees to 25 ft grown for the beauty of their flowers, berries, and foliage. White or pinkish flowers form in flattened clusters. *S. racemosa* (European red elder) 'Plumosa Aurea' has vivid yellow leaves.

Nativity: N. and S. America, Eurasia, N. and E. Africa, Australia

Uses: Specimens, hedges, woodland gardens, herb gardens

Toxicity: Leaves and raw berries contain sambunigrin, a glycoside that converts to cyanide ions during digestion, causing weakness, incoordination, labored respiration, seizures, and death. Cooking of berries removes toxins.

Propagation/Care: Take greenwood cuttings in early summer; hardwood cuttings in late fall. Plant seeds in autumn.

Preferences/Hardiness: Plant in full sun or partial shade in well-drained, moderately fertile soil with good humus. Zones 3–8.

Authorities: WA, WV; *S. canadensis* (American elder) 'Laciniata', PA; *S. racemosa* subspecies *pubens*, PA

Santolina chamaecyparissus
(Lavender cotton)

Satureja (Savory)

Scilla siberica (Siberian squill)

Santolina species

Lavender cotton

Aster family (ASTERACEAE)

Appearance: These evergreen shrubs are grown for ornamental value but are also used as an important ingredient in moth-repellent potpourris. The young shoots and leaves of *S. chamaecyparissus* (Lavender cotton) are soft gray-green and somewhat woolly looking. The flowers are yellow. Leaves of *S. pinnata* are gray-green in most cultivars and flowers are white or yellow.

Nativity: Mediterranean region

Uses: Herb gardens, mixed borders, wildflower gardens

Toxicity: Strong fragrance is a likely repellent.

Propagation/Care: Plant seeds indoors in early spring or in a cold frame in fall. Root semiripe cuttings in late summer.

Preferences/Hardiness: Plant in full sun in poor to moderately fertile soil that is extremely well-drained. Plants tolerate dry periods, particularly in winter when the light is low. Zones 6–9.

Authorities: AZ.u, CA.s, CA.u, MO, NC, NY.d, NY.r, OR, TX.a, WA, WV; *S. rosmarinifolia* = *S. virens* (Green santolina), OR, TX.a, WA

Satureja species

Savory

Mint family (LAMIACEAE)

Appearance: This genus includes annuals, perennials, and shrubs, including the culinary annual herbs *S. hortensis* (Summer savory) and *S. Montana* (Winter savory). The woody perennial *S. thymbra* is grown for its spikes of pink to purple flowers in the spring. It's hardy to Zone 6 and generally grows about 18 in. tall. Summer savory is an annual, but winter savory is a perennial in Zones 5–11.

Nativity: N. Hemisphere

Uses: Herb gardens, mixed borders, woodland and wildflower gardens

Toxicity: Our sources suggest no toxin issues.

Propagation/Care: Start seed indoors in early spring, or seed directly into the garden. Take greenwood cuttings of woody species in summer.

Preferences/Hardiness: Plant in full sun in well-drained, slightly alkaline soil with moderate fertility levels. Avoid overwatering in winter when the plants are resting. Zones 5–9.

Authorities: CA.u, IL, NY.d

> Abbreviations for **Authorities** can be found on page 234.

Scilla species

Scilla, Squill

Lily family (LILIACEAE)

Appearance: These bulbous perennials are a favorite early spring bloomer. Most species have relatively small star-shaped or bell-shaped flowers that grow on stalks that hold them just above the straplike green leaves. Flowers are usually blue or purple, although white, pink, and white cultivars are available. These plants look best when massed and multiply quickly.

Nativity: Europe, Africa, Asia

Uses: Bulb beds, under deciduous shrubs, woodland gardens, naturalized in grass

Toxicity: Cardioactive steroids throughout the plant can affect the heart and elevate blood potassium.

Propagation/Care: Plant bulbs in autumn. Divide offsets in autumn and replant. Plant seeds in containers and overwinter in a cold frame.

Preferences/Hardiness: Plant in full sun or partial shade in well-drained, moderately fertile soil.

Authorities: AZ.u, CA.u, NC; *S. peruviana* (Cuban lily, Peruvian jacinth), IL, NY.d; *S. siberica* (Siberian squill), MO, NY.l, NY.r, WV

Senecio cineraria 'Silver Queen' (Dusty miller) and *Zinnia elegans* 'Profusion Orange' (Zinnia)

Skimmia japonica (Japanese skimmia <female form>)

Solidago flexicaulis (Zigzag goldenrod)

Senecio cineraria

Dusty miller

Aster family (ASTERACEAE)

Appearance: This subshrub and cultivars are grown for their silvery leaves, which occasioned the Latinized species name, *cineraria,* meaning ash-gray. Most people grow them as annuals and so don't see the mustard-yellow flowers until they emerge the second year. The species grows to 2 ft. Dwarf cultivar 'Alice' grows to 1 ft. The 12- to 16-in. cultivars 'Silver Queen' and 'Silver Dust' have lacy leaves, and those of 'White Diamond' are oaklike.

Nativity: W. and C. Mediterranean

Uses: Mixed borders, edging plants

Toxicity: Many *Senecios* contain pyrrolizidine alkaloids. Concentrations may vary tenfold during the growing season. These alkaloids cause severe digestive discomfort and liver damage in livestock and humans.

Propagation/Care: Sow seed in spring. Take semiripe cuttings in mid- to late summer.

Preferences/Hardiness: Full sun and moderately fertile, well-drained soil. Zones 8–11.

Authorities: CA.u, GA.a, GA.u, NY.r; *S. aureus* (Golden groundsell), PA; *S. cineraria* (Dusty Miller), CA.u, GA.a, GA.u, MO, NC, OR, TX.a

Skimmia japonica

Japanese skimmia

Rue family (RUTACEAE)

Appearance: This creeping or dome-shaped to erect shrub to 20 ft tall is either male or female. Its dark green leaves are slightly aromatic. In late spring, fragrant ¼-inch white flowers are sometimes tinged with pink or red. If fertilized by a male plant, female flowers become red berries. Creeping *S.* 'Bowles Dwarf' grows only 6 in. tall and is available in both male and female clones. The species *S. reevesiana,* to 2 ft tall, can fertilize itself.

Nativity: China, Japan, S.E. Asia

Uses: Shrub borders, woodlands

Toxicity: Fruits cause stomach upset. Aromatic leaves may deter browsers.

Propagation/Care: Take semiripe cuttings in summer and root over heat. Plant seeds when they are ripe and feel dry to the touch and overwinter in a cold frame.

Preferences/Hardiness: Grow in partial to deep shade in well-drained, moist soil with high humus levels and moderate fertility. Zones 7–9.

Authorities: NY.d, OR

> Abbreviations for **Authorities** can be found on page 234.

Solidago species

Goldenrods

Aster family (ASTERACEAE)

Appearance: Contrary to popular belief, these woody perennials do not cause hay fever because the pollen isn't windborne. Goldenrods add beauty to late summer and fall gardens and make good cut flowers. Field identification can be challenging because the species hybridize. Various species can self-seed entirely too freely, but the cultivars tend to have fewer seeds.

Nativity: N. and S. America, Eurasia

Uses: Mixed borders, wildflower and cutting gardens

Toxicity: Goldenrods are rarely palatable to livestock. In sheep, they have caused excess salivation, uncontrolled mouth movement, hypersensitivity to touch and sound, quivering muscles, dazed wandering, seizures, and death. Fungus in goldenrods has poisoned horses.

Propagation/Care: Divide in autumn or early spring.

Preferences/Hardiness: Plant in full sun in well-drained, preferably sandy soil with moderate fertility. Zones 5–9.

Authorities: GA.a, GA.u, IL, MT, NY.d; *S.* 'Golden Baby', CA.s; *S.* hybrids, NY.l, NY.r; *S. rugosa* 'Fireworks' and *S. sphacelata* 'Golden Fleece', PA

Spiraea japonica = × *bumalda* 'Anthony Waterer' (Spirea)

Stachys byzantina 'Silver Carpet' (Lamb's ears)

Syringa vulgaris 'Paul Thirion' (Common lilac)

Spiraea species

Spirea, Bridalwreath

Rose family (ROSACEAE)

Appearance: These shrubs are deciduous or semi-evergreen and feature clusters of small white, pink, or yellow flowers that liberally clothe the branches in spring and early summer. Shrub sizes vary. *S. japonica* 'Alpina' and 'Alba' are only 16 to 24 in. tall.

Nativity: N. America, Europe, and Asia

Uses: Shrub borders, hedges, rock gardens, groundcovers

Toxicity: The leaves of *S. prunifolia* (Bridalwreath) create cyanide after ingestion. For more on Rose family cyanogenic poisoning, see page 274.

Propagation/Care: Divide suckering species in early spring or autumn. Take greenwood cuttings in summer.

Preferences/Hardiness: Plant in full sun in well-drained soil with good moisture-holding capacity, moderate to high fertility, and good humus levels. Zones 4–8.

Authorities: IL, NY.v, WA; *S. japonica* 'Alpina', CA.s; *S. prunifolia* (Bridalwreath), MT; *S.* × *bumalda* cultivars, *S. japonica*, *S. nipponica* cultivars, *S.* × *vanhouttei*, *S. dolchica*, *S. prunifolia*, NY.r; *S. cantoniensis* (Reeve's spirea), TX.a

Stachys byzantina

Lamb's ears, Woolly betony

Mint family (LAMIACEAE)

Appearance: This perennial is grown primarily for its silvery, hairy leaves. The small purple blooms are unspectacular on a spike that can grow to 2 ft high, so many gardeners remove it. The new version is *S. b.* 'Big Ears' = 'Helene von Stein', which is less rot-prone and seldom blooms.

Nativity: Caucasus to Iran

Uses: Edging plants, groundcovers

Toxicity: Deer are likely discouraged by the hairy leaves. Native *S. avensis* (Stagger weed) has caused diarrhea and incoordination in Australian livestock.

Propagation/Care: Plant seeds in spring or fall. Divide in spring when new growth begins. Cut back yellowing or ratty leaves. In fall, cut and remove leaves so they don't smother the crown in spring.

Preferences/Hardiness: Plant in full sun and well-drained, moderately fertile soil. Lamb's ears suffers in hot, rainy summers but needs water in dry spells. Zones 4–8.

Authorities: AZ.u, CA.s, CA.u, IL, NC, NY.l, NY.r, NY.s; *S. coccinea* (Texas betony), *S. palustris* (Marsh hedgenettle), PA

Syringa species

Lilacs

Olive family (OLEACEAE)

Appearance: These shrubs and one true tree to 30 ft tall (*Syringa reticulata*) are grown for their clusters of highly fragrant spring or summer flowers in whites, pinks, reds, purples, and blues. Like *S. vulgaris* (French lilac) and its many cultivars, most of the shrubs have heart-shaped leaves. *S. laciniata* (Cutleaf lilac) has short, narrow leaves.

Nativity: S.E. Europe, E. Asia

Uses: Shrub borders, specimens, woodland gardens

Toxicity: Our sources suggest no toxin issues, though Olive family members *Fraxinus* (ashes) and *Ligustrum* (privets) contain glycosides that cause digestive distress in livestock.

Propagation/Care: Take greenwood cuttings in early to midsummer; semiripe cuttings in mid- to late summer. *S. vulgaris* tolerates hard pruning.

Preferences/Hardiness: Grow in full sun in well-drained, fertile soil with high humus levels and a neutral to slightly alkaline pH. Zones 3–8.

Authorities: AZ.u, IL; *S.* × *persica* (Persian lilac), NY.d, WA; *S. reticulata*, IL

Tagetes tenuifolia 'Lemon Gem' (Marigold)

Tanacetum parthenium 'Aureum' (Feverfew)

Teucrium chamaedrys (Wall germander)

Tagetes species

Marigolds

Aster family (ASTERACEAE)

Appearance: This genus includes annuals and perennials. Most garden favorites are cultivars of annuals grouped by flower type: African (aka American), French, triploid, and signet. Single or double flowers are yellow, orange, red, cream, or bicolor. The lacy leaves may be green or gray-green and are strongly scented, as are the flowers of some species.

Nativity: N. and S. America

Uses: Mixed borders, vegetable gardens, herb gardens

Toxicity: Strong scent likely deters most browsers. In humans, skin contact can awaken allergies.

Propagation/Care: Plant seeds indoors in early spring, and transplant after frost. Plant successive crops in long-season climates.

Preferences/Hardiness: Grow in full sun in well-drained soil with moderate fertility. Deadhead to prolong blooming.

Authorities: GA.u, IL, WV; *T. lemonii* (Tangerine-scented marigold), *T. lucida* (Mexican tarragon, Sweet mace), TX.a; *Tagetes patula* (French marigold), NY.d

Site credit: Barbara Ellis garden

Tanacetum species

Feverfew, Tansy

Aster family (ASTERACEAE)

Appearance: The 70 *Tanacetum* species include annuals, subshrubs, and both evergreen and herbaceous perennials. Leaves are lacy or fernlike. Flowers are daisylike or buttonlike with white, pink, or red petals and a yellow or white center.

Nativity: N. temperate regions

Uses: Herb gardens, mixed borders, cutting gardens

Toxicity: Strong "chrysanthemum" scent likely deters browsing. In humans, *T. parthenium* (Feverfew) has caused mouth sores. *T. vulgare* (Tansy) oils and teas have caused cardiac arrest.

Propagation/Care: *T. vulgare* can take over the garden if it self-seeds, so deadhead promptly. Plant seeds indoors in early spring or overwinter in containers in a cold frame. Divide perennials in spring.

Preferences/Hardiness: Grow in full sun in well-drained, moderately fertile soil. Zones 5–9.

Authorities: IL; *T. coccinium* (Pyre-thrum), *T. densum* ssp. *amani* (Dwarf tansy), *T. parthenium* and *T. p.* 'Aureum' (Golden feverfew), CA.s *Note: T. vulgare* (Tansy) is highly invasive.

Teucrium species

Germanders

Mint family (LAMIACEAE)

Appearance: The perennials, subshrubs, and shrubs in this genus are grown for their attractive, aromatic foliage and delicate little flowers. Leaves are often silvery or grayish green, and flowers are generally a pale lavender-blue, dark blue, pink, or yellow. Some species are low-growing and trailing. Others are more upright.

Nativity: N. America, Mediterranean

Uses: Herb gardens, borders, hedges

Toxicity: Used medicinally, some species of *Teucrium,* including *T. chamaedrys,* cause serious liver damage, says James Duke.

Propagation/Care: Plant ripe seeds in a container set in a cold frame over winter. Take softwood cuttings in spring and semiripe cuttings in summer.

Preferences/Hardiness: Grow in full sun in well-drained, neutral to alkaline soils with moderate to low fertility. Zones 4–10.

Authorities: *T. canadense* (American germander), NY.r; *T. chamaedrys* (Wall germander), IL, NY.r; *T. chamaedrys* 'Compactum', *T. cossonii* ssp. *majoricum, T. polium,* CA.s; *T. fruticans* (Bush germander), CA.u, TX.a

Thelypteris noveboracensis
(New York fern)

Thymus vulgaris 'Argenteus' (Thyme)

Tiarella cordifolia (Foam flower)

Thelypteris noveboracensis

New York fern

Marsh Fern family (THELYPTERIDACEAE)

Appearance: This native has erect fronds with lower leaflets that taper abruptly into the stem. The delicate, lacy fronds contribute a soft feeling to any areas where they grow. *Caution: Avoid its invasive cousin, T. palustris* (Marsh fern), hailing from Europe and Asia, because its spreading rhizomes will soon overtake any area where it grows.

Nativity: From GA, AL, and TN to Newfoundland

Uses: Woodland gardens, beside water features, ponds, and streams

Toxicity: Our sources don't comment on this fern genus, though others can be very toxic. Bad taste may be key here. Deer having suffered toxic effects from one fern may avoid all.

Propagation/Care: Buy plants; divide roots when crowded.

Preferences/Hardiness: Plant in full sun to partial shade, in consistently moist, moderately fertile soil. Zones 2–8.

Authorities: Native-plant designer PA (Larry Weaner) and many others

Thymus species

Thymes

Mint family (LAMIACEAE)

Appearance: The 350 species are woody-based, aromatic perennials that serve as shrubs, subshrubs, ground covers, or culinary herbs. Flowers are pink, purple, or whitish. Leaves are small and grow opposite on the stem, sometimes dark or mid-green and sometimes yellow or variegated.

Nativity: Eurasia

Uses: Herb gardens, groundcovers, between pavers

Toxicity: Volatile oils likely discourage browsing. In humans, in quantity, thymol can irritate mucous membranes and digestive tract and cause dizziness, headache, convulsions, and cardiac/respiratory arrest. Thyme toothpaste may cause swollen tongue and lip cracks.

Propagation/Care: Start seed early indoors. Layer or divide in spring. Take semiripe cuttings in summer.

Preferences/Hardiness: Grow in full sun or partial shade in well-drained, neutral to alkaline soil with moderate fertility. Cut back in early spring and trim after bloom. Zones 3–9.

Authorities: AZ.u, CA.s, IL, NY.d, NY.r, NY.rug, TX.a, WA, WV; *T. cherlerioides,* CA.s

Tiarella species

Foam flowers

Saxifage family (SAXIFRAGACEAE)

Appearance: These perennials send up flower spikes in whites or pinks and have attractive lobed, basal leaves. "They've become the rage in breeding circles," says CT.n. Vigorously rhizomatous *T. cordifolia,* to 12 in. tall, spreads by stolons, its leaves turning bronze-red in autumn. Clump-forming and without spreading stolons, *T. trifoliata* from the northern Pacific region grows 20 in. tall, and *T. wherryi* from the Appalachians grows 8 in. tall and has maroon-tinted green leaves.

Nativity: N. America

Uses: Shady borders, groundcovers in woodlands

Toxicity: Our sources suggest no toxin issues.

Propagation/Care: Plant species seed when ripe or the following spring in a cold frame. Divide cultivars in spring.

Preferences/Hardiness: Zones 3–8, 7, or 9, per species sequence above.

Authorities: GA.a, NY.r; *T. cordifolia,* CT.n, NY.d, WV

Abbreviations for **Authorities** can be found on page 234.

Tropaeolum majus (Nasturtium)

Tulbaghia violacea (Society garlic, Pink agapanthus)

Vaccinium corymbosum (Highbush blueberry) and Northern cardinal

Tropaeolum species

Nasturtiums

Nasturtium family (TROPAEOLACEAE)

Appearance: This genus contains the popular annual *T. major* (Nasturtium) as well as perennials, such as *T. speciosum* (Scottish flame flower), and climbers, such as *T. peregrinum* (Canary creeper). Nasturtium flowers are edible as well as beautiful. Depending upon species, they may be yellow, orange, red, or rose—all with five petals, prominent spurs, and long stamens in an open throat. Leaves are often circular or lobed.

Nativity: C. and S. America

Uses: Mixed borders, containers, screens

Toxicity: Peppery flavor of leaves and flowers likely deters browsing during summer because milder-tasting plants are available. Watch out once fall comes!

Propagation/Care: Plant seeds indoors in peat pots or soil blocks in early spring to avoid disturbing the roots when you transplant, or direct-seed in midspring.

Preferences/Hardiness: Grow in full sun in well-drained, moist soil with moderate to low fertility. Zones 10–12.

Authorities: MO, NY.d, WV

Tulbaghia violacea

Society garlic, Pink agapanthus

Lily family (LILIACEAE)

Appearance: These graceful perennials are grown for their fragrant, light purple or white, tubular, almost trumpet-shaped flowers that form in groups on the ends of long stems. The leaves, which do smell like garlic, are straplike and sometimes grayish green. Even without flowers, this plant contributes both good color and a somewhat formal form to a mixed border.

Nativity: Southern Africa

Uses: Mixed borders, rock gardens

Toxicity: The garlic odor is the likely repellent.

Propagation/Care: Plant bulbs or rhizomes in spring or fall. Plant seeds in containers in a cold frame as soon as they are ripe and feel dry to the touch.

Preferences/Hardiness: Grow in full sun in well-drained, deep soil with high humus levels and moderate fertility. Plants do well with a winter dry period. Zones 7–10.

Authorities: GA.u, NC, OR

Abbreviations for **Authorities** can be found on page 234.

Vaccinium species

Blueberries, Cranberries

Erica family (ERICACEAE)

Appearance: A 7-ft highbush blueberry can steal the show for 5+ weeks in early summer as individual berries ripen at different paces, attracting chipmunks, catbirds, jays, cardinals, and even robins, and steal the show again in fall with red or yellow leaves. Resistance authorities also recommend box blueberries, to 12 ft, and cranberries, to 6 in.

Nativity: N. America

Uses: Anywhere in full sun

Toxicity: Our sources suggest no toxin issues.

Propagation/Care: Plant dormant hardwood cuttings in fall. Use acidic mulches such as pine needles. Prune neglected plants near ground. Best reference: *Backyard Fruits and Berries* by Miranda Smith.

Preferences/Hardiness: Full sun. All prefer humus-rich, well-drained acid soil (pH 4.0–5.0). Zones: 3–7 highbush blueberry, Zones 6–8 box blueberry, Z2–7 cranberry.

Authorities: *V. corymosum* (Highbush blueberry), NY.s; *V. macrocarpon* 'Pilgrim' (Cranberry), PA; *V. ovatum* (Box blueberry, California huckleberry), WA

Verbascum 'Helen Johnson' (Mullein)

Verbena × *hybrida* (Garden verbena)

Vernonia noveboracensis (Ironweed)

Verbascum species

Mulleins

Figwort family (SCROPHULARIACEAE)

Appearance: Most of the 350 species are biennials and produce rosettes of basal leaves the first year. There are also a few annuals, perennials, and subshrubs. Tall spikes of cream or yellow flowers in hybrids are showy, often with a contrasting eye. Leaves in some species are gray or silvery.

Nativity: Europe, N. Africa, W. and C. Asia

Uses: Mixed borders, herb gardens, rock gardens

Toxicity: Most mulleins have hairy or woolly leaves that discourage browsers. Our sources suggest no toxin issues.

Propagation/Care: Plant seeds in early spring to midsummer inside or in a nursery bed and set out where they will bloom in early fall. Divide perennials in spring.

Preferences/Hardiness: Grow in full sun in alkaline soil with poor to moderate fertility and excellent drainage. Support flower spikes if they threaten to topple. Zones 5–9.

Authorities: GA.a, IL, NY.l, NY.r *Note: V. blatteria* invasive NJ, OR, WA; others, mostly biennials, may be hard to control, says CT.n.

Verbena species

Vervains

Verbena family (VERBENACEAE)

Appearance: This genus includes annuals, perennials, and subshrubs. Most have clusters of small flowers that bloom at branch tips. Flower colors include pinks, purples, roses, and whites, sometimes with a contrasting eye. Leaves are variable, depending on species, but are generally attractive.

Nativity: N., C., and S. America, E. Europe

Uses: Mixed borders, herb gardens, containers

Toxicity: Our sources cite no toxic history for these plants themselves, but ethnobotanist James Duke says high doses of verbenalin can cause paralysis, convulsion, and stupor.

Propagation/Care: Plant seeds in early spring indoors or overwinter in a container in a cold frame. Divide perennials and take softwood cuttings in spring.

Preferences/Hardiness: Grow in full sun in moderately fertile, very well-drained, moist soil with good levels of organic matter. Zones 8–11.

Authorities: AZ.u, CA.s, CA.u, GA.u, NY.r; *V. bonariensis, V. rigida* (Vervain), CA.s

Vernonia noveboracensis

Ironweed

Aster family (ASTERACEAE)

Appearance: Members of this genus include plants of almost every category, including annuals, perennials, biennials, climbers, shrubs, and trees, although the only ironweeds you are likely to grow are herbaceous perennials that often hybridize. Tall native *V. noveboracensis* is admired for its fluffy, loose clusters of reddish purple or white "shaving-brush" flowers that bloom from late summer into autumn.

Nativity: N. America

Uses: Mixed borders

Toxicity: North American species contain lactones toxic to cells (cytotoxins) that can inactivate stomach enzymes and produce effects like an antihistamine that could in quantity have strong effects, say Burrows and Tyrl.

Propagation/Care: Plant seed indoors or in a cold frame in early spring. Divide in spring or autumn.

Preferences/Hardiness: Grow in full sun or partial shade in moderately fertile soil with good moisture levels. Deadhead to prolong blooming. Zones 4–8.

Authorities: NY.r

Veronicastrum virginicum = Veronica virginica (Culver's root)

Viburnum trilobum (Highbush cranberry)

Vinca minor 'La Grave' = 'Bowles' Blue' (Periwinkle)

Veronicastrum virginicum = *Veronica virginica*

Culver's root, Blackroot
Figwort family (SCROPHULARIACEAE)

Appearance: This native perennial can grow 6 ft tall in good conditions, making it a dramatic addition to a mixed border. The leaves are about 6 in. long and grow in whorls. The flower spikes are white to pink or blue-purple.

Nativity: N. America, Siberia

Uses: Mixed borders, screens

Toxicity: Veronica root tea induces vomiting and violent diarrhea. Our sources offer no comment on the leaves.

Propagation/Care: Divide in spring or autumn; plant seeds as soon as they are ripe (shown by a hardened seed coat) in a container and overwinter in a cold frame.

Preferences/Hardiness: Grow in full sun or partial shade in well-drained, moist soil with high humus levels and moderate fertility. Zones 4–8.

Authorities: NY.r

> Abbreviations for **Authorities** can be found on page 234.

Viburnum species

Viburnums
Honeysuckle family (CAPRIFOLIACEAE)

Appearance: The 150 deciduous, semi-evergreen, or evergreen species of viburnum shrubs and trees are grown for their graceful habits, ornamental foliage, intensely fragrant flowers, and berries. Flower clusters are white or pink. The purple, black, red, or yellow berries feed birds through late fall and early winter.

Nativity: N. America, N. temperate regions

Uses: Borders, focal points, hedgerows

Toxicity: Bark and berries may cause problems.

Propagation/Care: Take greenwood cuttings of deciduous species in early summer and semiripe cuttings of evergreens in mid- to late summer.

Preferences/Hardiness: Grow in full sun or partial shade in well-drained soil with good fertility and high humus content. Zones 4–8.

Authorities: AZ.u, GA.u, NY.r; *V. davidii*, CA.s; *V. opulus*, MT; *V. acerifolium* (Mapleleaf), *V.* × *burkwoodii* and cultivars, *V. lantanoides* (Hobblebush), *V. plicatum* var. *tomentosum* (Doublefile viburnum), *V.* × *sargentii* and cvs., NY.r

Vinca species

Periwinkle, Myrtle
Dogbane family (APOCYNACEAE)

Appearance: This genus of herbaceous and woody evergreen perennials includes the subshrub ground covers *Vinca major* (Periwinkle) and *V. minor* (Creeping myrtle, Lesser periwinkle). The species are invasive unless contained by barriers or mowing. Cultivars such as *V.* 'La Grave' (= 'Bowles') may be less aggressive.

Nativity: Europe, N. Africa, C. Asia

Uses: Groundcovers, woodlands

Toxicity: Concentrations of alkaloids and saponins depend on growing conditions but are capable of causing a drop in blood pressure. Although naturalized widely, vincas haven't been associated with livestock poisoning.

Propagation/Care: Divide in early spring. Take semiripe cuttings in summer.

Preferences/Hardiness: Plant in full sun or partial shade in moist soil with moderate to good humus levels. Plants flower more in full sun. Can spread prolifically; dig out if they exceed their boundaries. Zones 4–9.

Authorities: AZ.u; *V. major* (Greater periwinkle), MT, NY.l; *V. minor* (Creeping myrtle, Lesser periwinkle), GA.u, IL, NY.d, NY.r *Note:*

Viola sororia (Woolly blue violet) & *V. s.* forma *priceana* (Confederate violet)

Wisteria (Wisteria)

Woodwardia virginica (Virginia chain fern)

Viola species

Violets, Pansies

Violet family (VIOLACEAE)

Appearance: This genus includes 500 species, including pansies and violets. Flowers are blue, purple, pink, yellow, or bicolor, sometimes marked with contrasting splotches and whiskerlike stripes. Leaves are often heart-shaped.

Nativity: N. America; temperate regions worldwide

Uses: Bedding plants, naturalized in lawns, woodland gardens

Toxicity: Used medicinally, overdoses of *V. odorata* (English violet) can cause gastric distress and labored breathing. *V. tricolor* (Johnny-jump-ups) contains saponins toxic in large doses.

Propagation/Care: Plant seeds indoors in late winter or in fall in containers in a cold frame. Take semiripe cuttings in mid- to late summer. Many species, such as violets and Johnny-jump-ups, self-seed easily.

Preferences/Hardiness: Plant in full sun to partial shade in well-drained, fertile, and humus-rich soil. Zones 3–9.

Authorities: GA.a, IL; *V. odorata* (English violet), AZ.u, CA.s; *V. labradorica* (Labrador violet), CA.s, NY.l, NY.r, PA

Wisteria species

Wisteria

Pea family (FABACEAE)

Appearance: These woody, deciduous climbers feature pendent clusters of pealike fragrant flowers in shades of white and purple, followed by long seedpods. Alas, *W. floribunda* (Japanese wisteria) and *W. sinensis* (Chinese wisteria) are invasive in many states northward into Z6.

Nativity: S. United States, China, Korea, Japan

Uses: Focal points, over trellises

Toxicity: All parts are considered toxic. In humans, wistarine glycoside in seeds causes nausea, vomiting, weakness, cramps, and reddening of intestinal mucous membranes.

Propagation/Care: Layer in autumn. Graft in winter. Take basal cuttings in summer.

Preferences/Hardiness: Plant in full sun or partial shade in deep, fertile, moist soil with good humus and drainage. Plants can tolerate seasonal dry spells when they are dormant. Zones 5–9.

Authorities: AZ.u, GA.a, GA.u, IL, NY.d; *W. frutescens* 'Amethyst Falls' (American wisteria), PA; *W. macrostachya* (Kentucky wisteria) 'Clara Mack, Aunt Dee', PA

Woodwardia virginica, W. areolata

Virginia chain fern

Chain Fern family (BLECHNACEAE)

Appearance: Virginia chain fern is one of several fast-spreading native chain ferns that thrive in shaded swampy sites. *W. virginica's* outer fronds are 2 to 4 ft long when mature and glossy green. Fronds of narrow-leaved chain fern (*W. areolata*) are red when they first emerge but become glossy green by the time they reach their mature size of 2 ft long.

Nativity: N.E. United States

Uses: Swampy woodland gardens; moist, shady banks

Toxicity: Our sources don't comment on this fern genus, though others can be very toxic. Bad taste may be key here. Deer having suffered toxic effects from one fern may avoid all.

Propagation/Care: Divide underground stems in spring.

Preferences/Hardiness: Grow in light to deep shade in constantly damp, humus-rich soil. Many species tolerate acid conditions. Zones 4–10.

Authorities: Many

Yucca filamentosa 'Golden Sword' (Yucca)

Zauschneria californica (California fuchsia)

Zinnia elegans 'Profusion Orange' (Zinnia)

Yucca species

Yuccas

Agave family (AGAVACEAE)

Appearance: Garden species are 1–3 ft tall. Rosettes of stiff, lance-shaped leaves radiate 3–5 ft from the crown. Pendent, white or cream-colored flowers festoon tall spikes. Leaves may have bright yellow margins.

Nativity: N. and C. America, West Indies

Uses: Focal points, mixed borders, containers

Toxicity: Yuccas contain saponins. When chopped and fed to livestock, leaves have caused bloat and mild diarrhea. The roots are highly toxic. Still, the stiff, tough foliage likely discourages browsing.

Propagation/Care: Remove suckers with roots in spring. Take root cuttings in winter. Plant seeds indoors in early spring, using supplier's directions.

Preferences/Hardiness: Plant in full sun in extremely well-drained soil with moderate fertility. Yuccas tolerate dry periods. Most are tropical but *Y. filamentosa* is hardy in protected spots north to Zone 4. Zones 4–11.

Authorities: MT, NY.d, NY.l, NY.r; *Y. filamentosa*, TX.a, WV

Zauschneria californica = *Epilobium canum*

California fuchsia

Evening Primrose family (ONAGRACEAE)

Appearance: Also known as Hummingbird trumpet, this perennial is evergreen or semievergreen. Various subspecies, such as *Z. canna* 'Etteri', are deciduous and mat forming, although most cultivars are erect and grow to 1 to 2 ft tall. Flowers are trumpet-shaped and usually red, with prominent yellow stamens. Flowers appear late in the season, adding a note of brightness when few other plants are blooming. Leaves are gray-green and lance-shaped.

Nativity: Western N. America

Uses: Mixed borders, rock gardens

Toxicity: Our sources suggest no toxin issues.

Propagation/Care: Root basal cuttings in spring, over bottom heat. Plant seeds indoors in early spring and transplant after threat of frost has passed.

Preferences/Hardiness: Zones 8–11.

Authorities: AZ.u, CA.s, OR, WA

Abbreviations for **Authorities** can be found on page 234.

Zinnia species

Zinnias

Aster family (ASTERACEAE)

Appearance: Zinnias are grown for their brilliantly colored yellow, orange, red, purple, lilac, and white flowers, sometimes with contrasting eyes. Some resemble formal dahlias, some cactus-flowered dahlias.

Nativity: S.W. United States, Mexico, C. and S. America

Uses: Mixed borders, cutting gardens, containers, bedding

Toxicity: The leaves have a fine sandpaper-like texture that may reduce their appeal. Our sources suggest no toxin issues.

Propagation/Care: Collect seeds in autumn for broadcast in spring after soil has warmed to 55°F or start early indoors on a heating mat. Seedlings transplant well. Caterpillar damage to leaves is forgivable because caterpillars reappear the next year as beautiful butterflies.

Preferences/Hardiness: Full sun in fertile, humus-rich, well-drained soil. Seeds don't survive cold winters. Zones 9–11.

Authorities: GA.a, GA.u (*Z. elegans*), NY.s, TX.a, WA

Sources

All of these sources offer top-quality products and customer service. Most served as consultants for this book. None paid a dime for mention here, though two did provide an inexpensive product for photography.

PRODUCTS

Animal control, rescue, and exclusion products and equipment

Wildlife Control Supplies
Connecticut South Drive
Newgate One
PO Box 538
East Granby, CT 06026
(877) 684-7262
www.wildlifecontrolsupplies.com

Deer fencing, greenhouse supplies, groundcovers, more

Growers Supply
Division of FarmTek
1440 Filed of Dreams Way
Dyersville, IA 52040
(800) 476-9715
www.growerssupply.com

Fencing (electric and traditional wire)

Premier 1 Supplies
300th Street
Washington, IA 52353
(800) 282-6631 or (319) 653-7622
www.premier1supplies.com

Garbage cans, bear-proof

Dawg, Inc. (Doing Away With Grime)
25 Lassy Court
Terryville, CT 06786
(800) 935-3294
www.dawginc.com

Kit-framing for mammal-resistant vegetable gardens

Gardens To Gro
5640 Kearny Mesa Road, Ste. E
San Diego, CA 92111
(877) 476-8344
www.gardenstogro.com

Pet doors, raccoon-proof

Moore Pet Supplies
3170 Airport Road
La Crosse, WI 54603
(800) 829-7876
www.moorepet.com

Sherman live traps

H.B. Sherman Traps
3731 Peddie Drive
Tallahassee, FL. 32303
(850) 575-8727
www.shermantraps.com

PLANTS

One tip when ordering mail order: It's often wise to order woody plants from sources that grow plants approximately your hardiness zone and climate. You'll likely save in courier fees by ordering in large quantities. *Hint:* Get friends to join your order.

Forest Farm
990 Tetherow Road
Williams, OR 97544
(541) 846–7269
www.forestfarm.com
Ornamental plants from throughout the world

Johnny's Selected Seeds
955 Benton Avenue
Winslow, ME 04901-2601
(877) 564-6697
www.johnnyseeds.com
Also tools and equipment

North Creek Nurseries
388 North Creek Road
Landenberg, PA 19350
(877) ECO-PLUG or (610) 255–0100
www.northcreeknurseries.com
Although principally a wholesaler, will sell retail flats. Initial minimum order: $300.

WILDLIFE PHOTO PRINTS AND BOOKS

Rue Wildlife Photos
138 Millbrook Road
Hardwick, NJ 07825
(908) 362-8202
www.ruewildlifephotos.com
Fine art prints by Leonard Lee Rue III and Uschi Rue

Annotated Bibliography

PLANTS AND DEER RESISTANCE

Adler, Bill, Jr. *Outwitting Deer.* Guilford, CT: Lyons Press, 1999.

Armitage, Allan M. *Armitage's Native Plants for North American Gardens.* Portland, OR: Timber Press, 2006.

Bird, Richard. *A Gardener's Latin.* New York: Hearst Books, 1999.

Brickell, Christopher, and H. Mark Cathey, editors-in-chief. *The American Horticultural Society A–Z Encyclopedia of Garden Plants,* Revised US edition. London: DK Publishing, Inc., 2004.
A monumental full-color tome, my prime plant reference, 10 ¼ pounds!

Burrell, C. Colston. *Native Alternatives to Invasive Plants.* New York: Brooklyn Botanic Garden, 2006.
Many of these plants are also deer-resistant.

Coombes, Allen J. *Dictionary of Plant Names.* Portland, OR: Timber Press, 1985.
By a renowned British botanist whose pronunciations often remind us of George Bernard Shaw's observation that "England and America are two countries divided by a common language."

Cullina, William. *Native Ferns, Moss, and Grasses.* New York: Houghton Mifflin Co., 2008.
By the director of horticultural research at the New England Wildflower Society.

———. *Native Trees, Shrubs, and Vines.* New York: Houghton Mifflin Co., 2002.

Cutler, Karen Davis, and Barbara W. Ellis. *The Complete Flower Gardener.* Hoboken, NJ: Wiley Publishing, Inc., 2007.
By gardening authorities with impressive credentials.

Dirr, Michael A. *Dirr's Hardy Trees and Shrubs: An Illustrated Encyclopedia.* Portland, OR: Timber Press, 1997.
By the guru on woody plants.

———. *Viburnums.* Portland, OR: Timber Press, 2007.

Drzewucki, Vincent, Jr. *Gardening in Deer Country for Home and Garden.* New York: Brick Tower Press, 1998.
A Long Island authority.

Duke, James A. *The Green Pharmacy.* Rodale, 1997.
Top authority on the subject.

———. *Dr. Duke's Essential Herbs.* Rodale, 1999.

Elias, Thomas S. *Field Guide to North American Trees.* Revised edition. Grolier Book Clubs, Inc., 1989.
The best and easiest-to-use tree identification guide by the director of the National Arboretum in D.C. Includes natural history on all 652 native trees and more than 100 introduced trees, illustrated summer and winter identification keys, and more than 2,000 labeled drawings, including range maps (1,000 pages, alas out of print).

Ellis, Barbara W. *Complete Gardener's Dictionary.* New York: Barron's, 2000.
A richly reliable resource, also includes step-by-step techniques.

———. *Taylor's Guide to Growing North America's Favorite Plants.* New York: Houghton Mifflin Co., 1998.
The book my friend Barbara says she wishes she'd had available when she started gardening. Glad I researched plants for this book.

Gibbons, Euell. *Stalking the Wild Asparagus* and *Stalking the Healthful Herbs.* New York: David McKay Co., 1962.
Good reason these two books were national bestsellers. Delightfully written plant-by-plant foraging experiences!

Griffiths, Mark. *The New Royal Horticultural Dictionary: Index of Garden Plants.* Portland, OR: Timber Press, 1994.
Allows tracking of names and origins of even little-known plants.

Halpin, Anne. *Annuals, Perennials, and Bulbs.* Upper Saddle River, NJ: Creative Homeowner, 2001. *Esteemed gardening author and editor, as well as friend.*

———. *Homescaping: Designing Your Landscape to Match Your Home.* Rodale Inc., 2005. *A very sensible idea.*

———. *Seascape Gardening.* North Adams, MA: Storey Publishing, 2006. *Not your everyday plants.*

———, editor. *Sunset Northeastern Garden Book.* Menlo Park, CA: Sunset Books, 2001. *Anne's encyclopedic knowledge coming to bear.*

Hart, Rhonda Massingham. *Deerproofing Your Yard and Garden.* Second edition. North Adams, MA: Storey Publishing, 2005. *Hart's groundbreaking book, expanded and updated. Excellent.*

Hériteau, Jacqueline. *Complete Trees, Shrubs, and Hedges.* Revised and expanded edition. Upper Saddle River, NJ: Creative Homeowner, 2006. *Now with tips on deer-proofing, too.*

Holmes, Roger, Greg Grant, Rita Buchanan, and others. *Home Landscaping* series. Upper Saddle River, NJ: Creative Homeowner, 1998 to 2005. *Consisting of regionally selected plants by top regional designers, plus basics on hardscaping. It was my good fortune to help bring these books to publication.*

Johnson, Thomas H., editor. *The Letters of Emily Dickinson.* Cambridge, MA: Belknap Press of Harvard University Press, 1958, 1986. *Emily loved gardening. The best way to begin acquaintance with Emily, the person, is to read her letters, which include some of the easier poems. Next proceed to Marta McDowell's* Emily Dickinson's Gardens *and then Alfred Habegger's magisterial biography,* My Wars Are Laid Away in Books, *all leading to Emily's often challenging poems, now available in a revised 1998 chronology by Yale's R. W. Franklin.*

Leopold, Donald J. *Native Plants of the Northeast: A Guide for Gardening & Conservation.* Portland, OR: Timber Press, 2005. *By the distinguished teaching professor of Environmental Science & Forestry, State University of New York, Syracuse.*

Loewer, Peter. *Solving Deer Problems.* Guilford, CT: Lyons Press, 2003. *Author-illustrator of many gardening books, Loewer wisely begins by interviewing deer authority Leonard Lee Rue III before addressing deterrent options and his own deep knowledge of gardening.*

McDowell, Marta. *Emily Dickinson's Gardens: Celebration of a Poet and Gardener.* New York: McGraw Hill, 2005. *A compelling blend of Dickinson biography, gardening prose and poems, and McDowell's own gardening advice.*

McPhee, John. "A Forager," by Euell Gibbons, from *A Roomful of Hovings and Other Profiles.* New York: Farrar, Straus and Giroux, 1966. *Gibbons shows McPhee how to live by foraging in the Pennsylvania wilds for six bone-chilling days and nights in November, after which they've both gained weight.*

O'Sullivan, Penelope. *The Homeowner's Complete Tree & Shrub Handbook.* North Adams, MA: Storey Publishing, 2007. *Excellent, by landscape designer/author; photos mostly by the talented Karen Bussolini.*

Peterson, Roger Tory, and Margaret McKenny. *Wildflowers: Northeastern/North-Central North America.* New York: Houghton Mifflin Co., 1996. *Indispensable afield and in home gardens.*

Roddick, Christopher. *The Tree Care Primer.* New York: Brooklyn Botanic Garden, 2007. *Advice from the staff arborist at BBG, a consultant on mature tree preservation.*

Singer, Carolyn. *Deer in My Garden: Perennials and Subshrubs.* Volume 1. Grass Valley, CA: Garden Wisdom Press, 2006. *By a Sierra Nevada nursery owner and garden designer who has tested deer resistance for decades.*

———. *Deer in My Garden: Groundcovers and Edgers.* Volume 2. Grass Valley, CA: Garden Wisdom Press, 2006. *A third volume is in the works!*

Smith, Miranda. *Complete Home Gardening: Growing Secrets and Techniques.* Upper Saddle River, NJ: Creative Homeowner, 2006. *Market gardener extraordinaire, author, editor, teacher, and friend, Miranda also edited this book's manuscript and cowrote its plant profiles.*

———. *Backyard Fruits and Berries*. Rodale, Inc., 1997.

———. *Your Backyard Herb Garden*. Rodale, Inc., 1997.

Sunset editors. *Sunset Western Garden Book*. Menlo Park, CA: Sunset Publishing Corp., 1995.

Tallamy, Douglas W. *Bringing Nature Home: How Native Plants Sustain Wildlife in Our Gardens*. Portland, OR: Timber Press, 2007.
The book that is revolutionizing the way gardeners and landscape designers think about plant selection.

Wells, Diana. *100 Flowers and How They Got Their Names*. Chapel Hill, NC: Algonquin Books, 1997.
An elegantly written history in an elegant small package.

Internet Sources

nps.gov/plants/alien/list/WeedUS.xls: One of the largest listings of invasive plants in the United States, based on input from state agencies and the National Park Service.

plants/usda.gov: An enormous resource on native and alien plants.

Frederick D. Provenza, Utah State University professor of Forest, Range, and Wildlife Science: Use Fred's name in Internet searches to find his pioneering articles on browsing behaviors of livestock and deer.

PLANT TOXICITIES

Burrows, George E., and Ronald J. Tyrl. *Toxic Plants of North America*. Ames: Iowa State Press, 2001.
A monumental work, essential for veterinarians and emergency-room physicians, $6\frac{1}{2}$ pounds and commensurate price tag.

Duke, James A. *Handbook of Medicinal Herbs*. Second edition. Boca Raton, FL: CRC Press, 2002.
The definitive work on medicinal herbs by renowned ethnobotanist, herbal songwriter, and my first field mentor in foraging—he going barefoot.

Nelson, Lewis S., M.D., Richard D. Shih, M.D., Michael J. Balick, Ph.D. *Handbook of Poisonous and Injurious Plants*. Second edition. New York: Springer Science+Business, 2007.
The New York Botanical Garden's update of the AMA Handbook of Poisonous and Injurious Plants.

DEER BEHAVIORS

Geist, Valerius. *Deer of the World: Their Evolution, Behavior, and Ecology*. Mechanicsburg, PA: Stackpole Books, 1998.
Here the University of Calgary's professor emeritus of environmental science convincingly challenges 20th century theories, supported by his own extraordinary drawings.

Mackie, Richard J., John G. Kie, David F. Pac, and Kenneth L. Hamlin. "Mule Deer," *Wild Mammals of North America*. Second edition. Edited by George A. Feldhamer, Bruce C. Thomson, Joseph A. Chapman. Baltimore: Johns Hopkins University Press, 2003.
Representing one of the book-length chapters in this monumental $6\frac{1}{4}$-pound compendium.

Madson, John. "Deer Management," *The Outdoor Life Deer Hunter's Encyclopedia*. New York: Outdoor Life Books, 1985.
One of greatest rewards of editing this tome was working with this wonderful writer.

Miller, Karl V., Lisa I. Muller, and Stephen Demarai. "White-Tailed Deer," *Wild Mammals of North America*. Second edition. Edited by George A. Feldhamer, Bruce C. Thomson, Joseph A. Chapman. Baltimore: Johns Hopkins University Press, 2003.
Representing another of the book-length chapters in this monumental $6\frac{1}{4}$-pound compendium.

Provenza, Frederick D. *Foraging Behavior: Managing to Survive in a World of Change*. Logan, UT: Utah State University, 2003.
Google his name for pioneering articles on the subject.

Rue III, Leonard Lee. *The Deer of North America*. Guilford, CT: Lyons Press, 2004.
Nobody knows more about our deer or how to live life to the fullest.

———. *The Encyclopedia of Deer*. McGregor, MN: Voyageur Press, 2003.
Great photos, complementing Valerius Geist's book on deer worldwide.

———. *Whitetail Savvy* (scheduled for future publication)
It's been my privilege to read this informative and entertaining manuscript in progress, containing everything Lennie's learned in 60+ years of close study.

MAMMAL BEHAVIORS AND CONTROLS

Burroughs, John. *The Writings of John Burroughs: Wake-Robin*. New York: Houghton Mifflin Co, 1913.
The great naturalist-author and friend of John Muir and Teddy Roosevelt.

Curtis, Paul D., and Jill Shultz. *Best Practices for Wildlife Control Operators*. Clifton Park, NY: Thomson/Delmar Learning, 2008.
Primarily written for professional controlers in the Northeast, yet most applies continentwide.

Dillard, Annie. *Pilgrim at Tinker Creek*. New York: Harper & Row, 1974.
Annie deserved her Pulitzer for this book, reminding of Thoreau's Walden transported to the Blue Ridge Mountains but with more fireworks.

Elbroch, Mark. *Mammal Tracks & Sign: A Guide to North American Species*. Mechanicsburg, PA: Stackpole Books, 2003.
Astoundingly detailed field research, 784 full-color pages.

Feldhamer, George A., Bruce C. Thomson, and Joseph A. Chapman, editors. *Wild Mammals of North America*. Second edition. Baltimore: Johns Hopkins University Press, 2003.
My prime reference on mammals, with chapters usually by multiple national authorities (1,213 large-format pages in scholarly prose and small type, 6¼ pounds, with matching price tag).

Gould, Stephen Jay. All books in the series "Reflections in Natural History" (including *Ever Since Darwin, Eight Little Piggies,* and *Hen's Teeth and Horse's Toes*). New York: W.W. Norton & Co., 1977–2007.
Brilliant science, theorizing, and writing on antlers, endangered species, DNA, evolution, and much more, compiled from Gould's monthly columns in Natural History magazine until his untimely death.

Kanze, Edward M. *Over the Mountain and Home Again: Journeys of an Adirondack Naturalist*. Utica, NY: Nicholas Burns Publishing, 2006.
How to block mouse holes in an old house and more.

———. *The World of John Burroughs*. New York: Harry N. Abrams, Inc., 1993.
A photo-illustrated biography on author-naturalist Burroughs, impressively researched, written, and photographed by author-naturalist Kanze, whose body of work has begun to rival Burroughs' own.

Murie, Olaus J. *A Field Guide to Animal Tracks,* A Peterson Field Guide. New York: Houghton Mifflin Co., 1974.
The timeless classic.

Reid, Fiona A. *Mammals of North America,* A Peterson Field Guide. New York: Houghton-Mifflin Co., 2006.
For identifications and the latest in scientific reclassifications.

Rue III, Leonard Lee. *Complete Guide to Game Animals.* Outdoor Life Books, 1981.
Inimitable Rue, teeming with insights richly based on first-hand encounters.

Salmon, Terrell P., Desley A. Whisson, and Rex E. Marsh. *Wildlife Pest Control Around Gardens and Homes (*Publication 21385). Second edition. Davis, CA: University of California/Agricultural and Natural Resources, 2006.
Essential for Westerners, excellent illustrations.

Storer, Tracy I., Robert L. Usinger, and David Lukas. *Sierra Nevada Natural History.* Revised edition. Berkeley, CA: University of California Press, 2004.
Don't hit the trails there without it.

Whitaker, John O., Jr., and William J. Hamilton, Jr. *Mammals of the Eastern United States.* Third edition. Ithaca, NY: Comstock Publishing Associates/Cornell University Press, 1998.
Decades of scientific field research, reminding us that a mouse live-trapped and released a mile distant won't exactly beat us home but might return before our next oil change.

COMMUNICABLE DISEASES AND PARASITES

Though lacking in humor, these Internet sources often dispel myths about diseases and parasites that mammals can transmit to us. All remind that an ounce of prevention is worth a pound of cure, while reassuring that many cures are far surer than in the recent past. (See that chapter on page 210.)

apgea.army.mil: US Army Web site on health, especially good on the plague, transmitted by rodent fleas.

cdc/gov: U.S. Centers for Disease Control.

hrsa.gov: U.S. Dept. of Health and Human Services, Health Resources and Service Administration (HRSA).

webMD.com: A health resource for physicians and the public.

ADDITIONAL MAMMAL RESOURCES

animalremovalpro.com (Animal Removal Professionals): Allows search by zip code. Alternatively, use search words state/province name, wildlife, control, animal, nuisance, removal.

fawnrescue.org: Wildlife Fawn Rescue offers an afternoon's inspiring and informative reading by California's legendary Marjorie Davis; donations are tax-deductible.

nwrawildlife.org (National Wildlife Rehabilitators Association): If this Web site doesn't give you contact info on rehabilitators near you, search the Internet using state/province name and key words: wildlife, rehabilitator, rescue. Veterinarians can often recommend qualified rehabilitators.

MAMMAL WEB SITES, ARTICLES, AND BOOK CHAPTERS

Bears

bear.org and bearstudy.org: Web sites of Dr. Lynn Rogers, of Ely, Minnesota, "The Man Who Walks with Bears."

savebears.org: Tahoe Basin Web site founded by wildlife rights activist Ann Bryant.

Ebersole, Rene. "Black Bears on the Mind," *National Wildlife*, August/September 2005.

Hoagland, Edward. *The Edward Hoagland Reader.* New York: Vintage Books, 1979.
With "Bears, Bears, Bears," a chapter-length profile on bear researcher Lynn Rogers, selected from Hoagland's Of Red Wolves and Black Bears.

Tyson, Peter. "Secrets of Hibernation," www.pbs.org.

Beavers

beaversww.org: Articles on "How to Protect Trees from Beavers" and "Solutions to Beaver/Human Conflicts."

Chipmunks

Terres, John K. *Audubon Encyclopedia of North American Birds.* New York: Alfred A. Knopf, 1980.
See pages 140 to 142 for comparative weights of birds to small mammals.

Gophers, Pocket

FEMA. "Pocket Gopher Overview," *Technical Manual for Dam Owners, FEMA 473/Sept 2005,* U.S. Dept. of Homeland Security, pp 26–28.

France, John W., and Bill Moler (investigators). *Truckee Canal Failure on 5 January 2008*, prepared by URS Corp. for the U.S. Dept. of the Interior, Bureau of Reclamation, March 2008.

Knight, James E., extension wildlife specialist. "Guide to Pocket Gopher Control in Montana," Montana Guide Fact Sheet (montana.edu/wwwpb/pubs).

Salmon, Terrill P., et al. "Pocket Gophers," University of California Statewide Integrated Pest Management Program (ipm.ucdavis.edu/PMG/PESTNOTES).

Schalau, J. "Pocket Gopher Control," Arizona Cooperative Extension (cals.arizona.edu/Yavapai/anr/hort/gopher).

Virchow, Dallas R., et al. "Controlling Pocket Gophers in Nebraska," Wildlife Damage Management (ianrpubs.unl.edu/epublic/pages).

Moles

themoleman.com: Tom Schmidt, of Cincinnati—informative and entertaining.

Peccaries

Arizona Game and Fish Department. "Javelina," and "Living with Javelina." azgfd.com.

Internet Center for Wildlife Damage Management (Cornell, Clemson, University of NB, UT State). "Feral Pig, Javelina and Collared Pig Damage Management and Control." icwdm.org.

National Park Service, Big Bend National Park. "The Collared Peccary, or Javelina." nps.gov.

Sullivan, Lawrence M., extension specialist, University of Arizona. "Javelina Jassles: Living with Pesky Peccaries." Paper at Annual Meeting WCC-95, Reno, NV: 2001.

Texas Game & Fish Commission. "Specific Management Recommendation for Javelinas," *Wildlife Activities and Practices*. Bulletin 21. tpwd.state.tx.us/publications.

USDA, "Feral/Wild Pigs: Potential Problems for Farmers and Hunters," Agricultural Bulletin 299.

Rabbits

Salmon, Terrill P., et al. "Rabbits," University of California Statewide Integrated Pest Management Program (ipm.ucdavis.edu/PMG/PESTNOTES).

Rats and Mice

ratbehavior.org: Anne Hanson, Ph.D., animal behaviorist shares her research.

Skunks

Erickson, Rob. *Innovative Skunk Control* (R. J. E. Publications, 2005).

Woodchucks

urbanwildlifecontrol.com: Georgia Dept. of Natural Resources Wildlife Division bulletin.

Bellengier, Rene M., Jr. "Woodchucks," New Hampshire Animal Damage Control (www.ces.ncsu.edu/nreos/wild/pdf/wildlife/WOODCHUCKS.PDF).

Burroughs, John. "The Woodchuck," *The Writings of John Burroughs*: Volume 1. Wake-Robin (Elibron Classics) www.booksiread.org (release date: February 2005, EBook #7441).

Peterson, Cass. "In Gardens, Groundhogs Show Who's the Boss," *New York Times*, October 15, 2000.

Index

Boldface page numbers indicate photographs or illustrations. <u>Underscored</u> references indicate boxed text, tables or charts.

C